Analytic Philosophy

B

BLACKWELL PHILOSOPHY ANTHOLOGIES

Each volume in this outstanding series provides an authoritative and comprehensive collection of the essential primary readings from philosophy's main fields of study. Designed to complement the *Blackwell Companions to Philosophy* series, each volume represents an unparalleled resource in its own right, and will provide the ideal platform for course use.

Analytic Philosophy:
An Anthology

Edited by

A. P. Martinich and David Sosa
University of Texas at Austin

BLACKWELL
Publishers

Copyright © Blackwell Publishers Ltd 2001. Editorial arrangement and introduction copyright © A. P. Martinich and David Sosa 2001.

First published 2001

2 4 6 8 10 9 7 5 3 1

Blackwell Publishers Inc.
350 Main Street
Malden, Massachusetts 02148
USA

Blackwell Publishers Ltd
108 Cowley Road
Oxford OX4 1JF
UK

Library of Congress Cataloging-in-Publication Data

Analytic philosophy: an anthology/edited by A. P. Martinich and David Sosa.
     p.   cm. — (Blackwell philosophy anthologies; 13)
     Includes bibliographical references and index.
     ISBN 0-631-21646-4 (alk. paper) — ISBN 0-631-21647-2 (pb.: alk. paper)
     1. Analysis (Philosophy) I. Martinich, Aloysius. II. Sosa, David, 1966– III. Series.
B808.5. A52 2001
146′.4 — dc21   00-069789

British Library Cataloguing in Publication Data

A CIP catalogue record for this book is available from the British Library.

Typeset in 9 on 11pt Ehrhardt
by Graphicraft Limited, Hong Kong

Printed in Great Britain by T.J. International, Padstow, Cornwall
This book is printed on acid-free paper

Contents

Contents

Contents

Acknowledgments

We want to thank Steve Smith for originally suggesting this project and Beth Remmes for guiding us through it. We also thank all the colleagues, near and far, who advised us about the contents. Last, and not least, we thank Leslie Crooks and Laura Gentry for their help.

The editors and publishers would like to thank the following for permission to use copyright material:

George Allen & Unwin for entry 14; Blackwell Publishers for entries 1, 2, 15, 46; Cambridge University Press for entries 33, 36; Cornell University Press for entries 5, 25, 28, 31, 35, 37, 43, 44; the Editor of the Aristotelian Society for entries 9, 11, 42; Professor Edmund Gettier for entry 18; Victor Gollancz for entry 40; Nelson Goodman and Harvard University Press for entry 20; Harvard University Press for entry 26; Kluwer Academic Publishers for entry 6; Macmillan for entry 22; Marquette University Press for entry 17; University of Massachusetts Press for entry 24; University of Minnesota Press for entry 30; New York University Press for entry 7; Open Court Publishing Company for entries 38, 39; Oxford University Press for entries 4, 13, 16, 34; University of Pittsburgh Press for entries 23, 45; Prentice-Hall for entry 19; Professor W. V. Quine and Columbia University Press for entry 21; Routledge and Kegan Paul for entry 10; J. R. Searle and Harvard University Press for entry 27.

Every effort has been made to trace the copyright holders, but if any have been inadvertently overlooked, the publishers will be pleased to make the necessary arrangements at the first opportunity.

Introduction

A. P. Martinich and David Sosa

Analytic philosophy in the twentieth century is not easily defined by doctrine or method. Different philosophers of the period have held opposed positions and employed various methods, difficult to enumerate or to describe. Today, many methods overlap. Notwithstanding the nay-sayers who have declared analytic philosophy (or even more indiscriminately, philosophy in general) dead, it is flourishing.

Analytic philosophy would be easier to define if it had kept to its early form in Great Britain at the beginning of the century. Analysis, as it was originally understood, aimed at breaking down complex concepts into their simpler constituents, just as chemical analysis aimed at breaking down complex substances into simpler ones. For example, the concept of knowledge was decomposed into the concepts of truth, belief, and justification; knowledge was thus *analyzed* as justified true belief. Later, under the influence of Rudolf Carnap, explicit analyses were supposed to take the form of finding necessary and sufficient conditions for predicates or "open" sentences. If C is a necessary condition for something X, then anything that is X satisfies C; if C is a sufficient condition for something, then anything that satisfies C is X. For example:

A person K knows that p if and only if ("iff" or sometimes "$=_{df}$")

1   K believes that p;
2   K is justified in believing that p; and
3   it is true that p.

Philosophers thought for decades that this analysis of knowledge was correct as far as it went. However, they were not completely satisfied because the relevant notion of justification was not clear. Consequently, for decades philosophers worked on the concept of justification.

In 1963 Edmund Gettier (entry 18) caused a major stir in epistemology by giving some examples in which a person would have satisfied all the specified conditions for knowing something, but would not really know it. Confronted with a counterexample to the traditional analysis of knowledge, philosophers realized that they had been wrong about the nature of knowledge; this inspired them to new analyses. Indeed, years earlier Bertrand Russell had given an example that could have been turned to similar effect; see, for example, *The Problems of Philosophy* (Home University Library, 1912), chapter 13; but it was only with Gettier that philosophy appreciated the inadequacy of the traditional analysis.

Returning to its origins in Great Britain early in the twentieth century, analytic philosophy, in the hands of G. E. Moore, was a challenge to British idealism. He defended the mind-independence of the external world, the multiplicity of the world as against the indivisible unity of the mind, and the fundamentality of common-sense beliefs. Because Moore and Russell believed in multiple ultimately-irreducible objects, they thought of themselves as atomists, but because they were philosophers rather than physicists, Russell coined the term "Logical Atomism" for their general philosophy.

One of the greatest works of logical atomism was Ludwig Wittgenstein's *Tractatus Logico-Philosophicus*, of which the main positions are presented in entry 10. (See also entry 9.)

Though so far we have been discussing how analytic philosophy sprung up in English-speaking countries, we should emphasize that German-speaking countries represent a second font. ("Anglo-Germanic" philosophy might be less misleading than the standard "Anglo-American"; Michael Dummett has plugged "Anglo-Austrian" as better representing the significance of philosophers such as Bernard Bolzano, Franz Brentano, and Alexius Meinong.) Near the end of the nineteenth century, Gottlob Frege, a mathematician, revolutionized formal logic. This led him to study the foundations of language and thought (see entry 1). In his 1918 article, "Thought" (entry 2), Frege introduced many of the standard conceptual tools and distinctions analytic philosophers have used since. His most famous student was Carnap, who emigrated to the United States to escape political oppression in Germany. Other brilliant philosophers – Carl Hempel (see selection 19) is another notable example – also left Germany and later settled in the United States.

Beginning with the powerful effects of Frege on Russell, and then of the latter on the Austrian-born Wittgenstein, the cross-fertilization of German and English philosophy was broad and deeply important. To cite another example, Moritz Schlick organized in Vienna a group ("the Vienna Circle"), consisting mostly of scientists turned philosophers. Both A. J. Ayer, a brilliant young Englishman, and W. V. Quine, a brilliant young American, attended their discussions. When Ayer returned to England, he wrote *Language, Truth and Logic*, the most famous presentation of their philosophy: logical positivism (entry 40; see also 41). ("Positivism" comes from the phrase "empirical positivism," which was a nineteenth-century scientism promoted by Auguste Comte.)

No less impressed with the Vienna Circle than was Ayer, Quine turned his thought in a different direction when he returned to the United States. While he continued his work on formal logic, Quine importantly attacked what he called "two dogmas of empiricism" (entry 43; see also 44), which he saw as dogmas of logical positivism. The first dogma is that there is a significant distinction between analytic truths and synthetic truths. The second dogma is that "each meaningful statement is equivalent to some logical construct upon terms which refer to immediate experience." Quine's attack was on the foundations of conceptual analysis. If he is right that there is no principled distinction between analytic and synthetic propositions, then analysis is hopeless.

Quine's dissatisfaction with the empiricism of the logical positivists was part of a wave of critical interest from across the Atlantic, a wave that included Nelson Goodman and Morton White. At roughly the same time, two other schools, in England, were reflecting critically on positivist positions. One, at Oxford and led by Gilbert Ryle and J. L. Austin, thought that the criterion for meaningfulness dictated by the Logical Positivists was too confining. In "Performative Utterances" and most famously in *How To Do Things With Words*, Austin showed that ordinary sentences like "I christen thee the Queen Elizabeth," and "I promise to go to the store" are clearly cognitively meaningful, but do not pass the logical positivists' test for meaningfulness. This insight eventually led to the construction of speech-act theory, invented by Austin but perfected by John Searle and H. P. Grice (entry 5).

In addition, Austin and his band of "ordinary-language" philosophers believed that philosophical progress could be made by group investigation into the distinctions implicit in ordinary language (entry 42). In his own way, Gilbert Ryle investigated the scope and limits of ordinary language in order to chart the topography of human concepts; he did conceptual geography (see also his *The Concept of Mind*).

A second English school, headquartered in Cambridge (with an important outpost in Ithaca, New York) was led by Wittgenstein (selections 28 and 46 represent this group). He emphasized that meaning is an abstraction from speaking (or, more generally, from the "use" of language) and that speaking was inextricably linked to a non-linguistic context. Wittgenstein's work challenged basic assumptions concerning relations between mind, language, and the world, which lay at the root of almost all the analytic philosophy that had come before (including his own earlier work; cf. entries 10 and 46).

By 1970, logical atomism, logical positivism, and ordinary-language philosophy had had their day. At least three factors contributed to the decline. One was that the questions posed and the answers proffered were thought by their critics to be trivial. Second, some powerful new technical devices, notably possible-world semantics, promised to shed new light on substantive philosophical problems. Third, new philosophical theories, for example, causal theories of knowledge, perception, and language, not beholden to ordinary language or to science, were developed.

No one, two, or three ways of doing philosophy and no small class of problems dominated the last quarter century. A thousand philosophical flowers have bloomed. Metaphysics was reinvigorated by Strawson and by Chisholm (entries 11 and 17), ethics and political philosophy by John Rawls and others (entries 35–7), philosophy of mind by many (entries 22–7).

Moreover, even the variety of philosophical work included in this volume does not fully represent all that analytic philosophy has to offer. We have been unable to include work by Gustav Bergmann, for example, or by G. H. von Wright or other Scandinavian philosophers, by Gilbert Ryle, Frank Ramsey, or C. D. Broad. And the list goes on (Tarski, Gödel, Church . . .). Difficult choices were required. (Any damage is partly remedied,

we hope, by our *A Companion to Analytic Philosophy*, meant to accompany this anthology.)

Again, analytic philosophy (not to mention continental philosophy) is a cluster concept, encompassing a range of methods and doctrines. Many of these methods and doctrines bear a family resemblance to each other because they have the same ancestors; and, while analytic philosophy of the last quarter century encompasses many deep disagreements, it is also not an unhappy family, and it is creative and diverse.

This diversity makes it difficult to summarize or characterize philosophy today. Perhaps also we are too close to it in time to be able to see it clearly. However, what appears to us to be the case, if only as through a glass darkly, is a more widespread scientism. Although logical atomism and logical positivism were sympathetic to science, very little science actually appeared in the works of their adherents. Scientific results have become more important to philosophy, and philosophy overlaps with science now more than it has since the seventeenth century.

Further Reading

Coffa, J. Alberto, *The Semantic Tradition from Kant to Carnap: To the Vienna Station*, Cambridge: Cambridge University Press, 1991.

Dummett, Michael, *Origins of Analytic Philosophy*, Cambridge, MA: Harvard University Press, 1994.

Lewis, H. D., *Clarity is Not Enough*, London: George Allen & Unwin, 1963.

Martinich, A. P. and Sosa, David (eds.) *A Companion to Analytic Philosophy*, Malden, MA and Oxford: Blackwell Publishers, 2001.

Rorty, Richard, *The Linguistic Turn*, Chicago: University of Chicago Press, 1992.

Stroll, Avrum, *Twentieth Century Analytic Philosophy*, New York: Columbia University Press, 2000.

Urmson, J. O., *Philosophical Analysis: Its Development Between the Two World Wars*, London: Oxford University Press, 1956.

PART I

Philosophy of Language

1

On Sense and Reference

Gottlob Frege

Equality[1] gives rise to challenging questions which are not altogether easy to answer. Is it a relation? A relation between objects, or between names or signs of objects? In my *Begriffsschrift* I assumed the latter. The reasons which seem to favour this are the following: $a = a$ and $a = b$ are obviously statements of differing cognitive value; $a = a$ holds *a priori* and, according to Kant, is to be labelled analytic, while statements of the form $a = b$ often contain very valuable extensions of our knowledge and cannot always be established *a priori*. The discovery that the rising sun is not new every morning, but always the same, was one of the most fertile astronomical discoveries. Even today the identification of a small planet or a comet is not always a matter of course. Now if we were to regard equality as a relation between that which the names 'a' and 'b' designate, it would seem that $a = b$ could not differ from $a = a$ (i.e. provided $a = b$ is true). A relation would thereby be expressed of a thing to itself, and indeed one in which each thing stands to itself but to no other thing. What is intended to be said by $a = b$ seems to be that the signs or names 'a' and 'b' designate the same thing, so that those signs themselves would be under discussion; a relation between them would be asserted. But this relation would hold between the names or signs only in so far as they named or designated something. It would be mediated by the connexion

Previously published in *Translations from the Philosophical Writings of Gottlob Frege*, ed. Peter Geach and Max Black (Blackwell Publishers, Oxford, 1952).

of each of the two signs with the same designated thing. But this is arbitrary. Nobody can be forbidden to use any arbitrarily producible event or object as a sign for something. In that case the sentence $a = b$ would no longer refer to the subject matter, but only to its mode of designation; we would express no proper knowledge by its means. But in many cases this is just what we want to do. If the sign 'a' is distinguished from the sign 'b' only as object (here, by means of its shape), not as sign (i.e. not by the manner in which it designates something), the cognitive value of $a = a$ becomes essentially equal to that of $a = b$, provided $a = b$ is true. A difference can arise only if the difference between the signs corresponds to a difference in the mode of presentation of that which is designated. Let a, b, c be the lines connecting the vertices of a triangle with the midpoints of the opposite sides. The point of intersection of a and b is then the same as the point of intersection of b and c. So we have different designations for the same point, and these names ('point of intersection of a and b,' 'point of intersection of b and c') likewise indicate the mode of presentation; and hence the statement contains actual knowledge.

It is natural, now, to think of there being connected with a sign (name, combination of words, letter), besides that to which the sign refers, which may be called the reference of the sign, also what I should like to call the *sense* of the sign, wherein the mode of presentation is contained. In our example, accordingly, the reference of the expressions 'the point of intersection of a and b'

and 'the point of intersection of b and c' would be the same, but not their senses. The reference of 'evening star' would be the same as that of 'morning star,' but not the sense.

It is clear from the context that by 'sign' and 'name' I have here understood any designation representing a proper name, which thus has as its reference a definite object (this word taken in the widest range), but not a concept or a relation, which shall be discussed further in another article. The designation of a single object can also consist of several words or other signs. For brevity, let every such designation be called a proper name.

The sense of a proper name is grasped by everybody who is sufficiently familiar with the language or totality of designations to which it belongs;[2] but this serves to illuminate only a single aspect of the reference, supposing it to have one. Comprehensive knowledge of the reference would require us to be able to say immediately whether any given sense belongs to it. To such knowledge we never attain.

The regular connexion between a sign, its sense, and its reference is of such a kind that to the sign there corresponds a definite sense and to that in turn a definite reference, while to a given reference (an object) there does not belong only a single sign. The same sense has different expressions in different languages or even in the same language. To be sure, exceptions to this regular behaviour occur. To every expression belonging to a complete totality of signs, there should certainly correspond a definite sense; but natural languages often do not satisfy this condition, and one must be content if the same word has the same sense in the same context. It may perhaps be granted that every grammatically well-formed expression representing a proper name always has a sense. But this is not to say that to the sense there also corresponds a reference. The words 'the celestial body most distant from the Earth' have a sense, but it is very doubtful if they also have a reference. The expression 'the least rapidly convergent series' has a sense but demonstrably has no reference, since for every given convergent series, another convergent, but less rapidly convergent, series can be found. In grasping a sense, one is not certainly assured of a reference.

If words are used in the ordinary way, what one intends to speak of is their reference. It can also happen, however, that one wishes to talk about the words themselves or their sense. This happens, for instance, when the words of another are quoted. One's own words then first designate words of the other speaker, and only the latter have their usual reference. We then have signs of signs. In writing, the words are in this case enclosed in quotation marks. Accordingly, a word standing between quotation marks must not be taken as having its ordinary reference.

In order to speak of the sense of an expression 'A' one may simply use the phrase 'the sense of the expression "A".' In reported speech one talks about the sense, e.g., of another person's remarks. It is quite clear that in this way of speaking words do not have their customary reference but designate what is usually their sense. In order to have a short expression, we will say: In reported speech, words are used *indirectly* or have their *indirect* reference. We distinguish accordingly the *customary* from the *indirect* reference of a word; and its *customary* sense from its *indirect* sense. The indirect reference of a word is accordingly its customary sense. Such exceptions must always be borne in mind if the mode of connexion between sign, sense, and reference in particular cases is to be correctly understood.

The reference and sense of a sign are to be distinguished from the associated idea. If the reference of a sign is an object perceivable by the senses, my idea of it is an internal image,[3] arising from memories of sense impressions which I have had and acts, both internal and external, which I have performed. Such an idea is often saturated with feeling; the clarity of its separate parts varies and oscillates. The same sense is not always connected, even in the same man, with the same idea. The idea is subjective: one man's idea is not that of another. There result, as a matter of course, a variety of differences in the ideas associated with the same sense. A painter, a horseman, and a zoologist will probably connect different ideas with the name 'Bucephalus.' This constitutes an essential distinction between the idea and the sign's sense, which may be the common property of many and therefore is not a part or a mode of the individual mind. For one can hardly deny that mankind has a common store of thoughts which is transmitted from one generation to another.[4]

In the light of this, one need have no scruples in speaking simply of *the* sense, whereas in the case of an idea one must, strictly speaking, add to whom it belongs and at what time. It might perhaps be said: Just as one man connects this idea, and another that idea, with the same word, so also one man can associate this sense and another that sense. But there still remains a difference in the mode of connexion. They are not prevented from grasping the same sense; but they cannot have the same idea. *Si duo idem faciunt, non est idem.* If two persons picture the same thing, each still has his own idea. It is indeed sometimes possible to establish differences in the ideas, or even in the sensations, of different men; but an exact comparison is not possible, because we cannot have both ideas together in the same consciousness.

The reference of a proper name is the object itself which we designate by its means; the idea, which we have in that case, is wholly subjective; in between lies the sense, which is indeed no longer subjective like the idea, but is yet not the object itself. The following analogy will perhaps clarify these relationships. Somebody observes the Moon through a telescope. I compare the Moon itself to the reference; it is the object of the observation, mediated by the real image projected by the object glass in the interior of the telescope, and by the retinal image of the observer. The former I compare to the sense, the latter is like the idea or experience. The optical image in the telescope is indeed one-sided and dependent upon the standpoint of observation; but it is still objective, inasmuch as it can be used by several observers. At any rate it could be arranged for several to use it simultaneously. But each one would have his own retinal image. On account of the diverse shapes of the observers' eyes, even a geometrical congruence could hardly be achieved, and an actual coincidence would be out of the question. This analogy might be developed still further, by assuming A's retinal image made visible to B; or A might also see his own retinal image in a mirror. In this way we might perhaps show how an idea can itself be taken as an object, but as such is not for the observer what it directly is for the person having the idea. But to pursue this would take us too far afield.

We can now recognize three levels of difference between words, expressions, or whole sentences. The difference may concern at most the ideas, or the sense but not the reference, or, finally, the reference as well. With respect to the first level, it is to be noted that, on account of the uncertain connexion of ideas with words, a difference may hold for one person, which another

does not find. The difference between a translation and the original text should properly not overstep the first level. To the possible differences here belong also the colouring and shading which poetic eloquence seeks to give to the sense. Such colouring and shading are not objective, and must be evoked by each hearer or reader according to the hints of the poet or the speaker. Without some affinity in human ideas art would certainly be impossible; but it can never be exactly determined how far the intentions of the poet are realized.

In what follows there will be no further discussion of ideas and experiences; they have been mentioned here only to ensure that the idea aroused in the hearer by a word shall not be confused with its sense or its reference.

To make short and exact expressions possible, let the following phraseology be established:

A proper name (word, sign, sign combination, expression) *expresses* its sense, *stands for* or *designates* its reference. By means of a sign we express its sense and designate its reference.

Idealists or sceptics will perhaps long since have objected: 'You talk, without further ado, of the Moon as an object; but how do you know that the name "the Moon" has any reference? How do you know that anything whatsoever has a reference?' I reply that when we say 'the Moon,' we do not intend to speak of our idea of the Moon, nor are we satisfied with the sense alone, but we presuppose a reference. To assume that in the sentence 'The Moon is smaller than the Earth' the idea of the Moon is in question, would be flatly to misunderstand the sense. If this is what the speaker wanted, he would use the phrase 'my idea of the Moon.' Now we can of course be mistaken in the presupposition, and such mistakes have indeed occurred. But the question whether the presupposition is perhaps always mistaken need not be answered here; in order to justify mention of the reference of a sign it is enough, at first, to point out our intention in speaking or thinking. (We must then add the reservation: provided such reference exists.)

So far we have considered the sense and reference only of such expressions, words, or signs as we have called proper names. We now inquire concerning the sense and reference for an entire declarative sentence. Such a sentence contains a thought.[5] Is this thought, now, to be regarded as its sense or its reference? Let us assume for the time being that the sentence has reference. If we now replace one word of the sentence by another having the same reference, but a different sense, this can have no bearing upon the reference of the sentence. Yet we can see that in such a case the thought changes; since, e.g., the thought in the sentence 'The morning star is a body illuminated by the Sun' differs from that in the sentence 'The evening star is a body illuminated by the Sun.' Anybody who did not know that the evening star is the morning star might hold the one thought to be true, the other false. The thought, accordingly, cannot be the reference of the sentence, but must rather be considered as the sense. What is the position now with regard to the reference? Have we a right even to inquire about it? Is it possible that a sentence as a whole has only a sense, but no reference? At any rate, one might expect that such sentences occur, just as there are parts of sentences having sense but no reference. And sentences which contain proper names without reference will be of this kind. The sentence 'Odysseus was set ashore at Ithaca while sound asleep' obviously has a sense. But since it is doubtful whether the name 'Odysseus,' occurring therein, has reference, it is also doubtful whether the whole sentence has one. Yet it is certain, nevertheless, that anyone who seriously took the sentence to be true or false would ascribe to the name 'Odysseus' a reference, not merely a sense; for it is of the reference of the name that the predicate is affirmed or denied. Whoever does not admit the name has reference can neither apply nor withhold the predicate. But in that case it would be superfluous to advance to the reference of the name; one could be satisfied with the sense, if one wanted to go no further than the thought. If it were a question only of the sense of the sentence, the thought, it would be unnecessary to bother with the reference of a part of the sentence; only the sense, not the reference, of the part is relevant to the sense of the whole sentence. The thought remains the same whether 'Odysseus' has reference or not. The fact that we concern ourselves at all about the reference of a part of the sentence indicates that we generally recognize and expect a reference for the sentence itself. The thought loses value for us as soon as we recognize that the reference of one of its parts is missing. We are therefore justified in not being satisfied with the sense of a sentence, and in inquiring also as to its reference. But now why do we want every proper name to have not only a sense, but also a

reference? Why is the thought not enough for us? Because, and to the extent that, we are concerned with its truth value. This is not always the case. In hearing an epic poem, for instance, apart from the euphony of the language we are interested only in the sense of the sentences and the images and feelings thereby aroused. The question of truth would cause us to abandon aesthetic delight for an attitude of scientific investigation. Hence it is a matter of no concern to us whether the name 'Odysseus,' for instance, has reference, so long as we accept the poem as a work of art.[6] It is the striving for truth that drives us always to advance from the sense to the reference.

We have seen that the reference of a sentence may always be sought, whenever the reference of its components is involved; and that this is the case when and only when we are inquiring after the truth value.

We are therefore driven into accepting the *truth value* of a sentence as constituting its reference. By the truth value of a sentence I understand the circumstance that it is true or false. There are no further truth values. For brevity I call the one the True, the other the False. Every declarative sentence concerned with the reference of its words is therefore to be regarded as a proper name, and its reference, if it has one, is either the True or the False. These two objects are recognized, if only implicitly, by everybody who judges something to be true – and so even by a sceptic. The designation of the truth values as objects may appear to be an arbitrary fancy or perhaps a mere play upon words, from which no profound consequences could be drawn. What I mean by an object can be more exactly discussed only in connexion with concept and relation. I will reserve this for another article. But so much should already be clear, that in every judgment,[7] no matter how trivial, the step from the level of thoughts to the level of reference (the objective) has already been taken.

One might be tempted to regard the relation of the thought to the True not as that of sense to reference, but rather as that of subject to predicate. One can, indeed, say: 'The thought, that 5 is a prime number, is true.' But closer examination shows that nothing more has been said than in the simple sentence '5 is a prime number.' The truth claim arises in each case from the form of the declarative sentence, and when the latter lacks its usual force, e.g., in the mouth of an actor upon the stage, even the sentence 'The thought that 5 is a prime number is true' contains only a thought, and indeed the same thought as the simple '5 is a prime number.' It follows that the relation of the thought to the True may not be compared with that of subject to predicate. Subject and predicate (understood in the logical sense) are indeed elements of thought; they stand on the same level for knowledge. By combining subject and predicate, one reaches only a thought, never passes from sense to reference, never from a thought to its truth value. One moves at the same level but never advances from one level to the next. A truth value cannot be a part of a thought, any more than, say, the Sun can, for it is not a sense but an object.

If our supposition that the reference of a sentence is its truth value is correct, the latter must remain unchanged when a part of the sentence is replaced by an expression having the same reference. And this is in fact the case. Leibniz gives the definition: '*Eadem sunt, quae sibi mutuo substitui possunt, salva veritate.*' What else but the truth value could be found, that belongs quite generally to every sentence if the reference of its components is relevant, and remains unchanged by substitutions of the kind in question?

If now the truth value of a sentence is its reference, then on the one hand all true sentences have the same reference and so, on the other hand, do all false sentences. From this we see that in the reference of the sentence all that is specific is obliterated. We can never be concerned only with the reference of a sentence; but again the mere thought alone yields no knowledge, but only the thought together with its reference, i.e. its truth value. Judgments can be regarded as advances from a thought to a truth value. Naturally this cannot be a definition. Judgment is something quite peculiar and incomparable. One might also say that judgments are distinctions of parts within truth values. Such distinction occurs by a return to the thought. To every sense belonging to a truth value there would correspond its own manner of analysis. However, I have here used the word 'part' in a special sense. I have in fact transferred the relation between the parts and the whole of the sentence to its reference, by calling the reference of a word part of the reference of the sentence, if the word itself is a part of the sentence. This way of speaking can certainly be attacked, because the whole reference and one part of it do not

suffice to determine the remainder, and because the word 'part' is already used in another sense of bodies. A special term would need to be invented.

The supposition that the truth value of a sentence is its reference shall now be put to further test. We have found that the truth value of a sentence remains unchanged when an expression is replaced by another having the same reference; but we have not yet considered the case in which the expression to be replaced is itself a sentence. Now if our view is correct, the truth value of a sentence containing another as part must remain unchanged when the part is replaced by another sentence having the same truth value. Exceptions are to be expected when the whole sentence or its part is direct or indirect quotation; for in such cases, as we have seen, the words do not have their customary reference. In direct quotation, a sentence designates another sentence, and in indirect quotation a thought.

We are thus led to consider subordinate sentences or clauses. These occur as parts of a sentence complex, which is, from the logical standpoint, likewise a sentence – a main sentence. But here we meet the question whether it is also true of the subordinate sentence that its reference is a truth value. Of indirect quotation we already know the opposite. Grammarians view subordinate clauses as representatives of parts of sentences and divide them accordingly into noun clauses, adjective clauses, adverbial clauses. This might generate the supposition that the reference of a subordinate clause was not a truth value but rather of the same kind as the reference of a noun or adjective or adverb – in short, of a part of a sentence, whose sense was not a thought but only a part of a thought. Only a more thorough investigation can clarify the issue. In so doing, we shall not follow the grammatical categories strictly, but rather group together what is logically of the same kind. Let us first search for cases in which the sense of the subordinate clause, as we have just supposed, is not an independent thought.

The case of an abstract noun clause, introduced by 'that,' includes the case of indirect quotation, in which we have seen the words to have their indirect reference coinciding with what is customarily their sense. In this case, then, the subordinate clause has for its reference a thought, not a truth value; as sense not a thought, but the sense of the words 'the thought, that . . . ,' which is only a part of the thought in the entire complex sentence. This happens after 'say,' 'hear,' 'be of the opinion,' 'be convinced,' 'conclude,' and similar words.[8] There is a different, and indeed somewhat complicated, situation after words like 'perceive,' 'know,' 'fancy,' which are to be considered later.

That in the cases of the first kind the reference of the subordinate clause is in fact the thought can also be recognized by seeing that it is indifferent to the truth of the whole whether the subordinate clause is true or false. Let us compare, for instance, the two sentences 'Copernicus believed that the planetary orbits are circles' and 'Copernicus believed that the apparent motion of the Sun is produced by the real motion of the Earth.' One subordinate clause can be substituted for the other without harm to the truth. The main clause and the subordinate clause together have as their sense only a single thought, and the truth of the whole includes neither the truth nor the untruth of the subordinate clause. In such cases it is not permissible to replace one expression in the subordinate clause by another having the same customary reference, but only by one having the same indirect reference, i.e. the same customary sense. If somebody were to conclude: The reference of a sentence is not its truth value, for in that case it could always be replaced by another sentence of the same truth value; he would prove too much; one might just as well claim that the reference of 'morning star' is not Venus, since one may not always say 'Venus' in place of 'morning star.' One has the right to conclude only that the reference of a sentence is not *always* its truth value, and that 'morning star' does not always stand for the planet Venus, viz. when the word has its indirect reference. An exception of such a kind occurs in the subordinate clause just considered which has a thought as its reference.

If one says 'It seems that . . .' one means 'It seems to me that . . .' or 'I think that . . .' We therefore have the same case again. The situation is similar in the case of expressions such as 'to be pleased,' 'to regret,' 'to approve,' 'to blame,' 'to hope,' 'to fear.' If, toward the end of the battle of Waterloo, Wellington was glad that the Prussians were coming, the basis for his joy was a conviction. Had he been deceived, he would have been no less pleased so long as his illusion lasted; and before he became so convinced he could not have been pleased that the Prussians were coming – even though in fact they might have been already approaching.

Just as a conviction or a belief is the ground of a feeling, it can, as in inference, also be the ground of a conviction. In the sentence: 'Columbus inferred from the roundness of the Earth that he could reach India by travelling towards the west,' we have as the reference of the parts two thoughts, that the Earth is round, and that Columbus by travelling to the west could reach India. All that is relevant here is that Columbus was convinced of both, and that the one conviction was a ground for the other. Whether the Earth is really round and Columbus could really reach India by travelling west, as he thought, is immaterial to the truth of our sentence; but it is not immaterial whether we replace 'the Earth' by 'the planet which is accompanied by a moon whose diameter is greater than the fourth part of its own.' Here also we have the indirect reference of the words.

Adverbial final clauses beginning 'in order that' also belong here; for obviously the purpose is a thought; therefore: indirect reference for the words, subjunctive mood.

A subordinate clause with 'that' after 'command,' 'ask,' 'forbid,' would appear in direct speech as an imperative. Such a clause has no reference but only a sense. A command, a request, are indeed not thoughts, yet they stand on the same level as thoughts. Hence in subordinate clauses depending upon 'command,' 'ask,' etc., words have their indirect reference. The reference of such a clause is therefore not a truth value but a command, a request, and so forth.

The case is similar for the dependent question in phrases such as 'doubt whether,' 'not to know what.' It is easy to see that here also the words are to be taken to have their indirect reference. Dependent clauses expressing questions and beginning with 'who,' 'what,' 'where,' 'when,' 'how,' 'by what means,' etc., seem at times to approximate very closely to adverbial clauses in which words have their customary references. These cases are distinguished linguistically [in German] by the mood of the verb. With the subjunctive, we have a dependent question and indirect reference of the words, so that a proper name cannot in general be replaced by another name of the same object.

In the cases so far considered the words of the subordinate clauses had their indirect reference, and this made it clear that the reference of the subordinate clause itself was indirect, i.e. not a truth value but a thought, a command, a request, a question. The subordinate clause could be regarded as a noun, indeed one could say: as a proper name of that thought, that command, etc., which it represented in the context of the sentence structure.

We now come to other subordinate clauses, in which the words do have their customary reference without however a thought occurring as sense and a truth value as reference. How this is possible is best made clear by examples.

> Whoever discovered the elliptic form of the planetary orbits died in misery.

If the sense of the subordinate clause were here a thought, it would have to be possible to express it also in a separate sentence. But this does not work, because the grammatical subject 'whoever' has no independent sense and only mediates the relation with the consequent clause 'died in misery.' For this reason the sense of the subordinate clause is not a complete thought, and its reference is Kepler, not a truth value. One might object that the sense of the whole does contain a thought as part, viz. that there was somebody who first discovered the elliptic form of the planetary orbits; for whoever takes the whole to be true cannot deny this part. This is undoubtedly so; but only because otherwise the dependent clause 'whoever discovered the elliptic form of the planetary orbits' would have no reference. If anything is asserted there is always an obvious presupposition that the simple or compound proper names used have reference. If one therefore asserts 'Kepler died in misery,' there is a presupposition that the name 'Kepler' designates something; but it does not follow that the sense of the sentence 'Kepler died in misery' contains the thought that the name 'Kepler' designates something. If this were the case the negation would have to run not

> Kepler did not die in misery

but

> Kepler did not die in misery, or the name 'Kepler' has no reference.

That the name 'Kepler' designates something is just as much a presupposition for the assertion

> Kepler died in misery

as for the contrary assertion. Now languages have the fault of containing expressions which fail to designate an object (although their grammatical form seems to qualify them for that purpose) because the truth of some sentence is a prerequisite. Thus it depends on the truth of the sentence:

> There was someone who discovered the elliptic form of the planetary orbits

whether the subordinate clause

> Whoever discovered the elliptic form of the planetary orbits

really designates an object or only seems to do so while having in fact no reference. And thus it may appear as if our subordinate clause contained as a part of its sense the thought that there was somebody who discovered the elliptic form of the planetary orbits. If this were right the negation would run:

> Either whoever discovered the elliptic form of the planetary orbits did not die in misery or there was nobody who discovered the elliptic form of the planetary orbits.

This arises from an imperfection of language, from which even the symbolic language of mathematical analysis is not altogether free; even there combinations of symbols can occur that seem to stand for something but have (at least so far) no reference, e.g. divergent infinite series. This can be avoided, e.g., by means of the special stipulation that divergent infinite series shall stand for the number 0. A logically perfect language (*Begriffsschrift*) should satisfy the conditions, that every expression grammatically well constructed as a proper name out of signs already introduced shall in fact designate an object, and that no new sign shall be introduced as a proper name without being secured a reference. The logic books contain warnings against logical mistakes arising from the ambiguity of expressions. I regard as no less pertinent a warning against apparent proper names having no reference. The history of mathematics supplies errors which have arisen in this way. This lends itself to demagogic abuse as easily as ambiguity – perhaps more easily. 'The will of the people' can serve as an example; for it is easy to establish that there is at any rate no generally accepted reference for this expression. It is therefore by no means unimportant to eliminate the source of these mistakes, at least in science, once and for all. Then such objections as the one discussed above would become impossible, because it could never depend upon the truth of a thought whether a proper name had a reference.

With the consideration of these noun clauses may be coupled that of types of adjective and adverbial clauses which are logically in close relation to them.

Adjective clauses also serve to construct compound proper names, though, unlike noun clauses, they are not sufficient by themselves for this purpose. These adjective clauses are to be regarded as equivalent to adjectives. Instead of 'the square root of 4 which is smaller than 0,' one can also say 'the negative square root of 4.' We have here the case of a compound proper name constructed from the expression for a concept with the help of the singular definite article. This is at any rate permissible if the concept applies to one and only one single object.[9]

Expressions for concepts can be so constructed that marks of a concept are given by adjective clauses as, in our example, by the clause 'which is smaller than 0.' It is evident that such an adjective clause cannot have a thought as sense or a truth value as reference, any more than the noun clause could. Its sense, which can also be expressed in many cases by a single adjective, is only a part of a thought. Here, as in the case of the noun clause, there is no independent subject and therefore no possibility of reproducing the sense of the subordinate clause in an independent sentence.

Places, instants, stretches of time, are, logically considered, objects; hence the linguistic designation of a definite place, a definite instant, or a stretch of time is to be regarded as a proper name. Now adverbial clauses of place and time can be used for the construction of such a proper name in a manner similar to that which we have seen in the case of noun and adjective clauses. In the same way, expressions for concepts bringing in places, etc., can be constructed. It is to be noted here also that the sense of these subordinate clauses cannot be reproduced in an independent sentence, since an essential component, viz. the determination of place or time, is missing and is only indicated by a relative pronoun or a conjunction.[10]

In conditional clauses, also, there may usually be recognized to occur an indefinite indicator, having a similar correlate in the dependent clause. (We have already seen this occur in noun, adjective, and adverbial clauses.) In so far as each indicator refers to the other, both clauses together form a connected whole, which as a rule expresses only a single thought. In the sentence

If a number is less than 1 and greater than 0, its square is less than 1 and greater than 0

the component in question is 'a number' in the conditional clause and 'its' in the dependent clause. It is by means of this very indefiniteness that the sense acquires the generality expected of a law. It is this which is responsible for the fact that the antecedent clause alone has no complete thought as its sense and in combination with the consequent clause expresses one and only one thought, whose parts are no longer thoughts. It is, in general, incorrect to say that in the hypothetical judgment two judgments are put in reciprocal relationship. If this or something similar is said, the word 'judgment' is used in the same sense as I have connected with the word 'thought,' so that I would use the formulation: 'A hypothetical thought establishes a reciprocal relationship between two thoughts.' This could be true only if an indefinite indicator is absent;[11] but in such a case there would also be no generality.

If an instant of time is to be indefinitely indicated in both conditional and dependent clauses, this is often achieved merely by using the present tense of the verb, which in such a case however does not indicate the temporal present. This grammatical form is then the indefinite indicator in the main and subordinate clauses. An example of this is: 'When the Sun is in the tropic of Cancer, the longest day in the northern hemisphere occurs.' Here, also, it is impossible to express the sense of the subordinate clause in a full sentence, because this sense is not a complete thought. If we say: 'The Sun is in the tropic of Cancer,' this would refer to our present time and thereby change the sense. Just as little is the sense of the main clause a thought; only the whole, composed of main and subordinate clauses, has such a sense. It may be added that several common components in the antecedent and consequent clauses may be indefinitely indicated.

It is clear that noun clauses with 'who' or 'what' and adverbial clauses with 'where,' 'when,' 'wherever,' 'whenever' are often to be interpreted as having the sense of conditional clauses, e.g. 'who touches pitch, defiles himself.'

Adjective clauses can also take the place of conditional clauses. Thus the sense of the sentence previously used can be given in the form 'The square of a number which is less than 1 and greater than 0 is less than 1 and greater than 0.'

The situation is quite different if the common component of the two clauses is designated by a proper name. In the sentence:

Napoleon, who recognized the danger to his right flank, himself led his guards against the enemy position

two thoughts are expressed:

1 Napoleon recognized the danger to his right flank.
2 Napoleon himself led his guards against the enemy position.

When and where this happened is to be fixed only by the context, but is nevertheless to be taken as definitely determined thereby. If the entire sentence is uttered as an assertion, we thereby simultaneously assert both component sentences. If one of the parts is false, the whole is false. Here we have the case that the subordinate clause by itself has a complete thought as sense (if we complete it by indication of place and time). The reference of the subordinate clause is accordingly a truth value. We can therefore expect that it may be replaced, without harm to the truth value of the whole, by a sentence having the same truth value. This is indeed the case; but it is to be noticed that for purely grammatical reasons, its subject must be 'Napoleon,' for only then can it be brought into the form of an adjective clause belonging to 'Napoleon.' But if the demand that it be expressed in this form be waived, and the connexion be shown by 'and,' this restriction disappears.

Subsidiary clauses beginning with 'although' also express complete thoughts. This conjunction actually has no sense and does not change the sense of the clause but only illuminates it in a peculiar fashion.[12] We could indeed replace the concessive clause without harm to the truth of the whole by another of the same truth value; but the light in which the clause is placed by the conjunction might then easily appear unsuitable,

as if a song with a sad subject were to be sung in a lively fashion.

In the last cases the truth of the whole included the truth of the component clauses. The case is different if a conditional clause expresses a complete thought by containing, in place of an indefinite indicator, a proper name or something which is to be regarded as equivalent. In the sentence

If the Sun has already risen, the sky is very cloudy

the time is the present, that is to say, definite. And the place is also to be thought of as definite. Here it can be said that a relation between the truth values of conditional and dependent clauses has been asserted, viz. such that the case does not occur in which the antecedent stands for the True and the consequent for the False. Accordingly, our sentence is true if the Sun has not yet risen, whether the sky is very cloudy or not, and also if the Sun has risen and the sky is very cloudy. Since only truth values are here in question, each component clause can be replaced by another of the same truth value without changing the truth value of the whole. To be sure, the light in which the subject then appears would usually be unsuitable; the thought might easily seem distorted; but this has nothing to do with its truth value. One must always take care not to clash with the subsidiary thoughts, which are however not explicitly expressed and therefore should not be reckoned in the sense. Hence, also, no account need be taken of their truth values.[13]

The simple cases have now been discussed. Let us review what we have learned.

The subordinate clause usually has for its sense not a thought, but only a part of one, and consequently no truth value as reference. The reason for this is either that the words in the subordinate clause have indirect reference, so that the reference, not the sense, of the subordinate clause is a thought; or else that, on account of the presence of an indefinite indicator, the subordinate clause is incomplete and expresses a thought only when combined with the main clause. It may happen, however, that the sense of the subsidiary clause is a complete thought, in which case it can be replaced by another of the same truth value without harm to the truth of the whole – provided there are no grammatical obstacles.

Gottlob Frege

An examination of all the subordinate clauses which one may encounter will soon provide some which do not fit well into these categories. The reason, so far as I can see, is that these subordinate clauses have no such simple sense. Almost always, it seems, we connect with the main thoughts expressed by us subsidiary thoughts which, although not expressed, are associated with our words, in accordance with psychological laws, by the hearer. And since the subsidiary thought appears to be connected with our words of its own accord, almost like the main thought itself, we want it also to be expressed. The sense of the sentence is thereby enriched, and it may well happen that we have more simple thoughts than clauses. In many cases the sentence must be understood in this way, in others it may be doubtful whether the subsidiary thought belongs to the sense of the sentence or only accompanies it.[14] One might perhaps find that the sentence

Napoleon, who recognized the danger to his right flank, himself led his guards against the enemy position

expresses not only the two thoughts shown above, but also the thought that the knowledge of the danger was the reason why he led the guards against the enemy position. One may in fact doubt whether this thought is merely slightly suggested or really expressed. Let the question be considered whether our sentence be false if Napoleon's decision had already been made before he recognized the danger. If our sentence could be true in spite of this, the subsidiary thought should not be understood as part of the sense. One would probably decide in favour of this. The alternative would make for a quite complicated situation: We would have more simple thoughts than clauses. If the sentence

Napoleon recognized the danger to his right flank

were now to be replaced by another having the same truth value, e.g.

Napoleon was already more than 45 years old

not only would our first thought be changed, but also our third one. Hence the truth value of the latter might change – viz. if his age was not the reason for the decision to lead the guards against

the enemy. This shows why clauses of equal truth value cannot always be substituted for one another in such cases. The clause expresses more through its connexion with another than it does in isolation.

Let us now consider cases where this regularly happens. In the sentence:

Bebel fancies that the return of Alsace-Lorraine would appease France's desire for revenge

two thoughts are expressed, which are not however shown by means of antecedent and consequent clauses, viz.:

1 Bebel believes that the return of Alsace-Lorraine would appease France's desire for revenge
2 the return of Alsace-Lorraine would not appease France's desire for revenge.

In the expression of the first thought, the words of the subordinate clause have their indirect reference, while the same words have their customary reference in the expression of the second thought. This shows that the subordinate clause in our original complex sentence is to be taken twice over, with different reference, standing once for a thought, once for a truth value. Since the truth value is not the whole reference of the subordinate clause, we cannot simply replace the latter by another of equal truth value. Similar considerations apply to expressions such as 'know,' 'discover,' 'it is known that.'

By means of a subordinate causal clause and the associated main clause we express several thoughts, which however do not correspond separately to the original clauses. In the sentence: 'Because ice is less dense than water, it floats on water' we have

1 Ice is less dense than water;
2 If anything is less dense than water, it floats on water;
3 Ice floats on water.

The third thought, however, need not be explicitly introduced, since it is contained in the remaining two. On the other hand, neither the first and third nor the second and third combined would furnish the sense of our sentence. It can now be seen that our subordinate clause because ice is less dense than water

expresses our first thought, as well as a part of our second. This is how it comes to pass that our subsidiary clause cannot be simply replaced by another of equal truth value; for this would alter our second thought and thereby might well alter its truth value.

The situation is similar in the sentence

If iron were less dense than water, it would float on water.

Here we have the two thoughts that iron is not less dense than water, and that something floats on water if it is less dense than water. The subsidiary clause again expresses one thought and a part of the other.

If we interpret the sentence already considered

After Schleswig-Holstein was separated from Denmark, Prussia and Austria quarrelled

in such a way that it expresses the thought that Schleswig-Holstein was once separated from Denmark, we have first this thought, and secondly the thought that at a time, more closely determined by the subordinate clause, Prussia and Austria quarrelled. Here also the subordinate clause expresses not only one thought but also a part of another. Therefore it may not in general be replaced by another of the same truth value.

It is hard to exhaust all the possibilities given by language; but I hope to have brought to light at least the essential reasons why a subordinate clause may not always be replaced by another of equal truth value without harm to the truth of the whole sentence structure. These reasons arise:

1   when the subordinate clause does not stand for a truth value, inasmuch as it expresses only a part of a thought;

2   when the subordinate clause does stand for a truth value but is not restricted to so doing, inasmuch as its sense includes one thought and part of another.

The first case arises:

(a)   in indirect reference of words
(b)   if a part of the sentence is only an indefinite indicator instead of a proper name.

In the second case, the subsidiary clause may have to be taken twice over, viz. once in its customary reference, and the other time in indirect reference; or the sense of a part of the subordinate clause may likewise be a component of another thought, which, taken together with the thought directly expressed by the subordinate clause, makes up the sense of the whole sentence.

It follows with sufficient probability from the foregoing that the cases where a subordinate clause is not replaceable by another of the same value cannot be brought in disproof of our view that a truth value is the reference of a sentence having a thought as its sense.

Let us return to our starting point.

When we found '$a = a$' and '$a = b$' to have different cognitive values, the explanation is that for the purpose of knowledge, the sense of the sentence, viz., the thought expressed by it, is no less relevant than its reference, i.e. its truth value. If now $a = b$, then indeed the reference of 'b' is the same as that of 'a,' and hence the truth value of '$a = b$' is the same as that of '$a = a$.' In spite of this, the sense of 'b' may differ from that of 'a', and thereby the thought expressed in '$a = b$' differs from that of '$a = a$.' In that case the two sentences do not have the same cognitive value. If we understand by 'judgment' the advance from the thought to its truth value, as in the above paper, we can also say that the judgments are different.

Notes

1   I use this word in the sense of identity and understand '$a = b$' to have the sense of 'a is the same as b' or 'a and b coincide.'

2   In the case of an actual proper name such as 'Aristotle' opinions as to the sense may differ. It might, for instance, be taken to be the following: the pupil of Plato and teacher of Alexander the Great. Anybody who does this will attach another sense to the sentence 'Aristotle was born in Stagira' than will a man who takes as the sense of the name: the teacher of Alexander the Great who was born in Stagira. So long as the reference remains the same, such variations of sense may be tolerated, although they are to be avoided in the theoretical structure of a demonstrative science and ought not to occur in a perfect language.

3 We can include with ideas the direct experiences in which sense-impressions and acts themselves take the place of the traces which they have left in the mind. The distinction is unimportant for our purpose, especially since memories of sense-impressions and acts always go along with such impressions and acts themselves to complete the perceptual image. One may on the other hand understand direct experience as including any object, in so far as it is sensibly perceptible or spatial.

4 Hence it is inadvisable to use the word 'idea' to designate something so basically different.

5 By a thought I understand not the subjective performance of thinking but its objective content, which is capable of being the common property of several thinkers.

6 It would be desirable to have a special term for signs having only sense. If we name them, say, representations, the words of the actors on the stage would be representations; indeed the actor himself would be a representation.

7 A judgment, for me, is not the mere comprehension of a thought, but the admission of its truth.

8 In 'A lied in saying he had seen B,' the subordinate clause designates a thought which is said (1) to have been asserted by A (2) while A was convinced of its falsity.

9 In accordance with what was said above, an expression of the kind in question must actually always be assured of reference, by means of a special stipulation, e.g. by the convention that 0 shall count as its reference, when the concept applies to no object or to more than one.

10 In the case of these sentences, various interpretations are easily possible. The sense of the sentence, 'After Schleswig-Holstein was separated from Denmark, Prussia and Austria quarrelled' can also be rendered in the form 'After the separation of Schleswig-Holstein from Denmark, Prussia and Austria quarrelled.' In this version, it is surely sufficiently clear that the sense is not to be taken as having as a part the thought that Schleswig-Holstein was once separated from Denmark, but that this is the necessary presupposition in order for the expression 'after the separation of Schleswig-Holstein from Denmark' to have any reference at all. To be sure, our sentence can also be interpreted as saying that Schleswig-Holstein was once separated from Denmark. We then have a case which is to be considered later. In order to understand the difference more clearly, let us project ourselves into the mind of a Chinese who, having little knowledge of European history, believes it to be false that Schleswig-Holstein was ever separated from Denmark. He will take our sentence, in the first version, to be neither true nor false but will deny it to have any reference, on the ground of absence of reference for its subordinate clause. This clause would only apparently determine a time. If he interpreted our sentence in the second way, however, he would find a thought expressed in it which he would take to be false, beside a part which would be without reference for him.

11 At times an explicit linguistic indication is missing and must be read off from the entire context.

12 Similarly in the case of 'but,' 'yet.'

13 The thought of our sentence might also be expressed thus: 'Either the Sun has not risen yet or the sky is very cloudy' – which shows how this kind of sentence connexion is to be understood.

14 This may be important for the question whether an assertion is a lie, or an oath a perjury.

2

Thought

Gottlob Frege

Just as 'beautiful' points the way for aesthetics and 'good' for ethics, so do words like 'true' for logic. All sciences have truth as their goal; but logic is also concerned with it in a quite different way: logic has much the same relation to truth as physics has to weight or heat. To discover truths is the task of all sciences; it falls to logic to discern the laws of truth. The word 'law' is used in two senses. When we speak of moral or civil laws we mean [*meinen*] prescriptions, which ought to be obeyed but with which actual occurrences are not always in conformity. Laws of nature are general features of what happens in nature, and occurrences in nature are always in accordance with them. It is rather in this sense that I speak of laws of truth. Here of course it is not a matter of what happens but of what is. From the laws of truth there follow prescriptions about asserting, thinking, judging, inferring. And we may very well speak of laws of thought in this way too. But there is at once a danger here of confusing different things. People may very well interpret the expression 'law of thought' by analogy with 'law of nature' and then have in mind general features of thinking as a mental occurrence. A law of thought in this sense would be a psychological law. And so they might come to believe that logic deals with the mental process of thinking and with the psychological laws in accordance with which this takes

This translation originally published in *Frege's Writings*, ed. Michael Beaney (Blackwell Publishers, Oxford, 1997).

place. That would be misunderstanding the task of logic, for truth has not here been given its proper place. Error and superstition have causes just as much as correct cognition. Whether what you take for true is false or true, your so taking it comes about in accordance with psychological laws. A derivation from these laws, an explanation of a mental process that ends in taking something to be true, can never take the place of proving what is taken to be true. But may not logical laws also have played a part in this mental process? I do not want to dispute this, but if it is a question of truth this possibility is not enough. For it is also possible that something non-logical played a part in the process and made it swerve from the truth. We can decide only after we have come to know the laws of truth; but then we can probably do without the derivation and explanation of the mental process, if our concern is to decide whether the process terminates in *justifiably* taking something to be true. In order to avoid any misunderstanding and prevent the blurring of the boundary between psychology and logic, I assign to logic the task of discovering the laws of truth, not the laws of taking things to be true or of thinking. The *Bedeutung* of the word 'true' is spelled out in the laws of truth.

But first I shall attempt to outline roughly how I want to use 'true' ['*wahr*'] in this connection, so as to exclude irrelevant uses of the word. 'True' is not to be used here in the sense of 'genuine' ['*wahrhaftig*'] or 'veracious' ['*wahrheitsliebend*']; nor yet in the way it sometimes occurs in discussion of artistic questions, when, for example, people speak of truth in art, when truth is set up as the aim of art, when the truth of a work of art of true feeling is spoken of. Again, the word 'true' is prefixed to another word in order to show that the word is to be understood in its proper, unadulterated sense. This use too lies off the path followed here. What I have in mind is that sort of truth which it is the aim of science to discern.

Grammatically, the word 'true' looks like a word for a property. So we want to delimit more closely the region within which truth can be predicated, the region in which there is any question of truth. We find truth predicated of pictures, ideas, sentences, and thoughts. It is striking that visible and audible things turn up here along with things which cannot be perceived with the senses. This suggests that alterations in sense [*Verschiebungen des Sinnes*] have taken place. So indeed they have! Is a picture considered as a mere visible and tangible thing really true, and a stone or a leaf not true? Obviously we could not call a picture true unless there were an intention involved. A picture is meant to represent something. (Even an idea is not called true in itself, but only with respect to an intention that the idea should correspond to something.) It might be supposed from this that truth consists in a correspondence of a picture to what it depicts. Now a correspondence is a relation. But this goes against the use of the word 'true', which is not a relative term and contains no indication of anything else to which something is to correspond. If I do not know that a picture is meant to represent Cologne Cathedral then I do not know what to compare the picture with in order to decide on its truth. A correspondence, moreover, can only be perfect if the corresponding things coincide and so just are not different things. It is supposed to be possible to test the genuineness of a banknote by comparing it stereoscopically with a genuine one. But it would be ridiculous to try to compare a gold piece stereoscopically with a twenty-mark note. It would only be possible to compare an idea with a thing if the thing were an idea too. And then, if the first did correspond perfectly with the second, they would coincide. But this is not at all what people intend when they define truth as the correspondence of an idea with something real. For in this case it is essential precisely that the reality shall be distinct from the idea. But then there can be no complete correspondence, no complete truth. So nothing at all would be

true; for what is only half true is untrue. Truth does not admit of more or less. But could we not maintain that there is truth when there is correspondence in a certain respect? But which respect? For in that case what ought we to do so as to decide whether something is true? We should have to inquire whether it is *true* that an idea and a reality, say, correspond in the specified respect. And then we should be confronted by a question of the same kind, and the game could begin again. So the attempted explanation of truth as correspondence breaks down. And any other attempt to define truth also breaks down. For in a definition certain characteristics would have to be specified. And in application to any particular case the question would always arise whether it were *true* that the characteristics were present. So we should be going round in a circle. So it seems likely that the content of the word 'true' is *sui generis* and indefinable.

When we ascribe truth to a picture we do not really mean to ascribe a property which would belong to this picture quite independently of other things; we always have in mind some totally different object and we want to say that the picture corresponds in some way to this object. 'My idea corresponds to Cologne Cathedral' is a sentence, and now it is a matter of the truth of this sentence. So what is improperly called the truth of pictures and ideas is reduced to the truth of sentences. What is it that we call a sentence? A series of sounds, but only if it has a sense (which is not to say that *any* series of sounds that has a sense is a sentence). And when we call a sentence true we really mean [*meinen*] that its sense is true. And hence the only thing that raises the question of truth at all is the sense of sentences. Now is the sense of a sentence an idea? In any case, truth does not consist in correspondence of the sense with something else, for otherwise the question of truth would get reiterated to infinity.

Without offering this as a definition, I call a 'thought' something for which the question of truth can arise at all. So I count what is false among thoughts no less than what is true.[1] So I can say: thoughts are senses of sentences, without wishing to assert that the sense of every sentence is a thought. The thought, in itself imperceptible by the senses, gets clothed in the perceptible garb of a sentence, and thereby we are enabled to grasp it. We say a sentence *expresses* a thought.

A thought is something imperceptible: anything the senses can perceive is excluded from the realm of things for which the question of truth arises. Truth is not a quality that answers to a particular kind of sense impressions. So it is sharply distinguished from the qualities we call by the names 'red', 'bitter', 'lilac-smelling'. But do we not see that the Sun has risen? And do we not then also see that this is true? That the Sun has risen is not an object emitting rays that reach my eyes; it is not a visible thing like the Sun itself. That the Sun has risen is recognized to be true on the basis of sense impressions. But being true is not a sensible, perceptible, property. A thing's being magnetic is also recognized on the basis of sense impressions of the thing, although this property does not answer, any more than truth does, to a particular kind of sense impressions. So far these properties agree. However, we do need sense impressions in order to recognize a body as magnetic. On the other hand, when I find it is true that I do not smell anything at this moment, I do not do so on the basis of sense impressions.

All the same it is something worth thinking about that we cannot recognize a property of a thing without at the same time finding the thought *this thing has this property* to be true. So with every property of a thing there is tied up a property of a thought, namely truth. It is also worth noticing that the sentence 'I smell the scent of violets' has just the same content as the sentence 'It is true that I smell the scent of violets'. So it seems, then, that nothing is added to the thought by my ascribing to it the property of truth. And yet is it not a great result when the scientist after much hesitation and laborious researches can finally say 'My conjecture is true'? The *Bedeutung* of the word 'true' seems to be altogether *sui generis*. May we not be dealing here with something which cannot be called a property in the ordinary sense at all? In spite of this doubt I will begin by expressing myself in accordance with ordinary usage, as if truth were a property, until some more appropriate way of speaking is found.

In order to bring out more precisely what I want to call 'thought', I shall distinguish various kinds of sentences.[2] We should not wish to deny sense to a command, but this sense is not such that the question of truth could arise for it. Therefore I shall not call the sense of a command a thought. Sentences expressing wishes or

requests are ruled out in the same way. Only those sentences in which we communicate or assert something come into the question. But here I do not count exclamations in which one vents one's feelings, groans, sighs, laughs – unless it has been decided by some special convention that they are to communicate something. But how about interrogative sentences? In a word-question we utter an incomplete sentence, which is meant to be given a true sense just by means of the completion for which we are asking. Word-questions are accordingly left out of consideration here. Propositional questions are a different matter. We expect to hear 'yes' or 'no'. The answer 'yes' means [*besagt*] the same as an assertoric sentence, for in saying 'yes' the speaker presents as true the thought that was already completely contained in the interrogative sentence. This is how a propositional question can be formed from any assertoric sentence. And this is why an exclamation cannot be regarded as a communication: no corresponding propositional question can be formed. An interrogative sentence and an assertoric one contain the same thought; but the assertoric sentence contains something else as well, namely assertion. The interrogative sentence contains something more too, namely a request. Therefore two things must be distinguished in an assertoric sentence: the content, which it has in common with the corresponding propositional question; and assertion. The former is the thought or at least contains the thought. So it is possible to express a thought without laying it down as true. The two things are so closely joined in an assertoric sentence that it is easy to overlook their separability. Consequently we distinguish:

1 the grasp of a thought – thinking,
2 the acknowledgement of the truth of a thought – the act of judgement,[3]
3 the manifestation of this judgement – assertion.

We have already performed the first act when we form a propositional question. An advance in science usually takes place in this way: first a thought is grasped, and thus may perhaps be expressed in a propositional question; after appropriate investigations, this thought is finally recognized to be true. We express acknowledgement of truth in the form of an assertoric sentence. We do not need the word 'true' for this. And even when we do use it the properly assertoric force does not lie in it, but in the assertoric sentence-form; and where this form loses its assertoric force the word 'true' cannot put it back again. This happens when we are not speaking seriously. As stage thunder is only sham thunder and a stage fight only a sham fight, so stage assertion is only sham assertion. It is only acting, only fiction. When playing his part the actor is not asserting anything; nor is he lying, even if he says something of whose falsehood he is convinced. In poetry we have the case of thoughts being expressed without being actually put forward as true, in spite of the assertoric form of the sentence; although the poem may suggest to the hearer that he himself should make an assenting judgement. Therefore the question still arises, even about what is presented in the assertoric sentence-form, whether it really contains an assertion. And this question must be answered in the negative if the requisite seriousness is lacking. It is unimportant whether the word 'true' is used here. This explains why it is that nothing seems to be added to a thought by attributing to it the property of truth.

An assertoric sentence often contains, over and above a thought and assertion, a third component not covered by the assertion. This is often meant to act on the feelings and mood of the hearer, or to arouse his imagination. Words like 'regrettably' ['*leider*'] and 'fortunately' ['*gottlob*'] belong here. Such constitutents of sentences are more strongly prominent in poetry, but are seldom wholly absent from prose. They occur more rarely in mathematical, physical, or chemical expositions than in historical ones. What are called the humanities are closer to poetry, and are therefore less scientific, than the exact sciences, which are drier in proportion to being more exact; for exact science is directed toward truth and truth alone. Therefore all constitutents of sentences not covered by the assertoric force do not belong to scientific exposition; but they are sometimes hard to avoid, even for one who sees the danger connected with them. Where the main thing is to approach by way of intimation what cannot be conceptually grasped, these constitutents are fully justified. The more rigorously scientific an exposition is, the less the nationality of its author will be discernible and the easier it will be to translate. On the other hand, the constitutents of language to which I here want to call attention make the translation of poetry very difficult, indeed make

perfect translation almost always impossible, for it is just in what largely makes the poetic value that languages most differ.

It makes no difference to the thought whether I use the word 'horse' or 'steed' or 'nag' or 'prad'. The assertoric force does not cover the ways in which these words differ. What is called mood, atmosphere, illumination in a poem, what is portrayed by intonation and rhythm, does not belong to the thought.

Much in language serves to aid the hearer's understanding, for instance emphasizing part of a sentence by stress or word order. Here let us bear in mind words like 'still' and 'already'. Somebody using the sentence 'Alfred has still not come' actually says 'Alfred has not come', and at the same time hints – but only hints – that Alfred's arrival is expected. Nobody can say: Since Alfred's arrival is not expected, the sense of the sentence is false. The way that 'but' differs from 'and' is that we use it to intimate that what follows it contrasts with what was to be expected from what preceded it. Such conversational suggestions make no difference to the thought. A sentence can be transformed by changing the verb from active to passive and at the same time making the accusative into the subject. In the same way we may change the dative into the nominative and at the same time replace 'give' by 'receive'. Naturally such transformations are not trivial in every respect; but they do not touch the thought, they do not touch what is true or false. If the inadmissibility of such transformations were recognized as a principle, then any profound logical investigation would be hindered. It is just as important to ignore distinctions that do not touch the heart of the matter, as to make distinctions which concern essentials. But what is essential depends on one's purpose. To a mind concerned with the beauties of language, what is trivial to the logician may seem to be just what is important.

Thus the content of a sentence often goes beyond the thought expressed by it. But the opposite often happens too; the mere wording, which can be made permanent by writing or the gramophone, does not suffice for the expression of the thought. The present tense is used in two ways: first, in order to indicate a time; second, in order to eliminate any temporal restriction, where timelessness or eternity is part of the thought – consider for instance the laws of mathematics. Which of the two cases occurs is not expressed but must be divined. If a time-indication is conveyed by the present tense one must know when the sentence was uttered in order to grasp the thought correctly. Therefore the time of utterance is part of the expression of the thought. If someone wants to say today what he expressed yesterday using the word 'today', he will replace this word with 'yesterday'. Although the thought is the same its verbal expression must be different in order that the change of sense which would otherwise be effected by the differing times of utterance may be cancelled out. The case is the same with words like 'here' and 'there'. In all such cases the mere wording, as it can be preserved in writing, is not the complete expression of the thought; the knowledge of certain conditions accompanying the utterance, which are used as means of expressing the thought, is needed for us to grasp the thought correctly. Pointing the finger, hand gestures, glances may belong here too. The same utterance containing the word 'I' in the mouths of different men will express different thoughts of which some may be true, others false.

The occurrence of the word 'I' in a sentence gives rise to some further questions.

Consider the following case. Dr Gustav Lauben says, 'I was wounded'. Leo Peter hears this and remarks some days later, 'Dr Gustav Lauben was wounded'. Does this sentence express the same thought as the one Dr Lauben uttered himself? Suppose that Rudolph Lingens was present when Dr Lauben spoke and now hears what is related by Leo Peter. If the same thought was uttered by Dr Lauben and Leo Peter, then Rudolph Lingens, who is fully master of the language and remembers what Dr Lauben said in his presence, must now know at once from Leo Peter's report that he is speaking of the same thing. But knowledge of the language is a special thing when proper names are involved. It may well be the case that only a few people associate a definite thought with the sentence 'Dr Lauben was wounded'. For complete understanding one needs in this case to know the expression 'Dr Gustav Lauben'. Now if both Leo Peter and Rudolph Lingens understand by 'Dr Gustav Lauben' the doctor who is the only doctor living in a house known to both of them, then they both understand the sentence 'Dr Gustav Lauben was wounded' in the same way; they associate the same thought with it. But it is also possible that Rudolph Lingens does not know Dr Lauben

personally and does not know that it was Dr Lauben who recently said 'I was wounded'. In this case Rudolph Lingens cannot know that the same affair is in question. I say, therefore, in this case: the thought which Leo Peter expresses is not the same as that which Dr Lauben uttered.

Suppose further that Herbert Garner knows that Dr Gustav Lauben was born on 13 September 1875 in N.N. and this is not true of anyone else; suppose, however, that he does not know where Dr Lauben now lives nor indeed anything else about him. On the other had, suppose Leo Peter does not know that Dr Lauben was born on 13 September 1875 in N.N. Then as far as the proper name 'Dr Gustav Lauben' is concerned, Herbert Garner and Leo Peter do not speak the same language, although they do in fact designate the same man with this name; for they do not know that they are doing so. Therefore Herbert Garner does not associate the same thought with the sentence 'Dr Gustav Lauben was wounded' as Leo Peter wants to express with it. To avoid the awkwardness that Herbert Garner and Leo Peter are not speaking the same language, I shall suppose that Leo Peter uses the proper name 'Dr Lauben' and Herbert Garner uses the proper name 'Gustav Lauben'. Then it is possible that Herbert Garner takes the sense of the sentence 'Dr Lauben was wounded' to be true but is misled by false information into taking the sense of the sentence 'Gustav Lauben was wounded' to be false. So given our assumptions these thoughts are different.

Accordingly, with a proper name, it is a matter of the way that the object so designated is presented. This may happen in different ways, and to every such way there corresponds a special sense of a sentence containing the proper name. The different thoughts thus obtained from the same sentences correspond in truth-value, of course; that is to say, if one is true then all are true, and if one is false then all are false. Nevertheless the difference must be recognized. So we must really stipulate that for every proper name there shall be just one associated manner of presentation of the object so designated. It is often unimportant that this stipulation should be fulfilled, but not always.

Now everyone is presented to himself in a special and primitive way, in which he is presented to no one else. So, when Dr Lauben has the thought that he was wounded, he will probably be basing it on this primitive way in which he is presented to himself. And only Dr Lauben himself can grasp thoughts specified in this way. But now he may want to communicate with others. He cannot communicate a thought he alone can grasp. Therefore, if he now says 'I was wounded', he must use 'I' in a sense which can be grasped by others, perhaps in the sense of 'he who is speaking to you at this moment'; by doing this he makes the conditions accompanying his utterance serve towards the expression of a thought.[4]

Yet there is a doubt. Is it at all the same thought which first this and then that man expresses?

A man who is still unaffected by philosophy first of all gets to know things he can see and touch, can in short perceive with the senses, such as trees, stones and houses, and he is convinced that someone else can equally see and touch the same tree and the same stone as he himself sees and touches. Obviously a thought does not belong with these things. Now can it, nevertheless, like a tree be presented to people as the same?

Even an unphilosophical man soon finds it necessary to recognize an inner world distinct from the outer world, a world of sense impressions, of creations of his imagination, of sensations, of feelings and moods, a world of inclinations, wishes and decisions. For brevity's sake I want to use the word 'idea' ['Vorstellung'] to cover all these occurrences, except decisions.

Now do thoughts belong to this inner world? Are they ideas? They are obviously not decisions.

How are ideas distinct from the things of the outer world?

First: ideas cannot be seen, or touched, or smelled, or tasted, or heard.

I go for a walk with a companion. I see a green field, I thus have a visual impression of the green. I have it, but I do not see it.

Secondly: ideas are something we have. We have sensations, feelings, moods, inclinations, wishes. An idea that someone has belongs to the content of his consciousness.

The field and the frogs in it, the Sun which shines on them, are there no matter whether I look at them or not, but the sense impression I have of green exists only because of me, I am its owner. It seems absurd to us that a pain, a mood, a wish should go around the world without an owner, independently. A sensation is impossible without a sentient being. The inner world presupposes somebody whose inner world it is.

Thirdly: ideas need an owner. Things of the outer world are on the contrary independent.

My companion and I are convinced that we both see the same field; but each of us has a particular sense impression of green. I glimpse a strawberry among the green strawberry leaves. My companion cannot find it, he is colour-blind. The colour impression he gets from the strawberry is not noticeably different from the one he gets from the leaf. Now does my companion see the green leaf as red, or does he see the red berry as green, or does he see both with one colour which I am not acquainted with at all? These are unanswerable, indeed really nonsensical, questions. For when the word 'red' is meant not to state a property of things but to characterize sense impressions belonging to my consciousness, it is only applicable within the realm of my consciousness. For it is impossible to compare my sense impression with someone else's. For that, it would be necessary to bring together in one consciousness a sense impression belonging to one consciousness and a sense impression belonging to another consciousness. Now even if it were possible to make an idea disappear from one consciousness and at the same time make an idea appear in another consciousness, the question whether it is the same idea would still remain unanswerable. It is so much of the essence of any one of my ideas to be a content of my consciousness, that any idea someone else has is, just as such, different from mine. But might it not be possible that my ideas, the entire content of my consciousness, might be at the same time the content of a more embracing, perhaps divine consciousness? Only if I were myself part of the divine being. But then would they really be my ideas, would I be their owner? This so far oversteps the limits of human understanding that we must leave this possibility out of account. In any case it is impossible for us men to compare other people's ideas with our own. I pick the strawberry, I hold it between my fingers. Now my companion sees it too, this same strawberry; but each of us has his own idea. Nobody else has my idea, but many people can see the same thing. Nobody else has my pain. Someone may have sympathy with me, but still my pain belongs to me and his sympathy to him. He has not got my pain, and I have not got his feeling of sympathy.

Fourthly: every idea has only one owner; no two men have the same idea.

For otherwise it would exist independently of this man and independently of that man. Is that lime tree my idea? By using the expression 'that lime tree' in this question I am really already anticipating the answer, for I mean to use this expression to designate what I see and other people too can look at and touch. There are now two possibilities. If my intention is realized, if I do designate something with the expression 'that lime tree', then the thought expressed in the sentence 'That lime tree is my idea' must obviously be denied. But if my intention is not realized, if I only think I see without really seeing, if on that account the designation 'that lime tree' is empty, then I have wandered into the realm of fiction without knowing it or meaning to. In that case neither the content of the sentence 'That lime tree is my idea' nor the content of the sentence 'That lime tree is not my idea' is true, for in both cases I have a predication which lacks an object. So then I can refuse to answer the question, on the ground that the content of the sentence 'That lime tree is my idea' is fictional. I have, of course, got an idea then, but that is not what I am using the words 'that lime tree' to designate. Now someone might really want to designate one of his ideas with the words 'that lime tree'. He would then be the owner of that which he wants to designate with those words, but then he would not see that lime tree and no one else would see it or be its owner.

I now return to the question: is a thought an idea? If other people can assent to the thought I express in the Pythagorean theorem just as I do, then it does not belong to the content of my consciousness, I am not its owner; yet I can, nevertheless, acknowledge it as true. However, if what is taken to be the content of the Pythagorean theorem by me and by somebody else is not the same thought at all, we should not really say '*the* Pythagorean theorem', but '*my* Pythagorean theorem', '*his* Pythagorean theorem', and these would be different, for the sense necessarily goes with the sentence. In that case my thought may be the content of my consciousness and his thought the content of his. Could the sense of my Pythagorean theorem be true and the sense of his false? I said that the word 'red' was applicable only in the sphere of my consciousness if it was not meant to state a property of things but to characterize some of my own sense impressions. Therefore the words 'true' and 'false', as I understand them, might also be applicable

only in the realm of my consciousness, if they were not meant to apply to something of which I was not the owner, but to characterize in some way the content of my consciousness. Truth would then be confined to this content and it would remain doubtful whether anything at all similar occurred in the consciousness of others.

If every thought requires an owner and belongs to the contents of his consciousness, then the thought has this owner alone; and there is no science common to many on which many could work, but perhaps I have my science, a totality of thoughts whose owner I am, and another person has his. Each of us is concerned with contents of his own consciousness. No contradiction between the two sciences would then be possible, and it would really be idle to dispute about truth; as idle, indeed almost as ludicrous, as for two people to dispute whether a hundred-mark note were genuine, where each meant [*meinte*] the one he himself had in his pocket and understood the word 'genuine' in his own particular sense. If someone takes thoughts to be ideas, what he then accepts as true is, on his own view, the content of his consciousness, and does not properly concern other people at all. If he heard from me the opinion that a thought is not an idea he could not dispute it, for, indeed, it would not now concern him.

So the result seems to be: thoughts are neither things in the external world nor ideas.

A third realm must be recognized. Anything belonging to this realm has it in common with ideas that it cannot be perceived by the senses, but has it in common with things that it does not need an owner so as to belong to the contents of his consciousness. Thus for example the thought we have expressed in the Pythagorean theorem is timelessly true, true independently of whether anyone takes it to be true. It needs no owner. It is not true only from the time when it is discovered; just as a planet, even before anyone saw it, was in interaction with other planets.[5]

But I think I hear an odd objection. I have assumed several times that the same thing as I see can also be observed by other people. But what if everything were only a dream? If I only dreamed I was walking in the company of somebody else, if I only dreamed that my companion saw the green field as I did, if it were all only a play performed on the stage of my consciousness, it would be doubtful whether there were things of the external world at all. Perhaps the realm of things is empty and I do not see any things or any men, but only have ideas of which I myself am the owner. An idea, being something which can no more exist independently of me than my feeling of fatigue, cannot be a man, cannot look at the same field together with me, cannot see the strawberry I am holding. It is quite incredible that I really have only my inner world, instead of the whole environment in which I supposed myself to move and to act. And yet this is an inevitable consequence of the thesis that only what is my idea can be the object of my awareness. What would follow from this thesis if it were true? Would there then be other men? It would be possible, but I should know nothing of them. For a man cannot be my idea; consequently, if our thesis were true, he cannot be an object of my awareness either. And so this would undercut any reflections in which I assumed that something was an object for somebody else as it was for myself, for even if this were to happen I should know nothing of it. It would be impossible for me to distinguish something owned by myself from something I did not own. In judging something not to be my idea I would make it into the object of my thinking and, therefore, into my idea. On this view, is there a green field? Perhaps, but it would not be visible to me. For if a field is not my idea, it cannot, according to our thesis, be an object of my awareness. But if it is my idea it is invisible, for ideas are not visible. I can indeed have the idea of a green field; but this is not green, for there are no green ideas. Does a missile weighing a hundred kilogrammes exist, according to this view? Perhaps, but I could know nothing of it. If a missile is not my idea, then, according to our thesis, it cannot be an object of my awareness, of my thinking. But if a missile were my idea, it would have no weight. I can have an idea of a heavy missile. This then contains the idea of weight as a constituent idea. But this constituent idea is not a property of the whole idea, any more than Germany is a property of Europe. So the consequence is:

Either the thesis that only what is my idea can be the object of my awareness is false, or all my knowledge and perception is limited to the range of my ideas, to the stage of my consciousness. In this case I should have only an inner world and I should know nothing of other people.

It is strange how, in the course of such reflections, opposites turn topsy-turvy. There is, let us suppose, a physiologist of the senses. As is proper for someone investigating nature scientifically, he is at the outset far from supposing the things that he is convinced he sees and touches to be his own ideas. On the contrary, he believes that in sense impressions he has the most reliable evidence of things wholly independent of his feeling, imagining, thinking, which have no need of his consciousness. So little does he consider nerve fibres and ganglion cells to be the content of his consciousness that he is on the contrary inclined to regard his consciousness as dependent on nerve fibres and ganglion cells. He established that light rays, refracted in the eye, strike the visual nerve endings and there bring about a change, a stimulus. From this something is transmitted through nerve fibres to ganglion cells. Further processes in the nervous system perhaps follow upon this, and colour impressions arise, and these perhaps combine to make up what we call the idea of a tree. Physical, chemical and physiological occurrences get in between the tree and my idea. Only occurrences in my nervous system are immediately connected with my consciousness – or so it seems – and every observer of the tree has his particular occurrences in his particular nervous system. Now light rays, before they enter my eye, may be reflected by a mirror and diverge as if they came from places behind the mirror. The effects on the visual nerves and all that follows will now take place just as they would if the light rays had come from a tree behind the mirror and had been propagated undisturbed to the eye. So an idea of a tree will finally occur even though such a tree does not exist at all. The refraction of light too, with the mediation of the eye and nervous system, may give rise to an idea to which nothing at all corresponds. But the stimulation of the visual nerves need not even happen because of light. If lightning strikes near us, we believe we see flames, even though we cannot see the lightning itself. In this case the visual nerve is perhaps stimulated by electric currents occurring in our body as a result of the flash of lightning. If the visual nerve is stimulated by this means in just the way it would be stimulated by light rays coming from flames, then we believe we see flames. It just depends on the stimulation of the visual nerve, no matter how that itself comes about.

We can go a step further. Properly speaking this stimulation of the visual nerve is not immediately given; it is only an hypothesis. We believe that a thing independent of us stimulates a nerve and by this means produces a sense impression; but strictly speaking we experience only that end of the process which impinges on our consciousness. Might not this sense impression, this sensation, which we attribute to a nerve stimulation, have other causes also, just as the same nerve stimulation may arise in different ways? If we call what happens in our consciousness an idea, then we really experience only ideas, not their causes. And if the scientist wants to avoid all mere hypothesis, then he is left just with ideas; everything dissolves into ideas, even the light rays, nerve fibres and ganglion cells from which he started. So he finally undermines the foundations of his own construction. Is everything an idea? Does everything need an owner without which it could have no existence? I have considered myself as the owner of my ideas, but am I not myself an idea? It seems to me as if I were lying in a deck-chair, as if I could see the toes of a pair of polished boots, the front part of a pair of trousers, a waistcoat, buttons, parts of a jacket, in particular the sleeves, two hands, some hair of a beard, the blurred outline of a nose. Am I myself this entire complex of visual impressions, this aggregate idea? It also seems to me as if I saw a chair over there. That is an idea. I am not actually much different from the chair myself, for am I not myself just a complex of sense impressions, an idea? But where then is the owner of these ideas? How do I come to pick out one of these ideas and set it up as the owner of the rest? Why need this chosen idea be the idea I like to call 'I'? Could I not just as well choose the one that I am tempted to call a chair? Why, after all, have an owner for ideas at all? An owner would anyhow be something essentially different from ideas that were just owned; something independent, not needing any extraneous owner. If everything is idea, then there is no owner of ideas. And so now once again I experience opposites turning topsy-turvy. If there is no owner of ideas then there are also no ideas, for ideas need an owner and without one they cannot exist. If there is no ruler, there are also no subjects. The dependence which I found myself induced to ascribe to the sensation, as contrasted with the sentient being, disappears if there no longer is any owner. What I called ideas are then independent objects. No reason remains for granting an exceptional position to that object which I call 'I'.

But is that possible? Can there be an experience without someone to experience it? What would this whole play be without a spectator? Can there be a pain without someone who has it? Being felt necessarily goes with pain, and furthermore someone feeling it necessarily goes with its being felt. But then there *is* something which is not my idea and yet can be the object of my awareness, of my thinking; I myself am such a thing. Or can I be one part of the content of my consciousness, while another part is, perhaps, an idea of the Moon? Does this perhaps take place when I judge that *I* am looking at *the Moon*? Then this first part would have a consciousness, and part of the content of this consciousness would be I myself once more. And so on. Yet it is surely inconceivable that I should be inside myself like this in an infinite nest of boxes, for then there would not be just one I but infinitely many. I am not my own idea; and when I assert something about myself, e.g. that I am not feeling any pain at the moment, then my judgement concerns something which is not a content of my consciousness, is not an idea, namely myself. Therefore that about which I state something is not necessarily my idea. But someone perhaps objects: if I think I have no pain at the moment, does not the word 'I' answer to something in the content of my consciousness? And is that not an idea? That may be so. A certain idea in my consciousness may be associated with the idea of the word 'I'. But then this is one idea among other ideas, and I am its owner as I am the owner of the other ideas. I have an idea of myself, but I am not identical with this idea. What is a content of my consciousness, my idea, should be sharply distinguished from what is an object of my thinking. Therefore the thesis that only what belongs to the content of my consciousness can be the object of my awareness, of my thinking, is false.

Now the way is clear for me to acknowledge another man likewise as an independent owner of ideas. I have an idea of him, but I do not confuse it with him himself. And if I state something about my brother, I do not state it about the idea that I have of my brother.

The patient who has a pain is the owner of this pain, but the doctor who is treating him and reflects on the cause of this pain is not the owner of the pain. He does not imagine he can relieve the pain by anaesthetizing himself. There may very well be an idea in the doctor's mind that answers to the patient's pain, but that is not the pain, and is not what the doctor is trying to remove. The doctor might consult another doctor. Then one must distinguish: first, the pain, whose owner is the patient; secondly, the first doctor's idea of this pain; thirdly, the second doctor's idea of this pain. This last idea does indeed belong to the content of the second doctor's consciousness, but it is not the object of his reflection; it is rather an aid to reflection, as a drawing may be. The two doctors have as their common object [of thinking] the patient's pain, which they do not own. It may be seen from this that not only a thing but also an idea may be a common object of thinking for people who do not have the idea.

In this way, it seems to me, the matter becomes intelligible. If man could not think and could not take as the object of his thinking something of which he was not the owner, he would have an inner world but no environment. But may this not be based on a mistake? I am convinced that the idea I associate with the words 'my brother' corresponds to something that is not my idea and about which I can say something. But may I not be making a mistake about this? Such mistakes do happen. We then, against our will, lapse into fiction. Yes, indeed! By the step with which I win an environment for myself I expose myself to the risk of error. And here I come up against a further difference between my inner world and the external world. I cannot doubt that I have a visual impression of green, but it is not so certain that I see a lime leaf. So, contrary to widespread views, we find certainty in the inner world, while doubt never altogether leaves us in our excursions into the external world. But the probability is nevertheless in many cases hard to distinguish from certainty, so we can venture to judge about things in the external world. And we must make this venture even at the risk of error if we do not want to fall into far greater dangers.

As the result of these last considerations I lay down the following: not everything that can be the object of my acquaintance is an idea. I, as owner of ideas, am not myself an idea. Nothing now stops me from acknowledging other men to be owners of ideas, just as I am myself. And, once given the possibility, the probability is very great, so great that it is in my opinion no longer distinguishable from certainty. Would there be a science of history otherwise? Would not all moral theory, all law, otherwise collapse? What would

be left of religion? The natural sciences too could only be assessed as fables like astrology and alchemy. Thus the reflections I have set forth on the assumption that there are other men besides myself, who can make the same thing the object of their consideration, their thinking, remain in force without any essential weakening.

Not everything is an idea. Thus I can also acknowledge thoughts as independent of me; other men can grasp them just as much as I; I can acknowledge a science in which many can be engaged in research. We are not owners of thoughts as we are owners of our ideas. We do not *have* a thought as we have, say, a sense impression, but we also do not *see* a thought as we see, say, a star. So it is advisable to choose a special expression; the word 'grasp' suggests itself for the purpose.[6] To the grasping of thoughts there must then correspond a special mental capacity, the power of thinking. In thinking we do not produce thoughts, we grasp them. For what I have called thoughts stand in the closest connection with truth. What I acknowledge as true, I judge to be true quite apart from my acknowledging its truth or even thinking about it. That someone thinks it has nothing to do with the truth of a thought. 'Facts, facts, facts' cries the scientist if he wants to bring home the necessity of a firm foundation for science. What is a fact? A fact is a thought that is true. But the scientist will surely not acknowledge something to be the firm foundation of science if it depends on men's varying states of consciousness. The work of science does not consist in creation, but in the discovery of true thoughts. The astronomer can apply a mathematical truth in the investigation of long past events which took place when – on Earth at least – no one had yet recognized that truth. He can do this because the truth of a thought is timeless. Therefore that truth cannot have come to be only upon its discovery.

Not everything is an idea. Otherwise psychology would contain all the sciences within it, or at least it would be the supreme judge over all the sciences. Otherwise psychology would rule even over logic and mathematics. But nothing would be a greater misunderstanding of mathematics than making it subordinate to psychology. Neither logic nor mathematics has the task of investigating minds and contents of consciousness owned by individual men. Their task could perhaps be represented rather as the investigation of *the* mind; of *the* mind, not of minds.

The grasp of a thought presupposes someone who grasps it, who thinks. He is the owner of the thinking, not of the thought. Although the thought does not belong with the contents of the thinker's consciousness, there must be something in his consciousness that is aimed at the thought. But this should not be confused with the thought itself. Similarly Algol itself is different from the idea someone has of Algol.

A thought belongs neither to my inner world as an idea, nor yet to the external world, the world of things perceptible by the senses.

This consequence, however cogently it may follow from the exposition, will nevertheless perhaps not be accepted without opposition. It will, I think, seem impossible to some people to obtain information about something not belonging to the inner world except by sense perception. Sense perception indeed is often thought to be the most certain, even the sole, source of knowledge about everything that does not belong to the inner world. But with what right? For sense perception has as necessary constituents our sense impressions and these are a part of the inner world. In any case two men do not have the same sense impressions though they may have similar ones. Sense impressions alone do not reveal the external world to us. Perhaps there is a being that has only sense impressions without seeing or touching things. To have visual impressions is not to see things. How does it happen that I see the tree just there where I do see it? Obviously it depends on the visual impressions I have and on the particular sort which occur because I see with two eyes. On each of the two retinas there arises, physically speaking, a particular image. Someone else sees the tree in the same place. He also has two retinal images but they differ from mine. We must assume that these retinal images determine our impressions. Consequently the visual impressions we have are not only not the same, but markedly different from each other. And yet we move about in the same external world. Having visual impressions is certainly necessary for seeing things, but not sufficient. What must still be added is not anything sensible. And yet this is just what opens up the external world for us; for without this non-sensible something everyone would remain shut up in his inner world. So perhaps, since the decisive factor lies in the non-sensible, something non-sensible, even without the co-operation of sense impressions, could also lead us out of the inner world and enable us to grasp thoughts. Outside our inner world we should have to distinguish the external world proper of sensible, perceptible things and the realm of what is non-sensibly perceptible. We should need something non-sensible for the recognition of both realms; but for the sense perception of things we should need sense impressions as well, and these belong entirely to the inner world. So the distinction between the ways in which a thing and a thought are given mainly consists in something which is assignable, not to either of the two realms, but to the inner world. Thus I cannot find this distinction to be so great as to make impossible the presentation of a thought that does not belong to the inner world.

A thought, admittedly, is not the sort of thing to which it is usual to apply the term 'actual' ['*wirklich*']. The world of actuality is a world in which this acts [*wirkt*] on that and changes it and again undergoes reactions [*Gegenwirkungen*] itself and is changed by them. All this is a process in time. We will hardly admit what is timeless and unchangeable to be actual. Now is a thought changeable or is it timeless? The thought we express by the Pythagorean theorem is surely timeless, eternal, unvarying. But are there not thoughts which are true today but false in six months' time? The thought, for example, that the tree there is covered with green leaves, will surely be false in six months' time. No, for it is not the same thought at all. The words 'This tree is covered with green leaves' are not sufficient by themselves to constitute the expression of thought, for the time of utterance is involved as well. Without the time-specification thus given we have not a complete thought, i.e. we have no thought at all. Only a sentence with the time-specification filled out, a sentence complete in every respect, expresses a thought. But this thought, if it is true, is true not only today or tomorrow but timelessly. Thus the present tense in 'is true' does not refer to [*deutet . . . auf*] the speaker's present; it is, if the expression be permitted, a tense of timelessness. If we merely use the assertoric sentence-form and avoid the word 'true', two things must be distinguished, the expression of the thought and assertion. The time-specification that may be contained in the sentence belongs only to the expression of the thought; the truth, which we acknowledge by using the assertoric sentence-form, is timeless. To be sure the same words, on account of the variability of language with time, may take on another sense, express another thought; this change, however, relates only to the linguistic realm.

And yet what value could there be for us in the eternally unchangeable, which could neither be acted upon nor act on us? Something entirely and in every respect inactive would be quite unactual, and so far as we are concerned it would not be there. Even the timeless, if it is to be anything for us, must somehow be implicated with the temporal. What would a thought be for me if it were never grasped by me? But by grasping a thought I come into a relation to it, and it to me. It is possible that the same thought as is thought by me today was not thought by me yesterday. Of course this does away with strict timelessness. But we may be inclined to distinguish between essential and inessential properties and to regard something as timeless if the changes it undergoes involve only inessential properties. A property of a thought will be called inessential if it consists in, or follows from, the fact that this thought is grasped by a thinker.

How does a thought act? By being grasped and taken to be true. This is a process in the inner world of a thinker which may have further consequences in this inner world, and which may also encroach on the sphere of the will and make itself noticeable in the outer world as well. If, for example, I grasp the thought we express by the theorem of Pythagoras, the consequence may be that I recognize it to be true, and further that I apply it in making a decision, which brings about the acceleration of masses. This is how our actions are usually led up to by acts of thinking and judging. And so thoughts may indirectly influence the motion of masses. The influence of man on man is brought about for the most part by thoughts. People communicate thoughts. How do they do this? They bring about changes in the common external world, and these are meant to be perceived by someone else, and so give him a chance to grasp a thought and take it to be true. Could the great events of world history have come about without the communication of thoughts? And yet we are inclined to regard thoughts as unactual, because they appear to do nothing in relation to events, whereas thinking, judging, stating, understanding, in general doing things, are affairs that concern men. How very different the actuality of a hammer appears, compared with that of a thought! How different a process handing over a hammer is from communicating a thought! The hammer passes from one control to another, it is gripped, it undergoes pressure, and thus its density, the disposition of its parts, is locally changed. There is nothing of all this with a thought. It does not leave the control of the communicator by being communicated, for after all man has no power over it. When a thought is grasped, it at first only brings about changes in the inner world of the one who grasps it; yet it remains untouched in the core of its essence, for the changes it undergoes affect only inessential properties. There is lacking here something we observe everywhere in physical process – reciprocal action. Thoughts are not wholly unactual but their actuality is quite different from the actuality of things. And their action is brought about by a performance of the thinker; without this they would be inactive, at least as far as we can see. And yet the thinker does not create them but must take them as they are. They can be true without being grasped by a thinker; and they are not wholly unactual even then, at least if they *could* be grasped and so brought into action.

Notes

1 So, similarly, people have said 'a judgement is something which is either true or false'. In fact I use the word 'thought' more or less in the sense 'judgement' has in the writings of logicians. I hope it will become clear in what follows why I choose 'thought'. Such an explanation has been objected to on the ground that it makes a division of judgements into true and false judgements – perhaps the least significant of all possible divisions among judgements. But I cannot see that it is a logical fault that a division is given along with the explanation. As for the division's being significant, we shall perhaps find we must hold it in no small esteem, if, as I have said, it is the word 'true' that points the way for logic.

2 I am not using the word 'sentence' ['*Satz*'] here in quite the same sense as grammar does, which also includes subordinate clauses. An isolated subordinate clause does not always have a sense about which the question of truth can arise, whereas the complex sentence to which it belongs has such a sense.

3 It seems to me that thought and judgement have not hitherto been adequately distinguished. Perhaps language is misleading. For we have no particular

bit of assertoric sentences which corresponds to assertion; that something is being asserted is implicit rather in the assertoric form. We have the advantage in German that main and subordinate clauses are distinguished by the word order. However in this connection we must observe that a subordinate clause may also contain an assertion, and that often neither main nor subordinate clause expresses a complete thought by itself but only the complex sentence does.

4 I am not here in the happy position of a mineralogist who shows his audience a rock-crystal: I cannot put a thought in the hands of my readers with the request that they should examine it from all sides. Something in itself not perceptible by sense, the thought, is presented to the reader – and I must be content with that – wrapped up in a perceptible linguistic form. The pictorial aspect of language presents difficulties. The sensible always breaks in and makes expressions pictorial and so improper. So one fights against language, and I am compelled to occupy myself with language although it is not my proper concern here. I hope I have succeeded in making clear to my readers what I want to call 'thought'.

5 A person sees a thing, has an idea, grasps or thinks a thought. When he grasps or thinks a thought he does not create it but only comes to stand in a certain relation to what already existed – a different relation from seeing a thing or having an idea.

6 The expression 'grasp' is as metaphorical as 'content of consciousness'. The nature of language does not permit anything else. What I hold in my hand can certainly be regarded as the content of my hand; but all the same it is the content of my hand in quite another and a more extraneous way than are the bones and muscles of which the hand consists or again the tensions these undergo.

3

On Denoting

Bertrand Russell

By a 'denoting phrase' I mean a phrase such as any one of the following: a man, some man, any man, every man, all men, the present King of England, the present King of France, the center of mass in the solar system at the first instant of the twentieth century, the revolution of the earth round the sun, the revolution of the sun round the earth. Thus a phrase is denoting solely in virtue of its *form*. We may distinguish three cases: (1) A phrase may be denoting, and yet not denote anything; e.g., 'the present King of France'. (2) A phrase may denote one definite object, e.g., 'the present King of England' denotes a certain man. (3) A phrase may denote ambiguously; e.g., 'a man' denotes not many men, but an ambiguous man. The interpretation of such phrases is a matter of considerable difficulty; indeed, it is very hard to frame any theory not susceptible of formal refutation. All the difficulties with which I am acquainted are met, so far as I can discover, by the theory which I am about to explain.

The subject of denoting is of very great importance, not only in logic and mathematics, but also in theory of knowledge. For example, we know that the center of mass of the solar system at a definite instant is some definite point, and we can affirm a number of propositions about it; but we have no immediate *acquaintance* with this point, which is only known to us by description. The distinction between *acquaintance* and *knowledge about* is the distinction between the things

Originally published in *Mind* 14 (1905).

we have presentations of, and the things we can only reach by denoting phrases. It often happens that we know that a certain phrase denotes unambiguously, although we have no acquaintance with what it denotes; this occurs in the above case of the center of mass. In perception we have acquaintance with the objects of perception, and in thought we have acquaintance with objects of a more abstract logical character; but we do not necessarily have acquaintance with the objects denoted by phrases composed of words with whose meanings we are acquainted. To take a very important instance: there seems no reason to believe that we are ever acquainted with other people's minds, seeing that these are not directly perceived; hence what we know about them is obtained through denoting. All thinking has to start from acquaintance, but it succeeds in thinking *about* many things with which we have no acquaintance.

The course of my argument will be as follows. I shall begin by stating the theory I intend to advocate:[1] I shall then discuss the theories of Frege and Meinong, showing why neither of them satisfies me; then I shall give the grounds in favor of my theory; and finally I shall briefly indicate the philosophical consequences of my theory.

My theory, briefly, is as follows. I take the notion of the *variable* as fundamental; I use '$C(x)$' to mean a proposition[2] in which x is a constituent, where x, the variable, is essentially and wholly undetermined. Then we can consider the two notions '$C(x)$ is always true' and '$C(x)$ is sometimes true.'[3] Then *everything* and *nothing* and *something* (which are the most primitive of denoting phrases) are to be interpreted as follows:

C (everything) means '$C(x)$ is always true';
C (nothing) means ' "$C(x)$ is false" is always true';
C (something) means 'It is false that "$C(x)$ is false" is always true'.[4]

Here the notion '$C(x)$ is always true' is taken as ultimate and indefinable, and the others are defined by means of it. *Everything, nothing*, and *something* are not assumed to have any meaning in isolation, but a meaning is assigned to *every* proposition in which they occur. This is the principle of the theory of denoting I wish to advocate: that denoting phrases never have any meaning in themselves, but that every proposition in whose verbal expression they occur has a meaning. The difficulties concerning denoting are, I believe, all the result of a wrong analysis of propositions whose verbal expressions contain denoting phrases. The proper analysis, if I am not mistaken, may be further set forth as follows.

Suppose now we wish to interpret the proposition, 'I met a man'. If this is true, I met some definite man; but that is not what I affirm. What I affirm is, according to the theory I advocate:

' "I met x, and x is human" is not always false'.

Generally, defining the class of men as the class of objects having the predicate *human*, we say that:

'C (a man)' means ' "$C(x)$ and x is human" is not always false'. This leaves 'a man', by itself, wholly destitute of meaning, but gives a meaning to every proposition in whose verbal expression 'a man' occurs.

Consider next the proposition 'all men are mortal'. This proposition[5] is really hypothetical and states that *if* anything is a man, it is mortal. That is, it states that if x is a man, x is mortal, whatever x may be. Hence, substituting 'x is human' for 'x is a man', we find:

'All men are mortal' means ' "If x is human, x is mortal" is always true'.

This is what is expressed in symbolic logic by saying that 'all men are mortal' means ' "x is human" implies "x is mortal" for all values of x'. More generally, we say:

'C (all men)' means ' "If x is human, then C (x) is true" is always true'.

Similarly

'C (no men)' means ' "If x is human, then C (x) is false" is always true'.
'C (some men)' will mean the same as 'C (a man)',[6] and
'C (a man)' means 'It is false that "C (x) and x is human" is always false'.
'C (every man)' will mean the same as 'C (all men)'.

It remains to interpret phrases containing *the*. These are by far the most interesting and difficult of denoting phrases. Take as an example 'the father of Charles II was executed'. This asserts that there was an x who was the father of Charles II and was executed. Now, *the*, when it is strictly used, involves uniqueness; we do, it is true, speak of 'the son of So-and-so' even when So-and-so has several sons, but it would be more correct to say 'a son of So-and-so'. Thus for our purposes we take *the* as involving uniqueness. Thus when we say 'x was *the* father of Charles II' we not only assert that x had a certain relation to Charles II, but also that nothing else had this relation. The relation in question, without the assumption of uniqueness, and without any denoting phrases, is expressed by 'x begat Charles II'. To get an equivalent of 'x was the father of Charles II', we must add, 'If y is other than x, y did not beget Charles II', or what is equivalent, 'If y begat Charles II, y is identical with x'. Hence, 'x is the father of Charles II' becomes: 'x begat Charles II; and 'if y begat Charles II, y is identical with x' is always true of y'.

Thus 'the father of Charles II was executed' becomes:

'It is not always false of x that x begat Charles II and that x was executed and that "if y begat Charles II, y is identical with x" is always true of y'.

This may seem a somewhat incredible interpretation; but I am not at present giving reasons, I am merely *stating* the theory.

To interpret 'C (the father of Charles II)', where C stands for any statement about him, we have only to substitute $C(x)$ for 'x was executed' in the above. Observe that, according to the above interpretation C may be, 'C (the father of Charles II)' implies:

'It is not always false of x that "if y begat Charles II, y is identical with x" is always true of y',

which is what is expressed in common language by 'Charles II had one father and no more'. Consequently if this condition fails, *every* proposition of the form 'C (the father of Charles II)' is false. Thus e.g. every proposition of the form 'C (the present King of France)' is false. This is a great advantage in the present theory. I shall show later that it is not contrary to the law of contradiction, as might be at first supposed.

The above gives a reduction of all propositions in which denoting phrases occur to forms in which no such phrases occur. Why it is imperative to effect such a reduction, the subsequent discussion will endeavor to show.

The evidence for the above theory is derived from the difficulties which seem unavoidable if we regard denoting phrases as standing for genuine constituents of the propositions in whose verbal expressions they occur. Of the possible theories which admit such constituents the simplest is that of Meinong.[7] This theory regards any grammatically correct denoting phrase as standing for an *object*. Thus 'the present King of France', 'the round square', etc., are supposed to be genuine objects. It is admitted that such objects do not *subsist*, but nevertheless they are supposed to be objects. This is in itself a difficult view; but the chief objection is that such objects, admittedly, are apt to infringe the law of contradiction. It is contended, for example, that the existent present King of France exists, and also does not exist; that the round square is round, and also not round, etc. But this is intolerable; and if any theory can be found to avoid this result, it is surely to be preferred.

The above breach of the law of contradiction is avoided by Frege's theory. He distinguishes, in a denoting phrase, two elements, which we may call the *meaning* and the *denotation*.[8] Thus 'the center of mass of the solar system at the beginning of the twentieth century' is highly complex in *meaning*, but its *denotation* is a certain point, which is simple. The solar system, the twentieth century, etc., are constituents of the *meaning*; but the *denotation* has no constituents at all.[9] One advantage of this distinction is that it shows why it is often worthwhile to assert identity. If we say 'Scott is the author of *Waverley*', we assert an identity of denotation with a difference of meaning. I shall, however, not repeat the grounds in favor of this theory, as I have urged its claims elsewhere, and am now concerned to dispute those claims.

One of the first difficulties that confronts us, when we adopt the view that denoting phrases *express* a meaning and *denote* a denotation,[10] concerns the cases in which the denotation appears to be absent. If we say 'the King of England is bald', that is, it would seem, not a statement about the complex *meaning* 'the King of England', but about the actual man denoted by the meaning. But now consider 'the King of France is bald'. By parity of form, this also ought to be about the denotation of the phrase 'the King of France'. But this phrase, though it has a *meaning* provided 'the King of England' has a meaning, has certainly no denotation, at least in any obvious sense. Hence one would suppose that 'the King of France is bald' ought to be nonsense; but it is not nonsense, since it is plainly false. Or again consider such a proposition as the following: 'If u is a class which has only one member, then that one member is a member of u', or, as we may state it, 'If u is a unit class, the u is a u'. This proposition ought to be *always* true, since the conclusion is true whenever the hypothesis is true. But 'the u' is a denoting phrase, and it is the denotation, not the meaning, that is said to be a u. Now if u is *not* a unit class, 'the u' seems to denote nothing; hence our proposition would seem to become nonsense as soon as u is not a unit class.

Now it is plain that such propositions do *not* become nonsense merely because their hypotheses are false. The king in *The Tempest* might say, 'If Ferdinand is not drowned, Ferdinand is my only son'. Now 'my only son' is a denoting phrase, which, on the face of it, has a denotation when, and only when, I have exactly one son. But the above statement would nevertheless have remained true if Ferdinand had been in fact drowned. Thus we must either provide a denotation in cases in which it is at first sight absent, or we must abandon the view that the denotation is what is concerned in propositions which contain denotating phrases. The latter is the course that I advocate. The former course may be taken, as by Meinong, by admitting objects which do not subsist, and denying that they obey the law of contradiction; this, however, is to be avoided if possible. Another way of taking the same course (so far as our present alternative is concerned) is adopted by Frege, who provides by definition some purely conventional denotations for the cases in which otherwise there would be none. Thus 'the King of France' is to denote the null-class; 'the only son of Mr. So-and-so' (who has a fine family of ten), is to denote the class of all his sons; and so on. But this procedure, though it may not lead to actual logical error, is plainly artificial, and does not give an exact analysis of the matter. Thus if we allow that denoting phrases, in general, have the two sides of meaning and denotation, the cases where there seems to be no denotation cause difficulties both on the assumption that there really is a denotation and on the assumption that there really is none.

A logical theory may be tested by its capacity for dealing with puzzles, and it is a wholesome plan, in thinking about logic, to stock the mind with as many puzzles as possible, since these serve much the same purpose as is served by experiments in physical science. I shall therefore state three puzzles which a theory as to denoting ought to be able to solve; and I shall show later that my theory solves them.

(1) If a is identical with b, whatever is true of the one is true of the other, and either may be substituted for the other in any proposition without altering the truth or falsehood of that proposition. Now George IV wished to know whether Scott was the author of *Waverley*; and in fact Scott *was* the author of *Waverley*. Hence we may substitute *Scott* for *the author of 'Waverley'*, and thereby prove that George IV wished to know whether Scott was Scott. Yet an interest in the law of identity can hardly be attributed to the first gentleman of Europe.

(2) By the law of excluded middle, either 'A is B' or 'A is not B' must be true. Hence either 'the present King of France is bald' or 'the present King of France is not bald' must be true. Yet if we enumerated the things that are bald, and then the things that are not bald, we should not find the present King of France in either list. Hegelians, who love a synthesis, will probably conclude that he wears a wig.

(3) Consider the proposition 'A differs from B'. If this is true, there is a difference between A and B, which fact may be expressed in the form 'the difference between A and B subsists'. But if it is false that A differs from B, then there is no difference between A and B, which fact may be expressed in the form 'the difference between A and B does not subsist'. But how can a non-entity be the subject of a proposition? 'I think, therefore I am' is no more evident than 'I am the subject of a proposition, therefore I am', provided 'I am' is taken to assert subsistence or being,[11] not existence. Hence, it would appear, it must always be self-contradictory to deny the being of anything; but we have seen, in connection with Meinong, that to admit being also sometimes leads to contradictions. Thus, if A and B do not differ, to suppose either that there is, or that there is not, such an object as 'the difference between A and B' seems equally impossible.

The relation of the meaning to the denotation involves certain rather curious difficulties, which seem in themselves sufficient to prove that the theory which leads to such difficulties must be wrong.

When we wish to speak about the *meaning* of a denoting phrase, as opposed to its *denotation*, the natural mode of doing so is by inverted commas. Thus we say:

The center of mass of the solar system is a point, not a denoting complex;

'The center of mass of the solar system' is a denoting complex, not a point.

Or again,

The first line of Gray's Elegy states a proposition.

'The first line of Gray's Elegy' does not state a proposition. Thus taking any denoting phrase, say C, we wish to consider the relation between C and 'C', where the difference of the two is the kind exemplified in the above two instances.

We say, to begin with, that when C occurs it is the *denotation* that we are speaking about; but when 'C' occurs, it is the *meaning*. Now the relation of meaning and denotation is not merely linguistic through the phrase: there must be a logical relation involved, which we express by saying that the meaning denotes the denotation. But the difficulty which confronts us is that we cannot succeed in *both* preserving the connection of meaning and denotation *and* preventing them from being one and the same; also that the meaning cannot be got at except by means of denoting phrases. This happens as follows.

The one phrase C was to have both meaning and denotation. But if we speak of 'the meaning of C', that gives us the meaning (if any) of the denotation. 'The meaning of the first line of Gray's Elegy' is the same as 'The meaning of "The curfew tolls the knell of parting day",' and is not the same as 'The meaning of "the first line of Gray's Elegy".' Thus in order to get the meaning we want, we must speak not of 'the meaning of C', but of 'the meaning of "C",' which is the same as 'C' by itself. Similarly 'the denotation of C' does not mean the denotation we want, but means something which, if it denotes at all, denotes what is denoted by the denotation we want. For example, let 'C' be 'the denoting complex occurring in the second of the above instances'. Then C = 'the first line of Gray's Elegy', and the denotation of C = The curfew tolls the knell of parting day. But what we *meant* to have as the denotation was 'the first line of Gray's Elegy'. Thus we have failed to get what we wanted.

The difficulty in speaking of the meaning of a denoting complex may be stated thus: The moment we put the complex in a proposition, the proposition is about the denotation; and if we make a proposition in which the subject is 'the meaning of C', then the subject is the meaning (if any) of the denotation, which was not intended. This leads us to say that, when we distinguish meaning and denotation, we must be dealing with the meaning: the meaning has denotation and is a complex, and there is not something other than the meaning, which can be called the complex, and be said to *have* both meaning and denotation. The right phrase, on the view in question, is that some meanings have denotations.

But this only makes our difficulty in speaking of meanings more evident. For suppose C is our complex; then we are to say that C *is* the meaning of the complex. Nevertheless, whenever C occurs without inverted commas, what is said is not true of the meaning, but only of the denotation, as when we say: 'The center of mass of the solar system is a point'. Thus to speak of C itself, i.e., to make a proposition about the meaning, our subject must not be C, but something

which denotes C. Thus 'C', which is what we use when we want to speak of the meaning, must be not the meaning, but something which denotes the meaning. And C must not be a constituent of this complex (as it is of 'the meaning of C'); for if C occurs in the complex, it will be its denotation, not its meaning, that will occur, and there is no backward road from denotations to meanings, because every object can be denoted by an infinite number of different denoting phrases.

Thus it would seem that 'C' and C are different entities, such that 'C' denotes C; but this cannot be an explanation, because the relation of 'C' to C remains wholly mysterious; and where we are to find the denoting complex 'C' which is to denote C? Moreover, when C occurs in a proposition, it is not *only* the denotation that occurs (as we shall see in the next paragraph); yet, on the view in question, C is only the denotation, the meaning being wholly relegated to 'C'. This is an inextricable tangle and seems to prove that the whole distinction of meaning and denotation has been wrongly conceived.

That the meaning is relevant when a denoting phrase occurs in a proposition is formally proved by the puzzle about the author of *Waverley*. The proposition 'Scott was the author of *Waverley*' has a property not possessed by 'Scott was Scott', namely the property that George IV wished to know whether it was true. Thus the two are not identical propositions, hence the meaning of 'the author of *Waverley*' must be relevant as well as the denotation, if we adhere to the point of view to which this distinction belongs. Yet, as we have just seen, so long as we adhere to this point of view, we are compelled to hold that only the denotation can be relevant. Thus the point in question must be abandoned.

It remains to show how all the puzzles we have been considering are solved by the theory explained at the beginning of this article.

According to the view which I advocate, a denoting phrase is essentially *part* of a sentence, and does not, like most single words, have any significance on its own account. If I say 'Scott was a man', that is a statement of the form 'x was a man', and it has 'Scott' for its subject. But if I say 'the author of *Waverley* was a man', that is not a statement of the form 'x was a man', and does not have 'the author of *Waverley*' for its subject. Abbreviating the statement made at the beginning of this article, we may put, in place of 'the author of *Waverley* was a man', the following: 'One and only one entity wrote *Waverley*, and that one was a man'. (This is not so strictly what is meant as what was said earlier; but it is easier to follow.) And speaking generally, suppose we wish to say that the author of *Waverley* had the property ϕ, what we wish to say is equivalent to 'One and only one entity wrote *Waverley*, and that one had the property ϕ'.

The explanation of *denotation* is now as follows. Every proposition in which 'the author of *Waverley*' occurs being explained as above, the proposition 'Scott was the author of *Waverley*' (i.e., 'Scott was identical with the author of *Waverley*') becomes 'One and only one entity wrote *Waverley*, and Scott was identical with that one'; or, reverting to the wholly explicit form: 'It is not always false of x that x wrote *Waverley*, that it is always true of y that if y wrote *Waverley*, y is identical with x, and that Scott is identical with x'. Thus if 'C' is a denoting phrase, it may happen that there is one entity x (there cannot be more than one) for which the proposition 'x is identical with C' is true, this proposition being interpreted as above. We may then say that the entity x is the denotation of the phrase 'C'. Thus Scott is the denotation of 'the author of *Waverley*'. The 'C' in inverted commas will be merely the *phrase*, not anything that can be called the *meaning*. The phrase *per se* has no meaning, because in any proposition in which it occurs the proposition, fully expressed, does not contain the phrase, which has been broken up.

The puzzle about George IV's curiosity is now seen to have a very simple solution. The proposition 'Scott was the author of *Waverley*', which was written out in its unabbreviated form in the preceding paragraph, does not contain any constituent 'the author of *Waverley*' for which we could substitute 'Scott'. This does not interfere with the truth of inferences resulting from making what is *verbally* the substitution of 'Scott' for 'the author of *Waverley*', so long as 'the author of *Waverley*' has what I call a *primary* occurrence in the proposition considered. The difference of primary and secondary occurrences of denoting phrases is as follows:

When we say: 'George IV wished to know whether so-and-so', or when we say 'So-and-so is surprising' or 'So-and-so is true', etc., the 'so-and-so' must be a proposition. Suppose now that 'so-and-so' contains a denoting phrase. We may either eliminate this denoting phrase from the subordinate proposition 'so-and-so', or from the whole proposition in which 'so-and-so' is a mere constituent. Different propositions result according to which we do. I have heard of a touchy owner of a yacht to whom a guest, on first seeing it, remarked. 'I thought your yacht was larger than it is'; and the owner replied, 'No, my yacht is not larger than it is'. What the guest meant was, 'The size that I thought your yacht was is greater than the size your yacht is'; the meaning attributed to him is, 'I thought the size of your yacht was greater than the size of your yacht'. To return to George IV and *Waverley*, when we say 'George IV wished to know whether Scott was the author of *Waverley*', we normally mean 'George IV wished to know whether one and only one man wrote *Waverley* and Scott was that man'; but we *may* also mean: 'One and only one man wrote *Waverley*, and George IV wished to know whether Scott was that man'. In the latter, 'the author of *Waverley*' has a *primary* occurrence; in the former, a *secondary*. The latter might be expressed by 'George IV wished to know, concerning the man who in fact wrote *Waverley*, whether he was Scott'. This would be true, for example, if George IV had seen Scott at a distance, and had asked 'Is that Scott?'. A *secondary* occurrence of a denoting phrase may be defined as one in which the phrase occurs in a proposition p which is a mere constituent of the proposition we are considering, and the substitution for the denoting phrase is to be effected in p, not in the whole proposition concerned. The ambiguity as between primary and secondary occurrences is hard to avoid in language; but it does no harm if we are on our guard against it. In symbolic logic it is of course easily avoided.

The distinction of primary and secondary occurrences also enables us to deal with the question whether the present King of France is bald or not bald, and generally with the logical status of denoting phrases that denote nothing. If 'C' is a denoting phrase, say 'the term having the property F', then

> 'C has the property ϕ' means 'one and only one term has the property F, and that one has the property ϕ'.[12]

If now the property F belongs to no terms, or to several, it follows that 'C has the property ϕ' is false for *all* values of ϕ. Thus 'the present King of France is bald' is certainly false; and 'the present King of France is not bald' is false if it means

'There is an entity which is now King of France and is not bald'.

but is true if it means

'It is false that there is an entity which is now King of France and is bald'.

That is, 'the King of France is not bald' is false if the occurrence of 'the King of France' is *primary*, and true if it is *secondary*. Thus all propositions in which 'the King of France' has a primary occurrence are false; the denials of such propositions are true, but in them 'the King of France' has a secondary occurrence. Thus we escape the conclusion that the King of France has a wig.

We can now see also how to deny that there is such an object as the difference between A and B in the case when A and B do not differ. If A and B do differ, there is one and only one entity x such that 'x is the difference between A and B' is a true proposition; if A and B do not differ, there is no such entity x. Thus according to the meaning of denotation lately explained, 'the difference between A and B' has a denotation when A and B differ, but not otherwise. This difference applies to true and false propositions generally. If 'a R b' stands for 'a has the relation R to b', then when a R b is true, there is such an entity as the relation R between a and b; when a R b is false, there is no such entity. Thus out of any proposition we can make a denoting phrase, which denotes an entity if the proposition is true, but does not denote an entity if the proposition is false. E.g., it is true (at least we will suppose so) that the earth revolves around the sun, and false that the sun revolves around the earth; hence 'the revolution of the earth round the sun' denotes an entity, while 'the revolution of the sun round the earth' does not denote an entity.[13]

The whole realm of non–entities, such as 'the round square', 'the even prime other than 2', 'Apollo', 'Hamlet', etc., can now be satisfactorily dealt with. All these are denoting phrases which do not denote anything. A proposition about Apollo means what we get by substituting what the classical dictionary tells us is meant by Apollo, say 'the sun-god'. All propositions in which Apollo occurs are to be interpreted by the above rules for denoting phrases. If 'Apollo' has a primary occurrence, the proposition containing the occurrence is false; if the occurrence is secondary, the proposition may be true. So again 'the round square is round' means 'there is one and only one entity x which is round and square, and that entity is round', which is a false proposition, not, as Meinong maintains, a true one. 'The most perfect Being has all perfections; existence is a perfection; therefore the most perfect Being exists' becomes:

'There is one and only one entity x which is most perfect; that one has all perfections; existence is a perfection; therefore that one exists'. As a proof, this fails for want of a proof of the premise 'there is one and only one entity x which is most perfect'.[14]

Mr. MacColl (*Mind*, NS no. 54, and again no. 55, page 401) regards individuals as of two sorts, real and unreal; hence he defines the null-class as the class consisting of all unreal individuals. This assumes that such phrases as 'the present King of France', which do not denote a real individual, do, nevertheless, denote an individual, but an unreal one. This is essentially Meinong's theory, which we have seen reason to reject because it conflicts with the law of contradiction. With our theory of denoting, we are able to hold that there are no unreal individuals; so that the null-class is the class containing no members, not the class containing as members all unreal individuals.

It is important to observe the effect of our theory on the interpretation of definitions which proceed by means of denoting phrases. Most mathematical definitions are of this sort: for example '$m - n$ means the number which, added to n, gives m'. Thus $m - n$ is defined as meaning the same as a certain denoting phrase; but we agreed that denoting phrases have no meaning in isolation. Thus what the definition really ought to be is: 'Any proposition containing $m - n$ is to mean the proposition which results from substituting for "$m - n$" "the number which, added to n, gives m".' The resulting proposition is interpreted according to the rules already given for interpreting propositions whose verbal expression contains a denoting phrase. In the case where m and n are such that there is one and only one number x which, added to n, gives m, there is a number x which can be substituted for $m - n$ in any proposition containing $m - n$ without altering the truth or falsehood of the proposition.

But in other cases, all propositions in which '*m – n*' has a primary occurrence are false.

The usefulness of *identity* is explained by the above theory. No one outside a logic-book ever wishes to say '*x* is *x*', and yet assertions of identity are often made in such forms as 'Scott was the author of *Waverley*' or 'thou art the man'. The meaning of such propositions cannot be stated without the notion of identity, although they are not simply statements that Scott is identical with another term, the author of *Waverley*, or that thou art identical with another term, the man. The shortest statement of 'Scott is the author of *Waverley*' seems to be 'Scott wrote *Waverley*; and it is always true of *y* that if *y* wrote *Waverley*, *y* is identical with Scott'. It is in this way that identity enters into 'Scott is the author of *Waverley*'; and it is owing to such uses that identity is worth affirming.

One interesting result of the above theory of denoting is this: when there is anything with which we do not have immediate acquaintance, but only definition by denoting phrases, then the propositions in which this thing is introduced by means of a denoting phrase do not really contain this thing as a constituent, but contain instead the constituents expressed by the several words of the denoting phrase. Thus in every proposition that we can apprehend (i.e. not only in those whose truth or falsehood we can judge of, but in all that we can think about), all the constituents are really entities with which we have immediate acquaintance. Now such things as matter (in the sense in which matter occurs in physics) and the minds of other people are known to us only by denoting phrases, i.e. we are not *acquainted* with them, but we know them as what has such and such properties. Hence, although we can form propositional functions *C* (*x*) which must hold of such and such a material particle, or of So-and-so's mind, yet we are not acquainted with the propositions which affirm these things that we know must be true, because we cannot apprehend the actual entities concerned. What we know is 'So-and-so has a mind which has such and such properties', where *A* is the mind in question. In such a case, we know the properties of a thing without having acquaintance with the thing itself, and without, consequently, knowing any single proposition of which the thing itself is a constituent.

Of the many other consequences of the view I have been advocating, I will say nothing. I will only beg the reader not to make up his mind against the view – as he might be tempted to do, on account of its apparently excessive complication – until he has attempted to construct a theory of his own on the subject of denotation. This attempt, I believe, will convince him that, whatever the true theory may be, it cannot have such a simplicity as one might have expected beforehand.

Notes

1 I have discussed this subject in *Principles of Mathematics*, ch. v, and §476. The theory there advocated is very nearly the same as Frege's, and is quite different from the theory to be advocated in what follows.

2 More exactly, a propositional function.

3 The second of these can be defined by means of the first, if we take it to mean, 'It is not true that "*C* (*x*) is false" is always true'.

4 I shall sometimes use, instead of this complicated phrase, the phrase '*C* (*x*) is not always false', or '*C* (*x*) is sometimes true', supposed *defined* to mean the same as the complicated phrase.

5 As has been ably argued in Mr. Bradley's *Logic*, Book I, ch. II.

6 Psychologically '*C* (a man)' has a suggestion of *only* one, and '*C* (some men)' has a suggestion of *more than one*; but we may neglect these suggestions in a preliminary sketch.

7 See *Untersuchungen zur Gegenstandstheorie und Psychologie* (Leipzig, 1904) the first three articles (by Meinong, Ameseder, and Mally respectively).

8 See his "Ueber Sinn und Bedeutung," *Zeitschrift für Philosophie und Philosophische Kritik*, 100. [Reprinted as "On Sense and Reference" in this volume.]

9 Frege distinguishes the two elements of meaning and denotation everywhere, and not only in complex denoting phrases. Thus it is the *meanings* of the constituents of a denoting complex that enter into its *meaning*, not their *denotation*. In the proposition 'Mont Blanc is over 1,000 metres high', it is, according to him the *meaning* of 'Mont Blanc', not the actual mountain, that is a constituent of the *meaning* of the proposition.

10 In this theory, we shall say that the denoting phrase *expresses* a meaning; and we shall say both of the phrase and of the meaning that they *denote* a denotation. In the other theory, which I

advocate, there is no *meaning*, and only sometimes a *denotation*.

11 I use these as synonyms.

12 This is the abbreviated, not the stricter, interpretation.

13 The propositions from which such suppositions are derived are not identical either with these entities or with the propositions that these entities have being.

14 The argument can be made to prove validly that all members of the class of most perfect Beings exist; it can also be proved formally that this class cannot have *more* than one member; but, taking the definition of perfection as possession of all positive predicates, it can be proved almost equally formally that the class does not have even one member.

4

On Referring

P. F. Strawson

I

We very commonly use expressions of certain kinds to mention or refer to some individual person or single object or particular event or place or process, in the course of doing what we should normally describe as making a statement about that person, object, place, event, or process. I shall call this way of using expressions the "uniquely referring use". The classes of expressions which are most commonly used in this way are: singular demonstrative pronouns ("this" and "that"); proper names (e.g. "Venice", "Napoleon", "John"); singular personal and impersonal pronouns ("he", "she", "I", "you", "it"); and phrases beginning with the definite article followed by a noun, qualified or unqualified, in the singular (e.g. "the table", "the old man", "the king of France"). Any expression of any of these classes can occur as the subject of what would traditionally be regarded as a singular subject-predicate sentence; and would, so occurring, exemplify the use I wish to discuss.

I do not want to say that expressions belonging to these classes never have any other use than the one I want to discuss. On the contrary, it is obvious that they do. It is obvious that anyone who uttered the sentence, "The whale is a mammal", would be using the expression "the whale" in a way quite different from the way it would

Originally published in *Mind* 59 (1950). Reprinted by permission of Oxford University Press, Oxford.

be used by anyone who had occasion seriously to utter the sentence, "The whale struck the ship". In the first sentence one is obviously *not* mentioning, and in the second sentence one obviously *is* mentioning, a particular whale. Again if I said, "Napoleon was the greatest French soldier", I should be using the word "Napoleon" to mention a certain individual, but I should not be using the phrase, "the greatest French soldier", to mention an individual, but to say something about an individual I had already mentioned. It would be natural to say that in using this sentence I was talking *about* Napoleon and that what I was *saying* about him was that he was the greatest French soldier. But of course I *could* use the expression, "the greatest French soldier", to mention an individual; for example, by saying: "The greatest French soldier died in exile". So it is obvious that at least some expressions belonging to the classes I mentioned *can* have uses other than the use I am anxious to discuss. Another thing I do not want to say is that in any given sentence there is never more than one expression used in the way I propose to discuss. On the contrary, it is obvious that there may be more than one. For example, it would be natural to say that, in seriously using the sentence, "The whale struck the ship", I was saying something about both a certain whale and a certain ship, that I was using each of the expressions "the whale" and "the ship" to mention a particular object; or, in other words, that I was using each of these expressions in the uniquely referring

P. F. Strawson

way. In general, however, I shall confine my attention to cases where an expression used in this way occurs as the grammatical subject of a sentence.

I think it is true to say that Russell's Theory of Descriptions, which is concerned with the last of the four classes of expressions I mentioned above (i.e. with expressions of the form "the so-and-so") is still widely accepted among logicians as giving a correct account of the use of such expressions in ordinary language. I want to show, in the first place, that this theory, so regarded, embodies some fundamental mistakes.

What question or questions about phrases of the form "the so-and-so" was the Theory of Descriptions designed to answer? I think that at least one of the questions may be illustrated as follows. Suppose someone were now to utter the sentence, "The king of France is wise". No one would say that the sentence which had been uttered was meaningless. Everyone would agree that it was significant. But everyone knows that there is not at present a king of France. One of the questions the Theory of Descriptions was designed to answer was the question: how can such a sentence as "The king of France is wise" be significant even when there is nothing which answers to the description it contains, i.e., in this case, nothing which answers to the description "The king of France"? And one of the reasons why Russell thought it important to give a correct answer to this question was that he thought it important to show that another answer which might be given was wrong. The answer that he thought was wrong, and to which he was anxious to supply an alternative, might be exhibited as the conclusion of either of the following two fallacious arguments. Let us call the sentence "The king of France is wise" the sentence S. Then the first argument is as follows:

(1) The phrase, "the king of France", is the subject of the sentence S.
Therefore (2) if S is a significant sentence, S is a sentence *about* the king of France.
But (3) if there in no sense exists a king of France, the sentence is not about anything, and hence not about the king of France.
Therefore (4) since S is significant, there must in some sense (in some world) exist (or subsist) the king of France.

And the second argument is as follows:

(1) If S is significant, it is either true or false.
(2) S is true if the king of France is wise and false if the king of France is not wise.
(3) But the statement that the king of France is wise and the statement that the king of France is not wise are alike true only if there is (in some sense, in some world) something which is the king of France.
Hence (4) since S is significant, there follows the same conclusion as before.

These are fairly obviously bad arguments, and, as we should expect, Russell rejects them. The postulation of a world of strange entities, to which the king of France belongs, offends, he says, against "that feeling for reality which ought to be preserved even in the most abstract studies". The fact that Russell rejects these arguments is, however, less interesting than the extent to which, in rejecting their conclusion, he concedes the more important of their principles. Let me refer to the phrase, "the king of France", as the phrase D. Then I think Russell's reasons for rejecting these two arguments can be summarised as follows. The mistake arises, he says, from thinking that D, which is certainly the *grammatical* subject of S, is also the *logical* subject of S. But D is not the logical subject of S. In fact S, although grammatically it has a singular subject and a predicate, is not logically a subject-predicate sentence at all. The proposition it expresses is a complex kind of *existential* proposition, part of which might be described as a "uniquely existential" proposition. To exhibit the logical form of the proposition, we should re-write the sentence in a logically appropriate grammatical form; in such a way that the deceptive similarity of S to a sentence expressing a subject-predicate proposition would disappear, and we should be safeguarded against arguments such as the bad ones I outlined above. Before recalling the details of Russell's analysis of S, let us notice what his answer, as I have so far given it, seems to imply. His answer seems to imply that in the case of a sentence which is similar to S in that (1) it is grammatically of the subject-predicate form and (2) its grammatical subject does not refer to anything, then the only alternative to its being meaningless is that it should not really (i.e. logically) be of the subject-predicate form at all, but of some quite different form. And this in its turn seems to imply that if there are any sentences which are genuinely of the subject-predicate form, then the very fact of their being significant, having a meaning, guarantees that there *is* something referred to by the logical (and grammatical) subject. Moreover, Russell's answer seems to imply that there are such sentences. For if it is true that one may be misled by the grammatical similarity of S to other sentences into thinking that it is logically of the subject-predicate form, then surely there must be other sentences grammatically similar to S, which *are* of the subject-predicate form. To show not only that Russell's answer seems to imply these conclusions, but that he accepted at least the first two of them, it is enough to consider what he says about a class of expressions which he calls "logically proper names" and contrasts with expressions, like D, which he calls "definite descriptions". Of logically proper names Russell says or implies the following things:

(1) That they and they alone can occur as subjects of sentences which are genuinely of the subject-predicate form;

(2) that an expression intended to be a logically proper name is *meaningless* unless there is some single object for which it stands: for the *meaning* of such an expression just is the individual object which the expression designates. To be a name at all, therefore, it *must* designate something.

It is easy to see that if anyone believes these two propositions, then the only way for him to save the significance of the sentence S is to deny that it is a logically subject-predicate sentence. Generally, we may say that Russell recognises only two ways in which sentences which seem, from their grammatical structure, to be about some particular person or individual object or event, can be significant:

(1) The first is that their grammatical form should be misleading as to their logical form, and that they should be analysable, like S, as a special kind of existential sentence;

(2) The second is that their grammatical subject should be a logically proper name, of which the meaning is the individual thing it designates.

I think that Russell is unquestionably wrong in this, and that sentences which are significant, and which begin with an expression used in the uniquely referring way fall into neither of these

two classes. Expressions used in the uniquely referring way are never either logically proper names or descriptions, if what is meant by calling them "descriptions" is that they are to be analysed in accordance with the model provided by Russell's Theory of Descriptions.

There are no logically proper names and there are no descriptions (in this sense).

Let us now consider the details of Russell's analysis. According to Russell, anyone who asserted S would be asserting that:

(1) There is a king of France.
(2) There is not more than one king of France.
(3) There is nothing which is king of France and is not wise.

It is easy to see both how Russell arrived at this analysis, and how it enables him to answer the question with which we began, viz. the question: How can the sentence S be significant when there is no king of France? The way in which he arrived at the analysis was clearly by asking himself what would be the circumstances in which we would say that anyone who uttered the sentence S had made a true assertion. And it does seem pretty clear, and I have no wish to dispute, that the sentences (1)–(3) above do describe circumstances which are at least *necessary* conditions of anyone making a true assertion by uttering the sentence S. But, as I hope to show, to say this is not at all the same thing as to say that Russell has given a correct account of the use of the sentence S or even that he has given an account which, though incomplete, is correct as far as it goes; and is certainly not at all the same thing as to say that the model translation provided is a correct model for all (or for any) singular sentences beginning with a phrase of the form "the so-and-so".

It is also easy to see how this analysis enables Russell to answer the question of how the sentence S can be significant, even when there is no king of France. For, if this analysis is correct, anyone who utters the sentence S today would be jointly asserting three propositions, one of which (viz. that there is a king of France) would be false; and since the conjunction of three propositions, of which one is false, is itself false, the assertion as a whole would be significant, but false. So neither of the bad arguments for subsistent entities would apply to such an assertion.

II

As a step towards showing that Russell's solution of his problem is mistaken, and towards providing the correct solution, I want now to draw certain distinctions. For this purpose I shall, for the remainder of this section, refer to an expression which has a uniquely referring use as "an expression" for short; and to a sentence beginning with such an expression as "a sentence" for short. The distinctions I shall draw are rather rough and ready, and, no doubt, difficult cases could be produced which would call for their refinement. But I think they will serve my purpose. The distinctions are between:

(A1)   a sentence,
(A2)   a use of a sentence,
(A3)   an utterance of a sentence,

and, correspondingly, between:

(B1)   an expression,
(B2)   a use of an expression,
(B3)   an utterance of an expression.

Consider again the sentence, "The king of France is wise". It is easy to imagine that this sentence was uttered at various times from, say, the beginning of the seventeenth century onwards, during the reigns of each successive French monarch; and easy to imagine that it was also uttered during the subsequent periods in which France was not a monarchy. Notice that it was natural for me to speak of "the sentence" or "this sentence" being uttered at various times during this period; or, in other words, that it would be natural and correct to speak of *one and the same* sentence being uttered on all these various occasions. It is in the sense in which it would be correct to speak of one and the same sentence being uttered on all these various occasions that I want to use the expression (A1) "a sentence". There are, however, obvious differences between different *occasions of the use* of this sentence. For instance, if one man uttered it in the reign of Louis XIV and another man uttered it in the reign of Louis XV, it would be natural to say (to assume) that they were respectively talking about different people; and it might be held that the first man, in using the sentence, made a true assertion, while the second man, in using the same sentence, made a false assertion.

If on the other hand two different men simultaneously uttered the sentence (e.g. if one wrote it and the other spoke it) during the reign of Louis XIV, it would be natural to say (assume) that they were both talking about the same person, and, in that case, in using the sentence, they *must* either both have made a true assertion or both have made a false assertion. And this illustrates what I mean by *a use* of a sentence. The two men who uttered the sentence, one in the reign of Louis XV and one in the reign of Louis XIV, each made a different use of the same sentence; whereas the two men who uttered the sentence simultaneously in the reign of Louis XIV, made the same use[1] of the same sentence. Obviously in the case of this sentence, and equally obviously in the case of many others, we cannot talk of *the sentence* being true or false, but only of its being used to make a true or false assertion, or (if this is preferred) to express a true or a false proposition. And equally obviously we cannot talk of *the sentence* being *about* a particular person, for the same sentence may be used at different times to talk about quite different particular persons, but only of *a use* of the sentence to talk about a particular person. Finally it will make sufficiently clear what I mean by an utterance of a sentence if I say that the two men who simultaneously uttered the sentence in the reign of Louis XIV made two different utterances of the same sentence, though they made the same *use* of the sentence.

If we now consider not the whole sentence, "The king of France is wise", but that part of it which is the expression, "the king of France", it is obvious that we can make analogous, though not identical distinctions between (1) the expression, (2) a use of the expression and (3) an utterance of the expression. The distinctions will not be identical; we obviously cannot correctly talk of the expression "the king of France" being used to express a true or false proposition, since in general only sentences can be used truly or falsely; and similarly it is only by using a sentence and not by using an expression alone, that you can talk about a particular person. Instead, we shall say in this case that you *use* the expression to *mention* or *refer to* a particular person in the course of using the sentence to talk about him. But obviously in this case, and a great many others, the *expression* (B1) cannot be said to mention, or refer to, anything, any more than the *sentence* can be said to be true or false. The same expression can have different mentioning-uses, as the same sentence can be used to make statements with different truth-values. "Mentioning", or "referring", is not something an expression does; it is something that someone can use an expression to do. Mentioning, or referring to something is a characteristic of *a use* of an expression, just as "being about" something, and truth-or-falsity, are characteristics of *a use* of a sentence.

A very different example may help to make these distinctions clearer. Consider another case of an expression which has a uniquely referring use, viz. the expression "I"; and consider the sentence, "I am hot". Countless people may use this same sentence; but it is logically impossible for two different people to make *the same use* of this sentence: or, if this is preferred, to use it to express the same proposition. The expression "I" may correctly be used by (and only by) any one of innumerable people to refer to himself. To say this is to say something about the expression "I": it is, in a sense, to give its meaning. This is the sort of thing that can be said about *expressions*. But it makes no sense to say of the *expression* "I" that it refers to a particular person. This is the sort of thing that can be said only of a particular use of the expression.

Let me use "type" as an abbreviation for "sentence or expression". Then I am not saying that there are sentences and expression (types), *and* uses of them, *and* utterances of them, as there are ships *and* shoes *and* sealing-wax. I am saying that we cannot say *the same things* about types, uses of types, and utterances of types. And the fact is that we do talk about types; and that confusion is apt to result from the failure to notice the differences between what we can say about these and what we can say only about the *uses* of types. We are apt to fancy we are talking about sentences and expressions when we are talking about the uses of sentences and expressions.

This is what Russell does. Generally, as against Russell, I shall say this. Meaning (in at least one important sense) is a function of the sentence or expression; mentioning and referring and truth or falsity, are functions of the use of the sentence or expression. To give the meaning of an expression (in the sense in which I am using the word) is to give *general directions* for its use to refer to or mention particular objects or persons; to give the meaning of a sentence is to give *general directions* for its use in making true or false assertions. It is not to talk about any particular occasion of the use of the sentence or expression. The meaning of an expression cannot be identified with the object it is used, on a particular occasion, to refer to. The meaning of a sentence cannot be identified with the assertion it is used, on a particular occasion, to make. For to talk about the meaning of an expression or sentence is not to talk about its use on a particular occasion, but about the rules, habits, conventions governing its correct use, on all occasions, to refer or to assert. So the question of whether a sentence or expression *is significant or not* has nothing whatever to do with the question of whether the sentence, *uttered on a particular occasion*, is, on that occasion, being used to make a true-or-false assertion or not, or of whether the expression is, on that occasion, being used to refer to, or mention, anything at all.

The source of Russell's mistake was that he thought that referring or mentioning, if it occurred at all, must be meaning. He did not distinguish B1 from B2; he confused expressions with their use in a particular context; and so confused meaning with mentioning, with referring. If I talk about my handkerchief, I can, perhaps, produce the object I am referring to out of my pocket. I can't produce the meaning of the expression, "my handkerchief", out of my pocket. Because Russell confused meaning with mentioning, he thought that if there were any expressions having a uniquely referring use, which were what they seemed (i.e. logical subjects) and not something else in disguise, their meaning must *be* the particular object which they were used to refer to. Hence the troublesome mythology of the logically proper name. But if someone asks me the meaning of the expression "this" – once Russell's favourite candidate for this status – I do not hand him the object I have just used the expression to refer to, adding at the same time that the meaning of the word changes every time it is used. Nor do I hand him all the objects it ever has been, or might be, used to refer to. I explain and illustrate the conventions governing the use of the expression. This *is* giving the meaning of the expression. It is quite different from giving (in any sense of giving) the object to which it refers; for the expression itself does not refer to anything; though it can be used, on different occasions, to refer to innumerable things. Now as a matter of fact there is, in English, a sense of the word "mean" in which this word does approximate to "indicate, mention or refer to"; e.g. when somebody (unpleasantly) says, "I mean you"; or when I point and say, "That's the one I mean". But *the one I meant* is quite different from *the meaning of the expression* I used to talk of it. In this special sense of "mean", it is people who mean, not expressions. People use expressions to refer to particular things. But the meaning of an expression is not the set of things or the single thing it may correctly be used to refer to: the meaning is the set of rules, habits, conventions for its use in referring.

It is the same with sentences: even more obviously so. Every one knows that the sentence, "The table is covered with books", is significant, and every one knows what it means. But if I ask, "What object is that sentence about?" I am asking an absurd question – a question which cannot be asked about the sentence, but only about some use of the sentence: and in this case the sentence hasn't been used, it has only been taken as an example. In knowing what it means, you are knowing how it could correctly be used to talk about things: so knowing the meaning hasn't anything to do with knowing about any particular use of the sentence to talk about anything. Similarly, if I ask: "Is the sentence true or false?" I am asking an absurd question, which becomes no less absurd if I add, "It must be one or the other since it's significant". The question is absurd, because the *sentence* is neither true nor false any more than it's *about* some object. Of course the fact that it's significant is the same as the fact that it *can* correctly be used to talk about something and that, in so using it, someone will be making a true or false assertion. And I will add that it will be used to make a true or false assertion *only* if the person using it *is* talking about something. If, when he utters it, he is not talking about anything, then his use is not a genuine one, but a spurious or pseudo-use: he is not making either a true or a false assertion, though he may think he is. And this points the way to the correct answer to the puzzle to which the Theory of Descriptions gives a fatally incorrect answer. The important point is that the question of whether the sentence is significant or not is quite independent of the question that can be raised about a particular use of it, viz. the question whether it is a genuine or a spurious use, whether it is being used to talk about something, or in make-believe, or as an example in philosophy. The question whether the sentence

is significant or not is the question whether there exist such language habits, conventions or rules that the sentence logically could be used to talk about something; and is hence quite independent of the question whether it is being so used on a particular occasion.

III

Consider again the sentence, "The king of France is wise", and the true and false things Russell says about it.

There are at least two true things which Russell would say about the sentence:

(1) The first is that it is significant; that if anyone were now to utter it, he would be uttering a significant sentence.
(2) The second is that anyone now uttering the sentence would be making a true assertion only if there in fact at present existed one and only one king of France, and if he were wise.

What are the false things which Russell would say about the sentence? They are:

(1) That anyone now uttering it would be making a true assertion or a false assertion;
(2) That part of what he would be asserting would be that there at present existed one and only one king of France.

I have already given some reasons for thinking that these two statements are incorrect. Now suppose someone were in fact to say to you with a perfectly serious air: "The king of France is wise". Would you say, "That's untrue"? I think it's quite certain that you wouldn't. But suppose he went on to *ask* you whether you thought that what he had just said was true, or was false; whether you agreed or disagreed with what he had just said. I think you would be inclined, with some hesitation, to say that you didn't do either; that the question of whether his statement was true or false simply *didn't arise*, because there was no such person as the king of France.[2] You might, if he were obviously serious (had a dazed astray-in-the-centuries look), say something like: "I'm afraid you must be under a misapprehension. France is not a monarchy. There is no king of France." And this brings out the point that if a man seriously uttered the sentence, his uttering it would in some sense be *evidence* that he *believed* that there was a king of France. It would not be evidence for his believing this simply in the way in which a man's reaching for his raincoat is evidence for his believing that it is raining. But nor would it be evidence for his believing this in the way in which a man's saying, "It's raining" is evidence for his believing that it is raining. We might put it as follows. To say, "The king of France is wise" is, in some sense of "imply", to *imply* that there is a king of France. But this is a very special and odd sense of "imply". "Implies" in this sense is certainly not equivalent to "entails" (or "logically implies"). And this comes out from the fact that when, in response to his statement, we say (as we should) "There is no king of France", we should certainly *not* say we were *contradicting* the statement that the king of France is wise. We are certainly not saying that it's false. We are, rather, giving a reason for saying that the question of whether it's true or false simply doesn't arise.

And this is where the distinction I drew earlier can help us. The sentence, "The king of France is wise", is certainly significant; but this does not mean that any particular use of it is true or false. We use it truly or falsely when we use it to talk about someone; when, in using the expression, "The king of France", we are in fact mentioning someone. The fact that the sentence and the expression, respectively, are significant just is the fact that the sentence *could* be used, in certain circumstances, to say something true or false, that the expression *could* be used, in certain circumstances to mention a particular person; and to know their meaning is to know what sort of circumstances these are. So when we utter the sentence without in fact mentioning anybody by the use of the phrase, "The king of France", the sentence doesn't cease to be significant: we simply *fail* to say anything true or false because we simply fail to mention anybody by this particular use of that perfectly significant phrase. It is, if you like, a spurious use of the sentence, and a spurious use of the expression; though we may (or may not) mistakenly think it a genuine use.

And such spurious uses are very familiar. Sophisticated romancing, sophisticated fiction,[3] depend upon them. If I began, "The king of France is wise", and went on, "and he lives in a golden castle and has a hundred wives", and so on, a hearer would understand me perfectly well, without supposing *either* that I was talking about a particular person, *or* that I was making a false statement to the effect that there existed such a person as my words described. (It is worth adding that where the use of sentences and expressions is overtly fictional, the sense of the word "about" may change. As Moore said, it is perfectly natural and correct to say that some of the statements in *Pickwick Papers* are *about* Mr. Pickwick. But where the use of sentences and expressions is not overtly fictional, this use of "about" seems less correct; i.e. it would not *in general* be correct to say that a statement was about Mr. X or the so-and-so, unless there were such a person or thing. So it is where the romancing is in danger of being taken seriously that we might answer the question, "Who is he talking about?" with "He's not talking about anybody"; but, in saying this, we are not saying that what he is saying is either false or nonsense.)

Overtly fictional uses apart, however, I said just now that to use such an expression as "The king of France" at the beginning of a sentence was, in some sense of "imply", to imply that there was a king of France. When a man uses such an expression, he does not *assert*, nor does what he says *entail*, a uniquely existential proposition. But one of the conventional functions of the definite article is to act as a *signal* that a unique reference is being made – a signal, not a disguised assertion. When we begin a sentence with "the such-and-such" the use of "the" shows, but does not state, that we are, or intend to be, referring to one particular individual of the species "such-and-such". *Which* particular individual is a matter to be determined from context, time, place and any other features of the situation of utterance. Now, whenever a man uses any expression, the presumption is that he thinks he is using it correctly: so when he uses the expression, "the such-and-such", in a uniquely referring way, the presumption is that he thinks both that there is *some* individual of that species, and that the context of use will sufficiently determine which one he has in mind. To use the word "the" in this way is then to imply (in the relevant sense of "imply") that the existential conditions described by Russell are fulfilled. But to use "the" in this way is not to *state* that those conditions are fulfilled. If I begin a sentence with an expression of the form, "the so-and-so", and then am prevented from saying more, I have made no statement of any kind; but I may have succeeded in mentioning someone or something.

The uniquely existential assertion supposed by Russell to be part of any assertion in which a uniquely referring use is made of an expression of the form "the so-and-so" is, he observes, a compound of two assertions. To say that there is a ϕ is to say something compatible with there being several ϕs; to say there is not more than one ϕ is to say something compatible with there being none. To say there is one ϕ and one only is to compound these two assertions. I have so far been concerned mostly with the alleged assertion of existence and less with the alleged assertion of uniqueness. An example which throws the emphasis on to the latter will serve to bring out more clearly the sense of "implied" in which a uniquely existential assertion is implied, but not entailed, by the use of expressions in the uniquely referring way. Consider the sentence, "The table is covered with books". It is quite certain that in any normal use of this sentence, the expression "the table" would be used to make a unique reference, i.e. to refer to some one table. It is a quite strict use of the definite article, in the sense in which Russell talks on page 30 of *Principia Mathematica*, of using the article "*strictly*, so as to imply uniqueness". On the same page Russell says that a phrase of the form "the so-and-so", used strictly, "will only have an application in the event of there being one so-and-so and no more". Now it is obviously quite false that the phrase "the table" in the sentence "the table is covered with books", used normally, will "only have an application in the event of there being one table and no more". It is indeed tautologically true that, in such a use, the phrase will have an application only in the event of there being one table and no more *which is being referred to*, and that it will be understood to have an application only in the event of there being one table and no more which it is understood as being used to refer to. To use the sentence is not to assert, but it is (in the special sense discussed) to imply, that there is only one thing which is *both* of the kind specified (i.e. a table) *and is being referred to* by the speaker. It is obviously not to assert this. To refer is not to say you are referring. To say there is *some table or other* to which you are referring is not the same as referring to a particular table. We should have no use for such phrases as "the individual I referred to" unless there were something which counted as referring. (It would make no sense to say you had pointed if there were

nothing which counted as pointing.) So once more I draw the conclusion that referring to or mentioning a particular thing cannot be dissolved into any kind of assertion. To refer is not to assert, though you refer in order to go on to assert.

Let me now take an example of the uniquely referring use of an expression not of the form, "the so-and-so". Suppose I advance my hands, cautiously cupped, towards someone, saying, as I do so, "This is a fine red one". He, looking into my hands and seeing nothing there, may say: "What is? What are you talking about?" Or perhaps, "But there's nothing in your hands". Of course it would be absurd to say that in saying "But you've got nothing in your hands", he was *denying* or *contradicting* what I said. So "this" is not a disguised description in Russell's sense. Nor is it a logically proper name. For one must know what the sentence means in order to react in that way to the utterance of it. It is precisely because the significance of the word "this" is independent of any particular reference it may be used to make, though not independent of the way it may be used to refer, that I can, as in this example, use it to *pretend* to be referring to something.

The general moral of all this is that communication is much less a matter of explicit or disguised assertion than logicians used to suppose. The particular application of this general moral in which I am interested is its application to the case of making a unique reference. It is a part of the significance of expressions of the kind I am discussing that they can be used, in an immense variety of contexts, to make unique references. It is no part of their significance to assert that they are being so used or that the conditions of their being so used are fulfilled. So the wholly important distinction we are required to draw is between:

(1) using an expression to make a unique reference; and
(2) asserting that there is one and only one individual which has certain characteristics (e.g. is of a certain kind, or stands in a certain relation to the speaker, or both).

This is, in other words, the distinction between

(1) sentences containing an expression used to indicate or mention or refer to a particular person or thing; and
(2) uniquely existential sentences.

What Russell does is progressively to assimilate more and more sentences of class (1) to sentences of class (2), and consequently to involve himself in insuperable difficulties about logical subjects, and about values for individual variables generally: difficulties which have led him finally to the logically disastrous theory of names developed in the *Enquiry* and in *Human Knowledge*. That view of the meaning of logical-subject-expressions which provides the whole incentive to the Theory of Descriptions at the same time precludes the possibility of Russell's ever finding any satisfactory substitutes for those expressions which, beginning with substantival phrases, he progressively degrades from the status of logical subjects.[4] It is not simply, as is sometimes said, the fascination of the relation between a name and its bearer, that is the root of the trouble. Not even names come up to the impossible standard set. It is rather the combination of two more radical misconceptions: first, the failure to grasp the importance of the distinction (section II above) between what may be said of an expression and what may be said of a particular use of it; second, a failure to recognise the uniquely referring use of expressions for the harmless, necessary thing it is, distinct from, but complementary to, the predicative or ascriptive use of expressions. The expressions which can in fact occur as singular logical subjects are expressions of the class I listed at the outset (demonstratives, substantival phrases, proper names, pronouns): to say this is to say that these expressions, together with context (in the widest sense) are what one uses to make unique references. The point of the conventions governing the uses of such expressions is, along with the situation of utterance, to secure uniqueness of reference. But to do this, enough is enough. We do not, and we cannot, while referring, attain the point of complete explicitness at which the referring function is no longer performed. The actual unique reference made, if any, is a matter of the particular use in the particular context; the significance of the expression used is the set of rules or conventions which permit such references to be made. Hence we can, using significant expressions, pretend to refer, in make-believe or in fiction, or mistakenly think we are referring when we are not referring to anything.

This shows the need for distinguishing two kinds (among many others) of linguistic conventions or rules: rules for referring, and rules for attributing and ascribing; and for an investigation of the former. If we recognise this distinction of use for what it is, we are on the way to solving a number of ancient logical and metaphysical puzzles.

My last two sections are concerned, but only in the barest outline, with these questions.

IV

One of the main purposes for which we use language is the purpose of stating facts about things and persons and events. If we want to fulfil this purpose, we must have some way of forestalling the question, "What (who, which one) are you talking about?" as well as the question, "What are you saying about it (him, her)?" The task of forestalling the first question is the referring (or identifying) task. The task of forestalling the second is the attributive (or descriptive or classificatory or ascriptive) task. In the conventional English sentence which is used to state, or to claim to state, a fact about an individual thing or person or event, the performance of these two tasks can be roughly and approximately assigned to separable expressions.[5] And in such a sentence, this assigning of expressions to their separate roles corresponds to the conventional grammatical classification of subject and predicate. There is nothing sacrosanct about the employment of separable expressions for these two tasks. Other methods could be, and are, employed. There is, for instance, the method of uttering a single word or attributive phrase in the conspicuous presence of the object referred to; or that analogous method exemplified by, e.g. the painting of the words "unsafe for lorries" on a bridge, or the tying of a label reading "first prize" on a vegetable marrow. Or one can imagine an elaborate game in which one never used an expression in the uniquely referring way at all, but uttered only uniquely existential sentences, trying to enable the hearer to identify what was being talked of by means of an accumulation of relative clauses. (This description of the purposes of the game shows in what sense it would be a game: this is not the normal use we make of existential sentences.) Two points require emphasis. The first is that the necessity of performing these two tasks in order to state particular facts requires no transcendental explanation: to call attention to it is partly to elucidate the meaning of the phrase, "stating a fact". The second is that even this elucidation is made in terms derivative from the grammar of the conventional singular sentence; that even the overtly functional, linguistic distinction between the identifying and attributive roles that words may play in language is prompted by the fact that ordinary speech offers us separable expressions to which the different functions may be plausibly and approximately assigned. And this functional distinction has cast long philosophical shadows. The distinctions between particular and universal, between substance and quality, are such pseudo-material shadows, cast by the grammar of the conventional sentence, in which separable expressions play distinguishable roles.

To use a separate expression to perform the first of these tasks is to use an expression in the uniquely referring way. I want now to say something in general about the conventions of use for expressions used in this way, and to contrast them with conventions of ascriptive use. I then proceed to the brief illustration of these general remarks and to some further applications of them.

What in general is required for making a unique reference is, obviously, some device, or devices, for showing both *that* a unique reference is intended and *what* unique reference it is; some device requiring and enabling the hearer or reader to identify what is being talked about. In securing this result, the context of utterance is of an importance which it is almost impossible to exaggerate; and by "context" I mean, at least, the time, the place, the situation, the identity of the speaker, the subjects which form the immediate focus of interest, and the personal histories of both the speaker and those he is addressing. Besides context, there is, of course, convention – linguistic convention. But, except in the case of genuine proper names, of which I shall have more to say later, the fulfilment of more or less precisely stateable contextual conditions is *conventionally* (or, in a wide sense of the word, *logically*) required for the correct referring use of expressions in a sense in which this is not true of correct ascriptive uses. The requirement for the correct application of an expression in its ascriptive use to a certain thing is simply that the thing should be of a certain kind, have certain characteristics. The requirement for the correct application of an expression in its referring use to a certain thing is something over and above any

requirement derived from such ascriptive meaning as the expression may have; it is, namely, the requirement that the thing should be in a certain relation to the speaker and to the context of utterance. Let me call this the contextual requirement. Thus, for example, in the limiting case of the word "I" the contextual requirement is that the thing should be identical with the speaker; but in the case of most expressions which have a referring use this requirement cannot be so precisely specified. A further, and perfectly general, difference between conventions for referring and conventions for describing is one we have already encountered, viz. that the fulfilment of the conditions for a correct ascriptive use of an expression is a part of what is stated by such a use; but the fulfilment of the conditions for a correct referring use of an expression is never part of what is stated, though it is (in the relevant sense of "implied") implied by such a use.

Conventions for referring have been neglected or misinterpreted by logicians. The reasons for this neglect are not hard to see, though they are hard to state briefly. Two of them are, roughly: (1) the preoccupation of most logicians with definitions; (2) the preoccupation of some logicians with formal systems. (1) A definition, in the most familiar sense, is a specification of the conditions of the correct ascriptive or classificatory use of an expression. Definitions take no account of contextual requirements. So that in so far as the search for the meaning or the search for the analysis of an expression is conceived as the search for a definition, the neglect or misinterpretation of conventions other than ascriptive is inevitable. Perhaps it would be better to say (for I do not wish to legislate about "meaning" or "analysis") that logicians have failed to notice that problems of use are wider than problems of analysis and meaning. (2) The influence of the preoccupation with mathematics and formal logic is most clearly seen (to take no more recent examples) in the cases of Leibniz and Russell. The constructor of calculuses, not concerned or required to make factual statements, approaches applied logic with a prejudice. It is natural that he should assume that the types of convention with whose adequacy in one field he is familiar should be really adequate, if only one could see how, in a quite different field – that of statements of fact. Thus we have Leibniz striving desperately to make the uniqueness of unique references a matter of logic in the narrow sense, and Russell striving desperately to do the same thing, in a different way, both for the implication of uniqueness and for that of existence.

It should be clear that the distinction I am trying to draw is primarily one between different roles or parts that expressions may play in language, and not primarily one between different groups of expressions; for some expressions may appear in either role. Some of the kinds of words I shall speak of have predominantly, if not exclusively, a referring role. This is most obviously true of pronouns and ordinary proper names. Some can occur as wholes or parts of expressions which have a predominantly referring use, and as wholes or parts of expressions which have a predominantly ascriptive or classificatory use. The obvious cases are common nouns; or common nouns preceded by adjectives, including participial adjectives; or, less obviously, adjectives or participial adjectives alone. Expressions capable of having a referring use also differ from one another in at least the three following, not mutually independent, ways:

(1)   They differ in the extent to which the reference they are used to make is dependent on the context of their utterance. Words like "I" and "it" stand at one end of this scale – the end of maximum dependence – and phrases like "the author of Waverley" and "the eighteenth king of France" at the other.

(2)   They differ in the degree of "descriptive meaning" they possess: by "descriptive meaning" I intend "conventional limitation, in application, to things of a certain general kind, or possessing certain general characteristics". At one end of this scale stand the proper names we most commonly use in ordinary discourse; men, dogs and motor-bicycles may be called "Horace". The pure name has no descriptive meaning (except such as it may acquire *as a result of* some one of its uses as a name). A word like "he" has minimal descriptive meaning, but has some. Substantival phrases like "the round table" have the maximum descriptive meaning. An interesting intermediate position is occupied by 'impure' proper names like "The Round Table" – substantival phrases which have grown capital letters.

(3)   Finally, they may be divided into the following two classes:

(a)   those of which the correct referring use is regulated by some *general* referring-cum-ascriptive conventions. To this class belong both pronouns, which have the least descriptive meaning, and substantival phrases which have the most;

(b)   those of which the correct referring use is regulated by no general conventions, either of the contextual or the ascriptive kind, but by conventions which are *ad hoc* for each particular use (though not for each particular utterance). Roughly speaking, the most familiar kind of proper names belong to this class. Ignorance of a man's name is not ignorance of the language. This is why we do not speak of the meaning of proper names. (But it won't do to say they are meaningless.) Again an intermediate position is occupied by such phrases as "The Old Pretender". Only an old pretender may be so referred to; but to know which old pretender is not to know a general, but an *ad hoc*, convention.

In the case of phrases of the form "the so-and-so" used referringly, the use of "the" together with the position of the phrase in the sentence (i.e. at the beginning, or following a transitive verb or preposition) acts as a signal *that* a unique reference is being made; and the following noun, or noun and adjective, together with the context of utterance, shows *what* unique reference is being made. In general the functional difference between common nouns and adjectives is that the former are naturally and commonly used referringly, while the latter are not commonly, or so naturally, used in this way, except as qualifying nouns; though they can be and are, so used alone. And of course this functional difference is not independent of the descriptive force peculiar to each word. In general we should expect the descriptive force of nouns to be such that they are more efficient tools for the job of showing what unique reference is intended when such a reference is signalised; and we should also expect the descriptive force of the words we naturally and commonly use to make unique reference to mirror our interest in the salient, relatively permanent and behavioural characteristics of things. These two expectations are not independent of one another; and, if we look at the differences between the commoner sort of common nouns and the commoner sort of adjectives, we find them both fulfilled. These are differences of the kind that Locke quaintly reports, when he speaks of our ideas of substances being *collections* of simple ideas; when he says that "powers make up a great part of our ideas of substances"; and when he goes on to contrast the identity of real and nominal essence in the case of simple ideas with their lack of identity and the shiftingness of the nominal essence in the case of substances. "Substance" itself is the troublesome tribute Locke pays to his dim awareness of the difference in predominant linguistic function that lingered even when the noun had been expanded into a more or less indefinite string of adjectives. Russell repeats Locke's mistake with a difference when, admitting the inference from syntax to reality to the extent of feeling that he can get rid of this metaphysical unknown only if he can purify language of the referring function altogether, he draws up his programme for "abolishing particulars"; a programme, in fact, for abolishing the distinction of logical use which I am here at pains to emphasise.

The contextual requirement for the referring use of pronouns may be stated with the greatest precision in some cases (e.g. "I" and "you") and only with the greatest vagueness in others ("it" and "this"). I propose to say nothing further about pronouns, except to point to an additional symptom of the failure to recognise the uniquely referring use for what it is; the fact, namely, that certain logicians have actually sought to elucidate the nature of a variable by offering such *sentences* as "he is sick", "it is green", as examples of something in ordinary speech like a *sentential function*. Now of course it is true that the word "he" may be used on different occasions to refer to different people or different animals: so may the word "John" and the phrase "the cat". What deters such logicians from treating these two expressions as quasi-variables is, in the first case, the lingering superstition that a name is logically tied to a single individual, and, in the second case, the descriptive meaning of the word "cat". But "he", which has a wide range of applications and minimal descriptive force, only acquires a use as a referring word. It is this fact, together with the failure to accord to expressions used referringly, the place in logic which belongs to them (the place held open for the mythical logically proper name), that accounts for the misleading attempt to elucidate the nature of the variable by reference to such words as "he", "she", "it".

Of ordinary proper names it is sometimes said that they are essentially words each of which is used to refer to just one individual. This is obviously false. Many ordinary personal names – names *par excellence* – are correctly used to refer to numbers of people. An ordinary personal name,

is, roughly, a word, used referringly, of which the use is *not* dictated by any descriptive meaning the word may have, and is *not* prescribed by any such general rule for use as a referring expression (or a part of a referring expression) as we find in the case of such words as "I", "this" and "the", but is governed by *ad hoc* conventions for each particular set of applications of the word to a given person. The important point is that the correctness of such applications does not follow from any *general* rule or convention for the use of the word as such. (The limit of absurdity and obvious circularity is reached in the attempt to treat names as disguised description in Russell's sense; for what is in the special sense implied, but not entailed, by my now referring to someone by name is simply the existence of someone, *now being referred to*, who is *conventionally referred to* by that name.) Even this feature of names, however, is only a symptom of the purpose for which they are employed. At present our choice of names is partly arbitrary, partly dependent on legal and social observances. It would be perfectly possible to have a thoroughgoing *system* of names, based e.g. on dates of birth, or on a minute classification of physiological and anatomical differences. But the success of any such system would depend entirely on the convenience of the resulting name-allotments for the purpose of making unique references; and this would depend on the multiplicity of the classifications used and the degree to which they cut haphazard across normal social groupings. Given a sufficient degree of both, the selectivity supplied by context would do the rest; just as is the case with our present naming habits. Had we such a system, we could use name-words descriptively (as we do at present, to a limited extent and in a different way, with some famous names) as well as referringly. But it is by criteria derived from consideration of the requirements of the referring task that we should assess the adequacy of any system of naming. From the naming point of view, no kind of classification would be better or worse than any other simply because of the kind of classification – natal or anatomical – that it was.

I have already mentioned the class of quasi-names, of substantival phrases which grow capital letters, and of which such phrases as "the Glorious Revolution", "the Great War", "the Annunciation", "the Round Table" are examples. While the descriptive meaning of the words which follow

the definite article is still relevant to their referring role, the capital letters are a sign of that extralogical selectivity in their referring use, which
is characteristic of pure names. Such phrases are
found in print or in writing when one member
of some class of events or things is of quite
outstanding interest in a certain society. These
phrases are embryonic names. A phrase may, for
obvious reasons, pass into, and out of, this class
(e.g. "the Great War").

V

I want to conclude by considering, all too briefly,
three further problems about referring uses.

(a) *Indefinite references*. Not all referring uses of
singular expressions forestall the question "What
(who, which one) are you talking about?" There
are some which either invite this question, or
disclaim the intention or ability to answer it.
Examples are such sentence-beginnings as "A man
told me that . . .", "Someone told me that. . . ."
The orthodox (Russellian) doctrine is that such
sentences are existential, but not uniquely existential. This seems wrong in several ways. It is
ludicrous to suggest that part of what is asserted
is that the class of men or persons is not empty.
Certainly this is *implied* in the by now familiar
sense of implication; but the implication is also
as much an implication of the *uniqueness* of the
particular object of reference as when I begin a
sentence with such a phrase as "the table". The
difference between the use of the definite and
indefinite articles is, very roughly, as follows.
We use "the" either when a previous reference
has been made, and when "the" signalises that
the same reference is being made; or when, in
the absence of a previous indefinite reference, the
context (including the hearer's assumed knowledge) is expected to enable the hearer to tell
what reference is being made. We use "a" either
when these conditions are not fulfilled, or when,
although a definite reference *could* be made, we
wish to keep dark the identity of the individual
to whom, or to which, we are referring. This is
the *arch* use of such a phrase as "a certain person"
or "some one"; where it could be expanded, not
into "some one, but you wouldn't (or I don't)
know who" but into "some one, but I'm not
telling you who."

(b) *Identification statements*. By this label I intend statements like the following:

(i*a*) That is the man who swam the channel
        twice on one day.
(ii*a*) Napoleon was the man who ordered the
        execution of the Duc D'Enghien.

The puzzle about these statements is that their
grammatical predicates do not seem to be used
in a straightforwardly ascriptive way as are the
grammatical predicates of the statements:

(i*b*) That man swam the channel twice in
        one day.
(ii*b*) Napoleon ordered the execution of the
        Duc D'Enghien.

But if, in order to avoid blurring the difference
between (i*a*) and (i*b*) and (ii*a*) and (ii*b*), one says
that the phrases which form the grammatical
complements of (i*a*) and (ii*a*) are being used
referringly, one becomes puzzled about what is
being said in these sentences. We seem then to
be referring to the same person twice over and
either saying nothing about him and thus making no statement, or identifying him with himself and thus producing a trivial identity.

The bogey of triviality can be dismissed. This
only arises for those who think of the object
referred to by the use of an expression as its
meaning, and thus think of the subject and complement of these sentences as meaning the same
because they could be used to refer to the same
person.

I think the differences between sentences in
the (a) group and sentences in the (b) group can
best be understood by considering the differences between the circumstances in which you
would say (i*a*) and the circumstances in which
you would say (i*b*). You would say (i*a*) instead of
(i*b*) if you knew or believed that your hearer
knew or believed that *some one* had swum the
channel twice in one day. You say (i*a*) when you
take your hearer to be in the position of one
who can ask: "Who swam the channel twice in
one day?" (And in asking this, he is not saying
that anyone did, though his asking it implies –
in the relevant sense – that someone did.) Such
sentences are like answers to such questions.
They are better called "identification-statements"
than "identities". Sentence (i*a*) does not assert
more or less than sentence (i*b*). It is just that
you say (i*a*) to a man whom you take to know
certain things that you take to be unknown to
the man to whom you say (i*b*).

This is, in the barest essentials, the solution
to Russell's puzzle about "denoting phrases"
joining by "is"; one of the puzzles which he

claims for the Theory of Descriptions the merit of solving.

(c) *The logic of subjects and predicates.* Much of what I have said of the uniquely referring use of expressions can be extended, with suitable modifications, to the non-uniquely referring use of expressions; i.e. to some uses of expressions consisting of "the", "all the", "all", "some", "some of the", etc. followed by a noun, qualified or unqualified, in the *plural*; to some uses of "they", "them", "those", "these"; and to conjunctions of names. Expressions of the first kind have a special interest. Roughly speaking, orthodox modern criticism, inspired by mathematical logic, of such traditional doctrines as that of the Square of Opposition and of some of the forms of the syllogism traditionally recognised as valid, rests on the familiar failure to recognise the special sense in which existential assertions may be implied by the referring use of expressions. The universal propositions of the fourfold schedule, it is said, must *either* be given a negatively existential interpretation (e.g., for A, "there are no Xs which are not Ys") *or* they must be interpreted as conjunctions of negatively and positively existential statements of, e.g., the form (for A) "there are no Xs which are not Ys, and there are Xs". The I and O forms are normally given a positively existential interpretation. It is then seen that, whichever of the above alternat-ives is selected, some of the traditional laws have to be abandoned. The dilemma, however, is a bogus one. If we interpret the propositions of the schedule as neither positively, nor negatively, nor positively *and* negatively, existential, but as sentences such that *the question of whether they are being used to make true or false assertions does not arise except when the existential condition is fulfilled for the subject term*, then all the traditional laws hold good together. And this interpretation is far closer to the most common uses of expressions beginning with "all" and "some" that is any Russellian alternative. For these expressions are most commonly used in the referring way. A literal-minded and childless man asked whether all his children are asleep will certainly not answer "Yes" on the ground that he has none; but nor will he answer "No" on this ground. Since he has no children, the question does not arise. To say this is not to say that I may not use the sentence, "All my children are asleep", with the intention of letting someone know that I have children, or of deceiving him into thinking that I have. Nor is it any weakening of my thesis to concede that singular phrases of the form "the so-and-so" may sometimes be used with a similar purpose. Neither Aristotelian nor Russellian rules give the exact logic of any expression of ordinary language; for ordinary language has no exact logic.

Notes

1 This usage of 'use' is, of course, different from (a) the current usage in which 'use' (of a particular word, phrase, sentence) = (roughly) 'rules for using' = (roughly) 'meaning'; and from (b) my own usage in the phrase "uniquely referring use of expressions" in which 'use' = (roughly) 'way of using'.

2 Since this article was written, there has appeared a clear statement of this point by Mr Geach in *Analysis* 10/4 (March 1950).

3 The unsophisticated kind begins: "Once upon time there was . . .".

4 And this in spite of the danger-signal of that phrase, "*misleading* grammatical form".

5 I neglect relational sentences; for these require, not a modification in the principle of what I say, but a complication of the detail.

5

Meaning

H. P. Grice

Consider the following sentences:

'Those spots mean (meant) measles.'

'Those spots didn't mean anything to me, but to the doctor they meant measles.'

'The recent budget means that we shall have a hard year.'

(1) I cannot say, 'Those spots meant measles, but he hadn't got measles', and I cannot say, 'The recent budget means that we shall have a hard year, but we shan't have'. That is to say, in cases like the above, *x meant that p* and *x means that p* entail *p*.

(2) I cannot argue from 'Those spots mean (meant) measles' to any conclusion about 'what is (was) meant by those spots'; for example, I am not entitled to say, 'What was meant by those spots was that he had measles'. Equally I cannot draw from the statement about the recent budget the conclusion 'What is meant by the recent budget is that we shall have a hard year'.

(3) I cannot argue from 'Those spots meant measles' to any conclusion to the effect that somebody or other meant by those spots so-and-so. *Mutatis mutandis*, the same is true of the sentence about the recent budget.

(4) For none of the above examples can a restatement be found in which the verb 'mean' is followed by a sentence or phrase in inverted

Originally published in *Philosophical Review* 66 (1957). Copyright 1957 Cornell University. Reprinted by permission of the publisher.

commas. Thus 'Those spots meant measles' cannot be reformulated as 'Those spots meant "measles"' or as 'Those spots meant "he has measles"'.

(5) On the other hand, for all these examples an approximate restatement can be found beginning with the phrase 'The fact that . . .'; for example, 'The fact that he had those spots meant that he had measles' and 'The fact that the recent budget was as it was means that we shall have a hard year'.

Now contrast the above sentences with the following:

'Those three rings on the bell (of the bus) mean that the bus is full.'

'That remark, "Smith couldn't get on without his trouble and strife", meant that Smith found his wife indispensable.'

(1) I can use the first of these and go on to say, 'But it isn't in fact full – the conductor has made a mistake'; and I can use the second and go on, 'But in fact Smith deserted her seven years ago'. That is to say, here *x means that p* and *x meant that p* do not entail *p*.

(2) I can argue from the first to some statement about 'what is (was) meant' by the rings on the bell and from the second to some statement about 'what is (was) meant' by the quoted remark.

(3) I can argue from the first sentence to the conclusion that somebody (viz., the conductor) meant, or at any rate should have meant, by the

rings that the bus is full, and I can argue analogously for the second sentence.

(4) The first sentence can be restated in a form in which the verb 'mean' is followed by a phrase in inverted commas, that is, 'Those three rings on the bell mean "the bus is full"'. So also can the second sentence.

(5) Such a sentence as 'The fact that the bell has been rung three times means that the bus is full' is not a restatement of the meaning of the first sentence. Both may be true, but they do not have, even approximately, the same meaning.

When the expressions 'means', 'means something', 'means that' are used in the kind of way in which they are used in the first set of sentences, I shall speak of the sense, or senses, in which they are used, as the *natural* sense, or senses, of the expressions in question. When the expressions are used in the kind of way in which they are used, in the second set of sentences, I shall speak of the sense, or senses, in which they are used, as the *non-natural* sense, or senses, of the expressions in question. I shall use the abbreviation 'means$_{NN}$' to distinguish the non-natural sense or senses.

I propose, for convenience, also to include under the head of natural senses of 'mean' such senses of 'mean' as may be exemplified in sentences of the pattern '*A* means (meant) *to do* so-and-so (by *x*)', where *A* is a human agent. By contrast, as the previous examples show, I include under the head of non-natural senses of 'mean' any senses of 'mean' found in sentences of the patterns '*A* means (meant) something by *x*' or '*A* means (meant) by *x* that . . .' (This is over-rigid; but it will serve as an indication.)

I do not want to maintain that *all* our uses of 'mean' fall easily, obviously, and tidily into one of the two groups I have distinguished; but I think that in most cases we should be at least fairly strongly inclined to assimilate a use of 'mean' to one group rather than to the other. The question which now arises is this: 'What more can be said about the distinction between the cases where we should say that the word is applied in a natural sense and the cases where we should say that the word is applied in a non-natural sense?' Asking this question will not of course prohibit us from trying to give an explanation of 'meaning$_{NN}$' in terms of one or another natural sense of 'mean'.

This question about the distinction between natural and non-natural meaning is, I think, what people are getting at when they display an interest in a distinction between 'natural' and 'conventional' signs. But I think my formulation is better. For some things which can mean$_{NN}$ something are not signs (e.g., words are not), and some are not conventional in any ordinary sense (e.g., certain gestures); while some things which mean naturally are not signs of what they mean (cf. the recent budget example).

I want first to consider briefly, and reject, what I might term a causal type of answer to the question, 'What is meaning$_{NN}$?' We might try to say, for instance, more or less with C. L. Stevenson,[1] that for *x* to mean$_{NN}$ something, *x* must have (roughly) a tendency to produce in an audience some attitude (cognitive or otherwise) and a tendency, in the case of a speaker, to *be* produced *by* that attitude, these tendencies being dependent on 'an elaborate process of conditioning attending the use of the sign in communication'.[2] This clearly will not do.

(1) Let us consider a case where an utterance, if it qualifies at all as meaning$_{NN}$ something, will be of a descriptive or informative kind and the relevant attitude, therefore, will be a cognitive one, for example, a belief. (I use 'utterance' as a neutral word to apply to any candidate for meaning$_{NN}$; it has a convenient act/object ambiguity.) It is no doubt the case that many people have a tendency to put on a tail coat when they think they are about to go to a dance, and it is no doubt also the case that many people, on seeing someone put on a tail coat, would conclude that the person in question was about to go to a dance.

Does this satisfy us that putting on a tail coat means$_{NN}$ that one is about to go to a dance (or indeed means$_{NN}$ anything at all)? Obviously not. It is no help to refer to the qualifying phrase 'dependent on an elaborate process of conditioning . . .'. For if all this means is that the response to the sight of a tail coat being put on is in some way learned or acquired, it will not exclude the present case from being one of meaning$_{NN}$. But if we have to take seriously the second part of the qualifying phrase ('attending the use of the sign in communication'), then the account of meaning$_{NN}$ is obviously circular. We might just as well say, '*X* has meaning$_{NN}$ if it is used in communication', which, though true, is not helpful.

(2) If this is not enough, there is a difficulty – really the same difficulty, I think – which Stevenson recognizes: how we are to avoid saying, for example, that 'Jones is tall' is part of what is meant by 'Jones is an athlete', since to tell someone that Jones is an athlete would tend to make him believe that Jones is tall. Stevenson here resorts to invoking linguistic rules, namely, a permissive rule of language that 'athletes may be non-tall'. This amounts to saying that we are not prohibited by rule from speaking of 'non-tall athletes'. But why are we not prohibited? Not because it is not bad grammar, or is not impolite, and so on, but presumably because it is not meaningless (or, if this is too strong, does not in any way violate the rules of meaning for the expressions concerned). But this seems to involve us in another circle. Moreover, one wants to ask why, if it is legitimate to appeal here to rules to distinguish what is meant from what is suggested, this appeal was not made earlier, in the case of groans, for example, to deal with which Stevenson originally introduced the qualifying phrase about dependence on conditioning.

A further deficiency in a causal theory of the type just expounded seems to be that, even if we accept it as it stands, we are furnished with an analysis only of statements about the *standard* meaning, or the meaning in general, of a 'sign'. No provision is made for dealing with statements about what a particular speaker or writer means by a sign on a particular occasion (which may well diverge from the standard meaning of the sign); nor is it obvious how the theory could be adapted to make such provision. One might even go further in criticism and maintain that the causal theory ignores the fact that the meaning (in general) of a sign needs to be explained in terms of what users of the sign do (or should) mean by it on particular occasions; and so the latter notion, which is unexplained by the causal theory, is in fact the fundamental one. I am sympathetic to this more radical criticism, though I am aware that the point is controversial.

I do not propose to consider any further theories of the 'causal-tendency' type. I suspect no such theory could avoid difficulties analogous to those I have outlined without utterly losing its claim to rank as a theory of this type.

I will now try a different and, I hope, more promising line. If we can elucidate the meaning of

'x meant$_{NN}$ something (on a particular occasion)'
and
'x meant$_{NN}$ that so-and-so (on a particular occasion)'

and of

'A meant$_{NN}$ something by x (on a particular occasion)' and
'A meant$_{NN}$ by x that so-and-so (on a particular occasion)',

this might reasonably be expected to help us with

'x means$_{NN}$ (timeless) something (that so-and-so)',
'A means$_{NN}$ (timeless) by x something (that so-and-so)',

and with the explication of 'means the same as', 'understands', 'entails', and so on. Let us for the moment pretend that we have to deal only with utterances which might be informative or descriptive.

A first shot would be to suggest that 'x meant$_{NN}$ something' would be true if x was intended by its utterer to induce a belief in some 'audience' and that to say what the belief was would be to say what x meant$_{NN}$. This will not do. I might leave B's handkerchief near the scene of a murder in order to induce the detective to believe that B was the murderer; but we should not want to say that the handkerchief (or my leaving it there) meant$_{NN}$ anything or that I had meant$_{NN}$ by leaving it that B was the murderer. Clearly we must at least add that, for x to have meant$_{NN}$ anything, not merely must it have been 'uttered' with the intention of inducing a certain belief but also the utterer must have intended an 'audience' to recognize the intention behind the utterance.

This, though perhaps better, is not good enough. Consider the following cases:

(1) Herod presents Salome with the head of St. John the Baptist on a charger.
(2) Feeling faint, a child lets its mother see how pale it is (hoping that she may draw her own conclusions and help).
(3) I leave the china my daughter has broken lying around for my wife to see.

Here we seem to have cases which satisfy the conditions so far given for meaning$_{NN}$. For example,

Herod intended to make Salome believe that St. John the Baptist was dead and no doubt also intended Salome to recognize that he intended her to believe that St. John the Baptist was dead. Similarly for the other cases. Yet I certainly do not think that we should want to say that we have here cases of meaning$_{NN}$.

What we want to find is the difference between, for example, 'deliberately and openly letting someone know' and 'telling' and between 'getting someone to think' and 'telling'.

The way out is perhaps as follows. Compare the following two cases:

(1) I show Mr. X a photograph of Mr. Y displaying undue familiarity to Mrs. X.
(2) I draw a picture of Mr. Y behaving in this manner and show it to Mr. X.

I find that I want to deny that in (1) the photograph (or my showing it to Mr. X) mean$_{NN}$ anything at all; while I want to assert that in (2) the picture (or my drawing and showing it) meant$_{NN}$ something (that Mr. Y had been unduly unfamiliar), or at least that I had meant$_{NN}$ by it that Mr. Y had been unduly familiar. What is the difference between the two cases? Surely that in case (1) Mr. X's recognition of my intention to make him believe that there is something between Mr. Y and Mrs. X is (more or less) irrelevant to the production of this effect by the photograph. Mr. X would be led by the photograph at least to suspect Mrs. X even if instead of showing it to him I had left it in his room by accident; and I (the photograph shower) would not be unaware of this. But it will make a difference to the effect of my picture on Mr. X whether or not he takes me to be intending to inform him (make him believe something) about Mrs. X, and not to be just doodling or trying to produce a work of art.

But now we seem to be landed in a further difficulty if we accept this account. For consider now, say, frowning. If I frown spontaneously, in the ordinary course of events, someone looking at me may well treat the frown as a natural sign of displeasure. But if I frown deliberately (to convey my displeasure), an onlooker may be expected, provided he recognizes my intention, *still* to conclude that I am displeased. Ought we not then to say, since it could not be expected to make any difference to the onlooker's reaction whether he regards my frown as spontaneous or

as intended to be informative, that my frown (deliberate) does *not* mean$_{NN}$ anything? I think this difficulty can be met; for though in general a deliberate frown may have the same effect (as regards inducing belief in my displeasure) as a spontaneous frown, it can be expected to have the same effect only *provided* the audience takes it as intended to convey displeasure. That is, if we take away the recognition of intention, leaving the other circumstances (including the recognition of the frown as deliberate), the belief-producing tendency of the frown must be regarded as being impaired or destroyed.

Perhaps we may sum up what is necessary for A to mean something by x as follows. A must intend to induce by x a belief in an audience, and he must also intend his utterance to be recognized as so intended. But these intentions are not independent; the recognition is intended by A to play its part in inducing the belief, and if it does not do so something will have gone wrong with the fulfilment of A's intentions. Moreover, A's intending that the recognition should play this part implies, I think, that he assumes that there is some chance that it will in fact play this part, that he does not regard it as a foregone conclusion that the belief will be induced in the audience whether or not the intention behind the utterance is recognized. Shortly, perhaps, we may say that 'A meant something by x' is roughly equivalent to 'A uttered x with the intention of inducing a belief by means of the recognition of this intention'. (This seems to involve a reflexive paradox, but it does not really do so.)

Now perhaps it is time to drop the pretence that we have to deal only with 'informative' cases. Let us start with some examples of imperatives or quasi-imperatives. I have a very avaricious man in my room, and I want him to go; so I throw a pound note out of the window. Is there here any utterance with a meaning? No, because in behaving as I did, I did not intend his recognition of my purpose to be in any way effective in getting him to go. This is parallel to the photograph case. If on the other hand I had pointed to the door or given him a little push, then my behaviour might well be held to constitute a meaningful utterance, just because the recognition of my intention would be intended by me to be effective in speeding his departure. Another pair of cases would be (1) a policeman who stops a car by standing in its way and (2) a policeman who stops a car by waving.

Or, to turn briefly to another type of case, if as an examiner I fail a man, I may well cause him distress or indignation or humiliation; and if I am vindictive, I may intend this effect and even intend him to recognize my intention. But I should not be inclined to say that my failing him meant anything. On the other hand, if I cut someone in the street I do feel inclined to assimilate this to the cases of meaning, and this inclination seems to me dependent on the fact that I could not reasonably expect him to be distressed (indignant, humiliated) unless he recognized my intention to affect him in this way. (Cf., if my college stopped my salary altogether I should accuse them of ruining me; if they cut it by 2*s*. 6*d*. I might accuse them of insulting me; with some intermediate amounts I might not know quite what to say.)

Perhaps then we may make the following generalizations.

(1) '*A* meant something by *x*' is (roughly) equivalent to '*A* intended the utterance of *x* to produce some effect in an audience by means of the recognition of this intention'; and we may add that to ask what *A* meant is to ask for a specification of the intended effect (though, of course, it may not always be possible to get a straight answer involving a 'that' clause, for example, 'a belief that . . .').

(2) '*x* meant something' is (roughly) equivalent to 'Somebody meant something by *x*'. Here again there will be cases where this will not quite work. I feel inclined to say that (as regards traffic lights) the change to red meant that the traffic was to stop; but it would be very unnatural to say, 'Somebody (e.g., the Corporation) meant by the red-light change that the traffic was to stop.' Nevertheless, there seems to be *some* sort of reference to somebody's intentions.

(3) '*x* means$_{NN}$ (timeless) that so-and-so' might as a first shot be equated with some statement or disjunction of statements about what 'people' (vague) intend (with qualifications about 'recognition') to effect by *x*. I shall have a word to say about this.

Will any kind of intended effect do, or may there be cases where an effect is intended (with the required qualifications) and yet we should not want to talk of meaning$_{NN}$? Suppose I discovered some person so constituted that, when I told him that whenever I grunted in a special

way I wanted him to blush or to incur some physical malady, thereafter whenever he recognized the grunt (and with it my intention), he did blush or incur the malady. Should we then want to say that the grunt meant$_{NN}$ something? I do not think so. This points to the fact that for *x* to have meaning$_{NN}$, the intended effect must be something which in some sense is within the control of the audience, or that in some sense of 'reason' the recognition of the intention behind *x* is for the audience a reason and not merely a cause. It might look as if there is a sort of pun here ('reason for believing' and 'reason for doing'), but I do not think this is serious. For though no doubt from one point of view questions about reasons for believing are questions about evidence and so quite different from questions about reasons for doing, nevertheless to recognize an utterer's intention in uttering *x* (descriptive utterance), to have a reason for believing that so-and-so, is at least quite like 'having a motive for' accepting so-and-so. Decisions 'that' seem to involve decisions 'to' (and this is why we can 'refuse to believe' and also be 'compelled to believe'). (The 'cutting' case needs slightly different treatment, for one cannot in any straightforward sense 'decide' to be offended; but one can refuse to be offended.) It looks then as if the intended effect must be something within the control of the audience, or at least the *sort* of thing which is within its control.

One point before passing to an objection or two. I think it follows that from what I have said about the connexion between meaning$_{NN}$ and recognition of intention that (insofar as I am right) only what I may call the primary intention of an utterer is relevant to the meaning$_{NN}$ of an utterance. For if I utter *x*, intending (with the aid of the recognition of this intention) to induce an effect *E*, and intend this effect *E* to lead to a further effect *F*, then insofar as the occurrence of *F* is thought to be dependent solely on *E*, I cannot regard *F* as in the least dependent on recognition of my intention to induce *E*. That is, if (say) I intend to get a man to do something by giving him some information, it cannot be regarded as relevant to the meaning$_{NN}$ of my utterance to describe what I intend him to do.

Now some question may be raised about my use, fairly free, of such words as 'intention' and 'recognition'. I must disclaim any intention of peopling all our talking life with armies of complicated psychological occurrences. I do not hope to solve any philosophical puzzles about intending, but I do want briefly to argue that no special difficulties are raised by my use of the word 'intention' in connexion with meaning. First, there will be cases where an utterance is accompanied or preceded by a conscious 'plan', or explicit formulation of intention (e.g., I declare how I am going to use x, or ask myself how to 'get something across'). The presence of such an explicit 'plan' obviously counts fairly heavily in favour of the utterer's intention (meaning) being as 'planned'; though it is not, I think, conclusive; for example, a speaker who has declared an intention to use a familiar expression in an unfamiliar way may slip into the familiar use. Similarly in non-linguistic cases: if we are asking about an agent's intention, a previous expression counts heavily; nevertheless, a man might plan to throw a letter in the dustbin and yet take it to the post; when lifting his hand he might 'come to' and say *either* 'I didn't intend to do this at all' *or* 'I suppose I must have been intending to put it in'.

Explicitly formulated linguistic (or quasi-linguistic) intentions are no doubt comparatively rare. In their absence we would seem to rely on very much the same kinds of criteria as we do in the case of non-linguistic intentions where there is a general usage. An utterer is held to intend to convey what is normally conveyed (or normally intended to be conveyed), and we require a good reason for accepting that a particular use diverges from the general usage (e.g., he never

knew or had forgotten the general usage). Similarly in non-linguistic cases: we are presumed to intend the normal consequences of our actions.

Again, in cases where there is doubt, say, about which of two or more things an utterer intends to convey, we tend to refer to the context (linguistic or otherwise) of the utterance and ask which of the alternatives would be relevant to other things he is saying or doing, or which intention in a particular situation would fit in with some purpose he obviously has (e.g., a man who calls for a 'pump' at a fire would not want a bicycle pump). Non-linguistic parallels are obvious: context is a criterion in settling the question of why a man who has just put a cigarette in his mouth has put his hand in his pocket; relevance to an obvious end is a criterion in settling why a man is running away from a bull.

In certain linguistic cases we ask the utterer afterwards about his intention, and in a few of these cases (the very difficult ones, like a philosopher asked to explain the meaning of an unclear passage in one of his works), the answer is not based on what he remembers but is more like a decision, a decision about how what he said is to be taken. I cannot find a non-linguistic parallel here; but the case is so special as not to seem to contribute a vital difference.

All this is very obvious; but surely to show that the criteria for judging linguistic intentions are very like the criteria for judging non-linguistic intentions is to show that linguistic intentions are very like non-linguistic intentions.

Notes

1   *Ethics and Language* (New Haven, 1944), ch. III.
2   Ibid., p. 57.

6

Truth and Meaning

Donald Davidson

It is conceded by most philosophers of language, and recently even by some linguists, that a satisfactory theory of meaning must give an account of how the meanings of sentences depend upon the meanings of words. Unless such an account could be supplied for a particular language, it is argued, there would be no explaining the fact that we can learn the language: no explaining the fact that, on mastering a finite vocabulary and a finitely stated set of rules, we are prepared to produce and to understand any of a potential infinitude of sentences. I do not dispute these vague claims, in which I sense more than a kernel of truth.[1] Instead I want to ask what it is for a theory to give an account of the kind adumbrated.

One proposal is to begin by assigning some entity as meaning to each word (or other significant syntactical feature) of the sentence; thus we might assign Theaetetus to 'Theaetetus' and the property of flying to 'flies' in the sentence 'Theaetetus flies'. The problem then arises how the meaning of the sentence is generated from these meanings. Viewing concatenation as a significant piece of syntax, we may assign to it the relation of participating in or instantiating; however, it is obvious that we have here the start of an infinite regress. Frege sought to avoid the regress by saying that the entities corresponding to predicates (for example) are 'unsaturated' or 'incomplete' in contrast to the entities that correspond to names, but this doctrine seems to label a difficulty rather than solve it.

The point will emerge if we think for a moment of complex singular terms, to which Frege's theory applies along with sentences. Consider the expression 'the father of Annette'; how does the meaning of the whole depend on the meaning of the parts? The answer would seem to be that the meaning of 'the father of' is such that when this expression is prefixed to a singular term the result refers to the father of the person to whom the singular term refers. What part is played, in this account, by the unsaturated or incomplete entity for which 'the father of' stands? All we can think to say is that this entity 'yields' or 'gives' the father of x as value when the argument is x, or perhaps that this entity maps people onto their fathers. It may not be clear whether the entity for which 'the father of' is said to stand performs any genuine explanatory function as long as we stick to individual expressions; so think instead of the infinite class of expressions formed by writing 'the father of' zero or more times in front of 'Annette'. It is easy to supply a theory that tells, for an arbitrary one of these singular terms, what it refers to: if the term is 'Annette' it refers to Annette, while if the term is complex, consisting of 'the father of' prefixed to a singular term t, then it refers to the father of the person to whom t refers. It is obvious that no entity corresponding to 'the father of' is, or needs to be, mentioned in stating this theory.

It would be inappropriate to complain that this little theory *uses* the words 'the father of' in

Originally published in *Synthèse* 17 (1967). Reprinted by kind permission of Kluwer Academic Publishers, Dordrecht, The Netherlands.

Donald Davidson

giving the reference of expressions containing those words. For the task was to give the meaning of all expressions in a certain infinite set on the basis of the meaning of the parts; it was not in the bargain also to give the meanings of the atomic parts. On the other hand, it is now evident that a satisfactory theory of the meanings of complex expressions may not require entities as meanings of all the parts. It behooves us then to rephrase our demand on a satisfactory theory of meaning so as not to suggest that individual words must have meanings at all, in any sense that transcends the fact that they have a systematic effect on the meanings of the sentences in which they occur. Actually, for the case at hand we can do better still in stating the criterion of success: what we wanted, and what we got, is a theory that entails every sentence of the form 't refers to x' where 't' is replaced by a structural description[2] of a singular term, and 'x' is replaced by that term itself. Further, our theory accomplishes this without appeal to any semantical concepts beyond the basic 'refers to'. Finally, the theory clearly suggests an effective procedure for determining, for any singular term in its universe, what that term refers to.

A theory with such evident merits deserves wider application. The device proposed by Frege to this end has a brilliant simplicity: count predicates as a special case of functional expressions, and sentences as a special case of complex singular terms. Now, however, a difficulty looms if we want to continue in our present (implicit) course of identifying the meaning of a singular term with its reference. The difficulty follows upon making two reasonable assumptions: that logically equivalent singular terms have the same reference; and that a singular term does not change its reference if a contained singular term is replaced by another with the same reference. But now suppose that 'R' and 'S' abbreviate any two sentences alike in truth value. Then the following four sentences have the same reference:

(1) R
(2) $\hat{x}(x = x.R) = \hat{x}(x = x)$
(3) $\hat{x}(x = x.S) = \hat{x}(x = x)$
(4) S

For (1) and (2) are logically equivalent, as are (3) and (4), while (3) differs from (2) only in containing the singular term '$\hat{x}(x = x.S)$' where (2) contains '$\hat{x}(x = x.R)$' and these refer to the same thing if S and R are alike in truth value. Hence any two sentences have the same reference if they have the same truth value.[3] And if the meaning of a sentence is what it refers to, all sentences alike in truth value must be synonymous – an intolerable result.

Apparently we must abandon the present approach as leading to a theory of meaning. This is the natural point at which to turn for help to the distinction between meaning and reference. The trouble, we are told, is that questions of reference are, in general, settled by extra-linguistic facts, questions of meaning not, and the facts can conflate the references of expressions that are not synonymous. If we want a theory that gives the meaning (as distinct from reference) of each sentence, we must start with the meaning (as distinct from reference) of the parts.

Up to here we have been following in Frege's footsteps; thanks to him, the path is well known and even well worn. But now, I would like to suggest, we have reached an impasse: the switch from reference to meaning leads to no useful account of how the meanings of sentences depend upon the meanings of the words (or other structural features) that compose them. Ask, for example, for the meaning of 'Theaetetus flies'. A Fregean answer might go something like this: given the meaning of 'Theaetetus' as argument, the meaning of 'flies' yields the meaning of 'Theaetetus flies' as value. The vacuity of this answer is obvious. We wanted to know what the meaning of 'Theaetetus flies' is; it is no progress to be told that it is the meaning of 'Theaetetus flies'. This much we knew before any theory was in sight. In the bogus account just given, talk of the structure of the sentence and of the meanings of words was idle, for it played no role in producing the given description of the meaning of the sentence.

The contrast here between a real and pretended account will be plainer still if we ask for a theory, analogous to the miniature theory of reference of singular terms just sketched, but different in dealing with meanings in place of references. What analogy demands is a theory that has as consequences all sentences of the form 's means m' where 's' is replaced by a structural description of a sentence and 'm' is replaced by a singular term that refers to the meaning of that sentence; a theory, moreover, that provides an effective method for arriving at the meaning of an arbitrary sentence structurally described.

Clearly some more articulate way of referring to meanings than any we have seen is essential if these criteria are to be met.[4] Meanings as entities, or the related concept of synonymy, allow us to formulate the following rule relating sentences and their parts: sentences are synonymous whose corresponding parts are synonymous ('corresponding' here needs spelling out of course). And meanings as entities may, in theories such as Frege's, do duty, on occasion as references, thus losing their status as entities distinct from references. Paradoxically, the one thing meanings do not seem to do is oil the wheels of a theory of meaning – at least as long as we require of such a theory that it non-trivially give the meaning of every sentence in the language. My objection to meanings in the theory of meaning is not that they are abstract or that their identity conditions are obscure, but that they have no demonstrated use.

This is the place to scotch another hopeful thought. Suppose we have a satisfactory theory of syntax for our language, consisting of an effective method of telling, for an arbitrary expression, whether or not it is independently meaningful (i.e., a sentence), and assume as usual that this involves viewing each sentence as composed, in allowable ways, out of elements drawn from a fixed finite stock of atomic syntactical elements (roughly, words). The hopeful thought is that syntax, so conceived, will yield semantics when a dictionary giving the meaning of each syntactic atom is added. Hopes will be dashed, however, if semantics is to comprise a theory of meaning in our sense, for knowledge of the structural characteristics that make for meaningfulness in a sentence, plus knowledge of the meanings of the ultimate parts, does not add up to knowledge of what a sentence means. The point is easily illustrated by belief sentences. Their syntax is relatively unproblematic. Yet, adding a dictionary does not touch the standard semantic problem, which is that we cannot account for even as much as the truth conditions of such sentences on the basis of what we know of the meanings of the words in them. The situation is not radically altered by refining the dictionary to indicate which meaning or meanings an ambiguous expression bears in each of its possible contexts; the problem of belief sentences persists after ambiguities are resolved.

The fact that recursive syntax with dictionary added is not necessarily recursive semantics has been obscured in some recent writing on linguistics by the intrusion of semantic criteria into the discussion of purportedly syntactic theories. The matter would boil down to a harmless difference over terminology if the semantic criteria were clear; but they are not. While there is agreement that it is the central task of semantics to give the semantic interpretation (the meaning) of every sentence in the language, nowhere in the linguistic literature will one find, so far as I know, a straightforward account of how a theory performs this task, or how to tell when it has been accomplished. The contrast with syntax is striking. The main job of a modest syntax is to characterize *meaningfulness* (or sentencehood). We may have as much confidence in the correctness of such a characterization as we have in the representativeness of our sample and our ability to say when particular expressions are meaningful (sentences). What clear and analogous task and test exist for semantics?[5]

We decided a while back not to assume that parts of sentences have meanings except in the ontologically neutral sense of making a systematic contribution to the meaning of the sentences in which they occur. Since postulating meanings has netted nothing, let us return to that insight. One direction in which it points is a certain holistic view of meaning. If sentences depend for their meaning on their structure, and we understand the meaning of each item in the structure only as an abstraction from the totality of sentences in which it features, then we can give the meaning of any sentence (or word) only by giving the meaning of every sentence (and word) in the language. Frege said that only in the context of a sentence does a word have meaning; in the same vein he might have added that only in the context of the language does a sentence (and therefore a word) have meaning.

This degree of holism was already implicit in the suggestion that an adequate theory of meaning must entail *all* sentences of the form 's means m'. But now, having found no more help in meanings of sentences than in meanings of words, let us ask whether we can get rid of the troublesome singular terms supposed to replace 'm' and to refer to meanings. In a way, nothing could be easier: just write 's means that p', and imagine 'p' replaced by a sentence. Sentences, as we have seen, cannot name meanings, and sentences with 'that' prefixed are not names at all, unless we decide so. It looks as though we are in trouble on another count, however, for it is reasonable to expect that in wrestling with the logic of the apparently non-extensional 'means that' we will encounter problems as hard as, or perhaps identical with, the problems our theory is out to solve.

The only way I know to deal with this difficulty is simple, and radical. Anxiety that we are enmeshed in the intensional springs from using the words 'means that' as filling between description of sentence and sentence, but it may be that the success of our venture depends not on the filling but on what it fills. The theory will have done its work if it provides, for every sentence s in the language under study, a matching sentence (to replace 'p') that, in some way yet to be made clear, 'gives the meaning' of s. One obvious candidate for matching sentence is just s itself, if the object language is contained in the metalanguage; otherwise a translation of s in the metalanguage. As a final bold step, let us try treating the position occupied by 'p' extensionally: to implement this, sweep away the obscure 'means that', provide the sentence that replaces 'p' with a proper sentential connective, and supply the description that replaces 's' with its own predicate. The plausible result is

(T) s is T if and only if p.

What we require of a theory of meaning for a language L is that without appeal to any (further) semantical notions it place enough restrictions on the predicate 'is T' to entail all sentences got from schema T when 's' is replaced by a structural description of a sentence of L and 'p' by that sentence.

Any two predicates satisfying this condition have the same extension,[6] so if the metalanguage is rich enough, nothing stands in the way of putting what I am calling a theory of meaning into the form of an explicit definition of a predicate 'is T'. But whether explicitly defined or recursively characterized, it is clear that the sentences to which the predicate 'is T' applies will be just the true sentences of L, for the condition we have placed on satisfactory theories of meaning is in essence Tarski's Convention T that tests the adequacy of a formal semantical definition of truth.[7]

The path to this point has been tortuous, but the conclusion may be stated simply: a theory of meaning for a language L shows "how the meanings of sentences depend upon the meanings of words" if it contains a (recursive) definition of truth-in-L. And, so far at least, we have no other idea how to turn the trick. It is worth emphasizing that the concept of truth played no ostensible role in stating our original problem. That problem, upon refinement, led to the view that an adequate theory of meaning must characterize a predicate meeting certain conditions. It was in the nature of a discovery that such a predicate would apply exactly to the true sentences. I hope that what I am doing may be described in part as defending the philosophical importance of Tarski's semantical concept of truth. But my defense is only distantly related, if at all, to the question whether the concept Tarski has shown how to define is the (or a) philosophically interesting conception of truth, or the question whether Tarski has cast any light on the ordinary use of such words as 'true' and 'truth'. It is a misfortune that dust from futile and confused battles over these questions has prevented those with a theoretical interest in language – philosophers, logicians, psychologists, and linguists alike – from recognizing in the semantical concept of truth (under whatever name) the sophisticated and powerful foundation of a competent theory of meaning.

There is no need to suppress, of course, the obvious connection between a definition of truth of the kind Tarski has shown how to construct, and the concept of meaning. It is this: the definition works by giving necessary and sufficient conditions for the truth of every sentence, and to give truth conditions is a way of giving the meaning of a sentence. To know the semantic concept of truth for a language is to know what it is for a sentence – any sentence – to be true, and this amounts, in one good sense we can give to the phrase, to understanding the language. This at any rate is my excuse for a feature of the present discussion that is apt to shock old hands: my freewheeling use of the word 'meaning', for what I call a theory of meaning has after all turned out to make no use of meanings, whether of sentences or of words. Indeed since a Tarski-type truth definition supplies all we have asked so far of a theory of meaning, it is clear that such a theory falls comfortably within what Quine terms the 'theory of reference' as distinguished from what he terms the 'theory of meaning'. So much to the good for what I call a theory of meaning, and so much, perhaps, against my so calling it.[8]

A theory of meaning (in my mildly perverse sense) is an empirical theory, and its ambition it to account for the workings of a natural language. Like any theory, it may be tested by comparing some of its consequences with the facts. In the present case this is easy, for the theory has been characterized as issuing in an infinite flood of sentences each giving the truth conditions of a sentence; we only need to ask, in selected cases, whether what the theory avers to be the truth conditions for a sentence really are. A typical test case might involve deciding whether the sentence 'Snow is white' *is* true if and only if snow is white. Not all cases will be so simple (for reasons to be sketched), but it is evident that this sort of test does not invite counting noses. A sharp conception of what constitutes a theory in this domain furnishes an exciting context for raising deep questions about when a theory of language is correct and how it is to be tried. But the difficulties are theoretical, not practical. In application, the trouble is to get a theory that comes close to working; anyone can tell whether it is right.[9] One can see why this is so. The theory reveals nothing new about the conditions under which an individual sentence is true; it does not make those conditions any clearer than the sentence itself does. The work of the theory is in relating the known truth conditions of each sentence to those aspects ('words') of the sentence that recur in other sentences, and can be assigned identical roles in other sentences. Empirical power in such a theory depends on success in recovering the structure of a very complicated ability – the ability to speak and understand a language. We can tell easily enough when particular pronouncements of the theory comport with our understanding of the language; this is consistent with a feeble insight into the design of the machinery of our linguistic accomplishments.

The remarks of the last paragraph apply directly only to the special case where it is assumed that the language for which truth is being characterized is part of the language used and understood by the characterizer. Under these circumstances, the framer of a theory will as a matter of course avail himself when he can of the built-in convenience of metalanguage with a sentence guaranteed equivalent to each sentence in the object language. Still, this fact ought not to con us into thinking a theory any more correct that entails '"Snow is white" is true if and only if snow is white' than one that entails instead:

(S) 'Snow is white' is true if and only if grass is green,

provided, of course, we are as sure of the truth of (S) as we are of that of its more celebrated predecessor. Yet (S) may not encourage the same confidence that a theory that entails it deserves to be called a theory of meaning.

The threatened failure of nerve may be counteracted as follows. The grotesqueness of (S) is in itself nothing against a theory of which it is a consequence, provided the theory gives the correct results for every sentence (on the basis of its structure, there being no other way). It is not easy to see how (S) could be party to such an enterprise, but if it were – if, that is, (S) followed from a characterization of the predicate 'is true' that led to the invariable pairing of truths with truths and falsehoods with falsehoods – then there would not, I think, be anything essential to the idea of meaning that remained to be captured.[10]

What appears to the right of the biconditional in sentences of the form '*s* is true if and only if *p*' when such sentences are consequences of a theory of truth plays its role in determining the meaning of *s* not by pretending synonymy but by adding one more brush-stroke to the picture which, taken as a whole, tells what there is to know of the meaning of *s*; this stroke is added by virtue of the fact that the sentence that replaces '*p*' is true if and only if *s* is.

It may help to reflect that (S) is acceptable, if it is, because we are independently sure of the truth of 'Snow is white' and 'Grass is green'; but in cases where we are unsure of the truth of a sentence, we can have confidence in a characterization of the truth predicate only if it pairs that sentence with one we have good reason to believe equivalent. It would be ill advised for someone who had any doubts about the color of snow or grass to accept a theory that yielded (S), even if his doubts were of equal degree, unless he thought the color of the one was tied to the color of the other.[11] Omniscience can obviously afford more bizarre theories of meaning than ignorance; but then, omniscience has less need of communication.

It must be possible, of course, for the speaker of one language to construct a theory of meaning for the speaker of another, though in this case the empirical test of the correctness of the theory will no longer be trivial. As before, the aim of theory will be an infinite correlation of sentences alike in truth. But this time the theory-builder must not be assumed to have direct insight into likely equivalences between his own tongue and the alien. What he must do is find out, however he can, what sentences the alien holds true in his own tongue (or better, to what degree he holds them true). The linguist then will attempt to construct a characterization of truth-for-the-alien which yields, so far as possible, a mapping of sentences held true (or false) by the alien onto sentences held true (or false) by the linguist. Supposing no perfect fit is found, the residue of sentences held true translated by sentences held false (and vice versa) is the margin for error (foreign or domestic). Charity in interpreting the words and thoughts of others is unavoidable in another direction as well: just as we must maximize agreement, or risk not making sense of what the alien is talking about, so we must maximize the self-consistency we attribute to him, on pain of not understanding *him*. No single principle of optimum charity emerges; the constraints therefore determine no single theory. In a theory of radical translation (as Quine calls it) there is no completely disentangling questions of what the alien means from questions of what he believes. We do not know what someone means unless we know what he believes; we do not know what someone believes unless we know what he means. In radical translation we are able to break into this circle, if only incompletely, because we can sometimes tell that a person accedes to a sentence we do not understand.[12]

In the past few pages I have been asking how a theory of meaning that takes the form of a truth definition can be empirically tested, and have blithely ignored the prior question whether there is any serious chance such a theory can be given for a natural language. What are the prospects for a formal semantical theory of a natural language? Very poor, according to Tarski; and I believe most logicians, philosophers of language and linguists agree.[13] Let me do what I can to dispel the pessimism. What I can in a general and programmatic way, of course; for here the proof of the pudding will certainly be in the proof of the right theorems.

Tarski concludes the first section of his classic essay on the concept of truth in formalized languages with the following remarks, which he italicizes:

The very possibility of a consistent use of the expression 'true sentence' which is in harmony with the laws of logic and the spirit of everyday language seems to be very questionable, and consequently the same doubt attaches to the possibility of constructing a correct definition of this expression. (Language, Semantics, Metamathematics, p. 165)

Late in the same essay, he returns to the subject:

the concept of truth (as well as other semantical concepts) when applied to colloquial language in conjunction with the normal laws of logic leads inevitably to confusions and contradictions. Whoever wishes, in spite of all difficulties, to pursue the semantics of colloquial language with the help of exact methods will be driven first to undertake the thankless task of a reform of this language. He will find it necessary to define its structure, to overcome the ambiguity of the terms which occur in it, and finally to split the language into a series of languages of greater and greater extent, each of which stands in the same relation to the next in which a formalized language stands to its metalanguage. It may, however be doubted whether the language of everyday life, after being 'rationalized' in this way, would still preserve its naturalness and whether it would not rather take on the characteristic features of the formalized languages. (p. 267)

Two themes emerge: that the universal character of natural languages leads to contradiction (the semantic paradoxes), and that natural languages are too confused and amorphous to permit the direct application of formal methods. The first point deserves a serious answer, and I wish I had one. As it is, I will say only why I think we are justified in carrying on without having disinfected this particular source of conceptual anxiety, The semantic paradoxes arise when the range of the quantifiers in the object language is too generous in certain ways. But it is not really clear how unfair to Urdu or to Hindi it would be to view the range of their quantifiers as insufficient to yield an explicit definition of 'true-in-Urdu' or 'true-in-Hindi'. Or, to put the matter in another, if not more serious way, there may in the nature of the case always be something we grasp in understanding the language of another (the concept of truth) that we cannot communicate to him. In any case, most of the problems of general philosophical interest arise within a fragment of the relevant natural language that may be conceived as containing very little set theory. Of course these comments do not meet the claim that natural languages are universal. But it seems to me this claim, now that we know such universality leads to paradox, is suspect.

Tarski's second point is that we would have to reform a natural language out of all recognition before we could apply formal semantical methods. If this is true, it is fatal to my project, for the task of a theory of meaning as I conceive it is not to change, improve or reform a language, but to describe and understand it. Let us look at the positive side. Tarski has shown the way to giving a theory for interpreted formal languages of various kinds; pick one as much like English as possible. Since this new language has been explained in English and contains much English we not only may, but I think must, view it as part of English for those who understand it. For this fragment of English we have, *ex hypothesi*, a theory of the required sort. Not only that, but in interpreting this adjunct of English in old English we necessarily gave hints connecting old and new. Wherever there are sentences of old English with the same truth conditions as sentences in the adjunct we may extend the theory to cover them. Much of what is called for is just to mechanize as far as possible what we now do by art when we put ordinary English into one or another canonical notation. The point is not that canonical notation is better than the rough original idiom, but rather that if we know what idiom the canonical notation is canonical *for*, we have as good a theory for the idiom as for its kept companion.

Philosophers have long been at the hard work of applying theory to ordinary language by the device of matching sentences in the vernacular with sentences for which they have a theory. Frege's massive contribution was to show how 'all', 'some', 'every', 'each', 'none', and associated pronouns, in some of their uses, could be tamed; for the first time, it was possible to dream of a formal semantics for a significant part of a natural language. This dream came true in a sharp way with the work of Tarski. It would be a shame to miss the fact that as a result of these two magnificent achievements, Frege's and Tarski's, we have gained a deep insight into the structure of our mother tongues. Philosophers of a logical bent have tended to start where the theory was and work out towards the complications of natural language. Contemporary linguists, with an aim that cannot easily be seen to be different, start with the ordinary and work toward a general theory. If either party is successful, there must be a meeting. Recent work by Chomsky and others is doing much to bring the complexities of natural languages within the scope of serious semantic theory. To give an example: suppose success in giving the truth conditions for some significant range of sentences in the active voice. Then with a formal procedure for transforming each such sentence into a corresponding sentence in the passive voice, the theory of truth could be extended in an obvious way to this new set of sentences.[14]

One problem touched on in passing by Tarski does not, at least in all its manifestations, have to be solved to get ahead with theory: the existence in natural languages of 'ambiguous terms'. As long as ambiguity does not affect grammatical form, and can be translated, ambiguity for ambiguity, into the metalanguage, a truth definition will not tell us any lies. The trouble, for systematic semantics, with the phrase 'believes that' in English is not its vagueness, ambiguity, or unsuitability for incorporation in a serious science: let our metalanguage be English, and all *these* problems will be translated without loss or gain into the metalanguage. But the central problem of the logical grammar of 'believes that' will remain to haunt us.

The example is suited to illustrating another, and related, point, for the discussion of belief sentences has been plagued by failure to observe a fundamental distinction between tasks: uncovering the logical grammar or form of sentences (which is in the province of a theory of meaning as I construe it), and the analysis of individual words or expressions (which are treated as primitive by the theory). Thus Carnap, in the first edition of *Meaning and Necessity*, suggested we render 'John believes that the earth is round' as 'John responds affirmatively to "the earth is round" as an English sentence'. He gave this up when Mates pointed out that John might respond affirmatively to one sentence and not to another no matter how close in meaning.[15] But

Donald Davidson

there is a confusion here from the start. The semantic structure of a belief sentence, according to this idea of Carnap's, is given by a three-place predicate with places reserved for expressions referring to a person, a sentence, and a language. It is a different sort of problem entirely to attempt an analysis of this predicate, perhaps along behavioristic lines. Not least among the merits of Tarski's conception of a theory of truth is that the purity of method it demands of us follows from the formulation of the problem itself, not from the self-imposed restraint of some adventitious philosophical puritanism.

I think it is hard to exaggerate the advantages to philosophy of language of bearing in mind this distinction between questions of logical form or grammar, and the analysis of individual concepts. Another example may help advertise the point.

If we suppose questions of logical grammar settled, sentences like 'Bardot is good' raise no special problems for a truth definition. The deep differences between descriptive and evaluative (emotive, expressive, etc.) terms do not show here. Even if we hold there is some important sense in which moral or evaluative sentences do not have a truth value (for example, because they cannot be 'verified'), we ought not to boggle at ' "Bardot is good" is true if and only if Bardot is good'; in a theory of truth, this consequence should follow with the rest, keeping track, as must be done, of the semantic location of such sentences in the language as a whole – of their relation to generalizations, their role in such compound sentences as 'Bardot is good and Bardot is foolish', and so on. What is special to evaluative words is simply not touched: the mystery is transferred from the word 'good' in the object-language to its translation in the metalanguage.

But 'good' as it features in 'Bardot is a good actress' is another matter. The problem is not that the translation of this sentence is not in the metalanguage – let us suppose it is. The problem is to frame a truth definition such that ' "Bardot is a good actress" is true if and only if Bardot is a good actress' – and all other sentences like it – are consequences. Obviously 'good actress' does not mean 'good and an actress'. We might think of taking 'is a good actress' as an unanalyzed predicate. This would obliterate all connection between 'is a good actress' and 'is a good mother', and it would give us no excuse to think of 'good', in these uses, as a word or semantic element. But worse, it would bar us

from framing a truth definition at all, for there is no end to the predicates we would have to treat as logically simple (and hence accommodate in separate clauses in the definition of satisfaction): 'is a good companion to dogs', 'is a good 28-years-old conversationalist', and so forth. The problem is not peculiar to the case: it is the problem of attributive adjectives generally.

It is consistent with the attitude taken here to deem it usually a strategic error to undertake philosophical analysis of words or expressions which is not preceded by or at any rate accompanied by the attempt to get the logical grammar straight. For how can we have any confidence in our analyses of words like 'right', 'ought', 'can', and 'obliged', or the phrases we use to talk of actions, events and causes, when we do not know what (logical, semantical) parts of speech we have to deal with? I would say much the same about studies of the 'logic' of these and other words, and the sentences containing them. Whether the effort and ingenuity that has gone into the study of deontic logics, modal logics, imperative and erotetic logics has been largely futile or not cannot be known until we have acceptable semantic analyses of the sentences such systems purport to treat. Philosophers and logicians sometimes talk or work as if they were free to choose between, say, the truth-functional conditional and others, or free to introduce non-truth-functional sentential operators like 'Let it be the case that' or 'It ought to be the case that'. But in fact the decision is crucial. When we depart from idioms we can accommodate in a truth definition, we lapse into (or create) language for which we have no coherent semantical account – that is, no account at all of how such talk can be integrated into the language as a whole.

To return to our main theme: we have recognized that a theory of the kind proposed leaves the whole matter of what individual words mean exactly where it was. Even when the metalanguage is different from the object language, the theory exerts no pressure for improvement, clarification or analysis of individual words, except when, by accident of vocabulary, straightforward translation fails. Just as synonymy, as between expressions, goes generally untreated, so also synonymy of sentences, and analyticity. Even such sentences as 'A vixen is a female fox' bear no special tag unless it is our pleasure to provide it. A truth definition does not distinguish between analytic sentences and others, except for sentences that owe their truth to the presence alone of the constants that give the theory its grip on structure: the theory entails not only that these sentences are true but that they will remain true under all significant rewritings of their non-logical parts. A notion of logical truth thus given limited application, related notions of logical equivalence and entailment will tag along. It is hard to imagine how a theory of meaning could fail to read a logic into its object language to this degree; and to the extent that it does, our intuitions of logical truth, equivalence and entailment may be called upon in constructing and testing the theory.

I turn now to one more, and very large, fly in the ointment: the fact that the same sentence may at one time or in one mouth be true and at another time or in another mouth be false. Both logicians and those critical of formal methods here seem largely (though by no means universally) agreed that formal semantics and logic are incompetent to deal with the disturbances caused by demonstratives. Logicians have often reacted by downgrading natural language and trying to show how to get along without demonstratives; their critics react by downgrading logic and formal semantics. None of this can make me happy: clearly demonstratives cannot be eliminated from a natural language without loss or radical change, so there is no choice but to accommodate theory to them.

No logical errors result if we simply treat demonstratives as constants;[16] neither do any problems arise for giving a semantic truth definition. '"I am wise" is true if and only if I am wise', with its bland ignoring of the demonstrative element in 'I' comes off the assembly line along with '"Socrates is wise" is true if and only if Socrates is wise' with *its* bland indifference to the demonstrative element in 'is wise' (the tense).

What suffers in this treatment of demonstratives is not the definition of a truth predicate, but the plausibility of the claim that what has been defined is truth. For this claim is acceptable only if the speaker and circumstances of utterance of each sentence mentioned in the definition is matched by the speaker and circumstances of utterance of the truth definition itself. It could also be fairly pointed out that part of understanding demonstratives is knowing the rules by which they adjust their reference to circumstance; assimilating demonstratives to constant terms obliterates this feature. These complaints can be

met, I think, though only by a fairly far-reaching revision in the theory of truth. I shall barely suggest how this could be done, but bare suggestion is all that is needed: the idea is technically trivial, and quite in line with work being done on the logic of the tenses.[17]

We could take truth to be a property, not of sentences, but of utterances, or speech acts, or ordered triples of sentences, times and persons; but it is simplest just to view truth as a relation between a sentence, a person, and a time. Under such treatment, ordinary logic as now read applies as usual, but only to sets of sentences relativized to the same speaker and time; further logical relations between sentences spoken at different times and by different speakers may be articulated by new axioms. Such is not my concern. The theory of meaning undergoes a systematic but not puzzling change: corresponding to each expression with a demonstrative element there must in the theory be a phrase that relates the truth conditions of sentences in which the expression occurs to changing times and speakers. Thus the theory will entail sentences like the following:

'I am tired' is true as (potentially) spoken by p at t if and only if p is tired at t.
'That book was stolen' is true as (potentially) spoken by p at t if and only if the book demonstrated by p at t is stolen prior to t.[18]

Plainly, this course does not show how to eliminate demonstratives; for example, there is no suggestion that 'the book demonstrated by the speaker' can be substituted ubiquitously for 'that book' *salva veritate*. The fact that demonstratives are amenable to formal treatment ought greatly to improve hopes for a serious semantics of natural language, for it is likely that many outstanding puzzles, such as the analysis of quotations or sentences about propositional attitudes, can be solved if we recognize a concealed demonstrative construction.

Now that we have relativized truth to times and speakers, it is appropriate to glance back at the problem of empirically testing a theory of meaning for an alien tongue. The essence of the method was, it will be remembered, to correlate held-true sentences with held-true sentences by way of a truth definition, and within the bounds of intelligible error. Now the picture must be elaborated to allow for the fact that sentences are true, and held true, only relative to a speaker and a time. The real task is therefore to translate each sentence by another that is true for the same speakers at the same times. Sentences with demonstratives obviously yield a very sensitive test of the correctness of a theory of meaning, and constitute the most direct link between language and the recurrent macroscopic objects of human interest and attention.[19]

In this paper I have assumed that the speakers of a language can effectively determine the meaning or meanings of an arbitrary expression (if it has a meaning), and that it is the central task of a theory of meaning to show how this is possible. I have argued that a characterization of a truth predicate describes the required kind of structure, and provides a clear and testable criterion of an adequate semantics for a natural language. No doubt there are other reasonable demands that may be put on a theory of meaning. But a theory that does no more than define truth for a language comes far closer to consti-

tuting a complete theory of meaning than superficial analysis might suggest; so, at least, I have urged.

Since I think there is no alternative, I have taken an optimistic and programmatic view of the possibilities for a formal characterization of a truth predicate for a natural language. But it must be allowed that a staggering list of difficulties and conundrums remains. To name a few: we do not know the logical form of counterfactual or subjunctive sentences; nor of sentences about probabilities and about causal relations; we have no good idea what the logical role of adverbs is, nor the role of attributive adjectives; we have no theory for mass terms like 'fire', 'water' and 'snow', nor for sentences about belief, perception and intention, nor for verbs of action that imply purpose. And finally, there are all the sentences that seem not to have truth values at all: the imperatives, optatives, interrogatives, and a host more. A comprehensive theory of meaning for a natural language must cope successfully with each of these problems.[20]

Notes

1 See Essay 1 [in *Inquiries into Truth and Interpretation* (Oxford: Clarendon Press, 1984)].

2 A 'structural description' of an expression describes the expression as a concatenation of elements drawn from a fixed finite list (for example of words or letters).

3 The argument derives from Frege. See A. Church, *Introduction to Mathematical Logic*, vol. I (Princeton, NJ: Princeton University Press, 1956), pp. 24–5. It is perhaps worth mentioning that the argument does not depend on any particular identification of the entities to which sentences are supposed to refer.

4 It may be thought that Church, in 'A Formulation of the Logic of Sense and Denotation' (in *Structure, Method and Meaning: Essays in Honor of H. M. Sheffer*, ed. P. Henle, H. M. Kallen, and S. K. Langer (New York: Liberal Arts Press, 1951), has given a theory of meaning that makes essential use of meanings as entities. But this is not the case: Church's logics of sense and denotation are interpreted as being about meanings, but they do not mention expressions and so cannot of course be theories of meaning in the sense now under discussion.

5 For a recent statement of the role of semantics in linguistics, see Noam Chomsky, 'Topics in the Theory of Generative Grammar', in *Current Trends in Linguistics*, vol. III, ed. T. A. Sebeok (The Hague: Mouton, 1966). In this article, Chomsky

(1) emphasizes the central importance of semantics in linguistic theory, (2) argues for the superiority of transformational grammars over phrase-structure grammars largely on the grounds that, although phrase-structure grammars may be adequate to define sentencehood for (at least) some natural languages, they are inadequate as a foundation for semantics, and (3) comments repeatedly on the 'rather primitive state' of the concepts of semantics and remarks that the notion of semantic interpretation 'still resists any deep analysis'.

6 Assuming of course, that the extension of these predicates is limited to the sentences of L.

7 A. Tarski, 'The Concept of Truth in Formalized Languages', in *Logic, Semantics, Metamathematics*, 2nd edn., ed. John Corcoran (Indianapolis: Hackett, 1983).

8 But Quine may be quoted in support of my usage: 'in point of *meaning* . . . a word may be said to be determined to whatever extent the truth or falsehood of its contexts is determined' ('Truth by Convention', in *The Ways of Paradox* (New York: Random House, 1966), p. 82). Since a truth definition determines the truth value of every sentence in the object language (relative to a sentence in the metalanguage), it determines the meaning of every word and sentence. This would seem to justify the title Theory of Meaning.

9 To give a single example: it is clearly a count in favour of a theory that it entails ' "Snow is white" is true if and only if snow is white'. But to contrive a theory that entails this (and works for all related sentences) is not trivial. I do not know a wholly satisfactory theory that succeeds with this very case (the problem of 'mass terms').

10 Critics have often failed to notice the essential proviso mentioned in this paragraph. The point is that (S) could not belong to any reasonably simple theory that also gave the right truth conditions for 'That is snow' and 'This is white'. (See the discussion of indexical expressions below.) [Footnote added in 1982.]

11 This paragraph is confused. What it should say is that sentences of the theory are empirical generalizations about speakers, and so must not only be true but also lawlike. (S) presumably is not a law, since it does not support appropriate counterfactuals. It's also important that the evidence for accepting the (time and speaker relativized) truth conditions for 'That is snow' is based on the causal connection between a speaker's assent to the sentence and the demonstrative presentation of snow. For further discussion see Essay 12 [in *Inquiries into Truth and Interpretation*]. [Footnote added in 1982.]

12 This sketch of how a theory of meaning for an alien tongue can be tested obviously owes its inspiration to Quine's account of radical translation in ch. II of *Word and Object* (Cambridge, MA: MIT Press, 1960). In suggesting that an acceptable theory of radical translation take the form of a recursive characterization of truth, I go beyond Quine. Toward the end of this paper, in the discussion of demonstratives, another strong point of agreement will turn up.

13 So far as I am aware, there has been very little discussion of whether a formal truth definition can be given for a natural language. But in a more general vein, several people have urged that the concepts of formal semantics be applied to natural language. See, for example, the contributions of Yehoshua Bar-Hillel and Evert Beth to *The Philosophy of Rudolph Carnap*, ed. P. A. Schilpp, in the Library of Living Philosophers (LaSalle, IL: Open Court, 1963), and Bar-Hillel's 'Logical Syntax and Semantics in *Language* 30 (1954), pp. 230–7.

14 The *rapprochement* I prospectively imagine between transformational grammar and a sound theory of meaning has been much advanced by a recent change in the conception of transformational grammar described by Chomsky in the article referred to above (note 5). The structures generated by the phrase-structure part of the grammar, it has been realized for some time, are those suited to semantic interpretation: but this view is inconsistent with the idea, held by Chomsky until recently, that recursive operations are introduced only by the transformation rules. Chomsky now believes the phrase-structure rules are recursive. Since languages to which formal semantic methods directly and naturally apply are ones for which a (recursive) phrase-structure grammar is appropriate, it is clear that Chomsky's present picture of the relation between the structures generated by the phrase-structure part of the grammar, and the sentences of the language, is very much like the picture many logicians and philosophers have had of the relation between the richer formalized languages and ordinary language. (In these remarks I am indebted to Bruce Vermazen.)

15 B. Mates, 'Synonymity', in *Semantics and the Philosophy of Language*, ed. L. Linsky (Urbana, IL: University of Illinois Press, 1952).

16 See W. V. Quine, *Methods of Logic* (New York: H. Holt, 1960), p. 8.

17 This claim has turned out to be naively optimistic. For some serious work on the subject, see S. Weinstein, 'Truth and Demonstratives', *Noûs* 8 (1974), pp. 179–84. [Footnote added in 1982.]

18 There is more than an intimation of this approach to demonstratives and truth in J. L. Austin, 'Truth', from the symposium on Truth in *Proceedings of the Aristotelian Society*, suppl. vol. 24 (1950), reprinted in Austin's *Philosophical Papers* (Oxford: Oxford University Press, 1961), pp. 89–90.

19 These remarks derive from Quine's idea that 'occasion sentences' (those with a demonstrative element) must play a central role in constructing a translation manual.

20 For attempted solutions to some of these problems see Essays 6–10 of *Essays on Actions and Events*, and Essays 6–8 [of *Inquiries into Truth and Interpretation*]. There is further discussion in Essays 3, 4, 9, and 10, and reference to some progress in section 1 of Essay 9 [of *Inquiries*].

7

Identity and Necessity

Saul Kripke

A problem which has arisen frequently in contemporary philosophy is: "How are *contingent*
identity statements possible?" This question is
phrased by analogy with the way Kant phrased
his question "How are synthetic a priori judgments possible?" In both cases, it has usually
been taken for granted in the one case by Kant
that synthetic a priori judgments were possible,
and in the other case in contemporary philosophical literature that contingent statements of
identity are possible. I do not intend to deal
with the Kantian question except to mention this
analogy: After a rather thick book was written
trying to answer the question how synthetic a
priori judgments were possible, others came along
later who claimed that the solution to the problem was that synthetic a priori judgments were,
of course, impossible and that a book trying to
show otherwise was written in vain. I will not
discuss who was right on the possibility of synthetic a priori judgments. But in the case of
contingent statements of identity, most philosophers have felt that the notion of a contingent
identity statement ran into something like the
following paradox. An argument like the following can be given against the possibility of contingent identity statements:[1] First, the law of the
substitutivity of identity says that, for any objects
x and y, if x is identical to y, then if x has a
certain property F, so does y:

Previously published in *Identity and Individuation*,
ed. Milton K. Munitz (New York University Press,
New York, 1971).

$$(1) \quad (x)(y)[(x = y) \supset (Fx \supset Fy)]$$

On the other hand, every object surely is necessarily self-identical:

$$(2) \quad (x) \,\square\, (x = x)$$

But

$$(3) \quad (x)(y)(x = y) \supset [\square\, (x = x) \supset \square\, (x = y)]$$

is a substitution instance of (1), the substitutivity
law. From (2) and (3), we can conclude that, for
every x and y, if x equals y, then, it is necessary
that x equals y:

$$(4) \quad (x)(y)((x = y) \supset \square\, (x = y))$$

This is because the clause $\square\, (x = x)$ of the conditional drops out because it is known to be true.

This is an argument which has been stated
many times in recent philosophy. Its conclusion,
however, has often been regarded as highly paradoxical. For example, David Wiggins, in his paper, "Identity Statements," says,

> Now there undoubtedly exist contingent
> identity-statements. Let $a = b$ be one of them.
> From its simple truth and (5) [= (4) above]
> we can derive '$\square\, (a = b)$'. But how then can
> there be any contingent identity statements?[2]

He then says that five various reactions to this
argument are possible, and rejects all of these

reactions, and reacts himself. I do not want to discuss all the possible reactions to this statement, except to mention the second of those Wiggins rejects. This says,

> We might accept the result and plead that provided 'a' and 'b' are proper names nothing is amiss. The consequence of this is that no contingent identity-statements can be made by means of proper names.

And then he says that he is discontented with this solution and many other philosophers have been discontented with this solution, too, while still others have advocated it.

What makes the statement (4) seem surprising? It says, for any objects x and y, if x is y, then it is necessary that x is y. I have already mentioned that someone might object to this argument on the grounds that premise (2) is already false, that it is not the case that everything is necessarily self-identical. Well, for example, am I myself necessarily self-identical? Someone might argue that in some situations which we can imagine I would not even have existed and therefore the statement "Saul Kripke is Saul Kripke" would have been false or it would not be the case that I was self-identical. Perhaps, it would have been neither true nor false, in such a world, to say that Saul Kripke is self-identical. Well, that may be so, but really it depends on one's philosophical view of a topic that I will not discuss, that is, what is to be said about truth values of statements mentioning objects that do not exist in the actual world or any given possible world or counterfactual situation. Let us interpret necessity here weakly. We can count statements as necessary if whenever the objects mentioned therein exist, the statement would be true. If we wished to be very careful about this, we would have to go into the question of existence as a predicate and ask if the statement can be reformulated in the form: For every x it is necessary that, if x exists, then x is self-identical. I will not go into this particular form of subtlety here because it is not going to be relevant to my main theme. Nor am I really going to consider formula (4). Anyone who believes formula (2) is, in my opinion, committed to formula (4). If x and y are the same things and we can talk about modal properties of an object at all, that is, in the usual parlance, we can speak of modality *de re* and an object *necessarily* having certain prop-

erties as such, then formula (1), I think, has to hold. Where x is any property at all, including a property involving modal operators, and if x and y are the same object and x had a certain property F, then y has to have the same property F. And this is so even if the property F is itself of the form of necessarily having some other property G, in particular that of necessarily being identical to a certain object. Well, I will not discuss the formula (4) itself because by itself it does not assert, of any particular true statement of identity, that it is necessary. It does not say anything about *statements* at all. It says for every *object* x and *object* y, if x and y are the same object, then it is necessary that x and y are the same object. And this, I think, if we think about it (anyway, if someone does not think so, I will not argue for it here), really amounts to something very little different from the statement (2). Since x, by definition of identity, is the only object identical with x, "$(y)(y = x \supset Fy)$" seems to me to be little more than a garrulous way of saying 'Fx', and thus $(x)(y)(y = x \supset Fx)$ says the same as $(x)Fx$ no matter what 'F' is – in particular, even if 'F' stands for the property of necessary identity with x. So if x has this property (of necessary identity with x), trivially everything identical with x has it, as (4) asserts. But, from statement (4) one may apparently be able to deduce various particular statements of identity must be necessary and this is then supposed to be a very paradoxical consequence.

Wiggins says, "Now there undoubtedly exist contingent identity statements." One example of a contingent identity statement is the statement that the first Postmaster General of the United States is identical with the inventor of bifocals, or that both of these are identical with the man claimed by the *Saturday Evening Post* as its founder (*falsely* claimed, I gather, by the way). Now some such statements are plainly contingent. It plainly is a contingent fact that one and the same man both invented bifocals and took on the job of Postmaster General of the United States. How can we reconcile this with the truth of statement (4)? Well, that, too, is an issue I do not want to go into in detail except to be very dogmatic about it. It was I think settled quite well by Bertrand Russell in his notion of the scope of a description. According to Russell, one can, for example, say with propriety that the author of Hamlet might not have written "Hamlet," or even that the author of Hamlet might not have been the author of "Hamlet." Now here, of course, we do not deny the necessity of the identity of an object with itself; but we say it is true concerning a certain man that he in fact was the unique person to have written "Hamlet" and secondly that the man, who in fact was the man who wrote "Hamlet," might not have written "Hamlet." In other words, if Shakespeare had decided not to write tragedies, he might not have written "Hamlet." Under these circumstances, the man who in fact wrote "Hamlet" would not have written "Hamlet." Russell brings this out by saying that in such a statement, the first occurrence of the description "the author of 'Hamlet'" has large scope.[3] That is, we say "The author of 'Hamlet' has the following property: that he might not have written 'Hamlet.'" We *do not* assert that the following statement might have been the case, namely that the author of "Hamlet" did not write "Hamlet," for that is not true. That would be to say that it might have been the case that someone wrote "Hamlet" and yet did not write "Hamlet," which would be a contradiction. Now, aside from the details of Russell's particular formulation of it, which depends on his theory of descriptions, this seems to be the distinction that any theory of descriptions has to make. For example, if someone were to meet the President of Harvard and take him to be a Teaching Fellow, he might say: "I took the President of Harvard for a Teaching Fellow." By this he does not mean that he took the proposition "The President of Harvard is a Teaching Fellow" to be true. He could have meant this, for example, had he believed that some sort of democratic system had gone so far at Harvard that the President of it decided to take on the task of being a Teaching Fellow. But that probably is not what he means. What he means instead, as Russell points out, is "Someone is President of Harvard and I took him to be a Teaching Fellow." In one of Russell's examples someone says, "I thought your yacht is much larger than it is." And the other man replies, "No, my yacht is not much larger than it is."

Provided that the notion of modality *de re*, and thus of quantifying into modal contexts, makes any sense at all, we have quite an adequate solution to the problem of avoiding paradoxes if we substitute descriptions for the universal quantifiers in (4) because the only consequence we will draw,[4] for example, in the bifocals case, is that there is a man who both happened to have

invented bifocals and happened to have been the first Postmaster General of the United States, and is necessarily self-identical. There is an object x such that x invented bifocals, and as a matter of contingent fact an object y, such that y is the first Postmaster General of the United States, and finally, it is necessary, that x is y. What are x and y here? Here, x and y are both Benjamin Franklin, and it can certainly be necessary that Benjamin Franklin is identical with himself. So, there is no problem in the case of descriptions if we accept Russell's notion of scope.[5] And I just dogmatically want to drop that question here and go on to the question about names which Wiggins raises. And Wiggins says he might accept the result and plead that, provided a and b are proper names, nothing is amiss. And then he rejects this.

Now what is the special problem about proper names? At least if one is not familiar with the philosophical literature about this matter, one naively feels something like the following about proper names. First, if someone says "Cicero was an orator," then he uses the name 'Cicero' in that statement simply to pick out a certain object and then to ascribe a certain property to the object, namely, in this case, he ascribes to a certain man the property of having been an orator. If someone else uses another name, such as say 'Tully', he is still speaking about the same man. One ascribes the same property, if one says "Tully is an orator," to the same man. So to speak the fact, or state of affairs, represented by the statement is the same whether one says "Cicero is an orator" or one says "Tully is an orator." It would, therefore, seem that the function of names is *simply* to refer, and not to describe the objects so named by such properties as "being the inventor of bifocals" or "being the first Postmaster General." It would seem that Leibniz' law and the law (1) should not only hold in the universally quantified form, but also in the form "if $a = b$ and Fa, then Fb," wherever 'a' and 'b' stand in place of names and 'F' stands in place of a predicate expressing a genuine property of the object:

$$(a = b \cdot Fa) \supset Fb$$

We can run the same argument through again to obtain the conclusion where 'a' and 'b' replace any names, "if $a = b$, then necessarily $a = b$." And so, we could venture this conclusion: that whenever '*a*' and '*b*' are proper names, if *a* is *b*, that it is necessary that *a* is *b*. Identity statements between proper names have to be necessary if they are going to be true at all. This view in fact has been advocated, for example, by Ruth Barcan Marcus in a paper of hers on the philosophical interpretation of modal logic.[6] According to this view, whenever, for example, someone makes a correct statement of identity between two names, such as, for example, that Cicero is Tully, his statement has to be necessary if it is true. But such a conclusion *seems* plainly to be false. (I, like other philosophers, have a habit of understatement in which "it seems plainly false" means "it is plainly false." Actually, I think the view is true, though not quite in the form defended by Mrs. Marcus.) At any rate, it seems plainly false. One example was given by Professor Quine in his reply to Professor Marcus at the symposium: "I think I see trouble anyway in the contrast between proper names and descriptions as Professor Marcus draws it. The paradigm of the assigning of proper names is tagging. We may tag the planet Venus some fine evening with the proper name 'Hesperus'. We may tag the same planet again someday before sun rise with the proper name 'Phosphorus'." (Quine thinks that something like that actually was done once.) "When, at last, we discover that we have tagged the same planet twice, our discovery is empirical, and not because the proper names were descriptions." According to what we are told, the planet Venus seen in the morning was originally thought to be a star and was called "the Morning Star," or (to get rid of any question of using a description) was called 'Phosphorus'. One and the same planet, when seen in the evening, was thought to be another star, the Evening Star, and was called "Hesperus." Later on, astronomers discovered that Phosphorus and Hesperus were one and the same. Surely no amount of a priori ratiocination on their part could conceivably have made it possible for them to deduce that Phosphorus is Hesperus. In fact, given the information they had, it might have turned out the other way. Therefore, it is argued, the statement 'Hesperus is Phosphorus' has to be an ordinary contingent, empirical truth, one which might have come out otherwise, and so the view that true identity statements between names are necessary has to be false. Another example which Quine gives in *Word and Object* is taken from Professor Schrödinger, the famous pioneer of quantum mechanics: A certain mountain can be seen from both Tibet and Nepal. When seen from one direction it was called 'Gaurisanker'; when seen from another direction, it was called 'Everest'; and then, later on, the empirical discovery was made that Gaurisanker *is* Everest. (Quine further says that he gathers the example is actually geographically incorrect. I guess one should not rely on physicists for geographical information.)

Of course, one possible reaction to this argument is to deny that names like 'Cicero', 'Tully', 'Gaurisanker', and 'Everest' really are proper names. Look, someone might say (someone has said it: his name was 'Bertrand Russell'), just because statements like "Hesperus is Phosphorus" and "Gaurisanker is Everest" are contingent, we can see that the names in question are not really purely referential. You are not, in Mrs. Marcus' phrase, just 'tagging' an object; you are actually describing it. What does the contingent fact that Hesperus is Phosphorus amount to? Well, it amounts to the fact that *the* star in a certain portion of the sky in the evening is *the* star in a certain portion of the sky in the morning. Similarly, the contingent fact that Gaurisanker is Everest amounts to the fact that the mountain viewed from such and such an angle in Nepal is the mountain viewed from such and such another angle in Tibet. Therefore, such names as 'Hesperus' and 'Phosphorus' can only be abbreviations for descriptions. The term 'Phosphorus' *has* to mean "the star seen. . . ." or (let us be cautious because it actually turned out not to be a star), "the *heavenly body* seen from such and such a position at such and such a time in the morning," and the name 'Hesperus' has to mean "the heavenly body seen in such and such a position at such and such a time in the evening." So, Russell concludes, if we want to reserve the term "name" for things which really just name an object without describing it, the only real proper names we can have are names of our own immediate sense data, objects of our own 'immediate acquaintance'. The only such names which occur in language are demonstratives like "this" and "that." And it is easy to see that this requirement of necessity of identity, understood as exempting identities between names from all imaginable doubt, can indeed be guaranteed only for demonstrative names of immediate sense data; for only in such cases can an identity statement between two different names have a general immunity from Cartesian doubt. There are some other things Russell has sometimes allowed as objects of acquaintance, such as one's self; we need not go into details here. Other philosophers (for example, Mrs. Marcus in her reply, at least in the verbal discussion as I remember it – I do not know if this got into print, so perhaps this should not be 'tagged' on her[7]) have said, "If names are really just tags, genuine tags, then a good dictionary should be able to tell us that they are names of the same object." You have an object *a* and an object *b* with names 'John' and 'Joe'. Then, according to Mrs. Marcus, a dictionary should be able to tell you whether or not 'John' and 'Joe' are names of the same object. Of course, I do not know what ideal dictionaries should do, but ordinary proper names do not seem to satisfy this requirement. You certainly *can*, in the case of ordinary proper names, make quite empirical discoveries that, let's say, Hesperus is Phosphorus, though we thought otherwise. We can be in doubt as to whether Gaurisanker is Everest or Cicero is in fact Tully. Even now, we could conceivably discover that we were wrong in supposing that Hesperus was Phosphorus. Maybe the astronomers made an error. So it seems that this view is wrong and that if by a name we do not mean some artificial notion of names such as Russell's, but a proper name in the ordinary sense, then there can be contingent identity statements using proper names, and the view to the contrary seems plainly wrong.

In recent philosophy a large number of other identity statements have been emphasized as examples of contingent identity statements, different, perhaps, from either of the types I have mentioned before. One of them is, for example, the statement "Heat is the motion of molecules." First, science is supposed to have discovered this. Empirical scientists in their investigations have been supposed to discover (and, I suppose, they did) that the external phenomenon which we call "heat" is, in fact, molecular agitation. Another example of such a discovery is that water is H_2O, and yet other examples are that gold is the element with such and such an atomic number, that light is a stream of photons, and so on. These are all in some sense of "identity statement" identity statements. Second, it is thought, they are plainly contingent identity statements, just because they were scientific discoveries. After all, heat might have turned out not to have been the motion of molecules. There were other altern-

ative theories of heat proposed, for example, the caloric theory of heat. If these theories of heat had been correct, then heat would not have been the motion of molecules, but instead, some substance suffusing the hot object, called "caloric." And it was a matter of course of science and not of any logical necessity that the one theory turned out to be correct and the other theory turned out to be incorrect.

So, here again, we have, apparently, another plain example of a contingent identity statement. This has been supposed to be a very important example because of its connection with the mind–body problem. There have been many philosophers who have wanted to be materialists, and to be materialists in a particular form, which is known today as "the identity theory." According to this theory, a certain mental state, such as a person's being in pain, is identical with a certain state of his brain (or, perhaps, of his entire body, according to some theorists), at any rate, a certain material or neural state of his brain or body. And so, according to this theory, my being in pain at this instant, if I were, would be identical with my body's being or my brain's being in a certain state. Others have objected that this cannot be because, after all, we can imagine my pain existing even if the state of the body did not. We can perhaps imagine my not being embodied at all and still being in pain, or, conversely, we could imagine my body existing and being in the very same state even if there were no pain. In fact, conceivably, it could be in this state even though there were no mind 'back of it', so to speak, at all. The usual reply has been to concede that all of these things might have been the case, but to argue that these are irrelevant to the question of the identity of the mental state and the physical state. This identity, it is said, is just another contingent scientific identification, similar to the identification of heat with molecular motion, or water with H_2O. Just as we can imagine heat without any molecular motion, so we can imagine a mental state without any corresponding brain state. But, just as the first fact is not damaging to the identification of heat and the motion of molecules, so the second fact is not at all damaging to the identification of a mental state with the corresponding brain state. And so, many recent philosophers have held it to be very important for our theoretical understanding of the mind–body problem that there can be contingent identity statements of this form.

To state finally what *I* think, as opposed to what seems to be the case, or what others think, I think that in both cases, the case of names and the case of the theoretical identifications, the identity statements are necessary and not contingent. That is to say, they are necessary if *true*; of course, false identity statements are not necessary. How can one possibly defend such a view? Perhaps I lack a complete answer to this question, even though I am convinced that the view is true. But to begin an answer, let me make some distinctions that I want to use. The first is between a *rigid* and a *nonrigid designator*. What do these terms mean? As an example of a nonrigid designator, I can give an expression such as 'the inventor of bifocals'. Let us suppose it was Benjamin Franklin who invented bifocals, and so the expression, 'the inventor of bifocals', designates or refers to a certain man, namely, Benjamin Franklin. However, we can easily imagine that the world could have been different, that under different circumstances someone else would have come upon this invention before Benjamin Franklin did, and in that case, *he* would have been the inventor of bifocals. So, in this sense, the expression 'the inventor of bifocals' is nonrigid: Under certain circumstances one man would have been the inventor of bifocals; under other circumstances, another man would have. In contrast, consider the expression 'the square root of 25'. Independently of the empirical facts, we can give an arithmetical proof that the square root of 25 is in fact the number 5, and because we have proved this mathematically, what we have proved is necessary. If we think of numbers as entities at all, and let us suppose, at least for the purpose of this lecture, that we do, then the expression 'the square root of 25' necessarily designates a certain number, namely 5. Such an expression I call 'a *rigid* designator'. Some philosophers think that anyone who even uses the notions of rigid or nonrigid designator has already shown that he has fallen into a certain confusion or has not paid attention to certain facts. What do I mean by 'rigid designator'? I mean a term that designates the same object in all possible worlds. To get rid of one confusion which certainly is not mine, I do not use "might have designated a different object" to refer to the fact that language might have been used differently. For example, the expression 'the inventor of bifocals' might have been used by inhabitants of this planet always to refer to the man who corrupted Hadleyburg.

This would have been the case, if, first, the people on this planet had not spoken English, but some other language, which phonetically overlapped with English; and if, second, in that language the expression 'the inventor of bifocals' meant the 'man who corrupted Hadleyburg'. Then it would refer, of course, in their language, to whoever in fact corrupted Hadleyburg in this counterfactual situation. That is not what I mean. What I mean by saying that a description might have referred to something different, I mean that in *our* language as *we* use it in describing a counterfactual situation, there might have been a different object satisfying the descriptive conditions *we* give for reference. So, for example, we use the phrase 'the inventor of bifocals', when we are talking about another possible world or a counterfactual situation, to refer to whoever in that counterfactual situation would have invented bifocals, not to the person whom people *in* that counterfactual situation would have called the inventor of bifocals. *They* might have spoken a different language which phonetically overlapped with English in which 'the inventor of bifocals' is used in some other way. I am *not* concerned with that question here. For that matter, they might have been deaf and dumb, or there might have been no people at all. (There still could have been an inventor of bifocals even if there were no people – God, or Satan, will do.)

Second, in talking about the notion of a rigid designator, I do not mean to imply that the object referred to has to exist in all possible worlds, that is, that it has to necessarily exist. Some things, perhaps mathematical entities such as the positive integers, if they exist at all, necessarily exist. Some people have held that God both exists and necessarily exists; others, that He contingently exists; others, that He contingently fails to exist; and others, that He necessarily fails to exist:[8] all four options have been tried. But at any rate, when I use the notion of rigid designator, I do not imply that the object referred to necessarily exists. All I mean is that in any possible world where the object in question *does* exist, in any situation where the object *would* exist, we use the designator in question to designate that object. In a situation where the object does not exist, then we should say that the designator has no referent and that the object in question so designated does not exist.

As I said, many philosophers would find the very notion of rigid designator objectionable *per se*. And the objection that people make may be stated as follows: Look, you're talking about situations which are counterfactual, that is to say, you're talking about other possible worlds. Now these worlds are completely disjoint, after all, from the actual world which is not just another possible world; it is the actual world. So, before you talk about, let us say, such an object as Richard Nixon in another possible world at all, you have to say which object in this other possible world would *be* Richard Nixon. Let us talk about a situation in which, as *you* would say, Richard Nixon would have been a member of SDS. Certainly the member of SDS you are talking about is someone very different in many of his properties from Nixon. Before we even can say whether this man would have been Richard Nixon or not, we have to set up criteria of identity across possible worlds. Here are these other possible worlds. There are all kinds of objects in them with different properties from those of any actual object. Some of them resemble Nixon in some ways, some of them resemble Nixon in other ways. Well, which of these objects is Nixon? One has to give a criterion of identity. And this shows how the very notion of rigid designator runs in a circle. Suppose we designate a certain number as the number of planets. Then, if that is our favorite way, so to speak, of designating this number, then in any other possible worlds we will have to identify whatever number is the number of planets with the number 9, which in the actual world is the number of planets. So, it is argued by various philosophers, for example, implicitly by Quine, and explicitly by many others in his wake, we cannot really ask whether a designator is rigid or nonrigid because we first need a criterion of identity across possible worlds. An extreme view has even been held that, since possible worlds are so disjoint from our own, we cannot really say that any object in them is the *same* as an object existing now but only that there are some objects which resemble things in the actual world, more or less. We, therefore, should not really speak of what would have been true of Nixon in another possible world but, only of what 'counterparts' (the term which David Lewis uses[9]) of Nixon there would have been. Some people in other possible worlds have dogs whom they call 'Checkers'. Others favor the ABM but do not have any dog called Checkers. There are various people who resemble Nixon more or less, but none of them can really be said to be Nixon; they are only *counterparts* of Nixon, and you choose which one is the best counterpart by noting which resembles Nixon the most closely, according to your favorite criteria. Such views are widespread, both among the defenders of quantified modal logic and among its detractors.

All of this talk seems to me to have taken the metaphor of possible worlds much too seriously in some way. It is as if a 'possible world' were like a foreign country, or distant planet way out there. It is as if we see dimly through a telescope various actors on this distant planet. Actually David Lewis' view seems the most reasonable if one takes this picture literally. No one far away on another planet can be strictly identical with someone here. But, even if we have some marvelous methods of transportation to take one and the same person from planet to planet, we really need some epistemological criteria of identity to be able to say whether someone on this distant planet is the same person as someone here.

All of this seems to me to be a totally misguided way of looking at things. What it amounts to is the view that counterfactual situations have to be described purely qualitatively. So, we cannot say, for example, "If Nixon had only given a sufficient bribe to Senator X, he would have gotten Carswell through" because that refers to certain people, Nixon and Carswell, and talks about what things would be true of them in a counterfactual situation. We must say instead "If a man who has a hairline like such and such, and holds such and such political opinions had given a bribe to a man who was a senator and had such and such other qualities, then a man who was a judge in the South and had many other qualities resembling Carswell would have been confirmed." In other words, we must describe counterfactual situations purely qualitatively and then ask the question, "Given that the situation contains people or things with such and such qualities, which of these people is (or is a counterpart of) Nixon, which is Carswell, and so on?" This seems to me to be wrong. Who is to prevent us from saying "Nixon might have gotten Carswell through had he done certain things"? We are speaking of *Nixon* and asking what, in certain counterfactual situations, would have been true of *him*. We can say that if Nixon had done such and such, he would have lost the election to Humphrey. Those I am opposing would argue, "Yes, but how do you find out if the man you are talking about is in fact Nixon?" It would indeed be very hard to find out, if you were looking at the whole situation through a telescope, but that is not what we are doing here. Possible worlds are not something to which an epistemological question like this applies. And if the phrase 'possible worlds' is what makes anyone think some such question applies, he should just *drop* this phrase and use some other expression, say "counterfactual situation," which might be less misleading. If we say "If Nixon had bribed such and such a Senator, Nixon would have gotten Carswell through," what is *given* in the very description of that situation is that it is a situation in which we are speaking of Nixon, and of Carswell, and of such and such a Senator. And there seems to be no less objection to *stipulating* that we are speaking of certain *people* than there can be objection to stipulating that we are speaking of certain *qualities*. Advocates of the other view take speaking of certain qualities as unobjectionable. They do not say, "How do we know that this quality (in another possible world) is that of redness?" But they do find speaking of certain *people* objectionable. But I see no more reason to object in the one case than in the other. I think it really comes from the idea of possible worlds as existing out there, but very far off, viewable only through a special telescope. Even more objectionable is the view of David Lewis. According to Lewis, when we say "Under certain circumstances Nixon would have gotten Carswell through," we really mean "Some man, other than Nixon but closely resembling him, would have gotten some judge, other than Carswell but closely resembling him, through." Maybe that is so, that some man closely resembling Nixon could have gotten some man closely resembling Carswell through. But *that* would not comfort either Nixon or Carswell, nor would it make Nixon kick himself and say "*I* should have done such and such to get Carswell through." The question is whether under certain circumstances Nixon *himself* could have gotten *Carswell* through. And I think the objection is simply based on a misguided picture.

Instead, we can perfectly well talk about rigid and nonrigid designators. Moreover, we have a simple, intuitive test for them. We can say, for example, that the number of planets might have been a different number from the number it in fact is. For example, there might have been only seven planets. We can say that the inventor of bifocals might have been someone other than the man who *in fact* invented bifocals.[10] We cannot say, though, that the square root of 81 might have been a different number from the number it in fact is, for that number just has to be 9. If we apply this intuitive test to proper names, such as for example 'Richard Nixon', they would seem intuitively to come out to be rigid designators. First, when we talk even about the counterfactual situation in which we suppose Nixon to have done different things, we assume we are still talking about Nixon himself. We say, "If Nixon had bribed a certain Senator, he would have gotten Carswell through," and we assume that by 'Nixon' and 'Carswell' we are still referring to the very same people as in the actual world. And it seems that we cannot say "Nixon might have been a different man from the man he in fact was," unless, of course, we mean it metaphorically: he might have been a different *sort* of person (if you believe in free will and that people are not inherently corrupt). You might think the statement true in that sense, but Nixon could not have been in the other literal sense a different person from the person he, in fact, is, even though the thirty-seventh President of the United States might have been Humphrey. So the phrase "the thirty-seventh President" is nonrigid, but 'Nixon', it would seem, is rigid.

Let me make another distinction before I go back to the question of identity statements. This distinction is very fundamental and also hard to see through. In recent discussion, many philosophers who have debated the meaningfulness of various categories of truths, have regarded them as identical. Some of those who identify them are vociferous defenders of them, and others, such as Quine, say they are all identically meaningless. But usually they're not distinguished. These are categories such as 'analytic', 'necessary', 'a priori', and sometimes even 'certain'. I will not talk about all of these but only about the notions of a prioricity and necessity. Very often these are held to be synonyms. (Many philosophers probably should not be described as holding them to be synonyms; they simply *use* them interchangeably.) I wish to distinguish them. What do we mean by calling a statement *necessary*? We simply mean that the statement in question, first, is true, and, second, that it could not have been otherwise. When we say that something is *contingently* true, we mean that, though it is in fact the case, it could have been the case that things would have been otherwise. If we wish to assign this distinction to a branch of philosophy, we

Saul Kripke

should assign it to metaphysics. To the contrary, there is the notion of an *a priori truth*. An a priori truth is supposed to be one which can be *known* to be true independently of all experience. Notice that this does not in and of itself say anything about all possible worlds, unless this is put into the definition. All that it says is that it can be known to be true of the actual world, independently of all experience. It may, by some philosophical argument, follow from our knowing, independently of experience, that something is true of the actual world, that it has to be known to be true also of all possible worlds. But if this is to be established, it requires some philosophical argument to establish it. Now, *this* notion, if we were to assign it to a branch of philosophy, belongs, not to metaphysics, but to epistemology. It has to do with the way we can know certain things to be in fact true. Now, it may be the case, of course, that anything which is necessary is something which *can* be known a priori. (Notice, by the way, the notion a priori truth as thus defined has in it *another* modality: it *can* be known independently of all experience. It is a little complicated because there is a double modality here.) I will not have time to explore these notions in full detail here, but one thing we can see from the outset is that these two notions are by no means trivially the same. If they are coextensive, it takes some philosophical argument to establish it. As stated, they belong to different domains of philosophy. One of them has something to do with *knowledge*, of what can be known in certain ways about the *actual* world. The other one has to do with *metaphysics*, how the world *could* have been; given that it is the way it is, could it have been otherwise, in certain ways? Now I hold, as a matter of fact, that neither class of statements is contained in the other. But all we need to talk about here is this: Is everything that is necessary knowable a priori or known a priori? Consider the following example: the Goldbach conjecture. This says that every even number is the sum of two primes. It is a mathematical statement and if it is true at all, it has to be necessary. Certainly, one could not say that though in fact every even number is the sum of two primes, there could have been some extra number which was even and not the sum of two primes. What would that mean? On the other hand, the answer to the question whether every even number *is* in fact the sum of two primes is unknown, and we have no method

at present for deciding. So we certainly do not know, a priori or even a posteriori, that every even number is the sum of two primes. (Well, perhaps we have some evidence in that no counterexample has been found.) But we certainly do not know a priori anyway, that every even number is, in fact, the sum of two primes. But, of course, the definition just says "*can* be known independently of experience," and someone might say that if it is true, we *could* know it independently of experience. It is hard to see exactly what this claim means. It might be so. One thing it might mean is that if it were true we could *prove* it. This claim is certainly wrong if it is generally applied to mathematical statements and we have to work within some fixed system. This is what Gödel proved. And even if we mean an 'intuitive proof in general' it might just be the case (at least, this view is as clear and as probable as the contrary) that though the statement is true, there is just no way the human mind could ever prove it. Of course, one way an *infinite* mind might be able to prove it is by looking through each natural number one by one and checking. In this sense, of course, it can, perhaps, be known a priori, but only by an infinite mind, and then this gets into other complicated questions. I do not want to discuss questions about the conceivability of performing an infinite number of acts like looking through each number one by one. A vast philosophical literature has been written on this. Some have declared it is logically impossible; others that it is logically possible; and some do not know. The main point is that it is not trivial that just because such a statement is necessary it can be known a priori. Some considerable clarification is required before we decide that it can be so known. And so this shows that even if everything necessary is a priori in some sense, it should not be taken as a trivial matter of definition. It is a substantive philosophical thesis which requires some work.

Another example that one might give relates to the problem of essentialism. Here is a lectern. A question which has often been raised in philosophy is: What are its essential properties? What properties, aside from trivial ones like self-identity, are such that this object has to have them if it exists at all,[11] are such that if an object did not have it, it would not be this object?[12] For example, being made of wood, and not of ice, might be an essential property of this lectern. Let us just take the weaker statement that it is not made of ice. That will establish it as strongly as we need it, perhaps as dramatically. Supposing this lectern is in fact made of wood, could this very lectern have been made from the very beginning of its existence from ice, say frozen from water in the Thames? One has a considerable feeling that it could *not*, though in fact one certainly could have made a lectern of water from the Thames, frozen it into ice by some process, and put it right there in place of this thing. If one had done so, one would have made, of course, a *different* object. It would not have been *this very lectern*, and so one would not have a case in which this very lectern here was made of ice, or was made from water from the Thames. The question of whether it could afterward, say in a minute from now, turn into ice is something else. So, it would seem, if an example like this is correct – and this is what advocates of essentialism have held – that this lectern could not have been made of ice, that is in any counterfactual situation of which we would say that this lectern existed at all, we would have to say also that it was not made from water from the Thames frozen into ice. Some have rejected, of course, any such notion of essential property as meaningless. Usually, it is because (and I think this is what Quine, for example, would say) they have held that it depends on the notion of identity across possible worlds, and that this is itself meaningless. Since I have rejected this view already, I will not deal with it again. We can talk about *this very object*, and whether it could have had certain properties which it does not in fact have. For example, it could have been in another room from the room it in fact is in, even at this very time, but it could not have been made from the very beginning from water frozen into ice.

If the essentialist view is correct, it can only be correct if we sharply distinguish between the notions of a posteriori and a priori truth on the one hand, and contingent and necessary truth on the other hand, for although the statement that this table, if it exists at all, was not made of ice, is necessary, it certainly is not something that we know a priori. What we know is that first, lecterns usually are not made of ice, they are usually made of wood. This looks like wood. It does not feel cold and it probably would if it were made of ice. Therefore, I conclude, probably this is not made of ice. Here my entire judgment is a posteriori. I could find out that an ingenious trick has been played upon me and that, in fact,

this lectern is made of ice; but what I am saying is, given that it is in fact not made of ice, in fact is made of wood, one cannot imagine that under certain circumstances it could have been made of ice. So we have to say that though we cannot know a priori whether this table was made of ice or not, given that it is not made of ice, it is *necessarily* not made of ice. In other words, if *P* is the statement that the lectern is not made of ice, one knows by a priori philosophical analysis, some conditional of the form "if *P*, then necessarily *P*." If the table is not made of ice, it is necessarily not made of ice. On the other hand, then, we know by empirical investigation that *P*, the antecedent of the conditional, is true – that this table is not made of ice. We can conclude by *modus ponens*:

$$\frac{\begin{array}{l} P \supset \Box P \\ P \end{array}}{\Box P}$$

The conclusion – '$\Box P$' – is that it is necessary that the table not be made of ice, and this conclusion is known a posteriori, since one of the premises on which it is based is a posteriori. So, the notion of essential properties can be maintained only by distinguishing between the notions of a priori and necessary truth, and I do maintain it.

Let us return to the question of identities. Concerning the statement 'Hesperus is Phosphorus' or the statement 'Cicero is Tully', one can find all of these out by empirical investigation, and we might turn out to be wrong in our empirical beliefs. So, it is usually argued, such statements must therefore be contingent. Some have embraced the other side of the coin and have held "Because of this argument about necessity, identity statements between names have to be knowable a priori, so, only a very special category of names, possibly, really works as names; the other things are bogus names, disguised descriptions, or something of the sort. However, a certain very narrow class of statements of identity are known a priori, and these are the ones which contain the genuine names." If one accepts the distinctions that I have made, one need not jump to either conclusion. One can hold that certain statements of identity between names, though often known a posteriori, and maybe not knowable a priori, are in fact necessary, if true. So, we have some room to hold this. But, of course, to have some room to hold it does not mean that we should hold it. So let us see what the evidence is. First, recall the remark that I made that proper names seem to be rigid designators, as when we use the name 'Nixon' to talk about a certain man, even in counterfactual situations. If we say, "If Nixon had not written the letter to Saxbe, maybe he would have gotten Carswell through," we are in this statement talking about Nixon, Saxbe, and Carswell, the very same men as in the actual world, and what would have happened to them under certain counterfactual circumstances. If names are rigid designators, then there can be no question about identities being necessary, because '*a*' and '*b*' will be rigid designators of a certain man or thing *x*. Then even in every possible world, *a* and *b* will both refer to this same object *x*, and to no other, and so there will be no situation in which *a* might not have been *b*. That would have to be a situation in which the object which we are also now calling '*x*' would not have been identical with itself. Then one could not possibly have a situation in which Cicero would not have been Tully or Hesperus would not have been Phosphorus.[13]

Aside from the identification of necessity with a priority, what has made people feel the other way? There are two things which have made people feel the other way.[14] Some people tend to regard identity statements as metalinguistic statements, to identify the statement "Hesperus is Phosphorus" with the metalinguistic statement, "'Hesperus' and 'Phosphorus' are names of the same heavenly body." And that, of course, might have been false. We might have used the terms 'Hesperus' and 'Phosphorus' as names of *two* different heavenly bodies. But, of course, this has nothing to do with the necessity of identity. In the same sense "$2 + 2 = 4$" might have been false. The phrases "$2 + 2$" and "4" might have been used to refer to two different numbers. One can imagine a language, for example, in which "+", "2", and "=" were used in the standard way, but "4" was used as the name of, say, the square root of minus 1, as we should call it, "*i*." Then "$2 + 2 = 4$" would be false, for 2 plus 2 is not equal to the square root of minus 1. But this is not what we want. We do not want just to say that a certain statement which we in fact use to express something true could have expressed something false. We want to use the statement in *our* way and see if it could have been false. Let us do this. What is the idea people have?

They say, "Look, Hesperus might not have been Phosphorus. Here a certain planet was seen in the morning, and it was seen in the evening; and it just turned out later on as a matter of empirical fact that they were one and the same planet. If things had turned out otherwise, they would have been two different planets, or two different heavenly bodies, so how can you say that such a statement is necessary?"

Now there are two things that such people can mean. First, they can mean that we do not know a priori whether Hesperus is Phosphorus. This I have already conceded. Second, they may mean that they can actually imagine circumstances that they would call circumstances in which Hesperus would not have been Phosphorus. Let us think what would be such a circumstance, using these terms here as *names* of a planet. For example, it could have been the case that Venus did indeed rise in the morning in exactly the position in which we saw it, but that on the other hand, in the position which is in fact occupied by Venus in the evening, Venus was not there, and Mars took its place. This is all counterfactual because in fact Venus is there. Now one can also imagine that in this counterfactual other possible world, the earth would have been inhabited by people and that they should have used the names 'Phosphorus' for Venus in the morning and 'Hesperus' for Mars in the evening. Now, this is all very good, but would it be a situation in which Hesperus was not Phosphorus? Of course, it is a situation in which people would have been able to *say*, truly, "Hesperus is not Phosphorus"; but we are supposed to describe things in our language, not in theirs. So let us describe it in our language. Well, how could it actually happen that Venus would not be in that position in the evening? For example, let us say that there is some comet that comes around every evening and yanks things over a little bit. (That would be a very simple scientific way of imagining it: not really too simple – that is very hard to imagine actually.) It just happens to come around every evening, and things get yanked over a little bit. Mars gets yanked over to the very position where Venus is, then the comet yanks things back to their normal position in the morning. Thinking of this planet which we now call 'Phosphorus', what should we say? Well, we can say that the comet passes it and yanks Phosphorus over so that it is not in the position normally occupied by Phosphorus in the evening. If we do say this, and really use 'Phosphorus' as the name of a planet, then we have to say that, under such circumstances, Phosphorus in the evening would not be in the position where we, in fact, saw it; or alternatively, Hesperus in the evening would not be in the position in which we, in fact, saw it. We might say that under such circumstances, we would not have called Hesperus 'Hesperus' because Hesperus would have been in a different position. But that still would not make Phosphorus different from Hesperus; but what would then be the case instead is that Hesperus would have been in a different position from the position it in fact is and, perhaps, not in such a position that people would have called it 'Hesperus'. But that would not be a situation in which Phosphorus would not have been Hesperus.

Let us take another example which may be clearer. Suppose someone uses 'Tully' to refer to the Roman orator who denounced Cataline and uses the name 'Cicero' to refer to the man whose works he had to study in third-year Latin in high school. Of course, he may not know in advance that the very same man who denounced Cataline wrote these works, and that is a contingent statement. But the fact that this statement is contingent should not make us think that the statement that Cicero is Tully, if it is true, and it is in fact true, is contingent. Suppose, for example, that Cicero actually did denounce Cataline, but thought that this political achievement was so great that he should not bother writing any literary works. Would we say that these would be circumstances under which he would not have been Cicero? It seems to me that the answer is no, that instead we would say that, under such circumstances, Cicero would not have written any literary works. It is not a necessary property of Cicero – the way the shadow follows the man – that he should have written certain works; we can easily imagine a situation in which Shakespeare would not have written the works of Shakespeare, or one in which Cicero would not have written the works of Cicero. What may be the case is that we *fix the reference* of the term 'Cicero' by use of some descriptive phrase, such as 'the author of these works'. But once we have this reference fixed, we then use the name 'Cicero' *rigidly* to designate the man who in fact we have identified by his authorship of these works. We do not use it to designate whoever would have written these works in place of Cicero, if someone else wrote them. It might have been the case

that the man who wrote these works was not the man who denounced Cataline. Cassius might have written these works. But we would not then say that Cicero would have been Cassius, unless we were speaking in a very loose and metaphorical way. We would say that Cicero, whom we may have identified and come to know by his works, would not have written them, and that someone else, say Cassius, would have written them in his place.

Such examples are not grounds for thinking that identity statements are contingent. To take them as such grounds is to misconstrue the relation between a *name* and a *description used to fix its reference*, to take them to be *synonyms*. Even if we fix the reference of such a name as 'Cicero' as the man who wrote such and such works, in speaking of counterfactual situations, when we speak of Cicero, we do not then speak of whoever in such counterfactual situations *would* have written such and such works, but rather of Cicero, whom we have identified by the contingent property that he is the man who in fact, that is, in the actual world, wrote certain works.[15]

I hope this is reasonably clear in a brief compass. Now, actually I have been presupposing something I do not really believe to be, in general, true. Let us suppose that we do fix the reference of a name by a description. Even if we do so, we do not then make the name *synonymous* with the description, but instead we use the name *rigidly* to refer to the object so named, even in talking about counterfactual situations where the thing named would not satisfy the description in question. Now, this is what I think in fact is true for those cases of naming where the reference is fixed by description. But, in fact, I also think, contrary to most recent theorists, that the reference of names is rarely or almost never fixed by means of description. And by this I do not just mean what Searle says: "It's not a single description, but rather a cluster, a family of properties which fixes the reference." I mean that properties in this sense are not used *at all*. But I do not have the time to go into this here. So, let us suppose that at least one half of prevailing views about naming is true, that the reference is fixed by descriptions. Even were that true, the name would not be synonymous with the description, but would be used to *name* an object which we pick out by the contingent fact that it satisfies a certain description. And so, even though we can imagine a case where the man who wrote these works would not have been the man who denounced Cataline, we should not say that that would be a case in which Cicero would not have been Tully. We should say that it is a case in which Cicero did not write these works, but rather that Cassius did. And the identity of Cicero and Tully still holds.

Let me turn to the case of heat and the motion of molecules. Here surely is a case that is contingent identity! Recent philosophy has emphasized this again and again. So, if it is a case of contingent identity, then let us imagine under what circumstances it would be false. Now, concerning this statement I hold that the circumstances philosophers apparently have in mind as circumstances under which it would have been false are not in fact such circumstances. First, of course, it is argued that "Heat is the motion of molecules" is an a posteriori judgment; scientific investigation might have turned out otherwise. As I said before, this shows nothing against the view that it is necessary – at least if I am right. But here, surely, people had very specific circumstances in mind under which, so they thought, the judgment that heat is the motion of molecules would have been false. What were these circumstances? One can distill them out of the fact that we found out empirically that heat is the motion of molecules. How was this? What did we find out first when we found out that heat is the motion of molecules? There is a certain external phenomenon which we can sense by the sense of touch, and it produces a sensation which we call "the sensation of heat." We then discover that the external phenomenon which produces this sensation, which we sense, by means of our sense of touch, is in fact that of molecular agitation in the thing that we touch, a very high degree of molecular agitation. So, it might be thought, to imagine a situation in which heat would not have been the motion of molecules, we need only imagine a situation in which we would have had the very same sensation and it would have been produced by something other than the motion of molecules. Similarly, if we wanted to imagine a situation in which light was not a stream of photons, we could imagine a situation in which we were sensitive to something else in exactly the same way, producing what we call visual experiences, though not through a stream of photons. To make the case stronger, or to look at another side of the coin, we could also consider a situation in which we *are* concerned with

the motion of molecules but in which such motion does not give us the sensation of heat. And it might also have happened that we, or, at least, the creatures inhabiting this planet, might have been so constituted that, let us say, an increase in the motion of molecules did not give us this sensation but that, on the contrary, a slowing down of the molecules did give us the very same sensation. This would be a situation, so it might be thought, in which heat would not be the motion of molecules, or, more precisely, in which temperature would not be mean molecular kinetic energy.

But I think it would not be so. Let us think about the situation again. First, let us think about it in the actual world. Imagine right now the world invaded by a number of Martians, who do indeed get the very sensation that we call "the sensation of heat" when they feel some ice which has slow molecular motion, and who do not get a sensation of heat – in fact, maybe just the reverse – when they put their hand near a fire which causes a lot of molecular agitation. Would we say, "Ah, this casts some doubt on heat being the motion of molecules, because there are these other people who don't get the same sensation"? Obviously not, and no one would think so. We would say instead that the Martians somehow feel the very sensation we get when we feel heat when they feel cold and that they do not get a sensation of heat when they feel heat. But now let us think of a counterfactual situation.[16] Suppose the earth had from the very beginning been inhabited by such creatures. First, imagine it inhabited by no creatures at all: then there is no one to feel any sensations of heat. But we would not say that under such circumstances it would necessarily be the case that heat did not exist; we would say that heat might have existed, for example, if there were fires that heated up the air.

Let us suppose the laws of physics were not very different: fires do heat up the air. Then there would have been heat even though there were no creatures around to feel it. Now let us suppose evolution takes place, and life is created, and there are some creatures around. But they are not like us, they are more like the Martians. Now would we say that heat has suddenly turned to cold, because of the way the creatures of this planet sense it? No, I think we should describe this situation as a situation in which, though the creatures on this planet got our sensation of heat, they did not get it when they were exposed to heat. They got it when they were exposed to cold. And that is something we can surely well imagine. We can imagine it just as we can imagine our planet being invaded by creatures of this sort. Think of it in two steps. First there is a stage where there are no creatures at all, and one can certainly imagine the planet still having both heat and cold, though no one is around to sense it. Then the planet comes through an evolutionary process to be peopled with beings of different neural structure from ourselves. Then these creatures could be such that they were insensitive to heat; they did not feel it in the way we do; but on the other hand, they felt cold in much the same way that we feel heat. But still, heat would be heat, and cold would be cold. And particularly, then, this goes in no way against saying that in this counterfactual situation heat would still *be* the molecular motion, *be* that which is produced by fires, and so on, just as it would have been if there had been no creatures on the planet at all. Similarly, we could imagine that the planet was inhabited by creatures who got visual sensations when there were sound waves in the air. We should not therefore say, "Under such circumstances, sound would have been light." Instead we should say, "The planet was inhabited by creatures who were in some sense visually sensitive to sound, and maybe even visually sensitive to light." If this is correct, it can still be and will still be a necessary truth that heat is the motion of molecules and that light is a stream of photons.

To state the view succinctly: we use both the terms 'heat' and 'the motion of molecules' as rigid designators for a certain external phenomenon. Since heat is in fact the motion of molecules, and the designators are rigid, by the argument I have given here, it is going to be *necessary* that heat is the motion of molecules. What gives us the illusion of contingency is the fact we have identified the heat by the contingent fact that there happen to be creatures on this planet – (namely, ourselves) who are sensitive to it in a certain way, that is, who are sensitive to the motion of molecules or to heat – these are one and the same thing. And this is contingent. So we use the description, 'that which causes such and such sensations, or that which we sense in such and such a way', to identify heat. But in using this fact we use a contingent property of heat, just as we use the contingent

property of Cicero as having written such and such works to identify him. We then use the terms 'heat' in the one case and 'Cicero' in the other *rigidly* to designate the objects for which they stand. And of course the term 'the motion of molecules' is rigid; it always stands for the motion of molecules, never for any other phenomenon. So, as Bishop Butler said, "everything is what it is and not another thing." Therefore, "Heat is the motion of molecules" will be necessary, not contingent, and one only has the *illusion* of contingency in the way one could have the illusion of contingency in thinking that this table might have been made of ice. We might think one could imagine it, but if we try, we can see on reflection that what we are really imagining is just there being another lectern in this very position here which was in fact made of ice. The fact that we may identify this lectern by being the object we see and touch in such and such a position is something else.

Now how does this relate to the problem of mind and body? It is usually held that this is a contingent identity statement just like "Heat is the motion of molecules." That cannot be. It cannot be a contingent identity statement just like "Heat is the motion of molecules" because, if I am right, "Heat is the motion of molecules" is not a contingent identity statement. Let us look at this statement. For example, "My being in pain at such and such a time is my being in such and such a brain state at such and such a time," or, "Pain in general is such and such a neural (brain) state."

This is held to be contingent on the following grounds. First, we can imagine the brain state existing though there is no pain at all. It is only a scientific fact that whenever we are in a certain brain state we have a pain. Second, one might imagine a creature being in pain, but not being in any specified brain state at all, maybe not having a brain at all. People even think, at least prima facie, though they may be wrong, that they can imagine totally disembodied creatures, at any rate certainly not creatures with bodies anything like our own. So it seems that we can imagine definite circumstances under which this relationship would have been false. Now, if these circumstances are circumstances, notice that we cannot deal with them simply by saying that this is just an illusion, something we can apparently imagine, but in fact cannot in the way we thought erroneously that we could imagine a situation in which heat was not the motion of molecules. Because although we can say that we pick out heat contingently by the contingent property that it affects us in such and such a way, we cannot similarly say that we pick out pain contingently by the fact that it affects us in such and such a way. On such a picture there would be the brain state, and we pick it out by the contingent fact that it affects us as pain. Now that might be true of the brain state, but it cannot be true of the pain. The experience itself has to be *this experience*, and I cannot say that it is contingent property of the pain I now have that it is a pain.[17] In fact, it would seem that both the terms, 'my pain' and 'my being in such and such a brain state' are, first of all, both rigid designators. That is, whenever anything is such and such a pain, it is essentially that very object, namely, such and such a pain, and wherever anything is such and such a brain state, it is essentially that very object, namely, such and such a brain state. So both of these are rigid designators. One cannot say this pain might have been something else, some other state. These are both rigid designators.

Second, the way we would think of picking them out – namely, the pain by its being an experience of a certain sort, and the brain state by its being the state of a certain material object, being of such and such molecular configuration – both of these pick out their objects essentially and not accidentally, that is, they pick them out by essential properties. Whenever the molecules *are* in this configuration, we *do* have such and such a brain state. Whenever you feel *this*, you do have a pain. So it seems that the identity theorist is in some trouble, for, since we have two rigid designators, the identity statement in question is necessary. Because they pick out their objects essentially, we cannot say the case where you seem to imagine the identity statement false is really an illusion like the illusion one gets in

the case of heat and molecular motion, because that illusion depended on the fact that we pick out heat by a certain contingent property. So there is very little room to maneuver; perhaps none.[18] The identity theorist, who holds that pain is the brain state, also has to hold that it necessarily is the brain state. He therefore cannot concede, but has to deny, that there would have been situations under which one would have had pain but not the corresponding brain state. Now usually in arguments on the identity theory, this is very far from being denied. In fact, it is conceded from the outset by the materialist as well as by his opponent. He says, "Of course, it *could* have been the case that we had pains without the brain states. It is a contingent identity." But that cannot be. He has to hold that we are under some illusion in thinking that we can imagine that there could have been pains without brain states. And the only model I can think of for what the illusion might be, or at least the model given by the analogy the materialists themselves suggest, namely, heat and molecular motion, simply does not work in this case. So the materialist is up against a very stiff challenge. He has to show that these things we think we can see to be possible are in fact not possible. He has to show that these things which we can imagine are not in fact things we can imagine. And that requires some very different philosophical argument from the sort which has been given in the case of heat and molecular motion. And it would have to be a deeper and subtler argument than I can fathom and subtler than has ever appeared in any materialist literature that I have read. So the conclusion of this investigation would be that the analytical tools we are using go against the identity thesis and so go against the general thesis that mental states are just physical states.[19]

The next topic would be my own solution to the mind–body problem, but that I do not have.

Notes

1 This paper was presented orally, without a written text, to the New York University lecture series on identity which makes up the volume, *Identity and Individuation*, ed. M. K. Munitz (New York: New York University Press, 1971); see pp. 135–64. The lecture was taped, and the present paper represents a transcription of these tapes, edited only slightly with no attempt to change the style of the original. If the reader imagines the sentences of this paper as being delivered, extemporaneously, with proper pauses and emphases, this may facilitate his comprehension. Nevertheless, there may still be passages which are hard to follow, and the time allotted necessitated a condensed presentation of the argument. (A longer version of some of these views, still rather compressed and still representing a transcript of oral remarks, will appear elsewhere.) Occasionally, reservations,

amplifications, and gratifications of my remarks had to be repressed, especially in the discussion of theoretical identification and the mind–body problem. The footnotes, which were added to the original, would have become even more unwieldy if this had not been done.

2   R. J. Butler (ed.) *Analytical Philosophy*, second series (Oxford: Blackwell Publishers, 1965).

3   The second occurrence of the description has small scope.

4   In Russell's theory, $F(\imath x Gx)$ follows from $(x)Fx$ and $(\exists! x)Gx$, provided that the description in $F(\imath x Gx)$ has the entire context for its scope (in Russell's 1905 terminology, has a 'primary occurrence'). Only then is $F(\imath x Gx)$ 'about' the denotation of '$\imath x Gx$'. Applying this rule to (14), we get the results indicated in the text. Notice that, in the ambiguous form $\Box(\imath x Gx = \imath x Hx)$, if one or both of the descriptions have 'primary occurrences' the formula does not assert the necessity of $\imath x Gx = \imath x Hx$; if both have secondary occurrences, it does. Thus in a language without explicit scope indicators, descriptions must be construed with the smallest possible scope – only then will $\sim\!A$ be the negation of A, $\Box A$ the necessitation of A, and the like.

5   An earlier distinction with the same purpose was, of course, the medieval one of *de dicto–de re*. That Russell's distinction of scope eliminates modal paradoxes has been pointed out by many logicians, especially Smullyan.

So as to avoid misunderstanding, let me emphasize that I am of course not asserting that Russell's notion of scope solves Quine's problem of 'essentialism'; what it does show, especially in conjunction with modern model-theoretic approaches to modal logic, is that quantified modal logic need not deny the truth of all instances of $(x)(y)(x = y \cdot \supset \cdot Fx \supset Fy)$, nor of all instances of '$(x)(Gx \supset Ga)$' (where 'a' is to be replaced by a nonvacuous definite description whose scope is all of 'Ga'), in order to avoid making it a necessary truth that one and the same man invented bifocals and headed the original Postal Department. Russell's contextual definition of descriptions need not be adopted in order to ensure these results; but other logical theories, Fregean or other, which take descriptions as primitive must somehow express the same logical facts. Frege showed that a simple, non-iterated context containing a definite description with small scope, which cannot be interpreted as being 'about' the denotation of the description, can be interpreted as about its 'sense'. Some logicians have been interested in the question of the conditions under which, in an intensional context, a description with small scope is equivalent to the same one with large scope. One of the virtues of a Russellian treatment of descriptions in

modal logic is that the answer (roughly that the description be a 'rigid designator' in the sense of this lecture) then often follows from the other postulates for quantified modal logic; no special postulates are needed, as in Hintikka's treatment. Even if descriptions are taken as primitive, special postulation of when scope is irrelevant can often be deduced from more basic axioms.

6   "Modalities and Intensional Languages," *Boston Studies in the Philosophy of Science*, vol. 1 (New York: Humanities Press, 1963), pp. 71ff. See also the "Comments" by Quine and the ensuing discussion.

7   It should. See her remark on p. 115, "Modalities," in the discussion following the papers.

8   If there is no deity, and especially if the nonexistence of a deity is *necessary*, it is dubious that we can use "He" to refer to a deity. The use in the text must be taken to be non-literal.

9   David K. Lewis, "Counterpart Theory and Quantified Modal Logic," *Journal of Philosophy* 65 (1968), pp. 113ff.

10   Some philosophers think that definite descriptions, in English, are ambiguous, that sometimes 'the inventor of bifocals' rigidly designates the man who in fact invented bifocals. I am tentatively inclined to reject this view, construed as a thesis about English (as opposed to a possible hypothetical language), but I will not argue the question here.

What I do wish to note is that, contrary to some opinions, this alleged ambiguity cannot replace the Russellian notion of the scope of a description. Consider the sentence, "The number of planets might have been necessarily even." This sentence plainly can be read so as to express a truth; had there been eight planets, the number of planets would have been necessarily even. Yet without scope distinctions, both a 'referential' (rigid) and a non-rigid reading of the description will make the statement false. (Since the number of planets is nine, the rigid reading amounts to the falsity that nine might have been necessarily even.)

The 'rigid' reading is equivalent to the Russellian primary occurrence; the non-rigid, to innermost scope – some, following Donnellan, perhaps loosely, have called this reading the 'attributive' use. The possibility of intermediate scopes is then ignored. In the present instance, the intended reading of $\Diamond\Box$ (the number of planets is even) makes the scope of the description $\Box$ (the number of planets is even), neither the largest nor the smallest possible.

11   This definition is the usual formulation of the notion of essential property, but an exception must be made for existence itself; on the definition given, existence would be trivially essential. We should regard existence as essential to an object only if the object necessarily exists. Perhaps there

are other recherché properties, involving existence, for which the definition is similarly objectionable. (I thank Michael Slote for this observation.)

12 The two clauses of the sentence footnoted give equivalent definitions of the notion of essential property, since $\Box((\exists x)\ (x = a) \supset Fa)$ is equivalent to $\Box(x)\ (\sim Fx \supset x \neq a)$. The second formulation, however, has served as a powerful seducer in favor of theories of 'identification across possible worlds'. For it suggests that we consider 'an object b in another possible world' and test whether it is identifiable with a by asking whether it lacks any of the essential properties of a. Let me therefore emphasize that, although an essential property is (trivially) a property without which an object cannot be a, it by no means follows that the essential, purely qualitative properties of a jointly form a sufficient condition for being a, nor that *any* purely qualitative conditions are sufficient for an object to be a. Further, even if necessary and sufficient qualitative conditions for an object to be Nixon may exist, there would still be little justification for the demand for a purely qualitative description of all counterfactual situations. We can ask whether Nixon might have been a Democrat without engaging in these subtleties.

13 I thus agree with Quine, that "Hesperus is Phosphorus" is (or can be) an empirical discovery; with Marcus, that it is necessary. Both Quine and Marcus, according to the present standpoint, err in identifying the epistemological and the metaphysical issues.

14 The two confusions alleged, especially the second, are both related to the confusion of the metaphysical question of the necessity of "Hesperus is Phosphorus" with the epistemological question of its a prioricity. For if Hesperus is identified by its position in the sky in the evening, and Phosphorus by its position in the morning, an investigator may well know, in advance of empirical research, that Hesperus is Phosphorus if and only if one and the same body occupies position x in the evening and position y in the morning. The a priori material equivalence of the two statements, however, does not imply their strict (necessary) equivalence. (The same remarks apply to the case of heat and molecular motion below.) Similar remarks apply to some extent to the relationship between "Hesperus is Phosphorus" and "'Hesperus' and 'Phosphorus' name the same thing." A confusion that also operates is, of course, the confusion between what *we* would say of a counterfactual situation and how people *in* that situation would have described it; this confusion, too, is probably related to the confusion between a prioricity and necessity.

15 If someone protests, regarding the lectern, that it *could* after all have *turned out* to have been made of ice, and therefore could have been made of ice. I would reply that what he really means is that *a lectern* could have looked just like this one, and have been placed in the same position as this one, and yet have been made of ice. In short, I could have been in the *same epistemological situation* in relation to *a lectern made of ice* as I actually am in relation to *this* lectern. In the main text, I have argued that the same reply should be given to protests that Hesperus could have turned out to be other than Phosphorus, or Cicero other than Tully. Here, then, the notion of 'counterpart' comes into its own. For it is not this table, but an epistemic 'counterpart', which was hewn from ice; not Hesperus-Phosphorus-Venus, but two distinct counterparts thereof, in two of the roles Venus actually plays (that of Evening Star and Morning Star), which are different. Precisely because of this fact, it is not *this table* which could have been made of ice. Statements about the modal properties of *this table* never refer to counterparts. However, if someone confuses the epistemological and the metaphysical problems, he will be well on the way to the counterpart theory Lewis and others have advocated.

16 Isn't the situation I just described also counterfactual? At least it may well be, if such Martians never in fact invade. Strictly speaking, the distinction I wish to draw compares how we *would* speak *in* a (possibly counterfactual) situation, *if* it obtained, and how we *do* speak *of* a counterfactual situation, knowing that it does not obtain – i.e., the distinction between the language we would have used in a situation and the language we *do* use to describe it. (Consider the description: "Suppose we all spoke German." This description is in English.) The former case can be made vivid by imagining the counterfactual situation to be actual.

17 The most popular identity theories advocated today explicitly fail to satisfy this simple requirement. For these theories usually hold that a mental state is a brain state, and that what makes the brain state into a mental state is its 'causal role', the fact that it tends to produce certain behavior (as intentions produce actions, or pain, pain behavior) and to be produced by certain stimuli (e.g. pain, by pinpricks). If the relations between the brain state and its causes and effects are regarded as contingent, then *being such-and-such-a-mental state* is a contingent property of the brain state. Let X be a pain. The causal-role identity theorist holds (1) that X is a brain state, (2) that the fact that X is a pain is to be analyzed (roughly) as the fact that X is produced by certain stimuli and produces certain behavior. The fact mentioned in (2) is, of course, regarded *a phenomenon* in the same way we identify heat, namely, by feeling it by the sensation we call "the sensation

of heat," without the phenomenon being molecular motion. Further, the beings might not have been sensitive to molecular motion (i.e., to heat) by any neural mechanism whatsoever. It is impossible to explain the apparent possibility of C-fiber stimulations not having been pain in the same way. Here, too, we would have to suppose that we could have been in the same epistemological situation, and identify something in the same way we identify pain, without its corresponding to C-fiber stimulation. But the way we identify pain is by feeling it, and if a C-fiber stimulation could have occurred without our feeling any pain, then the C-fiber stimulation would have occurred without there *being* any pain, contrary to the necessity of the identity. The trouble is that although 'heat' is a rigid designator, heat is picked out by the contingent property of its being felt in a certain way; pain, on the other hand, is picked out by an essential (indeed necessary and sufficient) property. For a sensation to be *felt* as pain is for it to *be* pain.

18 A brief restatement of the argument may be helpful here. If "pain" and "C-fiber stimulation" are rigid designators of phenomena, one who identifies them must regard the identity as necessary. How can this necessity be reconciled with the apparent fact that C-fiber stimulation might have turned out not to be correlated with pain at all? We might try to reply by analogy to the case of heat and molecular motion; the latter identity, too, is necessary, yet someone may believe that, before scientific investigation showed otherwise, molecular motion might have turned out not to be heat. The reply is, of course, that what really is possible is that people (or some rational sentient beings) could have been in the *same epistemic situation* as we actually are, and identify as contingent; the brain state X might well exist and not tend to produce the appropriate behavior in the absence of other conditions. Thus (1) and (2) assert that a certain pain X might have existed, yet not have been a pain. This seems to me self-evidently absurd. Imagine any pain: is it possible that *it itself* could have existed, yet not have been a pain?

If $X = Y$, then X and Y share all properties, including modal properties. If X is a pain and Y the corresponding brain state, then *being a pain* is

an essential property of X, and *being a brain state* is an essential property of Y. If the correspondence relation is, in fact, identity, then it must be *necessary* of Y that it corresponds to a pain, and *necessary* of X that it correspond to a brain state, indeed to this particular brain state, Y. Both assertions seem false; it *seems* clearly possible that X should have existed without the corresponding brain state; or that the brain state should have existed without being felt as pain. Identity theorists cannot, contrary to their almost universal present practice, accept these intuitions; they must deny them, and explain them away. This is none too easy a thing to do.

19 All arguments against the identity theory which rely on the necessity of identity, or on the notion of essential property, are, of course, inspired by Descartes' argument for his dualism. The earlier arguments which superficially were rebutted by the analogies of heat and molecular motion, and the bifocals inventor who was also Postmaster General, had such an inspiration; and so does my argument here. R. Albritton and M. Slote have informed me that they independently have attempted to give essentialist arguments against the identity theory, and probably others have done so as well.

The simplest Cartesian argument can perhaps be restated as follows: Let 'A' be a *name* (rigid designator) of Descartes' body. Then Descartes argues that since he could exist even if A did not, $\Diamond$ (Descartes $\neq A$), hence Descartes $\neq A$. Those who have accused him of a modal fallacy have forgotten that 'A' is rigid. His argument is valid, and his conclusion is correct, provided its (perhaps dubitable) premise is accepted. On the other hand, provided that Descartes is regarded as having ceased to exist upon his death, "Descartes $\neq A$" can be established without the use of a modal argument; for if so, no doubt A survived Descartes when A was a corpse. Thus A had a property (existing at a certain time) which Descartes did not. The same argument can establish that a statue is not the hunk of stone, or the congery of molecules, of which it is composed. Mere non-identity, then, may be a weak conclusion. (See D. Wiggins, *Philosophical Review* 77 (1968), pp. 90ff.) The Cartesian modal argument, however, surely can be deployed to maintain relevant stronger conclusions as well.

8

Meaning and Reference

Hilary Putnam

Unclear as it is, the traditional doctrine that the notion "meaning" possesses the extension/intension ambiguity has certain typical consequences. The doctrine that the meaning of a term is a concept carried the implication that meanings are mental entities. Frege, however, rebelled against this "psychologism." Feeling that meanings are *public* property – that the *same* meaning can be "grasped" by more than one person and by persons at different times – he identified concepts (and hence "intensions" or meanings) with abstract entities rather than mental entities. However, "grasping" these abstract entities was still an individual psychological act. None of these philosophers doubted that understanding a word (knowing its intension) was just a matter of being in a certain psychological state (somewhat in the way in which knowing how to factor numbers in one's head is just a matter of being in a certain very complex psychological state).

Secondly, the timeworn example of the two terms 'creature with a kidney' and 'creature with a heart' does show that two terms can have the same extension and yet differ in intension. But it was taken to be obvious that the reverse is impossible: two terms cannot differ in extension and have the same intension. Interestingly, no argument for this impossibility was ever offered. Probably it reflects the tradition of the ancient and medieval philosophers, who assumed that the concept corresponding to a term was just a con-

junction of predicates, and hence that the concept corresponding to a term must *always* provide a necessary and sufficient condition for falling into the extension of the term. For philosophers like Carnap, who accepted the verifiability theory of meaning, the concept corresponding to a term provided (in the ideal case, where the term had "complete meaning") a *criterion* for belonging to the extension (not just in the sense of "necessary and sufficient condition," but in the strong sense of *way of recognizing* whether a given thing falls into the extension or not). So theory of meaning came to rest on two unchallenged assumptions:

(1) That knowing the meaning of a term is just a matter of being in a certain psychological state (in the sense of "psychological state," in which states of memory and belief are "psychological states"; no one thought that knowing the meaning of a word was a continuous state of consciousness, of course).

(2) That the meaning of a term determines its extension (in the sense that sameness of intension entails sameness of extension).

I shall argue that these two assumptions are not jointly satisfied by *any* notion, let alone any notion of meaning. The traditional concept of meaning is a concept which rests on a false theory.

Are Meanings in the Head?

For the purpose of the following science-fiction examples, we shall suppose that somewhere there

Originally published in *Journal of Philosophy* 70/19 (November 8, 1973).

is a planet we shall call Twin Earth. Twin Earth is very much like Earth: in fact, people on Twin Earth even speak *English*. In fact, apart from the differences we shall specify in our science-fiction examples, the reader may suppose that Twin Earth is *exactly* like Earth. He may even suppose that he has a *Doppelganger* – an identical copy – on Twin Earth, if he wishes, although my stories will not depend on this.

Although some of the people on Twin Earth (say, those who call themselves "Americans" and those who call themselves "Canadians" and those who call themselves "Englishmen," etc.) speak English, there are, not surprisingly, a few tiny differences between the dialects of English spoken on Twin Earth and standard English.

One of the peculiarities of Twin Earth is that the liquid called "water" is not H_2O but a different liquid whose chemical formula is very long and complicated. I shall abbreviate this chemical formula simply as XYZ. I shall suppose that XYZ is indistinguishable from water at normal temperatures and pressures. Also, I shall suppose that the oceans and lakes and seas of Twin Earth contain XYZ and not water, that it rains XYZ on Twin Earth and not water, etc.

If a space ship from Earth ever visits Twin Earth, then the supposition at first will be that 'water' has the same meaning on Earth and on Twin Earth. This supposition will be corrected when it is discovered that "water" on Twin Earth is XYZ, and the Earthian space ship will report somewhat as follows.

On Twin Earth the word 'water' means XYZ.

Symmetrically, if a space ship from Twin Earth ever visits Earth, then the supposition at first will be that the word 'water' has the same meaning on Twin Earth and on Earth. This supposition will be corrected when it is discovered that "water" on Earth is H_2O, and the Twin Earthian space ship will report:

On Earth the word 'water' means H_2O.

Note that there is no problem about the extension of the term 'water': the word simply has two different meanings (as we say); in the sense in which it is used on Twin Earth, the sense of water$_{TE}$, what *we* call "water" simply isn't water, while in the sense in which it is used on Earth,

the sense of water$_E$, what the Twin Earthians call "water" simply isn't water. The extension of 'water' in the sense of water$_E$ is the set of all wholes consisting of H_2O molecules, or something like that; the extension of water in the sense of water$_{TE}$ is the set of all wholes consisting of XYZ molecules, or something like that.

Now let us roll the time back to about 1750. The typical Earthian speaker of English did not know that water consisted of hydrogen and oxygen, and the typical Twin-Earthian speaker of English did not know that "water" consisted of XYZ. Let Oscar$_1$ be such a typical Earthian English speaker, and let Oscar$_2$ be his counterpart on Twin Earth. You may suppose that there is no belief that Oscar$_1$ had about water that Oscar$_2$ did not have about "water." If you like, you may even suppose that Oscar$_1$ and Oscar$_2$ were exact duplicates in appearance, feelings, thoughts, interior monologue, etc. Yet the extension of the term 'water' was just as much H_2O on Earth in 1750 as in 1950; and the extension of the term 'water' was just as much XYZ on Twin Earth in 1750 as in 1950. Oscar$_1$ and Oscar$_2$ understood the term 'water' differently in 1750 *although they were in the same psychological state*, and although, given the state of science at the time, it would have taken their scientific communities about fifty years to discover that they understood the term 'water' differently. Thus the extension of the term 'water' (and, in fact, its "meaning" in the intuitive preanalytical usage of that term) is *not* a function of the psychological state of the speaker by itself.[1]

But, it might be objected, why should we accept it that the term 'water' had the same extension in 1750 and in 1950 (on both Earths)? Suppose I point to a glass of water and say "this liquid is called water." My "ostensive definition" of water had the following empirical presupposition: that the body of liquid I am pointing to bears a certain sameness relation (say, *x is the same liquid as y*, or *x is the same$_L$ as y*) to most of the stuff I and other speakers in my linguistic community have on other occasions called "water." If this presupposition is false because, say, I am – unknown to me – pointing to a glass of gin and not a glass of water, then I do not intend my ostensive definition to be accepted. Thus the ostensive definition conveys what might be called a "defeasible" necessary and sufficient condition: the necessary and sufficient condition for being water is bearing the relation $same_L$ to the stuff in the glass; but this is the necessary and sufficient condition only if the empirical presupposition is satisfied. If it is not satisfied, then one of a series of, so to speak, "fallback" conditions becomes activated.

The key point is that the relation $same_L$ is a *theoretical* relation: whether something is or is not the same liquid as *this* may take an indeterminate amount of scientific investigation to determine. Thus, the fact that an English speaker in 1750 might have called XYZ "water," whereas he or his successors would not have called XYZ water in 1800 or 1850 does not mean that the "meaning" of 'water' changed for the average speaker in the interval. In 1750 or in 1850 or in 1950 one might have pointed to, say, the liquid in Lake Michigan as an example of "water." What changed was that in 1750 we would have mistakenly thought that XYZ bore the relation $same_L$ to the liquid in Lake Michigan, whereas in 1800 or 1850 we would have known that it did not.

Let us now modify our science-fiction story. I shall suppose that molybdenum pots and pans *can't* be distinguished from aluminum pots and pans save by an expert. (This could be true for all I know, and, *a fortiori*, it could be true for all I know by virtue of "knowing the meaning" of the words *aluminum* and *molybdenum*.) We will now suppose that molybdenum is as common on Twin Earth as aluminum is on Earth, and that aluminum is as rare on Twin Earth as molybdenum is on Earth. In particular, we shall assume that "aluminum" pots and pans are made of molybdenum on Twin Earth. Finally, we shall assume that the words 'aluminum' and 'molybdenum' are *switched* on Twin Earth: 'aluminum' is the name of *molybdenum*, and 'molybdenum' is the name of *aluminum*. If a space ship from Earth visited Twin Earth, the visitors from Earth probably would not suspect that the "aluminum" pots and pans on Twin Earth were not made of aluminum, especially when the Twin Earthians *said* they were. But there is one important difference between the two cases. An Earthian metallurgist could tell very easily that "aluminum" was molybdenum, and a Twin Earthian metallurgist could tell equally easily that aluminum was "molybdenum." (The shudder quotes in the preceding sentence indicate Twin Earthian usages.) Whereas in 1750 no one on either Earth or Twin Earth could have distinguished water

from "water," the confusion of aluminum with "aluminum" involves only a part of the linguistic communities involved.

This example makes the same point as the preceding example. If $Oscar_1$ and $Oscar_2$ are standard speakers of Earthian English and Twin Earthian English, respectively, and neither is chemically or metallurgically sophisticated, then there may be no difference at all in their psychological states when they use the world 'aluminum'; nevertheless, we have to say that 'aluminum' has the extension *aluminum* in the idiolect of $Oscar_1$ and the extension *molybdenum* in the idiolect of $Oscar_2$. (Also we have to say that $Oscar_1$ and $Oscar_2$ mean different things by 'aluminum'; that 'aluminum' has a different meaning on Earth than it does on Twin Earth, etc.) Again we see that the psychological state of the speaker does *not* determine the extension (*or* the "meaning," speaking preanalytically) of the word.

Before discussing this example further, let me introduce a *non*-science-fiction example. Suppose you are like me and cannot tell an elm from a beech tree. We will say that the extension of 'elm' in my idiolect is the same as the extension of 'elm' in anyone else's, viz., the set of all elm trees, and that the set of all beech trees is the extension of 'beech' in *both* of our idiolects. Thus 'elm' in my idiolect has a different extension from 'beech' in your idiolect (as it should). Is it really credible that this difference in extension is brought about by some difference in our *concepts*? My *concept* of an elm tree is exactly the same as my concept of a beech tree (I blush to confess). If someone heroically attempts to maintain that the difference between the extension of 'elm' and the extension of 'beech' in *my* idiolect is explained by a difference in my psychological state, then we can always refute him by constructing a "Twin Earth" example – just let the worlds 'elm' and 'beech' be switched on Twin Earth (the way 'aluminum' and 'molybdenum' were in the previous example). Moreover, suppose I have a *Doppelganger* on Twin Earth who is molecule for molecule "identical" with me. If you are a dualist, then also suppose my *Doppelganger* thinks the same verbalized thoughts I do, has the same sense data, the same dispositions, etc. It is absurd to think *his* psychological state is one bit different from mine: yet he 'means' *beech* when he says "elm," and *I* "mean" *elm* when I say "elm." Cut the pie any way you like, "meanings" just ain't in the *head*!

A Sociolinguistic Hypothesis

The last two examples depend upon a fact about language that seems, surprisingly, never to have been pointed out: that there is *division of linguistic labor*. We could hardly use such words as 'elm' and 'aluminum' if no one possessed a way of recognizing elm trees and aluminum metal; but not everyone to whom the distinction is important has to be able to make the distinction. Let us shift the example; consider *gold*. Gold is important for many reasons: it is a precious metal; it is a monetary metal; it has symbolic value (it is important to most people that the "gold" wedding ring they wear *really* consist of gold and not just *look* gold); etc. Consider our community as a "factory": in this "factory" some people have the "job" of *wearing gold wedding rings*; other people have the "job" of selling gold wedding rings; still other people have the job of *telling whether or not something is really gold*. It is not at all necessary or efficient that every one who wears a gold ring (or a gold cufflink, etc.), or discusses the "gold standard," etc., engage in buying and selling gold. Nor is it necessary or efficient that every one who buys and sells gold be able to tell whether or not something is really gold in a society where this form of dishonesty is uncommon (selling fake gold) and in which one can easily consult an expert in case of doubt. And it is *certainly* not necessary or efficient that every one who has occasion to buy or wear gold be able to tell with any reliability whether or not something is really gold.

The foregoing facts are just examples of mundane division of labor (in a wide sense). But they engender a division of linguistic labor: every one to whom gold is important for any reason has to *acquire* the word 'gold'; but he does not have to acquire the *method of recognizing* whether something is or is not gold. He can rely on a special subclass of speakers. The features that are generally thought to be present in connection with a general name – necessary and sufficient conditions for membership in the extension, ways of recognizing whether something is in the extension, etc. – are all present in the linguistic community *considered as a collective body*; but that collective body divides the "labor" of knowing and employing these various parts of the "meaning" of 'gold'.

This division of linguistic labor rests upon and presupposes the division of *non*linguistic labor,

of course. If only the people who know how to tell whether some metal is really gold or not have any reason to have the word 'gold' in their vocabulary, then the word 'gold' will be as the word 'water' was in 1750 with respect to that subclass of speakers, and the other speakers just won't acquire it at all. And some words do not exhibit any division of linguistic labor: 'chair', for example. But with the increase of division of labor in the society and the rise of science, more and more words begin to exhibit this kind of division of labor. 'Water', for example, did not exhibit it at all before the rise of chemistry. Today it is obviously necessary for every speaker to be able to recognize water (reliably under normal conditions), and probably most adult speakers even know the necessary and sufficient condition "water is H_2O," but only a few adult speakers could distinguish water from liquids that superficially resembled water. In case of doubt, other speakers would rely on the judgment of these "expert" speakers. Thus the way of recognizing possessed by these "expert" speakers is also, through them, possessed by the collective linguistic body, even though it is not possessed by each individual member of the body, and in this way the most *recherché* fact about water may become part of the *social* meaning of the word although unknown to almost all speakers who acquire the word.

It seems to me that this phenomenon of division of linguistic labor is one that it will be very important for sociolinguistics to investigate. In connection with it, I should like to propose the following hypothesis:

> *Hypothesis of the universality of the division of linguistic labor*: Every linguistic community exemplifies the sort of division of linguistic labor just described; that is, it possesses at least some terms whose associated "criteria" are known only to a subset of the speakers who acquire the terms, and whose use by the other speakers depends upon a structured cooperation between them and the speakers in the relevant subsets.

It is easy to see how this phenomenon accounts for some of the examples given above of the failure of the assumptions (1 and 2). When a term is subject to the division of linguistic labor, the "average" speaker who acquires it does not acquire anything that fixes its extension. In particular, his individual psychological state *certainly* does not fix its extension; it is only the sociolinguistic state of the collective linguistic body to which the speaker belongs that fixes the extension.

We may summarize this discussion by pointing out that there are two sorts of tools in the world: there are tools like a hammer or a screwdriver which can be used by one person; and there are tools like a steamship which require the cooperative activity of a number of persons to use. Words have been thought of too much on the model of the first sort of tool.

Indexicality and Rigidity

The first of our science-fiction examples – 'water' on Earth and on Twin Earth in 1750 – does not involve division of linguistic labor, or at least does not involve it in the same way the examples of 'aluminum' and 'elm' do. There were not (in our story, anyway) any "experts" on water on Earth in 1750, nor any experts on "water" on Twin Earth. The example *does* involve things which are of fundamental importance to the theory of reference and also to the theory of necessary truth, which we shall now discuss.

Let W_1 and W_2 be two possible worlds in which I exist and in which this glass exists and in which I am giving a meaning explanation by pointing to this glass and saying "This is water." Let us suppose that in W_1 the glass is full of H_2O and in W_2 the glass is full of XYZ. We shall also suppose that W_1 is the *actual* world, and that XYZ is the stuff typically called "water" in the world W_2 (so that the relation between English speakers in W_1 and English speakers in W_2 is exactly the same as the relation between English speakers on Earth and English speakers on Twin Earth). Then there are two theories one might have concerning the meaning of 'water':

(1)   One might hold that 'water' was *world-relative* but *constant* in meaning (i.e., the word has a constant relative meaning). On this theory, 'water' means the same in W_1 and W_2; it's just that water is H_2O in W_1, and water is XYZ in W_2.

(2)   One might hold that water is H_2O in all worlds (the stuff called "water" in W_2 isn't water), but 'water' doesn't have the same meaning in W_1 and W_2.

If what was said before about the Twin Earth case was correct, then (2) is clearly the correct theory. When I say "*this* (liquid) is water," the "this" is, so to speak, a *de re* "this" – i.e., the force of my explanation is that "water" is whatever bears a certain equivalence relation (the relation we called "*same$_L$*" above) to the piece of liquid referred to as "this" *in the actual world*.

We might symbolize the difference between the two theories as a "scope" difference in the following way. On theory (1), the following is true:

(1')   (For every world W) (for every x in W) (x is water $\equiv$ x bears *same$_L$* to the entity referred to as "this" in W)

while on theory (2):

(2')   (For every world W) (For every x in W) (x is water $\equiv$ x bears *same$_L$* to the entity referred to as "this" *in the actual world W_1*)

I call this a "scope" difference because in (1') 'the entity referred to as "this"' is within the scope of 'For every world W' – as the qualifying phrase 'in W' makes explicit – whereas in (2') 'the entity referred to as "this"' means "the entity referred to as 'this' *in the actual world*," and has thus a reference *independent* of the bound variable 'W'.

Kripke calls a designator "rigid" (in a given sentence) if (in that sentence) it refers to the same individual in every possible world in which the designator designates. If we extend this notion of rigidity to substance names, then we may express Kripke's theory and mine by saying that the term 'water' is *rigid*.

The rigidity of the term 'water' follows from the fact that when I give the "ostensive definition": "*this* (liquid) is water," I intend (2') and not (1').

We may also say, following Kripke, that when I give the ostensive definition "*this* (liquid) is water," the demonstrative 'this' is *rigid*.

What Kripke was the first to observe is that this theory of the meaning (or "use," or whatever) of the word 'water' (and other natural-kind terms as well) has startling consequences for the theory of necessary truth.

To explain this, let me introduce the notion of a *cross-world relation*. A two-term relation R will be called *cross-world* when it is understood in such a way that its extension is a set of ordered pairs of individuals *not all in the same possible world*. For example, it is easy to understand the relation *same height as* as a cross-world relation: just understand it so that, e.g., if *x* is an individual in a world W_1 who is 5 feet tall (in W_1) and *y* is an individual in W_2 who is 5 feet tall (in W_2), then the ordered pair *x,y* belongs to the extension of *same height as*. (Since an individual may have different heights in different possible worlds in which that same individual exists, strictly speaking, it is not the ordered pair *x,y* that constitutes an element of the extension of *same height as*, but rather the ordered pair *x-in-world-W_1, y-in-world-W_2*.)

Similarly, we can understand the relation $same_L$ (same liquid as) as a cross-world relation by understanding it so that a liquid in world W_1 which has the same important physical properties (in W_1) that a liquid in W_2 possesses (in W_2) bears $same_L$ to the latter liquid.

Then the theory we have been presenting may be summarized by saying that an entity *x*, in an arbitrary possible world, is *water* if and only if it bears the relation $same_L$ (construed as a cross-world relation) to the stuff *we* call "water" in the actual world.

Suppose, now, that I have not yet discovered what the important physical properties of water are (in the actual world) – i.e., I don't yet know that water is H_2O. I may have ways of *recognizing* water that are successful (of course, I may make a small number of mistakes that I won't be able to detect until a later stage in our scientific development), but not know the microstructure of water. If I agree that a liquid with the superficial properties of "water" but a different microstructure *isn't really water*, then my ways of recognizing water cannot be regarded as an analytical specification of what *it is to be* water. Rather, the operational definition, like the ostensive one, is simply a way of pointing out a standard – pointing out the stuff *in the actual world* such that, for *x* to be water, in *any* world, is for *x* to bear the relation $same_L$ to the *normal* members of the class of *local* entities that satisfy the operational definition. "Water" on Twin Earth is not water, even if it satisfies the operational definition, because it doesn't bear $same_L$ to the *local* stuff that satisfies the operational definition, and local stuff that satisfies the operational definition but has a microstructure different from the rest of the local stuff that satisfies the operational

definition isn't water either, because it doesn't bear $same_L$ to the *normal* examples of the local "water."

Suppose, now, that I discover the microstructure of water – that water is H_2O. At this point I will be able to say that the stuff on Twin Earth that I earlier *mistook* for water isn't really water. In the same way, if you describe, not another planet in the actual universe, but another possible universe in which there is stuff with the chemical formula XYZ which passes the "operational test" for *water*, we shall have to say that that stuff isn't water but merely XYZ. You will not have described a possible world in which "water is XYZ," but merely a possible world in which there are lakes of XYZ, people drink XYZ (and not water), or whatever. In fact, once we have discovered the nature of water, nothing counts as a possible world in which water doesn't have that nature. Once we have discovered that water (in the actual world) is H_2O, *nothing counts as a possible world in which water isn't H_2O*.

On the other hand, we can perfectly well imagine having experiences that would convince us (and that would make it rational to believe that) water *isn't* H_2O. In that sense, it is conceivable that water isn't H_2O. It is conceivable but it isn't possible! Conceivability is no proof of possibility.

Kripke refers to statements that are rationally unrevisable (assuming there are such) as *epistemically necessary*. Statements that are true in all possible worlds he refers to simply as necessary (or sometimes as "metaphysically necessary"). In this terminology, the point just made can be restated as: a statement can be (metaphysically) necessary and epistemically contingent. Human intuition has no privileged access to metaphysical necessity.

In this paper, our interest is in theory of meaning, however, and not in theory of necessary truth. Words like 'now', 'this', 'here' have long been recognized to be *indexical*, or *token-reflexive* – i.e., to have an extension which varies from context to context or token to token. For these words, no one has ever suggested the traditional theory that "intension determines extension." To take our Twin Earth example: if I have a *Doppelganger* on Twin Earth, then when I think "I have a headache," *he* thinks "I have a headache." But the extension of the particular token of 'I' in his verbalized thought is himself (or his unit class, to be precise), while the extension

Hilary Putnam

of the token of 'I' in *my* verbalized thought is *me* (or my unit class, to be precise). So the same word, 'I', has two different extensions in two different idiolects; but it does not follow that the concept I have of myself is in any way different from the concept my *Doppelganger* has of himself.

Now then, we have maintained that indexicality extends beyond the *obviously* indexical words and morphemes (e.g., the tenses of verbs). Our theory can be summarized as saying that words like 'water' have an unnoticed indexical component: "water" is stuff that bears a certain similarity relation to the water *around here*. Water at another time or in another place or even in another possible world has to bear the relation $same_L$ to *our* "water" *in order to be water*. Thus the theory that (1) words have "intensions," which are something like concepts associated with the words by speakers; and (2) intension determines extension – cannot be true of natural-kind words like 'water' for the same reason it cannot be true of obviously indexical words like 'I'.

The theory that natural-kind words like 'water' are indexical leaves it open, however, whether to say that 'water' in the Twin Earth dialect of English has the same *meaning* as 'water' in the Earth dialect and a different extension – which

is what we normally say about 'I' in different idiolects – thereby giving up the doctrine that "meaning (intension) determines extension," or to say, as we have chosen to do, that difference in extension is *ipso facto* a difference in meaning for natural-kind words, thereby giving up the doctrine that meanings are concepts, or, indeed, mental entities of *any* kind.[2]

It should be clear, however, that Kripke's doctrine that natural-kind words are rigid designators and our doctrine that they are indexical are but two ways of making the same point.

We have now seen that the extension of a term is not fixed by a concept that the individual speaker has in his head, and this is true both because extension is, in general, determined *socially* – there is division of linguistic labor as much as of "real" labor – and because extension is, in part, determined *indexically*. The extension of our terms depends upon the actual nature of the particular things that serve as paradigms, and this actual nature is not, in general, fully known to the speaker. Traditional semantic theory leaves out two contributions to the determination of reference – the contribution of society and the contribution of the real world; a better semantic theory must encompass both.

Notes

1 See note 2 and the corresponding text.
2 Our reasons for rejecting the first option – to say that 'water' has the same meaning on Earth and on Twin Earth, while giving up the doctrine that meaning determines reference – are presented in "The Meaning of 'Meaning'." They may be illustrated thus: Suppose 'water' has the same meaning on Earth and on Twin Earth. Now, let the word

'water' become phonemically different on Twin Earth – say, it becomes 'quaxel'. Presumably, this is not a change in meaning *per se*, on any view. So 'water' and 'quaxel' have the same meaning (although they refer to different liquids). But this is highly counterintuitive. Why not say, then, that 'elm' in my idiolect has the same meaning as 'beech' in your idiolect, although they refer to different trees?

Further reading in philosophy of language

Austin, J. L., *How to Do Things with Words*, 2nd edn., ed. J. O. Urmson and Marina Sbisa, Cambridge, MA: Harvard University Press, 1975.

Bach, Kent, *Thought and Reference*, Oxford: Clarendon Press, 1987.

Beaney, Michael, *The Frege Reader*, Oxford: Blackwell Publishers, 1997.

Devitt, Michael and Sterelny, Kim, *Language and Reality*, 2nd edn., Cambridge, MA: MIT Press, 1999.

Evans, Gareth, *The Varieties of Reference*, Oxford: Oxford University Press, 1982.

Grice, H. P., *Studies in the Way of Words*, Cambridge, MA: Harvard University Press, 1989.

Hale, Bob and Wright, Crispin (eds.) *A Companion to the Philosophy of Language*, Malden, MA: Blackwell Publishers, 1997.

Katz, Jerrold, *The Metaphysics of Meaning*, Cambridge, MA: MIT Press, 1992.

Kripke, Saul, *Naming and Necessity*, Cambridge, MA: Harvard University Press, 1980.

Martinich, A. P., "The Philosophy of Language," in *Philosophy of Meaning, Knowledge and Value in the Twentieth Century*, ed. John Canfield, London: Routledge, 1997, pp. 11–38.

——(ed.) *The Philosophy of Language*, 4th edn., New York: Oxford University Press, 2000.

Neale, Stephen, *Descriptions*, Cambridge, MA: MIT Press, 1990.

Putnam, Hilary, *Reason, Truth and History*, Cambridge: Cambridge University Press, 1981.

Quine, W. V., *Word and Object*, Cambridge, MA: MIT Press, 1992.

Salmon, Nathan, *Frege's Puzzle*, Atascadero, CA: Ridgeview Publishing, 1991 (reprint).

Searle, John, *Speech Acts*, Cambridge: Cambridge University Press, 1969.

——*Expression and Meaning*, Cambridge: Cambridge University Press, 1979.

Strawson, P. F., *Logico-Linguistic Papers*, London: Methuen, 1971.

PART II

Metaphysics

9

On the Relations of Universals and Particulars

Bertrand Russell

The purpose of the following paper is to consider whether there is a fundamental division of the objects with which metaphysics is concerned into two classes, universals and particulars, or whether there is any method of overcoming this dualism. My own opinion is that the dualism is ultimate; on the other hand, many men with whom, in the main, I am in close agreement, hold that it is not ultimate. I do not feel the grounds in favour of its ultimate nature to be very conclusive, and in what follows I should lay stress rather on the distinctions and considerations introduced during the argument than on the conclusion at which the argument arrives.

It is impossible to begin our discussion with sharp definitions of universals and particulars, though we may hope to reach such definitions in the end. At the beginning, we can only roughly indicate the kind of facts that we wish to analyse and the kind of distinctions that we wish to examine. There are several cognate distinctions which produce confusion by intermingling, and which it is important to disentangle before advancing into the heart of our problem.

The first distinction that concerns us is the distinction between percepts and concepts, i.e., between objects of acts of perception and objects of acts of conception. If there is a distinction between particulars and universals, percepts will

be among particulars, while concepts will be among universals. Opponents of universals, such as Berkeley and Hume, will maintain that concepts are derivable from percepts, as faint copies, or in some other way. Opponents of particulars will maintain that the apparent particularity of percepts is illusory, and that, though the act of perception may differ from the act of conception, yet its objects differ only by their greater complexity, and are really composed of constituents which are, or might be, concepts.

But the distinction of percepts and concepts is too psychological for an ultimate metaphysical distinction. Percepts and concepts are respectively the relata of two different relations, perception and conception, and there is nothing in their definitions to show whether, or how, they differ. Moreover, the distinction of percepts and concepts, in itself, is incapable of being extended to entities which are not objects of cognitive acts. Hence we require some other distinction expressing the intrinsic difference which we seem to feel between percepts and concepts.

A cognate distinction, which effects part at least of what we want, is the distinction between things which exist in time and things which do not. In order to avoid any question as to whether time is relative or absolute, we may say that an entity x 'exists in time' provided x is not itself a moment or part of time, and some such proposition as 'x is before y or simultaneous with y or after y' is true of x. (It is not to be assumed that *before*, *simultaneous*, and *after* are mutually exclusive: if x has duration, they will not be so.)

Originally published in *Proceedings of the Aristotelian Society* 12 (1911–12). Reprinted by courtesy of the Editor of the Aristotelian Society: © 1911–1912.

Prima facie, a percept exists in time, in the above sense, while a concept does not. The object of perception is simultaneous with the act of perception, while the object of conception seems indifferent to the time of conceiving and to all time. Thus, prima facie, we have here the non-psychological distinction of which we were in search. But the same controversies will break out as in the case of percepts and concepts. The man who reduces concepts to percepts will say that nothing is really out of time, and that the appearance of this in the case of concepts is illusory. The man who reduces percepts to concepts may either, like most idealists, deny that anything is in time, or, like some realists, maintain that concepts can and do exist in time.

In addition to the above distinction as regards time, there is a distinction as regards space which, as we shall find, is very important in connexion with our present question. Put as vaguely as possible, this is a distinction which divides entities into three classes: (a) those which are not in any place, (b) those which are in one place at one time, but never in more than one, (c) those which are in many places at once. To make this threefold division precise, we should have to discuss what we mean by a place, what we mean by 'in', and how the different kinds of space – visual, tactile, physical – produce different forms of this threefold division. For the present I will merely illustrate what I mean by examples. Relations, obviously, do not exist anywhere in space. Our bodies, we think, exist in one place at a time, but not in more than one. General qualities, such as whiteness, on the contrary, may be said to be in many places at once: we may say, in a sense, that whiteness is in every place where there is a white thing. This division of entities will be discussed later; for the present I merely wish to indicate that it requires examination.

In addition to the above psychological and metaphysical distinctions, there are two logical distinctions which are relevant in the present enquiry. In the first place, there is the distinction between relations and entities which are not relations. It has been customary for philosophers to ignore or reject relations, and speak as if all entities were either subjects or predicates. But this custom is on the decline, and I shall assume without further argument that there are such entities as relations. Philosophy has, so far as I know, no common name for all entities which are not relations. Among such entities are included

not only all the things that would naturally be called particulars, but also all the universals that philosophers are in the habit of considering when they discuss the relation of particulars to universals, for universals are generally conceived as common properties of particulars, in fact, as predicates. For our purpose it is hardly worth while to invent a technical term *ad hoc*; I shall therefore speak of entities which are not relations simply as *non-relations*.

The second logical distinction which we require is one which may or may not be identical in extension with that between relations and non-relations, but is certainly not identical in intention. It may be expressed as the distinction between verbs and substantives, or, more correctly, between the objects denoted by verbs and the objects denoted by substantives.[1] (Since this more correct expression is long and cumbrous, I shall generally use the shorter phrase to mean the same thing. Thus, when I speak of verbs, I mean the objects denoted by verbs, and similarly for substantives.) The nature of this distinction emerges from the analysis of complexes. In most complexes, if not in all, a certain number of different entities are combined into a single entity by means of a relation. '*A*'s hatred for *B*', for example, is a complex in which *hatred* combines *A* and *B* into one whole; '*C*'s belief that *A* hates *B*' is a complex in which *belief* combines *A* and *B* and *C* and hatred into one whole, and so on. A relation is distinguished as dual, triple, quadruple, etc., or dyadic, triadic, tetradic, etc., according to the number of terms which it unites in the simplest complexes in which it occurs. Thus in the above examples, hatred is a dual relation and belief is a quadruple relation. The capacity for combining terms into a single complex is the defining characteristic of what I call *verbs*. The question now arises: Are there complexes which consist of a single term and a verb? '*A* exists' might serve as an example of what is possibly such a complex. It is the possibility that there may be complexes of this kind which makes it impossible to decide off-hand that verbs are the same as relations. There may be verbs which are philosophically as well as grammatically intransitive. Such verbs, if they exist, may be called *predicates*, and the propositions in which they are attributed may be called subject-predicate propositions.

If there are no such verbs as those whose possibility we have been considering, i.e., if all verbs are relations, it will follow that subject-predicate propositions, if there are any, will express a *relation* of subject to predicate. Such propositions will then be definable as those that involve a certain relation called *predication*. Even if there are subject-predicate propositions in which the predicate is the verb, there will still be equivalent propositions in which the predicate is related to the subject; thus '*A* exists', for example, will be equivalent to '*A* has existence'. Hence the question whether predicates are verbs or not becomes unimportant. The more important question is whether there is a specific relation of predication, or whether what are grammatically subject-predicate propositions are really of many different kinds, no one of which has the characteristics one naturally associates with subject-predicate propositions. This question is one to which we shall return at a later stage.

The above logical distinctions are relevant to our enquiry because it is natural to regard particulars as entities which can only be subjects or terms of relations, and cannot be predicates or relations. A particular is naturally conceived as a *this* or something intrinsically analogous to a *this*; and such an entity seems incapable of being a predicate or a relation. A universal, on this view, will be anything that is a predicate or a relation. But if there is no specific relation of predication, so that there is no class of entities which can properly be called predicates, then the above method of distinguishing particulars and universals fails. The question whether philosophy must recognize two ultimately distinct kinds of entities, particulars and universals, turns, as we shall see more fully later on, on the question whether non-relations are of two kinds, subjects and predicates, or rather terms which can only be subjects and terms which may be either subjects or predicates. And this question turns on whether there is an ultimate simple asymmetrical relation which may be called predication, or whether all apparent subject-predicate propositions are to be analysed into propositions of other forms, which do not require a radical difference of nature between the apparent subject and the apparent predicate.

The decision of the question whether there is a simple relation of predication ought perhaps to be possible by inspection, but for my part I am unable to come to any decision in this way. I think, however, that it can be decided in favour of predication by the analysis of *things* and by

considerations as to spatio-temporal diversity. This analysis and these considerations will also show the way in which our purely logical question is bound up with the other questions as to particulars and universals which I raised at the beginning of this paper.

The common-sense notion of things and their qualities is, I suppose, the source of the conception of subject and predicate, and the reason why language is so largely based on this conception. But the thing, like other common-sense notions, is a piece of half-hearted metaphysics, which neither gives crude data nor gives a tenable hypothesis as to a reality behind the data. A thing, of the everyday sort, is constituted by a bundle of sensible qualities belonging to various senses, but supposed all to coexist in one continuous portion of space. But the common space which should contain both visual and tactile qualities is not the space of either visual or tactile perception: it is a constructed 'real' space, belief in which has, I suppose, been generated by association. And in crude fact, the visual and tactile qualities of which I am sensible are not in a common space, but each in its own space. Hence if the thing is to be impartial as between sight and touch, it must cease to have the actual qualities of which we are sensible, and become their common cause or origin or whatever vaguer word can be found. Thus the road is opened to the metaphysical theories of science and to the metaphysical theories of philosophy: the thing may be a number of electric charges in rapid motion, or an idea in the mind of God, but it is certainly not what the senses perceive.

The argument against things is trite, and I need not labour it. I introduce it here only in order to illustrate a consequence which is sometimes overlooked. Realists who reject particulars are apt to regard a thing as reducible to a number of qualities coexisting in one place. But, apart from other objections to this view, it is doubtful whether the different qualities in question ever do coexist in one place. If the qualities are sensible, the place must be in a sensible space; but this makes it necessary that the qualities should belong to only one sense, and it is not clear that genuinely different qualities belonging to one sense ever coexist in a single place in a perceptual space. If, on the other hand, we consider what may be called 'real' space, i.e. the inferred space containing the 'real' objects which we suppose to be the causes of our perceptions, then we no longer know what is the nature of the qualities, if any, which exist in this 'real' space, and it is natural to replace the bundle of qualities by a collection of pieces of matter having whatever characteristics the science of the moment may prescribe. Thus in any case the bundle of coexisting qualities in the same place is not an admissible substitute for the thing.

For our purposes, the 'real' object by which science or philosophy replaces the thing is not important. We have rather to consider the relations of sensible objects in a single sensible space, say that of sight.

The theory of sensible qualities which dispenses with particulars will say, if the same shade of colour is found in two different places, that what exists is the shade of colour itself, and that what exists in the one place is identical with what exists in the other. The theory which admits particulars will say, on the contrary, that two numerically different *instances* of the shade of colour exist in the two places: in this view, the shade of colour itself is a universal and a predicate of both the instances, but the universal does not exist in space and time. Of the above two views, the first, which does not introduce particulars, dispenses altogether with predication as a fundamental relation: according to this view, when we say 'this thing is white', the fundamental fact is that whiteness exists here. According to the other view, which admits particulars, what exists here is something of which whiteness is a predicate – not, as for common sense, the thing with many other qualities, but an instance of whiteness, a particular of which whiteness is the only predicate except shape and brightness and whatever else is necessarily connected with whiteness.

Of the above two theories, one admits only what would naturally be called universals, while the other admits both universals and particulars. Before examining them, it may be as well to examine and dismiss the theory which admits only particulars, and dispenses altogether with universals. This is the theory advocated by Berkeley and Hume in their polemic against 'abstract ideas'. Without tying ourselves down to their statements, let us see what can be made of this theory. The general name 'white', in this view, is defined for a given person at a given moment by a particular patch of white which he sees or imagines; another patch is called white if it has exact likeness in

colour to the standard patch. In order to avoid making the colour a universal, we have to suppose that 'exact likeness' is a simple relation, not analysable into community of predicates; moreover, it is not the general relation of likeness that we require, but a more special relation, that of colour-likeness, since two patches might be exactly alike in shape or size but different in colour. Thus, in order to make the theory of Berkeley and Hume workable, we must assume an ultimate relation of colour-likeness, which holds between two patches which would commonly be said to have the same colour. Now, prima facie, this relation of colour-likeness will itself be a universal or an 'abstract idea', and thus we shall still have failed to avoid universals. But we may apply the same analysis to colour-likeness. We may take a standard particular case of colour-likeness, and say that anything else is to be called a colour-likeness if it is exactly like our standard case. It is obvious, however, that such a process leads to an endless regress: we explain the likeness of two terms as consisting in the likeness which their likeness bears to the likeness of two other terms, and such a regress is plainly vicious. Likeness at least, therefore, must be admitted as a universal, and, having admitted one universal, we have no longer any reason to reject others. Thus the whole complicated theory, which had no motive except to avoid universals, falls to the ground. Whether or not there are particulars, there must be relations which are universals in the sense that (a) they are concepts, not percepts; (b) they do not exist in time; (c) they are verbs, not substantives.

It is true that the above argument does not prove that there are universal qualities as opposed to universal relations. On the contrary, it shows that universal qualities *can*, so far as logic can show, be replaced by exact likenesses of various kinds between particulars. This view has, so far as I know, nothing to recommend it beyond its logical possibility. But from the point of view of the problem whether there are particulars, it has no bearing on the argument. It is a view which is only possible if there are particulars, and it demands only an easy re-statement of subject-predicate propositions: instead of saying that an entity has such and such a predicate, we shall have to say that there are entities to which it has such and such a specific likeness. I shall therefore in future ignore this view, which in any case assumes our main thesis, namely, the existence of particulars. To the grounds in favour of this thesis we must now return.

When we endeavoured to state the two theories as to sensible qualities, we had occasion to consider two white patches. On the view which denies particulars, whiteness itself exists in both patches: a numerically single entity, whiteness, exists in all places that are white. Nevertheless, we speak of *two* white patches, and it is obvious that, in some sense, the patches are two, not one. It is this spatial plurality which makes the difficulty of the theory that denies particulars.

Without attempting, as yet, to introduce all the necessary explanations and distinctions, we may state the argument for particulars roughly as follows. It is logically possible for two exactly similar patches of white, of the same size and shape, to exist simultaneously in different places. Now, whatever may be the exact meaning of 'existing in different places', it is self-evident that, in such a case, there are two different patches of white. Their diversity might, if we adopted the theory of absolute position, be regarded as belonging, not to the white itself which exists in the two places, but to the complexes 'whiteness in this place' and 'whiteness in that place'. This would derive their diversity from the diversity of this place and that place; and since places cannot be supposed to differ as to qualities, this would require that the places should be particulars. But if we reject absolute position, it will become impossible to distinguish the two patches as two, unless each, instead of being the universal whiteness, is an *instance* of whiteness. It might be thought that the two might be distinguished by means of other qualities in the same place as the one but not in the same place as the other. This, however, presupposes that the two patches are already distinguished as numerically diverse, since otherwise what is in the same place as the one must be in the same place as the other. Thus the fact that it is logically possible for precisely similar things to coexist in two different places, but that things in different places at the same time cannot be numerically identical, forces us to admit that it is particulars, i.e., *instances* of universals, that exist in places, and not universals themselves.

The above is the outline of our argument. But various points in it have to be examined and expanded before it can be considered conclusive.

In the first place, it is not necessary to assert that there ever are two exactly similar existents. It is only necessary to perceive that our judgment that this and that are two different existents is not necessarily based on any difference of qualities, but may be based on difference of spatial position alone; and that difference of qualities, whether or not it always in fact accompanies numerical difference, is not logically necessary in order to insure numerical difference where there is difference of spatial position.

Again, it is not easy to state exactly what sort of spatial distribution in perceived space warrants us in asserting plurality. Before we can use space as an argument for particulars, we must be clear on this point. We are accustomed to concede that a thing cannot be in two places at once, but this common-sense maxim, unless very carefully stated, will lead us into inextricable difficulties. Our first business, therefore, is to find out how to state this maxim in an unobjectionable form.

In rational dynamics, where we are concerned with matter and 'real' space, the maxim that nothing can be in two places at once is taken rigidly, and any matter occupying more than a point of space is regarded as at least theoretically divisible. Only what occupies a bare point is simple and single. This view is straightforward, and raises no difficulties as applied to 'real' space.

But as applied to perceived space, such a view is quite inadmissible. The immediate object of (say) visual perception is always of finite extent. If we suppose it to be, like the matter corresponding to it in 'real' space, composed of a collection of entities, one for each point which is not empty, we shall have to suppose two things, both of which seem incredible, namely: (1) that every immediate object of visual (or tactile) perception is infinitely complex; (2) that every such object is always composed of parts which are by their very nature imperceptible. It seems quite impossible that the immediate object of perception should have these properties. Hence we must suppose that an indivisible object of visual perception may occupy a finite extent of visual space. In short, we must, in dividing any complex object of visual perception, reach, after a finite number of steps, a *minimum sensibile*, which contains no plurality although it is of finite extent. Visual space may, in a sense, be infinitely *divisible*, for, by attention alone, or by the microscope, the immediate object of perception can be changed in a way which introduces complexity where formerly there was simplicity; and to this process no clear limit can be set. But this is a process which substitutes a new immediate object in place of the old one, and the new object, though more subdivided than the old one, will still consist of only a finite number of parts. We must therefore admit that the space of perception is not infinitely divided, and does not consist of points, but is composed of a finite though constantly varying number of surfaces or volumes, continually breaking up or joining together according to the fluctuations of attention. If there is a 'real' geometrical space corresponding to the space of perception, an infinite number of points in the geometrical space will have to correspond to a single simple entity in the perceived space.

It follows from this that, if we are to apply to the immediate objects of perception the maxim that a thing cannot be in two places at once, a 'place' must not be taken to be a point, but must be taken to be the extent occupied by a single object of perception. A white sheet of paper, for example, may be seen as a single undivided object, or as an object consisting of two parts, an upper and a lower or a right hand and a left hand part, or again as an object consisting of four parts, and so on. If we on this account consider that, even when the sheet appeared as an undivided object, its upper and lower halves were in different places, then we shall have to say that the undivided object was in both these places at once. But it is better to say that, when the sheet appeared as an undivided object, this object occupied only one 'place', though the place corresponded to what were afterwards two places. Thus a 'place' may be defined as the space occupied by one undivided object of perception.

With this definition, the maxim that a thing cannot be in two places at once might seem to reduce to a tautology. But this maxim, though it may need re-wording, will still have a substantial significance, to be derived from the consideration of spatial relations. It is obvious that perceived spatial relations cannot hold between points, but must hold between the parts of a single complex object of perception. When the sheet of paper is perceived as consisting of two halves, an upper and a lower, these two halves are combined into a complex whole by means of a spatial relation which holds directly between the two halves, not between supposed smaller subdivisions which in

fact do not exist in the immediate object of perception. Perceived spatial relations, therefore, must have a certain roughness, not the neat smooth properties of geometrical relations between points. What, for example, shall we say of distance? The distance between two simultaneously perceived objects will have to be defined by the perceived objects between them; in the case of two objects which touch, like the two halves of the sheet of paper, there is no distance between them. What remains definite is a certain order; by means of right and left, up and down, and so on, the parts of a complex object of perception acquire a spatial order, which is definite, though not subject to quite the same laws as geometrical order. The maxim that a thing cannot be in two places at once will then become the maxim that every spatial relation implies diversity of its terms, i.e., that nothing is to the right of itself, or above itself, and so on. In that case, given two white patches, one of which is to the right of the other, it will follow that there is not a single thing, whiteness, which is to the right of itself, but that there are two different things, instances of whiteness, of which one is to the right of the other. In this way our maxim will support the conclusion that there must be particulars as well as universals. But the above outline of an argument needs some amplification before it can be considered conclusive. Let us therefore examine, one by one, the steps of the argument.

Let us suppose, for the sake of definiteness, that within one field of vision we perceive two separated patches of white on a ground of black. It may then be taken as quite certain that the two patches are two and not one. The question is: Can we maintain that there are two if what exists in each is the universal whiteness?

If absolute space is admitted, we can of course say that it is the difference of place that makes the patches two; there is whiteness in this place, and whiteness in that place. From the point of view of our main problem, which is as to the existence of particulars, such a view would prove our thesis, since this place and that place would be or imply particulars constituting absolute space. But from the point of view of our immediate problem, which is concerned with plurality in perceived space, we may reject the above view on the ground that, whatever may be the case with 'real' space, perceived space is certainly not absolute, i.e., absolute positions are not among objects of perception. Thus the whiteness here and the whiteness there cannot be distinguished as complexes of which this place and that place are respectively constituents.

Of course the whitenesses may be of different shapes, say one round and one square, and then they could be distinguished by their shapes. It will be observed that, with the view adopted above as to the nature of perceived space, it is perfectly possible for a simple object of perception to have a shape: the shape will be a quality like another. Since a simple object of perception may be of finite extent, there is no reason to suppose that a shape must imply spatial divisibility in the object of perception. Hence our two patches may be respectively round and square, and yet not be spatially divisible. It is obvious, however, that this method of distinguishing the two patches is altogether inadequate. The two patches are just as easily distinguished if both are square or both are round. So long as we can see both at once, no degree of likeness between them causes the slightest difficulty in perceiving that there are two of them. Thus difference of shape, whether it exists or not, is not what makes the patches two entities instead of one.

It may be said that the two patches are distinguished by the difference in their relations to other things. For example, it may happen that a patch of red is to the right of one and to the left of the other. But this does not imply that the patches are two unless we know that one thing cannot be both to the right and to the left of another. This, it might be said, is obviously false. Suppose a surface of black with a small white space in the middle. Then the whole of the black may form only one simple object of perception, and would seem to be both to the right and to the left of the white space which it entirely surrounds. I think it would be more true to say, in this case, that the black is neither to the right nor to the left of the white. But right and left are complicated relations involving the body of the percipient. Let us take some other simpler relation, say that of surrounding, which the black surface has to the white patch in our example. Suppose we have another white patch, of exactly the same size and shape, entirely surrounded by red. Then, it may be said, the two patches of white are distinguished by difference of relation, since one is surrounded by black and the other by red. But if this ground of distinction is to be valid, we must know that it is impossible for one entity to be both wholly and

immediately surrounded by black and wholly and immediately surrounded by red. I do not mean to deny that we do know this. But two things deserve notice – first, that it is not an analytic proposition; second, that it presupposes the numerical diversity of our two patches of white.

We are so accustomed to regarding such relations as 'inside' and 'outside' as incompatible that it is easy to suppose a *logical* incompatibility, although in fact the incompatibility is a characteristic of space, not a result of logic. I do not know what are the unanalysable spatial relations of objects of perception, whether visual or tactile, but whatever they are they must have the kind of characteristics which are required in order to generate an order. They, or some of them, must be asymmetrical, i.e., such that they are incompatible with their converses: for example, supposing 'inside' to be one of them, a thing which is inside another must not also be outside it. They, or some of them, must also be transitive, i.e., such that, for example, if x is inside y and y is inside z, then x is inside z – supposing, for the sake of illustration, 'inside' to be among fundamental spatial relations. Probably some further properties will be required, but these at least are essential, in view of the fact that there is such a thing as spatial order. It follows that some at least of the fundamental spatial relations must be such as no entity can have to itself. It is indeed self-evident that spatial relations fulfil these conditions. But these conditions are not demonstrable by purely logical considerations: they are synthetic properties of perceived spatial relations.

It is in virtue of these self-evident properties that the numerical diversity of the two patches of white is self-evident. They have the relation of being outside each other, and this requires that they should be two, not one. They may or may not have intrinsic differences – of shape, or size, or brightness, or any other quality – but whether they have or not they are two, and it is obviously logically possible that they should have no intrinsic differences whatever. It follows from this that the terms of spatial relations cannot be universals or collections of universals, but must be particulars capable of being exactly alike and yet numerically diverse.

It is very desirable, in such discussions as that on which we are at present engaged, to be able to talk of 'places' and of things or qualities 'occupying' places, without implying absolute position. It must be understood that, on the view which adopts relative position, a 'place' is not a precise notion. But its usefulness arises as follows: Suppose a set of objects, such as the walls and furniture of a room, to retain their spatial relations unchanged for a certain length of time, while a succession of other objects, say people who successively sit in a certain chair, have successively a given set of spatial relations to the relatively fixed objects. Then the people have, one after the other, a given set of properties, consisting in spatial relations to the walls and furniture. Whatever has this given set of properties at a given moment is said to 'occupy' a certain place, the 'place' itself being merely a fixed set of spatial relations to certain objects whose spatial relations to each other do not change appreciably during the time considered. Thus when we say that one thing can only be in one place at one time, we mean that it can only have one set of spatial relations to a given set of objects at one time.

It might be argued that, since we have admitted that a simple object of perception may be of finite extent, we have admitted that it may be in many places at once, and therefore may be outside itself. This, however, would be a misunderstanding. In perceived space, the finite extent occupied by a simple object of perception is not divided into many places. It is a single place occupied by a single thing. There are two different ways in which this place may 'correspond' to many places. First, if there is such a thing as 'real' space with geometrical properties, the one place in perceived space will correspond to an infinite number of points in 'real' space, and the single entity which is the object of perception will correspond to many physical entities in 'real' space. Secondly, there is a more or less partial correspondence between perceived space at one time and perceived space at another. Suppose that we attend closely to our white patch, and meanwhile no other noticeable changes occur in the field of vision. Our white patch may, and often does, change as the result of attention – we may perceive differences of shade or other differentiations, or, without differences of quality, we may merely observe parts in it which make it complex and introduce diversity and spatial relations within it. We consider, naturally, that we are still looking at the same thing as before, and that what we see now was there all along. Thus we conclude that our apparently simple white patch was not really simple. But, in fact, the

object of perception is not the same as it was before; what may be the same is the physical object supposed to correspond to the object of perception. This physical object is, of course, complex. And the perception which results from attention will be in one sense more correct than that which perceived a simple object, because, if attention reveals previously unnoticed differences, it may be assumed that there are corresponding differences in the 'real' object which corresponds to the object of perception. Hence the perception resulting from attention gives more information about the 'real' object than the other perception did: but the object of perception itself is no more and no less real in the one case than in the other – that is to say, in both cases it is an object which exists when perceived, but which there is no reason to believe existent except when it is perceived.

In perceived space, the spatial unit is not a point, but a simple object of perception or an ultimate constituent in a complex object of perception. This is the reason why, although two patches of white which are visibly separated from each other must be two, a continuous area of white may not be two. A continuous area, if not too large, may be a single object of perception not consisting of parts, which is impossible for two visibly separated areas. The spatial unit is variable, constantly changing its size, and subject to every fluctuation of attention, but it must occupy a continuous portion of perceived space, since otherwise it would be perceived as plural.

The argument as to numerical diversity which we have derived from perceived space may be reinforced by a similar argument as regards the contents of different minds. If two people are both believing that two and two are four, it is at least theoretically possible that the meanings they attach to the words *two* and *and* and *are* and *four* are the same, and that therefore, so far as the objects of their beliefs are concerned, there is nothing to distinguish the one from the other. Nevertheless, it seems plain that there are two entities, one the belief of the one man and the other the belief of the other. A particular belief is a complex of which something which we may call a subject is a constituent; in our case, it is the diversity of the subjects that produces the diversity of the beliefs. But these subjects cannot be mere bundles of general qualities. Suppose one of our men is characterized by benevolence, stupidity, and love of puns. It would not be correct to say: 'Benevolence, stupidity, and love of puns believe that two and two are four'. Nor would this become correct by the addition of a larger number of general qualities. Moreover, however many qualities we add, it remains possible that the other subject may also have them; hence qualities cannot be what constitutes the diversity of the subjects. The only respect in which two different subjects *must* differ is in their relations to particulars: for example, each will have to the other relations which he does not have to himself. But it is not logically impossible that everything concerning one of the subjects and otherwise only concerning universals might be true of the other subject. Hence, even when differences in regard to such propositions occur, it is not these differences that constitute the diversity of the two subjects. The subjects, therefore, must be regarded as particulars, and as radically different from any collection of those general qualities which may be predicated of them.

It will be observed that, according to the general principles which must govern any correspondence of real things with objects of perception, any principle which introduces diversity among objects of perception must introduce a corresponding diversity among real things. I am not now concerned to argue as to what grounds exist for assuming a correspondence, but, if there is such a correspondence, it must be supposed that diversity in the effects – i.e., the perceived objects – implies diversity in the causes – i.e., the real objects. Hence if I perceive two objects in the field of vision, we must suppose that at least two real objects are concerned in causing my perception.

The essential characteristic of particulars, as they appear in perceived space, is that they cannot be in two places at once. But this is an unsatisfactory way of stating the matter, owing to the doubt as to what a 'place' is. The more correct statement is that certain perceptible spatial relations imply diversity of their terms; for example, if x is above y, x and y must be different entities. So long, however, as it is understood that this is what is meant, no harm is done by the statement that a thing cannot be in two places at once.

We may now return to the question of particulars and universals with a better hope of being able to state precisely the nature of the opposition between them. It will be remembered that we began with three different oppositions: (1) that of percept and concept, (2) that of entities existing in time and entities not existing in time, (3) that of substantives and verbs. But in the course of our discussion a different opposition developed itself, namely, (4) that between entities which can be in one place, but not in more than one, at a given time, and entities which either cannot be anywhere or can be in several places at one time. What makes a particular patch of white particular, whereas whiteness is universal, is the fact that the particular patch cannot be in two places simultaneously, whereas the whiteness, if it exists at all, exists wherever there are white things. This opposition, as stated, might be held not to apply to thoughts. We might reply that a man's thoughts are in his head; but without going into this question, we may observe that there certainly is some relation between a man's thoughts and his head (or some part of it) which there is not between his thoughts and other things in space. We may extend our definition of particulars so as to cover this relation. We may say that a man's thought 'belongs to' the place where his head is. We may then define a particular in our fourth sense as an entity which cannot be in or belong to more than one place at one time, and a universal as an entity which either cannot be in or belong to any place, or can be in or belong to many places at once. This opposition has certain affinities with the three earlier oppositions, which must be examined.

(1) Owing to the admission of particulars in our fourth sense, we can make an absolute division between percepts and concepts. The universal whiteness is a concept, whereas a particular white patch is a percept. If we had not admitted particulars in our fourth sense, percepts would have been identical with certain concepts.

(2) For the same reason, we are able to say that such general qualities as whiteness never exist in time, whereas the things that do exist in time are all particulars in our fourth sense. The converse, that all particulars in our fourth sense exist in time, holds in virtue of their definition. Hence the second and fourth senses of the opposition of particulars and universals are co-extensive.

(3) The third opposition, that of substantives and verbs, presents more difficulties, owing to the doubt whether predicates are verbs or not. In order to evade this doubt, we may substitute

another opposition, which will be co-extensive with substantives and verbs if predicates are verbs, but not otherwise. This other opposition puts predicates and relations on one side, and everything else on the other. What is not a predicate or relation is, according to one traditional definition, a substance. It is true that, when substance was in vogue, it was supposed that a substance must be indestructible, and this quality will not belong to our substances. For example, what a man sees when he sees a flash of lightning is a substance in our sense. But the importance of indestructibility was metaphysical, not logical. As far as logical properties are concerned, our substances will be fairly analogous to traditional substances. Thus we have the opposition of substances on the one hand and predicates and relations on the other hand. The theory which rejects particulars allows entities commonly classed as predicates – e.g. white – to exist; thus the distinction between substances and predicates is obliterated by this theory. Our theory, on the contrary, preserves the distinction. In the world we know, substances are identical with particulars in our fourth sense, and predicates and relations with universals.

It will be seen that, according to the theory which assumes particulars, there is a specific relation of subject to predicate, unless we adopt the view – considered above in connexion with Berkeley and Hume – that common sensible qualities are really derivative from specific kinds of likeness. Assuming this view to be false, ordinary sensible qualities will be predicates of the particulars which are instances of them. The sensible qualities themselves do not exist in time in the same sense in which the instances do. Predication is a relation involving a fundamental logical difference between its two terms. Predicates may themselves have predicates, but the predicates of predicates will be radically different from the predicates of substances. The predicate, on this view, is never part of the subject, and thus no true subject-predicate proposition is analytic. Propositions of the form 'All A is B' are not really subject-predicate propositions, but express relations of predicates; such propositions may be analytic, but the traditional confusion of them with true subject-predicate propositions has been a disgrace to formal logic.

The theory which rejects particulars, and assumes that, e.g., whiteness itself exists wherever (as common sense would say) there are white things, dispenses altogether with predication as a fundamental relation. 'This is white', which, on the other view, expresses a relation between a particular and whiteness, will, when particulars are rejected, really state that whiteness is one of the qualities in this place, or has certain spatial relations to certain other qualities. Thus the question whether predication is an ultimate simple relation may be taken as distinguishing the two theories; it is ultimate if there are particulars, but not otherwise. And if predication is an ultimate relation, the best definition of particulars is that they are entities which can only be subjects of predicates or terms of relations, i.e., that they are (in the logical sense) substances. This definition is preferable to one introducing space or time, because space and time are accidental characteristics of the world with which we happen to be acquainted, and therefore are destitute of the necessary universality belonging to purely logical categories.

We have thus a division of all entities into two classes: (1) particulars, which enter into complexes only as the subjects of predicates or the terms of relations, and, if they belong to the world of which we have experience, exist in time, and cannot occupy more than one place at one time in the space to which they belong; (2) universals, which can occur as predicates or relations in complexes, do not exist in time, and have no relation to one place which they may not simultaneously have to another. The ground for regarding such a division as unavoidable is the self-evident fact that certain spatial relations imply diversity of their terms, together with the self-evident fact that it is logically possible for entities having such spatial relations to be wholly indistinguishable as to predicates.

The argument in the above article in favour of the existence of particulars no longer seems to me valid for reasons which I have explained in *Human Knowledge: its scope and limits*. The gist of the matter arises out of the last sentence in the above article. I no longer think that there are any spatial or temporal relations which always and necessarily imply diversity. This does not prove that the theory which asserts particulars is wrong, but only that it cannot be proved to be right. The theory which asserts particulars and the theory which denies them would seem equally tenable. If so, the latter has the merit of logical parsimony. [Note added in 1955]

Notes

The thesis of the present paper is closely similar to that of Mr. Moore's paper 'Identity', read before the Aristotelian Society in 1900–1901. My chief reason for thinking that the question demands a fresh discussion is that the statement of the grounds for the thesis appears to require some examination of the nature of sensible space as opposed to physical space.

1 This is the distinction which I formerly spoke of as the distinction between *things* and *concepts*, but these terms no longer seem to me appropriate. Cf. *Principles of Mathematics*, §48.

10

From the *Tractatus Logico-Philosophicus*

Ludwig Wittgenstein

1	The world is everything that is the case.*
1.1	The world is the totality of facts, not of things.
1.11	The world is determined by the facts, and by these being *all* the facts.
1.12	For the totality of facts determines both what is the case, and also all that is not the case.
1.13	The facts in logical space are the world.
1.2	The world divides into facts.
1.21	Any one can either be the case or not be the case, and everything else remain the same.
2	What is the case, the fact, is the existence of atomic facts.
2.01	An atomic fact is a combination of objects (entities, things).
2.011	It is essential to a thing that it can be a constituent part of an atomic fact.
2.012	In logic nothing is accidental: if a thing *can* occur in an atomic fact the possibility of that atomic fact must already be prejudged in the thing.
2.0121	It would, so to speak, appear as an accident, when to a thing that could exist alone on its own account, subsequently a state of affairs could be made to fit.
	If things can occur in atomic facts, this possibility must already lie in them.
	(A logical entity cannot be merely possible. Logic treats of every possibility, and all possibilities are its facts.)
	Just as we cannot think of spatial objects at all apart from space, or temporal objects apart from time, so we cannot think of *any* object apart from the possibility of its connexion with other things.
	If I can think of an object in the context of an atomic fact, I cannot think of it apart from the *possibility* of this context.
2.0122	The thing is independent, in so far as it can occur in all *possible* circumstances, but this form of independence is a form of connexion with the atomic fact, a form of dependence. (It is impossible for words to occur in two different ways, alone and in the proposition.)
2.0123	If I know an object, then I also know all the possibilities of its occurrence in atomic facts. (Every such possibility must lie in the nature of the object.)
	A new possibility cannot subsequently be found.

Originally published in *Tractatus Logico-Philosophicus*, trans. C. K. Ogden (Routledge and Kegan Paul, London, 1922).

* The decimal figures as numbers of the separate propositions indicate the logical importance of the propositions, the emphasis laid upon them in my exposition. The propositions *n*.1, *n*.2, *n*.3, etc., are comments on proposition No. *n*; the propositions *n.m*1, *n.m*2, etc., are comments on the proposition No. *n.m*; and so on. [LW]

2.01231　In order to know an object, I must know not its external but all its internal qualities.

2.0124　If all objects are given, then thereby are all *possible* atomic facts also given.

2.013　Every thing is, as it were, in a space of possible atomic facts. I can think of this space as empty, but not of the thing without the space.

2.0131　A spatial object must lie in infinite space. (A point in space is an argument place.)

A speck in a visual field need not be red, but it must have a colour; it has, so to speak, a colour space round it. A tone must have *a* pitch, the object of the sense of touch *a* hardness, etc.

2.014　Objects contain the possibility of all states of affairs.

2.0141　The possibility of its occurrence in atomic facts is the form of the object.

2.02　The object is simple.

2.0201　Every statement about complexes can be analysed into a statement about their constituent parts, and into those propositions which completely describe the complexes.

2.021　Objects form the substance of the world. Therefore they cannot be compound.

2.0211　If the world had no substance, then whether a proposition had sense would depend on whether another proposition was true.

2.0212　It would then be impossible to form a picture of the world (true or false).

2.022　It is clear that however different from the real one an imagined world may be, it must have something – a form – in common with the real world.

2.023　This fixed form consists of the objects.

2.0231　The substance of the world *can* only determine a form and not any material properties. For these are first presented by the propositions – first formed by the configuration of the objects.

2.0232　Roughly speaking: objects are colourless.

2.0233　Two objects of the same logical form are – apart from their external properties – only differentiated from one another in that they are different.

2.02331　Either a thing has properties which no other has, and then one can distinguish it straight away from the others by a description and refer to it; or, on the other hand, there are several things which have the totality of their properties in common, and then it is quite impossible to point to any one of them.

For if a thing is not distinguished by anything, I cannot distinguish it – for otherwise it would be distinguished.

2.024　Substance is what exists independently of what is the case.

2.025　It is form and content.

2.0251　Space, time and colour (colouredness) are forms of objects.

2.026　Only if there are objects can there be a fixed form of the world.

2.027　The fixed, the existent and the object are one.

2.0271　The object is the fixed, the existent; the configuration is the changing, the variable.

2.0272　The configuration of the objects forms the atomic fact.

2.03　In the atomic fact objects hang one in another, like the links of a chain.

2.031　In the atomic fact the objects are combined in a definite way.

2.032　The way in which objects hang together in the atomic fact is the structure of the atomic fact.

2.033　The form is the possibility of the structure.

2.034　The structure of the fact consists of the structures of the atomic facts.

2.04　The totality of existent atomic facts is the world.

2.05　The totality of existent atomic facts also determines which atomic facts do not exist.

2.06　The existence and non-existence of atomic facts is the reality.

(The existence of atomic facts we also call a positive fact, their non-existence a negative fact.)

2.061　Atomic facts are independent of one another.

2.062　From the existence or non-existence of an atomic fact we cannot infer the existence or non-existence of another.

2.063　The total reality is the world.

2.1　We make to ourselves pictures of facts.

2.11   The picture presents the facts in logical space, the existence and non-existence of atomic facts.

2.12   The picture is a model of reality.

2.13   To the objects correspond in the picture the elements of the picture.

2.131   The elements of the picture stand, in the picture, for the objects.

2.14   The picture consists in the fact that its elements are combined with one another in a definite way.

2.141   The picture is a fact.

2.15   That the elements of the picture are combined with one another in a definite way, represents that the things are so combined with one another.
       This connexion of the elements of the picture is called its structure, and the possibility of this structure is called the form of representation of the picture.

2.151   The form of representation is the possibility that the things are combined with one another as are the elements of the picture.

2.1511   Thus the picture is linked with reality; it reaches up to it.

2.1512   It is like a scale applied to reality.

2.15121   Only the outermost points of the dividing lines *touch* the object to be measured.

2.1513   According to this view the representing relation which makes it a picture, also belongs to the picture.

2.1514   The representing relation consists of the co-ordinations of the elements of the picture and the things.

2.1515   These co-ordinations are as it were the feelers of its elements with which the picture touches reality.

2.16   In order to be a picture a fact must have something in common with what it pictures.

2.161   In the picture and the pictured there must be something identical in order that the one can be a picture of the other at all.

2.17   What the picture must have in common with reality in order to be able to represent it after its manner – rightly or falsely – is its form of representation.

2.171   The picture can represent every reality whose form it has.
       The spatial picture, everything spatial, the coloured, everything coloured, etc.

2.172   The picture, however, cannot represent its form of representation; it shows it forth.

2.173   The picture represents its object from without (its standpoint is its form of representation), therefore the picture represents its object rightly or falsely.

2.174   But the picture cannot place itself outside of its form of representation.

2.18   What every picture, of whatever form, must have in common with reality in order to be able to represent it at all – rightly or falsely – is the logical form, that is, the form of reality.

2.181   If the form of representation is the logical form, then the picture is called a logical picture.

2.182   Every picture is *also* a logical picture. (On the other hand, for example, not every picture is spatial.)

2.19   The logical picture can depict the world.

2.2   The picture has the logical form of representation in common with what it pictures.

2.201   The picture depicts reality by representing a possibility of the existence and non-existence of atomic facts.

2.202   The picture represents a possible state of affairs in logical space.

2.203   The picture contains the possibility of the state of affairs which it represents.

2.21   The picture agrees with reality or not; it is right or wrong, true or false.

2.22   The picture represents what it represents, independently of its truth or falsehood, through the form of representation.

2.221   What the picture represents is its sense.

2.222   In the agreement or disagreement of its sense with reality, its truth or falsity consists.

2.223   In order to discover whether the picture is true or false we must compare it with reality.

2.224   It cannot be discovered from the picture alone whether it is true or false.

2.225   There is no picture which is a priori true.

3	The logical picture of the facts is the thought.
3.001	"An atomic fact is thinkable" – means: we can imagine it.
3.01	The totality of true thoughts is a picture of the world.
3.02	The thought contains the possibility of the state of affairs which it thinks.
	What is thinkable is also possible.
3.03	We cannot think anything unlogical, for otherwise we should have to think unlogically.
3.031	It used to be said that God could create everything, except what was contrary to the laws of logic. The truth is, we could not *say* of an "unlogical" world how it would look.
3.032	To present in language anything which "contradicts logic" is as impossible as in geometry to present by its co-ordinates a figure which contradicts the laws of space; or to give the co-ordinates of a point which does not exist.
3.0321	We could present spatially an atomic fact which contradicted the laws of physics, but not one which contradicted the laws of geometry.
3.04	An a priori true thought would be one whose possibility guaranteed its truth.
3.05	We could only know a priori that a thought is true if its truth was to be recognized from the thought itself (without an object of comparison).
3.1	In the proposition the thought is expressed perceptibly through the senses.
3.11	We use the sensibly perceptible sign (sound or written sign, etc.) of the proposition as a projection of the possible state of affairs.
	The method of projection is the thinking of the sense of the proposition.
3.12	The sign through which we express the thought I call the propositional sign. And the proposition is the propositional sign in its projective relation to the world.
3.13	To the proposition belongs everything which belongs to the projection; but not what is projected.
	Therefore the possibility of what is projected but not this itself.
	In the proposition, therefore, its sense is not yet contained, but the possibility of expressing it.
	("The content of the proposition" means the content of the significant proposition.)
	In the proposition the form of its sense is contained, but not its content.
3.14	The propositional sign consists in the fact that its elements, the words, are combined in it in a definite way.
	The propositional sign is a fact.
3.141	The proposition is not a mixture of words (just as the musical theme is not a mixture of tones).
	The proposition is articulate.
3.142	Only facts can express a sense, a class of names cannot.
3.143	That the propositional sign is a fact is concealed by the ordinary form of expression, written or printed.
	(For in the printed proposition, for example, the sign of a proposition does not appear essentially different from a word. Thus it was possible for Frege to call the proposition a compounded name.)
3.1431	The essential nature of the propositional sign becomes very clear when we imagine it made up of spatial objects (such as tables, chairs, books) instead of written signs.
	The mutual spatial position of these things then expresses the sense of the proposition.
3.1432	We must not say, "The complex sign '*aRb*' says '*a* stands in relation R to *b*'"; but we must say, "*That* '*a*' stands in a certain relation to '*b*' says *that aRb*".
3.144	States of affairs can be described but not *named*.
	(Names resemble points; propositions resemble arrows, they have sense.)
3.2	In propositions thoughts can be so expressed that to the objects of the thoughts correspond the elements of the propositional sign.
3.201	These elements I call "simple signs" and the proposition "completely analysed".
3.202	The simple signs employed in propositions are called names.
3.203	The name means the object. The object is its meaning. ("*A*" is the same sign as "*A*".)

3.21   To the configuration of the simple signs in the propositional sign corresponds the configu-
          ration of the objects in the state of affairs.
3.22   In the proposition the name represents the object.
3.221   Objects I can only *name*. Signs represent them. I can only speak *of* them. I cannot *assert*
          them. A proposition can only say *how* a thing is, not *what* it is.
3.23   The postulate of the possibility of the simple signs is the postulate of the determinateness
          of the sense.
3.25   There is one and only one complete analysis of the proposition.
3.251   The proposition expresses what it expresses in a definite and clearly specifiable way: the
          proposition is articulate.
3.26   The name cannot be analysed further by any definition. It is a primitive sign.
3.261   Every defined sign signifies *via* those signs by which it is defined, and the definitions show
          the way.
          Two signs, one a primitive sign, and one defined by primitive signs, cannot signify in
          the same way. Names cannot be taken to pieces by definition (nor any sign which alone and
          independently has a meaning).

3.3   Only the proposition has sense; only in the context of a proposition has a name meaning.
3.31   Every part of a proposition which characterizes its sense I call an expression (a symbol).
          (The proposition itself is an expression.)
          Expressions are everything – essential for the sense of the proposition – that propositions
          can have in common with one another.
          An expression characterizes a form and a content.

3.314   An expression has meaning only in a proposition. Every variable can be conceived as a
          propositional variable.

3.318   I conceive the proposition – like Frege and Russell – as a function of the expressions
          contained in it.

3.322   It can never indicate the common characteristic of two objects that we symbolize them with
          the same signs but by different *methods of symbolizing*. For the sign is arbitrary. We could
          therefore equally well choose two different signs and where then would be what was common
          in the symbolization.
3.323   In the language of everyday life it very often happens that the same word signifies in two
          different ways – and therefore belongs to two different symbols – or that two words, which
          signify in different ways, are apparently applied in the same way in the proposition.
          Thus the word "is" appears as the copula, as the sign of equality, and as the expression of
          existence; "to exist" as an intransitive verb like "to go"; "identical" as an adjective; we speak
          of *something* but also of the fact of *something* happening.
          (In the proposition "Green is green" – where the first word is a proper name and the last
          an adjective – these words have not merely different meanings but they are *different symbols*.)
3.324   Thus there easily arise the most fundamental confusions (of which the whole of philosophy
          is full).
3.325   In order to avoid these errors, we must employ a symbolism which excludes them, by not
          applying the same sign in different symbols and by not applying signs in the same way which
          signify in different ways. A symbolism, that is to say, which obeys the rules of *logical* grammar
          – of logical syntax.
          (The logical symbolism of Frege and Russell is such a language, which, however, does still
          not exclude all errors.)
3.326   In order to recognize the symbol in the sign we must consider the significant use.
3.327   The sign determines a logical form only together with its logical syntactic application.

3.328   If a sign is *not necessary* then it is meaningless. That is the meaning of Occam's razor.
(If everything in the symbolism works as though a sign had meaning, then it has meaning.)

3.33   In logical syntax the meaning of a sign ought never to play a role; it must admit of being established without mention being thereby made of the *meaning* of a sign; it ought to presuppose *only* the description of the expressions.

3.331   From this observation we get a further view – into Russell's *Theory of Types*. Russell's error is shown by the fact that in drawing up his symbolic rules he has to speak about the things his signs mean.

3.332   No proposition can say anything about itself, because the propositional sign cannot be contained in itself (that is the "whole theory of types").

3.333   A function cannot be its own argument, because the functional sign already contains the prototype of its own argument and it cannot contain itself.
If, for example, we suppose that the function $F(fx)$ could be its own argument, then there would be a proposition "$F(F(fx))$", and in this the outer function F and the inner function F must have different meanings; for the inner has the form $\phi(fx)$, the outer the form $\psi(\phi(fx))$. Common to both functions is only the letter "F", which by itself signifies nothing.
This is at once clear, if instead of "$F(F(u))$" we write "$(\exists\phi) : F(\phi u) \cdot \phi u = Fu$".
Herewith Russell's paradox vanishes.

3.334   The rules of logical syntax must follow of themselves, if we only know how every single sign signifies.

3.34   A proposition possesses essential and accidental features.
Accidental are the features which are due to a particular way of producing the propositional sign. Essential are those which alone enable the proposition to express its sense.

3.341   The essential in a proposition is therefore that which is common to all propositions which can express the same sense.
And in the same way in general the essential in a symbol is that which all symbols which can fulfil the same purpose have in common.

3.343   Definitions are rules for the translation of one language into another. Every correct symbolism must be translatable into every other according to such rules. It is *this* which all have in common.

3.5   The applied, thought, propositional sign is the thought.

4   The thought is the significant proposition.

4.001   The totality of propositions is the language.

4.002   Man possesses the capacity of constructing languages, in which every sense can be expressed, without having an idea how and what each word means – just as one speaks without knowing how the single sounds are produced.
Colloquial language is a part of the human organism and is not less complicated than it.
From it is humanly impossible to gather immediately the logic of language.
Language disguises the thought; so that from the external form of the clothes one cannot infer the form of the thought they clothe, because the external form of the clothes is constructed with quite another object than to let the form of the body be recognized.
The silent adjustments to understand colloquial language are enormously complicated.

4.003   Most propositions and questions, that have been written about philosophical matters, are not false, but senseless. We cannot, therefore, answer questions of this kind at all, but only state their senselessness. Most questions and propositions of the philosophers result from the fact that we do not understand the logic of our language.
(They are of the same kind as the question whether the Good is more or less identical than the Beautiful.)
And so it is not to be wondered at that the deepest problems are really *no* problems.

4.0031   All philosophy is "Critique of language" (but not at all in Mauthner's sense). Russell's merit is to have shown that the apparent logical form of the proposition need not be its real form.

4.01   The proposition is a picture of reality.

The proposition is a model of the reality as we think it is.

4.011   At the first glance the proposition – say as it stands printed on paper – does not seem to be a picture of the reality of which it treats. But nor does the musical score appear at first sight to be a picture of a musical piece; nor does our phonetic spelling (letters) seem to be a picture of our spoken language. And yet these symbolisms prove to be pictures – even in the ordinary sense of the word – of what they represent.

4.012   It is obvious that we perceive a proposition of the form aRb as a picture. Here the sign is obviously a likeness of the signified.

4.016   In order to understand the essence of the proposition, consider hieroglyphic writing, which pictures the facts it describes.

And from it came the alphabet without the essence of the representation being lost.

4.021   The proposition is a picture of reality, for I know the state of affairs presented by it, if I understand the proposition. And I understand the proposition, without its sense having been explained to me.

4.022   The proposition *shows* its sense.

The proposition *shows* how things stand, *if* it is true. And it *says*, that they do so stand.

4.024   To understand a proposition means to know what is the case, if it is true.

(One can therefore understand it without knowing whether it is true or not.)

One understands it if one understands its constituent parts.

4.027   It is essential to propositions, that they can communicate a *new* sense to us.

4.0312 The possibility of propositions is based upon the principle of the representation of objects by signs.

My fundamental thought is that the "logical constants" do not represent. That the *logic* of the facts cannot be represented.

4.032   The proposition is a picture of its state of affairs, only in so far as it is logically articulated.

(Even the proposition "ambulo" is composite, for its stem gives a different sense with another termination, or its termination with another stem.)

4.04   In the proposition there must be exactly as many things distinguishable as there are in the state of affairs, which it represents.

They must both possess the same logical (mathematical) multiplicity (cf. Hertz's *Mechanics*, on Dynamic Models).

4.05   Reality is compared with the proposition.

4.06   Propositions can be true or false only by being pictures of the reality.

4.1   A proposition presents the existence and non-existence of atomic facts.

4.11   The totality of true propositions is the total natural science (or the totality of the natural sciences).

4.111   Philosophy is not one of the natural sciences.

(The word "philosophy" must mean something which stands above or below, but not beside the natural sciences.)

4.112   The object of philosophy is the logical clarification of thoughts.

Philosophy is not a theory but an activity.

A philosophical work consists essentially of elucidations.

The result of philosophy is not a number of "philosophical propositions", but to make propositions clear.

Philosophy should make clear and delimit sharply the thoughts which otherwise are, as it were, opaque and blurred.

4.116   Everything that can be thought at all can be thought clearly. Everything that can be said can be said clearly.

4.12   Propositions can represent the whole reality, but they cannot represent what they must have in common with reality in order to be able to represent it – the logical form.

To be able to represent the logical form, we should have to be able to put ourselves with the propositions outside logic, that is outside the world.

4.121   Propositions cannot represent the logical form: this mirrors itself in the propositions.

That which mirrors itself in language, language cannot represent.

That which expresses *itself* in language, *we* cannot express by language.

The propositions *show* the logical form of reality.

They exhibit it.

4.1211   Thus a proposition "*fa*" shows that in its sense the object *a* occurs, two propositions "*fa*" and "*ga*" that they are both about the same object.

If two propositions contradict one another, this is shown by their structure; similarly if one follows from another, etc.

4.1212   What *can* be shown *cannot* be said.

4.126   In the sense in which we speak of formal properties we can now speak also of formal concepts.

(I introduce this expression in order to make clear the confusion of formal concepts with proper concepts which runs through the whole of the old logic.)

That anything falls under a formal concept as an object belonging to it, cannot be expressed by a proposition. But it is shown in the symbol for the object itself. (The name shows that it signifies an object, the numerical sign that it signifies a number, etc.)

Formal concepts cannot, like proper concepts, be presented by a function.

For their characteristics, the formal properties, are not expressed by the functions.

The expression of a formal property is a feature of certain symbols.

The sign that signifies the characteristics of a formal concept is, therefore, a characteristic feature of all symbols, whose meanings fall under the concept.

4.21   The simplest proposition, the elementary proposition, asserts the existence of an atomic fact.

4.211   It is a sign of an elementary proposition, that no elementary proposition can contradict it.

4.22   The elementary proposition consists of names. It is a connexion, a concatenation, of names.

4.221   It is obvious that in the analysis of propositions we must come to elementary propositions, which consist of names in immediate combination.

The question arises here, how the propositional connexion comes to be.

4.23   The name occurs in the proposition only in the context of the elementary proposition.

4.25   If the elementary proposition is true, the atomic fact exists; if it is false the atomic fact does not exist.

4.26   The specification of all true elementary propositions describes the world completely. The world is completely described by the specification of all elementary propositions plus the specification, which of them are true and which false.

4.46   Among the possible groups of truth-conditions there are two extreme cases.

In the one case the proposition is true for all the truth-possibilities of the elementary propositions. We say that the truth-conditions are *tautological.*

In the second case the proposition is false for all the truth-possibilities. The truth-conditions are *self-contradictory.*

In the first case we call the proposition a tautology, in the second case a contradiction.

4.461   The proposition shows what it says, the tautology and the contradiction that they say nothing.

The tautology has no truth-conditions, for it is unconditionally true; and the contradiction is on no condition true.

Tautology and contradiction are without sense.

(Like the point from which two arrows go out in opposite directions.)

(I know, e.g. nothing about the weather, when I know that it rains or does not rain.)

5   Propositions are truth-functions of elementary propositions.

(An elementary proposition is a truth-function of itself.)

5.01   The elementary propositions are the truth-arguments of propositions.

5.124   A proposition asserts every proposition which follows from it.

5.1241   "$p \cdot q$" is one of the propositions which assert "p" and at the same time one of the propositions which assert "q".

Two propositions are opposed to one another if there is no significant proposition which asserts them both.

Every proposition which contradicts another, denies it.

5.13   That the truth of one proposition follows from the truth of other propositions, we perceive from the structure of the propositions.

5.621   The world and life are one.

5.63   I am my world. (The microcosm.)

5.631   The thinking, presenting subject; there is no such thing.

If I wrote a book "The world as I found it", I should also have therein to report on my body and say which members obey my will and which do not, etc. This then would be a method of isolating the subject or rather of showing that in an important sense there is no subject: that is to say, of it alone in this book mention could *not* be made.

5.632   The subject does not belong to the world but it is a limit of the world.

5.633   *Where in* the world is a metaphysical subject to be noted?

You say that this case is altogether like that of the eye and the field of sight. But you do *not* really see the eye.

And from nothing *in the field of sight* can it be concluded that it is seen from an eye.

6.1   The propositions of logic are tautologies.

6.11   The propositions of logic therefore say nothing. (They are the analytical propositions.)

6.13   Logic is not a theory but a reflexion of the world.

Logic is transcendental.

6.2   Mathematics is a logical method.

The propositions of mathematics are equations, and therefore pseudo-propositions.

6.21   Mathematical propositions express no thoughts.

6.2322   The identity of the meaning of two expressions cannot be *asserted*. For in order to be able to assert anything about their meaning, I must know their meaning, and if I know their meaning, I know whether they mean the same or something different.

6.4   All propositions are of equal value.

6.41   The sense of the world must lie outside the world. In the world everything is as it is and happens as it does happen. *In* it there is no value – and if there were, it would be of no value.

If there is a value which is of value, it must lie outside all happening and being-so. For all happening and being-so is accidental.

What makes it non-accidental cannot lie *in* the world, for otherwise this would again be accidental.

It must lie outside the world.

6.42   Hence also there can be no ethical propositions.
        Propositions cannot express anything higher.
6.421   It is clear that ethics cannot be expressed.
        Ethics is transcendental.
        (Ethics and æsthetics are one.)

6.4311 Death is not an event of life. Death is not lived through.
        If by eternity is understood not endless temporal duration but timelessness, then he lives eternally who lives in the present.
        Our life is endless in the way that our visual field is without limit.

6.44   Not *how* the world is, is the mystical, but *that* it is.
6.45   The contemplation of the world sub specie aeterni is its contemplation as a limited whole.
        The feeling of the world as a limited whole is the mystical feeling.

6.51   Scepticism is *not* irrefutable, but palpably senseless, if it would doubt where a question cannot be asked.
        For doubt can only exist where there is a question; a question only where there is an answer, and this only where something *can* be *said*.

6.522   There is indeed the inexpressible. This *shows* itself; it is the mystical.
6.53   The right method of philosophy would be this. To say nothing except what can be said, i.e. the propositions of natural science, i.e. something that has nothing to do with philosophy: and then always, when someone else wished to say something metaphysical, to demonstrate to him that he had given no meaning to certain signs in his propositions. This method would be unsatisfying to the other – he would not have the feeling that we were teaching him philosophy – but it would be the only strictly correct method.
6.54   My propositions are elucidatory in this way: he who understands me finally recognizes them as senseless, when he has climbed out through them, on them, over them. (He must so to speak throw away the ladder, after he has climbed up on it.)
        He must surmount these propositions; then he sees the world rightly.
7   Whereof one cannot speak, thereof one must be silent.

11

Particular and General

P. F. Strawson

1. There is a certain philosophical question which, if antiquity confers respectability, is as respectable as any. It was not long ago discussed by Ramsey in the form "What is the difference between a particular and a universal?",[1] and more recently by Ayer in the form "What is the difference between properties and individuals?"[2] Ramsey decided that there was no ultimate difference; but perhaps he set the standard for an ultimate difference higher than we should wish to, or drew it from a theory we no longer wish to hold. Ayer, after some interesting suggestions, changed the subject, and discussed instead two other questions: viz., what is the difference in function between indicator words and predicates, and could we in principle say what we want to say without using the former?[3] It may be that the original question is made easier to start on, and more difficult to settle, by an initial failure to make even fairly clear what types or classes of things are to be included in the two general categories between which a satisfying difference is sought. The words of the questions I quoted are not very helpful. Universals are said to include qualities and relations. But if, for example, we take the words "quality," "relation" and "property" in their current uses, much that we should no doubt wish to include on the side of the general, as opposed to the particular, would be left out; and if we do not take them in their current

uses, it is not clear how we are to take them. Thus snow, gold and clothing are not properties; nor is man, nor any other species; nor is chess nor furniture; nor is the Union Jack – by which I mean, not the tattered specimen the porter keeps in a drawer, but the flag designed in the nineteenth century, examples of which are taken from drawers by porters and hung from windows. But all these are things which we might well wish to classify with properties correctly so-called, like inflammability, or with qualities correctly so-called, like prudence, when we contrast these latter with individuals or particulars. For there are individual flakes or drifts or falls of snow, pieces of gold, articles of clothing or furniture, games of chess,[4] members of species; and there are hundreds of Union Jacks. These are all (are they not?) particular instances of the general things named in *their* names. Sometimes the unlikeness of these general things to properties or qualities correctly so-called is masked by the introduction of expresssions like "being (a piece of) gold," "being snow," "being a man," "being a Union Jack," "being a chair," "being a game of chess" – phrases like these being said to name properties. Now such expressions no doubt have a participial use; and some (e.g., "being a man") may have a use as noun-phrases, as singular terms. But it is dubious whether many of them have a use as singular terms; and it is dubious whether any of them can be regarded as names of properties. And however we resolve these doubts in different cases, the following dilemma arises in each. Either these verbal nouns (where

Originally published in *Proceedings of the Aristotelian Society* 54 (1953–4). Reprinted by courtesy of the Editor of the Aristotelian Society: © 1953–1954.

they are nouns) have the same use as the general names they incorporate – and in that case they may as well be discarded in favour of those general names, which are more familiar, and about the use of which we are consequently less liable to be misled; or they have a different use from those general names – and in this case we still have on our hands, to be differentiated, like properties correctly so-called, from particulars, the general things designated by those familiar general names.

2. This initial unclarity about the limits of the two great categories of general and particular shows itself also in that arbitrary narrowing of the field which must be presumed to occur whenever certain answers to our question seem plausible. I shall consider again some of these answers, which were dismissed by Ayer or Ramsey or both, not so much on the ground that they thought them false as on the ground that they did not think them fundamental. There is, for example, the suggestion that general, unlike particular, things cannot be perceived by means of the senses; and this seems most plausible if one is thinking of the things designated by certain abstract nouns. It is not with the eyes that one is said to see hope. But one can quite literally smell blood or bacon, watch cricket, hear music or thunder; and there are, on the other hand, certain particulars which it makes dubious sense to say one perceives. Then there is the suggestion that general, unlike particular, things can be in several places at once. There can be influenza in London as well as in Birmingham, and gold in Australia as well as in Africa. But then so can many particulars be scattered over the surface of the table or the globe. Moreover, it makes dubious sense to say of some general things (e.g., solubility) that they are in any place, let alone in many; and equally dubious sense to say of some particular things (a sudden thought, a mental image, the constitution of France) that they have a particular spatial location. It may be said that I have missed the point of both these theories; that, first, when we say we perceive general things, what we really perceive is individual instances of them, not the general things themselves; and, second, to say that general things can be in several places at once is to say that they may have different instances, differently located; whereas it makes no sense to speak of different instances of individuals. But so to explain these theories is to

give them up. It is to fall back on saying that general things may have instances, and individual instances of general things may not. This is, perhaps, an unexceptionable statement of the general distinction between the two categories, but scarcely seems to count as an explanation of it.

A third suggestion is that individual things, unlike general things, have dates or histories. But similar objections apply to this. We may speak of the history of dress or engineering, the origins of civilisation, the invention of golf and the evolution of man. This theory, like the others (when taken at their face value), may draw a logically interesting distinction; but, like them, does not draw one that coincides with the categorial line between particular and general.

A doctrine which might appear more promising, because more general, than these, is that individuals can function in propositions only as subjects, never as predicates; whereas general things can function as both. But it is not clear what this doctrine amounts to. Suppose, first, it is a grammatical point. Then if it says that the names of individuals never have adjectival or verbal forms, whereas names of general things do, it is false. If it says that individual names never form parts of grammatical predicates, or alternatively, never stand by themselves after the word "is" in a grammatical predicate, it is equally false. In any case, a grammatical point could scarcely be fundamental, since it is easy to imagine the elimination of those distinctions upon which such points must rely, in favour of the device of merely coupling names of appropriate types, in any order, in a singular sentence. We should not, by so doing, eliminate the category-distinction. For we might imagine changing the language once more, requiring that our names should stand on one side or the other of the phrase "is an instance of," and then simply distinguishing the individual names as those that could never stand on the right of this phrase.[5] So I think we must conclude that the point misleadingly made in the languages of grammar is simply once more the point that individuals, unlike general things, cannot have instances. To say that general things, unlike individuals, can be predicated of other things, is simply to paraphrase this; and neither expression seems more perspicuous than the other.

3. But will the word "instance" itself really bear the weight of this distinction? Of course, as

P. F. Strawson

a philosopher's word, understood in terms of that distinction, it cannot fail to bear it; but then it ceases to explain the distinction for us. If we ask what expressions we actually use to refer to or describe an individual thing as an instance of a general thing, we find that they are many; and that perhaps none of them is appropriate in every case. They include: "a case of," "an example of," "a specimen of," "a member of," "a piece of," "a quantity of," "a copy of," "a performance of," "a game of," "an article of," and so on. Though each can be followed by the name of a general thing, many can also be followed by expressions we should hesitate to regard as the names of general things. This is true of the phrase "an instance of" itself. We may speak of a signal instance of generosity; but we may also speak of a signal instance of Smith's generosity. Similarly we may speak not only of a piece of gold and an article of clothing, but of a piece of Smith's gold and an article of Smith's clothing. So if we seek to draw our distinction in terms of the words actually used to play the part of the philosopher's word "instance" – including the word "instance" itself – then it will not be enough to say that general things may have instances. For so may non-general things.

The point here may be put roughly as follows. We are tempted to explain the distinction between two types of things, T_1 and T_2, by means of a certain relation R; by saying, that is, that only things belonging to T_2 can appear as the second term of this relation, whereas both things belonging to T_2 and things belonging to T_1 can appear as its first term. R is something like, but more general than, *is characterised by* or *is a member of* or the converse of *is predicated of.* But then it appears that we really have no notion of R except one which is useless for explanatory purposes since it is itself to be explained in terms of the difference between T_1 and T_2; this is what I called the philosopher's notion of "an instance of." What we have instead is a lot of notions which are either too restricted to serve our purpose (e.g., "has the property of"), or fail to be restricted in precisely the way in which we want them to be, or both. As a member of this set of notions, preeminent for its abstract character, we may take the logician's idea of class-membership. The difficulty is, roughly, that we can form closed classes on what principle we please; we could count almost any particular we are likely to mention as such a class, and hence

as the second term of our relation. (These remarks are very rough and schematic; but they serve, I hope, to make the point in a general form.) Consequently, we shall have to give up the idea of explaining the difference between the particular and the general in terms of such a relation. This will not lead us, as it perhaps led Ramsey, to despise the philosopher's notion of an instance, and to think that there is nothing in it; for it is easy enough to teach anyone the application of it, without precise explanations. But it will lead us to look further for such explanations.

4. To begin with, I want to draw a rough distinction between three classes of nouns, all of which would traditionally be regarded either as themselves the names of universals (general things) or – in the case of the nouns of group (2) – as closely linked to such names. The distinctions are indicated only by examples; and the three classes are by no means exhaustive of the field. But this does not matter for my purpose.

(1) Examples of the first class are such partitive nouns as "gold," "snow," "water," "jam," "music." These I shall call *material-names*, and what they name, *materials.*

(2) Examples of the second are certain articulative nouns such as "(a) man," "(an) apple," "(a) cat." These I shall call *substance-names*, and what they apply to, *substances.*

(3) Examples of the third are such abstract nouns as "redness," (or "red"), "roundness," "anger," "wisdom." These I shall call *quality-* or *property-names*, and what they name, *qualities* or *properties.*[6] These three classes of nouns may be compared and contrasted with one another in a number of ways. But the contrast on which I wish to lay most emphasis is

(i) The contrast between the nouns of group (3) and those of groups (1) and (2). The nouns of group (3) are the most sophisticated and the most dispensable. They are derived from adjectives and the general things they name usually enter our talk by way of the adjectives from which their names are derived. When we consider the things which philosophers are prepared to count as individual instances of these general things, we find a considerable latitude in the categories of the things to which these instances may belong. Thus an instance of wisdom may be a man, a remark or an action. An instance of the colour red may be a material thing like a pillar-box, an event like a sunset, or a mental thing like an image. A word, a gesture, an expression, a man may all be instances of anger. In contrast, unsystematic ambiguities aside, there is no latitude at all about what category of thing can be an individual instance of a cat or an apple. There is some latitude, but one would often hesitate to call it a category-latitude, about what can be an individual instance of the general things named by the nouns of group (1). An instance of gold may be a vein, a piece or a quantity of gold; an instance of snow may be a drift, an expanse, a piece, and even a fall, of snow.

(ii) Next I want to emphasise a respect in which the nouns of group (2) differ from those of groups (1) and (3). Philosophers may speak of "an individual (particular) instance (example, specimen) of ϕ," where "ϕ" is replaced by a noun from any of these three groups. Suppose the noun is drawn from group (2). Then we have such phrases as "an instance of a horse" or "an instance of an apple." It is to be noticed that what follows the expression "an instance of" is a phrase which can and does *by itself* function as an indefinite designation of an individual instance. (An instance of a horse is the same as a horse.) This is not the case if the nouns are drawn from groups (1) or (3). (Gold is not the same as a piece of gold.) It seems as if, when we say that x is an instance of y, then when y is such that there is no choice about the sort of thing we can count as an instance of it, we feel no need of a true general-thing name for y, i.e., of a name differing from an indefinite designation of an individual instance of y. (It is true that we have the expressions "*the* horse," "*the* apple," etc., names of species or kinds, obvious collectors of homogeneous individuals; but these follow less naturally after the expression "an instance of" than does the phrase containing the indefinite article). Philosophers have felt this difference, and tried to blur it with the invention of such expressions as "horseness" (cf. "being a horse"). But it should rather be treated as a clue until proved an anomaly.

(iii) Finally, I want to note the existence of a special class of individual instances of general things whose names belong to group (3). The simplest, though not the only recipe, for forming the names of members of this class is as follows: in the formula "the ... of ... ," fill the first gap with the property-name in question and the second gap with the definite designation of a suit-able individual. Thus we may speak of *the wisdom of Socrates* as an instance of wisdom; of *the redness of Smith's face* as an instance of redness; and we may also speak of *Jones' present mental state* as an instance of anger. This class of individual instances of properties, or property-like things, will include the "particular qualities" which Stout defended. And an analogy may be found between referring to a horse as "an instance of a horse" and referring to Jones' present stage of anger as "an instance of anger."

5. Next, I want to make some general, and still propaedeutic, remarks about the notion of an individual or particular.

(1) The idea of an individual is the idea of an individual instance *of* something general. There is no such thing as a pure particular. (This truth is too old to need the support of elaboration.)

(2) The idea of an individual instance of ϕ is the idea of something which we are able in principle

(a) to distinguish from other instances of ϕ; and

(b) to recognise as the same instance at different times (where this notion is applicable). So, to have the idea of a particular instance of ϕ, we need (in general)

(a) criteria of distinctness,

(b) criteria of identity

for a particular instance of ϕ. On the need for these criteria the following comments must be made:

(i) It might be supposed that the distinction between the two kinds of criteria is a mistake; that there is no such distinction. For identity and difference are two sides of the same coin. It is possible, however, at least in some cases, to consider separately the criteria by which we distinguish and enumerate objects of the same sort, in a situation in which the question of identifying any one of them as, or distinguishing it from, the one which had such-and-such a history, does not arise or is not considered. It is to criteria of this kind that I give the name "criteria of distinctness". They might also be called "criteria of enumeration."[7]

(ii) What the criteria of distinctness and identity for instances of ϕ may be is obviously closely connected with what ϕ is; but is not wholly determined by it in every case. That it is not so determined is obvious in the case of properties, qualities, states, etc.; we have already seen how wide a range of categories their instances may be drawn from (4(i)). It is less obvious, but still true, in the case of general things named by material-names. The *general* question of the criteria of distinctness and identity of individual instances of snow or gold cannot be raised or, if raised, be satisfactorily answered. We have to wait until we know whether we are talking of *veins*, *pieces* or *quantities* of gold, or of *falls*, *drifts* or *expanses* of snow. There are cases, however, where this indeterminateness regarding the criteria of identity and distinctness does not seem to exist, where it seems that once ϕ is given, the criteria are given, too. And among these cases are those where "ϕ" is a substance-name (4(ii)). It should once more be noted that these are the cases where we do not find a true name of a general thing following the phrase "an instance of," but instead an expression which can by itself function as an indefinite designation of an individual instance (e.g., "a horse").

(3)   When it has been said that a particular must be an instance of something general, and that there must be criteria of distinctness and (where applicable) of identity for individual instances of a general thing, something of central importance still remains unsaid. In giving the relevant criteria – or sets of criteria – for individual instances of a certain general thing, we do not indicate how such particulars are brought into our discourse. Nor do we bring a particular into our discourse by mentioning these criteria. (To mention them is still to talk *in general*.) We bring a particular into our discourse only when we determine, select, *a point of application* for such criteria, only when we mention, refer to, something to which these criteria are to be applied; and no theory of particulars can be adequate which does not take account of the means by which we determine such a point of application *as* a point of application for these criteria.

6.   In the rest of this paper I shall try to do two things. First, I shall try to show how, in the case of *certain kinds* of particulars (particular instances of *certain kinds* of general things), the notion of a particular may be seen as something logically complex in relation to other notions (a kind of compound of these notions). That is, I shall try to produce a partial explanation (analysis) of the notion of an individual instance, for certain cases; and then I shall try to show how this notion, as explained for these cases, may be used in the

explanation of the notion of individual instances of *other* sorts of general things, and in the explanation of the notions of those other types of general things themselves. So in this part of the paper (sections 6–9), no general account is offered of the distinction we are concerned with. The procedure is essentially one of indicating, step by step, how certain types of notion can be seen as depending upon others; and it makes no claim at all to completeness. Second (section 12), this procedure is found to suggest a possible general account of the distinction we are concerned with; though the acceptability or otherwise of this general account seems to be independent of that of the step-by-step schema of explanation.

Now it might seem that the difficulty of finding an explanation of the notion of an individual instance arises from the fact that the category distinction between general and individual is so fundamental that there is nothing logically simpler, or more fundamental, in terms of which this notion could be explained. But I think this view can be challenged for a certain range of important cases, which can then perhaps serve as the basis for the explanation of others. To challenge it successfully we have to envisage the possibility of making statements which (a) do not make use of the notion of individual instances, and (b) do not presuppose the existence of statements which do make use of this notion. The second condition may be held to rule out general statements; for though many general statements make no direct mention of individuals, they have often and plausibly been held in some sense to presuppose the existence of statements which do. So what we have to consider is the possibility of singular statements which make no mention of (i.e., contain no names for, or other expressions definitely or indefinitely referring to) individual instances of general things. Now there certainly does exist, in ordinary use, a range of empirical singular statements answering to this description. I suggest, as examples, the following:

It is (has been) raining.
Music can be heard in the distance.
Snow is falling.
There is gold here.
There is water here.

All these sentences contain either the material-name of a general thing ("music," "snow") or a corresponding verb; but none contains any expression which can be construed as serving to make a definite or indefinite mention of individual instances of those general things (i.e., falls or drops of rain, pieces of gold, pools of water and so on). Of course, when these sentences are used, the combination of the circumstances of their use with the tense of the verb and the demonstrative adverbs, if any, which they contain, provides an indication of the incidence of the general thing in question. Such an indication must be provided somehow, if empirical singular statements are to be made at all. But it is important that it can be provided by means of utterance-centred indications which do not include noun-expressions referring definitely or indefinitely to individual instances. *Such sentences as these do not bring particulars into our discourse.*

Languages imagined on the model of such sentences are sometimes called "property-location" languages. But I think the word "property" is objectionable here because (a) the general things which figure in my examples are not properties, and (b) the idea of a property belongs, with the idea of an individual instance itself, to a level of logical complexity we are trying to get below. So I propose to substitute the less philosophically committed word "feature"; and to speak of feature-placing sentences.

Though feature-placing sentences do not introduce particulars into our discourse, they provide the materials for this introduction. Suppose we compare a feature-placing *sentence* ("There is snow here") with a *phrase* ("This (patch of) snow") in the use of which an individual instance of the feature is mentioned. It seems possible, in this case, to regard the notion of the individual instance as something logically complex in relation to the two simpler notions of the feature and of placing. The logical complexity may be brought out in the following way. In making the feature-placing statement, we utter a completed sentence without mentioning individuals. If we *merely* mention the individual without going on to say anything about it, we fail to utter a completed sentence; yet what the feature-placing sentence does explicitly is, in a sense, implicit in this mere mention. So, as the basic step in an explanatory schema, we may regard the notion of a particular instance of *certain sorts* of general things as a kind of logical compound of the simpler notions of a feature and of placing.

But what about the criteria of distinctness and identity which were said in general to be necessary to the notion of an individual instance of a general thing? The *basis* for the criteria of dis-

tinctness can already be introduced at the feature-placing level, without yet introducing particulars. For where we can say "There is snow here" or "There is gold here," we can also, perhaps, more exactly, though not more correctly, say "There is snow (gold) *here* – and *here* – and *here*." And when we can say "It snowed to-day," we can also, perhaps, more exactly, but not more correctly, say "It snowed twice to-day." The considerations which determine multiplicity of placing become, when we introduce particulars, the criteria for distinguishing this *patch of* snow from that, or the first *fall of* snow from the second. Of criteria of identity I shall say more in general later.

It might be objected that it is absurd to speak of an imagined transition from feature-placing sentences to substantival expressions definitely designating particular instances of features as the *introduction* of particulars; that it is absurd to represent this imagined transition as part of a possible analysis of the notion of a particular instance, even for these simple cases of material-names which seem the most favourable; and that at most what is achieved is the indication of a possible way of looking at certain *designations* of certain particulars. For are not the particulars as much a relevant part of the situation in which a feature-placing sentence is employed as they are of a situation in which a substantival particular-designation is employed? To this I would reply by asking what philosophical question there would be about particulars if we did not designate them, could not make lists of them, did not predicate qualities of them and so on. What we have to explain is a certain mode of speech.

7. When we turn from material-names to substance-names, the attempt to provide an analogous explanation of the notion of an individual instance seems much harder. But though it is harder, it is perhaps worth making; for if it succeeds, we may find we have then an adequate basis for the explanation of the notion of an individual instance in other cases, and for the explanation of further kinds of general things. In order for the attempt to succeed, we must be able to envisage a situation in which, instead of operating with the notion of an individual instance of a cat or an apple, we operate with the notions of a corresponding feature and of placing. Ordinary language does not seem to provide us, in these cases, with feature-placing sentences. And it might

be argued that the idea of such sentences was, in these cases, absurd. For (1) it might be pointed out that an all-important difference between such things as snow and such things as cats lay in the fact that different instances of snow are, in a sense, indefinitely additive, can be counted together as one instance of snow; while this is not true in the case of instances of cats; and it might be suggested that herein lay a reason for the possibility of feature-placing sentences in the case of snow and for their impossibility in the case of cats. And (2) it might be added that we have no name for a general thing which could count as the required feature in the case of cats. It is true that we speak of *the cat* in general; but "the cat" ranks as a species-name, and the notion of a species as surely presupposes the notion of individual members as the notion of a property involves that of individual things to which the property belongs or might belong. It is also true that we may speak of an instance (specimen) of *a* cat, as we may speak of an instance of gold; but here what follows the phrase "an instance of" is not, as "gold" is, a general-thing name which could figure in a merely feature-placing sentence, but an expression which also serves as an indefinite designation of an individual. Does not all this strongly suggest that there *could* be no concept of the "cat-feature" such as would be required for the analysis to work, that any general idea of cat must be the idea of *a* cat, i.e., must involve criteria of identity and distinctness for cats as individuals and hence the notion of an individual instance?

These objections have great force and importance; but I do not think them decisive. For they do not show that it is logically absurd to suppose that we might recognise the presence of cat or signs of the past or future presence of cat, without ever having occasion to distinguish one cat from another as the cat on the left, or identify a cat as ours or as Felix.[8] The second argument merely reminds us that the resources of our language are such that on any actual occasion of this kind we in fact use, not a partitive noun, but the indefinite forms ("cats" or "a cat") of the articulative noun. But this fact can be explained in a way consistent with the advocated analysis (see section 10). Nevertheless, these arguments show something. The point about the species-name, for example, is sound; the notion of a species, like that of a property, belongs to a level of logical complexity we are trying to get

below. Second, and more immediately important, the first argument shows that if there is to be a general concept of the cat-feature, corresponding in the required way to the notion of an individual instance, it must already include in itself the *basis* for the criteria of *distinctness* which we apply to individual cats. (Roughly, the idea of cat, unlike that of snow, would include the idea of a characteristic shape). But to concede this is not to concede the impossibility of the analysis. It is worth adding that sometimes we do find verbal indications of our use of feature-concepts such as those we are trying to envisage; as, e.g., when we speak of "smelling cat" or "hunting lion," using the noun in the singular without the article.

There might seem to exist a more general objection to this whole procedure. For it seems that it would always be possible in practice to paraphrase a given feature-placing sentence in use, by means of a sentence incorporating *indefinite* designations of particular instances; e.g., "There is gold here" by "There is *a quantity of* gold here"; "Snow has fallen twice" by "There have been *two falls of* snow"; "There is snow here – and here" by "There are *patches* (*expanses*) *of* snow here and here"; and so on. And if sentences incorporating definite *or* indefinite designations of particular instances bring particulars into our discourse; and if statements made by the use of feature-placing sentences are *equivalent* to statements made by the use of sentences incorporating indefinite designations of particular instances; then do not feature-placing sentences themselves bring particulars into our discourse? But this argument can be turned in favour of the explanation it is directed against. Suppose there is a statement S made by means of a feature-placing sentence; and an equivalent statement S′ made by means of a sentence incorporating an indefinite particular-designation; and a statement T made by means of a sentence incorporating a definite designation of the particular indefinitely designated in S′. *Now only if a language admits of statements like T can it admit of statements correctly described as I have described S′.* (There are no *indefinite* designations of particulars where there are no *definite* designations of particulars.) But a language might admit of statements like S without admitting of statements like T. So the existence of statements like S′, in a language which admits of both statements like S and statements like T, is not destructive of the analysis, but is a proof of its correctness.

8. If the argument so far is acceptable, then at least in the case of some materials and some substances, we can regard the notion of an individual instance as partially explained in terms of the logical composition of the two notions of a feature and of placing. When we turn to properties and qualities, we may make use of a different kind of explanation which is also, in a sense, the completion of the first kind. I shall not, that is to say, try to explain the notion of individual instances of anger or wisdom or red in terms of the logical composition of a feature, such as *anger* or *red*, and placing. But nor shall I maintain that it would be wrong or impossible to do so. We *might* think of such general things as anger (or red) *not* primarily as qualities, properties, states or conditions of persons or things, but primarily as instantiated in, say, situations (or patches) which acquired their status as individuals from just such a logical composition. But though this is how we might think, it is not, for the most part, how we do think. It is natural, rather, to regard those general things which are properly called qualities, conditions, etc., as belonging at least to the same level of logical complexity as the idea of individual instances of the kinds we have so far been concerned with; to regard them, that is, as feature-*like* things, the incidence of which, however, is primarily indicated, not by placing, but by their *ascription* to individual instances of material or substantial features the incidence of which *is* primarily indicated by placing.[9] We have seen that the notion of an individual instance of some materials and substances can be regarded as a logical compound of the notions of a feature and of placing. We have now to see the ascription of a quality (etc.) to such an individual as an operation *analogous* to the placing of a feature. Indeed, we may find in the possibility of this operation the point – or one important point – of that logical composition which yields us the particular. The individual instance of the simply placeable feature emerges as a possible location-point for general things other than the feature of which it is primarily an instance, and hence as also an individual instance of *these* general things, its properties or qualities or states. One might exaggeratedly say: the *point* of having the idea of individual instances of material or substantial features is that they may be represented as individual instances of property-like features. The individuals are distinguished as individuals in order to be contrasted and compared.

Other notions call for other treatment. I consider two more.

(a) I mentioned, at 4(iii), a rather special class of individual instances of properties or property-like things. We form the notion of such an instance when, for example, we speak not of a man or an action as an instance of wisdom or anger, but of the wisdom of Socrates as an individual (a case of wisdom) or of Jones' present mental state as an individual instance of anger. Here the notion of the individual instance can be seen as a new kind of logical compound, namely, a compound which includes as elements both the notion of the general thing (property) in question and that of the material or substantial individual which is an instance of it; it may sometimes include a further element of temporal placing (cf. "his *present* state of anger").

(b) Instances of events, processes and changes I have so far scarcely mentioned. Most of our most familiar words for happenings strike us essentially as names for the actions and undergoings of individual instances of material or substantial features. But there is a difference between these happening words and quality or state-words. A wise man is an instance of wisdom, but a dead or dying man is not an instance of death. Only a death is that. As regards such happening-words as these, then, we have to see the idea of an individual instance as reached by a kind of logical composition analogous to that considered in the paragraph immediately above: an individual instance of a material or substantial feature is an element in the compound. But these, though perhaps the most important, are not the only kinds of happening-words.

9. The general form of these explanations may be roughly indicated as follows. The notion of placing a feature is taken as basic, as consisting of the logically simplest elements with which we are to operate. It is pointed out that neither of these elements involves the notion of an individual instance, nor therefore the notions of certain types of general things, such as properties and species; and it is shown that the idea of operating solely with these simplest elements can be made intelligible for certain cases. (Features in fact of course belong to the class of general things; but so long as we remain at the feature-placing level, they cannot be assigned to it; for there is nothing to contrast the general with.) From this basis we proceed by composition and

analogy. The designations of individual instances of (some) material and substantial features are first introduced, as expressions, not themselves complete sentences, which include placing-indications; and, complementarily, certain types of general things (e.g., properties and types of happening) are introduced as items the designations of which do not include placing-indications and which are ascribed to material or substantial individuals. The ascription of such a thing as a property to a substantial individual is represented simply as an operation analogous to the placing of a feature; so no circularity attends the word "ascription." Individuals of certain other types (e.g., events happening to substances, states of substances and "particularised" qualities) are then introduced as the designata of expressions which include the designations of individuals of earlier types, and hence indirectly include the notion of placing.

There are many types of individual and of general thing besides these here considered. Some may admit of analogous treatment; and it might be possible to introduce others, on the basis already provided, by other methods of construction and explanation. But every introduction of a particular, in terms of such a schema, will either directly contain the notion of placing or will preserve, by way of individuals already introduced, the original link with this notion. Of course the value of this suggestion, as it stands, is small. For the notion of an individual instance extends itself indefinitely, by way of far more complicated connexions than I have so far indicated; and the limits of plausibility for the kinds of construction-procedure I have used would, no doubt, soon be reached, if they are not already overpassed. Nevertheless, I think this sketch of a procedure has certain merits:

(1)   Some of the difficulties which attend any attempt to elucidate the category-distinction between the particular and the general arise from the fact that these two classes include so many different category-distinctions within themselves. This fact creates a dilemma for the theorist of the distinction. On the one hand, he is tempted, in a way illustrated at the beginning of this paper, into drawing distinctions which indeed separate one or more sub-categories of one class from one or more sub-categories of the other, but which fail to yield the desired result if applied over the whole field. Or, on the other hand, in the effort to escape from this domination by

irrelevant category differences, he is tempted by the prospect of a purely formal distinction, drawing for this purpose on the terms and concepts of grammar or of formal logic. But distinctions so drawn can only seem to succeed by forfeiting their formal character and silently incorporating the problematic category-distinction. The present procedure offers at least a hope of escape from this difficulty. For it fully allows for the differences between types of general thing and of individual; and instead of producing one single explanation, the same for every case, it offers a serial method of explaining later types of general or particular things on the basis of earlier ones, while preserving a continuous general differentiation between the two major categories in the course of the explanation. Too much must not be claimed for the suggested procedure, however; in particular, it must not be thought that it has been so described as to provide a *criterion* for the distinction we are concerned with.

(2)   Another characteristic of the schema of explanation is that it accords a central place to the notion of an individual instance of certain kinds of general things, viz., of material and substantial features. This (see section 8) is not an essential characteristic; it could be modified. But there is reason to think that it corresponds to our actual way of thinking; that these individuals *are* the "basic particulars." Why this should be so, and whether it might not be otherwise, are questions which I shall not now consider.

(3)   Finally, while not itself providing a criterion of general and particular, the schema points the way to a possible general distinction which might be defensible even if the procedure which suggests it should prove unsatisfactory. This general distinction I shall outline in section 12. Before I do so, some further points remain to be considered.

10.   Something further must first be said on the subject of criteria of identity for individual instances of a general thing. We saw (5(2)) how in many cases the question of the criteria of distinctness and identity of an individual instance of a general thing was incompletely determined when the general thing was named. This was particularly evident in the case of some properties and was evident also in the case of materials. Where substance-names were concerned, however, this indeterminateness seemed not to exist; when the name was given, the criteria were fixed.

And this was connected with the fact that in these cases there seemed to exist no true general-thing name, apart from expressions which ranked as species-names and obviously presupposed certain definite criteria of identity for individual members. As far as criteria of distinctness are concerned, this raises no particular difficulty. We saw, for example, how the idea of a simply placeable feature might include – might indeed *be* – the idea of a characteristic shape, and in this way provide a basis for criteria of distinctness for individual instances of the feature. But it is not so easy to account for the apparent determinateness of criteria of identity. The explanatory schema advanced required that we should theoretically be able to form concepts of some substance-features which were logically prior to, and independent of, the corresponding concepts of an individual instance of such features; and this requirement seems to clash with the apparent determinateness of the criteria of identity for such individuals. A parallel answer to that given in the case of criteria of distinctness is theoretically available, but is unattractively unplausible. If we reject this answer, and cannot find an alternative, then we must at least radically revise, though in a not unfamiliar direction, the basis of the explanatory schema. (The difficulty is essentially a more specific form of that encountered already in section 7.)

I think, however, that an acceptable alternative can be found. For in all cases where a feature-concept can be assumed to be possible, the criteria of identity (and of distinctness) for an instance of the general thing in question – or the sets of such criteria, where there is more than one set – can be seen as determined by a *combination* of factors, viz., the nature of the feature itself, the ways in which the feature empirically manifests itself in the world, and – to adopt a possibly misleading mode of expression – the kind of incentives[10] that exist for having a notion of an individual instance of the feature in question. The relevance of this third factor even, perhaps, gives us the right to say that there is something arbitrary about the criteria we adopt, something which, given the other two factors, is – in at any rate a stretched sense – a matter of choice. In extreme cases this is obvious. Even those who had witnessed the whole of the affair under discussion might, for example, give varying answers to such a question as: Is this the same quarrel going on now as was going on when I left? The

answer we choose may depend on just what distinctions we are interested in; and one can imagine many situations for this example, and many different things which might influence us. There may, on the other hand, be very many cases of features where the adoption of a certain particular set of criteria of identity (and distinctness) for their instances is so utterly natural that it would seem to be stretching the phrase "matter of choice" intolerably to apply it to them. But, even in these cases, the naturalness may still be seen as depending on the combination of factors I mentioned; and, if we bear this in mind, we can sometimes imagine the possibility of alternatives. (Here is a question which might with advantage be explored for many different types of case.)

It seems reasonable to view substantial features as cases of this kind. If this view is acceptable, we can find in it an explanation of that difference between substance-names and certain other true general-thing names to which I have several times referred. Given a true general-thing name, like "gold" or "wisdom," the question of the criteria of identity of its instances cannot be answered until the kind of instance is specified, by such a phrase as "a *piece* of gold" or "a wise *action*". But where one set of criteria of identity is peculiarly dominant, its adoption peculiarly compelling, we find no such non-committal general name in current, adult, unsophisticated use. All that we might wish to do with it, we can equally well do without it, by the use of the indefinite singular or plural forms of the ordinary substance-name (e.g., "a horse" or "horses").

11. It is, perhaps, necessary to guard briefly against a misunderstanding. Of course, I am not denying that we can very well use individual-designations as such without being, or ever having been, in a position to make a relevant placing of some feature which, in terms of the explanatory schema I have defended, is immediately or ultimately relevant to the explanation of the type of instance concerned. To deny this would be absurd. It would be to deny, for example, that when we talk about remoter historical characters, we are really talking about individuals. But the view I am defending does not require such a denial. For this view seeks merely to explain the notion of an individual instance of a general thing in terms, ultimately, of feature-placing. It does not at all imply that we cannot make use of this notion in situations other than those in terms

P. F. Strawson

of which it is explained. In fact, of course, the expansiveness of our talk about individuals is in marked contrast with the restrictedness of our contacts with them. Both the possibility of, and the incentives to, this expansiveness have an empirical ground; in the variousness of individuals, the non-repetitiveness of situations. But this fact may nevertheless mislead us, may make the theoretical problem of individuation look more difficult than it is by distracting our attention from an essential element in the notion of an individual instance. The problem would scarcely seem difficult for the case of an imagined universe in which all that happened was the repetition of a single note, varying, perhaps, in volume. Individual instances could then be described only as, say, "the third before now" or "the next one to come". But in such a universe the incentives to forming the notion of an individual instance would be small. We might say that, in general, what is essential to the notion of an individual instance is not what is interesting about individuals.

12. To conclude. I remarked earlier that the explanatory schema I have sketched points the way to a possible general distinction between the two major categories we are concerned with. To recall, first, some vague, figurative and unsatisfactory terms I have already used: the schema suggests that the notion of a particular individual always includes, directly or indirectly, that of placing, whereas the notion of a general thing does not. Now placing is characteristically effected by the use of expressions the *reference* of which is in part determined by the context of their use and not by their *meaning*, if any, alone. And this suggests the possibility of formulating a general distinction in a more satisfactory way. We may say: *it is a necessary condition for a thing's being a general thing that it can be referred to by a singular substantival expression, a unique reference for which is determined solely by the meaning of the words making up that expression; and it is a necessary condition of a thing's being a particular thing that it cannot be referred to by a singular substantival expression, a unique reference for which is determined solely by the meaning of the words making up that expression.* This specification of mutually exclusive necessary conditions could be made to yield definitions by stipulating that the conditions were not only necessary, but also sufficient. But there is point in refraining from doing so. For as we consider substantival expressions increas-

ingly remote from the simplest cases, there may be increasing reluctance to apply the distinction at all. Nor is this reluctance quite irrational; for the simplest cases are those which form the basis of the general distinction. (Hence, roughly, the association of particularity with concreteness.) We may admit that the traditional distinction was vague as well as unclear, and respect its well-founded vagueness in this way.

To elucidate this quasi-definition of particular and general, I add some miscellaneous comments of varying degrees of importance.

(1) It might be objected to the conditions given that expressions like "The third tallest man who ever lived or lives or will live" answer to the specifications for a general-thing designation. If they did, it would perhaps not be difficult to legislate them out, by suitable amendments of those specifications. But in fact they do not. For their meaning does not suffice to determine for them a unique object of reference. It is, if true, contingently true that there is a single thing answering to such a description. This case, however, does raise a problem about how the words "expression a unique reference for which is determined solely by the meaning" are to be construed. If we construe them as "expression the *existence* of just one object of reference for which is *guaranteed* by the meaning," we may find ourselves in (possibly circumventable) trouble over, e.g., "phlogiston" and "the unicorn." Yes this is the construction at first suggested by the present case.[11] It will be better, therefore, to construe them as follows: "expression the (or a) meaning of which is such that it is both logically impossible for it to refer to more than one thing (in that meaning)[12] and logically impossible for the expression to fail to have reference because of the existence of competing candidates for the title." And the sense of "competing candidates" can be explained as follows: x, y and z are competing candidates (and the only competing candidates) for the title D if, if any two of them had not existed, D would apply to the third.

(2) It may seem, perhaps, a more troublesome fact that the names we commonly employ for certain *types*, like Beethoven's Fifth Symphony, do not answer to the specifications given for a general-thing designation, although we may be more than half inclined to count such types as general things; for these names include, as a part of themselves or of their explanation, proper names like "Beethoven." We have, however, an

132

easy remedy here. We can regard the pattern of sounds in question as a general thing for which there might (perhaps does) exist a general description the meaning of which uniquely determines its reference; and then it will appear as the contingent truth it is that Beethoven stands to the general thing so designated in a certain special relation. This does not commit us to saying that it is a contingent truth that Beethoven's Fifth Symphony was composed by Beethoven; but the necessity here is simply a consequence of the fact that we ordinarily and naturally refer to the general thing in question by means of an expression which incorporates a reference to a particular individual who stands in a special relation to it. Analogous considerations apply to many other types. Of course, the alternative is always open to us of declining to apply the criterion in such cases.

(3) It is clear that numbers, if we apply our criterion to them, will emerge as general things. But this is a result which will disturb few, and will certainly disturb no one who continues to feel the charm of the class-of-classes analysis.

(4) If we choose to apply the test to facts, we get the not wholly unappealing result that, e.g., the facts that $2 + 2 = 4$, that all crows are black and that crows exist (in one use of "exist") are general things, while the facts that Brutus killed Caesar and that all the people in this room are philosophers are particular things. For propositions, of course, the result is similar. The distinction will correspond roughly to the old distinction between those propositions (or facts) which are "truly universal" and those which are not. In the case of facts and propositions, however, we may well feel a *very* strong reluctance to classify in this way at all; and, if we do, there is no reason why we should struggle to overcome it.[13]

Some points of more general significance remain.

(5) As historical evidence for the general correctness of this doctrine, we may note that Russell who, for so large a part of his philosophical life, showed an anxiety to equate meaning and reference in the case of *names*, finally inclined to the conclusion that the only true names are those of universals.[14] We do not, of course, need to adopt his idiosyncratic use of the word "name," in acknowledging the correctness of his implied view of universals.

(6) It will be clear that the quasi-definition I am suggesting has points of contact with some of those more familiar ways of marking the distinction which turn out to be more or less unsatisfactory. For instance, it will not do to say that general things do not have spatio-temporal positions and limits, whereas particular things do. Some general things, those of appropriate categories, like gold, do have spatial distribution; and some may have temporal limits. It is rather that when we refer to general things, we abstract from their actual distribution and limits, if they have any, as we cannot do when we refer to particulars. Hence, with general things, meaning suffices to determine reference. And with this is connected the tendency, on the whole dominant, to ascribe superior reality to particular things. Meaning is not enough, in their case, to determine the reference of their designations; the extra, contextual element is essential. They are, in a quite precise sense, less abstract; and we are, on the whole, so constituted as to count the less abstract as the more real.

(7) Finally, we may, if we choose, revert to the original philosophical way of marking the distinction in terms of the concept of an instance, and give it a sense in terms of the final definition. Instantiability, in the philosophers' sense, ends precisely at the point at which contextual dependence of referring expressions begins, or where referring expressions, as being proper names of individuals, have meaning only in a sense in which it is altogether divorced from reference. So general things may have instances, while particular things may not.

Notes

I am much indebted to Mr. H. P. Grice for his criticisms of an earlier version of this paper; and I owe much to the stimulus of an unpublished paper by Mr. Michael Dummett. For the errors and obscurities which remain in the present paper I am alone responsible.

1 F. P. Ramsey, *Foundations of Mathematics*, ed. R. B. Braithwaite (London: Routledge and Kegan Paul, 1931), pp. 112–34.
2 A. J. Ayer, "Individuals", *Mind* 41 (1952).
3 To the second question Ayer's answer was affirmative; and, things being as they are, this is no doubt

correct as a matter of what is theoretically practicable. Ayer also acknowledges (a) that in actual practice we could scarcely dispense with indicator words, and (b) that the attempt to do so would always involve a theoretical failure to individuate, since no elaboration of predicates rules out the theoretical possibility of reduplication. But I doubt if the original question can be answered unless we take these two facts more seriously than he does.

4   But a game of chess *may* be something which itself has instances.

5   Ramsey seems to suggest that this would simply be to manufacture an empty verbal distinction. (Cf. *Foundations of Mathematics*, pp. 132–3.) But it would not. For it would not be an arbitrary matter to decide which names to put on which side of the coupling phrase.

6   The terminology, evidently, is not to be taken too seriously. Anger is a state, not a property or quality.

7   It might be true, if intelligible, that *if* we had so time-indifferent a perspective of things as to see them as four-dimensional objects in space-time, then there would be no point in giving separate consideration to criteria of distinctness. But we do not have such a perspective.

8   Cf. H. H. Price, *Thinking and Experience* (London and New York: Hutchinson's University Library, 1953), pp. 40–1, on identity of individuals and of characteristics.

9   These remarks, of course, apply only to some of the things correctly called properties, states, qualities, etc.

10   What I mean by "incentives" here may be illustrated from the convenience of the institution of property. Suppose there is a general feature, ϕ, which human beings wish to make use of. Even if there is enough ϕ for all, friction may be avoided if criteria are used for distinguishing my ϕ from yours. ("Mine" is indeed one of the earliest individuating words used by children.)

11   This difficulty was pointed out to me by Mr. H. P. Grice.

12   This qualification allows for the possible case where there is no convenient unambiguous designation of the general thing in question; but is not strictly necessary since an unambiguous designation could always be framed.

13   What I have said here of facts and propositions must not lead us to suppose that we should obtain a similar result for *sentences*. These, and expression-*types* generally, will emerge as general things (e.g., in virtue of the conventions for the use of inverted commas, the expression "the word 'and'" may be said to determine, by meaning alone, a unique object of reference).

14   See *Inquiry into Meaning and Truth* (London: George Allen & Unwin, 1940) and *Human Knowledge: Its Scope and Limits* (London: George Allen & Unwin, 1948).

12

On What There Is

W. V. Quine

A curious thing about the ontological problem is its simplicity. It can be put in three Anglo-Saxon monosyllables: 'What is there?' It can be answered, moreover, in a word – 'Everything' – and everyone will accept this answer as true. However, this is merely to say that there is what there is. There remains room for disagreement over cases; and so the issue has stayed alive down the centuries.

Suppose now that two philosophers, McX and I, differ over ontology. Suppose McX maintains there is something which I maintain there is not. McX can, quite consistently with his own point of view, describe our difference of opinion by saying that I refuse to recognize certain entities. I should protest, of course, that he is wrong in his formulation of our disagreement, for I maintain that there are no entities, of the kind which he alleges, for me to recognize; but my finding him wrong in his formulation of our disagreement is unimportant, for I am committed to considering him wrong in his ontology anyway.

When *I* try to formulate our difference of opinion, on the other hand, I seem to be in a predicament. I cannot admit that there are some things which McX countenances and I do not, for in admitting that there are such things I should be contradicting my own rejection of them.

It would appear, if this reasoning were sound, that in any ontological dispute the proponent of

Originally published in *Review of Metaphysics* 2/1 (1948).

the negative side suffers the disadvantage of not being able to admit that his opponent disagrees with him.

This is the old Platonic riddle of nonbeing. Nonbeing must in some sense be, otherwise what is it that there is not? This tangled doctrine might be nicknamed *Plato's beard*; historically it has proved tough, frequently dulling the edge of Occam's razor.

It is some such line of thought that leads philosophers like McX to impute being where they might otherwise be quite content to recognize that there is nothing. Thus, take Pegasus. If Pegasus *were* not, McX argues, we should not be talking about anything when we use the word; therefore it would be nonsense to say even that Pegasus is not. Thinking to show thus that the denial of Pegasus cannot be coherently maintained, he concludes that Pegasus is.

McX cannot, indeed, quite persuade himself that any region of space-time, near or remote, contains a flying horse of flesh and blood. Pressed for further details on Pegasus, then, he says that Pegasus is an idea in men's minds. Here, however, a confusion begins to be apparent. We may for the sake of argument concede that there is an entity, and even a unique entity (though this is rather implausible), which is the mental Pegasus-idea; but this mental entity is not what people are talking about when they deny Pegasus.

McX never confuses the Parthenon with the Parthenon-idea. The Parthenon is physical; the Parthenon-idea is mental (according anyway to McX's version of ideas, and I have no better to offer). The Parthenon is visible; the Parthenon-idea is invisible. We cannot easily imagine two things more unlike, and less liable to confusion, than the Parthenon and the Parthenon-idea. But when we shift from the Parthenon to Pegasus, the confusion sets in – for no other reason than that McX would sooner be deceived by the crudest and most flagrant counterfeit than grant the nonbeing of Pegasus.

The notion that Pegasus must be, because it would otherwise be nonsense to say even that Pegasus is not, has been seen to lead McX into an elementary confusion. Subtler minds, taking the same precept as their starting point, come out with theories of Pegasus which are less patently misguided than McX's, and correspondingly more difficult to eradicate. One of these subtler minds is named, let us say, Wyman. Pegasus, Wyman maintains, has his being as an unactualized possible. When we say of Pegasus that there is no such thing, we are saying, more precisely, that Pegasus does not have the special attribute of actuality. Saying that Pegasus is not actual is on a par, logically, with saying that the Parthenon is not red; in either case we are saying something about an entity whose being is unquestioned.

Wyman, by the way, is one of those philosophers who have united in ruining the good old word 'exist'. Despite his espousal of unactualized possibles, he limits the word 'existence' to actuality – thus preserving an illusion of ontological agreement between himself and us who repudiate the rest of his bloated universe. We have all been prone to say, in our common-sense usage of 'exist', that Pegasus does not exist, meaning simply that there is no such entity at all. If Pegasus existed he would indeed be in space and time, but only because the word 'Pegasus' has spatio-temporal connotations, and not because 'exists' has spatio-temporal connotations. If spatio-temporal reference is lacking when we affirm the existence of the cube root of 27, this is simply because a cube root is not a spatio-temporal kind of thing, and not because we are being ambiguous in our use of 'exist'.[1] However, Wyman, in an ill-conceived effort to appear agreeable, genially grants us the nonexistence of Pegasus and then, contrary to what *we* meant by nonexistence of Pegasus, insists that Pegasus *is*. Existence is one thing, he says, and subsistence is another. The only way I know of coping with this obfuscation of issues is to *give* Wyman the word 'exist'. I'll try not to use it again; I still have 'is'. So

much for lexicography; let's get back to Wyman's ontology.

Wyman's overpopulated universe is in many ways unlovely. It offends the aesthetic sense of us who have a taste for desert landscapes, but this is not the worst of it. Wyman's slum of possibles is a breeding ground for disorderly elements. Take, for instance, the possible fat man in that doorway; and, again, the possible bald man in that doorway. Are they the same possible man, or two possible men? How do we decide? How many possible men are there in that doorway? Are there more possible thin ones than fat ones? How many of them are alike? Or would their being alike make them one? Are no *two* possible things alike? Is this the same as saying that it is impossible for two things to be alike? Or, finally, is the concept of identity simply inapplicable to unactualized possibles? But what sense can be found in talking of entities which cannot meaningfully be said to be identical with themselves and distinct from one another? These elements are well-nigh incorrigible. By a Fregean therapy of individual concepts, some effort might be made at rehabilitation; but I feel we'd do better simply to clear Wyman's slum and be done with it.

Possibility, along with the other modalities of necessity and impossibility and contingency, raises problems upon which I do not mean to imply that we should turn our backs. But we can at least limit modalities to whole statements. We may impose the adverb 'possibly' upon a statement as a whole, and we may well worry about the semantical analysis of such usage; but little real advance in such analysis is to be hoped for in expanding our universe to include so-called *possible entities*. I suspect that the main motive for this expansion is simply the old notion that Pegasus, for example, must be because otherwise it would be nonsense to say even that he is not.

Still, all the rank luxuriance of Wyman's universe of possibles would seem to come to naught when we make a slight change in the example and speak not of Pegasus but of the round square cupola on Berkeley College. If, unless Pegasus were, it would be nonsense to say that he is not, then by the same token, unless the round square cupola on Berkeley College were, it would be nonsense to say that it is not. But, unlike Pegasus, the round square cupola on Berkeley College cannot be admitted even as an unactualized *possible*. Can we drive Wyman now to admitting also a realm of unactualizable impossibles? If so, a good many embarrassing questions could be asked about them. We might hope even to trap Wyman in contradictions, by getting him to admit that certain of these entities are at once round and square. But the wily Wyman chooses the other horn of the dilemma and concedes that it is nonsense to say that the round square cupola on Berkeley College is not. He says that the phrase 'round square cupola' is meaningless.

Wyman was not the first to embrace this alternative. The doctrine of the meaninglessness of contradictions runs away back. The tradition survives, moreover, in writers who seem to share none of Wyman's motivations. Still, I wonder whether the first temptation to such a doctrine may not have been substantially the motivation which we have observed in Wyman. Certainly the doctrine has no intrinsic appeal; and it has led its devotees to such quixotic extremes as that of challenging the method of proof by *reductio ad absurdum* – a challenge in which I sense a *reductio ad absurdum* of the doctrine itself.

Moreover, the doctrine of meaninglessness of contradictions has the severe methodological drawback that it makes it impossible, in principle, ever to devise an effective test of what is meaningful and what is not. It would be forever impossible for us to devise systematic ways of deciding whether a string of signs made sense – even to us individually, let alone other people – or not. For it follows from a discovery in mathematical logic, due to Church,[2] that there can be no generally applicable test of contradictoriness.

I have spoken disparagingly of Plato's beard, and hinted that it is tangled. I have dwelt at length on the inconveniences of putting up with it. It is time to think about taking steps.

Russell, in his theory of so-called singular descriptions, showed clearly how we might meaningfully use seeming names without supposing that there be the entities allegedly named. The names to which Russell's theory directly applies are complex descriptive names such as 'the author of *Waverley*', 'the present King of France', 'the round square cupola on Berkeley College'. Russell analyzes such phrases systematically as fragments of the whole sentences in which they occur. The sentence 'The author of *Waverley* was a poet', for example, is explained as a whole as meaning 'Someone (better: something) wrote *Waverley* and was a poet, and nothing else wrote *Waverley*'. (The point of this added clause is to affirm the uniqueness which is implicit in the word 'the', in '*the* author of *Waverley*'.) The sentence 'The round square cupola on Berkeley College is pink' is explained as 'Something is round and square and is a cupola on Berkeley College and is pink, and nothing else is round and square and a cupola on Berkeley College'.

The virtue of this analysis is that the seeming name, a descriptive phrase, is paraphrased *in context* as a so-called incomplete symbol. No unified expression is offered as an analysis of the descriptive phrase, but the statement as a whole which was the context of that phrase still gets its full quota of meaning – whether true or false.

The unanalyzed statement 'The author of *Waverley* was a poet' contains a part, 'the author of *Waverley*', which is wrongly supposed by McX and Wyman to demand objective reference in order to be meaningful at all. But in Russell's translation, 'Something wrote *Waverley* and was a poet and nothing else wrote *Waverley*', the burden of objective reference which had been put upon the descriptive phrase is now taken over by words of the kind that logicians call bound variables, variables of quantification: namely, words like 'something', 'nothing', 'everything'. These words, far from purporting to be names specifically of the author of *Waverley*, do not purport to be names at all; they refer to entities generally, with a kind of studied ambiguity peculiar to themselves. These quantificational words or bound variables are, of course a basic part of language, and their meaningfulness, at least in context, is not to be challenged. But their meaningfulness in no way presupposes there being either the author of *Waverley* or the round square cupola on Berkeley College or any other specifically preassigned objects.

Where descriptions are concerned, there is no longer any difficulty in affirming or denying being. 'There *is* the author of *Waverley*' is explained by Russell as meaning 'Someone (or, more strictly, something) wrote *Waverley* and nothing else wrote *Waverley*'. 'The author of *Waverley* is not' is explained, correspondingly, as the alternation 'Either each thing failed to write *Waverley* or two or more things wrote *Waverley*'. This alternation is false, but meaningful; and it contains no expression purporting to name the author of *Waverley*. The statement 'The round square cupola on Berkeley College is not' is analyzed in similar fashion. So the old notion that statements of nonbeing defeat themselves goes by the board. When a statement of being or nonbeing

W. V. Quine

is analyzed by Russell's theory of descriptions, it ceases to contain any expression which even purports to name the alleged entity whose being is in question, so that the meaningfulness of the statement no longer can be thought to presuppose that there be such an entity.

Now what of 'Pegasus'? This being a word rather than a descriptive phrase, Russell's argument does not immediately apply to it. However, it can easily be made to apply. We have only to rephrase 'Pegasus' as a description, in any way that seems adequately to single out our idea; say, 'the winged horse that was captured by Bellerophon'. Substituting such as phrase for 'Pegasus', we can then proceed to analyze the statement 'Pegasus is', or 'Pegasus is not', precisely on the analogy of Russell's analysis of 'The author of *Waverley* is' and 'The author of *Waverley* is not'.

In order thus to subsume a one-word name or alleged name such as 'Pegasus' under Russell's theory of description, we must, of course, be able first to translate the word into a description. But this is no real restriction. If the notion of Pegasus had been so obscure or so basic a one that no pat translation into a descriptive phrase had offered itself along familiar lines, we could still have availed ourselves of the following artificial and trivial-seeming device: we could have appealed to the *ex hypothesi* unanalyzable, irreducible attribute of *being Pegasus*, adopting, for its expression, the verb 'is-Pegasus', or 'pegasizes'. The noun 'Pegasus' itself could then be treated as derivative, and identified after all with a description: 'the thing that is-Pegasus', 'the thing that pegasizes'.

If the importing of such a predicate as 'pegasizes' seems to commit us to recognizing that there is a corresponding attribute, pegasizing, in Plato's heaven or in the minds of men, well and good. Neither we nor Wyman nor McX have been contending, thus far, about the being or nonbeing of universals, but rather about that of Pegasus. If in terms of pegasizing we can interpret the noun 'Pegasus' as a description subject to Russell's theory of descriptions, then we have disposed of the old notion that Pegasus cannot be said not to be without presupposing that in some sense Pegasus is.

Our argument is now quite general. McX and Wyman supposed that we could not meaningfully affirm a statement of the form 'So-and-so is not', with a simple or descriptive singular noun in place of 'so-and-so', unless so-and-so is.

This supposition is now seen to be quite generally groundless, since the singular noun in question can always be expanded into a singular description, trivially or otherwise, and then analyzed out *à la* Russell.

We commit ourselves to an ontology containing numbers when we say there are prime numbers larger than a million; we commit ourselves to an ontology containing centaurs when we say there are centaurs; and we commit ourselves to an ontology containing Pegasus when we say Pegasus is. But we do not commit ourselves to an ontology containing Pegasus or the author of *Waverley* or the round square cupola on Berkeley College when we say that Pegasus or the author of *Waverley* or the cupola in question is *not*. We need no longer labor under the delusion that the meaningfulness of a statement containing a singular term presupposes an entity named by the term. A singular term need not name to be significant.

An inkling of this might have dawned on Wyman and McX even without benefit of Russell if they had only noticed – as so few of us do – that there is a gulf between *meaning* and *naming* even in the case of a singular term which is genuinely a name of an object. The following example from Frege will serve.[3] The phrase 'Evening Star' names a certain large physical object of spherical form, which is hurtling through space some scores of millions of miles from here. The phrase 'Morning Star' names the same thing, as was probably first established by some observant Babylonian. But the two phrases cannot be regarded as having the same meaning; otherwise that Babylonian could have dispensed with his observations and contented himself with reflecting on the meanings of his words. The meanings, then, being different from one another, must be other than the named object, which is one and the same in both cases.

Confusion of meaning with naming not only made McX think he could not meaningfully repudiate Pegasus; a continuing confusion of meaning with naming no doubt helped engender his absurd notion that Pegasus is an idea, a mental entity. The structure of his confusion is as follows. He confused the alleged *named object* Pegasus with the *meaning* of the word 'Pegasus', therefore concluding that Pegasus must be in order that the word have meaning. But what sorts of things are meanings? This is a moot point; however, one might quite plausibly explain meanings as ideas in the mind, supposing we can make clear sense in turn of the idea of ideas in the mind. Therefore Pegasus, initially confused with a meaning, ends up as an idea in the mind. It is the more remarkable that Wyman, subject to the same initial motivation as McX, should have avoided this particular blunder and wound up with unactualized possibles instead.

Now let us turn to the ontological problem of universals: the question whether there are such entities as attributes, relations, classes, numbers, functions. McX, characteristically enough, thinks there are. Speaking of attributes, he says: 'There are red houses, red roses, red sunsets; this much is prephilosophical common sense in which we must all agree. These houses, roses, and sunsets, then, have something in common; and this which they have in common is all I mean by the attribute of redness.' For McX, thus, there being attributes is even more obvious and trivial than the obvious and trivial fact of there being red houses, roses, and sunsets. This, I think, is characteristic of metaphysics, or at least of that part of metaphysics called ontology: one who regards a statement on this subject as true at all must regard it as trivially true. One's ontology is basic to the conceptual scheme by which he interprets all experiences, even the most commonplace ones. Judged within some particular conceptual scheme – and how else is judgment possible? – an ontological statement goes without saying, standing in need of no separate justification at all. Ontological statements follow immediately from all manner of casual statements of commonplace fact, just as – from the point of view, anyway, of McX's conceptual scheme – 'There is an attribute' follows from 'There are red houses, red roses, red sunsets'.

Judged in another conceptual scheme, an ontological statement which is axiomatic to McX's mind may, with equal immediacy and triviality, be adjudged false. One may admit that there are red houses, roses, and sunsets, but deny, except as a popular and misleading manner of speaking, that they have anything in common. The words 'houses', 'roses', and 'sunsets' are true of sundry individual entities which are houses and roses and sunsets, and the word 'red' or 'red object' is true of each of sundry individual entities which are red houses, red roses, red sunsets; but there is not, in addition, any entity whatever, individual or otherwise, which is named by the word 'redness', nor, for that matter, by the word 'househood', 'rosehood', 'sunsethood'. That the

houses and roses and sunsets are all of them red may be taken as ultimate and irreducible, and it may be held that McX is no better off, in point of real explanatory power, for all the occult entities which he posits under such names as 'redness'.

One means by which McX might naturally have tried to impose his ontology of universals on us was already removed before we turned to the problem of universals. McX cannot argue that predicates such as 'red' or 'is-red', which we all concur in using, must be regarded as names each of a single universal entity in order that they be meaningful at all. For we have seen that being a name of something is a much more special feature than being meaningful. He cannot even charge us – at least not by *that* argument – with having posited an attribute of pegasizing by our adoption of the predicate 'pegasizes'.

However, McX hits upon a different strategem. 'Let us grant,' he says, 'this distinction between meaning and naming of which you make so much. Let us even grant that "is red", "pegasizes", etc., are not names of attributes. Still, you admit they have meanings. But these *meanings*, whether they are *named* or not, are still universals, and I venture to say that some of them might even be the very things that I call attributes, or something to much the same purpose in the end.'

For McX, this is an unusually penetrating speech; and the only way I know to counter it is by refusing to admit meanings. However, I feel no reluctance toward refusing to admit meanings, for I do not thereby deny that words and statements are meaningful. McX and I may agree to the letter in our classification of linguistic forms into the meaningful and the meaningless, even though McX construes meaningfulness as the *having* (in some sense of 'having') of some abstract entity which he calls a meaning, whereas I do not. I remain free to maintain that the fact that a given linguistic utterance is meaningful (or *significant*, as I prefer to say so as not to invite hypostasis of meanings as entities) is an ultimate and irreducible matter of fact; or, I may undertake to analyze it in terms directly of what people do in the presence of the linguistic utterance in question and other utterances similar to it.

The useful ways in which people ordinarily talk or seem to talk about meanings boil down to two: the *having* of meanings, which is significance, and *sameness* of meaning, or synonymy. What is called *giving* the meaning of an utterance is simply the uttering of a synonym, couched, ordinarily, in clearer language than the original. If we are allergic to meanings as such, we can speak directly of utterances as significant or insignificant, and as synonymous or heteronymous one with another. The problem of explaining these adjectives 'significant' and 'synonymous' with some degree of clarity and rigor – preferably, as I see it, in terms of behavior – is as difficult as it is important.[4] But the explanatory value of special and irreducible intermediary entities called meanings is surely illusory.

Up to now I have argued that we can use singular terms significantly in sentences without presupposing that there are the entities which those terms purport to name. I have argued further that we can use general terms, for example, predicates, without conceding them to be names of abstract entities. I have argued further that we can view utterances as significant, and as synonymous or heteronymous with one another, without countenancing a realm of entities called meanings. At this point McX begins to wonder whether there is any limit at all to our ontological immunity. Does *nothing* we may say commit us to the assumption of universals or other entities which we may find unwelcome?

I have already suggested a negative answer to this question, in speaking of bound variables, or variables of quantification, in connection with Russell's theory of descriptions. We can very easily involve ourselves in ontological commitments by saying, for example, that *there is something* (bound variable) which red houses and sunsets have in common; or that *there is something* which is a prime number larger than a million. But this is, essentially, the *only* way we can involve ourselves in ontological commitments: by our use of bound variables. The use of alleged names is no criterion, for we can repudiate their namehood at the drop of a hat unless the assumption of a corresponding entity can be spotted in the things we affirm in terms of bound variables. Names are, in fact, altogether immaterial to the ontological issue, for I have shown, in connection with 'Pegasus' and 'pegasize', that names can be converted to descriptions, and Russell has shown that descriptions can be eliminated. Whatever we say with the help of names can be said in a language which shuns names altogether. To be assumed as an entity is, purely and simply, to be reckoned as the value of a variable. In terms of the categories of traditional grammar, this amounts roughly to saying that to be is to be in the range of reference of a pronoun. Pronouns are the basic media of reference; nouns might better have been named propronouns. The variables of quantification, 'something', 'nothing', 'everything', range over our whole ontology, whatever it may be; and we are convicted of a particular ontological presupposition if, and only if, the alleged presupposition has to be reckoned among the entities over which our variables range in order to render one of our affirmations true.

We may say, for example, that some dogs are white and not thereby commit ourselves to recognizing either doghood or whiteness as entities. 'Some dogs are white' says that some things that are dogs are white; and, in order that this statement be true, the things over which the bound variable 'something' ranges must include some white dogs, but need not include doghood or whiteness. On the other hand, when we say that some zoological species are cross-fertile, we are committing ourselves to recognizing as entities the several species themselves, abstract though they are. We remain so committed at least until we devise some way of so paraphrasing the statement as to show that the seeming reference to species on the part of our bound variable was an avoidable manner of speaking.[5]

Classical mathematics, as the example of primes larger than a million clearly illustrates, is up to its neck in commitments to an ontology of abstract entities. Thus it is that the great medieval controversy over universals has flared up anew in the modern philosophy of mathematics. The issue is clearer now than of old, because we now have a more explicit standard whereby to decide what ontology a given theory or form of discourse is committed to: a theory is committed to those and only those entities to which the bound variables of the theory must be capable of referring in order that the affirmations made in the theory be true.

Because this standard of ontological presupposition did not emerge clearly in the philosophical tradition, the modern philosophical mathematicians have not on the whole recognized that they were debating the same old problem of universals in a newly clarified form. But the fundamental cleavages among modern points of view on foundations of mathematics do come down pretty explicitly to disagreements as to the range of entities to which the bound variables should be permitted to refer.

The three main medieval points of view regarding universals are designated by historians as *realism*, *conceptualism*, and *nominalism*. Essentially these same three doctrines reappear in twentieth-century surveys of the philosophy of mathematics under the new names *logicism, intuitionism*, and *formalism*.

Realism, as the word is used in connection with the medieval controversy over universals, is the Platonic doctrine that universals or abstract entities have being independently of the mind; the mind may discover them but cannot create them. *Logicism*, represented by Frege, Russell, Whitehead, Church, and Carnap, condones the use of bound variables to refer to abstract entities known and unknown, specifiable and unspecifiable, indiscriminately.

Conceptualism holds that there are universals but they are mind-made. *Intuitionism*, espoused in modern times in one form or another by Poincaré, Brouwer, Weyl, and others, countenances the use of bound variables to refer to abstract entities only when those entities are capable of being cooked up individually from ingredients specified in advance. As Fraenkel has put it, logicism holds that classes are discovered while intuitionism holds that they are invented – a fair statement indeed of the old opposition between realism and conceptualism. This opposition is no mere quibble; it makes an essential difference in the amount of classical mathematics to which one is willing to subscribe. Logicists, or realists, are able on their assumptions to get Cantor's ascending orders of infinity; intuitionists are compelled to stop with the lowest order of infinity, and, as an indirect consequence, to abandon even some of the classical laws of real numbers. The modern controversy between logicism and intuitionism arose, in fact, from disagreements over infinity.

Formalism, associated with the name of Hilbert, echoes intuitionism in deploring the logicist's unbridled recourse to universals. But formalism also finds intuitionism unsatisfactory. This could happen for either of two opposite reasons. The formalist might, like the logicist, object to the crippling of classical mathematics; or he might, like the *nominalists* of old, object to admitting abstract entities at all, even in the restrained sense of mind-made entities. The upshot is the same: the formalist keeps classical mathematics as a play of insignificant notations. This play of notations can still be of utility – whatever utility it has already shown itself to have as a crutch for physicists and technologists. But utility need not imply significance, in any literal linguistic sense. Nor need the marked success of mathematicians in spinning out theorems, and in finding objective bases for agreement with one another's results, imply significance. For an adequate basis for agreement among mathematicians can be found simply in the rules which govern the manipulation of the notations – these syntactical rules being, unlike the notations themselves, quite significant and intelligible.[6]

I have argued that the sort of ontology we adopt can be consequential – notably in connection with mathematics, although this is only an example. Now how are we to adjudicate among rival ontologies? Certainly the answer is not provided by the semantical formula 'To be is to be the value of a variable'; this formula serves rather, conversely, in testing the conformity of a given remark or doctrine to a prior ontological standard. We look to bound variables in connection with ontology not in order to know what there is, but in order to know what a given remark or doctrine, ours or someone else's, *says* there is; and this much is quite properly a problem involving language. But what there is is another question.

In debating over what there is, there are still reasons for operating on a semantical plane. One reason is to escape from the predicament noted at the beginning of this essay: the predicament of my not being able to admit that there are things which McX countenances and I do not. So long as I adhere to my ontology, as opposed to McX's, I cannot allow my bound variables to refer to entities which belong to McX's ontology and not to mine. I can, however, consistently describe our disagreement by characterizing the statements which McX affirms. Provided merely that my ontology countenances linguistic forms, or at least concrete inscriptions and utterances, I can talk about McX's sentences.

Another reason for withdrawing to a semantical plane is to find common ground on which to argue. Disagreement in ontology involves basic disagreement in conceptual schemes; yet McX and I, despite these basic disagreements, find that our conceptual schemes converge sufficiently in their intermediate and upper ramifications to enable us to communicate successfully on such topics as politics, weather, and, in particular, language. Insofar as our basic controversy over ontology can be translated upward into a semantical controversy about words and what to do with them, the collapse of the controversy into question-begging may be delayed.

It is no wonder, then, that ontological controversy should tend into controversy over language. But we must not jump to the conclusion that what there is depends on words. Translatability of a question into semantical terms is no indication that the question is linguistic. To see Naples is to bear a name which, when prefixed to the words 'sees Naples', yields a true sentence; still there is nothing linguistic about seeing Naples.

Our acceptance of an ontology is, I think, similar in principle to our acceptance of a scientific theory, say a system of physics: we adopt, at least insofar as we are reasonable, the simplest conceptual scheme into which the disordered fragments of raw experience can be fitted and arranged. Our ontology is determined once we have fixed upon the overall conceptual scheme which is to accommodate science in the broadest sense; and the considerations which determine a reasonable construction of any part of that conceptual scheme, for example, the biological or the physical part, are not different in kind from the considerations which determine a reasonable construction of the whole. To whatever extent the adoption of any system of scientific theory may be said to be a matter of language, the same – but no more – may be said of the adoption of an ontology.

But simplicity, as a guiding principle in constructing conceptual schemes, is not a clear and unambiguous idea; and it is quite capable of presenting a double or multiple standard. Imagine, for example, that we have devised the most economical set of concepts adequate to the play-by-play reporting of immediate experience. The entities under this scheme – the values of bound variables – are, let us suppose, individual subjective events of sensation or reflection. We should still find, no doubt, that a physicalistic conceptual scheme, purporting to talk about external objects, offers great advantages in simplifying our overall reports. By bringing together scattered sense events and treating them as perceptions of one object, we reduce the complexity of our stream of experience to a manageable conceptual simplicity. The rule of simplicity is indeed our guiding maxim in assigning sense-data to objects: we associate an earlier and a later round sensum with the same so-called penny, or with two different so-called pennies, in obedience to the demands of maximum simplicity in our total world-picture.

Here we have two competing conceptual schemes, a phenomenalistic one and a physicalistic one. Which should prevail? Each has its advantages; each has its special simplicity in its own way. Each, I suggest, deserves to be developed. Each may be said, indeed, to be the more fundamental, though in different senses: the one is epistemologically, the other physically, fundamental.

The physical conceptual scheme simplifies our account of experience because of the way myriad scattered sense events come to be associated with single so-called objects; still there is no likelihood that each sentence about physical objects can actually be translated, however deviously and complexly, into the phenomenalistic language. Physical objects are postulated entities which round out and simplify our account of the flux of experience, just as the introduction of irrational numbers simplifies laws of arithmetic. From the point of view of the conceptual scheme of the elementary arithmetic of rational numbers alone, the broader arithmetic of rational and irrational numbers would have the status of a convenient myth, simpler than the literal truth (namely, the arithmetic of rationals) and yet containing that literal truth as a scattered part. Similarly, from a phenomenalistic point of view, the conceptual scheme of physical objects is a convenient myth, simpler than the literal truth and yet containing that literal truth as a scattered part.[7]

Now what of classes or attributes of physical objects, in turn? A platonistic ontology of this sort is, from the point of view of a strictly physicalistic conceptual scheme, as much a myth as that physicalistic conceptual scheme itself is for phenomenalism. This higher myth is a good and useful one, in turn, insofar as it simplifies our account of physics. Since mathematics is an integral part of this higher myth, the utility of this myth for physical science is evident enough. In speaking of it nevertheless as a myth, I echo that philosophy of mathematics to which I alluded earlier under the name of formalism. But an attitude of formalism may with equal justice be adopted toward the physical conceptual scheme, in turn, by the pure aesthete or phenomenalist.

The analogy between the myth of mathematics and the myth of physics is, in some additional and perhaps fortuitous ways, strikingly close. Consider, for example, the crisis which was precipitated in the foundations of mathematics, at the turn of the century, by the discovery of Russell's paradox and other antinomies of set theory. These contradictions had to be obviated by unintuitive, *ad hoc* devices; our mathematical myth-making became deliberate and evident to all. But what of physics? An antinomy arose between the undular and the corpuscular accounts of light; and if this was not as out-and-out a contradiction as Russell's paradox, I suspect that the reason is that physics is not as out-and-out as mathematics. Again, the second great modern crisis in the foundations of mathematics – precipitated in 1931 by Gödel's proof that there are bound to be undecidable statements in arithmetic[8] – has its companion piece in physics in Heisenberg's indeterminacy principle.

In earlier pages I undertook to show that some common arguments in favor of certain ontologies are fallacious. Further, I advanced an explicit standard whereby to decide what the ontological commitments of a theory are. But the question what ontology actually to adopt still stands open, and the obvious counsel is tolerance and an experimental spirit. Let us by all means see how much of the physicalistic conceptual scheme can be reduced to a phenomenalistic one; still, physics also naturally demands pursuing, irreducible *in toto* though it be. Let us see how, or to what degree, natural science may be rendered independent of platonistic mathematics; but let us also pursue mathematics and delve into its platonistic foundations.

From among the various conceptual schemes best suited to these various pursuits, one – the phenomenalistic – claims epistemological priority. Viewed from within the phenomenalistic conceptual scheme, the ontologies of physical objects and mathematical objects are myths. The quality of myth, however, is relative; relative, in this case, to the epistemological point of view. This point of view is one among various, corresponding to one among our various interests and purposes.

Notes

1 The impulse to distinguish terminologically between existence as applied to objects actualized somewhere in space-time and existence (or subsistence or being) as applied to other entities arises in part, perhaps, from an idea that the observation of nature is relevant only to questions of existence of the first kind. But this idea is readily refuted by counter-instances such as 'the ratio of the number of centaurs to the number of unicorns'. If there were such a ratio, it would be an abstract entity, viz., a number. Yet it is only by studying nature that we conclude that the number of centaurs and the number of unicorns are both 0 and hence that there is no such ratio.
2 Alonzo Church, 'A Note on the *Entscheidungsproblem*', *Journal of Symbolic Logic* 1 (1936), pp. 40–1, 101–2.
3 Gottlob Frege, 'On Sense and Nominatum', in Herbert Feigl and Wilfrid Sellars (eds.) *Readings in Philosophical Analysis* (New York: Appleton-Century-Crofts, 1949), pp. 85–102.
4 See 'Two Dogmas of Empiricism' and 'The Problem of Meaning in Linguistics', in W. V. Quine, *From a Logical Point of View* (Cambridge, MA: Harvard University Press, 1953).
5 W. V. Quine, 'Logic and the Reification of Universals', in *From a Logical Point of View*.
6 See Nelson Goodman and W. V. Quine, 'Steps toward a Constructive Nominalism', *Journal of Symbolic Logic* 12 (1947), pp. 105–22.
7 The arithmetical analogy is due to Philip Frank, *Modern Science and its Philosophy* (Cambridge, MA: Harvard University Press, 1949), pp. 108f.
8 Kurt Gödel, 'Über formal unertscheidbare Sätze der Principia Mathematica und verwandter Systeme', *Monatshefte für Mathematik und Physik* 38 (1931), pp. 173–98.

13

The Identity of Indiscernibles

Max Black

A. The principle of the Identity of Indiscernibles seems to me obviously true. And I don't see how we are going to define identity or establish the connexion between mathematics and logic without using it.

B. It seems to me obviously false. And your troubles as a mathematical logician are beside the point. If the principle is false you have no right to use it.

A. You simply *say* it's false – and even if you said so three times that wouldn't make it so.

B. Well, you haven't done anything more yourself than assert the principle to be true. As Bradley once said, "assertion can demand no more than counter-assertion; and what is affirmed on the one side, we on the other can simply deny".

A. How will this do for an argument? If two things, *a* and *b*, are given, the first has the property of being identical with *a*. Now *b* cannot have this property, for else *b* would be *a*, and we should have only one thing, not two as assumed. Hence *a* has at least one property, which *b* does not have, that is to say the property of being identical with *a*.

B. This is a roundabout way of saying nothing, for "*a* has the property of being identical with *a*" means no more than "*a* is *a*". When you begin to say "*a* is ..." I am supposed to know what thing you are referring to as '*a*' and I expect to be told something about that thing.

Originally published in *Mind* 61 (1952). Reprinted by permission of Oxford University Press, Oxford.

But when you end the sentence with the words "... is *a*" I am left still waiting. The sentence "*a* is *a*" is a useless tautology.

A. Are you as scornful about difference as about identity? For *a* also has, and *b* does not have, the property of being different from *b*. This is a second property that the one thing has but not the other.

B. All you are saying is that *b* is different from *a*. I think the form of words "*a* is different from *b*" does have the advantage over "*a* is *a*" that it might be used to give information. I might learn from hearing it used that '*a*' and '*b*' were applied to different things. But this is not what you want to say, since you are trying to use the names, not mention them. When I already know what '*a*' and '*b*' stand for, "*a* is different from *b*" tells me nothing. It, too, is a useless tautology.

A. I wouldn't have expected you to treat 'tautology' as a term of abuse. Tautology or not, the sentence has a philosophical use. It expresses the necessary truth that different things have at least one property not in common. Thus different things must be discernible; and hence, by contraposition, indiscernible things must be identical. Q.E.D.

B. Why obscure matters by this old-fashioned language? By "indiscernible" I suppose you mean the same as "having all properties in common". Do you claim to have proved that two things having all their properties in common are identical?

A. Exactly.

B. Then this is a poor way of stating your conclusion. If *a* and *b* are identical, there is just one thing having the two names '*a*' and '*b*'; and in that case it is absurd to say that *a* and *b* are two. Conversely, once you have supposed there are *two* things having all their properties in common, you can't without contradicting yourself say that *they* are "identical".

A. I can't believe you were really misled. I simply meant to say it is logically impossible for two things to have all their properties in common. I showed that *a* must have at least two properties – the property of being identical with *a*, and the property of being different from *b* – neither of which can be a property of *b*. Doesn't this prove the principle of Identity of Indiscernibles?

B. Perhaps you have proved something. If so, the nature of your proof should show us exactly what you have proved. If you want to call "being identical with *a*" a "property" I suppose I can't prevent you. But you must then accept the consequences of this way of talking. All you mean when you say "*a* has the property of being identical with *a*" is that *a* is *a*. And all you mean when you say "*b* does not have the property of being identical with *a*" is that *b* is not *a*. So what you have "proved" is that *a* is *a* and *b* is not *a*, that is to say, *b* and *a* are different. Similarly, when you said that *a*, but not *b*, had the property of being different from *b*, you were simply saying that *a* and *b* were different. In fact you are merely redescribing the hypothesis that *a* and *b* are different by calling it a case of "difference of properties". Drop the misleading description and your famous principle reduces to the truism that different things are different. How true! And how uninteresting!

A. Well, the properties of identity and difference may be uninteresting, but they *are* properties. If I had shown that grass was green, I suppose you would say I hadn't shown that grass was coloured.

B. You certainly would not have shown that grass had any colour *other than* green.

A. What it comes to is that you object to the conclusion of my argument *following* from the premise that *a* and *b* are different.

B. No, I object to the triviality of the conclusion. If you want to have an interesting principle to defend, you must interpret "property" more narrowly – enough so, at any rate, for "identity" and "difference" not to count as properties.

A. Your notion of an interesting principle seems to be one which I shall have difficulty in establishing. Will you at least allow me to include among "properties" what are sometimes called "relational characteristics" – like *being married to Caesar* or *being at a distance from London*?

B. Why not? If you are going to defend the principle, it is for you to decide what version you wish to defend.

A. In that case, I don't need to count identity and difference as properties. Here is a different argument that seems to me quite conclusive. The only way we can discover that two different things exist is by finding out that one has a quality not possessed by the other or else that one has a relational characteristic that the other hasn't.

If *both* are blue and hard and sweet and so on, and have the same shape and dimensions and are in the same relations to everything in the universe, it is logically impossible to tell them apart. The supposition that in such a case there might really be two things would be unverifiable *in principle*. Hence it would be meaningless.

B. You are going too fast for me.

A. Think of it this way. If the principle were false, the fact that I can see only two of your hands would be no proof that you had just two. And even if every conceivable test agreed with the supposition that you had two hands, you might all the time have three, four, or any number. You might have nine hands, different from one another and all indistinguishable from your left hand, and nine more all different from each other but indistinguishable from your right hand. And even if you really did have just two hands, and no more, neither you nor I nor anybody else could ever know that fact. This is too much for me to swallow. This is the kind of absurdity you get into, as soon as you abandon verifiability as a test of meaning.

B. Far be it from me to abandon your sacred cow. Before I give you a direct answer, let me try to describe a counter-example.

Isn't it logically possible that the universe should have contained nothing but two exactly similar spheres? We might suppose that each was made of chemically pure iron, had a diameter of one mile, that they had the same temperature, colour, and so on, and that nothing else existed. Then every quality and relational characteristic of the one would also be a property of the other. Now if what I am describing is logically possible, it is not impossible for two things to have all their properties in common. This seems to me to *refute* the principle.

A. Your supposition, I repeat, isn't verifiable and therefore can't be regarded as meaningful. But supposing you *have* described a possible world, I still don't see that you have refuted the principle. Consider one of the spheres, *a*, . . .

B. How can I, since there is no way of telling them apart? *Which* one do you want me to consider?

A. This is very foolish. I mean either of the two spheres, leaving you to decide which one you wished to consider. If I were to say to you "Take any book off the shelf" it would be foolish on your part to reply "Which?"

B. It's a poor analogy. I know how to take a book off a shelf, but I don't know how to identify one of two spheres supposed to be alone in space and so symmetrically placed with respect to each other that neither has any quality or character the other does not also have.

A. All of which goes to show as I said before, the unverifiability of your supposition. Can't you imagine that one sphere has been designated as '*a*'?

B. I can imagine only what is logically possible. Now it is logically possible that somebody should enter the universe I have described, see one of the spheres on his left hand and proceed to call it '*a*'. I can imagine that all right, if that's enough to satisfy you.

A. Very well, now let me try to finish what I began to say about *a* . . .

B. I still can't let you, because you, in your present situation, have no right to talk about *a*. All I have conceded is that if something were to happen to introduce a change into my universe, so that an observer entered and could see the two spheres, one of them could then have a name. But this would be a different supposition from the one I wanted to consider. My spheres don't yet have names. If an observer were to enter the scene, he could perhaps put a red mark on one of the spheres. You might just as well say "By '*a*' I mean the sphere which would be the first to be marked by a red mark if anyone were to arrive and were to proceed to make a red mark!" You might just as well ask me to consider the first daisy in my lawn that would be picked by a child, if a child were to come along and do the picking. This doesn't now distinguish any daisy from the others. You are just pretending to use a name.

A. And I think you are just pretending not to understand me. All I am asking you to do is to think of one of your spheres, no matter which, so that I may go on to say something about it when you give me a chance.

B. You talk as if naming an object and then thinking about it were the easiest thing in the world. But it isn't so easy. Suppose I tell you to name any spider in my garden: if you can catch one first or describe one uniquely you can name it easily enough. But you can't pick one out, let alone "name" it, by just thinking. You remind me of the mathematicians who thought that talking about an Axiom of Choice would really allow them to choose a single member of a collection when they had no criterion of choice.

A. At this rate you will never give me a chance to say anything. Let me try to make my point without using names. Each of the spheres will surely differ from the other in being at some distance from that other one, but at no distance from itself – that is to say, it will bear at least one relation to itself – *being at no distance from*, or *being in the same place as* – that it does not bear to the other. And this will serve to distinguish it from the other.

B. Not at all. *Each* will have the relational characteristic *being at a distance of two miles*, say, *from the centre of a sphere one mile in diameter*, etc. And each will have the relational characteristic (if you want to call it that) of *being in the same place as itself*. The two are alike in this respect as in all others.

A. But look here. Each sphere occupies a different place; and this at least will distinguish them from one another.

B. This sounds as if you thought the places had some independent existence, though I don't suppose you really think so. To say the spheres are in "different places" is just to say that there is a distance between the two spheres; and we have already seen that will not serve to distinguish them. Each is at a distance – indeed the same distance – from the other.

A. When I said they were at different places I didn't mean simply that they were at a distance from one another. That one sphere is in a certain place does not entail the existence of any *other* sphere. So to say that one sphere is in its place, and the other in its place, and then to add that these places are different seems to me different from saying the spheres are at a distance from one another.

B. What does it mean to say "a sphere is in its place"? Nothing at all, so far as I can see. Where else could it be? *All* you are saying is that the spheres are in different places.

A. Then my retort is. What does it mean to say "Two spheres are in different places"? Or, as you so neatly put it, "Where else could they be?"

B. You have a point. What I should have said was that your assertion that the spheres occupied different places said nothing at all, unless you were drawing attention to the necessary truth that different physical objects must be in different places. Now if two spheres must be in different places, as indeed they must, to say that the spheres occupy different places is to say no more than they are two spheres.

A. This is like a point you made before. You won't allow me to deduce anything from the supposition that there are two spheres.

B. Let me put it another way. In the two-sphere universe, the only reason for saying that the places occupied were different would be that different things occupied them. So in order to show the places were different you would first have to show, in some other way, that the spheres were different. You will never be able to distinguish the spheres by means of the places they occupy.

A. A minute ago, you were willing to allow that somebody might give your spheres different names. Will you let me suppose that some traveller has visited your monotonous "universe" and has named one sphere "Castor" and the other "Pollux"?

B. All right – provided you don't try to use those names yourself.

A. Wouldn't the traveller, at least, have to recognise that *being at a distance of two miles from Castor* was not the same property as being at a distance of two miles *from Pollux*?

B. I don't see why. If he were to see that Castor and Pollux had exactly the same properties, he would see that "being at a distance of two miles from Castor" meant exactly the same as "being at a distance of two miles from Pollux".

A. They couldn't mean the same. If they did, "*being at a distance of two miles from Castor and at the same time not being at a distance of two miles from Pollux*" would be a self-contradictory description. But plenty of bodies could answer to this description. Again if the two expressions meant the same, anything which was two miles

from Castor would have to be two miles from Pollux – which is clearly false. So the two expressions don't mean the same and the two spheres have at least two properties not in common.

B. Which?

A. *Being at a distance of two miles from Castor* and *being at a distance of two miles from Pollux*.

B. But now you are *using* the words "Castor" and "Pollux" as if they really stood for something. They are just our old friends '*a*' and '*b*' in disguise.

A. You surely don't want to say that the arrival of the name-giving traveller creates spatial properties? Perhaps we can't name your spheres and therefore can't name the corresponding properties; but the properties must be there.

B. What can this mean? The traveller has not visited the spheres, and the spheres have no names – neither 'Castor', nor 'Pollux', nor '*a*', nor '*b*', nor any others. Yet you still want to say they have certain properties which cannot be referred to without using names for the spheres. You want to say "the property of being at a distance from Castor" though it is logically impossible for you to talk in this way. You can't speak, but you won't be silent.

A. How eloquent, and how unconvincing! But since you seem to have convinced yourself, at least, perhaps you can explain another thing that bothers me: I don't see that you have a right to talk as you do about places or spatial relations in connexion with your so-called "universe". So long as we are talking about our own universe – *the* universe – I know what you mean by "distance", "diameter", "place" and so on. But in what you want to call a universe, even though it contains only two objects, I don't see what such words could mean. So far as I can see, you are applying these spatial terms in their present usage to a hypothetical situation which contradicts the presuppositions of that usage.

B. What do you mean by "presupposition"?

A. Well, you spoke of measured distances, for one thing. Now this presupposes some means of measurement. Hence your "universe" must contain at least a third thing – a ruler or some other measuring device.

B. Are you claiming that a universe must have at least three things in it? What is the least number of things required to make a world?

A. No, all I am saying is that you cannot describe a configuration as *spatial* unless it includes at least three objects. This is part of the meaning of "spatial" – and it is no more mysterious than saying you can't have a game of chess without there existing at least thirty-five things (thirty-two pieces, a chess-board, and two players).

B. If this is all that bothers you, I can easily provide for three or any number of things without changing the force of my counter-example. The important thing, for my purpose, was that the configuration of two spheres was symmetrical. So long as we preserve this feature of the imaginary universe, we can now allow any number of objects to be found in it.

A. You mean any *even* number of objects.

B. Quite right. Why not imagine a plane running clear through space, with everything that happens on one side of it always exactly duplicated at an equal distance in the other side.

A. A kind of cosmic mirror producing real images.

B. Yes, except that there wouldn't be any mirror! The point is that in *this* world we can imagine any degree of complexity and change to occur. No reason to exclude rulers, compasses, and weighing machines. No reason, for that matter, why the Battle of Waterloo shouldn't happen.

A. Twice over, you mean – with Napoleon surrendering later in two different places simultaneously!

B. Provided you wanted to call both of them "Napoleon".

A. So your point is that everything could be duplicated on the other side of the non-existent Looking Glass. I suppose whenever a man got married, his identical twin would be marrying the identical twin of the first man's fiancée?

B. Exactly.

A. Except that "identical twins" wouldn't be *numerically* identical?

B. You seem to be agreeing with me.

A. Far from it. This is just a piece of gratuitous metaphysics. If the inhabitants of your world had enough sense to know what was sense and what wasn't, they would never suppose all the events in their world were duplicated. It would be much more sensible for them to regard the "second" Napoleon as a mere mirror image – and similarly for all the other supposed "duplicates".

B. But they could walk through the "mirror" and find water just as wet, sugar just as sweet, and grass just as green on the other side.

A. You don't understand me. They would not postulate "another side". A man looking at the

"mirror" would be seeing *himself*, not a duplicate. If he walked in a straight line toward the "mirror" he would eventually find himself back at his starting point, not at a duplicate of his starting point. This would involve their having a different geometry from ours – but that would be preferable to the logician's nightmare of the reduplicated universe.

B. They might think so – until the twins really began to behave differently for the first time!

A. Now it's you who are tinkering with your supposition. You can't have your universe and change it too.

B. All right, I retract.

A. The more I think about your "universe" the queerer it seems. What would happen when a man crossed your invisible "mirror"? While he was actually crossing, his body would have to change shape, in order to preserve the symmetry. Would it gradually shrink to nothing and then expand again?

B. I confess I hadn't thought of that.

A. And here is something that explodes the whole notion. Would you say that one of the two Napoleons in your universe had his heart in the right place – literally, I mean?

B. Why, of course.

A. In that case his "mirror-image" twin would have the heart on the opposite side of the body. One Napoleon would have his heart on the left of his body, and the other would have it on the right of his body.

B. It's a good point, though it would still make objects like spheres indistinguishable. But let me try again. Let me abandon the original idea of a *plane* of symmetry and to suppose instead that we have only a *centre* of symmetry. I mean that everything that happened at any place would be exactly duplicated at a place an equal distance on the opposite side of the centre of symmetry. In short, the universe would be what the mathematicians call "radially symmetrical". And to avoid complications we could suppose that the centre of symmetry itself was physically inaccessible, so that it would be impossible for any material body to pass through it. Now in *this* universe, identical twins would have to be either both right-handed or both left-handed.

A. Your universes are beginning to be as plentiful as blackberries. You are too ingenious to see the force of my argument about verifiability. Can't you see that your supposed description of a universe in which everything has its "identical twin" doesn't describe anything verifiably different from a corresponding universe without such duplication? This must be so, no matter what kind of symmetry your universe manifested.

B. You are assuming that in order to verify that there are two things of a certain kind, it must be possible to show that one has a property not possessed by the other. But this is not so. A pair of very close but similar magnetic poles produce a characteristic field of force which assures me that there are two poles, even if I have no way of examining them separately. The presence of two exactly similar stars at a great distance might be detected by some resultant gravitational effect or by optical interference – or in some such similar way – even though we had no way of inspecting one in isolation from the other. Don't physicists say something like this about the electrons inside an atom? We can verify *that* there are two, that is to say a certain property of the whole configuration, even though there is no way of detecting any character that uniquely characterises any element of the configuration.

A. But if you were to approach your two stars one would have to be on your left and one on the right. And this would distinguish them.

B. I agree. Why shouldn't we say that the two stars are distinguishable – meaning that it would be possible for an observer to see one on his left and the other on his right, or more generally, that it would be *possible* for one star to come to have a relation to a third object that the second star would not have to that third object.

A. So you agree with me after all.

B. Not if you mean that the two stars do not have all their properties in common. All I said was that it was logically possible for them to enter into different relationships with a third object. But this would be a change in the universe.

A. If you are right, nothing unobserved would be observable. For the presence of an observer would always change it, and the observation would always be an observation of something else.

B. I don't say that every observation changes what is observed. My point is that there isn't any *being to the right* or *being to the left* in the two-sphere universe until an observer is introduced, that is to say until a real change is made.

A. But the spheres themselves wouldn't have changed.

B. Indeed they would: they would have acquired new relational characteristics. In the absence of any asymmetric observer, I repeat, the spheres would have all their properties in common (including, if you like, he power to enter into different relations with other objects). Hence the principle of Identity of Indiscernibles is false.

A. So perhaps you really do have twenty hands after all?

B. Not a bit of it. Nothing that I have said prevents me from holding that we can verify *that* there are exactly two. But we could know *that* two things existed without there being any way to distinguish one from the other. The Principle is false.

A. I am not surprised that you ended in this way, since you assumed it in the description of your fantastic "universe".

Of course, if you began by assuming that the spheres were numerically different though qualitatively alike, you could end by "proving" what you first assumed.

B. But I wasn't "proving" anything. I tried to support my contention that it is logically possible for two things to have all their properties in common by giving an illustrative description. (Similarly, if I had to show it is logically possible for nothing at all to be seen I would ask you to imagine a universe in which everybody was blind.) It was for you to show that my description concealed some hidden contradiction. And you haven't done so.

A. All the same I am not convinced.

B. Well, then, you ought to be.

Notes

The following notes and references might be helpful to anybody wishing to make up his own mind on the questions raised:

The Definition of Identity: See *Principia Mathematica*, vol. I, definition 13.01. The theory of types required Whitehead and Russell to say x and y are identical if and only if the same predicative functions are satisfied by both. For a similar definition see W. V. Quine,

Mathematical Logic (New York: Norton, 1940), definition D 10 (p. 136). See also G. Frege, *The Foundations of Arithmetic* (Oxford, 1940), p. 76.

Self-evidence of the Principle: "I think it is obvious that the principle of Identity of Indiscernibles is not true" (G. E. Moore, *Philosophical Studies*, (New York: Harcourt Brace, 1922), p. 307). "Leibniz's 'principles of indiscernibles' is all nonsense. No doubt, all things differ; but there is no logical necessity for it" (C. S. Peirce, *Collected Papers*, 4.311). "Russell's definition of '=' won't do; because according to it one cannot say that two objects have all their properties in common (even if this proposition is never true, it is nevertheless *significant*)" (L. Wittgenstein, *Tractatus Logico-Philosophicus*, 5.5302). See also C. H. Langford, "Otherness and Dissimilarity," in *Mind* 39 (1930), pp. 454–61.

Bradley's remark: Not made in connexion with *this* topic. See *Ethical Studies*, 2nd edn. (Oxford: Clarendon Press, 1927), p. 165. Bradley affirmed what he called "the Axiom of the Identity of Indiscernibles" (*The Principles of Logic*, 2nd edn. (Oxford: Oxford University Press, 1928), p. 288).

Identity as a relational property: ". . . numerical identity, which is a dyadic relation of a subject to itself of which nothing but an existent individual is capable" (C. S. Peirce, *Collected Papers*, 1.461).

The proof of the principle by treating identity as a property: "It should be observed that by 'indiscernibles' he [Leibniz] cannot have meant two objects which agree as to *all* their properties, for one of the properties of x is to be identical with x, and therefore this property would necessarily belong to y if x and y agreed in *all* their properties. Some limitation of the common

properties necessary to make things indiscernible is therefore implied by the necessity of an axiom" (*Principia Mathematica*, vol. I (Cambridge: Cambridge University Press, 1910), p. 51). Cf. K. Grelling, "Identitas indiscernibilium," in *Erkenntnis* 6 (1936), pp. 252–9.

Counter-examples: C. D. Broad tries to refute McTaggart's form of the principle ("The dissimilarity of the diverse") by the example of a universe consisting of two minds, without bodies, that are exactly alike in all respects (*Examination of McTaggart's Philosophy*, vol. I (Cambridge: Cambridge University Press, 1933), p. 176). Broad holds however, that "either spatial or temporal separation involves dissimilarity" (p. 173).

The argument from verifiability: "To say that B and C are 'really' two, although they seem one, is to say something which, if B and C are totally indistinguishable, seems wholly devoid of meaning" (B. Russell, *An Inquiry into Meaning and Truth* (London: George Allen & Unwin, 1940), p. 127).

The distinguishability of asymmetric bodies and their mirror images: There is a famous discussion of this in Kant's *Critique of Pure Reason*. See, for instance, H. Vaihinger, *Kommentar zur Kant's Kritik der reinen Vernunft*, vol. II (Stuttgart: Union Deutsche Verlagsgesellschaft, 1922), pp. 518–32 ("Anhang – Das Paradoxon der symmetrischen Gegenstände").

Further reading in metaphysics

Armstrong, David, *A Theory of Universals*, Cambridge: Cambridge University Press, 1978.

Griffin, James, *Wittgenstein's Logical Atomism*, Oxford: Oxford University Press, 1964.

Jubien, Michael, *Contemporary Metaphysics*, Malden, MA: Blackwell Publishers, 1997.

Kim, Jaegwon and Sosa, Ernest (eds.) *A Companion to Metaphysics*, Malden, MA: Blackwell Publishers, 1995.

—— ——(eds.) *Metaphysics: An Anthology*, Malden, MA: Blackwell Publishers, 1999.

Lewis, David, *On the Plurality of Worlds*, Oxford: Blackwell Publishers, 1986.

——*Papers in Metaphysics and Epistemology*, Cambridge: Cambridge University Press, 1999.

Rea, Michael (ed.) *Material Constitution*, Boston: Rowman and Littlefield, 1997.

Sosa, Ernest and Tooley, Michael (eds.) *Causation*, Oxford: Oxford University Press, 1993.

Strawson, P. F., *Individuals*, London: Methuen, 1959.

——*Analysis and Metaphysics*, Oxford: Oxford University Press, 1992.

Wiggins, David, *Sameness and Substance*, Cambridge, MA: Harvard University Press, 1980.

Wright, Crispin, *Truth and Objectivity*, Cambridge, MA: Harvard University Press, 1992.

PART III

Epistemology

14

Four Forms of Scepticism

G. E. Moore

My object in this lecture is to discuss four different philosophical views, each of which may, I think, be properly called a form of Scepticism. Each of these views consists in holding, with regard to one particular *sort* of thing, that no human being ever knows with complete certainty anything whatever of that sort; and they differ from one another only in respect of the sort of thing with regard to which each of them holds this.

I hope that nobody will be misled by my use of the word "thing" in the above statement. I was not using it in the sense in which this pencil is one "thing" and this piece of paper another. I was using it in the sense in which it is used, for instance, if one says: "I know very little about American history, but there are two *things* I do know about it, namely that Washington was the first President of the United States, and that Lincoln was President at the time of the Civil War." This use of "thing" seems to me to be perfectly good and idiomatic English, and I intend to continue to use the word in this way; but obviously it is quite a different use of the word from that in which chairs or tables are "things": nobody would say that "*that* Washington was the first President of the United States" is a "thing" in the same sense in which this pencil is a thing.

At first sight it may seem as if, in this use, "thing" is a mere synonym for "fact," and as if, therefore, instead of speaking of four sorts of

"things," I might just as well have spoken of four sorts of *facts*. That Washington was the first President of the United States is a fact; and there is nothing strange in this use of the word "fact." But the use of "thing" with which I am concerned is not only one in which it makes sense to say, e.g. "That the sun is larger than the moon is a thing which I know for certain," but also one in which it makes sense to say "That the sun is larger than the moon is a thing which *nobody knows for certain*." Indeed, as we shall see, one of the four forms of scepticism with which I am concerned holds that the latter proposition is true; and though perhaps this is nonsense in the sense that it is obviously untrue, it is not nonsense in the peculiar sense in which, if we substituted the word "fact" for the word "thing" in this sentence, we should get a nonsensical statement. Consider the form of words "That the sun is larger than the moon is a *fact* which nobody knows for certain." Here the proposition "That the sun is larger than the moon is a fact" is logically equivalent to the proposition "The sun is larger than the moon." But the proposition "Nobody knows for certain that the sun is larger than the moon" is logically equivalent to the proposition "It is possible that the sun is not larger than the moon." Hence the combination of the two gives us "The sun is larger than the moon, but it's possible that it's not" or "That the sun is larger than the moon is a fact, but possibly it's not a fact." And these are a peculiar kind of nonsense like "I am at present sitting down, but possibly I'm not" or like "I'm

Previously published in *Philosophical Papers* (George Allen & Unwin, London, 1959).

at present sitting down, but I don't believe I am." But the person who says "That the sun is larger than the moon is a *thing* which nobody knows for certain," though he may be talking nonsense, is certainly not talking *this sort* of nonsense. And hence it follows that this is a sentence in which "thing" is not a mere synonym for "fact" – a sentence in which the word "fact" cannot be substituted for the word "thing," without changing the meaning of the sentence.

Once it is realized that the word "thing" in this usage is not a synonym for "fact," it is natural to suggest that perhaps it is a synonym for "proposition." But this also, I think, will not do, for the following reason. "I don't know that the sun is larger than the moon" certainly is logically equivalent to "I don't know that the proposition that the sun is larger than the moon *is true*"; but it seems to me that it is not good English to use the expression "I don't know the proposition that the sun is larger than the moon" to mean the same as the latter or to mean anything which is logically equivalent to the latter. This is a respect in which our use of the word "know" differs from our use of the word "believe." Whenever a man believes a given proposition p, we can also rightly say that he believes that p is true; but from the fact that a boy *knows* the fifth proposition of Euclid, it by no means follows that he knows that that proposition is *true*. Hence for the expression "That the sun is larger than the moon is a *thing* which I know" we cannot rightly substitute "That the sun is larger than the moon is a *proposition* which I know"; since the former is logically equivalent to ". . . is a proposition which I know *to be true*," while the latter is not. I may "know" a given proposition in the sense of being perfectly familiar with it, and yet *not* know it to be true. We can, I think, say that the usage of "thing" with which we are concerned is one in which the expression "That the sun is larger than the moon is a *thing* which nobody knows for certain" is short for ". . . is a proposition which nobody knows for certain *to be true*"; but we cannot always, in the case of this usage, simply substitute the word "proposition" for the word "thing," since it is not good English to use an expression of the form "I know the proposition p" as short for the corresponding expression of the form "I know that the proposition p is true."

Assuming then, that my use of the word "thing" is understood, we can say that I am so using the term "scepticism" that anybody who *denies* that we ever know for certain "things" of a certain sort can be said to be "sceptical" about our *knowledge* of "things" of that sort. And I think that this is *one* correct usage of the words "scepticism" and "sceptical." But it is worth noting that, if it is so, then to say that a man is sceptical about certain sorts of things, or holds certain forms of scepticism, does not necessarily imply that he is *in doubt* about anything whatever. I think this is worth noting because people seem very commonly to assume that doubt is essential to any form of scepticism. But, if I am right in my use of the word, it is obvious that this is a mistake. For a man who *denies* that we ever know for certain things of a certain sort, obviously need not feel any doubt about that which he asserts – namely, that no human being ever does know for certain a thing of the sort in question; and in fact many who have made this sort of denial seem to have felt no doubt at all that they were right: they have been as dogmatic about it as any dogmatist. And also, curiously enough, a man who denies that we ever know for certain things of a certain sort, need not necessarily feel any doubt whatever about *particular* things of the sort in question. A man who, like Bertrand Russell, believes with the utmost confidence that he never knows for certain such a thing as that he is sitting down, may nevertheless feel perfectly sure, without a shadow of doubt, on thousands of occasions, that he is sitting down. And yet his view that we never do know for certain things of that sort can, I think, be obviously quite rightly called a form of scepticism – scepticism about our knowledge of things of that sort. In the case of all the four forms of scepticism with which I shall be concerned, it is, I think, the case that those who have held them have constantly felt no doubt at all about particular things of the very sort with regard to which they have held that nobody knows for certain things of that sort. Even if, on a particular occasion, such a man remembers his philosophical view that such things are never known for certain, and accordingly says quite sincerely e.g. "I don't know for certain that I am at present sitting down," it by no means follows that he doubts in the least degree that he is sitting down. It is true that if he really believes that he doesn't know for certain that he is, he can also be truly said to believe that *it is doubtful* whether he is. But from the fact that he sincerely believes that it is doubtful whether he is, it certainly does not follow that he *doubts* whether he is. I think that the common opinion that doubt is essential to scepticism arises from the mistaken opinion that if a man sincerely believes that a thing is doubtful he must doubt it. In the case of sincere philosophical opinions this seems to me to be certainly not the case. Accordingly I think that all that is *necessary* for a man to be properly called a sceptic with regard to our knowledge of certain kinds of things is that he should sincerely hold the view that things of that kind are always doubtful; and that this is a thing which he may do both without having any doubt at all that such things always are doubtful and also without ever doubting any particular thing of the sort. There is, therefore, a sort of scepticism which is *compatible* with a complete absence of doubt on any subject whatever. But, of course, though it is compatible with a complete absence of doubt, it is also quite compatible with doubt. A man who sincerely holds that certain kinds of things are always doubtful *may* nevertheless doubt whether he is right in this opinion: he need not necessarily be dogmatic about it: and also he *may* sometimes be in actual doubt about particular things of the sort. All that I think is true is that he *need* not have any doubt of either of those kinds: from the fact that he does hold that all things of a certain kind are doubtful it does not logically follow that he has any doubts at all. At all events, whether or not I am right as to this, I wish it to be clearly understood that I am so using the term "scepticism" that all that is necessary for a man to be a sceptic in this sense with regard to our knowledge of certain things is that he should hold the view (whether doubtfully or not) that no human being ever knows for certain a thing of the sort in question. It is only with scepticism in this sense that I shall be concerned.

All four of the sceptical views with which I shall be concerned have, I believe, been held in the past, and still are held, by a good many philosophers. But I am going to illustrate them exclusively by reference to two books of Russell's – his *Analysis of Matter*[1] and the book which in the English edition was called *An Outline of Philosophy*, and in the American edition *Philosophy*. When he wrote these books, Russell held, so far as I can make out, with regard to each of the four kinds of "things" which I shall describe, that no human being has ever known for certain anything of that kind, and I shall give you quota-

tions from these books to show why I think that this was his view. Now I can't help thinking that I myself have often known for certain things of all the four kinds, with regard to which Russell declares that no human being has ever known any such thing for certain; and when he says that no human being has ever known such things, I think he implies that I haven't, and that therefore I am wrong in thinking that I have. And the question I want to discuss is simply this: Was he right in thinking that I haven't, or am I right in thinking that I have? Of course, if I am right in thinking that *I* have, I think it is quite certain that other people, including Russell himself, often have too – that all of you, for instance, have very, very often known for certain things of each of these sorts with regard to which he asserts that no human being has ever known for certain anything whatever of that sort. But I don't want to discuss whether other people have, nor yet the very interesting question *why* it's certain that, if I have, other people have too. The question I want to raise is merely whether I am right in thinking that *I* have, or Russell is right in thinking that I never have.

I will now try to state what these four sorts of things are with regard to which Russell implies that I have never known for certain anything whatever of any of these sorts, whereas I can't help thinking that I have often known for certain things of all four sorts.

1. The first sort is this. I have, according to him, never known with complete certainty anything whatever about *myself*. I do not, according to him, know now with certainty even that I am "having a white percept,"[2] and I never have known any such thing. This is a view which is implied by him in two different passages in the *Outline*. The first is where (on page 171), having raised the question whether Dr. Watson or Descartes is right as to "the region of *minimum* doubtfulness," he goes on to say: "What, from his own point of view, [Descartes] should profess to know is not '*I* think' but 'there is thinking' . . . To translate this into '*I* think' is to assume a great deal that a previous exercise in scepticism ought to have taught him to call in question." That is to say, Russell is saying: "Your proposition '*I* am having a white visual percept' is not so certainly true as the proposition 'There is a white visual percept'; it is not a proposition of *minimum* doubtfulness." From which, of course,

it will follow that "I am having a white percept" is not a thing which I know with complete certainty. And the same is implied in a later passage (page 214) where he says that the difference between two such propositions as *"There's a triangle!"* and *"I see a triangle"* is only "as to surroundings *of which we are not certain.*" All that is *quite* certain, he says, is something common to both, namely, something which could be properly expressed by "There is a visual triangle," where "There is" means the same as *"Es gibt"* (page 216), not, as in the second expression, the same as *"Da ist."* That is to say, *"I* am seeing a white percept" includes, according to him, besides something which is quite certain, something else which is not.

2.   The second class of things with regard to which he seems to imply that I have never known with certainty any such things is a class to which he refers as if it embraced all those things, and those things only, which I have at some time remembered. That is to say, he implies that, when I seem to remember, at a given time, e.g. that there was "a white visual percept" a little while ago, I never know with complete certainty that there was. Thus, according to him I do not even know with certainty now that a sound like "ago" existed a little while ago; still less, of course (because that involves the first point also), that *I* heard such a sound; and still less (because that involves a third point also) that I have been uttering words for some time past.

This view seems to me to be implied by him in the following passages.

Take first a passage in the *Analysis of Matter* (page 26). He there says: "The inference from a recollection (which occurs now) to what is recollected (which occurred at a former time) appears to me to be essentially similar to the inferences in physics. The grounds for the trustworthiness of memory seem to be of the same kind as those for the trustworthiness of perception."

Now he has repeatedly insisted that inferences in physics cannot give complete certainty; and I think, therefore, that when he wrote this he must have meant to accept the implication that I cannot be completely certain now even of such a thing as there there was a white visual percept a little while ago.

But a much stronger and clearer statement of this view is to be found in the *Outline*. The passage in which he gives this strong statement occurs in the place before mentioned (page 171), where he is considering whether Descartes or Dr. Watson is right as to the "region of *minimum* doubtfulness." He here (page 174) uses these words: "In dreams we often remember things that never happened; at best therefore we *can be sure* of our present momentary experience, *not of anything that happened even half a minute ago* [my italics]. And before we can so fix our momentary experience as to make it the basis of a philosophy, it will be past, *and therefore uncertain.* When Descartes said 'I think,' he may have had certainty; but by the time he said 'therefore I am,' he was relying on memory, and *may have been deceived.*"

3.   The third kind of thing about which he implies that I can never know anything of that kind with certainty, is the sort of thing which I might express on a particular occasion by pointing at a particular person and saying "That person is seeing something," "That person is hearing something"; or "That person saw something just now" or "That person heard something just now"; or, more definitely, "That person is seeing now, or saw just now, a white visual percept"; or "That person is hearing, or heard just now, the sound 'that.'"

There can, I think, be no doubt whatever that Russell holds the view that I never do know for certain anything of this sort. I may refer first to a passage in the *Analysis*, in the chapter on what he calls "The Causal Theory of Perception," where he is expressly dealing with the question: "What grounds have we for inferring that our percepts and what we recollect do not constitute the entire universe?" (page 200). He here says: "Someone says 'There's Jones,' and you look round and see Jones. It would seem odd to suppose that the words you heard were not caused by a perception analogous to what you had when you looked round. Or your friend says, 'Listen,' and after he has said it you hear distant thunder. Such experiences lead irresistibly to the conclusion that the percepts *you call other people* are associated with percepts which you do not have, but which are like those you would have if you were in their place" [my italics]. And it is obvious, I think, that the imaginary instances to which he refers in the first three sentences, are instances in which you might be either believing or knowing things of just the sort to which I have referred. In the first case, if, at the time when you saw Jones, you were seeing also the person who had just said "There's Jones," you would either be believing or knowing something which might be naturally expressed by pointing at the person who said it and saying "That person saw just now a visual percept resembling this one" – where this one is the one you are now having in seeing Jones. And in the second case, if at the time when you heard the distant thunder you are also seeing your friend who has just said "Listen"; you would similarly be *either* believing or knowing what would be expressed by pointing at your friend and saying "That person heard just now a rumbling sound like this." And if, in these cases, Russell would say, as we shall see he would, that you would not, under *any* circumstances, be knowing *for certain* that that person did see a visual percept like this or that this one did hear a rumbling sound like this, we may, I think, safely conclude that he would say that nothing of *any* of the kinds of which I have given instances is ever known for certain by any of us.

But in the case of Russell's last sentence, there is an important ambiguity to which I wish to call attention. He says that such experiences "lead irresistibly" to a certain "conclusion"; the conclusion, namely, "that the percepts you call other people are associated with percepts which you do not have, but which are like what you would have if you were in their place." And it is quite impossible to infer from this language whether what he means is that each such experience leads irresistibly to a conclusion different in each case and a conclusion which belongs to our class of things, namely the first to the conclusion "That person saw just now a visual percept like this," the second to the conclusion "That person heard just now a rumbling sound like the this," and so on. Or whether what he means is that a number of such experiences *taken together* lead irresistibly to the *general conclusion: Sometimes* other people have percepts which I don't have. Of course, neither of these things is what he actually says. In what he says he is implying, what seems to me certainly false, that it is *percepts of your own* which you call "other people," i.e. that if I say now, pointing at Professor Stace, "That person heard just now the sound 'Stace,'" it is a *percept* of my own which I am calling "that person" – that it is of a visual percept of mine that I am saying that *it had* an auditory percept of the kind "Stace." Surely this is absurd; and it

is perhaps because Russell himself felt it to be absurd that he uses the queer expression "other people are *associated with* percepts which you don't have," where what he seems to mean is merely "other people *have* percepts which you don't have." There is no absurdity in saying that a visual percept is *associated with* an auditory percept, nor in saying that another person *has* an auditory percept; but there is an absurdity in saying that a visual percept *has* an auditory percept; and these facts perhaps make it clear that it is certainly false that we ever "call" a percept another person.

But this mistake which Russell makes, and his queer use of "is associated with" to mean "has," do not affect my present point. My present point is to call attention to the difference between the *general* conclusion "Other people sometimes have percepts which I don't have but which are similar to percepts which I have had," and *particular* conclusions of the form "This person had just now a percept which I did not have, but which was similar to that one which I did have." I want to call attention to this difference, partly because the question whether we ever know for certain the *general* conclusion is, I think, easily confused with the question whether we ever know for certain any *particular* conclusion of the sort indicated; and I want to make it quite clear that in my view I often know for certain not merely the general conclusion, but particular conclusions of the sort "This person had just now a percept of this sort." And I call attention to it also partly because I gather from what immediately follows in Russell, that his view is that the *general* conclusion is *more* certain than *any* particular conclusion of the form in question ever is; from which it would, of course, follow that in his view I never do know with complete certainty any particular thing of the kind we are now concerned with, since the degree of certainty with which I know such a thing is always, according to him, less than some degree of certainty with which I know the general conclusion.

But that Russell does hold that I never do know with complete certainty any particular thing of this sort is, I think, directly drawn from many things he says. He says, for instance, immediately after (page 205): "We *may* be mistaken in any given instance." And here, I think, clearly the force of "may" is, what it often is, i.e. he is saying: In *no* particular instance do I *know for certain* that I am not mistaken. Moreover, he has

G. E. Moore

just said that "the argument is not demonstrative" in any of these cases; and it is clear that what he means by "not demonstrative," is what he has expressed on page 200 by saying that "it has not the type of cogency that we should demand in pure mathematics"; and he then says that what he means by saying that an argument has not this type of cogency is that its conclusion is *only* probable.

But here are three passages from the *Outline*, which seem to make it clear that this is his view.

The first is on pages 8–10, where he says:

"I ask a policeman the way, and he says: 'Fourth to the right, third to the left.' That is to say, I hear these sounds, and perhaps I see what I interpret as his lips moving. I assume that he has a mind more or less like my own, and has uttered these sounds with the same intention as I should have had if I had uttered them, namely to convey information. In ordinary life, all this is not, in any proper sense, an inference; it is a belief which arises in us on the appropriate occasion. But, if we are challenged, we have to substitute inference for spontaneous belief, and the more the inference is examined the more shaky it looks." He concludes on page 10 with the words "The inference to the policeman's mind certainly *may* be wrong."

In these concluding words I think he certainly means by "may" the same as before; i.e. he is saying that in no such case does anyone ever know for certain that the policeman was conscious.

The second passage in the *Outline* to which I wish to call attention is on page 157, where he says:

"For the present, I shall take it for granted that we may accept testimony, with due precautions. In other words, I shall assume that what we hear, when, as we believe, others are speaking to us, does in fact have 'meaning' to the speaker and not only to us; with a corresponding assumption as regards writing. This assumption will be examined at a later stage. For the present, I will merely emphasize that it *is* an assumption, and that it may possibly be false, since people seem to speak to us in dreams, and yet, on waking, we become persuaded that we invented the dream. It is impossible to prove by a demonstrative argument, that we are not dreaming; the best we can hope is a proof that this is improbable."

In this passage, it seems to me, Russell clearly means to say *both* that when in any particular case I either believe or think I know "That person

meant this," I *may* be wrong, i.e. that I never know for certain "That person did mean this," *and also* that I never know for certain even the general proposition "Sometimes other people have meant something." And when he says I cannot *prove* this proposition to be more than probable, he means, I think, as usual, that, *since* I cannot prove it to be more than probable, it follows that I do not *know for certain* that it is true; since it is a kind of thing which, according to him, cannot be *known for certain* unless it can be proved by a demonstrative argument.

Finally I will quote a passage from the chapter on "The Validity of Inference," to which I think he must have been referring when he said on page 157 "This assumption will be examined at a later stage," since I cannot find any other place in which he does seem to examine the assumption in question.

He here says (page 278):

"The belief in external objects is a learned reaction acquired in the first months of life, and it is the duty of the philosopher to treat it as an inference whose validity must be tested. A very little consideration shows that, logically, the inference cannot be demonstrative, but must be at best probable. It is not *logically impossible* that my life may be one long dream, in which I merely imagine all the objects that I believe to be external to me. If we are to reject this view, we must do so on the basis of an inductive or analogical argument, which cannot give *complete certainty*. We perceive other people behaving in a manner analogous to that in which we behave, and we assume that they have had similar stimuli. We may hear a whole crowd say 'Oh' at the moment when we see a rocket burst, and it is natural to suppose that the crowd saw it too." And he concludes with the words "It remains possible . . . that there is no crowd watching the rocket; my percepts *may* be all that is happening in such cases"; where, I think, he clearly means that I never do know for certain in such a case "There were other percepts, not mine, like those of mine," far less, therefore, such a thing as "*That* person had just now a percept like this of mine."

I think, therefore, it is pretty clear that Russell did hold, when he wrote both books, not only that I never know for certain any things of the sort I have stated, but also that I never know for certain even the general proposition that some people have had percepts which I have not had, but like mine, or even that there have been percepts other than mine.

4.   The fourth class of things of which I think I have often known for certain particular specimens, whereas Russell seems to have thought that no human being had ever known for certain anything whatever of the kind, is as follows. It consists of such things as that this is a pencil; that this is a piece of paper, that this pencil is much longer than it's thick; that this piece of paper is longer than it's broad, and that its thickness is very much less than either its length or its breadth; that this pencil is now nearer to this piece of paper than it is to my left hand; and that now, again, it is moving towards this piece of paper, etc. etc. All these things that I have mentioned I think I knew with certainty at the time when I mentioned them; and though Russell does not talk very much *expressly* about things of this sort, there can, I think, be no doubt he did hold that no human being has ever known for certain anything whatever of the sort.

I will give references only from the *Outline*, where he comes nearest to expressly mentioning things of the sort in question. We have already seen that he raises the question whether Descartes or Dr. Watson is right as to "the region of *minimum* doubtfulness"; and it is precisely in things of this sort (though Russell does not *expressly* say so) that Dr. Watson, according to him, finds the region of minimum doubtfulness. Russell gives as an example of the kind of thing which Dr. Watson takes to be particularly certain, what he calls "the movements of rats in mazes," and says that a lover of paradox might sum up Watson's philosophy by saying that, whereas Descartes said "I think, therefore I am," Dr. Watson says "There are rats in mazes, therefore I don't think" (page 176). And here is a passage (page 140) in which he expressly deals, quite seriously, with Watson's view about rats in mazes. "Even," he says, "when we assume the truth of physics, what we know most indubitably through perception is not the movements of matter, but certain events in ourselves which are connected, in a manner not quite invariable, with the movements of matter. To be specific, when Dr. Watson watches rats in mazes, what he knows, apart from difficult inferences, are certain events in himself. The behaviour of the rats can only be inferred by the help of physics, and is by no means to be accepted as something accurately

knowable by direct observation." What interests us here is that the kind of thing which Watson (according to Russell) takes himself to know with certainty when he watches rats in mazes is obviously (though Russell does not expressly say so) just the kind of thing I have illustrated: it is, e.g., "This rat is now running down that passage" (which includes, of course, "This is a rat" and "That is a passage"), etc. etc. And we see Russell here says that such things are *never* what Watson is knowing most *indubitably; never* therefore things he is quite certain of, because there are other things of which he is more certain. And he says also that these things are things which can only be inferred *by difficult inferences*; the inferences meant being obviously of the kind we have seen he has already so often referred to, and which he says at best yield probability and not certainty. I think this leaves no doubt at all that he does hold that *nothing* of the kind I have mentioned is ever known by me *with certainty*.

But I will give one other example. On page 156, he tells us: "When my boy was three years old, I showed him Jupiter and told him that Jupiter was larger than the earth. He insisted that I must be speaking of some other Jupiter, because, as he patiently explained, the one he was seeing was obviously quite small. After some efforts, I had to give it up and leave him unconvinced." Now here what Russell said to his son must have been just one of the things with which I am now concerned: he must have pointed at the planet and said "That is Jupiter," just as I now point at this pencil and say "This is a pencil." And while he is telling this story Russell speaks, you see, as if he himself entertained no doubt whatever that we sometimes do know for certain things of this sort as well as of all the other three *sorts* which we have found he really thinks no human being ever does know for certain. He speaks as if there were no doubt whatever that he *did* point out Jupiter to his son; that is to say as if at the moment when he said "That is Jupiter," he knew for certain "That is Jupiter." He speaks, again, as if, when telling the story, he knew for certain that an incident of the kind he describes really did occur in the past, i.e. knew for certain something which he then remembered. He speaks, again, as if he knew for certain things about himself – that *he* did in the past see Jupiter, say the words "That is Jupiter," etc. etc. And finally, as if, at the time of the incident in question, he knew for certain "This boy is seeing Jupiter," "This boy is having a very small percept," etc. etc. Yet we have seen that, as regards the two latter points at all events, he certainly holds that he *cannot* have known for certain any such thing. If, therefore, in telling the story he had been concerned to relate only what he thought he really knew, he would have had to have said: *It is highly probable* that, when my boy was three years old, I showed him Jupiter and told him that it was larger than the earth; but *perhaps* I didn't. It is highly probable that he insisted that I must be speaking of some other Jupiter; but *perhaps* he didn't. It is highly probable that after some efforts I had to give it up; but *perhaps* I never made such efforts. And we have now to see that he holds similarly that, if he ever did say in the past to his boy "That is Jupiter," he did not know for certain that it was Jupiter. For he goes on to say, in the next sentence: "In the case of the heavenly bodies, adults have got used to the idea that what is really there can only be *inferred* from what they see; but where rats in mazes are concerned, they still tend to think that they are seeing what is happening in the physical world. The difference, however, is only one of degree." He holds, that is to say, that if he ever did say "That is Jupiter," what he thereby expressed was only something which he had *inferred*, and *inferred* by the same kind of process by which Dr. Watson infers "That is a rat, and that is a passage in a maze, and that rat is running down that passage" – a kind of information which we have seen he clearly holds can only give *probability*, not certainty. He holds, therefore, that he did not know for certain "That is Jupiter," when (if ever) he said "That is Jupiter." And the same appears, I think, very clearly from what he says two pages later, viz.:

"A lamp at the top of a tall building might produce the same visual stimulus as Jupiter, or at any rate one practically indistinguishable from that produced by Jupiter. A blow on the nose might make us 'see stars.' Theoretically, it should be possible to apply a stimulus to the optic nerve, which should give us a visual sensation. Thus when we think we see Jupiter, we may be mistaken. We are less likely to be mistaken if we say that the surface of the eye is being stimulated in a certain way, and still less likely to be mistaken if we say that the optic nerve is being stimulated in a certain way. We do not eliminate the risk of error completely unless we confine ourselves to saying that an event of a certain sort is happen-

ing in the brain: this statement may still be true if we see Jupiter in a dream" (page 138). Here, I think, he clearly means: *Always*, when we think we see Jupiter, we *may* be mistaken; and by this again: In no case do we know for certain that we are not mistaken; from whence it will follow: In no case does any human being know *for certain* "That is Jupiter." We have seen, then, that Russell implies that I have never at any time known for certain any things of any of the following four classes: viz. (1) anything whatever about *myself*, i.e. anything whatever which I could properly express by the use of the words "I" or "me"; (2) anything whatever which I remember; (3) any such thing as "That person has or had a visual percept or an auditory percept of this kind"; nor even the truth of the *general* proposition; "Some people have had percepts which I have not had but which were like what I have had"; and (4) any such thing as "This is a pencil," "This is a sheet of paper," "This pencil is moving towards this sheet of paper," etc. etc.

Now I cannot help thinking that I have often known *with complete certainty* things of all these four sorts. And I want to raise the question: Is Russell right with regard to this, or am I? Obviously it is a logical possibility that he should be right with regard to some of these four classes of things, and I with regard to others. And it seems to me that, in respect of the arguments which he brings forward for his position, there is an important difference between those which he brings forward for saying that he is right as to the first two classes, and those which he brings forward for saying that he is right as to the last two. I propose, therefore, first to consider the first two classes separately.

To begin with the first. Russell says that I do not know with complete certainty now even that I am having a white percept; *only* that there *is* a white percept. And the only argument I can discover which he brings forward in favour of this position is the one already mentioned: "the meaning of the word 'I' evidently depends on memory and expectation" (page 215). If this premiss is to yield the desired result that I do not know for certain now that I am having a white percept, what it must mean is that in asserting that I have a white percept I am asserting something both with regard to the past and with regard to the future; and the argument must be: Since I don't know with certainty anything with regard to the past or with regard to the future it follows that a *part* of what I am asserting in asserting that I have a white percept is something that I don't know with certainty. Russell is therefore assuming two distinct things both with regard to the past and with regard to the future. With regard to the past he is assuming: (1) In asserting "I have a white percept now" you are asserting something or other with regard to the past, and (2) You don't know for certain *that* (whatever it is) which you are asserting with regard to the past. And even if we grant, what I must confess seems to me by no means so evident as Russell thinks it is, that I *am* asserting something with regard to the past; I should maintain that there is no reason whatever why what I am asserting with regard to the past shouldn't be something which I do know with certainty. Russell's reasons for saying that it is not, must be those which he has for saying that I don't know for certain anything which I remember; so that so far as the past is concerned, the validity of his argument for saying that I don't know with certainty anything about myself entirely depends on the validity of his argument for saying that I don't know with certainty anything which I remember – to which I shall presently come. The only independent argument here offered is, therefore, that with regard to the future: and here again he is making two assumptions. He is assuming (1) that part of what I assert in asserting "I am now having a white visual percept" is a proposition with regard to the future and (2) that *that* (whatever it is) which I am asserting with regard to the future is something which I do not know with certainty to be true. Now here, if it were true that in asserting "I am now having a white visual percept," I were asserting anything whatever with regard to the future, I should be inclined to agree with him that that part of what I assert must be something that I do not know for certain: since it does seem to me very certain that I know little, if anything, with certainty with regard to the future. But Russell's first assumption that in asserting that I am seeing a white percept I *am* asserting anything whatever with regard to the future, seems to me a purely preposterous assumption, for which there is nothing whatever to be said. I now assert "I am now having a white visual percept." The moment at which I asserted that is already past, but it seems to me quite evident that the whole of what I then asserted is something which might

quite well have been true, *whatever* happened subsequently to it, and even if nothing happened subsequently at all: even if that had been the last moment of the Universe. I cannot conceive any good reason for asserting the contrary.

The only argument, independent of the question whether I ever know with certainty what I remember, which Russell brings forward in favour of the view that I never know with certainty anything about myself, seems to me, therefore, to be extremely weak. But there is another argument, which he might have used, and which he hints at in the *Analysis of Mind*, though so far as I know he has not expressly mentioned it in either of these two books; and I want just to mention it, because it raises a question, about which there really seems to me some doubt, and which is of great importance in philosophy. You all know, probably, that there is a certain type of philosophers, who are fond of insisting that myself includes my body as well as my mind; that I am a sort of union of the two – a "psychophysical organism." And if we were to take this view strictly, it would follow that *part* of what I am asserting whenever I assert anything about myself, is something about my body. It would follow, therefore, again that I cannot know for certain anything about myself, without knowing for certain something about my body; and hence that I cannot know for certain anything about myself, unless I can know for certain some things of my fourth class. For of course the propositions "This is a body," "This body has eyes," etc. etc., are just as much propositions of my fourth class, as the proposition "That is a human body." If this were so, then Russell's arguments to prove that I cannot know with certainty anything of my fourth class would, if they proved this, also prove that I cannot know with certainty anything of this first one – anything about myself. This, of course, does not seem to me to prove that I don't know with certainty anything about myself, since as I have said I think I do know with certainty things of my fourth class. But it seems to me important to point out that the two questions are possibly connected in this way: that, *if* the dogma that I am a psychophysical organism were true, then I could not know for certain anything about myself, without knowing for certain things of my fourth class, and that hence any arguments which appear to show that I can't know for certain things of this class would be relevant to the question whether

I can know for certain anything about myself. For my part I feel extremely doubtful of the proposition that when I assert "I am now seeing a white visual percept," I am asserting anything at all about my body. Those who take this view seem to me to have overlooked one consequence of it, which constitutes a very strong argument against it. So far as I can see, if this view were true, then it would follow that the proposition "This body is *my* body" was a tautology: and it seems to me that it is not a tautology. But nevertheless I don't feel perfectly confident that their view may not possibly be true.

However, so far as the arguments actually brought forward by Russell in the *Outline* are concerned, it seems to me he has no good reason whatever for the view that I do not know with certainty anything whatever about myself, *unless* he has good reasons for his second proposition that I do not know with certainty anything whatever that I remember.

Let us then now turn to consider this.

When I first described this second form of Scepticism (above), I said that the class of things which it denies that I have ever known for certain is one to which Russell refers as if it embraced all those things, and those things only, which I have at some time remembered; and I have since myself adopted his way of expressing this second sceptical view: I have spoken of it as if it really were the view that I have never known for certain anything whatever that I remembered. But I think that, in fact, this is a very incorrect way of expressing the view which Russell really holds and which constitutes this second form of Scepticism. For if, in the sentence "We never know for certain anything that we remember," the word "remember" were being used in accordance with ordinary English usage, the proposition expressed by this sentence would, I think, be a self-contradictory one. We ordinarily so use the word "remember" that *part* of what is asserted by expressions of the form "I remember that *p*" is "I know for certain that *p*"; so that anybody who were to say, e.g., "I remembered that I had promised to dine with you on Tuesday, but I didn't know for certain that I had" would be asserting the self-contradictory proposition "I knew for certain that I had promised, but I didn't know for certain that I had." Suppose you were to ask a friend who had failed to keep an engagement "Didn't you remember that you had promised to come?," and he were to answer,

"Oh yes, I remembered all right that I had promised to come, but I didn't know for certain that I had promised," what would you think of such an answer? I think you would be entitled to say: "What on earth do you mean? What an absurd thing to say! If you did remember that you had promised, of course you knew for certain that you had; and if you didn't know for certain that you had, you can't possibly have *remembered* that you had, though you may possibly have *thought* you remembered it." I think, therefore, that if the word "remember" were being correctly used, the sentence "We never know for certain what we remember" would express a self-contradictory proposition. But I have no doubt that the view which Russell intended to express was not a self-contradictory one. It follows, therefore, if I am right as to the correct use of "remember," that he was not expressing his view correctly.

It is also worth notice that, although towards the beginning of the *Outline* (page 16) Russell says truly that the word "memory" has a variety of meanings, he never, so far as I can discover, even tries to tell us to which of these various meanings his sceptical view is supposed by him to apply. I think, however, that there is one well-understood sense in which the word is used, which is the one in which he is using it in stating his sceptical view. It is a use which we can perhaps call "personal memory," and which can be defined as that meaning in which nobody can be properly said to "remember" that so-and-so was the case, unless he (or she) himself (or herself) either witnessed or experienced that it was the case. That this is a different sense of the word from others which are in common use can be seen from the fact that I can properly be said to "remember" that 7×9 *is* 63, which differs from the usage in question in respect of the fact that we cannot properly say that 7×9 *was* 63, or, to use an expression used by Russell, that 7×9 *is* 63 is not something which "happened" in the past; and we can also quite properly say we "remember" that the Battle of Hastings happened in 1066, yet, though the Battle of Hastings was a thing which "happened," no living person can have either witnessed or experienced that it happened at that time; in other words, this is not a "personal" memory of any living person.

But where Russell gives as a reason for his sceptical view, as he does in my second quotation, that, in a dream we often "remember" what never happened; he is, it seems to me, merely making a mistake. For though, in relating a dream, it is perfectly correct to say that I (or he or she) "remembered" a thing which never happened, it is, it seems to me, a mere mistake to think that we are here using "remember" in the sense defined above. In relating a dream, it seems to me, we use "remember" in a special sense, namely as short for I (or he or she) *dreamt* that I (or he or she) remembered, which is not identical with any sense in which we ordinarily use the word; just as, in relating a dream, it is correct to use, e.g., "I saw John" as short for "I dreamt that I saw John." And there is no difficulty in understanding why, in relating a dream, we should use "remembered" in this special sense, since it is obvious that once we have made it quite plain that it is a dream which we are relating, it is unnecessary and would be tiresome to repeat with regard to every item in the dream the full phrase "I (or he or she) *dreamt* that so-and-so was the case." In place of this, it is natural to say "I (or he or she) remembered" or "saw John," etc. etc. It follows, if I am right, that the use we make of the word "remember" in relating a dream, is one of that "variety of meanings" in which Russell rightly declares that we use the word "memory." Yet this obvious possibility seems never to have occurred to him. He says that "dreams would have supplied a sufficient argument" for his sceptical view (page 172). But if it is true, as I think it is, that the use of "remember," in relating a dream, is different from any ordinary use, it is not true that dreams would have supplied a sufficient argument, for any ordinary use.

But even if, as I think, the reference to dreams as a proof of his scepticism is a mistake on Russell's part, because when we use "remembered," in relating a dream, we are using "remember" in a special sense, not identical with any ordinary sense, it is nevertheless true, that even when they are using "remember" in the sense defined above, many people do (as Russell does not fail to point out) think they remember what, in fact, never happened. What is Russell's reason, based on this fact, for holding his sceptical view that it is always only probable, never quite certain, that what we think we remember to have happened did in fact happen?

He seems to come nearest to suggesting a reason in a passage in which he suggests that we can only know with certainty that so-and-so is

true, if the "so-and-so" in question belongs to some class of which it is true that no member of that class ever "leads us into error." This seems to be the principle to which he is appealing when he suggests that perhaps we can each be sure of "our present momentary experience"; though he does not seem quite sure that we can be certain even of this, since he goes on to say only that "there is no reason" to suppose that our present momentary experience ever leads us into error. But is it true that we can be certain of our present momentary experience and of nothing else? Russell seems to suppose that his sceptical conclusion follows *directly* from this principle. But does it? If the principle is true at all, that it is true seems to require some further argument, which Russell does not supply. To me it seems certain that sometimes we do know with certainty things of classes which, like the class of what we think we remember, do sometimes lead us into error.

The truth seems to be that Russell has never noticed the fact that, sometimes at least, we use the word "remember" in such a sense that if a thing did not actually happen we say that any person who thinks he remembers that it happened *only* thinks that he remembers its happening but does not in fact remember it. In other words we so use the word that it is *logically impossible* that what did not in fact occur should be remembered; since to say that it did not occur, but nevertheless is remembered, is to be guilty of a contradiction. This is certainly the case if we so use the word that in saying that a person remembers that so-and-so happened, we are not only saying something about that person's state of mind at the moment, but are also saying that the so-and-so in question did in fact happen in the past. Russell, on the contrary, expressly says that it is logically possible that "acts of remembrance" should occur which are of things which never happened (*Outline*, page 7). This is certainly a mistake if, as I think, we often use the word "remember" in such a sense that when we say that a person remembers that so-and-so was the case, part (but, of course, *only* a part) of what we are saying is something not concerned merely with what his state was at the moment, but also that the so-and-so which he thinks he remembers to have happened did actually occur in the past. If Russell was using "remember" to include such cases, we must say that what he here calls "acts of remembrance" are not "acts of remembrance" at all, but only the sort of act which we perform when we *think* we remember that so-and-so was the case, but do not in fact remember that it was the case. He seems constantly to assume that whether a person "remembers" what he thinks he remembers depends only on what his state was at the moment, never at all on whether what he thought he remembered actually occurred. And this assumption of his is, no doubt, partly responsible for his view that "dreams would have supplied a sufficient argument" to prove his sceptical conclusion (*Outline*, page 172), a view which we have seen to be false, because, in relating a dream, it is correct to use "I (or he or she) remembered" in the special sense "I (or he or she) *dreamt that* I (or he or she) remembered." So far as I can see, the only sense in which "remember" can correctly be used (other than the special sense) whenever, as happens so often, the words "remembers" or "remembered" are followed by a clause beginning with "that," is that sense in which, in saying that a person "remembers" or "remembered" so-and-so to have happened, we are not merely saying something about the person's state at the moment, but are also saying that what the person (I or he or she) "remembers" or "remembered" did in fact happen at some time previous to that at which the memory occurred. When, on the other hand, the word "remember" is followed by a noun, as often happens, it seems not incorrect to speak of remembering "correctly" or "incorrectly"; but such cases, so far as I can see, can always be analysed into cases where the word "remember" is followed by one or more that-clauses, the memory being "correct," if *all* the that-clauses say what is true, i.e. are remembered, and "incorrect" if some of them say what is false, i.e. say what the person in question *only* thought he remembered, but did not in fact "remember."

If, therefore, we are to discuss whether Russell is right in the view which he expresses by saying that I have never known for certain anything whatever which I remembered, we must try to find out what view he is expressing in this self-contradictory way: we must try to find out in *what* unusual way he is using the word "remember"; and I do not think that this is quite an easy thing to do. The natural way of trying to express it is to say that his view is: When we *think* that we remember so-and-so, we never do in fact know for certain the so-and-so in question, i.e. we never do in fact remember it. But

obviously this is inaccurate, since the immense majority of the cases he really wants to consider are cases where we don't really *think* we remember, but simply either do remember or else do something else which is just what has got to be defined.

The best way I can find of stating what he means to say is this. He is saying that: In cases in which, *if* the question happened to occur to us whether we are remembering or not that so-and-so happened, we should feel very sure that we are remembering, we are never really knowing for certain that the thing in question did happen. I intend to speak of all such cases as cases where we *feel just as if we were remembering* a thing, using this expression in such a way that whenever (if ever) we *are* remembering the thing in question it is always true that we feel as if we were, though we sometimes feel as if we were when in fact we are not. Using this language, then, if I am right as to the proper use of "remember," we can say Russell's view is that when we feel as if we were remembering, we *never* are in fact remembering.

Assuming that this, or something like it, is what he means, what arguments does he give for his view? In the *Analysis* he does not profess, so far as I can see, to bring forward any arguments at all in favour of the view there put forward, which, as we saw, implies this view; and in the *Outline* I can find only one argument, and that a very short one, which seems to be definitely put forward as an argument for this view. But, though short, it is, I think, very important to consider it carefully; because it is, if I'm not mistaken, of the same nature as one of the chief arguments put forward by Russell in favour of his view that I never know for certain things of the two last classes, which we are presently to consider.

The argument occurs in the passage I quoted before. And it is this: "In dreams we often remember things that never happened. At best, *therefore*, we can be sure of our present momentary experience, not of anything that happened even half a minute ago." That is all. What precisely is the nature of this argument, and is it a good one? Russell says to me: "You don't now know for certain that you heard the sound 'Russell' a little while ago, not even that there *was* such a sound, *because* in dreams we often remember things that never happened." In what way could the alleged reason, if true, be a reason for the conclusion? This alleged reason is, of course, according to me, badly expressed; since if the word "remember" were being properly used, it would be self-contradictory. If a thing didn't happen, it follows that I can't remember it. But what Russell means is quite clearly not self-contradictory. What he means is roughly: In dreams we often feel as if we were remembering things which in fact never happened. And that we do sometimes, not only in dreams, but also in waking life, feel as if we remembered things which in fact never happened, I fully grant. That this is true I don't feel at all inclined to question. What I do feel inclined to question is that this fact is in any way *incompatible* with the proposition that I do now know for certain that I heard a sound like "Russell" a little while ago. Suppose I have had experiences which resembled this one in the respect that I felt as if I remembered hearing a certain sound a little while before, while yet it is not true that a little while before I did hear the sound in question. Does that prove that I don't know for certain *now* that I did hear the sound "Russell" just now? It seems to me that the idea that it does is a mere fallacy, resting partly at least on a confusion between two different uses of the words "possible" or "may."

What really does follow from the premiss is this: That it is possible for an experience of a sort, of which my present experience is an example, i.e. one which resembles my present experience in a certain respect, *not* to have been preceded within a certain period by the sound "Russell." Whereas the conclusion alleged to follow is: It is possible that *this* experience was not preceded within that period by the sound "Russell." Now in the first of these sentences the meaning of "possible" is such that the whole sentence means merely: Some experiences of feeling as if one remembered a certain sound are not preceded by the sound in question. But in the conclusion: It is possible that this experience was not preceded by the word "Russell"; or This experience *may* not have been preceded by the word "Russell"; "possible" and "may" are being used in an entirely different sense. Here the whole expression merely means the same as: "*It is not known* for certain that this experience was preceded by that sound." And how from "Some experiences of this kind were not preceded" can we possibly be justified in inferring "It is not known that this one was preceded"? The argument seems to me to be precisely on a par with the following: It is possible

for a human being to be of the female sex; (but) I am a human thing; *therefore* it is possible that I am of the female sex. The two premisses here are perfectly true, and yet obviously it does not follow from them that I do not know that I am not of the female sex. I do (in my view) happen to know this, in spite of the fact that the two premisses are both true; but whether I know it or not the two premisses certainly don't prove that I don't. The conclusion *seems* to follow from the premisses because the premiss "It is possible for a human being to be of the female sex" or "Human beings may be of the female sex" is so easily falsely taken to be of the same form as "Human beings are mortal," i.e. to mean "In the case of *every* human being, it is possible that the human being in question is of the female sex," or "*Every* human being *may* be of the female sex." If, and only if, it did mean this, then, from the combination of this with the minor premiss "I am a human being" would the conclusion follow: It is possible that I am of the female sex; or *I may* be of the female sex. But in fact the premiss "Human beings *may* be of the female sex" does not mean "Every human being *may* be," but only "Some human beings *are*." "May" is being used in a totally different sense from any in which you could possibly assert of a particular human being "This human being *may* be so-and-so." And so soon as this is realized, it is surely quite plain that from this, together with the premiss "I am a human being," there does not follow "I may be of the female sex." There may perhaps be something more than this simple fallacy in the argument that because experiences of this sort are sometimes not preceded by the sound of which they feel as if they were a memory, and this is an experience of this sort, therefore this experience *may* not have been preceded by that sound, i.e. that I do not know for certain that it *was* so preceded. But I cannot see that there is anything more in it.

The only argument, therefore, which Russell seems to bring forward to persuade me that I don't know for certain that I heard the word "Russell" just now, does not seem to me one to which it is reasonable to attach any weight whatever. I cannot, therefore, find in him any good reason for doubting that I do know for certain things of both my first two classes; that I do know for certain things about myself; and that I also know for certain things about the past – in short that I *do* remember things.

But let us now turn to consider my third and fourth class of things. I take them together, because, so far as I can see, his arguments in both cases are the same. What arguments has he in favour of the view that I never know for certain such things as "That person is seeing," "That person is hearing" etc.?

Now here I think it is extremely difficult to discover what his reasons are: and in trying to distinguish them I shall very likely omit some or make mistakes. There is no passage, so far as I can discover, in which he tells us quite clearly "These are the arguments in favour of this view," and, so far as I can see, he uses in different places arguments of very different orders, without being conscious of the difference between them. All I can do is to try to distinguish and consider separately each of the arguments which seem to me to differ in an important way.

I will begin by quoting three from the *Analysis* (page 205) which are the ones which lead up to his conclusion before quoted that "we may be mistaken in any given instance." The thing to be proved, I may remind you, is that when you hear your friend say "There's Jones" and look round and see Jones, you can never be *quite* certain that your friend did just before have a visual percept like the one you're now having. And these are the supposed proofs: "A conjurer might make a waxwork man with a gramophone inside, and arrange a series of little mishaps of which the gramophone would give the audience warning. In dreams, people give evidence of being alive which is similar in kind to that which they give when they are awake; yet the people we see in dreams are supposed to have no external existence. Descartes's malicious demon is a logical possibility." "For these reasons," says Russell, "we may be mistaken in any given instance."

Each of these three arguments seems to me to differ from the other two in important respects. I will take each separately, and try to explain what the differences are; beginning with the second, because that seems to me of exactly the same nature as the argument just considered in the case of memory.

Russell is trying to persuade me that I don't know for certain now that that person is conscious; and his argument is: In dreams you have evidence of the same kind for the proposition "That person is conscious"; yet in that case the proposition is *supposed* not to be true. Now it seems to me quite certain that in dreams the

proposition in question often *is* not true; and that nevertheless I have then evidence for it of the same kind *in certain respects* as what I now have for saying that person is. I admit, further, that sometimes when I am awake I have evidence of the same kind *in certain respects* for "That person is conscious" when yet the proposition is not true. I have actually, at Mme. Tussaud's, mistaken a waxwork for a human being. I admit, therefore, the proposition: This percept of mine is of a kind such that percepts of that kind are in fact sometimes (to use Russell's phrase) *not* associated with a percept that belongs to someone else. But from the general proposition "Percepts of this kind *may* fail to be associated with a percept that belongs to someone else," which means merely "Some percepts of this kind are in fact not so associated," I entirely deny that there follows the conclusion "*This* percept *may* not be so associated," which means "It's not known for certain that it is associated." It seems to me a pure fallacy to argue that it does; and I have nothing more to say about *that* argument, if that is all that is meant. I don't see any reason to abandon my view that I do know for certain (to use Russell's language) that this percept which I have in looking at Professor Stace *is* associated with a percept that is not mine; I suspect that Russell may be at least partly influenced by the same fallacious argument when he tells me (as he does tell me, *Outline*, page 157) that I *may* now be dreaming. I think I know for certain that I am not dreaming now. And the mere proposition, which I admit, that percepts of the same kind *in certain respects* do sometimes occur in dreams, is, I am quite certain, no good reason for saying: this percept *may* be one which is occurring in a dream.

I pass next to the argument beginning "A conjurer *might* make a waxwork." The important difference between this argument and the last, is that Russell does not here say that a conjurer now *has* made a waxwork of the kind supposed and fulfilled the other supposed conditions; he is not therefore saying: Percepts like this in a certain respect *may* fail to be associated, meaning "are sometimes actually not associated"; but merely "Percepts like this *might* fail to be associated." In that respect this argument is like one that he uses in the *Outline* on page 173, in dealing with our fourth class of cases, when he says: "It would be theoretically possible to stimulate the optic nerve artificially in just the way in which light coming from the moon stimulates it; in this case, we should have the same experience as when we 'see the moon' but should be deceived as to its external source." He does not say that such a percept ever *has* been produced in this way; but only that it is theoretically possible that it *might* be. And obviously he might have used the same argument here. He might have said: "It would be theoretically possible to stimulate the optic nerve artificially in such a way as to produce a percept like this one of yours, which would then *not* be associated with a percept belonging to another person." But it is, I think, quite obviously just as fallacious to argue directly from "Percepts like this *might* not be associated with a percept of another form" to "*This* percept *may* not be so associated" meaning "It is not known that it is so associated": as from "Percepts like this sometimes are not associated" to the same conclusion.

We pass next to the argument: "Descartes's malicious demon is a logical possibility." This is obviously quite different from both the two preceding. Russell does not say that any percepts *are* produced by Descartes's malicious demon; nor does he mean that it is practically or theoretically possible for Descartes's malicious demon to produce in me percepts like this, in the sense in which it is (perhaps) practically possible that a conjurer should, and theoretically possible that a physiologist should by stimulating the optic nerve. He only says it is a *logical possibility*. But what exactly does this mean? It is, I think, an argument which introduces quite new considerations, of which I have said nothing so far, and which lead us to the root of the difference between Russell and me. I take it that Russell is here asserting that it is *logically possible* that this particular percept of mine, which I think I know to be associated with a percept belonging to someone else, was in fact produced in me by a malicious demon when there was no such associated percept: and that, therefore, I cannot know for certain what I think I know. It is, of course, being assumed that, *if* it was produced by a malicious demon, then it follows that it is not associated with a percept belonging to someone else, in the way in which I think I know it is: that is how the phrase "was produced by a malicious demon" is being used. The questions we have to consider are, then, simply these three: What is meant by saying that it is *logically possible* that this percept was produced by a malicious

demon? Is it *true* that this is logically possible? And: If it is true, does it follow that I don't know for certain that it was *not* produced by a malicious demon?

Now there are three different things which might be meant by saying that this proposition is logically possible. The first is that it is not a self-contradictory proposition. This I readily grant. But from the mere fact that it is not self-contradictory, it certainly does not follow that I don't know for certain that it is false. This Russell grants. He holds that I do know for certain to be false, propositions about my percepts which are not self-contradictory. He holds, for instance, that I do know for certain that there is a white visual percept now; and yet the proposition that there isn't is certainly not self-contradictory.

He must, therefore, in his argument, be using "logically possible" in some other sense. And one sense in which it might naturally be used is this: Not logically incompatible with anything that I know. If, however, he were using it in this sense, he would be simply begging the question. For the very thing I am claiming to know is that this percept was *not* produced by a malicious demon: and of course the proposition that it was produced by a malicious demon *is* incompatible with the proposition that it was *not*.

There remains one sense, which is, I think, the sense in which he is actually using it. Namely he is saying: The proposition "This percept was produced by a malicious demon" is *not* logically incompatible with anything you know *immediately*. And if this is what he means, I own that I think Russell is right. This is a matter about which I suppose many philosophers would disagree with us. There are people who suppose that I *do* know immediately, in certain cases, such things as: That person is conscious; at least, they use this language, though whether they mean exactly what I am here meaning by "know immediately" may be doubted. I can, however, not help agreeing with Russell that I never do know *immediately* that that person is conscious, nor anything else that is *logically incompatible* with "This percept was produced by a malicious demon." Where, therefore, I differ from him is in supposing that I do know of certain things which I do not know immediately and which also do *not* follow logically from anything which I do know immediately.

This seems to me to be the fundamental question at issue in considering my classes (3) and

(4) and what distinguishes them from cases (1) and (2). I think I do know *immediately* things about myself and such things as "There was a sound like 'Russell' a little while ago" – that is, I think that memory is *immediate* knowledge and that much of my knowledge about myself is immediate. But I cannot help agreeing with Russell that I never know immediately such a thing as "That person is conscious" or "This is a pencil," and that also the truth of such propositions never follows logically from anything which I do know immediately, and yet I think that I do know such things for certain. Has he any argument for his view that if their falsehood is *logically possible* (i.e. if I do not know *immediately* anything logically incompatible with their falsehood) then I do *not* know them for certain? This is a thing which he certainly constantly assumes; but I cannot find that he anywhere gives any distinct arguments for it.

So far as I can gather, his reasons for holding it are the two assumptions which he expresses when he says: "If (I am to reject the view that my life is one long dream) I must do so on the basis of an analogical or inductive argument, which cannot give complete certainty" (*Outline*, page 218). That is to say he assumes: (1) My belief or knowledge that this is a pencil is, *if* I do not know it immediately, and if also the proposition does not follow logically from anything that I know immediately, in some sense "based on" an analogical or inductive argument; and (2) What is "based on" an analogical or inductive argument is never certain knowledge, but only more or less probable belief. And with regard to these assumptions, it seems to me that the first must be true in some sense or other, though it seems to

me terribly difficult to say exactly what the sense is. What I am inclined to dispute, therefore, is the second: I am inclined to think that what is "based on" an analogical or inductive argument, in the sense in which my knowledge or belief that this is a pencil is so, may nevertheless be certain knowledge and *not* merely more or less probable belief.

What I want, however, finally to emphasize is this: Russell's view that I do not know for certain that this is a pencil or that you are conscious rests, if I am right, on no less than four distinct assumptions: (1) That I don't know these things immediately; (2) That they don't follow logically from any thing or things that I do know immediately; (3) That, *if* (1) and (2) are true, my belief in or knowledge of them must be "based on an analogical or inductive argument"; and (4) That what is so based cannot be *certain knowledge*. And what I can't help asking myself is this: Is it, in fact, as certain that all these four assumptions are true, as that I *do* know that this is a pencil and that you are conscious? I cannot help answering: It seems to me *more* certain that I *do* know that this is a pencil and that you are conscious, than that any single one of these four assumptions is true, let alone all four. That is to say, though, as I have said, I agree with Russell that (1), (2) and (3) *are* true; yet of no one even of these three do I feel *as* certain as that I do know for certain that this is a pencil. Nay more: I do not think it is *rational* to be as certain of any one of these four propositions, as of the proposition that I do know that this is a pencil. And how on earth is it to be decided which of the two things it is *rational* to be most certain of?

Notes

1 Bertrand Russell: *Analysis of Matter* and *An Outline of Philosophy* (London: George Allen & Unwin, 1927).
2 It should be noted that in the *Outline* Russell uses the word "percept" in such a sense that by no means everything which would commonly be said to be "perceived" is a "percept." I have, e.g., perceived each instance of the word "the" which I have written on this paper; but no instance of the word "the," though it is "perceived," is a "percept" in Russell's sense. It is a physical object, and no physical object is identical with what he means by a "percept." He uses the word "percept" in the same sense in which others have used the word "sense-datum," except that the word "sense-datum" of course implies that sense-data are given, whereas his view seems to be that "percepts" are not "given," or at least that it's not certain that they are – two very different views, which he seems, in this case, not very clearly to distinguish from one another.

15

From *On Certainty*

Ludwig Wittgenstein

1. If you do know that *here is one hand*,[1] we'll grant you all the rest.

   When one says that such and such a proposition can't be proved, of course that does not mean that it can't be derived from other propositions; any proposition can be derived from other ones. But they may be no more certain than it is itself. (On this a curious remark by H. Newman.)

2. From its *seeming* to me – or to everyone – to be so, it doesn't follow that it *is* so.

   What we can ask is whether it can make sense to doubt it.

3. If e.g. someone says "I don't know if there's a hand here" he might be told "Look closer". – This possibility of satisfying oneself is part of the language-game. Is one of its essential features.

4. "I know that I am a human being." In order to see how unclear the sense of this proposition is, consider its negation. At most it might be taken to mean "I know I have the organs of a human". (E.g. a brain which, after all, no one has ever yet seen.) But what about such a proposition as "I know I have a brain"? Can I doubt it? Grounds for *doubt* are lacking! Everything speaks in its favour, nothing against it. Nevertheless it is imaginable that my skull should turn out empty when it was operated on.

Originally published in *On Certainty* (Blackwell Publishers, Oxford, 1963).

5. Whether a proposition can turn out false after all depends on what I make count as determinants for that proposition.

6. Now, can one enumerate what one knows (like Moore)? Straight off like that, I believe not. – For otherwise the expression "I know" gets misused. And through this misuse a queer and extremely important mental state seems to be revealed.

7. My life shews that I know or am certain that there is a chair over there, or a door, and so on. – I tell a friend e.g. "Take that chair over there", "Shut the door", etc. etc.

8. The difference between the concept of 'knowing' and the concept of 'being certain' isn't of any great importance at all, except where "I know" is meant to mean: I *can't* be wrong. In a law-court, for example, "I am certain" could replace "I know" in every piece of testimony. We might even imagine its being forbidden to say "I know" there. [A passage in *Wilhelm Meister*, where "You know" or "You knew" is used in the sense "You were certain", the facts being different from what he knew.]

9. Now do I, in the course of my life, make sure I know that here is a hand – my own hand, that is?

10. I know that a sick man is lying here? Nonsense! I am sitting at his bedside, I am looking

Ludwig Wittgenstein

attentively into his face. – So I don't know, then, that there is a sick man lying here? Neither the question nor the assertion makes sense. Any more than the assertion "I am here", which I might yet use at any moment, if suitable occasion presented itself. – Then is "2 × 2 = 4" nonsense in the same way, and not a proposition of arithmetic, apart from particular occasions? "2 × 2 = 4" is a true proposition of arithmetic – not "on particular occasions" nor "always" – but the spoken or written sentence "2 × 2 = 4" in Chinese might have a different meaning or be out and out nonsense, and from this is seen that it is only in use that the proposition has its sense. And "I know that there's a sick man lying here", used in an *unsuitable* situation, seems not to be nonsense but rather seems matter-of-course, only because one can fairly easily imagine a situation to fit it, and one thinks that the words "I know that . . ." are always in place where there is no doubt, and hence even where the expression of doubt would be unintelligible.

11.   We just do not see how very specialized the use of "I know" is.

12.   – For "I know" seems to describe a state of affairs which guarantees what is known, guarantees it as a fact. One always forgets the expression "I thought I knew".

13.   For it is not as though the proposition "It is so" could be inferred from someone else's utterance: "I know it is so". Nor from the utterance together with its not being a lie. – But can't I infer "It is so" from my own utterance "I know etc."? Yes; and also "There is a hand there" follows from the proposition "He knows that there's a hand there". But from his utterance "I know . . ." it does not follow that he does know it.

14.   That he does know takes some shewing.

15.   It needs to be *shewn* that no mistake was possible. Giving the assurance "I know" doesn't suffice. For it is after all only an assurance that I can't be making a mistake, and it needs to be *objectively* established that I am not making a mistake about *that*.

16.   "If I know something, then I also know that I know it, etc." amounts to: "I know that" means "I am incapable of being wrong about

that". But whether I am so needs to be established objectively.

17.   Suppose now I say "I'm incapable of being wrong about this: that is a book" while I point to an object. What would a mistake here be like? And have I any *clear* idea of it?

18.   "I know" often means: I have the proper grounds for my statement. So if the other person is acquainted with the language-game, he would admit that I know. The other, if he is acquainted with the language-game, must be able to imagine *how* one may know something of the kind.

19.   The statement "I know that here is a hand" may then be continued: "for it's *my* hand that I'm looking at". Then a reasonable man will not doubt that I know. – Nor will the idealist; rather he will say that he was not dealing with the practical doubt which is being dismissed, but there is a further doubt *behind* that one. – That this is an *illusion* has to be shewn in a different way.

20.   "Doubting the existence of the external world" does not mean for example doubting the existence of a planet, which later observations proved to exist. – Or does Moore want to say that knowing that here is his hand is different in kind from knowing the existence of the planet Saturn? Otherwise it would be possible to point out the discovery of the planet Saturn to the doubters and say that its existence has been proved, and hence the existence of the external world as well.

21.   Moore's view really comes down to this: the concept 'know' is analogous to the concepts 'believe', 'surmise', 'doubt', 'be convinced' in that the statement "I know . . ." can't be a mistake. And if that *is* so, then there can be an inference from such an utterance to the truth of an assertion. And here the form "I thought I knew" is being overlooked. – But if this latter is inadmissible, then a mistake in the *assertion* must be logically impossible too. And anyone who is acquainted with the language-game must realize this – an assurance from a reliable man that he *knows* cannot contribute anything.

22.   It would surely be remarkable if we had to believe the reliable person who says "I can't be wrong"; or who says "I am not wrong".

23. If I don't know whether someone has two hands (say, whether they have been amputated or not) I shall believe his assurance that he has two hands, if he is trustworthy. And if he says he *knows* it, that can only signify to me that he has been able to make sure, and hence that his arms are e.g. not still concealed by coverings and bandages, etc. etc. My believing the trustworthy man stems from my admitting that it is possible for him to make sure. But someone who says that perhaps there are no physical objects makes no such admission.

24. The idealist's question would be something like: "What right have I not to doubt the existence of my hands?" (And to that the answer can't be: I *know* that they exist.) But someone who asks such a question is overlooking the fact that a doubt about existence only works in a language-game. Hence, that we should first have to ask: what would such a doubt be like?, and don't understand this straight off.

25. One may be wrong even about "there being a hand here". Only in particular circumstances is it impossible. – "Even in a calculation one can be wrong – only in certain circumstances one can't."

26. But can it be seen from a *rule* what circumstances logically exclude a mistake in the employment of rules of calculation?

What use is a rule to us here? Mightn't we (in turn) go wrong in applying it?

27. If, however, one wanted to give something like a rule here, then it would contain the expression "in normal circumstances". And we recognize normal circumstances but cannot precisely describe them. At most, we can describe a range of abnormal ones.

28. What is 'learning a rule'? – *This.*

What is 'making a mistake in applying it'? – *This.* And what is pointed to here is something indeterminate.

29. Practice in the use of the rule also shews what is a mistake in its employment.

30. When someone has made sure of something, he says: "Yes, the calculation is right", but he did not infer that from his condition of certainty. One does not infer how things are from one's own certainty.

Certainty is *as it were* a tone of voice in which one declares how things are, but one does not infer from the tone of voice that one is justified.

31. The propositions which one comes back to again and again as if bewitched – these I should like to expunge from philosophical language.

32. It's not a matter of *Moore's* knowing that there's a hand there, but rather we should not understand him if he were to say "Of course I may be wrong about this". We should ask "What is it like to make such a mistake as that?" – e.g. what's it like to discover that it was a mistake?

33. Thus we expunge the sentences that don't get us any further.

34. If someone is taught to calculate, is he also taught that he can rely on a calculation of his teacher's? But these explanations must after all sometime come to an end. Will he also be taught that he can trust his senses – since he is indeed told in many cases that in such and such a special case you *cannot* trust them? –

Rule and exception.

35. But can't it be imagined that there should be no physical objects? I don't know. And yet "There are physical objects" is nonsense. Is it supposed to be an empirical proposition? –

And is *this* an empirical proposition: "There seem to be physical objects"?

36. "A is a physical object" is a piece of instruction which we give only to someone who doesn't yet understand either what "A" means, or what "physical object" means. Thus it is instruction about the use of words, and "physical object" is a logical concept. (Like colour, quantity, . . .) And that is why no such proposition as: "There are physical objects" can be formulated.

Yet we encounter such unsuccessful shots at every turn.

37. But is it an adequate answer to the scepticism of the idealist, or the assurances of the realist, to say that "There are physical objects" is nonsense? For them after all it is not nonsense. It would, however, be an answer to say:

this assertion, or its opposite is a misfiring attempt to express what can't be expressed like that. And that it does misfire can be shewn; but that isn't the end of the matter. We need to realize that what presents itself to us as the first expression of a difficulty, or of its solution, may as yet not be correctly expressed at all. Just as one who has a just censure of a picture to make will often at first offer the censure where it does not belong, and an *investigation* is needed in order to find the right point of attack for the critic.

38. Knowledge in mathematics: Here one has to keep on reminding oneself of the unimportance of the 'inner process' or 'state' and ask "Why should it be important? What does it matter to me?" What is interesting is how we *use* mathematical propositions.

39. *This* is how calculation is done, in such circumstances a calculation is *treated* as absolutely reliable, as certainly correct.

40. Upon "I know that here is my hand" there may follow the question "How do you know?" and the answer to that presupposes that *this* can be known in *that* way. So, instead of "I know that here is my hand", one might say "Here is my hand", and then add *how* one knows.

41. "I know where I am feeling pain", "I know that I feel it *here*" is as wrong as "I know that I am in pain". But "I know where you touched my arm" is right.

42. One can say "He believes it, but it isn't so", but not "He knows it, but it isn't so". Does this stem from the difference between the mental states of belief and of knowledge? No. – One may for example call "mental state" what is expressed by tone of voice in speaking, by gestures etc. It would thus be *possible* to speak of a mental state of conviction, and that may be the same whether it is knowledge or false belief. To think that different states must correspond to the words "believe" and "know" would be as if one believed that different people had to correspond to the word "I" and the name "Ludwig", because the concepts are different.

43. What sort of proposition is this: "We *cannot* have miscalculated in $12 \times 12 = 144$"? It must surely be a proposition of logic. – But now, is it

not the same, or doesn't it come to the same, as the statement $12 \times 12 = 144$?

44. If you demand a rule from which it follows that there can't have been a miscalculation here, the answer is that we did not learn this through a rule, but by learning to calculate.

45. We got to know the *nature* of calculating by learning to calculate.

46. But then can't it be described how we satisfy ourselves of the reliability of a calculation? O yes! Yet no rule emerges when we do so. – But the most important thing is: The rule is not needed. Nothing is lacking. We do calculate according to a rule, and that is enough.

47. *This* is how one calculates. Calculating is *this*. What we learn at school, for example. Forget this transcendent certainty, which is connected with your concept of spirit.

48. However, out of a host of calculations certain ones might be designated as reliable once for all, others as not yet fixed. And now, is this a *logical* distinction?

49. But remember: even when the calculation is something fixed for me, this is only a decision for a practical purpose.

50. When does one say, I know that $\ldots \times \ldots = \ldots$? When one has checked the calculation.

51. What sort of proposition is: "What could a mistake here be like!"? It would have to be a logical proposition. But it is a logic that is not used, because what it tells us is not learned through propositions. – It is a logical proposition; for it does describe the conceptual (linguistic) situation.

52. This situation is thus not the same for a proposition like "At this distance from the sun there is a planet" and "Here is a hand" (namely my own hand). The second can't be called a hypothesis. But there isn't a sharp boundary line between them.

53. So one might grant that Moore was right, if he is interpreted like this: a proposition saying that here is a physical object may have the same

logical status as one saying that here is a red patch.

54. For it is not true that a mistake merely gets more and more improbable as we pass from the planet to my own hand. No: at some point it has ceased to be conceivable.

This is already suggested by the following: if it were not so, it would also be conceivable that we should be wrong in *every* statement about physical objects; that any we ever make are mistaken.

55. So is the *hypothesis* possible, that all the things around us don't exist? Would that not be like the hypothesis of our having miscalculated in all our calculations?

56. When one says: "Perhaps this planet doesn't exist and the light-phenomenon arises in some other way", then after all one needs an example of an object which does exist. This doesn't exist, – as *for example* does. . . .

Or are we to say that *certainty* is merely a constructed point to which some things approximate more, some less closely? No. Doubt gradually loses its sense. This language-game just *is* like that.

And everything descriptive of a language-game is part of logic.

57. Now might not "I *know*, I am not just surmising, that here is my hand" be conceived as a proposition of grammar? Hence *not* temporally. –

But in that case isn't it like *this* one: "I know, I am not just surmising, that I am seeing red"?

And isn't the consequence "So there are physical objects" like: "So there are colours"?

58. If "I know etc." is conceived as a grammatical proposition, of course the "I" cannot be important. And it properly means "There is no such thing as a doubt in this case" or "The expression 'I do not know' makes no sense in this case". And of course it follows from this that "I *know*" makes no sense either.

59. "I know" is here a *logical* insight. Only realism can't be proved by means of it.

60. It is wrong to say that the 'hypothesis' that *this* is a bit of paper would be confirmed or disconfirmed by later experience, and that, in "I know that this is a bit of paper," the "I know" either relates to such an hypothesis or to a logical determination.

61. . . . A meaning of a word is a kind of employment of it.

For it is what we learn when the word is incorporated into our language.

62. That is why there exists a correspondence between the concepts 'rule' and 'meaning'.

63. If we imagine the facts otherwise than as they are, certain language-games lose some of their importance, while others become important. And in this way there is an alteration – a gradual one – in the use of the vocabulary of a language.

64. Compare the meaning of a word with the 'function' of an official. And 'different meanings' with 'different functions'.

65. When language-games change, then there is a change in concepts, and with the concepts the meanings of words change.

———

66. I make assertions about reality, assertions which have different degrees of assurance. How does the degree of assurance come out? What consequences has it?

We may be dealing, for example, with the certainty of memory, or again of perception. I may be sure of something, but still know what test might convince me of error. I am e.g. quite sure of the date of a battle, but if I should find a different date in a recognized work of history, I should alter my opinion, and this would not mean I lost all faith in judging.

67. Could we imagine a man who keeps on making mistakes where we regard a mistake as ruled out, and in fact never encounter one?

E.g. he says he lives in such and such a place, is so and so old, comes from such and such a city, and he speaks with the same certainty (giving all the tokens of it) as I do, but he is wrong.

But what is his relation to this error? What am I to suppose?

68. The question is: what is the logician to say here?

69. I should like to say: "If I am wrong about *this*, I have no guarantee that anything I say is true." But others won't say that about me, nor will I say it about other people.

70. For months I have lived at address A, I have read the name of the street and the number of the house countless times, have received countless letters here and given countless people the address. If I am wrong about it, the mistake is hardly less than if I were (wrongly) to believe I was writing Chinese and not German.

71. If my friend were to imagine one day that he had been living for a long time past in such and such a place, etc. etc., I should not call this a *mistake*, but rather a mental disturbance, perhaps a transient one.

72. Not every false belief of this sort is a mistake.

73. But what is the difference between mistake and mental disturbance? Or what is the difference between my treating it as a mistake and my treating it as mental disturbance?

74. Can we say: a *mistake* doesn't only have a cause, it also has a ground? I.e., roughly: when someone makes a mistake, this can be fitted into what he knows aright.

75. Would this be correct: If I merely believed wrongly that there is a table here in front of me, this might still be a mistake; but if I believe wrongly that I have seen this table, or one like it, every day for several months past, and have regularly used it, that isn't a mistake?

76. Naturally, my aim must be to say what statements one would like to make here, but cannot make significantly.

77. Perhaps I shall do a multiplication twice to make sure, or perhaps get someone else to work it over. But shall I work it over again twenty times, or get twenty people to go over it? And is that some sort of negligence? Would the certainty really be greater for being checked twenty times?

78. And can I give a *reason* why it isn't?

79. That I am a man and not a woman can be verified, but if I were to say I was a woman, and

then tried to explain the error by saying I hadn't checked the statement, the explanation would not be accepted.

80. The *truth* of my statements is the test of my *understanding* of these statements.

81. That is to say: if I make certain false statements, it becomes uncertain whether I understand them.

82. What counts as an adequate test of a statement belongs to logic. It belongs to the description of the language-game.

83. The *truth* of certain empirical propositions belongs to our frame of reference.

84. Moore says he *knows* that the earth existed long before his birth. And put like that it seems to be a personal statement about him, even if it is in addition a statement about the physical world. Now it is philosophically uninteresting whether Moore knows this or that, but it is interesting that, and how, it can be known. If Moore had informed us that he knew the distance separating certain stars, we might conclude from that that he had made some special investigations, and we shall want to know what these were. But Moore chooses precisely a case in which we all seem to know the same as he, and without being able to say how. I believe e.g. that I know as much about this matter (the existence of the earth) as Moore does, and if he knows that it is as he says, then *I* know it too. For it isn't, either, as if he had arrived at his proposition by pursuing some line of thought which, while it is open to me, I have not in fact pursued.

85. And what goes into someone's knowing this? Knowledge of history, say? He must know what it means to say: the earth has already existed for such and such a length of time. For not *any* intelligent adult must know that. We see men building and demolishing houses, and are led to ask: "How long has this house been here?" But how does one come on the idea of asking this about a mountain, for example? And have all men the notion of the earth as a *body*, which may come into being and pass away? Why shouldn't I think of the earth as flat, but extending without end in every direction (including depth)? But in that case one might still say "I know that

this mountain existed long before my birth." – But suppose I met a man who didn't believe that?

86. Suppose I replaced Moore's "I know" by "I am of the unshakeable conviction"?

87. Can't an assertoric sentence, which was capable of functioning as an hypothesis, also be used as a foundation for research and action? I.e. can't it simply be isolated from doubt, though not according to any explicit rule? It simply gets assumed as a truism, never called in question, perhaps not even ever formulated.

88. It may be for example that *all enquiry on our part* is set so as to exempt certain propositions from doubt, if they are ever formulated. They lie apart from the route travelled by enquiry.

89. One would like to say: "Everything speaks for, and nothing against the earth's having existed long before. . . ."

Yet might I not believe the contrary after all? But the question is: What would the practical effects of this belief be? – Perhaps someone says: "That's not the point. A belief is what it is whether it has any practical effects or not." One thinks: It is the same adjustment of the human mind anyway.

90. "I know" has a primitive meaning similar to and related to "I see" ("wissen", "videre"). And "I knew he was in the room, but he wasn't in the room" is like "I saw him in the room, but he wasn't there". "I know" is supposed to express a relation, not between me and the sense of a proposition (like "I believe") but between me and a fact. So that the *fact* is taken into my consciousness. (Here is the reason why one wants to say that nothing that goes on in the outer world is really known, but only what happens in the domain of what are called sense-data.) This would give us a picture of knowing as the perception of an outer event through visual rays which project it as it is into the eye and the consciousness. Only then the question at once arises whether one can be *certain* of this projection. And this picture does indeed show how our *imagination* presents knowledge, but not what lies at the bottom of this presentation.

91. If Moore says he knows the earth existed etc., most of us will grant him that it has existed

all that time, and also believe him when he says he is convinced of it. But has he also got the right *ground* for his conviction? For if not, then after all he doesn't *know* (Russell).

92. However, we can ask: May someone have telling grounds for believing that the earth has only existed for a short time, say since his own birth? – Suppose he had always been told that, – would he have any good reason to doubt it? Men have believed that they could make rain; why should not a king be brought up in the belief that the world began with him? And if Moore and this king were to meet and discuss, could Moore really prove his belief to be the right one? I do not say that Moore could not convert the king to his view, but it would be a conversion of a special kind; the king would be brought to look at the world in a different way.

Remember that one is sometimes convinced of the *correctness* of a view by its *simplicity* or *symmetry*, i.e., these are what induce one to go over to this point of view. One then simply says something like: "*That's* how it must be."

93. The propositions presenting what Moore '*knows*' are all of such a kind that it is difficult to imagine *why* anyone should believe the contrary. E.g. the proposition that Moore has spent his whole life in close proximity to the earth. – Once more I can speak of myself here instead of speaking of Moore. What could induce me to believe the opposite? Either a memory, or having been told. – Everything that I have seen or heard gives me the conviction that no man has ever been far from the earth. Nothing in my picture of the world speaks in favour of the opposite.

94. But I did not get my picture of the world by satisfying myself of its correctness; nor do I have it because I am satisfied of its correctness. No: it is the inherited background against which I distinguish between true and false.

95. The propositions describing this world-picture might be part of a kind of mythology. And their role is like that of rules of a game; and the game can be learned purely practically, without learning any explicit rules.

96. It might be imagined that some propositions, of the form of empirical propositions, were hardened and functioned as channels for such

empirical propositions as were not hardened but fluid; and that this relation altered with time, in that fluid propositions hardened, and hard ones became fluid.

97. The mythology may change back into a state of flux, the river-bed of thoughts may shift. But I distinguish between the movement of the waters on the river-bed and the shift of the bed itself; though there is not a sharp division of the one from the other.

98. But if someone were to say "So logic too is an empirical science" he would be wrong. Yet this is right: the same proposition may get treated at one time as something to test by experience, at another as a rule of testing.

99. And the bank of that river consists partly of hard rock, subject to no alteration or only to an imperceptible one, partly of sand, which now in one place now in another gets washed away, or deposited.

100. The truths which Moore says he knows, are such as, roughly speaking, all of us know, if he knows them.

101. Such a proposition might be e.g. "My body has never disappeared and reappeared again after an interval."

102. Might I not believe that once, without knowing it, perhaps in a state of unconsciousness, I was taken far away from the earth – that other people even know this, but do not mention it to me? But this would not fit into the rest of my convictions at all. Not that I could describe the system of these convictions. Yet my convictions do form a system, a structure.

103. And now if I were to say "It is my unshakeable conviction that etc.", this means in the present case too that I have not consciously arrived at the conviction by following a particular line of thought, but that it is anchored in all my *questions and answers*, so anchored that I cannot touch it.

104. I am for example also convinced that the sun is not a hole in the vault of heaven.

105. All testing, all confirmation and disconfirmation of a hypothesis takes place already within a system. And this system is not a more or less arbitrary and doubtful point of departure for all our arguments: no, it belongs to the essence of what we call an argument. The system is not so much the point of departure, as the element in which arguments have their life.

106. Suppose some adult had told a child that he had been on the moon. The child tells me the story, and I say it was only a joke, the man hadn't been on the moon; no one has ever been on the moon; the moon is a long way off and it is impossible to climb up there or fly there. – If now the child insists, saying perhaps there is a way of getting there which I don't know, etc. what reply could I make to him? What reply could I make to the adults of a tribe who believe that people sometimes go to the moon (perhaps that is how they interpret their dreams), and who indeed grant that there are no ordinary means of climbing up to it or flying there? – But a child will not ordinarily stick to such a belief and will soon be convinced by what we tell him seriously.

107. Isn't this altogether like the way one can instruct a child to believe in a God, or that none exists, and it will accordingly be able to produce apparently telling grounds for the one or the other?

108. "But is there then no objective truth? Isn't it true, or false, that someone has been on the moon?" If we are thinking within our system, then it is certain that no one has ever been on the moon. Not merely is nothing of the sort ever seriously reported to us by reasonable people, but our whole system of physics forbids us to believe it. For this demands answers to the questions "How did he overcome the force of gravity?" "How could he live without an atmosphere?" and a thousand others which could not be answered. But suppose that instead of all these answers we met the reply: "We don't know *how* one gets to the moon, but those who get there know at once that they are there; and even you can't explain everything." We should feel ourselves intellectually very distant from someone who said this.

109. "An empirical proposition can be *tested*" (we say). But how? and through what?

110. What *counts* as its test? – "But is this an adequate test? And, if so, must it not be recognizable as such in logic?" – As if giving grounds

did not come to an end sometime. But the end is not an ungrounded presupposition: it is an ungrounded way of acting.

111. "I *know* that I have never been on the moon." That sounds quite different in the circumstances which actually hold, to the way it would sound if a good many men had been on the moon, and some perhaps without knowing it. In *this* case one could give grounds for this knowledge. Is there not a relationship here similar to that between the general rule of multiplying and particular multiplications that have been carried out?

I want to say: my not having been on the moon is as sure a thing for me as any grounds I could give for it.

112. And isn't that what Moore wants to say, when he says he *knows* all these things? – But is his knowing it really what is in question, and not rather that some of these propositions must be solid for us?

113. When someone is trying to teach us mathematics, he will not begin by assuring us that he *knows* that a + b = b + a.

114. If you are not certain of any fact, you cannot be certain of the meaning of your words either.

115. If you tried to doubt everything you would not get as far as doubting anything. The game of doubting itself presupposes certainty.

116. Instead of "I know ...", couldn't Moore have said: "It stands fast for me that ..."? And further: "It stands fast for me and many others. ..."

117. Why is it not possible for me to doubt that I have never been on the moon? And how could I try to doubt it?

First and foremost, the supposition that perhaps I have been there would strike me as *idle*. Nothing would follow from it, nothing be explained by it. It would not tie in with anything in my life.

When I say "Nothing speaks for, everything against it," this presupposes a principle of speaking for and against. That is, I must be able to say what *would* speak for it.

118. Now would it be correct to say: So far no one has opened my skull in order to see whether there is a brain inside; but everything speaks for, and nothing against, its being what they would find there?

119. But can it also be said: Everything speaks for, and nothing against the table's still being there when no one sees it? For what does speak for it?

120. But if anyone were to doubt it, how would his doubt come out in practice? And couldn't we peacefully leave him to doubt it, since it makes no difference at all?

121. Can one say: "Where there is no doubt there is no knowledge either"?

122. Doesn't one need grounds for doubt?

123. Wherever I look, I find no ground for doubting that. ...

124. I want to say: We use judgments as principles of judgment.

125. If a blind man were to ask me "Have you got two hands?" I should not make sure by looking. If I were to have any doubt of it, then I don't know why I should trust my eyes. For why shouldn't I test my *eyes* by looking to find out whether I see my two hands? *What* is to be tested by *what*? (Who decides *what* stands fast?)

And what does it mean to say that such and such stands fast?

126. I am not more certain of the meaning of my words than I am of certain judgments. Can I doubt that this colour is called "blue"?

(My) doubts form a system.

127. For how do I know that someone is in doubt? How do I know that he uses the words "I doubt it" as I do?

128. From a child up I learnt to judge like this. *This is* judging.

129. This is how I learned to judge; *this* I got to know *as* judgment.

130. But isn't it experience that teaches us to judge like *this*, that is to say, that it is correct to

judge like this? But how does experience *teach* us, then? *We* may derive it from experience, but experience does not direct us to derive anything from experience. If it is the *ground* of our judging like this, and not just the cause, still we do not have a ground for seeing this in turn as a ground.

131. No, experience is not the ground for our game of judging. Nor is its outstanding success.

132. Men have judged that a king can make rain; *we* say this contradicts all experience. To-day they judge that aeroplanes and the radio etc. are means for the closer contact of peoples and the spread of culture.

133. Under ordinary circumstances I do not satisfy myself that I have two hands by seeing how it looks. *Why* not? Has experience shown it to be unnecessary? Or (again): Have we in some way learnt a universal law of induction, and do we trust it here too? – But why should we have learnt one *universal* law first, and not the special one straight away?

134. After putting a book in a drawer, I assume it is there, unless. . . . "Experience always proves me right. There is no well attested case of a book's (simply) disappearing." It has *often* happened that a book has never turned up again, although we thought we knew for certain where it was. – But experience does really teach that a book, say, does not vanish away. (E.g. gradually evaporate.) But is it this experience with books etc. that leads us to assume that such a book has not vanished away? Well, suppose we were to find that under particular novel circumstances books did vanish away. – Shouldn't we alter our assumption? Can one give the lie to the effect of experience on our system of assumption?

135. But do we not simply follow the principle that what has always happened will happen again (or something like it)? What does it mean to follow this principle? Do we really introduce it into our reasoning? Or is it merely the *natural law* which our inferring apparently follows? This latter it may be. It is not an item in our considerations.

136. When Moore says he *knows* such and such, he is really enumerating a lot of empirical pro-

positions which we affirm without special testing; propositions, that is, which have a peculiar logical role in the system of our empirical propositions.

137. Even if the most trustworthy of men assures me that he *knows* things are thus and so, this by itself cannot satisfy me that he does know. Only that he believes he knows. That is why Moore's assurance that he knows . . . does not interest us. The propositions, however, which Moore retails as examples of such known truths are indeed interesting. Not because anyone knows their truth, or believes he knows them, but because they all have a *similar* role in the system of our empirical judgments.

138. We don't, for example, arrive at any of them as a result of investigation.
There are e.g. historical investigations and investigations into the shape and also the age of the earth, but not into whether the earth has existed during the last hundred years. Of course many of us have information about this period from our parents and grandparents; but mayn't they be wrong? – "Nonsense!" one will say. "How should all these people be wrong?" – But is that an argument? Is it not simply the rejection of an idea? And perhaps the determination of a concept? For if I speak of a possible mistake here, this changes the role of "mistake" and "truth" in our lives.

139. Not only rules, but also examples are needed for establishing a practice. Our rules leave loop-holes open, and the practice has to speak for itself.

140. We do not learn the practice of making empirical judgments by learning rules: we are taught *judgments* and their connexion with other judgments. *A totality* of judgments is made plausible to us.

141. When we first begin to *believe* anything, what we believe is not a single proposition, it is a whole system of propositions. (Light dawns gradually over the whole.)

142. It is not single axioms that strike me as obvious, it is a system in which consequences and premises give one another *mutual* support.

143. I am told, for example, that someone climbed this mountain many years ago. Do I

always enquire into the reliability of the teller of this story, and whether the mountain did exist years ago? A child learns there are reliable and unreliable informants much later than it learns facts which are told it. It doesn't learn *at all* that that mountain has existed for a long time: that is, the question whether it is so doesn't arise at all. It swallows this consequence down, so to speak, together with *what* it learns.

144.   The child learns to believe a host of things. I.e. it learns to act according to these beliefs. Bit by bit there forms a system of what is believed, and in that system some things stand unshakeably fast and some are more or less liable to shift. What stands fast does so, not because it is intrinsically obvious or convincing; it is rather held fast by what lies around it.

145.   One wants to say "*All* my experiences shew that it is so". But how do they do that? For that proposition to which they point itself belongs to a particular interpretation of them.

"That I regard this proposition as certainly true also characterizes my interpretation of experience."

146.   We form *the picture* of the earth as a ball floating free in space and not altering essentially in a hundred years. I said "We form the *picture* etc." and this picture now helps us in the judgment of various situations.

I may indeed calculate the dimensions of a bridge, sometimes calculate that here things are more in favour of a bridge than a ferry, etc. etc., – but somewhere I must begin with an assumption or a decision.

147.   The picture of the earth as a ball is a *good* picture, it proves itself everywhere, it is also a simple picture – in short, we work with it without doubting it.

148.   Why do I not satisfy myself that I have two feet when I want to get up from a chair? There is no why. I simply don't. This is how I act.

149.   My judgments themselves characterize the way I judge, characterize the nature of judgment.

150.   How does someone judge which is his right and which his left hand? How do I know that my judgment will agree with someone else's? How do I know that this colour is blue? If I

don't trust *myself* here, why should I trust anyone else's judgment? Is there a why? Must I not begin to trust somewhere? That is to say: somewhere I must begin with not-doubting; and that is not, so to speak, hasty but excusable: it is part of judging.

151.   I should like to say: Moore does not *know* what he asserts he knows, but it stands fast for him, as also for me; regarding it as absolutely solid is part of our *method* of doubt and enquiry.

152.   I do not explicitly learn the propositions that stand fast for me. I can *discover* them subsequently like the axis around which a body rotates. This axis is not fixed in the sense that anything holds it fast, but the movement around it determines its immobility.

153.   No one ever taught me that my hands don't disappear when I am not paying attention to them. Nor can I be said to presuppose the truth of this proposition in my assertions etc., (as if they rested on it) while it only gets sense from the rest of our procedure of asserting.

154.   There are cases such that, if someone gives signs of doubt where we do not doubt, we cannot confidently understand his signs as signs of doubt.

I.e.: if we are to understand his signs of doubt as such, he may give them only in particular cases and may not give them in others.

155.   In certain circumstances a man cannot make a *mistake*. ("Can" is here used logically, and the proposition does not mean that a man cannot say anything false in those circumstances.) If Moore were to pronounce the opposite of those propositions which he declares certain, we should not just not share his opinion: we should regard him as demented.

156.   In order to make a mistake, a man must already judge in conformity with mankind.

157.   Suppose a man could not remember whether he had always had five fingers or two hands? Should we understand him? Could we be sure of understanding him?

158.   Can I be making a mistake, for example, in thinking that the words of which this sentence

is composed are English words whose meaning I know?

159. As children we learn facts; e.g., that every human being has a brain, and we take them on trust. I believe that there is an island, Australia, of such-and-such a shape, and so on and so on; I believe that I had great-grandparents, that the people who gave themselves out as my parents really were my parents, etc. This belief may never have been expressed; even the thought that it was so, never thought.

160. The child learns by believing the adult. Doubt comes *after* belief.

161. I learned an enormous amount and accepted it on human authority, and then I found some things confirmed or disconfirmed by my own experience.

162. In general I take as true what is found in text-books, of geography for example. Why? I say: All these facts have been confirmed a hundred times over. But how do I know that? What is my evidence for it? I have a world-picture. Is it true or false? Above all it is the substratum of all my enquiring and asserting. The propositions describing it are not all equally subject to testing.

163. Does anyone ever test whether this table remains in existence when no one is paying attention to it?

We check the story of Napoleon, but not whether all the reports about him are based on sense-deception, forgery and the like. For whenever we test anything, we are already presupposing something that is not tested. Now am I to say that the experiment which perhaps I make in order to test the truth of a proposition presupposes the truth of the proposition that the apparatus I believe I see is really there (and the like)?

164. Doesn't testing come to an end?

165. One child might say to another: "I know that the earth is already hundreds of years old" and that would mean: I have learnt it.

166. The difficulty is to realize the groundlessness of our believing.

167. It is clear that our empirical propositions do not all have the same status, since one can lay down such a proposition and turn it from an empirical proposition into a norm of description.

Think of chemical investigations. Lavoisier makes experiments with substances in his laboratory and now he concludes that this and that takes place when there is burning. He does not say that it might happen otherwise another time. He has got hold of a definite world-picture – not of course one that he invented: he learned it as a child. I say world-picture and not hypothesis, because it is the matter-of-course foundation for his research and as such also goes unmentioned.

168. But now, what part is played by the pre-supposition that a substance A always reacts to a substance B in the same way, given the same circumstances? Or is that part of the definition of a substance?

169. One might think that there were propositions declaring that chemistry is *possible*. And these would be propositions of a natural science. For what should they be supported by, if not by experience?

170. I believe what people transmit to me in a certain manner. In this way I believe geographical, chemical, historical facts etc. That is how I *learn* the sciences. Of course learning is based on believing.

If you have learnt that Mont Blanc is 4000 metres high, if you have looked it up on the map, you say you *know* it.

And can it now be said: we accord credence in this way because it has proved to pay?

171. A principal ground for Moore to assume that he never was on the moon is that no one ever was on the moon or *could* come there; and this we believe on grounds of what we learn.

172. Perhaps someone says "There must be some basic principle on which we accord credence", but what can such a principle accomplish? Is it more than a natural law of 'taking for true'?

173. Is it maybe in my power what I believe? or what I unshakeably believe?

I believe that there is a chair over there. Can't I be wrong? But, can I believe that I am wrong? Or can I so much as bring it under consideration? – And mightn't I also hold fast to my belief whatever I learned later on?! But is my belief then *grounded*?

174. I act with *complete* certainty. But this certainty is my own.

175. "I know it" I say to someone else; and here there is a justification. But there is none for my belief.

176. Instead of "I know it" one may say in some cases "That's how it is – rely upon it." In some cases, however "I learned it years and years ago"; and sometimes: "I am sure it is so."

177. What I know, I believe.

178. The wrong use made by Moore of the proposition "I know . . ." lies in his regarding it as an utterance as little subject to doubt as "I am in pain". And since from "I know it is so" there follows "It is so", then the latter can't be doubted either.

179. It would be correct to say: "I believe . . ." has subjective truth; but "I know . . ." not.

180. Or again "I believe . . ." is an 'expression', but not "I know . . .".

181. Suppose Moore had said "I swear . . ." instead of "I know . . .".

182. The more primitive idea is that the earth *never* had a beginning. No child has reason to ask himself how long the earth has existed, because all change takes place *on* it. If what is called the earth really came into existence at some time – which is hard enough to picture – then one naturally assumes the beginning as having been an inconceivably long time ago.

183. "It is certain that after the battle of Austerlitz Napoleon . . . Well, in that case it's surely also certain that the earth existed then."

184. "It is certain that we didn't arrive on this planet from another one a hundred years ago." Well, it's as certain as such things *are*.

185. It would strike me as ridiculous to want to doubt the existence of Napoleon; but if someone doubted the existence of the earth 150 years ago, perhaps I should be more willing to listen, for now he is doubting our whole system of evidence. It does not strike me as if this system were more certain than a certainty within it.

186. "I might suppose that Napoleon never existed and is a fable, but not that the *earth* did not exist 150 years ago."

187. "Do you *know* that the earth existed then?" – "Of course I know that. I have it from someone who certainly knows all about it."

188. It strikes me as if someone who doubts the existence of the earth at that time is impugning the nature of all historical evidence. And I cannot say of this latter that it is definitely *correct*.

189. At some point one has to pass from explanation to mere description.

190. What we call historical evidence points to the existence of the earth a long time before my birth; – the opposite hypothesis has *nothing* on its side.

191. Well, if everything speaks for an hypothesis and nothing against it – is it then certainly true? One may designate it as such. – But does it certainly agree with reality, with the facts? – With this question you are already going round in a circle.

192. To be sure there is justification; but justification comes to an end.

---

193. What does this mean: the truth of a proposition is *certain*?

194. With the word "certain" we express complete conviction, the total absence of doubt, and thereby we seek to convince other people. That is *subjective* certainty.
But when is something objectively certain? When a mistake is not possible. But what kind of possibility is that? Mustn't mistake be *logically* excluded?

195. If I believe that I am sitting in my room when I am not, then I shall not be said to have *made a mistake*. But what is the essential difference between this case and a mistake?

196. Sure evidence is what we *accept* as sure, it is evidence that we go by in *acting* surely, acting without any doubt.

What we call "a mistake" plays a quite special part in our language-games, and so too does what we regard as certain evidence.

197. It would be nonsense to say that we regard something as sure evidence because it is certainly true.

198. Rather, we must first determine the role of deciding for or against a proposition.

199. The reason why the use of the expression "true or false" has something misleading about it is that it is like saying "it tallies with the facts or it doesn't", and the very thing that is in question is what "tallying" is here.

200. Really "The proposition is either true or false" only means that it must be possible to decide for or against it. But this does not say what the ground for such a decision is like.

201. Suppose someone were to ask: "Is it really right for us to rely on the evidence of our memory (or our senses) as we do?"

Note

1 See G. E. Moore, "Proof of an External World" and "A Defence of Common Sense", in his *Philo-* *sophical Papers* (London: George Allen & Unwin, 1959). [*Editors.*]

16

Knowledge by Acquaintance and Knowledge by Description

Bertrand Russell

. . . We have seen that there are two sorts of knowledge: knowledge of things, and knowledge of truths. In this chapter we shall be concerned exclusively with knowledge of things, of which in turn we shall have to distinguish two kinds. Knowledge of things, when it is of the kind we call knowledge by *acquaintance*, is essentially simpler than any knowledge of truths, and logically independent of knowledge of truths, though it would be rash to assume that human beings ever, in fact, have acquaintance with things without at the same time knowing some truth about them. Knowledge of things by *description*, on the contrary, always involves, as we shall find in the course of the present chapter, some knowledge of truths as its source and ground. But first of all we must make clear what we mean by 'acquaintance' and what we mean by 'description'.

We shall say that we have *acquaintance* with anything of which we are directly aware, without the intermediary of any process of inference or any knowledge of truths. Thus in the presence of my table I am acquainted with the sense-data that make up the appearance of my table – its colour, shape, hardness, smoothness, etc.; all these are things of which I am immediately conscious when I am seeing and touching my table. The particular shade of colour that I am seeing may have many things said about it – I may say that it is brown, that it is rather dark, and so on. But such statements, though they make me know

Previously published in *The Problems of Philosophy* (Oxford University Press, London, 1959).

truths *about* the colour, do not make me know the colour itself any better than I did before: so far as concerns knowledge of the colour itself, as opposed to knowledge of truths about it, I know the colour perfectly and completely when I see it, and no further knowledge of it itself is even theoretically possible. Thus the sense-data which make up the appearance of my table are things with which I have acquaintance, things immediately known to me just as they are.

My knowledge of the table as a physical object, on the contrary, is not direct knowledge. Such as it is, it is obtained through acquaintance with the sense-data that make up the appearance of the table. We have seen that it is possible, without absurdity, to doubt whether there is a table at all, whereas it is not possible to doubt the sense-data. My knowledge of the table is of the kind which we shall call 'knowledge by description'. The table is 'the physical object which causes such-and-such sense-data'. This *describes* the table by means of the sense-data. In order to know anything at all about the table, we must know truths connecting it with things with which we have acquaintance: we must know that 'such-and-such sense-data are caused by a physical object'. There is no state of mind in which we are directly aware of the table; all our knowledge of the table is really knowledge of *truths*, and the actual thing which is the table is not, strictly speaking, known to us at all. We know a description, and we know that there is just one object to which this description applies, though the object itself is not directly known to us. In such a case, we say that our knowledge of the object is knowledge by description.

All our knowledge, both knowledge of things and knowledge of truths, rests upon acquaintance as its foundation. It is therefore important to consider what kinds of things there are with which we have acquaintance.

Sense-data, as we have already seen, are among the things with which we are acquainted; in fact, they supply the most obvious and striking example of knowledge by acquaintance. But if they were the sole example, our knowledge would be very much more restricted than it is. We should only know what is now present to our senses: we could not know anything about the past – not even that there was a past – nor could we know any truths about our sense-data, for all knowledge of truths, as we shall show, demands acquaintance with things which are of an essentially different character from sense-data, the things which are sometimes called 'abstract ideas', but which we shall call 'universals'. We have therefore to consider acquaintance with other things besides sense-data if we are to obtain any tolerably adequate analysis of our knowledge.

The first extension beyond sense-data to be considered is acquaintance by *memory*. It is obvious that we often remember what we have seen or heard or had otherwise present to our senses, and that in such cases we are still immediately aware of what we remember, in spite of the fact that it appears as past and not as present. This immediate knowledge by memory is the source of all our knowledge concerning the past: without it, there could be no knowledge of the past by inference, since we should never know that there was anything past to be inferred.

The next extension to be considered is acquaintance by *introspection*. We are not only aware of things, but we are often aware of being aware of them. When I see the sun, I am often aware of my seeing the sun; thus 'my seeing the sun' is an object with which I have acquaintance. When I desire food, I may be aware of my desire for food; thus 'my desiring food' is an object with which I am acquainted. Similarly we may be aware of our feeling pleasure or pain, and generally of the events which happen in our minds. This kind of acquaintance, which may be called self-consciousness, is the source of all our knowledge of mental things. It is obvious that it is only what goes on in our own minds that can be thus known immediately. What goes on in the minds of others is known to us through our perception of their bodies, that is, through the sense-data in us which are associated with their bodies. But for our acquaintance with the contents of our own minds, we should be unable to imagine the minds of others, and therefore we could never arrive at the knowledge that they have minds. It seems natural to suppose that self-consciousness is one of the things that distinguish men from animals: animals, we may suppose, though they have acquaintance with sense-data, never become aware of this acquaintance. I do not mean that they *doubt* whether they exist, but that they have never become conscious of the fact that they have sensations and feelings, nor therefore of the fact that they, the subjects of their sensations and feelings, exist.

We have spoken of acquaintance with the contents of our minds as *self*-consciousness, but it is not, of course, consciousness of our *self*: it is consciousness of particular thoughts and feelings. The question whether we are also acquainted with our bare selves, as opposed to particular thoughts and feelings, is a very difficult one, upon which it would be rash to speak positively. When we try to look into ourselves we always seem to come upon some particular thought or feeling, and not upon the 'I' which has the thought or feeling. Nevertheless there are some reasons for thinking that we are acquainted with the 'I', though the acquaintance is hard to disentangle from other things. To make clear what sort of reason there is, let us consider for a moment what our acquaintance with particular thoughts really involves.

When I am acquainted with 'my seeing the sun', it seems plain that I am acquainted with two different things in relation to each other. On the one hand there is the sense-datum which represents the sun to me, on the other hand there is that which sees this sense-datum. All acquaintance, such as my acquaintance with the sense-datum which represents the sun, seems obviously a relation between the person acquainted and the object with which the person is acquainted. When a case of acquaintance is one with which I can be acquainted (as I am acquainted with my acquaintance with the sense-datum representing the sun), it is plain that the person acquainted is myself. Thus, when I am acquainted with my seeing the sun, the whole fact with which I am acquainted is 'Self-acquainted-with-sense-datum'.

Further, we know the truth 'I am acquainted with this sense-datum'. It is hard to see how we could know this truth, or even understand what is meant by it, unless we were acquainted with something which we call 'I'. It does not seem necessary to suppose that we are acquainted with a more or less permanent person, the same to-day as yesterday, but it does seem as though we must be acquainted with that thing, whatever its nature, which sees the sun and has acquaintance with sense-data. Thus, in some sense it would seem we must be acquainted with our Selves as opposed to our particular experiences. But the question is difficult, and complicated arguments can be adduced on either side. Hence, although acquaintance with ourselves seems *probably* to occur, it is not wise to assert that it undoubtedly does occur.

We may therefore sum up as follows what has been said concerning acquaintance with things that exist. We have acquaintance in sensation with the data of the outer senses, and in introspection with the data of what may be called the inner sense – thoughts, feelings, desires, etc.; we have acquaintance in memory with things which have been data either of the outer senses or of the inner sense. Further, it is probable, though not certain, that we have acquaintance with Self, as that which is aware of things or has desires towards things.

In addition to our acquaintance with particular existing things, we also have acquaintance with what we shall call *universals*, that is to say, general ideas, such as *whiteness, diversity, brotherhood*, and so on. Every complete sentence must contain at least one word which stands for a universal, since all verbs have a meaning which is universal. We shall return to universals later on . . . ; for the present, it is only necessary to guard against the supposition that whatever we can be acquainted with must be something particular and existent. Awareness of universals is called *conceiving*, and a universal of which we are aware is called a *concept*.

It will be seen that among the objects with which we are acquainted are not included physical objects (as opposed to sense-data), nor other people's minds. These things are known to us by what I call 'knowledge by description', which we must now consider.

By a 'description' I mean any phrase of the form 'a so-and-so' or 'the so-and-so'. A phrase of the form 'a so-and-so' I shall call an 'ambiguous' description; a phrase of the form 'the so-and-so' (in the singular) I shall call a 'definite' description. Thus 'a man' is an ambiguous description, and 'the man with the iron mask' is a definite description. There are various problems connected with ambiguous descriptions, but I pass them by, since they do not directly concern the matter we are discussing, which is the nature of our knowledge concerning objects in cases where we know that there is an object answering to a definite description, though we are not *acquainted* with any such object. This is a matter which is concerned exclusively with *definite* descriptions. I shall therefore, in the sequel, speak simply of 'descriptions' when I mean 'definite descriptions'. Thus a description will mean any phrase of the form 'the so-and-so' in the singular.

We shall say that an object is 'known by description' when we know that it is 'the so-and-so', i.e. when we know that there is one object, and no more, having a certain property; and it will generally be implied that we do not have knowledge of the same object by acquaintance. We know that the man with the iron mask existed, and many propositions are known about him; but we do not know who he was. We know that the candidate who gets the most votes will be elected, and in this case we are very likely also acquainted (in the only sense in which one can be acquainted with some one else) with the man who is, in fact, the candidate who will get most votes; but we do not know which of the candidates he is, i.e. we do not know any proposition of the form 'A is the candidate who will get most votes' where A is one of the candidates by name. We shall say that we have 'merely descriptive knowledge' of the so-and-so when, although we know that the so-and-so exists, and although we may possibly be acquainted with the object which is, in fact, the so-and-so, yet we do not know any proposition '*a* is the so-and-so', where *a* is something with which we are acquainted.

When we say 'the so-and-so exists', we mean that there is just one object which is the so-and-so. The proposition '*a* is the so-and-so' means that *a* has the property so-and-so, and nothing else has. 'Mr. A. is the Unionist candidate for this constituency' means 'Mr. A. is a Unionist candidate for this constituency, and no one else is'. 'The Unionist candidate for this constituency exists' means 'some one is a Unionist candidate for this constituency, and no one else is'. Thus, when we are acquainted with an object which is the so-and-so, we know that the so-and-so exists;

but we may know that the so-and-so exists when we are not acquainted with any object which we know to be the so-and-so, and even when we are not acquainted with any object which, in fact, is the so-and-so.

Common words, even proper names, are usually really descriptions. That is to say, the thought in the mind of a person using a proper name correctly can generally only be expressed explicitly if we replace the proper name by a description. Moreover, the description required to express the thought will vary for different people, or for the same person at different times. The only thing constant (so long as the name is rightly used) is the object to which the name applies. But so long as this remains constant, the particular description involved usually makes no difference to the truth or falsehood of the proposition in which the name appears.

Let us take some illustrations. Suppose some statement made about Bismarck. Assuming that there is such a thing as direct acquaintance with oneself, Bismarck himself might have used his name directly to designate the particular person with whom he was acquainted. In this case, if he made a judgement about himself, he himself might be a constituent of the judgement. Here the proper name has the direct use which it always wishes to have, as simply standing for a certain object, and not for a description of the object. But if a person who knew Bismarck made a judgement about him, the case is different. What this person was acquainted with were certain sense-data which he connected (rightly, we will suppose) with Bismarck's body. His body, as a physical object, and still more his mind, were only known as the body and the mind connected with these sense-data. That is, they were known by description. It is, of course, very much a matter of chance which characteristics of a man's appearance will come into a friend's mind when he thinks of him; thus the description actually in the friend's mind is accidental. The essential point is that he knows that the various descriptions all apply to the same entity, in spite of not being acquainted with the entity in question.

When we, who did not know Bismarck, make a judgement about him, the description in our minds will probably be some more or less vague mass of historical knowledge – far more, in most cases, than is required to identify him. But, for the sake of illustration, let us assume that we think of him as 'the first Chancellor of the German Empire'. Here all the words are abstract except 'German'. The word 'German' will, again, have different meanings for different people. To some it will recall travels in Germany, to some the look of Germany on the map, and so on. But if we are to obtain a description which we know to be applicable, we shall be compelled, at some point, to bring in a reference to a particular with which we are acquainted. Such reference is involved in any mention of past, present, and future (as opposed to definite dates), or of here and there, or of what others have told us. Thus it would seem that, in some way or other, a description known to be applicable to a particular must involve some reference to a particular with which we are acquainted, if our knowledge about the thing described is not to be merely what follows *logically* from the description. For example, 'the most long-lived of men' is a description involving only universals, which must apply to some man, but we can make no judgements concerning this man which involve knowledge about him beyond what the description gives. If, however, we say, 'The first Chancellor of the German Empire was an astute diplomatist', we can only be assured of the truth of our judgement in virtue of something with which we are acquainted – usually a testimony heard or read. Apart from the information we convey to others, apart from the fact about the actual Bismarck, which gives importance to our judgement, the thought we really have contains the one or more particulars involved, and otherwise consists wholly of concepts.

All names of places – London, England, Europe, the Earth, the Solar System – similarly involve, when used, descriptions which start from some one or more particulars with which we are acquainted. I suspect that even the Universe, as considered by metaphysics, involves such a connexion with particulars. In logic, on the contrary, where we are concerned not merely with what does exist, but with whatever might or could exist or be, no reference to actual particulars is involved.

It would seem that, when we make a statement about something only known by description, we often *intend* to make our statement, not in the form involving the description, but about the actual thing described. That is to say, when we say anything about Bismarck, we should like, if we could, to make the judgement which Bismarck alone can make, namely, the judgement of which he himself is a constituent. In this we are necessarily defeated, since the actual Bismarck is unknown to us. But we know that there is an object B, called Bismarck, and that B was an astute diplomatist. We can thus *describe* the proposition we should like to affirm, namely, 'B was an astute diplomatist', where B is the object which was Bismarck. If we are describing Bismarck as 'the first Chancellor of the German Empire', the proposition we should like to affirm may be described as 'the proposition asserting, concerning the actual object which was the first Chancellor of the German Empire, that this object was an astute diplomatist'. What enables us to communicate in spite of the varying descriptions we employ is that we know there is a true proposition concerning the actual Bismarck, and that however we may vary the description (so long as the description is correct) the proposition described is still the same. This proposition, which is described and is known to be true, is what interests us; but we are not acquainted with the proposition itself, and do not know *it*, though we know it is true.

It will be seen that there are various stages in the removal from acquaintance with particulars: there is Bismarck to people who knew him; Bismarck to those who only know of him through history; the man with the iron mask; the longest-lived of men. These are progressively further removed from acquaintance with particulars; the first comes as near to acquaintance as is possible in regard to another person; in the second, we shall still be said to know 'who Bismarck was'; in the third, we do not know who was the man with the iron mask, though we can know many propositions about him which are not logically deducible from the fact that he wore an iron mask; in the fourth, finally, we know nothing beyond what is logically deducible from the definition of the man. There is a similar hierarchy in the region of universals. Many universals, like many particulars, are only known to us by description. But here, as in the case of particulars, knowledge concerning what is known by description is ulti-

mately reducible to knowledge concerning what is known by acquaintance.

The fundamental principle in the analysis of propositions containing descriptions is this: *Every proposition which we can understand must be composed wholly of constituents with which we are acquainted.*

We shall not at this stage attempt to answer all the objections which may be urged against this fundamental principle. For the present, we shall merely point out that, in some way or other, it must be possible to meet these objections, for it is scarcely conceivable that we can make a judgement or entertain a supposition without knowing what it is that we are judging or supposing about. We must attach *some* meaning to the words we use, if we are to speak significantly and not utter mere noise; and the meaning we attach to our words must be something with which we are acquainted. Thus when, for example, we make a statement about Julius Caesar, it is plain that Julius Caesar himself is not before our minds, since we are not acquainted with him. We have in mind some *description* of Julius Caesar: 'the man who was assassinated on the Ides of March', 'the founder of the Roman Empire', or, perhaps, merely 'the man whose name was *Julius Caesar*'. (In this last description, *Julius Caesar* is a noise or shape with which we are acquainted.) Thus our statement does not mean quite what it seems to mean, but means something involving, instead of Julius Caesar, some description of him which is composed wholly of particulars and universals with which we are acquainted.

The chief importance of knowledge by description is that it enables us to pass beyond the limits of our private experience. In spite of the fact that we can only know truths which are wholly composed of terms which we have experienced in acquaintance, we can yet have knowledge by description of things which we have never experienced. In view of the very narrow range of our immediate experience, this result is vital, and until it is understood, much of our knowledge must remain mysterious and therefore doubtful.

17

The Problem of the Criterion

Roderick Chisholm

1

"The problem of the criterion" seems to me to be one of the most important and one of the most difficult of all the problems of philosophy. I am tempted to say that one has not begun to philosophize until one has faced this problem and has recognized how unappealing, in the end, each of the possible solutions is. I have chosen this problem as my topic for the Aquinas Lecture because what first set me to thinking about it (and I remain obsessed by it) were two treatises of twentieth-century scholastic philosophy. I refer first to P. Coffey's two-volume work, *Epistemology or the Theory of Knowledge*, published in 1917.[1] This led me in turn to the treatises of Coffey's great teacher, Cardinal D. J. Mercier: *Critériologie générale ou théorie générale de la certitude*.[2]

Mercier and, following him, Coffey set the problem correctly, I think, and have seen what is necessary for its solution. But I shall not discuss their views in detail. I shall formulate the problem; then note what, according to Mercier, is necessary if we are to solve the problem; then sketch my own solution; and, finally, note the limitations of my approach to the problem.

Originally the Aquinas Lecture, published by Marquette University Press, 1973. Reprinted from *The Foundations of Knowing* (University of Minnesota Press, 1982).

2

What is the problem, then? It is the ancient problem of "the diallelus" – the problem of "the wheel" or "the vicious circle." It was put very neatly by Montaigne is his *Essays*. So let us begin by paraphrasing his formulation of the puzzle. To know whether things really are as they seem to be, we must have a *procedure* for distinguishing appearances that are true from appearances that are false. But to know whether our procedure is a good procedure, we have to know whether it really *succeeds* in distinguishing appearances that are true from appearances that are false. And we cannot know whether it does really succeed unless we already know which appearances are *true* and which ones are *false*. And so we are caught in a circle.[3]

Let us try to see how one gets into a situation of this sort.

The puzzles begin to form when you ask yourself, "What can I really know about the world?" We all are acquainted with people who think they know a lot more than in fact they do know. I'm thinking of fanatics, bigots, mystics, various types of dogmatists. And we have all heard of people who claim at least to know a lot less than what in fact they do know. I'm thinking of those people who call themselves "skeptics" and who like to say that people cannot know what the world is really like. People tend to become skeptics, temporarily, after reading books on popular science: the authors tell us we cannot know what things are like really (but they make use of a vast amount of knowledge, or a vast amount of what is claimed to be knowledge, to support this skeptical conclusion). And as we know, people tend to become dogmatists, temporarily, as a result of the effects of alcohol, or drugs, or religious and emotional experiences. Then they claim to have an inside view of the world and they think they have a deep kind of knowledge giving them a key to the entire workings of the universe.

If you have a healthy common sense, you will feel that something is wrong with both of these extremes and that the truth is somewhere in the middle: we can know far more than the skeptic says we can know and far less than the dogmatist or the mystic says that he can know. But how are we to decide these things?

3

How do we decide, in any particular case, whether we have a genuine item of knowledge? Most of us are ready to confess that our beliefs far transcend what we really know. There are things we believe that we don't in fact know. And we can say of many of these things that we know that we don't know them. I believe that Mrs. Jones is honest, say, but I don't know it, and I know that I don't know it. There are other things that we don't know, but they are such that we don't know that we don't know them. Last week, say, I thought I knew that Mr. Smith was honest, but he turned out to be a thief. I didn't know that he was a thief, and, moreover, I didn't know that I didn't know that he was a thief; I thought I knew that he was honest. And so the problem is: How are we to distinguish the real cases of knowledge from what only seem to be cases of knowledge? Or, as I put it before, how are we to decide in any particular case whether we have genuine items of knowledge?

What would be a satisfactory solution to our problem? Let me quote in detail what Cardinal Mercier says:

If there is any knowledge which bears the mark of truth, if the intellect does have a way of distinguishing the true and the false, in short, *if there is* a criterion of truth, then this criterion should satisfy three conditions: it should be *internal*, *objective*, and *immediate*.

It should be *internal*. No reason or rule of truth that is provided by an *external authority* can serve as an ultimate criterion. For the reflective doubts that are essential to criteriology can and should be applied to this authority itself. The mind cannot attain to certainty until it has found *within itself* a sufficient reason for adhering to the testimony of such an authority.

The criterion should be *objective*. The ultimate reason for believing cannot be a merely *subjective* state of the thinking subject. A man is aware that he can reflect upon his psychological states in order to control them. Knowing that he has this ability, he does not, so long as he has not made use of it, have the right to be sure. The ultimate ground of certitude cannot consist in a subjective feeling. It can be found only in that which, objectively, produces this feeling and is adequate to reason.

Finally, the criterion must be *immediate*. To be sure, a certain conviction may rest upon many different reasons some of which are subordinate to others. But if we are to avoid an infinite regress, then we must find a ground of assent that presupposes no other. We must find an *immediate* criterion of certitude.

Is there a criterion of truth that satisfies these three conditions? If so, what is it?[4]

4

To see how perplexing our problem is, let us consider a figure that Descartes had suggested and that Coffey takes up in his dealings with the problem of the criterion.[5] Descartes' figure comes to this.

Let us suppose that you have a pile of apples and you want to sort out the good ones from the bad ones. You want to put the good ones in a pile by themselves and throw the bad ones away. This is a useful thing to do, obviously, because the bad apples tend to infect the good ones and then the good ones become bad, too. Descartes thought our beliefs were like this. The bad ones tend to infect the good ones, so we should look them over very carefully, throw out the bad ones if we can, and then – or so Descartes hoped – we would be left with just a stock of good beliefs on which we could rely completely. But how are we to do the sorting? If we are to sort out the good ones from the bad ones, then, of course, we must have a way of recognizing the good ones. Or at least we must have a way of recognizing the bad ones. And – again, of course – you and I do have a way of recognizing good apples and also of recognizing bad ones. The good ones have their own special feel, look, and taste, and so do the bad ones.

But when we turn from apples to beliefs, the matter is quite different. In the case of the apples, we have a method – a criterion – for distinguishing the good ones from the bad ones. But in the case of the beliefs, we do not have a method or a criterion for distinguishing the good ones from the bad ones. Or, at least, we don't have one yet. The question we started with was: How *are* we to tell the good ones from the bad ones? In other words, we were asking: What is the proper method for deciding which are the good beliefs and which are the bad ones – which beliefs are genuine cases of knowledge and which beliefs are not?

And now, you see, we are on the wheel. First, we want to find out which are the good beliefs and which are the bad ones. To find this out we have to have some way – some method – of deciding which are the good ones and which are the bad ones. But there are good and bad methods – good and bad ways – of sorting out the good beliefs from the bad ones. And so we now have a new problem: How are we to decide which are the good methods and which are the bad ones?

If we could fix on a good method for distinguishing between good and bad methods, we might be all set. But this, of course, just moves the problem to a different level. How are we to distinguish between a good method for choosing good methods? If we continue in this way, of course, we are led to an infinite regress and we will never have the answer to our original question.

What do we do in fact? We do know that there are fairly reliable ways of sorting out good beliefs from bad ones. Most people will tell you, for example, that if you follow the procedures of science and common sense – if you tend carefully to your observations and if you make use of the canons of logic, induction, and the theory of probability – you will be following the best possible procedure for making sure that you will have more good beliefs than bad ones. This is doubtless true. But how do we know that it is? How do we know that the procedures of science,

reason, and common sense are the best methods that we have?

If we do know this, it is because we know that these procedures work. It is because we know that these procedures do in fact enable us to distinguish the good beliefs from the bad ones. We say: "See – these methods turn out good beliefs." But *how* do we know that they do? It can only be that we already know how to tell the difference between the good beliefs and the bad ones.

And now you can see where the skeptic comes in. He'll say this: "You said you wanted to sort out the good beliefs from the bad ones. Then to do this, you apply the canons of science, common sense, and reason. And now, in answer to the question, 'How do you know that that's the right way to do it?', you say 'Why, I can see that the ones it picks out are the good ones and the ones it leaves behind are the bad ones.' But if you can *see* which ones are the good ones and which ones are the bad ones, why do you think you need a general method for sorting them out?"

5

We can formulate some of the philosophical issues that are involved here by distinguishing two pairs of questions. These are:

(A) "*What* do we know? What is the *extent* of our knowledge?"

(B) "How are we to decide *whether* we know? What are the *criteria* of knowledge?"

If you happen to know the answers to the first of these pairs of questions, you may have some hope of being able to answer the second. Thus, if you happen to know which are the good apples and which are the bad ones, then maybe you could explain to some other person how he could go about deciding whether or not he has a good apple or a bad one. But if you don't know the answer to the first of these pairs of questions – if you don't know what things you know or how far your knowledge extends – it is difficult to see how you could possibly figure out an answer to the second.

On the other hand, *if*, somehow, you already know the answers to the second of these pairs of questions, then you may have some hope of being able to answer the first. Thus, if you happen to have a good set of directions for telling whether apples are good or bad, then maybe you can go about finding a good one – assuming, of course, that there are some good apples to be found. But if you don't know the answer to the second of these pairs of questions – if you don't know how to go about deciding whether or not you know, if you don't know what the criteria of knowing are – it is difficult to see how you could possibly figure out an answer to the first.

And so we can formulate the position of *the skeptic* on these matters. He will say: "You cannot answer question A until you have answered question B. And you cannot answer question B until you have answered question A. Therefore you cannot answer either question. You cannot know what, if anything, you know, and there is no possible way for you to decide in any particular case." Is there any reply to this?

6

Broadly speaking, there are at least two other possible views. So we may choose among three possibilities.

There are people – philosophers – who think that they do have an answer to B and that, given their answer to B, they can then figure out their answer to A. And there are other people – other philosophers – who have it the other way around: they think that they have an answer to A and that, given their answer to A, they can then figure out the answer to B.

There don't seem to be any generally accepted names for these two different philosophical positions. (Perhaps this is just as well. There are more than enough names, as it is, for possible philosophical views.) I suggest, for the moment, we use the expressions "methodists" and "particularists." By "methodists," I mean, not the followers of John Wesley's version of Christianity, but those who think they have an answer to B, and who then, in terms of it, work out their answer to A. By "particularists" I mean those who have it the other way around.

7

Thus John Locke was a methodist – in our present, rather special sense of the term. He was able to arrive – somehow – at an answer to B.

He said, in effect: "The way you decide whether or not a belief is a good belief – that is to say, the way you decide whether a belief is likely to be a genuine case of knowledge – is to see whether it is derived from sense experience, to see, for example, whether it bears certain relations to your sensations." Just what these relations to our sensations might be is a matter we may leave open, for present purposes. The point is: Locke felt that if a belief is to be credible, it must bear certain relations to the believer's sensations – but he never told us *how* he happened to arrive at this conclusion. This, of course, is the view that has come to be known as "empiricism." David Hume followed Locke in this empiricism and said that empiricism gives us an effective criterion for distinguishing the good apples from the bad ones. You can take this criterion to the library, he said. Suppose you find a book in which the author makes assertions that do not conform to the empirical criterion. Hume said: "Commit it to the flames: for it can contain nothing but sophistry and illusion."

8

Empiricism, then, was a form of what I have called "methodism." The empiricist – like other types of methodist – begins with a criterion and then he uses it to throw out the bad apples. There are two objections, I would say, to empiricism. The first – which applies to every form of methodism (in our present sense of the word) – is that the criterion is very broad and far-reaching and at the same time completely arbitrary. How can one *begin* with a broad generalization? It seems especially odd that the empiricist – who wants to proceed cautiously, step by step, from experience – begins with such a generalization. He leaves us completely in the dark so far as concerns what *reasons* he may have for adopting this particular criterion rather than some other. The second objection applies to empiricism in particular. When we apply the empirical criterion – at least, as it was developed by Hume, as well as by many of those in the nineteenth and twentieth centuries who have called themselves "empiricists" – we seem to throw out, not only the bad apples but the good ones as well, and we are left, in effect, with just a few parings or skins with no meat behind them. Thus Hume virtually conceded that, if you are going to be empiricist, the only matters of fact that you can really know about pertain to the existence of sensations. "'Tis vain," he said, "to ask whether there be body." He meant you cannot know whether any physical things exist – whether there are trees, or houses, or bodies, much less whether there are atoms or other such microscopic particles. All you can know is that there are and have been certain sensations. You cannot know whether there is any you who experiences those sensations – much less whether any other people exist who experience sensations. And I think, if he had been consistent in his empiricism, he would also have said you cannot really be sure whether there have been any sensations in the past; you can know only that certain sensations exist here and now.

9

The great Scottish philosopher, Thomas Reid, reflected on all this in the eighteenth century. He was serious about philosophy and man's place in the world. He finds Hume saying things implying that we can know only of the existence of certain sensations here and now. One can imagine him saying: "Good Lord! What kind of nonsense is this?" What he did say, among other things, was this: "A traveller of good judgment may mistake his way, and be unawares led into a wrong track; and while the road is fair before him, he may go on without suspicion and be followed by others but, when it ends in a coal pit, it requires no great judgment to know that he hath gone wrong, nor perhaps to find out what misled him."[6]

Thus Reid, as I interpret him, was not an empiricist; nor was he, more generally, what I have called a "methodist." He was a "particularist." That is to say, he thought that he had an answer to question A, and in terms of the answer to question A, he then worked out kind of an answer to question B.[7] An even better example of a "particularist" is the great twentieth-century English philosopher, G. E. Moore.

Suppose, for a moment, you were tempted to go along with Hume and say "The only thing about the world I can really know is that there are now sensations of a certain sort. There's a sensation of a man, there's the sound of a voice, and there's a feeling of bewilderment or boredom. But that's all I can really know about." What

would Reid say? I can imagine him saying something like this: "Well, you can talk that way if you want to. But you know very well that it isn't true. You know that you are there, that you have a body of such and such a sort and that other people are here, too. And you know about this building and where you were this morning and all kinds of other things as well." G. E. Moore would raise his hand at this point and say: "I know very well this is a hand, and so do you. If you come across some philosophical theory that implies that you and I cannot know that this is a hand, then so much the worse for the theory." I think that Reid and Moore are right, myself, and I'm inclined to think that the "methodists" are wrong.

Going back to our questions A and B, we may summarize the three possible views as follows: there is skepticism (you cannot answer either question without presupposing an answer to the other, and therefore the questions cannot be answered at all); there is "methodism" (you begin with an answer to B); and there is "particularism" (you begin with an answer to A). I suggest that the third possibility is the most reasonable.

10

I would say – and many reputable philosophers would disagree with me – that, to find out whether you know such a thing as that this is a hand, you don't have to apply any test or criterion. Spinoza has it right. "In order to know," he said, "there is no need to know that we know, much less to know that we know that we know."[8]

This is part of the answer, it seems to me, to the puzzle about the diallelus. There are many things that, quite obviously, we do know to be true. If I report to you the things I now see and hear and feel – or, if you prefer, the things I now think I see and hear and feel – the chances are that my report will be correct; I will be telling you something I know. And so, too, if you report the things that you think you now see and hear and feel. To be sure, there are hallucinations and illusions. People often think they see or hear or feel things that in fact they do not see or hear or feel. But from this fact – that our senses do sometimes deceive us – it hardly follows that your senses and mine are deceiving you and me right now. One may say similar things about what we remember.

Having these good apples before us, we can look them over and formulate certain criteria of goodness. Consider the senses, for example. One important criterion – one epistemological principle – was formulated by St. Augustine. It is more reasonable, he said, to trust the senses than to distrust them. Even though there have been illusions and hallucinations, the wise thing, when everything seems all right, is to accept the testimony of the senses. I say "when everything seems all right." If on a particular occasion something about *that* particular occasion makes you suspect that particular report of the senses, if, say, you seem to remember having been drugged or hypnotized, or brainwashed, then perhaps you should have some doubts about what you think you see, or hear, or feel, or smell. But if nothing about this particular occasion leads you to suspect what the senses report on this particular occasion, then the wise thing is to take such a report at its face value. In short the senses should be regarded as innocent until there is some positive reason, on some particular occasion, for thinking that they are guilty on that particular occasion.

One might say the same thing of memory. If, on any occasion, you think you remember that such-and-such an event occurred, then the wise thing is to assume that that particular event did occur – unless something special about this particular occasion leads you to suspect your memory.

We have then a kind of answer to the puzzle about the diallelus. We start with particular cases of knowledge and then from those we generalize and formulate criteria of goodness – criteria telling us what it is for a belief to be epistemologically respectable. Let us now try to sketch somewhat more precisely this approach to the problem of the criterion.

11

The theory of evidence, like ethics and the theory of value, presupposes an objective right and wrong. To explicate the requisite senses of "right" and "wrong," we need the concept of *right preference* – or, more exactly, the concept of one state of mind being *preferable*, epistemically, to another. One state of mind may be *better*, epistemically, than another. This concept of epistemic preferability is what Cardinal Mercier called an *objective* concept. It is one thing to say, objectively, that one state of mind is *to be preferred* to another. It is quite another thing to say, subjectively, that one state of mind is in fact preferred to another – that someone or other happens to prefer the one state of mind to the other. If a state of mind A is to be preferred to a state of mind B, if it is, as I would like to say, intrinsically preferable to B, then anyone who prefers B to A is *mistaken* in his preference.

Given this concept of epistemic preferability, we can readily explicate the basic concepts of the theory of evidence. We could say, for example, that a proposition p is *beyond reasonable doubt* provided only that believing p is then epistemically preferable for S to withholding p – where by "withholding p" we mean the state of neither accepting p nor its negation. It is evident to me, for example, that many people are here. This means it is epistemically preferable for me to believe that many people are here than for me neither to believe nor to disbelieve that many people are here.

A proposition is *evident* for a person if it is beyond reasonable doubt for that person and is such that his including it among the propositions upon which he bases his decisions is preferable to his not so including it. A proposition is *acceptable* if withholding it is *not* preferable to believing it. And a proposition is *unacceptable* if withholding it *is* preferable to believing it.

Again, some propositions are not beyond reasonable doubt but they may be said to have *some presumption in their favor*. I suppose that the proposition that each of us will be alive an hour from now is one that has some presumption in its favor. We could say that a proposition is of this sort provided only that believing the proposition is epistemically preferable to believing its negation.

Moving in the other direction in the epistemic hierarchy, we could say that a proposition is *certain*, absolutely certain, for a given subject at a given time, if that proposition is then evident to that subject and if there is no other proposition that is such that believing that other proposition is then epistemically preferable for him to believing the given proposition. It is certain for me, I would say, that there seem to be many people here and that 7 and 5 are 12. If this is so, then each of the two propositions is evident to me and there are no other propositions that are such that it would be even better, epistemically, if I were to believe those other propositions.

This concept of epistemic preferability can be axiomatized and made the basis of a system of epistemic logic exhibiting the relations among these and other concepts of the theory of evidence.[9] For present purposes, let us simply note how they may be applied in our approach to the problem of the criterion.

12

Let us begin with the most difficult of the concepts to which we have just referred – that of a proposition being *certain* for a man at a given time. Can we formulate *criteria* of such certainty? I think we can.

Leibniz had said that there are two kinds of immediately evident proposition – the "first truths of fact" and the "first truths of reason." Let us consider each of these in turn.

Among the "first truths of fact," for any man at any given time, I would say, are various propositions about his own state of mind at that time – his thinking certain thoughts, his entertaining certain beliefs, his being in a certain sensory or emotional state. These propositions all pertain to certain states of the man that may be said to manifest or present themselves to him at that time. We could use Meinong's term and say that certain states are "self-presenting," where this concept might be marked off in the following way.

A man's being in a certain state is *self-presenting* to him at a given time provided only that (1) he is in that state at that time and (2) it is necessarily true that if he is in that state at that time then it is evident to him that he is in that state at that time.

The states of mind just referred to are of this character. Wishing, say, that one were on the moon is a state that is such that a man cannot be in that state without it being evident to him that he is in that state. And so, too, for thinking certain thoughts and having certain sensory or emotional experiences. These states present themselves and are, so to speak, marks of their own evidence. They cannot occur unless it is evident that they occur. I think they are properly called the "first truths of fact." Thus St. Thomas could say that "the intellect knows that it possesses the truth by reflecting on itself."[10]

Perceiving external things and remembering are not states that present themselves. But thinking that one perceives (or seeming to perceive) and thinking that one remembers (or seeming to remember) *are* states of mind that present themselves. And in presenting themselves they may, at least under certain favorable conditions, present something else as well.

Coffey quotes Hobbes as saying that "the inn of evidence has no sign-board."[11] I would prefer saying that these self-presenting states are sign-boards – of the inn of indirect evidence. But these sign-boards need no further sign-boards in order to be presented, for they present themselves.

13

What of the first truths of reason? These are the propositions that some philosophers have called "a priori" and that Leibniz, following Locke, referred to as "maxims" or "axioms." These propositions are all necessary and have a further characteristic that Leibniz described in this way: "You will find in a hundred places that the Scholastics have said that these propositions are evident, *ex terminis*, as soon as the terms are understood, so that they were persuaded that the force of conviction was grounded in the nature of the terms, i.e., in the connection of their ideas."[12] Thus St. Thomas referred to propositions that are "manifest through themselves."[13]

An axiom, one might say, is a necessary proposition such that one cannot understand it without thereby knowing that it is true. Since one cannot know a proposition unless it is evident and one believes it, and since one cannot believe a proposition unless one understands it, we might characterize these first truths of reason in the following way:

A proposition is *axiomatic* for a given subject at a given time provided only that (1) the proposition is one that is necessarily true and (2) it is also necessarily true that if the person then believes that proposition, the proposition is then evident to him.

We might now characterize the *a priori* somewhat more broadly by saying that a proposition is a priori for a given subject at a given time provided that one or the other of these two things is true: either (1) the proposition is one that is axiomatic for that subject at that time, or else (2) the proposition is one such that it is evident to the man at that time that the proposition is entailed by a set of propositions that are axiomatic for him at that time.

In characterizing the "first truths of fact" and the "first truths of reason," I have used the expression "evident." But I think it is clear that such truths are not only evident but also certain. And they may be said to be *directly*, or *immediately*, evident.

What, then, of the indirectly evident?

14

I have suggested in rather general terms above what we might say about memory and the senses. These ostensible sources of knowledge are to be treated as innocent until there is positive ground for thinking them guilty. I will not attempt to develop a theory of the indirectly evident at this point. But I will note at least the *kind* of principle to which we might appeal in developing such a theory.

We could *begin* by considering the following two principles, M and P; M referring to memory, and P referring to perception or the senses.

(M)   For any subject S, if it is evident to S that she seems to remember that *a* was F, then it is beyond reasonable doubt for S that *a* was F.

(P)   For any subject S, if it is evident to S that she thinks she perceives that *a* is F, then it is evident to S that *a* is F.

"She seems to remember" and "she thinks she perceives" here refer to certain self-presenting states that, in the figure I used above, could be said to serve as sign-boards for the inn of indirect evidence.

But principles M and P, as they stand, are much too latitudinarian. We will find that it is necessary to make qualifications and add more and more conditions. Some of these will refer to the subject's sensory state; some will refer to certain of her other beliefs; and some will refer to the relations of confirmation and mutual support. To set them forth in adequate detail would require a complete epistemology.[14]

So far as our problem of the criterion is concerned, the essential thing to note is this. In formulating such principles we will simply proceed as Aristotle did when he formulated his rules for the syllogism. As "particularists" in our approach to the problem of the criterion, we will fit our rules to the cases – to the apples we know to be good and to the apples we know to be bad. Knowing what we do about ourselves and the world, we have at our disposal certain instances that our rules or principles should countenance, and certain other instances that our rules or principles should rule out or forbid. And, as rational beings, we assume that by investigating these instances we can formulate criteria that any instance must satisfy if it is to be countenanced and we can formulate other criteria that any instance must satisfy if it is to be ruled out or forbidden.

If we proceed in this way we will have satisfied Cardinal Mercier's criteria for a theory of evidence or, as he called it, a theory of certitude. He said that any criterion, or any adequate set of criteria, should be internal, objective, and immediate. The type of criteria I have referred to are certainly *internal*, in his sense of the term. We have not appealed to any external authority as constituting the ultimate test of evidence. (Thus we haven't appealed to "science" or to "the scientists of our culture circle" as constituting the touchstone of what we know.) I would say that our criteria are *objective*. We have formulated them in terms of the concept of epistemic preferability – where the location "*p* is epistemically preferable to *q* for S" is taken to refer to an objective relation that obtains independently of the actual preferences of any particular subject. The criteria that we formulate, if they are adequate, will be principles that are necessarily true. And they are also *immediate*. Each of them is such that, if it is applicable at any particular time, then the fact that it is then applicable is capable of being directly evident to that particular subject at that particular time.

15

But in all of this I have presupposed the approach I have called "particularism." The "methodist" and the "skeptic" will tell us that we have started in the wrong place. If now we try to reason with them, then, I am afraid, we will be back on the wheel.

What few philosophers have had the courage to recognize is this: we can deal with the problem only by begging the question. It seems to me that, if we do recognize this fact, as we should, then it is unseemly for us to try to pretend that it isn't so.

One may object: "Doesn't this mean, then, that the skeptic is right after all?" I would answer: "Not at all. His view is only one of the three possibilities and in itself has no more to recommend it than the others do. And in favor of our approach there is the fact that we *do* know many things, after all."

Notes

1 Published in London in 1917 by Longmans, Green and Co.

2 The eighth edition of this work was published in 1923 in Louvain by the Institut Supérieur de Philosophie, and in Paris by Félix Alcan. The first edition was published in 1884. It has been translated into Spanish, Polish, Portuguese and perhaps still other languages, but unfortunately not yet into English.

3 The quotation is a paraphrase. What Montaigne wrote was: "Pour juger des apparences que nous recevons des subjects, il nous faudroit un instrument judicatoire; pour verifier cet instrument, il nous y faut de la demonstration; pour verifier la demonstration, un instrument; nous voylà au rouet. Puisque les sens ne peuvent arrester notre dispute, éstans pleins eux-mesmes d'incertitude, il faut que se soit la raison; aucune raison s'establira sans une autre raison: nous voylà à reculons jusques à l'infiny." The passage appears in Book 2, Chapter 12 ("An Apologie of Raymond Sebond"); it may be found on page 544 of the Modern Library edition of *The Essays of Montaigne*.

4 *Critériologie*, 8th edn., p. 234.

5 See the reply to the VIIth set of Objections and Coffey, vol. 1, p. 127.

6 Thomas Reid, *Inquiry into the Human Mind*, ch. 1, sec. 8.

7 Unfortunately Cardinal Mercier takes Reid to be what I have called a "methodist." He assumes, incorrectly I think, that Reid defends certain principles (principles that Reid calls principles of "common sense") on the ground that these principles happen to be the deliverance of a faculty called "common sense." See Mercier, pp. 179–81.

8 *On Improvement of the Understanding*, in *Chief Works of Benedict de Spinoza*, vol. 2, trans. R. H. M. Elwes, rev. edn. (London: George Bell and Sons, 1898), p. 13.

9 The logic of these concepts, though with a somewhat different vocabulary, is set forth in Roderick M. Chisholm and Robert Keim, "A System of Epistemic Logic," *Ratio* 15 (1973).

10 *The Disputed Questions on Truth*, trans. Robert W. Mulligan (Chicago: Henry Regnery Company, 1952), Question One, Article 9.

11 Coffey, vol. 1, p. 146. I have been unable to find this quotation in Hobbes.

12 *New Essays concerning Human Understanding*, book 4, ch. 7, n. 1.

13 *Exposition of the Posterior Analytics of Aristotle*, trans. Pierre Conway (Quebec: M. Doyon, 1956), Lectio 4, No. 10.

14 I have attempted to do this to some extent in *Theory of Knowledge* (Englewood Cliffs, NJ: Prentice-Hall, 1966). Revisions and corrections may be found in my essay "On the Nature of Empirical Evidence" in Roderick M. Chisholm and Robert J. Swartz (eds.) *Empirical Knowledge* (Englewood Cliffs, NJ: Prentice-Hall, 1973).

18

Is Justified True Belief Knowledge?

Edmund Gettier

Various attempts have been made in recent years to state necessary and sufficient conditions for someone's knowing a given proposition. The attempts have often been such that they can be stated in a form similar to the following:

(a) S knows that P
  IFF
  (i) P is true.
  (ii) S believes that P, and
  (iii) S is justified in believing that P.[1]

For example, Chisholm has held that the following gives the necessary and sufficient conditions for knowledge:[2]

(b) S knows that P
  IFF
  (i) S accepts P,
  (ii) S has adequate evidence for P, and
  (iii) P is true.

Ayer has stated the necessary and sufficient conditions for knowledge as follows:[3]

(c) S knows that P
  IFF
  (i) P is true.
  (ii) S is sure that P is true, and
  (iii) S has the right to be sure that P is true.

Originally published in *Analysis* 23 (1966). Reprinted by kind permission of Professor Edmund Gettier.

I shall argue that (a) is false in that the conditions stated therein do not constitute a *sufficient* condition for the truth of the proposition that S knows that P. The same argument will show that (b) and (c) fail if "has adequate evidence for" or "has the right to be sure that" is substituted for "is justified in believing that" throughout.

I shall begin by noting two points. First, in that sense of "justified" in which S's being justified in believing P is a necessary condition of S's knowing that P, it is possible for a person to be justified in believing a proposition which is in fact false. Secondly, for any proposition P, if S is justified in believing P and P entails Q and S deduces Q from P and accepts Q as a result of this deduction, then S is justified in believing Q. Keeping these two points in mind, I shall now present two cases in which the conditions stated in (a) are true for some proposition, though it is at the same time false that the person in question knows that proposition.

Case I

Suppose that Smith and Jones have applied for a certain job. And suppose that Smith has strong evidence for the following conjunctive proposition:

(d) Jones is the man who will get the job, and Jones has ten coins in his pocket.

Smith's evidence for (d) might be that the president of the company assured him that Jones would in the end be selected, and that he, Smith, had counted the coins in Jones's pocket ten minutes ago. Proposition (d) entails:

(e)   The man who will get the job has ten coins in his pocket.

Let us suppose that Smith sees the entailment from (d) to (e), and accepts (e) on the grounds of (d), for which he has strong evidence. In this case, Smith is clearly justified in believing that (e) is true.

But imagine, further, that unknown to Smith, he himself, not Jones, will get the job. And, also, unknown to Smith, he himself has ten coins in his pocket. Proposition (e) is then true, though proposition (d), from which Smith inferred (e), is false. In our example, then, all of the following are true: (1) (e) is true, (2) Smith believes that (e) is true, and (3) Smith is justified in believing that (e) is true. But it is equally clear that Smith does not *know* that (e) is true; for (e) is true in virtue of the number of coins in Smith's pocket, while Smith does not know how many coins are in Smith's pocket, and bases his belief in (e) on a count of the coins in Jones's pocket, whom he falsely believes to be the man who will get the job.

Case II

Let us suppose that Smith has strong evidence for the following proposition:

(f)   Jones owns a Ford.

Smith's evidence might be that Jones has at all times in the past within Smith's memory owned a car, and always a Ford, and that Jones has

just offered Smith a ride while driving a Ford. Let us imagine, now, that Smith has another friend, Brown, of whose whereabouts he is totally ignorant. Smith selects three place names quite at random and constructs the following three propositions:

(g)   Either Jones owns a Ford, or Brown is in Boston.
(h)   Either Jones owns a Ford, or Brown is in Barcelona.
(i)   Either Jones owns a Ford, or Brown is in Brest-Litovsk.

Each of these propositions is entailed by (f). Imagine that Smith realizes the entailment of each of these propositions he has constructed by (f), and proceeds to accept (g), (h), and (i) on the basis of (f). Smith has correctly inferred (g), (h), and (i) from a proposition for which he has strong evidence. Smith is therefore completely justified in believing each of these three propositions. Smith, of course, has no idea where Brown is.

But imagine now that two further conditions hold. First, Jones does *not* own a Ford, but is at present driving a rented car. And secondly, by the sheerest coincidence, and entirely unknown to Smith, the place mentioned in proposition (h) happens really to be the place where Brown is. If these two conditions hold, then Smith does *not* know that (h) is true, even though (1) (h) is true, (2) Smith does believe that (h) is true, and (3) Smith is justified in believing that (h) is true.

These two examples show that definition (a) does not state a *sufficient* condition for someone's knowing a given proposition. The same cases, with appropriate changes, will suffice to show that neither definition (b) nor definition (c) do so either.

Notes

1   Plato seems to be considering some such definition at *Theaetetus* 201, and perhaps accepting one at *Meno* 98.

2   Roderick M. Chisholm, *Perceiving: A Philosophical Study* (Ithaca, NY, 1957), p. 16.
3   A. J. Ayer, *The Problem of Knowledge* (London, 1956).

19

Laws and their Role in Scientific Explanation

Carl G. Hempel

Two Basic Requirements for Scientific Explanations

To explain the phenomena of the physical world is one of the primary objectives of the natural sciences. Indeed, almost all of the scientific investigations that served as illustrations in the preceding chapters [in *Philosophy of Natural Science*] were aimed not at ascertaining some particular fact but at achieving some explanatory insight; they were concerned with questions such as how puerperal fever is contracted, why the water-lifting capacity of pumps has its characteristic limitation, why the transmission of light conforms to the laws of geometrical optics, and so forth. In this chapter . . . we will examine in some detail the character of scientific explanations and the kind of insight they afford.

That man has long and persistently been concerned to achieve some understanding of the enormously diverse, often perplexing, and sometimes threatening occurrences in the world around him is shown by the manifold myths and metaphors he has devised in an effort to account for the very existence of the world and of himself, for life and death, for the motions of the heavenly bodies, for the regular sequence of day and night, for the changing seasons, for thunder and lightning, sunshine and rain. Some of these explanatory ideas are based on anthropomorphic conceptions of the forces of nature, others invoke hidden

Previously published in *Philosophy of Natural Science* (Prentice-Hall, Englewood Cliffs, NJ, 1966).

powers or agents, still others refer to God's inscrutable plans or to fate.

Accounts of this kind undeniably may give the questioner a sense of having attained some understanding; they may resolve his perplexity and in this sense "answer" his question. But however satisfactory these answers may be psychologically, they are not adequate for the purposes of science, which, after all, is concerned to develop a conception of the world that has a clear, logical bearing on our experience and is thus capable of objective test. Scientific explanations must, for this reason, meet two systematic requirements, which will be called the requirement of explanatory relevance and the requirement of testability.

The astronomer Francesco Sizi offered the following argument to show why, contrary to what his contemporary, Galileo, claimed to have seen through his telescope, there could be no satellites circling around Jupiter:

> There are seven windows in the head, two nostrils, two ears, two eyes and a mouth; so in the heavens there are two favorable stars, two unpropitious, two luminaries, and Mercury alone undecided and indifferent. From which and many other similar phenomena of nature such as the seven metals, etc., which it were tedious to enumerate, we gather that the number of planets is necessarily seven. . . . Moreover, the satellites are invisible to the naked eye and therefore can have no influence on the earth and therefore would be useless and therefore do not exist.[1]

The crucial defect of this argument is evident: the "facts" it adduces, even if accepted without question, are entirely irrelevant to the point at issue; they do not afford the slightest reason for the assumption that Jupiter has no satellites; the claim of relevance suggested by the barrage of words like 'therefore', 'it follows', and 'necessarily' is entirely spurious.

Consider by contrast the physical explanation of a rainbow. It shows that the phenomenon comes about as a result of the reflection and refraction of the white light of the sun in spherical droplets of water such as those that occur in a cloud. By reference to the relevant optical laws, this account shows that the appearance of a rainbow is to be expected whenever a spray or mist of water droplets is illuminated by a strong white light behind the observer. Thus, even if we happened never to have seen a rainbow, the explanatory information provided by the physical account would constitute good grounds for expecting or believing that a rainbow will appear under the specified circumstances. We will refer to this characteristic by saying that the physical explanation meets the *requirement of explanatory relevance*: the explanatory information adduced affords good grounds for believing that the phenomenon to be explained did, or does, indeed occur. This condition must be met if we are to be entitled to say: "That explains it – the phenomenon in question was indeed to be expected under the circumstances!"

The requirement represents a necessary condition for an adequate explanation, but not a sufficient one. For example, a large body of data showing a red-shift in the spectra of distant galaxies provides strong grounds for believing *that* those galaxies recede from our local one at enormous speeds, yet it does not explain *why*.

To introduce the second basic requirement for scientific explanations, let us consider once more the conception of gravitational attraction as manifesting a natural tendency akin to love. As we noted earlier, this conception has no test implications whatever. Hence, no empirical finding could possibly bear it out or disconfirm it. Being thus devoid of empirical content, the conception surely affords no grounds for expecting the characteristic phenomena of gravitational attraction: it lacks objective explanatory power. Similar comments apply to explanations in terms of an inscrutable fate: to invoke such an idea is not to achieve an especially profound insight, but to give up the

attempt at explanation altogether. By contrast, the statements on which the physical explanation of a rainbow is based do have various test implications; these concern, for example, the conditions under which a rainbow will be seen in the sky, and the order of the colors in it; the appearance of rainbow phenomena in the spray of a wave breaking on the rocks and in the mist of a lawn sprinkler; and so forth. These examples illustrate a second condition for scientific explanations, which we will call the *requirement of testability*: the statements constituting a scientific explanation must be capable of empirical test.

It has already been suggested that since the conception of gravitation in terms of an underlying universal affinity has no test implications, it can have no explanatory power: it cannot provide grounds for expecting that universal gravitation will occur, nor that gravitational attraction will show such and such characteristic features; for if it did imply such consequences either deductively or even in a weaker, inductive-probabilistic sense, then it would be testable by reference to those consequences. As this example shows, the two requirements just considered are interrelated: a proposed explanation that meets the requirement of relevance also meets the requirement of testability. (The converse clearly does not hold.)

Now let us see what forms scientific explanations take, and how they meet the two basic requirements.

Deductive-nomological Explanation

Consider once more Périer's finding in the Puy-de-Dôme experiment, that the length of the mercury column in a Torricelli barometer decreased with increasing altitude. Torricelli's and Pascal's ideas on atmospheric pressure provided an explanation for this phenomenon; somewhat pedantically, it can be spelled out as follows:

(a) At any location, the pressure that the mercury column in the closed branch of the Torricelli apparatus exerts upon the mercury below equals the pressure exerted on the surface of the mercury in the open vessel by the column of air above it.

(b) The pressures exerted by the columns of mercury and of air are proportional to their weights; and the shorter the columns, the smaller their weights.

(c) As Périer carried the apparatus to the top of the mountain, the column of air above the open vessel became steadily shorter.

(d) (Therefore,) the mercury column in the closed vessel grew steadily shorter during the ascent.

Thus formulated, the explanation is an argument to the effect that the phenomenon to be explained, as described by the sentence (d), is just what is to be expected in view of the explanatory facts cited in (a), (b), and (c); and that, indeed, (d) follows deductively from the explanatory statements. The latter are of two kinds; (a) and (b) have the character of general laws expressing uniform empirical connections; whereas (c) describes certain particular facts. Thus, the shortening of the mercury column is here explained by showing that it occurred in accordance with certain laws of nature, as a result of certain particular circumstances. The explanation fits the phenomenon to be explained into a pattern of uniformities and shows that its occurrence was to be expected, given the specified laws and the pertinent particular circumstances.

The phenomenon to be accounted for by an explanation will henceforth also be referred to as the *explanandum phenomenon*; the sentence describing it, as the *explanandum sentence*. When the context shows which is meant, either of them will simply be called the explanandum. The sentences specifying the explanatory information – (a), (b), (c) in our example – will be called the *explanans sentences*; jointly they will be said to form the *explanans*.

As a second example, consider the explanation of a characteristic of image formation by reflection in a spherical mirror; namely, that generally $1/u + 1/v = 2/r$, where u and v are the distances of object-point and image-point from the mirror, and r is the mirror's radius of curvature. In geometrical optics, this uniformity is explained with the help of the basic law of reflection in a plane mirror, by treating the reflection of a beam of light at any one point of a spherical mirror as a case of reflection in a plane tangential to the spherical surface. The resulting explanation can be formulated as a deductive argument whose conclusion is the explanandum sentence, and whose premises include the basic laws of reflection and of rectilinear propagation, as well as the statement that the surface of the mirror forms a segment of a sphere.[2]

A similar argument, whose premises again include the law for reflection in a plane mirror, offers an explanation of why the light of a small light source placed at the focus of a paraboloidal mirror is reflected in a beam parallel to the axis of the paraboloid (a principle technologically applied in the construction of automobile headlights, searchlights, and other devices).

The explanations just considered may be conceived, then, as deductive arguments whose conclusion is the explanandum sentence, E, and whose premiss-set, the explanans, consists of general laws, $L_1, L_2, \ldots, L_r$ and of other statements, $C_1, C_2, \ldots, C_k$, which make assertions about particular facts. The form of such arguments, which thus constitute one type of scientific explanation, can be represented by the following schema:

$$(\text{D-N}) \quad \left. \begin{array}{l} L_1, L_2, \ldots, L_r \\[4pt] C_1, C_2, \ldots, C_k \end{array} \right\} \text{Explanans sentences}$$
$$\frac{}{E} \quad \begin{array}{l} \text{Explanandum} \\ \text{sentence} \end{array}$$

Explanatory accounts of this kind will be called explanations by deductive subsumption under general laws, or *deductive-nomological explanations*. (The root of the term 'nomological' is the Greek word 'nomos', for law.) The laws invoked in a scientific explanation will also be called *covering laws* for the explanandum phenomenon, and the explanatory argument will be said to subsume the explanandum under those laws.

The explanandum phenomenon in a deductive-nomological explanation may be an event occurring at a particular place and time, such as the outcome of Périer's experiment. Or it may be some regularity found in nature, such as certain characteristics generally displayed by rainbows; or a uniformity expressed by an empirical law such as Galileo's or Kepler's laws. Deductive explanations of such uniformities will then invoke laws of broader scope, such as the laws of reflection and refraction, or Newton's laws of motion and of gravitation. As this use of Newton's laws illustrates, empirical laws are often explained by means of theoretical principles that refer to structures and processes underlying the uniformities in question. . . .

Deductive-nomological explanations satisfy the requirement of explanatory relevance in the strongest possible sense: the explanatory information they provide implies the explanandum sentence deductively and thus offers logically conclusive grounds why the explanandum phenomenon is to be expected. (We will soon encounter other scientific explanations, which fulfill the requirement only in a weaker, inductive, sense.) And the testability requirement is met as well, since the explanans implies among other things that under the specified conditions, the explanandum phenomenon occurs.

Some scientific explanations conform to the pattern (D-N) quite closely. This is so, particularly, when certain quantitative features of a phenomenon are explained by mathematical derivation from covering general laws, as in the case of reflection in spherical and paraboloidal mirrors. Or take the celebrated explanation, propounded by Leverrier (and independently by Adams), of peculiar irregularities in the motion of the planet Uranus, which on the current Newtonian theory could not be accounted for by the gravitational attraction of the other planets then known. Leverrier conjectured that they resulted from the gravitational pull of an as yet undetected outer planet, and he computed the position, mass, and other characteristics which that planet would have to possess to account in quantitative detail for the observed irregularities. His explanation was strikingly confirmed by the discovery, at the predicted location, of a new planet, Neptune, which had the quantitative characteristics attributed to it by Leverrier. Here again, the explanation has the character of a deductive argument whose premises include general laws – specifically, Newton's laws of gravitation and of motion – as well as statements specifying various quantitative particulars about the disturbing planet.

Not infrequently, however, deductive-nomological explanations are stated in an elliptical form: they omit mention of certain assumptions that are presupposed by the explanation but are simply taken for granted in the given context. Such explanations are sometimes expressed in the form 'E because C', where E is the event to be explained and C is some antecedent or concomitant event or state of affairs. Take, for example, the statement: 'The slush on the sidewalk remained liquid during the frost because it had been sprinkled with salt'. This explanation does not explicitly mention any laws, but it tacitly presupposes at least one: that the freezing point of water is lowered whenever salt is dissolved in it. Indeed, it is precisely by virtue of this law that the sprinkling of salt acquires the explanatory,

and specifically causative, role that the elliptical because-statement ascribes to it. That statement, incidentally, is elliptical also in other respects; for example, it tacitly takes for granted, and leaves unmentioned, certain assumptions about the prevailing physical conditions, such as the temperature's not dropping to a very low point. And if nomic and other assumptions thus omitted are added to the statement that salt had been sprinkled on the slush, we obtain the premises for a deductive-nomological explanation of the fact that the slush remained liquid.

Similar comments apply to Semmelweis's explanation that childbed fever was caused by decomposed animal matter introduced into the bloodstream through open wound surfaces. Thus formulated, the explanation makes no mention of general laws; but it presupposes that such contamination of the bloodstream generally leads to blood poisoning attended by the characteristic symptoms of childbed fever, for this is implied by the assertion that the contamination *causes* puerperal fever. The generalization was no doubt taken for granted by Semmelweis, to whom the cause of Kolletschka's fatal illness presented no etiological problem: given that infectious matter was introduced into the bloodstream, blood poisoning would result. (Kolletschka was by no means the first one to die of blood poisoning resulting from a cut with an infected scalpel. And by a tragic irony, Semmelweis himself was to suffer the same fate.) But once the tacit premiss is made explicit, the explanation is seen to involve reference to general laws.

As the preceding examples illustrate, corresponding general laws are always presupposed by an explanatory statement to the effect that a particular event of a certain kind G (e.g., expansion of a gas under constant pressure; flow of a current in a wire loop) was *caused* by an event of another kind, F (e.g., heating of the gas; motion of the loop across a magnetic field). To see this, we need not enter into the complex ramifications of the notion of cause; it suffices to note that the general maxim "Same cause, same effect", when applied to such explanatory statements, yields the implied claim that whenever an event of kind F occurs, it is accompanied by an event of kind G.

To say that an explanation rests on general laws is not to say that its discovery required the discovery of the laws. The crucial new insight achieved by an explanation will sometimes lie in the discovery of some particular fact (e.g., the presence of an undetected outer planet; infectious matter adhering to the hands of examining physicians) which, by virtue of antecedently accepted general laws, accounts for the explanandum phenomenon. In other cases, such as that of the lines in the hydrogen spectrum, the explanatory achievement does lie in the discovery of a covering law (Balmer's) and eventually of an explanatory theory (such as Bohr's); in yet other cases, the major accomplishment of an explanation may lie in showing that, and exactly how, the explanandum phenomenon can be accounted for by reference to laws and data about particular facts that are already available: this is illustrated by the explanatory derivation of the reflection laws for spherical and paraboloidal mirrors from the basic law of geometrical optics in conjunction with statements about the geometrical characteristics of the mirrors.

An explanatory problem does not by itself determine what kind of discovery is required for its solution. Thus, Leverrier discovered deviations from the theoretically expected course also in the motion of the planet Mercury; and as in the case of Uranus, he tried to explain these as resulting from the gravitational pull of an as yet undetected planet, Vulcan, which would have to be a very dense and very small object between the sun and Mercury. But no such planet was found, and a satisfactory explanation was provided only much later by the general theory of relativity, which accounted for the irregularities not by reference to some disturbing particular factor, but by means of a new system of laws.

Universal Laws and Accidental Generalizations

As we have seen, laws play an essential role in deductive-nomological explanations. They provide the link by reason of which particular circumstances (described by $C_1, C_2, \ldots, C_k$) can serve to explain the occurrence of a given event. And when the explanandum is not a particular event, but a uniformity such as those represented by characteristics mentioned earlier of spherical and paraboloidal mirrors, the explanatory laws exhibit a system of more comprehensive uniformities, of which the given one is but a special case.

The laws required for deductive-nomological explanations share a basic characteristic: they are, as we shall say, statements of universal form. Broadly speaking, a statement of this kind asserts a uniform connection between different empirical phenomena or between different aspects of an empirical phenomenon. It is a statement to the effect that whenever and wherever conditions of a specified kind F occur, then so will, always and without exception, certain conditions of another kind, G. (Not all scientific laws are of this type. In the sections that follow, we will encounter laws of probabilistic form, and explanations based on them.)

Here are some examples of statements of universal form: whenever the temperature of a gas increases while its pressure remains constant, its volume increases; whenever a solid is dissolved in a liquid, the boiling point of the liquid is raised; whenever a ray of light is reflected at a plane surface, the angle of reflection equals the angle of incidence; whenever a magnetic iron rod is broken in two, the pieces are magnets again; whenever a body falls freely from rest in a vacuum near the surface of the earth, the distance it covers in t seconds is $16t^2$ feet. Most of the laws of the natural sciences are quantitative: they assert specific mathematical connections between different quantitative characteristics of physical systems (e.g., between volume, temperature, and pressure of a gas) or of processes (e.g., between time and distance in free fall in Galileo's law; between the period of revolution of a planet and its mean distance from the sun, in Kepler's third law; between the angles of incidence and refraction in Snell's law).

Strictly speaking, a statement asserting some uniform connection will be considered a law only if there are reasons to assume it is true: we would not normally speak of false laws of nature. But if this requirement were rigidly observed, then the statements commonly referred to as Galileo's and Kepler's laws would not qualify as laws; for according to current physical knowledge, they hold only approximately; and as we shall see later, physical theory explains why this is so. Analogous remarks apply to the laws of geometrical optics. For example, even in a homogeneous medium, light does not move strictly in straight lines: it can bend around corners. We shall therefore use the word 'law' somewhat liberally, applying the term also to certain statements of the kind here referred to, which, on theoretical grounds, are known to hold only approximately and with certain qualifications. . . .

We saw that the laws invoked in deductive-nomological explanations have the basic form: 'In all cases when conditions of kind F are realized, conditions of kind G are realized as well'. But, interestingly, not all statements of this universal form, even if true, can qualify as laws of nature. For example, the sentence 'All rocks in this box contain iron' is of universal form (F is the condition of being a rock in the box, G that of containing iron); yet even if true, it would not be regarded as a law, but as an assertion of something that "happens to be the case", as an "accidental generalization". Or consider the statement: 'All bodies consisting of pure gold have a mass of less than 100,000 kilograms'. No doubt all bodies of gold ever examined by man conform to it; thus, there is considerable confirmatory evidence for it and no disconfirming instances are known. Indeed, it is quite possible that never in the history of the universe has there been or will there be a body of pure gold with a mass of 100,000 kilograms or more. In this case, the proposed generalization would not only be well confirmed, but true. And yet, we would presumably regard its truth as accidental, on the ground that nothing in the basic laws of nature as conceived in contemporary science precludes the possibility of there being – or even the possibility of our producing – a solid gold object with a mass exceeding 100,000 kilograms.

Thus, a scientific law cannot be adequately defined as a true statement of universal form: this characterization expresses a necessary, but not a sufficient, condition for laws of the kind here under discussion.

What distinguishes genuine laws from accidental generalizations? This intriguing problem has been intensively discussed in recent years. Let us look briefly at some of the principal ideas that have emerged from the debate, which is still continuing.

One telling and suggestive difference, noted by Nelson Goodman,[3] is this: a law can, whereas an accidental generalization cannot, serve to support *counterfactual conditionals*, i.e., statements of the form 'If A were (had been) the case, then B would be (would have been) the case', where in fact A is not (has not been) the case. Thus, the assertion 'If this paraffin candle had been put into a kettle of boiling water, it would have melted' could be supported by adducing the law that paraffin is liquid above 60 degrees centigrade (and the fact that the boiling point of

water is 100 degrees centigrade). But the statement 'All rocks in this box contain iron' could not be used similarly to support the counterfactual statement 'If this pebble had been put into the box, it would contain iron'. Similarly, a law, in contrast to an accidentally true generalization, can support *subjunctive conditionals*, i.e., sentences of the type 'If A should come to pass, then so would B', where it is left open whether or not A will in fact come to pass. The statement 'If this paraffin candle should be put into boiling water then it would melt' is an example.

Closely related to this difference is another one, which is of special interest to us: a law can, whereas an accidental generalization cannot, serve as a basis for an explanation. Thus, the melting of a particular paraffin candle that was put into boiling water can be explained, in conformity with the schema (D-N), by reference to the particular facts just mentioned and to the law that paraffin melts when its temperature is raised above 60 degrees centigrade. But the fact that a particular rock in the box contains iron cannot be analogously explained by reference to the general statement that all rocks in the box contain iron.

It might seem plausible to say, by way of a further distinction, that the latter statement simply serves as a conveniently brief formulation of a finite conjunction of this kind: 'Rock r_1 contains iron, and rock r_2 contains iron, ..., and rock r_{63} contains iron'; whereas the generalization about paraffin refers to a potentially infinite set of particular cases and therefore cannot be paraphrased by a finite conjunction of statements describing individual instances. This distinction is suggestive, but it is overstated. For to begin with, the generalization 'All rocks in this box contain iron' does not in fact tell us how many rocks there are in the box, nor does it name any particular rocks r_1, r_2, etc. Hence, the general sentence is not logically equivalent to a finite conjunction of the kind just mentioned. To formulate a suitable conjunction, we need additional information, which might be obtained by counting and labeling the rocks in the box. Besides, our generalization 'All bodies of pure gold have a mass of less than 100,000 kilograms' would not count as a law even if there were infinitely many bodies of gold in the world. Thus, the criterion we have under consideration fails on several grounds.

Finally, let us note that a statement of universal form may qualify as a law even if it actually has no instances whatever. As an example, consider the sentence: 'On any celestial body that has the same radius as the earth but twice its mass, free fall from rest conforms to the formula $s = 32t^2$'. There might well be no celestial object in the entire universe that has the specified size and mass, and yet the statement has the character of a law. For it (or rather, a close approximation of it, as in the case of Galileo's law) follows from the Newtonian theory of gravitation and of motion in conjunction with the statement that the acceleration of free fall on the earth is 32 feet per second per second; thus, it has strong theoretical support, just like our earlier law for free fall on the moon.

A law, we noted, can support subjunctive and counterfactual conditional statements about potential instances, i.e., about particular cases that might occur, or that might have occurred but did not. In similar fashion, Newton's theory supports our general statement in a subjunctive version that suggests its lawlike status, namely: 'On any celestial body that there may be which has the same size as the earth but twice its mass, free fall would conform to the formula $s = 32t^2$'. By contrast, the generalization about the rocks cannot be paraphrased as asserting that any rock that might be in this box would contain iron, nor of course would this latter claim have any theoretical support.

Similarly, we would not use our generalization about the mass of gold bodies – let us call it H – to support statements such as this: 'Two bodies of pure gold whose individual masses add up to more than 100,000 kilograms cannot be fused to form one body; or if fusion should be possible, then the mass of the resulting body will be less than 100,000 kg', for the basic physical and chemical theories of matter that are currently accepted do not preclude the kind of fusion here considered, and they do not imply that there would be a mass loss of the sort here referred to. Hence, even if the generalization H should be true, i.e., if no exceptions to it should ever occur, this would constitute a mere accident or coincidence as judged by current theory, which permits the occurrence of exceptions to H.

Thus, whether a statement of universal form counts as a law will depend in part upon the scientific theories accepted at the time. This is not to say that "empirical generalizations" – statements of universal form that are empirically well confirmed but have no basis in theory –

never qualify as laws: Galileo's, Kepler's, and Boyle's laws, for example, were accepted as such before they received theoretical grounding. The relevance of theory is rather this: a statement of universal form, whether empirically confirmed or as yet untested, will qualify as a law if it is implied by an accepted theory (statements of this kind are often referred to as theoretical laws); but even if it is empirically well confirmed and presumably true in fact, it will not qualify as a law if it rules out certain hypothetical occurrences (such as the fusion of two gold bodies with a resulting mass of more than 100,000 kilograms, in the case of our generalization H) which an accepted theory qualifies as possible.[4]

Probabilistic Explanation: Fundamentals

Not all scientific explanations are based on laws of strictly universal form. Thus, little Jim's getting the measles might be explained by saying that he caught the disease from his brother, who had a bad case of the measles some days earlier. This account again links the explanandum event to an earlier occurrence, Jim's exposure to the measles; the latter is said to provide an explanation because there is a connection between exposure to the measles and contracting the disease. That connection cannot be expressed by a law of universal form, however; for not every case of exposure to the measles produces contagion. What can be claimed is only that persons exposed to the measles will contract the disease with high probability, i.e., in a high percentage of all cases. General statements of this type, which we shall soon examine more closely, will be called *laws of probabilistic form* or *probabilistic laws*, for short.

In our illustration, then, the explanans consists of the probabilistic law just mentioned and the statement that Jim was exposed to the measles. In contrast to the case of deductive-nomological explanation, these explanans statements do not deductively imply the explanandum statement that Jim got the measles; for in deductive inferences from true premises, the conclusion is invariably true, whereas in our example, it is clearly possible that the explanans statements might be true and yet the explanandum statement false. We will say, for short, that the explanans implies the explanandum, not with "deductive certainty", but only with near-certainty or with high probability.

The resulting explanatory argument may be schematized as follows:

> The probability for persons exposed to the measles to catch the disease is high.
> Jim was exposed to the measles.
> ═══════════════ [makes highly probable]
> Jim caught the measles.

In the customary presentation of a deductive argument, which was used, for example, in the schema (D-N) above, the conclusion is separated from the premises by a single line, which serves to indicate that the premises logically imply the conclusion. The double line used in our latest schema is meant to indicate analogously that the "premises" (the explanans) make the "conclusion" (the explanandum sentence) more or less probable; the degree of probability is suggested by the notation in brackets.

Arguments of this kind will be called *probabilistic explanations*. As our discussion shows, a probabilistic explanation of a particular event shares certain basic characteristics with the corresponding deductive-nomological type of explanation. In both cases, the given event is explained by reference to others, with which the explanandum event is connected by laws. But in one case, the laws are of universal form; in the other, of probabilistic form. And while a deductive explanation shows that, on the information contained in the explanans, the explanandum was to be expected with "deductive certainty", an inductive explanation shows only that, on the information contained in the explanans, the explanandum was to be expected with high probability, and perhaps with "practical certainty"; it is in this manner that the latter argument meets the requirement of explanatory relevance.

Statistical Probabilities and Probabilistic Laws

We must now consider more closely the two differentiating features of probabilistic explanation that have just been noted: the probabilistic laws they invoke and the peculiar kind of probabilistic implication that connects the explanans with the explanandum.

Suppose that from an urn containing many balls of the same size and mass, but not necessarily of the same color, successive drawings are made. At each drawing, one ball is removed, and its color is noted. Then the ball is returned to the urn, whose contents are thoroughly mixed before the next drawing takes place. This is an example of a so-called random process or random experiment, a concept that will soon be characterized in more detail. Let us refer to the procedure just described as experiment U, to each drawing as one performance of U, and to the color of the ball produced by a given drawing as the result, or the outcome, of that performance.

If all the balls in an urn are white, then a statement of strictly universal form holds true of the results produced by the performance of U: every drawing from the urn yields a white ball, or yields the result W, for short. If only some of the balls – say, 600 of them – are white, whereas the others – say 400 – are red, then a general statement of probabilistic form holds true of the experiment: the probability for a performance of U to produce a white ball, or outcome W, is 0.6; in symbols:

[5a] $P(W,U) = 0.6$

Similarly, the probability of obtaining heads as a result of the random experiment C of flipping a fair coin is given by

[5b] $P(H,C) = 0.5$

and the probability of obtaining an ace as a result of the random experiment D of rolling a regular die is

[5c] $P(A,D) = 1/6$

What do such probability statements mean? According to one familiar view, sometimes called the "classical" conception of probability, the statement (5a) would have to be interpreted as follows: each performance of the experiment U effects a choice of one from among 1,000 basic possibilities, or basic alternatives, each represented by one of the balls in the urn; of these possible choices, 600 are "favorable" to the outcome W; and the probability of drawing a white ball is simply the ratio of the number of favorable choices available to the number of all possible choices, i.e., 600/1,000. The classical interpretation of the probability statements (5b) and (5c) follows similar lines.

Yet this characterization is inadequate; for if before each drawing, the 400 red balls in the urn were placed on top of the white ones, then in this new kind of urn experiment – let us call it U' – the ratio of favorable to possible basic alternatives would remain the same, but the probability of drawing a white ball would be smaller than in the experiment U, in which the balls are thoroughly mixed before each drawing. The classical conception takes account of this difficulty by requiring that the basic alternatives referred to in its definition of probability must be "equipossible" or "equiprobable" – a requirement presumably violated in the case of experiment U'.

This added proviso raises the question of how to define equipossibility or equiprobability. We will pass over this notoriously troublesome and controversial issue, because – even assuming that equiprobability can be satisfactorily characterized – the classical conception would still be inadequate, since probabilities are assigned also to the outcomes of random experiments for which no plausible way is known of marking off equiprobable basic alternatives. Thus, for the random experiment D of rolling a regular die, the six faces might be regarded as representing such equiprobable alternatives; but we attribute probabilities to such results as rolling an ace, or an odd number of points, etc., also in the case of a loaded die, even though no equiprobable basic outcomes can be marked off here.

Similarly – and this is particularly important – science assigns probabilities to the outcomes of certain random experiments or random processes encountered in nature, such as the step-by-step decay of the atoms of radioactive substances, or the transition of atoms from one energy state to another. Here again, we find no equiprobable basic alternatives in terms of which such probabilities might be classically defined and computed.

To arrive at a more satisfactory construal of our probability statements, let us consider how one would ascertain the probability of the rolling of an ace with a given die that is not known to be regular. This would obviously be done by making a large number of throws with the die and ascertaining the *relative frequency*, i.e., the proportion, of those cases in which an ace turns up. If, for example, the experiment D' of rolling the given die is performed 300 times and an ace turns up in 62 cases, then the relative frequency, $62/300$, would be regarded as an approximate value of the probability $p(A, D')$ of rolling an ace with the given die. Analogous procedures would

be used to estimate the probabilities associated with the flipping of a given coin, the spinning of a roulette wheel, and so on. Similarly, the probabilities associated with radioactive decay, with the transitions between different atomic energy states, with genetic processes, etc., are determined by ascertaining the corresponding relative frequencies; however, this is often done in highly indirect ways rather than by simply counting individual atomic or other events of the relevant kinds.

The interpretation in terms of relative frequencies applies also to probability statements such as (5b) and (5c), which concern the results of flipping a fair (i.e., homogeneous and strictly cylindrical) coin or tossing a regular (homogeneous and strictly cubical) die: what the scientist (or the gambler, for that matter) is concerned with in making a probability statement is the relative frequency with which a certain outcome O can be expected in long series of repetitions of some random experiment R. The counting of "equiprobable" basic alternatives and of those among them which are "favorable" to O may be regarded as a heuristic device for guessing at the relative frequency of O. And indeed when a regular die or a fair coin is tossed a large number of times, the different faces tend to come up with equal frequency. One might expect this on the basis of symmetry considerations of the kind frequently used in forming physical hypotheses, for our empirical knowledge affords no grounds on which to expect any of the faces to be favored over any other. But while such considerations often are heuristically useful, they must not be regarded as certain or as self-evident truths: some very plausible symmetry assumptions, such as the principle of parity, have been found not to be generally satisfied at the subatomic level. Assumptions about equiprobabilities are therefore always subject to correction in the light of empirical data concerning the actual relative frequencies of the phenomena in question. This point is illustrated also by the statistical theories of gases developed by Bose and Einstein and by Fermi and Dirac, respectively, which rest on different assumptions concerning what distributions of particles over a phase space are equiprobable.

The probabilities specified in the probabilistic laws, then, represent relative frequencies. They cannot, however, be strictly defined as relative frequencies in long series of repetitions of the relevant random experiment. For the proportion, say, of aces obtained in throwing a given die will change, if perhaps only slightly, as the series of throws is extended; and even in two series of exactly the same length, the number of aces will usually differ. We do find, however, that as the number of throws increases, the relative frequency of each of the different outcomes tends to change less and less, even though the results of successive throws continue to vary in an irregular and practically unpredictable fashion. This is what generally characterizes a random experiment R with outcomes $O_1, O_2, \ldots O_n$: successive performances of R yield one or another of those outcomes in an irregular manner; but the relative frequencies of the outcomes tend to become stable as the number of performances increases. And the probabilities of the outcomes, $p(O_1, R)$, $p(O_2, R)$, $\ldots$, $p(O_n, R)$, may be regarded as ideal values that the actual frequencies tend to assume as they become increasingly stable. For mathematical convenience, the probabilities are sometimes defined as the mathematical *limits* toward which the relative frequencies converge as the number of performances increases indefinitely. But this definition has certain conceptual shortcomings, and in some more recent mathematical studies of the subject, the intended empirical meaning of the concept of probability is deliberately, and for good reasons, characterized more vaguely by means of the following so-called *statistical interpretation of probability*:[5]

The statement

$$p(O, R) = r$$

means that in a long series of performances of random experiment R, the proportion of cases with outcome O is almost certain to be close to r.

The concept of *statistical probability* thus characterized must be carefully distinguished from the concept of *inductive or logical probability.* . . . Logical probability is a quantitative logical relation between definite *statements*; the sentence

$$c(H, K) = r$$

asserts that the hypothesis H is supported, or made probable, to degree r by the evidence formulated in statement K. Statistical probability is a quantitative relation between repeatable *kinds of events*: a certain kind of outcome, O, and a certain kind of random process, R; it represents, roughly speaking, the relative frequency with

which the result O tends to occur in a long series of performances of R.

What the two concepts have in common are their mathematical characteristics: both satisfy the basic principles of mathematical probability theory:

(a) The possible numerical values of both probabilities range from 0 to 1:

$$0 \leq p(O, R) \leq 1$$
$$0 \leq c(H, K) \leq 1$$

(b) The probability for one of two mutually exclusive outcomes of R to occur is the sum of the probabilities of the outcomes taken separately; the probability, on any evidence K, for one or the other of two mutually exclusive hypotheses to hold is the sum of their respective probabilities:

If O_1, O_2 are mutually exclusive, then
$$p(O_1 \text{ or } O_2, R) = p(O_1, R) + p(O_2, R)$$
If H_1, H_2 are logically exclusive hypotheses, then
$$c(H_1 \text{ or } H_2, K) = c(H_1, K) + c(H_2, K)$$

(c) The probability of an outcome that necessarily occurs in all cases – such as O or not O – is 1; the probability, on any evidence, of a hypothesis that is logically (and in this sense necessarily) true, such as H or not H, is 1:

$$p(O \text{ or not } O, R) = 1$$
$$c(H \text{ or not } H, K) = 1$$

Scientific hypotheses in the form of statistical probability statements can be, and are, tested by examining the long-run relative frequencies of the outcomes concerned; and the confirmation of such hypotheses is then judged, broadly speaking, in terms of the closeness of the agreement between hypothetical probabilities and observed frequencies. The logic of such tests, however, presents some intriguing special problems, which call for at least brief examination.

Consider the hypothesis, H, that the probability of rolling an ace with a certain die is 0.15; or briefly, that $p(A, D) = 0.15$, where D is the random experiment of rolling the given die. The hypothesis H does not deductively imply any test implications specifying how many aces will occur in a finite series of throws of the die. It does not imply, for example, that exactly 75 among the first 500 throws will yield an ace, nor even that the number of aces will lie between 50 and 100, say. Hence, if the proportion of aces actually obtained in a large number of throws differs considerably from 0.15, this does not refute *H* in the sense in which a hypothesis of strictly universal form, such as 'All swans are white', can be refuted, in virtue of the *modus tollens* argument, by reference to one counter-instance, such as a black swan. Similarly, if a long run of throws of the given die yields a proportion of aces very close to 0.15, this does not confirm *H* in the sense in which a hypothesis is confirmed by the finding that a test sentence *I* that it logically implies is in fact true. For in this latter case, the hypothesis asserts *I* by logical implication, and the test result is thus confirmatory in the sense of showing that a certain part of what the hypothesis asserts is indeed true; but nothing strictly analogous is shown for *H* by confirmatory frequency data; for *H* does *not* assert by implication that the frequency of aces in some long run will definitely be very close to 0.15.

But while *H* does not logically preclude the possibility that the proportion of aces obtained in a long series of throws of the given die may depart widely from 0.15, it does logically imply that such departures are highly improbable in the statistical sense; i.e., that if the experiment of performing a long series of throws (say, 1,000 of them per series) is repeated a large number of times, then only a tiny proportion of those long series will yield a proportion of aces that differs considerably from 0.15. For the case of rolling a die, it is usually assumed that the results of successive throws are "statistically independent"; this means roughly that the probability of obtaining an ace in a throw of the die does not depend on the result of the preceding throw. Mathematical analysis shows that in conjunction with this independence assumption, our hypothesis *H* deductively determines the statistical probability for the proportion of aces obtained in *n* throws to differ from 0.15 by no more than a specified amount. For example, *H* implies that for a series of 1,000 throws of the die here considered, the probability is about 0.976 that the proportion of aces will lie between 0.125 and 0.175; and similarly, that for a run of 10,000 throws the probability is about 0.995 that the proportion of aces will be between 0.14 and 0.16. Thus, we may say that if *H* is true, then it is practically certain that in a long trial run the observed proportion of aces will differ by very little from the hypothetical probability value 0.15. Hence, if the observed

long-run frequency of an outcome is not close to the probability assigned to it by a given probabilistic hypothesis, then that hypothesis is very likely to be false. In this case, the frequency data count as disconfirming the hypothesis, or as reducing its credibility; and if sufficiently strong disconfirming evidence is found, the hypothesis will be considered as practically, though not logically, refuted and will accordingly be rejected. Similarly, close agreement between hypothetical probabilities and observed frequencies will tend to confirm a probabilistic hypothesis and may lead to its acceptance.

If probabilistic hypotheses are to be accepted or rejected on the basis of statistical evidence concerning observed frequencies, then appropriate standards are called for. These will have to determine (a) what deviations of observed frequencies from the probability stated by a hypothesis are to count as grounds for rejecting the hypothesis, and (b) how close an agreement between observed frequencies and hypothetical probability is to be required as a condition for accepting the hypothesis. The requirements in question can be made more or less strict, and their specification is a matter of choice. The stringency of the chosen standards will normally vary with the context and the objectives of the research in question. Broadly speaking, it will depend on the importance that is attached, in the given context, to avoiding two kinds of error that might be made: rejecting the hypothesis under test although it is true, and accepting it although it is false. The importance of this point is particularly clear when acceptance or rejection of the hypothesis is to serve as a basis for practical action. Thus, if the hypothesis concerns the probable effectiveness and safety of a new vaccine, then the decision about its acceptance will have to take into account not only how well the statistical test results accord with the probabilities specified by the hypothesis, but also how serious would be the consequences of accepting the hypothesis and acting on it (e.g., by inoculating children with the vaccine) when in fact it is false, and of rejecting the hypothesis and acting accordingly (e.g., by destroying the vaccine and modifying or discontinuing the process of manufacture) when in fact the hypothesis is true. The complex problems that arise in this context form the subject matter of the theory of statistical tests and decisions, which has been developed in recent decades on the basis of the mathematical theory of probability and statistics.[6]

Carl G. Hempel

Many important laws and theoretical principles in the natural sciences are of probabilistic character, though they are often of more complicated form than the simple probability statements we have discussed. For example, according to current physical theory, radioactive decay is a random phenomenon in which the atoms of each radioactive element possess a characteristic probability of disintegrating during a specified period of time. The corresponding probabilistic laws are usually formulated as statements giving the "half-life" of the element concerned. Thus, the statements that the half-life of radium^{226} is 1,620 years and that of polonium^{218} is 3.05 minutes are laws to the effect that the probability for a radium^{226} atom to decay within 1,620 years, and for an atom of polonium^{218} to decay within 3.05 minutes, are both one-half. According to the statistical interpretation cited earlier, these laws imply that of a large number of radium^{226} atoms or of polonium^{218} atoms given at a certain time, very close to one-half will still exist 1,620 years, or 3.05 minutes, later; the others having disintegrated by radioactive decay.

Again, in the kinetic theory various uniformities in the behavior of gases, including the laws of classical thermodynamics, are explained by means of certain assumptions about the constituent molecules; and some of these are probabilistic hypotheses concerning statistical regularities in the motions and collisions of those molecules.

A few additional remarks concerning the notion of a probabilistic law are indicated. It might seem that all scientific laws should be qualified as probabilistic since the supporting evidence we have for them is always a finite and logically inconclusive body of findings, which can confer upon them only a more or less high probability. But this argument misses the point that the distinction between laws of universal form and laws of probabilistic form does not refer to the strength of the evidential support for the two kinds of statements, but to their form, which reflects the logical character of the claim they make. A law of universal form is basically a statement to the effect that in *all* cases where conditions of kind F are realized, conditions of kind G are realized as well; a law of probabilistic form asserts, basically, that under certain conditions, constituting the performance of a random experiment R, a certain kind of outcome will occur in a specified percentage of cases. No matter whether true or false, well supported or poorly supported, these

two types of claims are of a logically different character, and it is on this difference that our distinction is based.

As we saw earlier, a law of the universal form "Whenever F then G" is by no means a brief, telescoped equivalent of a report stating for each occurrence of F so far examined that it was associated with an occurrence of G. Rather, it implies assertions also for all unexamined cases of F, past as well as present and future; also, it implies counterfactual and hypothetical conditionals which concern, so to speak "possible occurrences" of F: and it is just this characteristic that gives such laws their explanatory power. Laws of probabilistic form have an analogous status. The law stating that the radioactive decay of radium^{226} is a random process with an associated half-life of 1,620 years is plainly not tantamount to a report about decay rates that have been observed in certain samples of radium^{226}. It concerns the decaying process of any body of radium^{226} – past, present, or future; and it implies subjunctive and counterfactual conditionals, such as: if two particular lumps of radium^{226} were to be combined into one, the decay rates would remain the same as if the lumps had remained separate. Again, it is this characteristic that gives probabilistic laws their predictive and their explanatory force.

The Inductive Character of Probabilistic Explanation

One of the simplest kinds of probabilistic explanation is illustrated by our earlier example of Jim's catching the measles. The general form of that explanatory argument may be stated thus:

$p(0,R)$ is close to 1
i is a case of R
————————— [makes highly probable]
i is a case of 0

Now the high probability which, as indicated in brackets, the explanans confers upon the explanandum is surely not a statistical probability, for it characterizes a relation between sentences, not between (kinds of) events. . . . we might say that the probability in question represents the rational credibility of the explanandum, given the information provided by the explanans; and as we noted earlier, in so far as this notion can

212

be construed as a probability, it represents a logical or inductive probability.

In some simple cases, there is a natural and obvious way of expressing that probability in numerical terms. In an argument of the kind just considered, if the numerical value of $p(O,R)$ is specified, then it is reasonable to say that the inductive probability that the explanans confers upon the explanandum has the same numerical value. The resulting probabilistic explanation has the form:

$$p(0,R) = r$$
$$\frac{i \text{ is a case of } R}{i \text{ is a case of } 0} \; [r]$$

If the explanans is more complex, the determination of corresponding inductive probabilities for the explanandum raises difficult problems, which in part are still unsettled. But whether or not it is possible to assign definite numerical probabilities to all such explanations, the preceding considerations show that when an event is explained by reference to probabilistic laws, the explanans confers upon the explanandum only more or less strong inductive support. Thus, we may distinguish deductive-nomological from probabilistic explanations by saying that the former effect a deductive subsumption under laws of universal form, the latter an inductive subsumption under laws of probabilistic form.

It is sometimes said that precisely because of its inductive character, a probabilistic account does not explain the occurrence of an event, since the explanans does not logically preclude its nonoccurrence. But the important, steadily expanding role that probabilistic laws and theories play in science and its applications, makes it preferable to view accounts based on such principles as affording explanations as well, though of a less stringent kind than those of deductive-nomological form. Take, for example, the radioactive decay of a sample of one milligram of polonium[218]. Suppose that what is left of this initial amount after 3.05 minutes is found to have a mass that falls within the interval from 0.499 to 0.501 milligrams. This finding can be explained by the probabilistic law of decay for polonium[218]; for that law, in combination with the principles of mathematical probability, deductively implies that given the huge number of atoms in a milligram of polonium[218], the probability of the specified outcome is overwhelmingly large, so that in a particular case its occurrence may be expected with "practical certainty".

Or consider the explanation offered by the kinetic theory of gases for an empirically established generalization called Graham's law of diffusion. The law states that at fixed temperature and pressure, the rates at which different gases in a container escape, or diffuse, through a thin porous wall are inversely proportional to the square roots of their molecular weights; so that the amount of a gas that diffuses through the wall per second will be the greater, the lighter its molecules. The explanation rests on the consideration that the mass of a given gas that diffuses through the wall per second will be proportional to the average velocity of its molecules, and that Graham's law will therefore have been explained if it can be shown that the average molecular velocities of different pure gases are inversely proportional to the square roots of their molecular weights. To show this, the theory makes certain assumptions broadly to the effect that a gas consists of a very large number of molecules moving in random fashion at different speeds that frequently change as a result of collisions, and that this random behavior shows certain probabilistic uniformities – in particular, that among the molecules of a given gas at specified temperature and pressure, different velocities will occur with definite, and different, probabilities. These assumptions make it possible to compute the probabilistically expected values – or, as we might briefly say, the "most probable" values – that the average velocities of different gases will possess at equal temperatures and pressures. These most probable average values, the theory shows, are indeed inversely proportional to the square roots of the molecular weights of the gases. But the actual diffusion rates, which are measured experimentally and are the subject of Graham's law, will depend on the actual values that the average velocities have in the large but finite swarms of molecules constituting the given bodies of gas. And the actual average values are related to the corresponding probabilistically estimated, or "most probable", values in a manner that is basically analogous to the relation between the proportion of aces occurring in a large but finite series of tossings of a given die and the corresponding probability of rolling an ace with that die. From the theoretically derived conclusion concerning the probabilistic estimates, it follows only that in view of the very large number of molecules involved, it is overwhelmingly *probable* that at any given time the actual average speeds will have values very close to their probability estimates and that, therefore, it is *practically certain* that they will be, like the latter, inversely proportional to the square roots of their molecular masses, thus satisfying Graham's law.[7]

It seems reasonable to say that this account affords an explanation, even though "only" with very high associated probability, of why gases display the uniformity expressed by Graham's law; and in physical texts and treatises, theoretical accounts of this probabilistic kind are indeed very widely referred to as explanations.

Notes

1 From Holton and Roller, *Foundations of Modern Physical Science* (Reading, MA: Addison-Wesley, 1958), p. 160.
2 The derivation of the laws of reflection for the curved surfaces referred to in this example and in the next one is simply and lucidly set forth in ch. 17 of Morris Kline, *Mathematics and the Physical World* (New York: Thomas Y. Crowell, 1959).
3 In his essay, "The Problem of Counterfactual Conditionals," reprinted as the first chapter of his book, *Fact, Fiction, and Forecast*, 2nd edn. (Indianapolis: Bobbs-Merrill, 1965). This work raises fascinating basic problems concerning laws, counterfactual statements, and inductive reasoning, and examines them from an advanced analytic point of view.
4 For a fuller analysis of the concept of law, and for further bibliographic references, see E. Nagel, *The Structure of Science* (New York: Harcourt, Brace & World, 1961), ch. 4.
5 Further details on the concept of statistical probability and on the limit-definition and its shortcomings will be found in E. Nagel's monograph, *Principles of the Theory of Probability* (Chicago: University of Chicago Press, 1939). Our version of the statistical interpretation follows that given by H. Cramer on pp. 148–9 of his book, *Mathematical Methods of Statistics* (Princeton, NJ: Princeton University Press, 1946).
6 On this subject, see R. D. Luce and H. Raiffa, *Games and Decisions* (New York: John Wiley & Sons, 1957).
7 The "average" velocities here referred to are technically defined as root-mean square velocities. Their values do not differ very much from those of average velocities in the usual sense of the arithmetic mean. A succinct outline of the theoretical explanation of Graham's law can be found in ch. 25 of Holton and Roller, *Foundations of Modern Physical Science*. The distinction, not explicitly mentioned in that presentation, between the average value of a quantity for some finite number of cases and the probabilistically estimated or expected value of that quantity is briefly discussed in ch. 6 (especially section 4) of R. P. Feynman, R. B. Leighton, and M. Sands, *The Feynman Lectures on Physics* (Reading, MA: Addison-Wesley, 1963).

20

The New Riddle of Induction

Nelson Goodman

The Old Problem of Induction

At the close of the preceding lecture, I said that today I should examine how matters stand with respect to the problem of induction. In a word, I think they stand ill. But the real difficulties that confront us today are not the traditional ones. What is commonly thought of as the Problem of Induction has been solved, or dissolved; and we face new problems that are not as yet very widely understood. To approach them, I shall have to run as quickly as possible over some very familiar ground.

The problem of the validity of judgments about future or unknown cases arises, as Hume pointed out, because such judgments are neither reports of experience nor logical consequences of it. Predictions, of course, pertain to what has not yet been observed. And they cannot be logically inferred from what has been observed; for what *has* happened imposes no logical restrictions on what *will* happen. Although Hume's dictum that there are no necessary connections of matters of fact has been challenged at times, it has withstood all attacks. Indeed, I should be inclined not merely to agree that there are no necessary connections of matters of fact, but to ask whether there are any necessary connections at all[1] – but that is another story.

Reprinted by permission of the publisher from *Fact, Fiction and Forecast,* 4th edn., by Nelson Goodman (Harvard University Press, Cambridge, Mass.). Copyright © 1979, 1983 by Nelson Goodman.

Hume's answer to the question how predictions are related to past experience is refreshingly non-cosmic. When an event of one kind frequently follows upon an event of another kind in experience, a habit is formed that leads the mind, when confronted with a new event of the first kind, to pass to the idea of an event of the second kind. The idea of necessary connection arises from the felt impulse of the mind in making this transition.

Now if we strip this account of all extraneous features, the central point is that to the question "Why one prediction rather than another?", Hume answers that the elect prediction is one that accords with a past regularity, because this regularity has established a habit. Thus among alternative statements about a future moment, one statement is distinguished by its consonance with habit and thus with regularities observed in the past. Prediction according to any other alternative is errant.

How satisfactory is this answer? The heaviest criticism has taken the righteous position that Hume's account at best pertains only to the source of predictions, not their legitimacy; that he sets forth the circumstances under which we make given predictions – and in this sense explains why we make them – but leaves untouched the question of our license for making them. To trace origins, runs the old complaint, is not to establish validity: the real question is not why a prediction is in fact made but how it can be justified. Since this seems to point to the awkward conclusion that the greatest of modern philosophers completely missed the point of his own problem, the idea has developed that he did not really take his solution very seriously, but regarded the main problem as unsolved and perhaps as insoluble. Thus we come to speak of 'Hume's problem' as though he propounded it as a question without answer.

All this seems to me quite wrong. I think Hume grasped the central question and considered his answer to be passably effective. And I think his answer is reasonable and relevant, even if it is not entirely satisfactory. I shall explain presently. At the moment, I merely want to record a protest against the prevalent notion that the problem of justifying induction, when it is so sharply dissociated from the problem of describing how induction takes place, can fairly be called Hume's problem.

I suppose that the problem of justifying induction has called forth as much fruitless discussion as has any half-way respectable problem of modern philosophy. The typical writer begins by insisting that some way of justifying predictions must be found; proceeds to argue that for this purpose we need some resounding universal law of the Uniformity of Nature, and then inquires how this universal principle itself can be justified. At this point, if he is tired, he concludes that the principle must be accepted as an indispensable assumption; or if he is energetic and ingenious, he goes on to devise some subtle justification for it. Such an invention, however, seldom satisfies anyone else; and the easier course of accepting an unsubstantiated and even dubious assumption much more sweeping than any actual predictions we make seems an odd and expensive way of justifying them.

Dissolution of the Old Problem

Understandably, then, more critical thinkers have suspected that there might be something awry with the problem we are trying to solve. Come to think of it, what precisely would constitute the justification we seek? If the problem is to explain how we know that certain predictions will turn out to be correct, the sufficient answer is that we don't know any such thing. If the problem is to *find* some way of distinguishing antecedently between true and false predictions, we are asking for prevision rather than for philosophical explanation. Nor does it help matters much to say that we are merely trying to show

that or why certain predictions are *probable*. Often it is said that while we cannot tell in advance whether a prediction concerning a given throw of a die is true, we can decide whether the prediction is a probable one. But if this means determining how the prediction is related to actual frequency distributions of future throws of the die, surely there is no way of knowing or proving this in advance. On the other hand, if the judgment that the prediction is probable has nothing to do with subsequent occurrences, then the question remains in what sense a probable prediction is any better justified than an improbable one.

Now obviously the genuine problem cannot be one of attaining unattainable knowledge or of accounting for knowledge that we do not in fact have. A better understanding of our problem can be gained by looking for a moment at what is involved in justifying non-inductive inferences. How do we justify a *deduction*? Plainly, by showing that it conforms to the general rules of deductive inference. An argument that so conforms is justified or valid, even if its conclusion happens to be false. An argument that violates a rule is fallacious even if its conclusion happens to be true. To justify a deductive conclusion therefore requires no knowledge of the facts it pertains to. Moreover, when a deductive argument has been shown to conform to the rules of logical inference, we usually consider it justified without going on to ask what justifies the rules. Analogously, the basic task in justifying an inductive inference is to show that it conforms to the general rules of *in*duction. Once we have recognized this, we have gone a long way towards clarifying our problem.

Yet, of course, the rules themselves must eventually be justified. The validity of a deduction depends not upon conformity to any purely arbitrary rules we may contrive, but upon conformity to valid rules. When we speak of *the* rules of inference we mean the valid rules — or better, *some* valid rules, since there may be alternative sets of equally valid rules. But how is the validity of rules to be determined? Here again we encounter philosophers who insist that these rules follow from some self-evident axiom, and others who try to show that the rules are grounded in the very nature of the human mind. I think the answer lies much nearer the surface. Principles of deductive inference are justified by their conformity with accepted deductive practice. Their validity depends upon accordance with the particular deductive inferences we actually make and sanction. If a rule yields inacceptable inferences, we drop it as invalid. Justification of general rules thus derives from judgments rejecting or accepting particular deductive inferences.

This looks flagrantly circular. I have said that deductive inferences are justified by their conformity to valid general rules, and that general rules are justified by their conformity to valid inferences. But this circle is a virtuous one. The point is that rules and particular inferences alike are justified by being brought into agreement with each other. *A rule is amended if it yields an inference we are unwilling to accept; an inference is rejected if it violates a rule we are unwilling to amend.* The process of justification is the delicate one of making mutual adjustments between rules and accepted inferences; and in the agreement achieved lies the only justification needed for either.

All this applies equally well to induction. An inductive inference, too, is justified by conformity to general rules, and a general rule by conformity to accepted inductive inferences. Predictions are justified if they conform to valid canons of induction; and the canons are valid if they accurately codify accepted inductive practice.

A result of such analysis is that we can stop plaguing ourselves with certain spurious questions about induction. We no longer demand an explanation for guarantees that we do not have, or seek keys to knowledge that we cannot obtain. It dawns upon us that the traditional smug insistence upon a hard-and-fast line between justifying induction and describing ordinary inductive practice distorts the problem. And we owe belated apologies to Hume. For in dealing with the question how normally accepted inductive judgments are made, he was in fact dealing with the question of inductive validity.[2] The validity of a prediction consisted for him in its arising from habit, and thus in its exemplifying some past regularity. His answer was incomplete and perhaps not entirely correct; but it was not beside the point. The problem of induction is not a problem of demonstration but a problem of defining the difference between valid and invalid predictions.

This clears the air but leaves a lot to be done. As principles of *deductive* inference, we have the familiar and highly developed laws of logic; but there are available no such precisely stated and well-recognized principles of inductive inference. Mill's canons hardly rank with Aristotle's

rules of the syllogism, let alone with *Principia Mathematica*. Elaborate and valuable treatises on probability usually leave certain fundamental questions untouched. Only in very recent years has there been any explicit and systematic work upon what I call the constructive task of confirmation theory.

The Constructive Task of Confirmation Theory

The task of formulating rules that define the difference between valid and invalid inductive inferences is much like the task of defining any term with an established usage. If we set out to define the term "tree", we try to compose out of already understood words an expression that will apply to the familiar objects that standard usage calls trees, and that will not apply to objects that standard usage refuses to call trees. A proposal that plainly violates either condition is rejected; while a definition that meets these tests may be adopted and used to decide cases that are not already settled by actual usage. Thus the interplay we observed between rules of induction and particular inductive inferences is simply an instance of this characteristic dual adjustment between definition and usage, whereby the usage informs the definition, which in turn guides extension of the usage.

Of course this adjustment is a more complex matter than I have indicated. Sometimes, in the interest of convenience or theoretical utility, we deliberately permit a definition to run counter to clear mandates of common usage. We accept a definition of "fish" that excludes whales. Similarly we may decide to deny the term "valid induction" to some inductive inferences that are commonly considered valid, or apply the term to others not usually so considered. A definition may modify as well as extend ordinary usage.[3]

Some pioneer work on the problem of defining confirmation or valid induction has been done by Professor Hempel.[4] Let me remind you briefly of a few of his results. Just as deductive logic is concerned primarily with a relation between statements – namely the consequence relation – that is independent of their truth or falsity, so inductive logic as Hempel conceives it is concerned primarily with a comparable relation of confirmation between statements. Thus the problem is to define the relation that obtains between any statement S_1 and another S_2 if and only if S_1 may properly be said to confirm S_2 in any degree.

With the question so stated, the first step seems obvious. Does not induction proceed in just the opposite direction from deduction? Surely some of the evidence-statements that inductively support a general hypothesis are consequences of it. Since the consequence relation is already well defined by deductive logic, will we not be on firm ground in saying that confirmation embraces the converse relation? The laws of deduction in reverse will then be among the laws of induction.

Let's see where this leads us. We naturally assume further that whatever confirms a given statement confirms also whatever follows from that statement.[5] But if we combine this assumption with our proposed principle, we get the embarrassing result that every statement confirms every other. Surprising as it may be that such innocent beginnings lead to such an intolerable conclusion, the proof is very easy. Start with any statement S_1. It is a consequence of, and so by our present criterion confirms, the conjunction of S_1 and any statement whatsoever – call it S_2. But the confirmed conjunction, $S_1 \cdot S_2$, of course has S_2 as a consequence. Thus every statement confirms all statements.

The fault lies in careless formulation of our first proposal. While some statements that confirm a general hypothesis are consequences of it, not all its consequences confirm it. This may not be immediately evident; for indeed we do in some sense furnish support for a statement when we establish one of its consequences. We settle one of the questions about it. Consider the heterogeneous conjunction:

8497 is a prime number and the other side of the moon is flat and Elizabeth the First was crowned on a Tuesday.

To show that any one of the three component statements is true is to support the conjunction by reducing the net undetermined claim. But support[6] of this kind is not confirmation; for establishment of one component endows the whole statement with no credibility that is transmitted to other component statements. Confirmation of a hypothesis occurs only when an instance imparts to the hypothesis some credibility that is conveyed to other instances. Appraisal of hypotheses, indeed, is incidental to prediction, to the judgment of new cases on the basis of old ones.

Our formula thus needs tightening. This is readily accomplished, as Hempel points out, if we observe that a hypothesis is genuinely confirmed only by a statement that is an instance of it in the special sense of entailing not the hypothesis itself but its relativization or restriction to the class of entities mentioned by that statement. The relativization of a general hypothesis to a class results from restricting the range of its universal and existential quantifiers to the members of that class. Less technically, what the hypothesis says of all things the evidence statement says of one thing (or of one pair or other n-ad of things). This obviously covers the confirmation of the conductivity of all copper by the conductivity of a given piece; and it excludes confirmation of our heterogeneous conjunction by any of its components. And, when taken together with the principle that what confirms a statement confirms all its consequences, this criterion does not yield the untoward conclusion that every statement confirms every other.

New difficulties promptly appear from other directions, however. One is the infamous paradox of the ravens. The statement that a given object, say this piece of paper, is neither black nor a raven confirms the hypothesis that all non-black things are non-ravens. But this hypothesis is logically equivalent to the hypothesis that all ravens are black. Hence we arrive at the unexpected conclusion that the statement that a given object is neither black nor a raven confirms the hypothesis that all ravens are black. The prospect of being able to investigate ornithological theories without going out in the rain is so attractive that we know there must be a catch in it. The trouble this time, however, lies not in faulty definition, but in tacit and illicit reference to evidence not stated in our example. Taken by itself, the statement that the given object is neither black nor a raven confirms the hypothesis that everything that is not a raven is not black as well as the hypothesis that everything that is not black is not a raven. We tend to ignore the former hypothesis because we know it to be false from abundant other evidence – from all the familiar things that are not ravens but are black. But we are required to assume that no such evidence is available. Under this circumstance, even a much stronger hypothesis is also obviously confirmed: that nothing is either black or a raven. In the light of this confirmation of the hypothesis that there are no ravens, it is no longer surprising that under the artificial restrictions of the example, the hypothesis that all ravens are black is also confirmed. And the prospects for indoor ornithology vanish when we notice that under these same conditions, the contrary hypothesis that no ravens are black is equally well confirmed.[7]

On the other hand, our definition does err in not forcing us to take into account all the *stated* evidence. The unhappy results are readily illustrated. If two compatible evidence statements confirm two hypotheses, then naturally the conjunction of the evidence statements should confirm the conjunction of the hypotheses.[8] Suppose our evidence consists of the statements E_1 saying that a given thing b is black, and E_2 saying that a second thing c is not black. By our present definition, E_1 confirms the hypothesis that everything is black, and E_2 the hypothesis that everything is non-black. The conjunction of these perfectly compatible evidence statements will then confirm the self-contradictory hypothesis that everything is both black and non-black. Simple as this anomaly is, it requires drastic modification of our definition. What given evidence confirms is not what we arrive at by generalizing from separate items of it, but – roughly speaking – what we arrive at by generalizing from the total stated evidence. The central idea for an improved definition is that, within certain limitations, what is asserted to be true for the narrow universe of the evidence statements is confirmed for the whole universe of discourse. Thus if our evidence is E_1 and E_2, neither the hypothesis that all things are black nor the hypothesis that all things are non-black is confirmed; for neither is true for the evidence-universe consisting of b and c. Of course, much more careful formulation is needed, since some statements that are true of the evidence-universe – such as that there is only one black thing – are obviously not confirmed for the whole universe. These matters are taken care of by the studied formal definition that Hempel develops on this basis; but we cannot and need not go into further detail here.

No one supposes that the task of confirmation-theory has been completed. But the few steps I have reviewed – chosen partly for their bearing on what is to follow – show how things move along once the problem of definition displaces the problem of justification. Important and long-unnoticed questions are brought to light and answered; and we are encouraged to expect that the many remaining questions will in time yield to similar treatment.

But our satisfaction is shortlived. New and serious trouble begins to appear.

The New Riddle of Induction

Confirmation of a hypothesis by an instance depends rather heavily upon features of the hypothesis other than its syntactical form. That a given piece of copper conducts electricity increases the credibility of statements asserting that other pieces of copper conduct electricity, and thus confirms the hypothesis that all copper conducts electricity. But the fact that a given man now in this room is a third son does not increase the credibility of statements asserting that other men now in this room are third sons, and so does not confirm the hypothesis that all men now in this room are third sons. Yet in both cases our hypothesis is a generalization of the evidence statement. The difference is that in the former case the hypothesis is a *lawlike* statement; while in the latter case, the hypothesis is a merely contingent or accidental generality. Only a statement that is *lawlike* – regardless of its truth or falsity or its scientific importance – is capable of receiving confirmation from an instance of it; accidental statements are not. Plainly, then, we must look for a way of distinguishing lawlike from accidental statements.

So long as what seems to be needed is merely a way of excluding a few odd and unwanted cases that are inadvertently admitted by our definition of confirmation, the problem may not seem very hard or very pressing. We fully expect that minor defects will be found in our definition and that the necessary refinements will have to be worked out patiently one after another. But some further examples will show that our present difficulty is of a much graver kind.

Suppose that all emeralds examined before a certain time t are green.[9] At time t, then, our observations support the hypothesis that all emeralds are green; and this is in accord with our definition of confirmation. Our evidence statements assert that emerald a is green, that emerald b is green, and so on; and each confirms the general hypothesis that all emeralds are green. So far, so good.

Now let me introduce another predicate less familiar than "green". It is the predicate "grue" and it applies to all things examined before t just in case they are green but to other things just in case they are blue. Then at time t we have, for each evidence statement asserting that a given emerald is green, a parallel evidence statement asserting that that emerald is grue. And the statements that emerald a is grue, that emerald b is grue, and so on, will each confirm the general hypothesis that all emeralds are grue. Thus according to our definition, the prediction that all emeralds subsequently examined will be green and the prediction that all will be grue are alike confirmed by evidence statements describing the same observations. But if an emerald subsequently examined is grue, it is blue and hence not green. Thus although we are well aware which of the two incompatible predictions is genuinely confirmed, they are equally well confirmed according to our present definition. Moreover, it is clear that if we simply choose an appropriate predicate, then on the basis of these same observations we shall have equal confirmation, by our definition, for any prediction whatever about other emeralds – or indeed about anything else.[10] As in our earlier example, only the predictions subsumed under lawlike hypotheses are genuinely confirmed; but we have no criterion as yet for determining lawlikeness. And now we see that without some such criterion, our definition not merely includes a few unwanted cases, but is so completely ineffectual that it virtually excludes nothing. We are left once again with the intolerable result that anything confirms anything. This difficulty cannot be set aside as an annoying detail to be taken care of in due course. It has to be met before our definition will work at all.

Nevertheless, the difficulty is often slighted because on the surface there seem to be easy ways of dealing with it. Sometimes, for example, the problem is thought to be much like the paradox of the ravens. We are here again, it is pointed out, making tacit and illegitimate use of information outside the stated evidence: the information, for example, that different samples of one material are usually alike in conductivity, and the information that different men in a lecture audience are usually not alike in the number of their older brothers. But while it is true that such information is being smuggled in, this does not by itself settle the matter as it settles the matter of the ravens. There the point was that when the smuggled information is forthrightly declared, its effect upon the confirmation of the

hypothesis in question is immediately and properly registered by the definition we are using. On the other hand, if to our initial evidence we add statements concerning the conductivity of pieces of other materials or concerning the number of older brothers of members of other lecture audiences, this will not in the least affect the confirmation, according to our definition, of the hypothesis concerning copper or of that concerning this lecture audience. Since our definition is insensitive to the bearing upon hypotheses of evidence so related to them, even when the evidence is fully declared, the difficulty about accidental hypotheses cannot be explained away on the ground that such evidence is being surreptitiously taken into account.

A more promising suggestion is to explain the matter in terms of the effect of this other evidence not directly upon the hypothesis in question but *in*directly through other hypotheses that *are* confirmed, according to our definition, by such evidence. Our information about other materials does by our definition confirm such hypotheses as that all pieces of iron conduct electricity, that no pieces of rubber do, and so on; and these hypotheses, the explanation runs, impart to the hypothesis that all pieces of copper conduct electricity (and also to the hypothesis that none do) the character of lawlikeness – that is, amenability to confirmation by direct positive instances when found. On the other hand, our information about other lecture audiences *dis*confirms many hypotheses to the effect that all the men in one audience are third sons, or that none are; and this strips any character of lawlikeness from the hypothesis that all (or the hypothesis that none) of the men in *this* audience are third sons. But clearly if this course is to be followed, the circumstances under which hypotheses are thus related to one another will have to be precisely articulated.

The problem, then, is to define the relevant way in which such hypotheses must be alike. Evidence for the hypothesis that all iron conducts electricity enhances the lawlikeness of the hypothesis that all zirconium conducts electricity, but does not similarly affect the hypothesis that all the objects on my desk conduct electricity. Wherein lies the difference? The first two hypotheses fall under the broader hypothesis – call it "H" – that every class of things of the same material is uniform in conductivity; the first and third fall only under some such hypothesis as – call it "K" – that every class of things that are either all of the same material or all on a desk is uniform in conductivity. Clearly the important difference here is that evidence for a statement affirming that one of the classes covered by H has the property in question increases the credibility of any statement affirming that another such class has this property; while nothing of the sort holds true with respect to K. But this is only to say that H is lawlike and K is not. We are faced anew with the very problem we are trying to solve: the problem of distinguishing between lawlike and accidental hypotheses.

The most popular way of attacking the problem takes its cue from the fact that accidental hypotheses seem typically to involve some spatial or temporal restriction, or reference to some particular individual. They seem to concern the people in some particular room, or the objects on some particular person's desk; while lawlike hypotheses characteristically concern all ravens or all pieces of copper whatsoever. Complete generality is thus very often supposed to be a sufficient condition of lawlikeness; but to define this complete generality is by no means easy. Merely to require that the hypothesis contain no term naming, describing, or indicating a particular thing or location will obviously not be enough. The troublesome hypothesis that all emeralds are grue contains no such term; and where such a term does occur, as in hypotheses about men in *this room*, it can be suppressed in favor of some predicate (short or long, new or old) that contains no such term but applies only to exactly the same things. One might think, then, of excluding not only hypotheses that actually contain terms for specific individuals but also all hypotheses that are equivalent to others that do contain such terms. But, as we have just seen, to exclude only hypotheses of which *all* equivalents contain such terms is to exclude nothing. On the other hand, to exclude all hypotheses that have *some* equivalent containing such a term is to exclude everything; for even the hypothesis

All grass is green

has as an equivalent

All grass in London or elsewhere is green.

The next step, therefore, has been to consider ruling out predicates of certain kinds. A syntactically universal hypothesis is lawlike, the proposal

runs, if its predicates are 'purely qualitative' or 'non-positional'.[11] This will obviously accomplish nothing if a purely qualitative predicate is then conceived either as one that is equivalent to some expression free of terms for specific individuals, or as one that is equivalent to no expression that contains such a term; for this only raises again the difficulties just pointed out. The claim appears to be rather that at least in the case of a simple enough predicate we can readily determine by direct inspection of its meaning whether or not it is purely qualitative. But even aside from obscurities in the notion of 'the meaning' of a predicate, this claim seems to me wrong. I simply do not know how to tell whether a predicate is qualitative or positional, except perhaps by completely begging the question at issue and asking whether the predicate is 'well-behaved' – that is, whether simple syntactically universal hypotheses applying it are lawlike.

This statement will not go unprotested. "Consider", it will be argued, "the predicates 'blue' and 'green' and the predicate 'grue' introduced earlier, and also the predicate 'bleen' that applies to emeralds examined before time t just in case they are blue and to other emeralds just in case they are green. Surely it is clear", the argument runs, "that the first two are purely qualitative and the second two are not; for the meaning of each of the latter two plainly involves reference to a specific temporal position." To this I reply that indeed I do recognize the first two as well-behaved predicates admissible in lawlike hypotheses, and the second two as ill-behaved predicates. But the argument that the former but not the latter are purely qualitative seems to me quite unsound. True enough, if we start with "blue" and "green", then "grue" and "bleen" will be explained in terms of "blue" and "green" and a temporal term. But equally truly, if we start with "grue" and "bleen", then "blue" and "green" will be explained in terms of "grue" and "bleen" and a temporal term; "green", for example, applies to emeralds examined before time t just in case they are grue, and to other emeralds just in case they are bleen. Thus qualitativeness is an entirely relative matter and does not by itself establish any dichotomy of predicates. This relativity seems to be completely overlooked by those who contend that the qualitative character of a predicate is a criterion for its good behavior.

Of course, one may ask why we need worry about such unfamiliar predicates as "grue" or about accidental hypotheses in general, since we are unlikely to use them in making predictions. If our definition works for such hypotheses as are normally employed, isn't that all we need? In a sense, yes; but only in the sense that we need no definition, no theory of induction, and no philosophy of knowledge at all. We get along well enough without them in daily life and in scientific research. But if we seek a theory at all, we cannot excuse gross anomalies resulting from a proposed theory by pleading that we can avoid them in practice. The odd cases we have been considering are clinically pure cases that, though seldom encountered in practice, nevertheless display to best advantage the symptoms of a widespread and destructive malady.

We have so far neither any answer nor any promising clue to an answer to the question what distinguishes lawlike or confirmable hypotheses from accidental or non-confirmable ones; and what may at first have seemed a minor technical difficulty has taken on the stature of a major obstacle to the development of a satisfactory theory of confirmation. It is this problem that I call the new riddle of induction.

The Pervasive Problem of Projection

At the beginning of this lecture, I expressed the opinion that the problem of induction is still unsolved, but that the difficulties that face us today are not the old ones; and I have tried to outline the changes that have taken place. The problem of justifying induction has been displaced by the problem of defining confirmation, and our work upon this has left us with the residual problem of distinguishing between confirmable and non-confirmable hypotheses. One might say roughly that the first question was "Why does a positive instance of a hypothesis give any grounds for predicting further instances?"; that the newer question was "What is a positive instance of a hypothesis?"; and that the crucial remaining question is "What hypotheses are confirmed by their positive instances?"

The vast amount of effort expended on the problem of induction in modern times has thus altered our afflictions but hardly relieved them. The original difficulty about induction arose from the recognition that anything may follow upon anything. Then, in attempting to define confirmation in terms of the converse of the consequence

relation, we found ourselves with the distressingly similar difficulty that our definition would make any statement confirm any other. And now, after modifying our definition drastically, we still get the old devastating result that any statement will confirm any statement. Until we find a way of exercising some control over the hypotheses to be admitted, our definition makes no distinction whatsoever between valid and invalid inductive inferences.

The real inadequacy of Hume's account lay not in his descriptive approach but in the imprecision of his description. Regularities in experience, according to him, give rise to habits of expectation; and thus it is predictions conforming to past regularities that are normal or valid. But Hume overlooks the fact that some regularities do and some do not establish such habits; that predictions based on some regularities are valid while predictions based on other regularities are not. Every word you have heard me say has occurred prior to the final sentence of this lecture; but that does not, I hope, create any expectation that every word you will hear me say will be prior to that sentence. Again, consider our case of emeralds. All those examined before time t are green; and this leads us to expect, and confirms the prediction, that the next one will be green. But also, all those examined are grue; and this does not lead us to expect, and does not confirm the prediction, that the next one will be grue. Regularity in greenness confirms the prediction of further cases; regularity in grueness does not. To say that valid predictions are those based on past regularities, without being able to say *which* regularities, is thus quite pointless. Regularities are where you find them, and you can find them anywhere. As we have seen, Hume's failure to recognize and deal with this problem has been shared even by his most recent successors.

As a result, what we have in current confirmation theory is a definition that is adequate for certain cases that so far can be described only as those for which it is adequate. The theory works where it works. A hypothesis is confirmed by statements related to it in the prescribed way provided it is so confirmed. This is a good deal like having a theory that tells us that the area of a plane figure is one-half the base times the altitude, without telling us for what figures this holds. We must somehow find a way of distinguishing lawlike hypotheses, to which our definition of confirmation applies, from accidental hypotheses, to which it does not.

Today I have been speaking solely of the problem of induction, but what has been said applies equally to the more general problem of projection. As pointed out earlier, the problem of prediction from past to future cases is but a narrower version of the problem of projecting from any set of cases to others. We saw that a whole cluster of troublesome problems concerning dispositions and possibility can be reduced to this problem of projection. That is why the new riddle of induction, which is more broadly the problem of distinguishing between projectible and non-projectible hypotheses, is as important as it is exasperating.

Our failures teach us, I think, that lawlike or projectible hypotheses cannot be distinguished on any merely syntactical grounds or even on the ground that these hypotheses are somehow purely general in meaning. Our only hope lies in re-examining the problem once more and looking for some new approach. This will be my course in the final lecture.

Notes

1. Although this remark is merely an aside, perhaps I should explain for the sake of some unusually sheltered reader that the notion of a necessary connection of ideas, or of an absolutely analytic statement, is no longer sacrosanct. Some, like Quine and White, have forthrightly attacked the notion; others, like myself, have simply discarded it; and still others have begun to feel acutely uncomfortable about it.

2. A hasty reader might suppose that my insistence here upon identifying the problem of justification with a problem of description is out of keeping with my parenthetical insistence in the preceding lecture that the goal of philosophy is something quite different from the mere description of ordinary or scientific procedure. Let me repeat that the point urged there was that the organization of the explanatory account need not reflect the manner or order in which predicates are adopted in practice. It surely must describe practice, however, in the sense that the extensions of predicates as explicated must conform in certain ways to the extensions of the same predicates as applied in practice. Hume's account is a description in just this sense. For it is an attempt to set forth the circumstances under which those inductive judgments are made that are normally accepted as valid; and to do that is to state necessary and sufficient conditions for, and thus to define, valid induction. What I am maintaining above is that the problem of justifying induction is not something over and above the problem of describing or defining valid induction.

3. For a fuller discussion of definition in general see ch. I of *The Structure of Appearance*, 2nd edn. (Indianapolis: Bobbs-Merrill, 1966).

4. The basic article is 'A Purely Syntactical Definition of Confirmation', cited in *Journal of Symbolic Logic* 8 (1943), pp. 122–43. A much less technical account is given in 'Studies in the Logic of Confirmation', *Mind*, NS 54 (1945), pp. 1–26 and 97–121. Later work by Hempel and others on defining *degree* of confirmation does not concern us here.

5. I am not here asserting that this is an indispensable requirement upon a definition of confirmation. Since our commonsense assumptions taken in combination quickly lead us to absurd conclusions, some of these assumptions have to be dropped; and different theorists may make different decisions about which to drop and which to preserve. Hempel gives up the converse consequence condition, while Carnap (*Logical Foundations of Probability* (Chicago and London, 1950), pp. 474–6) drops both the consequence condition and the converse consequence condition. Such differences of detail between different treatments of confirmation do not affect the central points I am making in this lecture.

6. Any hypothesis is 'supported' by its own positive instances; but support – or better, direct factual support – is only one factor in confirmation. This factor has been separately studied by John G. Kemeny and Paul Oppenheim in 'Degree of Factual Support', *Philosophy of Science* 19 (1952), pp. 307–24. As will appear presently, my concern in these lectures is primarily with certain other important factors in confirmation, some of them quite generally neglected.

7. An able and thorough exposition of this paragraph is given by Israel Scheffler in his *Anatomy of Inquiry* (New York, 1963), pp. 286–91.

8. The status of the conjunction condition is much like that of the consequence condition – see note 5, above. Although Carnap drops the conjunction condition also (*Logical Foundations*, p. 394), he adopts for different reasons the requirement we find needed above: that the total available evidence must always be taken into account (pp. 211–13).

9. Although the example used is different, the argument to follow is substantially the same as that set

forth in my note 'A Query on Confirmation', cited in *Journal of Philosophy* 43 (1946), pp. 383–5.

10 For instance, we shall have equal confirmation, by our present definition, for the prediction that roses subsequently examined will be blue. Let "emerose" apply just to emeralds examined before time t, and to roses examined later. Then all emeroses so far examined are grue, and this confirms the hypothesis that all emeroses are grue and hence the prediction that roses subsequently examined will be blue. The problem raised by such antecedents

has been little noticed, but is no easier to meet than that raised by similarly perverse consequents.

11 Carnap took this course in his paper 'On the Application of Inductive Logic', *Philosophy and Phenomenological Research* 8 (1947), pp. 133–47, which is in part a reply to my 'A Query on Confirmation', cited in note 9. The discussion was continued in my note 'On Infirmities of Confirmation Theory', *Philosophy and Phenomenological Research* 8 (1947), pp. 149–51; and in Carnap's 'Reply to Nelson Goodman', same journal, same volume, pp. 461–2.

21

Epistemology Naturalized

W. V. Quine

Epistemology is concerned with the foundations of science. Conceived thus broadly, epistemology includes the study of the foundations of mathematics as one of its departments. Specialists at the turn of the century thought that their efforts in this particular department were achieving notable success: mathematics seemed to reduce altogether to logic. In a more recent perspective this reduction is seen to be better describable as a reduction to logic and set theory. This correction is a disappointment epistemologically, since the firmness and obviousness that we associate with logic cannot be claimed for set theory. But still the success achieved in the foundations of mathematics remains exemplary by comparative standards, and we can illuminate the rest of epistemology somewhat by drawing parallels to this department.

Studies in the foundations of mathematics divide symmetrically into two sorts, conceptual and doctrinal. The conceptual studies are concerned with meaning, the doctrinal with truth. The conceptual studies are concerned with clarifying concepts by defining them, some in terms of others. The doctrinal studies are concerned with establishing laws by proving them, some on the basis of others. Ideally the obscurer concepts would be defined in terms of the clearer ones so as to maximize clarity, and the less obvious laws would

Previously published in *Ontological Relativity and Other Essays* (Columbia University Press, 1969). Reprinted by kind permission of Professor W. V. Quine.

be proved from the more obvious ones so as to maximize certainty. Ideally the definitions would generate all the concepts from clear and distinct ideas, and the proofs would generate all the theorems from self-evident truths.

The two ideals are linked. For, if you define all the concepts by use of some favored subset of them, you thereby show how to translate all theorems into these favored terms. The clearer these terms are, the likelier it is that the truths couched in them will be obviously true, or derivable from obvious truths. If in particular the concepts of mathematics were all reducible to the clear terms of logic, then all the truths of mathematics would go over into truths of logic; and surely the truths of logic are all obvious or at least potentially obvious, i.e., derivable from obvious truths by individually obvious steps.

This particular outcome is in fact denied us, however, since mathematics reduces only to set theory and not to logic proper. Such reduction still enhances clarity, but only because of the interrelations that emerge and not because the end terms of the analysis are clearer than others. As for the end truths, the axioms of set theory, these have less obviousness and certainty to recommend them than do most of the mathematical theorems that we would derive from them. Moreover, we know from Gödel's work that no consistent axiom system can cover mathematics even when we renounce self-evidence. Reduction in the foundations of mathematics remains mathematically and philosophically fascinating, but it does not do what the epistemologist would like of it: it does not reveal the ground of mathematical knowledge, it does not show how mathematical certainty is possible.

Still there remains a helpful thought, regarding epistemology generally, in that duality of structure which was especially conspicuous in the foundations of mathematics. I refer to the bifurcation into a theory of concepts, or meaning, and a theory of doctrine, or truth; for this applies to the epistemology of natural knowledge no less than to the foundations of mathematics. The parallel is as follows. Just as mathematics is to be reduced to logic, or logic and set theory, so natural knowledge is to be based somehow on sense experience. This means explaining the notion of body in sensory terms; here is the conceptual side. And it means justifying our knowledge of truths of nature in sensory terms; here is the doctrinal side of the bifurcation.

Hume pondered the epistemology of natural knowledge on both sides of the bifurcation, the conceptual and the doctrinal. His handling of the conceptual side of the problem, the explanation of body in sensory terms, was bold and simple: he identified bodies outright with the sense impressions. If common sense distinguishes between the material apple and our sense impressions of it on the ground that the apple is one and enduring while the impressions are many and fleeting, then, Hume held, so much the worse for common sense; the notion of its being the same apple on one occasion and another is a vulgar confusion.

Nearly a century after Hume's *Treatise*, the same view of bodies was espoused by the early American philosopher Alexander Bryan Johnson.[1] "The word iron names an associated sight and feel," Johnson wrote.

What then of the doctrinal side, the justification of our knowledge of truths about nature? Here, Hume despaired. By his identification of bodies with impressions he did succeed in construing some singular statements about bodies as indubitable truths, yes; as truths about impressions, directly known. But general statements, also singular statements about the future, gained no increment of certainty by being construed as about impressions.

On the doctrinal side, I do not see that we are farther along today than where Hume left us. The Humean predicament is the human predicament. But on the conceptual side there has been progress. There the crucial step forward was made already before Alexander Bryan Johnson's day, although Johnson did not emulate it. It was made by Bentham in his theory of fictions. Bentham's step was the recognition of contextual definition, or what he called paraphrasis. He recognized that to explain a term we do not need to specify an object for it to refer to, nor even specify a synonymous word or phrase; we need only show, by whatever means, how to translate all the whole sentences in which the term is to be used. Hume's and Johnson's desperate measure of identifying bodies with impressions ceased to be the only conceivable way of making sense of talk of bodies, even granted that impressions were the only reality. One could undertake to explain talk of bodies in terms of talk of impressions by translating one's whole sentences about bodies into whole sentences about impressions, without equating the bodies themselves to anything at all.

This idea of contextual definition, or recognition of the sentence as the primary vehicle of meaning, was indispensable to the ensuing developments in the foundations of mathematics. It was explicit in Frege, and it attained its full flower in Russell's doctrine of singular descriptions as incomplete symbols.

Contextual definition was one of two resorts that could be expected to have a liberating effect upon the conceptual side of the epistemology of natural knowledge. The other is resort to the resources of set theory as auxiliary concepts. The epistemologist who is willing to eke out his austere ontology of sense impressions with these set-theoretic auxiliaries is suddenly rich: he has not just his impressions to play with, but sets of them, and sets of sets, and so on up. Constructions in the foundations of mathematics have shown that such set-theoretic aids are a powerful addition; after all, the entire glossary of concepts of classical mathematics is constructible from them. Thus equipped, our epistemologist may not need either to identify bodies with impressions or to settle for contextual definition; he may hope to find in some subtle construction of sets upon sets of sense impressions a category of objects enjoying just the formula properties that he wants for bodies.

The two resorts are very unequal in epistemological status. Contextual definition is unassailable. Sentences that have been given meaning as wholes are undeniably meaningful, and the use they make of their component terms is therefore meaningful, regardless of whether any translations are offered for those terms in isolation. Surely Hume and A. B. Johnson would have used contextual definition with pleasure if they had thought of it. Recourse to sets, on the other hand, is a drastic ontological move, a retreat from the austere ontology of impressions. There are philosophers who would rather settle for bodies outright than accept all these sets, which amount, after all, to the whole abstract ontology of mathematics.

This issue has not always been clear, however, owing to deceptive hints of continuity between elementary logic and set theory. This is why mathematics was once believed to reduce to logic, that is, to an innocent and unquestionable logic, and to inherit these qualities. And this is probably why Russell was content to resort to sets as well as to contextual definition when in *Our Knowledge of the External World* and elsewhere he addressed himself to the epistemology of natural knowledge, on its conceptual side.

To account for the external world as a logical construct of sense data – such, in Russell's terms, was the program. It was Carnap, in his *Der logische Aufbau der Welt* of 1928, who came nearest to executing it.

This was the conceptual side of epistemology; what of the doctrinal? There the Humean predicament remained unaltered. Carnap's constructions, if carried successfully to completion, would have enabled us to translate all sentences about the world into terms of sense data, or observation, plus logic and set theory. But the mere fact that a sentence is *couched* in terms of observation, logic, and set theory does not mean that it can be *proved* from observation sentences by logic and set theory. The most modest of generalizations about observable traits will cover more cases than its utterer can have had occasion actually to observe. The hopelessness of grounding natural science upon immediate experience in a firmly logical way was acknowledged. The Cartesian quest for certainty had been the remote motivation of epistemology, both on its conceptual and its doctrinal side; but that quest was seen as a lost cause. To endow the truths of nature with the full authority of immediate experience was as forlorn a hope as hoping to endow the truths of mathematics with the potential obviousness of elementary logic.

What then could have motivated Carnap's heroic efforts on the conceptual side of epistemology, when hope of certainty on the doctrinal

side was abandoned? There were two good reasons still. One was that such constructions could be expected to elicit and clarify the sensory evidence for science, even if the inferential steps between sensory evidence and scientific doctrine must fall short of certainty. The other reason was that such constructions would deepen our understanding of our discourse about the world, even apart from questions of evidence; it would make all cognitive discourse as clear as observation terms and logic and, I must regretfully add, set theory.

It was sad for epistemologists, Hume and others, to have to acquiesce in the impossibility of strictly deriving the science of the external world from sensory evidence. Two cardinal tenets of empiricism remained unassailable, however, and so remain to this day. One is that whatever evidence there *is* for science *is* sensory evidence. The other, to which I shall recur, is that all inculcation of meanings of words must rest ultimately on sensory evidence. Hence the continuing attractiveness of the idea of a *logischer Aufbau* in which the sensory content of discourse would stand forth explicitly.

If Carnap had successfully carried such a construction through, how could he have told whether it was the right one? The question would have had no point. He was seeking what he called a *rational reconstruction*. Any construction of physicalistic discourse in terms of sense experience, logic, and set theory would have been seen as satisfactory if it made the physicalistic discourse come out right. If there is one way there are many, but any would be a great achievement.

But why all this creative reconstruction, all this make-believe? The stimulation of his sensory receptors is all the evidence anybody has had to go on, ultimately, in arriving at his picture of the world. Why not just see how this construction really proceeds? Why not settle for psychology? Such a surrender of the epistemological burden to psychology is a move that was disallowed in earlier times as circular reasoning. If the epistemologist's goal is validation of the grounds of empirical science, he defeats his purpose by using psychology or other empirical science in the validation. However, such scruples against circularity have little point once we have stopped dreaming of deducing science from observations. If we are out simply to understand the link between observation and science, we are well advised to use any available information, including that provided by

W. V. Quine

the very science whose link with observation we are seeking to understand.

But there remains a different reason, unconnected with fears of circularity, for still favoring creative reconstruction. We should like to be able to *translate* science into logic and observation terms and set theory. This would be a great epistemological achievement, for it would show all the rest of the concepts of science to be theoretically superfluous. It would legitimize them – to whatever degree the concepts of set theory, logic, and observation are themselves legitimate – by showing that everything done with the one apparatus could in principle be done with the other. If psychology itself could deliver a truly translational reduction of this kind, we should welcome it; but certainly it cannot, for certainly we did not grow up learning definitions of physicalistic language in terms of a prior language of set theory, logic, and observation. Here, then, would be good reason for persisting in a rational reconstruction: we want to establish the essential innocence of physical concepts, by showing them to be theoretically dispensable.

The fact is, though, that the construction which Carnap outlined in *Der logische Aufbau der Welt* does not give translational reduction either. It would not even if the outline were filled in. The crucial point comes where Carnap is explaining how to assign sense qualities to positions in physical space and time. These assignments are to be made in such a way as to fulfill, as well as possible, certain desiderata which he states, and with growth of experience the assignments are to be revised to suit. This plan, however illuminating, does not offer any key to *translating* the sentences of science into terms of observation, logic, and set theory.

We must despair of any such reduction. Carnap had despaired of it by 1936, when, in "Testability and Meaning,"[2] he introduced so-called *reduction forms* of a type weaker than definition. Definitions had shown always how to translate sentences into equivalent sentences. Contextual definition of a term showed how to translate sentences containing the term into equivalent sentences lacking the term. Reduction forms of Carnap's liberalized kind, on the other hand, do not in general give equivalences; they give implications. They explain a new term, if only partially, by specifying some sentences which are implied by sentences containing the term, and other sentences which imply sentences containing the term.

It is tempting to suppose that the countenancing of reduction forms in this liberal sense is just one further step of liberalization comparable to the earlier one, taken by Bentham, of countenancing contextual definition. The former and sterner kind of rational reconstruction might have been represented as a fictitious history in which we imagined our ancestors introducing the terms of physicalistic discourse on a phenomenalistic and set-theoretic basis by a succession of contextual definitions. The new and more liberal kind of rational reconstruction is a fictitious history in which we imagine our ancestors introducing those terms by a succession rather of reduction forms of the weaker sort.

This, however, is a wrong comparison. The fact is rather that the former and sterner kind of rational reconstruction, where definition reigned, embodied no fictitious history at all. It was nothing more nor less than a set of directions – or would have been, if successful – for accomplishing everything in terms of phenomena and set theory that we now accomplish in terms of bodies. It would have been a true reduction by translation, a legitimation by elimination. *Definire est eliminare*. Rational reconstruction by Carnap's later and looser reduction forms does none of this.

To relax the demand for definition, and settle for a kind of reduction that does not eliminate, is to renounce the last remaining advantage that we supposed rational reconstruction to have over straight psychology; namely, the advantage of translational reduction. If all we hope for is a reconstruction that links science to experience in explicit ways short of translation, then it would seem more sensible to settle for psychology. Better to discover how science is in fact developed and learned than to fabricate a fictitious structure to a similar effect.

The empiricist made one major concession when he despaired of deducing the truths of nature from sensory evidence. In despairing now even of translating those truths into terms of observation and logico-mathematical auxiliaries, he makes another major concession. For suppose we hold, with the old empiricist Peirce, that the very meaning of a statement consists in the difference its truth would make to possible experience. Might we not formulate, in a chapter-length sentence in observational language, all the difference that the truth of a given statement might make to experience, and might we not then take all this as the translation? Even if the difference that the truth of the statement would make to experience ramifies indefinitely, we might still hope to embrace it all in the logical implications of our chapter-length formulation, just as we can axiomatize an infinity of theorems. In giving up hope of such translation, then, the empiricist is conceding that the empirical meanings of typical statements about the external world are inaccessible and ineffable.

How is this inaccessibility to be explained? Simply on the ground that the experiential implications of a typical statement about bodies are too complex for finite axiomatization, however lengthy? No; I have a different explanation. It is that the typical statement about bodies has no fund of experiential implications it can call its own. A substantial mass of theory, taken together, will commonly have experiential implications; this is how we make verifiable predictions. We may not be able to explain why we arrive at theories which make successful predictions, but we do arrive at such theories.

Sometimes also an experience implied by a theory fails to come off; and then, ideally, we declare the theory false. But the failure falsifies only a block of theory as a whole, a conjunction of many statements. The failure shows that one or more of those statements is false, but it does not show which. The predicted experiences, true and false, are not implied by any one of the component statements of the theory rather than another. The component statements simply do not have empirical meanings, by Peirce's standard; but a sufficiently inclusive portion of theory does. If we can aspire to a sort of *logischer Aufbau der Welt* at all, it must be to one in which the texts slated for translation into observational and logico-mathematical terms are mostly broad theories taken as wholes, rather than just terms or short sentences. The translation of a theory would be a ponderous axiomatization of all the experiential difference that the truth of the theory would make. It would be a queer translation, for it would translate the whole but none of the parts. We might better speak in such a case not of translation but simply of observational evidence for theories; and we may, following Peirce, still fairly call this the empirical meaning of the theories.

These considerations raise a philosophical question even about ordinary unphilosophical translation, such as from English into Arunta or Chinese. For, if the English sentences of a theory have

their meaning only together as a body, then we can justify their translation into Arunta only together as a body. There will be no justification for pairing off the component English sentences with component Arunta sentences, except as these correlations make the translation of the theory as a whole come out right. Any translations of the English sentences into Arunta sentences will be as correct as any other, so long as the net empirical implications of the theory as a whole are preserved in translation. But it is to be expected that many different ways of translating the component sentences, essentially different individually, would deliver the same empirical implications for the theory as a whole; deviations in the translation of one component sentence could be compensated for in the translation of another component sentence. Insofar, there can be no ground for saying which of two glaringly unlike translations of individual sentences is right.[3]

For an uncritical mentalist, no such indeterminacy threatens. Every term and every sentence is a label attached to an idea, simple or complex, which is stored in the mind. When on the other hand we take a verification theory of meaning seriously, the indeterminacy would appear to be inescapable. The Vienna Circle espoused a verification theory of meaning but did not take it seriously enough. If we recognize with Peirce that the meaning of a sentence turns purely on what would count as evidence for its truth, and if we recognize with Duhem that theoretical sentences have their evidence not as single sentences but only as larger blocks of theory, then the indeterminacy of translation of theoretical sentences is the natural conclusion. And most sentences, apart from observation sentences, are theoretical. This conclusion, conversely, once it is embraced, seals the fate of any general notion of propositional meaning or, for that matter, state of affairs.

Should the unwelcomeness of the conclusion persuade us to abandon the verification theory of meaning? Certainly not. The sort of meaning that is basic to translation, and to the learning of one's own language, is necessarily empirical meaning and nothing more. A child learns his first words and sentences by hearing and using them in the presence of appropriate stimuli. These must be external stimuli, for they must act both on the child and on the speaker from whom he is learning.[4] Language is socially inculcated and controlled; the inculcation and control turn strictly on the keying of sentences to shared stimulation.

Internal factors may vary *ad libitum* without prejudice to communication as long as the keying of language to external stimuli is undisturbed. Surely one has no choice but to be an empiricist so far as one's theory of linguistic meaning is concerned.

What I have said of infant learning applies equally to the linguist's learning of a new language in the field. If the linguist does not lean on related languages for which there are previously accepted translation practices, then obviously he has no data but the concomitances of native utterance and observable stimulus situation. No wonder there is indeterminacy of translation – for of course only a small fraction of our utterances report concurrent external stimulation. Granted, the linguist will end up with unequivocal translations of everything; but only by making many arbitrary choices – arbitrary even though unconscious – along the way. Arbitrary? By this I mean that different choices could still have made everything come out right that is susceptible in principle to any kind of check.

Let me link up, in a different order, some of the points I have made. The crucial consideration behind my argument for the indeterminacy of translation was that a statement about the world does not always or usually have a separable fund of empirical consequences that it can call its own. That consideration served also to account for the impossibility of an epistemological reduction of the sort where every sentence is equated to a sentence in observational and logico-mathematical terms. And the impossibility of that sort of epistemological reduction dissipated the last advantage that rational reconstruction seemed to have over psychology.

Philosophers have rightly despaired of translating everything into observational and logico-mathematical terms. They have despaired of this even when they have not recognized, as the reason for this irreducibility, that the statements largely do not have their private bundles of empirical consequences. And some philosophers have seen in this irreducibility the bankruptcy of epistemology. Carnap and the other logical positivists of the Vienna Circle had already pressed the term "metaphysics" into pejorative use, as connoting meaninglessness; and the term "epistemology" was next. Wittgenstein and his followers, mainly at Oxford, found a residual philosophical vocation in therapy: in curing philosophers of the delusion that there were epistemological problems.

But I think that at this point it may be more useful to say rather that epistemology still goes on, though in a new setting and a clarified status. Epistemology, or something like it, simply falls into place as a chapter of psychology and hence of natural science. It studies a natural phenomenon, viz., a physical human subject. This human subject is accorded a certain experimentally controlled input – certain patterns of irradiation in assorted frequencies, for instance – and in the fullness of time the subject delivers as output a description of the three-dimensional external world and its history. The relation between the meager input and the torrential output is a relation that we are prompted to study for somewhat the same reasons that always prompted epistemology; namely, in order to see how evidence relates to theory, and in what ways one's theory of nature transcends any available evidence.

Such a study could still include, even, something like the old rational reconstruction, to whatever degree such reconstruction is practicable; for imaginative constructions can afford hints of actual psychological processes, in much the way that mechanical simulations can. But a conspicuous difference between old epistemology and the epistemological enterprise in this new psychological setting is that we can now make free use of empirical psychology.

The old epistemology aspired to contain, in a sense, natural science; it would construct it somehow from sense data. Epistemology in its new setting, conversely, is contained in natural science, as a chapter of psychology. But the old containment remains valid too, in its way. We are studying how the human subject of our study posits bodies and projects his physics from his data, and we appreciate that our position in the world is just like his. Our very epistemological enterprise, therefore, and the psychology wherein it is a component chapter, and the whole of natural science wherein psychology is a component book – all this is our own construction or projection from stimulations like those we were meting out to our epistemological subject. There is thus reciprocal containment, though containment in different senses: epistemology in natural science and natural science in epistemology.

This interplay is reminiscent again of the old threat of circularity, but it is all right now that we have stopped dreaming of deducing science from sense data. We are after an understanding of science as an institution or process in the world, and we do not intend that understanding to be any better than the science which is its object. This attitude is indeed one that Neurath was already urging in Vienna Circle days, with his parable of the mariner who has to rebuild his boat while staying afloat in it.

One effect of seeing epistemology in a psychological setting is that it resolves a stubborn old enigma of epistemological priority. Our retinas are irradiated in two dimensions, yet we see things as three-dimensional without conscious inference. Which is to count as observation – the unconscious two-dimensional reception or the conscious three-dimensional apprehension? In the old epistemological context the conscious form had priority, for we were out to justify our knowledge of the external world by rational reconstruction, and that demands awareness. Awareness ceased to be demanded when we gave up trying to justify our knowledge of the external world by rational reconstruction. What to count as observation now can be settled in terms of the stimulation of sensory receptors, let consciousness fall where it may.

The Gestalt psychologists' challenge to sensory atomism, which seemed so relevant to epistemology forty years ago, is likewise deactivated. Regardless of whether sensory atoms or Gestalten are what favor the forefront of our consciousness, it is simply the stimulations of our sensory receptors that are best looked upon as the input to our cognitive mechanism. Old paradoxes about unconscious data and inference, old problems about chains of inference that would have to be completed too quickly – these no longer matter.

In the old anti-psychologistic days the question of epistemological priority was moot. What is epistemologically prior to what? Are Gestalten prior to sensory atoms because they are noticed, or should we favor sensory atoms on some more subtle ground? Now that we are permitted to appeal to physical stimulation, the problem dissolves; A is epistemologically prior to B if A is causally nearer than B to the sensory receptors. Or, what is in some ways better, just talk explicitly in terms of causal proximity to sensory receptors and drop the talk of epistemological priority.

Around 1932 there was debate in the Vienna Circle over what to count as observation sentences, or *Protokollsätze*.[5] One position was that they had the form of reports of sense impressions. Another was that they were statements of an elementary sort about the external world, e.g.,

"A red cube is standing on the table." Another, Neurath's, was that they had the form of reports of relations between percipients and external things: "Otto now sees a red cube on the table." The worst of it was that there seemed to be no objective way of settling the matter: no way of making real sense of the question.

Let us now try to view the matter unreservedly in the context of the external world. Vaguely speaking, what we want of observation sentences is that they be the ones in closest causal proximity to the sensory receptors. But how is such proximity to be gauged? The idea may be rephrased this way: observation sentences are sentences which, as we learn language, are most strongly conditioned to concurrent sensory stimulation rather than to stored collateral information. Thus let us imagine a sentence queried for our verdict as to whether it is true or false; queried for our assent or dissent. Then the sentence is an observation sentence if our verdict depends only on the sensory stimulation present at the time.

But a verdict cannot depend on present stimulation to the exclusion of stored information. The very fact of our having learned the language evinces much storing of information, and of information without which we should be in no position to give verdicts on sentences however observational. Evidently then we must relax our definition of observation sentence to read thus: a sentence is an observation sentence if all verdicts on it depend on present sensory stimulation and on no stored information beyond what goes into understanding the sentence.

This formulation raises another problem: how are we to distinguish between information that goes into understanding a sentence and information that goes beyond? This is the problem of distinguishing between analytic truth, which issues from the mere meanings of words, and synthetic truth, which depends on more than meanings. Now I have long maintained that this distinction is illusory. There is one step toward such a distinction, however, which does make sense: a sentence that is true by mere meanings of words should be expected, at least if it is simple, to be subscribed to by all fluent speakers in the community. Perhaps the controversial notion of analyticity can be dispensed with, in our definition of observation sentence, in favor of this straightforward attribute of community-wide acceptance.

This attribute is of course no explication of analyticity. The community would agree that there have been black dogs, yet none who talk of analyticity would call this analytic. My rejection of the analyticity notion just means drawing no line between what goes into the mere understanding of the sentences of a language and what else the community sees eye-to-eye on. I doubt that an objective distinction can be made between meaning and such collateral information as is community-wide.

Turning back then to our task of defining observation sentences, we get this: an observation sentence is one on which all speakers of the language give the same verdict when given the same concurrent stimulation. To put the point negatively, an observation sentence is one that is not sensitive to differences in past experience within the speech community.

This formulation accords perfectly with the traditional role of the observation sentence as the court of appeal of scientific theories. For by our definition the observation sentences are the sentences on which all members of the community will agree under uniform stimulation. And what is the criterion of membership in the same community? Simply general fluency of dialogue. This criterion admits of degrees, and indeed we may usefully take the community more narrowly for some studies than for others. What count as observation sentences for a community of specialists would not always so count for a larger community.

There is generally no subjectivity in the phrasing of observation sentences, as we are now conceiving them; they will usually be about bodies. Since the distinguishing trait of an observation sentence is intersubjective agreement under agreeing stimulation, a corporeal subject matter is likelier than not.

The old tendency to associate observation sentences with a subjective sensory subject matter is rather an irony when we reflect that observation sentences are also meant to be the intersubjective tribunal of scientific hypotheses. The old tendency was due to the drive to base science on something firmer and prior in the subject's experience; but we dropped that project.

The dislodging of epistemology from its old status of first philosophy loosed a wave, we saw, of epistemological nihilism. This mood is reflected somewhat in the tendency of Polányi, Kuhn, and the late Russell Hanson to belittle the role of evidence and to accentuate cultural relativism. Hanson ventured even to discredit the idea of observation, arguing that so-called observations vary from observer to observer with the amount of knowledge that the observers bring with them. The veteran physicist looks at some apparatus and sees an x-ray tube. The neophyte, looking at the same place, observes rather "a glass and metal instrument replete with wires, reflectors, screws, lamps, and pushbuttons."[6] One man's observation is another man's closed book or flight of fancy. The notion of observation as the impartial and objective source of evidence for science is bankrupt. Now my answer to the x-ray example was already hinted a little while back: what counts as an observation sentence varies with the width of community considered. But we can also always get an absolute standard by taking in all speakers of the language, or most.[7] It is ironical that philosophers, finding the old epistemology untenable as a whole, should react by repudiating a part which has only now moved into clear focus.

Clarification of the notion of observation sentence is a good thing, for the notion is fundamental in two connections. These two correspond to the duality that I remarked upon early in this lecture: the duality between concept and doctrine, between knowing what a sentence means and knowing whether it is true. The observation sentence is basic to both enterprises. Its relation to doctrine, to our knowledge of what is true, is very much the traditional one: observation sentences are the repository of evidence for scientific hypotheses. Its relation to meaning is fundamental too, since observation sentences are the ones we are in a position to learn to understand first, both as children and as field linguists. For observation sentences are precisely the ones that we can correlate with observable circumstances of the occasion of utterance or assent, independently of variations in the past histories of individual informants. They afford the only entry to a language.

The observation sentence is the cornerstone of semantics. For it is, as we just saw, fundamental to the learning of meaning. Also, it is where meaning is firmest. Sentences higher up in theories have no empirical consequences they can call their own; they confront the tribunal of sensory evidence only in more or less inclusive aggregates. The observation sentence, situated at the sensory periphery of the body scientific, is the minimal verifiable aggregate; it has an empirical content all its own and wears it on its sleeve.

The predicament of the indeterminacy of translation has little bearing on observation sentences. The equating of an observation sentence of our language to an observation sentence of another language is mostly a matter of empirical generalization; it is a matter of identity between the range of stimulations that would prompt assent to the one sentence and the range of stimulations that would prompt assent to the other.[8]

It is no shock to the preconceptions of old Vienna to say that epistemology now becomes semantics. For epistemology remains centered as always on evidence, and meaning remains centered as always on verification; and evidence is verification. What is likelier to shock preconceptions is that meaning, once we get beyond observation sentences, ceases in general to have any clear applicability to single sentences; also that epistemology merges with psychology, as well as with linguistics.

This rubbing out of boundaries could contribute to progress, it seems to me, in philosophically interesting inquiries of a scientific nature. One possible area is perceptual norms. Consider, to begin with, the linguistic phenomenon of phonemes. We form the habit, in hearing the myriad variations of spoken sounds, of treating each as an approximation to one or another of a limited number of norms – around thirty altogether – constituting so to speak a spoken alphabet. All speech in our language can be treated in practice as sequences of just those thirty elements, thus rectifying small deviations. Now outside the realm of language also there is probably only a rather limited alphabet of perceptual norms altogether, toward which we tend unconsciously to rectify all perceptions. These, if experimentally identified, could be taken as epistemological building blocks, the working elements of experience. They might prove in part to be culturally variable, as phonemes are, and in part universal.

Again there is the area that the psychologist Donald T. Campbell calls evolutionary epistemology.[9] In this area there is work by Hüseyin Yilmaz, who shows how some structural traits of color perception could have been predicted from survival value.[10] And a more emphatically epistemological topic that evolution helps to clarify is induction, now that we are allowing epistemology the resources of natural science.[11]

Notes

1   A. B. Johnson, *A Treatise on Language* (New York, 1836; Berkeley, 1947).

2   *Philosophy of Science* 3 (1936), pp. 419–71; 4 (1937), pp. 1–40.

3   See W. V. Quine, *Ontological Relativity and Other Essays* (New York: Columbia University Press, 1969), pp. 2ff.

4   See Quine, *Ontological Relativity*, p. 28.

5   R. Carnap and O. Neurath in *Erkenntnis* 3 (1932), pp. 204–28.

6   N. R. Hanson, "Observation and Interpretation," in *Philosophy of Science Today* ed. S. Morgenbesser (New York: Basic Books, 1966).

7   This qualification allows for occasional deviants such as the insane or the blind. Alternatively, such cases might be excluded by adjusting the level of fluency of dialogue whereby we define sameness of language. (For prompting this note and influencing the development of this paper also in more substantial ways I am indebted to Burton Dreben.)

8   Cf. W. V. Quine, *Word and Object* (Cambridge, MA: MIT Press, 1960), pp. 31–46, 68.

9   D. T. Campbell, "Methodological Suggestions from a Comparative Psychology of Knowledge Processes," *Inquiry* 2 (1959), pp. 152–82.

10 Hüseyin Yilmaz, "On Color Vision and a New Approach to General Perception," in *Biological Prototypes and Synthetic Systems*, ed. E. E. Bernard and M. R. Kare (New York: Plenum, 1962); "Perceptual Invariance and the Psychophysical Law," *Perception and Psychophysics* 2 (1967), pp. 533–8.

11 See "Natural Kinds," ch. 5 in Quine, *Ontological Relativity*.

Further reading in epistemology

Bonjour, Laurence, *The Structure of Empirical Knowledge*, Cambridge, MA: Harvard University Press, 1985.

Chisholm, Roderick, *Theory of Knowledge*, Englewood Cliffs, NJ: Prentice-Hall, 1966; 2nd edn. 1977, 3rd edn. 1989.

Dancy, Jonathan and Sosa, Ernest (eds.) *A Companion to Epistemology*, Malden, MA: Blackwell Publishers, 1992.

Davidson, Donald, "A Coherence Theory of Truth and Knowledge," in *Kant oder Hegel*, ed. D. Henrich, Stuttgart: Klett-Cotta, 1983.

Goldman, Alvin, *Epistemology and Cognition*, Cambridge, MA: Harvard University Press, 1986.

Harman, Gilbert, *Change in View*, Cambridge, MA: MIT Press, 1986; 2nd edn. 1989.

Lehrer, Keith, *Theory of Knowledge*, Boulder, CO: Westview Press, 1990.

Martinich, A. P. and Stroll, Avrum, "Epistemology," in *Encyclopedia Britannica*, 15th edn., vol. 18, Chicago: Encyclopedia Britannica, Inc., 1990, pp. 466–88.

Nagel, Thomas, *The View From Nowhere*, New York: Oxford University Press, 1986.

Nozick, Robert, *Philosophical Explanations*, Cambridge, MA: Harvard University Press, 1981.

Plantinga, Alvin, *Warrant and Proper Function*, New York: Oxford University Press, 1993.

Russell, Bertrand, *Logic and Knowledge: Essays 1901–1950*, ed. Robert Marsh, London: George Allen & Unwin, 1956.

Sosa, Ernest, "The Raft and the Pyramid," *Midwest Studies in Philosophy*, vol. 5, ed. P. A. French, T. E. Uehling, Jr., H. K. Wettstein, Minneapolis: University of Minnesota Press, 1980.

Sosa, Ernest, and Kim, Jaegwon, *Epistemology: An Anthology*, Malden, MA: Blackwell Publishers, 2000.

Stroud, Barry, *The Significance of Philosophical Scepticism*, Oxford: Oxford University Press, 1984.

PART IV

Philosophy of Mind

22

The Nature of Mind

D. M. Armstrong

Men have minds, that is to say, they perceive, they have sensations, emotions, beliefs, thoughts, purposes, and desires. What is it to have a mind? What is it to perceive, to feel emotion, to hold a belief, or to have a purpose? In common with many other modern philosophers, I think that the best clue we have to the nature of mind is furnished by the discoveries and hypotheses of modern science concerning the nature of man.

What does modern science have to say about the nature of man? There are, of course, all sorts of disagreements and divergencies in the views of individual scientists. But I think it is true to say that one view is steadily gaining ground, so that it bids fair to become established scientific doctrine. This is the view that we can give a complete account of man *in purely physico-chemical terms*. This view has received a tremendous impetus in the last decade from the new subject of molecular biology, a subject which promises to unravel the physical and chemical mechanisms which lie at the basis of life. Before that time, it received great encouragement from pioneering work in neurophysiology pointing to the likelihood of a purely electro-chemical account of the working of the brain. I think it is fair to say that those scientists who still reject the physico-chemical account of man do so primarily for philosophical, or moral, or religious reasons, and only secondarily, and half-heartedly, for reasons of scientific detail. This is not to say that in the future new

Previously published in *The Mind/Brain Identity Theory*, ed. C. V. Borst (Macmillan, London, 1970).

evidence and new problems may not come to light which will force science to reconsider the physico-chemical view of man. But at present the drift of scientific thought is clearly set towards the physico-chemical hypothesis. And we have nothing better to go on than the present.

For me, then, and for many philosophers who think like me, the moral is clear. We must try to work out an account of the nature of mind which is compatible with the view that man is nothing but a physico-chemical mechanism.

And in this paper I shall be concerned to do just this: to sketch (in barest outline) what may be called a Materialist or Physicalist account of the mind.

But before doing this I should like to go back and consider a criticism of my position which must inevitably occur to some. What reason have I, it may be asked, for taking my stand on science? Even granting that I am right about what is the currently dominant scientific view of man, why should we concede science a special authority to decide questions about the nature of man? What of the authority of philosophy, of religion, of morality, or even of literature and art? Why do I set the authority of science above all these? Why this 'scientism'?

It seems to me that the answer to this question is very simple. If we consider the search for truth, in all its fields, we find that it is only in science that men versed in their subject can, after investigation that is more or less prolonged, and which may in some cases extend beyond a single human lifetime, reach substantial agreement about what is the case. It is only as a result of scientific investigation that we ever seem to reach an intellectual consensus about controversial matters.

In the Epistle Dedicatory to his *De Corpore* Hobbes wrote of William Harvey, the discoverer of the circulation of the blood, that he was 'the only man I know, that conquering envy, hath established a new doctrine in his life-time'.

Before Copernicus, Galileo and Harvey, Hobbes remarks, 'there was nothing certain in natural philosophy'. And, we might add, with the exception of mathematics, there was nothing certain in any other learned discipline.

These remarks of Hobbes are incredibly revealing. They show us what a watershed in the intellectual history of the human race the seventeenth century was. Before that time inquiry proceeded, as it were, in the dark. Men could not hope to see their doctrine *established*, that is to say, accepted by the vast majority of those properly versed in the subject under discussion. There was no intellectual consensus. Since that time, it has become a commonplace to see new doctrines, sometimes of the most far-reaching kind, established to the satisfaction of the learned, often within the lifetime of their first proponents. Science has provided us with a method of deciding disputed questions. This is not to say, of course, that the consensus of those who are learned and competent in a subject cannot be mistaken. Of course such a consensus can be mistaken. Sometimes it has been mistaken. But, granting fallibility, what better authority have we than such a consensus?

Now this is of the utmost importance. For in philosophy, in religion, in such disciplines as literary criticism, in moral questions in so far as they are thought to be matters of truth and falsity, there has been a notable failure to achieve an intellectual consensus about disputed questions among the learned. Must we not then attach a peculiar authority to the discipline that can achieve a consensus? And if it presents us with a certain vision of the nature of man, is this not a powerful reason for accepting that vision?

I will not take up here the deeper question *why* it is that the methods of science have enabled us to achieve an intellectual consensus about so many disputed matters. That question, I think, could receive no brief or uncontroversial answer. I am resting my argument on the simple and uncontroversial fact that, as a result of scientific investigation, such a consensus has been achieved.

It may be replied – it often is replied – that while science is all very well in its own sphere – the sphere of the physical, perhaps – there are matters of fact on which it is not competent to pronounce. And among such matters, it may be claimed, is the question what is the whole nature of man. But I cannot see that this reply has much force. Science has provided us with an island of truths, or, perhaps one should say, a raft of truths, to bear us up on the sea of our disputatious ignorance. There may have to be revisions and refinements, new results may set old findings in a new perspective, but what science has given us will not be altogether superseded. Must we not therefore appeal to these relative certainties for guidance when we come to consider uncertainties elsewhere? Perhaps science cannot help us to decide whether or not there is a God, whether or not human beings have immortal souls, or whether or not the will is free. But if science cannot assist us, what can? I conclude that it is the scientific vision of man, and not the philosophical or religious or artistic or moral vision of man, that is the best clue we have to the nature of man. And it is rational to argue from the best evidence we have.

Having in this way attempted to justify my procedure, I turn back to my subject: the attempt to work out an account of mind, or, if you prefer, of mental process, within the framework of the physico-chemical, or, as we may call it, the Materialist view of man.

Now there is one account of mental process that is at once attractive to any philosopher sympathetic to a Materialist view of man: this is Behaviourism. Formulated originally by a psychologist, J. B. Watson, it attracted widespread interest and considerable support from scientifically oriented philosophers. Traditional philosophy had tended to think of the mind as a rather mysterious inward arena that lay behind, and was responsible for, the outward or physical behaviour of our bodies. Descartes thought of this inner arena as a *spiritual substance*, and it was this conception of the mind as spiritual object that Gilbert Ryle attacked, apparently in the interest of Behaviourism, in his important book *The Concept of Mind*. He ridiculed the Cartesian view as the dogma of 'the ghost in the machine'. The mind was not something behind the behaviour of the body, it was simply part of that physical behaviour. My anger with you is not some modification of a spiritual substance which somehow brings about aggressive behaviour; rather it is the aggressive behaviour itself: my addressing strong words to you, striking you, turning my back on you, and so on. Thought is not an inner process that lies behind, and brings about, the words I speak and write: it is my speaking and writing. The mind is not an inner arena, it is outward act.

It is clear that such a view of mind fits in very well with a completely Materialistic or Physicalist view of man. If there is no need to draw a distinction between mental processes and their expression in physical behaviour, but if instead the mental processes are identified with their so-called 'expressions', then the existence of mind stands in no conflict with the view that man is nothing but a physico-chemical mechanism.

However, the version of Behaviourism that I have just sketched is a very crude version, and its crudity lays it open to obvious objections. One obvious difficulty is that it is our common experience that there can be mental processes going on although there is no behaviour occurring that could possibly be treated as expressions of these processes. A man may be angry, but give no bodily sign; he may think, but say or do nothing at all.

In my view, the most plausible attempt to refine Behaviourism with a view to meeting this objection was made by introducing the notion of *a disposition to behave*. (Dispositions to behave play a particularly important part in Ryle's account of the mind.) Let us consider the general notion of disposition first. Brittleness is a disposition, a disposition possessed by materials like glass. Brittle materials are those which, when subjected to relatively small forces, break or shatter easily. But breaking and shattering easily is not brittleness, rather it is the *manifestation* of brittleness. Brittleness itself is the tendency or liability of the material to break or shatter easily. A piece of glass may never shatter or break throughout its whole history, but it is still the case that it is brittle: it is liable to shatter or break if dropped quite a small way or hit quite lightly. Now a disposition to *behave* is simply a tendency or liability of a person to behave in a certain way under certain circumstances. The brittleness of glass is a disposition that the glass retains throughout its history, but clearly there could also be dispositions that come and go. The dispositions to behave that are of interest to the Behaviourist are, for the most part, of this temporary character.

Now how did Ryle and others use the notion of a disposition to behave to meet the obvious objection to Behaviourism that there can be mental processes going on although the subject is engaging in no relevant behaviour? Their strategy was to argue that in such cases, although the subject was not behaving in any relevant way, he or she was *disposed* to behave in some relevant way. The glass does not shatter, but it is still brittle. The man does not behave, but he does have a disposition to behave. We can say he thinks although he does not speak or act because at that time he was disposed to speak or act in a certain way. *If* he had been asked, perhaps, he would have spoken or acted. We can say he is angry although he does not behave angrily, because he is disposed so to behave. *If* only one more word had been addressed to him, he would have burst out. And so on. In this way it was hoped that Behaviourism could be squared with the obvious facts.

It is very important to see just how these thinkers conceived of dispositions. I quote from Ryle:

> To possess a dispositional property *is not to be in a particular state, or to undergo a particular change*; it is to be bound or liable to be in a particular state, or to undergo a particular change, when a particular condition is realised. (*The Concept of Mind*, p. 43, my italics)[1]

So to explain the breaking of a lightly struck glass on a particular occasion by saying it was brittle is, on this view of dispositions, simply to say that the glass broke because it is the sort of thing that regularly breaks when quite lightly struck. The breaking was the normal behaviour, or not abnormal behaviour, of such a thing. The brittleness is not to be conceived of as a *cause* for the breakage, or even, more vaguely, a *factor* in bringing about the breaking. Brittleness is just the fact that things of that sort break easily.

But although in this way the Behaviourists did something to deal with the objection that mental processes can occur in the absence of behaviour, it seems clear, now that the shouting and the dust have died, that they did not do enough. When I think, but my thoughts do not issue in any action, it seems as obvious as anything is obvious that there is something actually going on in me which constitutes my thought. It is not simply that I would speak or act if some conditions that are unfulfilled were to be fulfilled. Something is currently going on, in the strongest and most literal sense of 'going on', and this something is my thought. Rylean Behaviourism denies this, and so it is unsatisfactory as a theory of mind. Yet I know of no version of Behaviourism that is more satisfactory. The moral for those of us who wish to take a purely physicalistic view of man is that we must look for some other account of the nature of mind and of mental processes.

But perhaps we need not grieve too deeply about the failure of Behaviourism to produce a satisfactory theory of mind. Behaviourism is a profoundly unnatural account of mental processes. If somebody speaks and acts in certain ways it is natural to speak of this speech and action as the *expression* of his thought. It is not at all natural to speak of his speech and action as identical with his thought. We naturally think of the thought as something quite distinct from the speech and action which, under suitable circumstances, brings the speech and action about. Thoughts are not to be identified with behaviour, we think, they lie behind behaviour. A man's behaviour constitutes the *reason* we have for attributing certain mental processes to him, but the behaviour cannot be identified with the mental processes.

This suggests a very interesting line of thought about the mind. Behaviourism is certainly wrong, but perhaps it is not altogether wrong. Perhaps the Behaviourists are wrong in identifying the mind and mental occurrences with behaviour, but perhaps they are right in thinking that our notion of a mind and of individual mental states is *logically tied to behaviour*. For perhaps what we mean by a mental state is some state of the person which, under suitable circumstances, *brings about* a certain range of behaviour. Perhaps mind can be defined not as behaviour, but rather as the inner *cause* of certain behaviour. Thought is not speech under suitable circumstances, rather it is something within the person which, in suitable circumstances, brings about speech. And, in fact, I believe that this is the true account, or, at any rate, a true first account, of what we mean by a mental state.

How does this line of thought link up with a purely physicalist view of man? The position is,

I think, that while it does not make such a physicalist view inevitable, it does make it *possible*. It does not entail, but it is compatible with, a purely physicalist view of man. For if our notion of the mind and mental states is nothing but that of a cause within the person of certain ranges of behaviour, then it becomes a scientific question, and not a question of logical analysis, what in fact the intrinsic nature of that cause is. The cause might be, as Descartes thought it was, a spiritual substance working through the pineal gland to produce the complex bodily behaviour of which men are capable. It might be breath, or specially smooth and mobile atoms dispersed throughout the body; it might be many other things. But in fact the verdict of modern science seems to be that the sole cause of mind-betokening behaviour in man and the higher animals is the physicochemical workings of the central nervous system. And so, assuming we have correctly characterised our concept of a mental state as nothing but the cause of certain sorts of behaviour, then we can identify these mental states with purely physical states of the central nervous system.

At this point we may stop and go back to the Behaviourists' dispositions. We saw that, according to them, the brittleness of glass or, to take another example, the elasticity of rubber, is not a state of the glass or the rubber, but is simply the fact that things of that sort behave in the way they do. But now let us consider how a scientist would think about brittleness or elasticity. Faced with the phenomenon of breakage under relatively small impacts, or the phenomenon of stretching when a force is applied followed by contraction when the force is removed, he will assume that there is some current *state* of the glass or the rubber which is responsible for the characteristic behaviour of samples of these two materials. At the beginning he will not know what this state is, but he will endeavour to find out, and he may succeed in finding out. And when he has found out he will very likely make remarks of this sort: We have discovered that the brittleness of glass is in fact a certain sort of pattern in the molecules of the glass.' That is to say, he will *identify* brittleness with the state of the glass that is responsible for the liability of the glass to break. For him, a disposition of an object is a state of the object. What makes the state a state of brittleness is the fact that it gives rise to the characteristic manifestations of brittleness. But the disposition itself is distinct from its manifestations:

it is the state of the glass that gives rise to these manifestations in suitable circumstances.

You will see that this way of looking at dispositions is very different from that of Ryle and the Behaviourists. The great difference is this: If we treat dispositions as actual states, as I have suggested that scientists do, even if states whose intrinsic nature may yet have to be discovered, then we can say that dispositions are actual *causes*, or causal factors, which, in suitable circumstances, actually bring about those happenings which are the manifestations of the disposition. A certain molecular constitution of glass which constitutes its brittleness is actually *responsible* for the fact that, when the glass is struck, it breaks.

Now I shall not argue the matter here, because the detail of the argument is technical and difficult,[2] but I believe that the view of dispositions as states, which is the view that is natural to science, is the correct one. I believe it can be shown quite strictly that, to the extent that we admit the notion of dispositions at all, we are committed to the view that they are actual *states* of the object that has the disposition. I may add that I think that the same holds for the closely connected notions of capacities and powers. Here I will simply assume this step in my argument.

But perhaps it can be seen that the rejection of the idea that mind is simply a certain range of man's behaviour in favour of the view that mind is rather the inner *cause* of that range of man's behaviour is bound up with the rejection of the Rylean view of dispositions in favour of one that treats disposition as states of objects and so as having actual causal power. The Behaviourists were wrong to identify the mind with behaviour. They were not so far off the mark when they tried to deal with cases where mental happenings occur in the absence of behaviour by saying that these are dispositions to behave. But in order to reach a correct view, I am suggesting, they would have to conceive of these dispositions as actual *states* of the person who has the disposition, states that have actual power to bring about behaviour in suitable circumstances. But to do this is to abandon the central inspiration of Behaviourism: that in talking about the mind we do not have to go behind outward behaviour to inner states.

And so two separate but interlocking lines of thought have pushed me in the same direction. The first line of thought is that it goes pro-

foundly against the grain to think of the mind as behaviour. The mind is, rather, that which stands behind and brings about our complex behaviour. The second line of thought is that the Behaviourists' dispositions, properly conceived, are really states that underlie behaviour, and, under suitable circumstances, bring about behaviour. Putting these two together, we reach the conception of a mental state as *a state of the person apt for producing certain ranges of behaviour*. This formula: a mental state is a state of the person apt for producing certain ranges of behaviour, I believe to be a very illuminating way of looking at the concept of a mental state. I have found it very fruitful in the search for detailed logical analyses of the individual mental concepts.

Now, I do not think that Hegel's dialectic has much to tell us about the nature of reality. But I think that human thought often moves in a dialectical way, from thesis to antithesis and then to the synthesis. Perhaps thought about the mind is a case in point. I have already said that classical philosophy tended to think of the mind as an inner arena of some sort. This we may call the Thesis. Behaviourism moved to the opposite extreme: the mind was seen as outward behaviour. This is the Antithesis. My proposed Synthesis is that the mind is properly conceived as an inner principle, but a principle that is identified in terms of the outward behaviour it is apt for bringing about. This way of looking at the mind and mental states does not itself entail a Materialist or Physicalist view of man, for nothing is said in this analysis about the intrinsic nature of these mental states. But if we have, as I have asserted that we do have, general scientific grounds for thinking that man is nothing but a physical mechanism, we can go on to argue that the mental states are in fact nothing but physical states of the central nervous system.

Along these lines, then, I would look for an account of the mind that is compatible with a purely Materialist theory of man. I have tried to carry out this programme in detail in *A Materialist Theory of the Mind*. There are, as may be imagined, all sorts of powerful objections that can be made to this view. But in the rest of this paper I propose to do only one thing. I will develop one very important objection to my view of the mind – an objection felt by many philosophers – and then try to show how the objection should be met.

D. M. Armstrong

The view that our notion of mind is nothing but that of an inner principle apt for bringing about certain sorts of behaviour may be thought to share a certain weakness with Behaviourism. Modern philosophers have put the point about Behaviourism by saying that although Behaviourism may be a satisfactory account of the mind from an *other-person point of view*, it will not do as a *first-person* account. To explain. In our encounters with other people, all we ever observe is their behaviour: their actions, their speech, and so on. And so, if we simply consider other people, Behaviourism might seem to do full justice to the facts. But the trouble about Behaviourism is that it seems so unsatisfactory as applied to our *own* case. In our own case, we seem to be aware of so much more than mere behaviour.

Suppose that now we conceive of the mind as an inner principle apt for bringing about certain sorts of behaviour. This again fits the other-person cases very well. Bodily behaviour of a very sophisticated sort is observed, quite different from the behaviour that ordinary physical objects display. It is inferred that this behaviour must spring from a very special sort of inner cause in the object that exhibits this behaviour. This inner cause is christened 'the mind', and those who take a physicalist view of man argue that it is simply the central nervous system of the body observed. Compare this with the case of glass. Certain characteristic behaviour is observed: the breaking and shattering of the material when acted upon by relatively small forces. A special inner state of the glass is postulated to explain this behaviour. Those who take a purely physicalist view of glass then argue that this state is a *natural* state of the glass. It is, perhaps, an arrangement of its molecules, and not, say, the peculiarly malevolent disposition of the demons that dwell in glass.

But when we turn to our own case, the position may seem less plausible. We are conscious, we have experiences. Now can we say that to be conscious, to have experiences, is simply for something to go on within us apt for the causing of certain sorts of behaviour? Such an account does not seem to do any justice to the phenomena. And so it seems that our account of the mind, like Behaviourism, will fail to do justice to the first-person case.

In order to understand the objection better it may be helpful to consider a particular case. If you have driven for a very long distance without a break, you may have had experience of a curious state of automatism, which can occur in these conditions. One can suddenly 'come to' and realise that one has driven for long distances without being aware of what one was doing, or, indeed, without being aware of anything. One has kept the car on the road, used the brake and the clutch perhaps, yet all without any awareness of what one was doing.

Now, if we consider this case it is obvious that *in some sense* mental processes are still going on when one is in such an automatic state. Unless one's will was still operating in some way, and unless one was still perceiving in some way, the car would not still be on the road. Yet, of course, *something* mental is lacking. Now, I think, when it is alleged that an account of mind as an inner principle apt for the production of certain sorts of behaviour leaves out consciousness or experience, what is alleged to have been left out is just whatever is missing in the automatic driving case. It is conceded that an account of mental processes as states of the person apt for the production of certain sorts of behaviour may very possibly be adequate to deal with such cases as that of automatic driving. It may be adequate to deal with most of the mental processes of animals, who perhaps spend a good deal of their lives in this state of automatism. But, it is contended, it cannot deal with the consciousness that we normally enjoy.

I will now try to sketch an answer to this important and powerful objection. Let us begin in an apparently unlikely place, and consider the way that an account of mental processes of the sort I am giving would deal with *sense-perception*.

Now psychologists, in particular, have long realised that there is a very close logical tie between sense-perception and *selective behaviour*. Suppose we want to decide whether an animal can perceive the difference between red and green. We might give the animal a choice between two pathways, over one of which a red light shines and over the other of which a green light shines. If the animal happens by chance to choose the green pathway we reward it; if it happens to choose the other pathway we do not reward it. If, after some trials, the animal systematically takes the green-lighted pathway, and if we become assured that the only relevant differences in the two pathways are the differences in the colour of the lights, we are entitled to say that the animal can see this colour difference. Using its eyes, it selects between red-lighted and green-lighted pathways. So we say it can see the difference between red and green.

Now a Behaviourist would be tempted to say that the animal's regularly selecting the green-lighted pathway *was* its perception of the colour difference. But this is unsatisfactory, because we all want to say that perception is something that goes on within the person or animal – within its mind – although, of course, this mental event is normally *caused* by the operation of the environment upon the organism. Suppose, however, that we speak instead of *capacities* for selective behaviour towards the current environment, and suppose we think of these capacities, like dispositions, as actual inner states of the organism. We can then think of the animal's perception as a state within the animal apt, if the animal is so impelled, for selective behaviour between the red- and green-lighted pathways.

In general, we can think of perceptions as inner states or events apt for the production of certain sorts of selective behaviour towards our environment. To perceive is like acquiring a key to a door. You do not have to use the key: you can put it in your pocket and never bother about the door. But if you do want to open the door the key may be essential. The blind man is a man who does not acquire certain keys, and, as a result, is not able to operate in his environment in the way that somebody who has his sight can operate. It seems, then, a very promising view to take of perceptions that they are inner states defined by the sorts of selective behaviour that they enable the perceiver to exhibit, if so impelled.

Now how is this discussion of perception related to the question of consciousness or experience, the sort of thing that the driver who is in a state of automatism has not got, but which we normally do have? Simply this. My proposal is that consciousness, in this sense of the word, is nothing but *perception or awareness of the state of our own mind*. The driver in a state of automatism perceives, or is aware of, the road. If he did not, the car would be in a ditch. But he is not currently aware of his awareness of the road. He perceives the road, but he does not perceive his perceiving, or anything else that is going on in his mind. He is not, as we normally are, conscious of what is going on in his mind.

And so I conceive of consciousness or experience, in this sense of the words, in the way that Locke and Kant conceived it, as like perception. Kant, in a striking phrase, spoke of 'inner sense'. We cannot directly observe the minds of others, but each of us has the power to observe directly our own minds, and 'perceive' what is going on there. The driver in the automatic state is one whose 'inner eye' is shut: who is not currently aware of what is going on in his own mind.

Now if this account is along the right lines, why should we not give an account of this inner observation along the same lines as we have already given of perception? Why should we not conceive of it as an inner state, a state in this case directed towards other inner states and not to the environment, which enables us, if we are so impelled, to behave in a selective way *towards our own states of mind*? One who is aware, or conscious, of his thoughts or his emotions is one who has the capacity to make discriminations between his different mental states. His capacity might be exhibited in words. He might say that he was in an angry state of mind when, and only when, he *was* in an angry state of mind. But such verbal behaviour would be the mere *expression* or *result* of the awareness. The awareness itself would be an inner state: the sort of inner state that gave the man a capacity for such behavioural expressions.

So I have argued that consciousness of our own mental state may be assimilated to *perception* of our own mental state, and that, like other perceptions, it may then be conceived of as an inner state or event giving a capacity for selective behaviour, in this case selective behaviour towards our own mental state. All this is meant to be simply a logical analysis of consciousness, and none of it entails, although it does not rule out, a purely physicalist account of what these inner states are. But if we are convinced, on general scientific grounds, that a purely physical account of man is likely to be the true one, then there seems to be no bar to our identifying these inner states with purely physical states of the central nervous system. And so consciousness of our own mental state becomes simply the scanning of one part of our central nervous system by another. Consciousness is a self-scanning mechanism in the central nervous system.

As I have emphasised before, I have done no more than sketch a programme for a philosophy of mind. There are all sorts of expansions and elucidations to be made, and all sorts of doubts

D. M. Armstrong

and difficulties to be stated and overcome. But I hope I have done enough to show that a purely physicalist theory of the mind is an exciting and plausible intellectual option.

Notes

Inaugural lecture of the Challis Professor of Philosophy at the University of Sydney (1965); slightly amended (1968) and published in *The Mind/Brain Identity Theory* (London: Macmillan, 1970), pp. 67–79.

1 *The Concept of Mind* (New York: Barnes & Noble, University Paperbacks, 1949). (Published by special arrangement with Hutchinson & Co., London.)
2 It is presented in my book *A Materialist Theory of the Mind* (London: Routledge, 1968), ch. 6, sec. VI.

23

The Nature of Mental States

Hilary Putnam

The typical concerns of the Philosopher of Mind might be represented by three questions: (1) How do we know that other people have pains? (2) Are pains brain states? (3) What is the analysis of the concept *pain*? I do not wish to discuss questions (1) and (3) in this paper. I shall say something about question (2).[1]

Identity Questions

"Is pain a brain state?" (Or, "Is the property of having a pain at time t a brain state?"[2]) It is impossible to discuss this question sensibly without saying something about the peculiar rules which have grown up in the course of the development of "analytical philosophy" – rules which, far from leading to an end to all conceptual confusions, themselves represent considerable conceptual confusion. These rules – which are, of course, implicit rather than explicit in the practice of most analytical philosophers – are (1) that a statement of the form "being A is being B" (e.g., "being in pain is being in a certain brain state") can be *correct* only if it follows, in some sense, from the meaning of the terms A and B; and (2) that a statement of the form "being A is being B" can be philosophically *informative* only

Originally published as "Psychological Predicates," by Hilary Putnam in *Art, Mind, and Religion*, ed. W. H. Capitan and D. D. Merrill, © 1967 by the University of Pittsburgh Press. Reprinted by permission of the University of Pittsburgh Press.

if it is in some sense reductive (e.g. "being in pain is having a certain unpleasant sensation" is not philosophically informative, "being in pain is having a certain behavior disposition" is, if true, philosophically informative). These rules are excellent rules if we still believe that the program of reductive analysis (in the style of the 1930s) can be carried out; if we don't, then they turn analytical philosophy into a mug's game, at least so far as "is" questions are concerned.

In this paper I shall use the term 'property' as a blanket term for such things as being in pain, being in a particular brain state, having a particular behavior disposition, and also for magnitudes such as temperature, etc. – i.e., for things which can naturally be represented by one-or-more-place predicates or functors. I shall use the term 'concept' for things which can be identified with synonymy-classes of expressions. Thus the concept *temperature* can be identified (I maintain) with the synonymy-class of the word 'temperature.'[3] (This is like saying that the number 2 can be identified with the class of all pairs. This is quite a different statement from the peculiar statement that 2 is the class of all pairs. I do not maintain that concepts *are* synonymy-classes, whatever that might mean, but that they can be identified with synonymy-classes, for the purpose of formalization of the relevant discourse.)

The question "What is the concept *temperature*?" is a very "funny" one. One might take it to mean "What is temperature? Please take my question as a conceptual one." In that case an answer might be (pretend for a moment 'heat' and 'temperature' are synonyms) "temperature is heat," or even "the concept of temperature is the same concept as the concept of heat." Or one might take it to mean "What are *concepts*, really? For example, what is 'the concept of temperature'?" In that case heaven knows what an "answer" would be. (Perhaps it would be the statement that concepts *can be identified with* synonymy-classes.)

Of course, the question "What is the property temperature?" is also "funny." And one way of interpreting it is to take it as a question about the concept of temperature. But this is not the way a physicist would take it.

The effect of saying that the property P_1 can be identical with the property P_2 only if the terms P_1, P_2 are in some suitable sense "synonyms" is, to all intents and purposes, to collapse the two notions of "property" and "concept" into a single notion. The view that concepts (intensions) *are* the same as properties has been explicitly advocated by Carnap (e.g., in *Meaning and Necessity*). This seems an unfortunate view, since "temperature is mean molecular kinetic energy" appears to be a perfectly good example of a true statement of identity of properties, whereas "the concept of temperature is the same concept as the concept of mean molecular kinetic energy" is simply false.

Many philosophers believe that the statement "pain is a brain state" violates some rules or norms of English. But the arguments offered are hardly convincing. For example, if the fact that I can know that I am in pain without knowing that I am in brain state S shows that pain cannot be brain state S, then, by exactly the same argument, the fact that I can know that the stove is hot without knowing that the mean molecular kinetic energy is high (or even that molecules exist) shows that it is *false* that temperature is mean molecular kinetic energy, physics to the contrary. In fact, all that immediately follows from the fact that I can know that I am in pain without knowing that I am in brain state S is that the concept of pain is not the same concept as the concept of being in brain state S. But either pain, or the state of being in pain, or some pain, or some pain state, might still be brain state S. After all, the concept of temperature is not the same concept as the concept of mean molecular kinetic energy. But temperature is mean molecular kinetic energy.

Some philosophers maintain that both 'pain is a brain state' and 'pain states are brain states' are unintelligible. The answer is to explain to these philosophers, as well as we can, given the vagueness of all scientific methodology, what sorts of considerations lead one to make an empirical reduction (i.e., to say such things as "water is H_2O," "light is electro-magnetic radiation," "temperature is mean molecular kinetic energy"). If, without giving reasons, he still maintains in the face of such examples that one cannot imagine parallel circumstances for the use of 'pains are brain states' (or, perhaps, 'pain states are brain states') one has grounds to regard him as perverse.

Some philosophers maintain that "P_1 is P_2" is something that can be true, when the 'is' involved is the 'is' of empirical reduction, only when the properties P_1 and P_2 are (a) associated with a spatio-temporal region; and (b) the region is one and the same in both cases. Thus "temperature is mean molecular kinetic energy" is an admissible empirical reduction, since the temperature and the molecular energy are associated with the same space-time region, but "having a pain in my arm is being in a brain state" is not, since the spatial regions involved are different.

This argument does not appear very strong. Surely no one is going to be deterred from saying that mirror images are light reflected from an object and then from the surface of a mirror by the fact that an image can be "located" three feet *behind* the mirror. (Moreover, one can always find *some* common property of the reductions one is willing to allow – e.g., temperature is mean molecular kinetic energy – which is not a property of some one identification one wishes to disallow. This is not very impressive unless one has an argument to show that the very purposes of such identification depend upon the common property in question.)

Again, other philosophers have contended that all the predictions that can be derived from the conjunction of neurophysiological laws with such statements as "pain states are such-and-such brain states" can equally well be derived from the conjunction of the same neurophysiological laws with "being in pain is correlated with such-and-such brain states," and hence (sic!) there can be no methodological grounds for saying that pains (or pain states) *are* brain states, as opposed to saying that they are *correlated* (invariantly) with brain states. This argument, too, would show that light is only correlated with electromagnetic radiation. The mistake is in ignoring the fact that, although the theories in question may indeed lead to the same predictions, they open and exclude different *questions*. "Light is invariantly correlated with electromagnetic radiation" would leave open the questions "What is the light then, if it isn't the same as the electromagnetic radiation?" and "What makes the light accompany the electromagnetic radiation?" – questions which are excluded by saying that the light *is* the electromagnetic radiation. Similarly, the purpose of saying that pains are brain states is precisely to exclude from empirical meaningfulness the questions "What is the pain, then, if it isn't the same as the brain state?" and "What makes the pain accompany the brain state?" If there are grounds to suggest that these questions represent, so to speak, the wrong way to look at the matter, then those grounds are grounds for a theoretical identification of pains with brain states.

If all arguments to the contrary are unconvincing, shall we then conclude that it is meaningful (and perhaps true) to say either that pains are brain states or that pain states are brain states?

1   It is perfectly meaningful (violates no "rule of English," involves no "extension of usage") to say "pains are brain states."
2   It is not meaningful (involves a "changing of meaning" or "an extension of usage," etc.) to say "pains are brain states."

My own position is not expressed by either (1) or (2). It seems to me that the notions "change of meaning" and "extension of usage" are simply so ill-defined that one cannot in fact say *either* (1) or (2). I see no reason to believe that either the linguist, or the man-on-the-street, or the philosopher possesses today a notion of "change of meaning" applicable to such cases as the one we have been discussing. The *job* for which the notion of change of meaning was developed in the history of the language was just a *much* cruder job than this one.

But, if we don't assert either (1) or (2) – in other words, if we regard the "change of meaning" issue as a pseudo-issue in this case – then how are we to discuss the question with which we started? "Is pain a brain state?"

The answer is to allow statements of the form "pain is *A*," where 'pain' and '*A*' are in no sense synonyms, and to see whether any such statement can be found which might be acceptable on empirical and methodological grounds. This is what we shall now proceed to do.

Is Pain a Brain State?

We shall discuss "Is pain a brain state?," then. And we have agreed to waive the "change of meaning" issue.

Since I am discussing not what the concept of pain comes to, but what pain is, in a sense of 'is' which requires empirical theory-construction (or, at least, empirical speculation), I shall not apologize for advancing an empirical hypothesis. Indeed, my strategy will be to argue that pain is *not* a brain state, not on *a priori* grounds, but on the grounds that another hypothesis is more plausible. The detailed development and verification of my hypothesis would be just as Utopian a task as the detailed development and verification of the brain-state hypothesis. But the putting-forward, not of detailed and scientifically "finished" hypotheses, but of schemata for hypotheses, has long been a function of philosophy. I shall, in short, argue that pain is not a brain state, in the sense of a physical-chemical state of the brain (or even the whole nervous system), but another *kind* of state entirely. I propose the hypothesis that pain, or the state of being in pain, is a functional state of a whole organism.

To explain this it is necessary to introduce some technical notions. In previous papers I have explained the notion of a Turing Machine and discussed the use of this notion as a model for an organism. The notion of a Probabilistic Automaton is defined similarly to a Turing Machine, except that the transitions between "states" are allowed to be with various probabilities rather than being "deterministic." (Of course, a Turing Machine is simply a special kind of Probabilistic Automaton, one with transition probabilities 0, 1.) I shall assume the notion of a Probabilistic Automaton has been generalized to allow for "sensory inputs" and "motor outputs" – that is, the Machine Table specifies, for every possible combination of a "state" and a complete set of "sensory inputs," an "instruction" which determines the probability of the next "state," and also the probabilities of the "motor outputs." (This replaces the idea of the Machine as printing on a tape.) I shall also assume that the physical realization of the sense organs responsible for the various inputs, and of the motor organs, is specified, but that the "states" and the "inputs" themselves are, as usual, specified only "implicitly" – i.e., by the set of transition probabilities given by the Machine Table.

Since an empirically given system can simultaneously be a "physical realization" of many different Probabilistic Automata, I introduce the notion of a *Description* of a system. A Description of S where S is a system, is any true statement to the effect that S possesses distinct states $S_1, S_2, \ldots, S_n$ which are related to one another and to the motor outputs and sensory inputs by the transition probabilities given in such-and-such a Machine Table. The Machine Table mentioned in the Description will then be called the Functional Organization of S relative to that Description, and the S_i such that S is in state S_i at a given time will be called the Total State of S (at that time) relative to that Description. It should be noted that knowing the Total State of a system relative to a Description involves knowing a good deal about how the system is likely to "behave," given various combinations of sensory inputs, but does *not* involve knowing the physical realization of the S_i as, e.g., physical-chemical states of the brain. The S_i, to repeat, are specified only *implicitly* by the Description – i.e., specified *only* by the set of transition probabilities given in the Machine Table.

The hypothesis that "being in pain is a functional state of the organism" may now be spelled out more exactly as follows:

1   All organisms capable of feeling pain are Probabilistic Automata.
2   Every organism capable of feeling pain possesses at least one Description of a certain kind (i.e., being capable of feeling pain *is* possessing an appropriate kind of Functional Organization).
3   No organism capable of feeling pain possesses a decomposition into parts which separately possess Descriptions of the kind referred to in (2).
4   For every Description of the kind referred to in (2), there exists a subset of the sensory inputs such that an organism with that Description is in pain when and only when some of its sensory inputs are in that subset.

This hypothesis is admittedly vague, though surely no vaguer than the brain-state hypothesis in its present form. For example, one would like to know more about the kind of Functional Organization that an organism must have to be capable of feeling pain, and more about the marks that distinguish the subset of the sensory inputs

referred to in (4). With respect to the first question, one can probably say that the Functional Organization must include something that resembles a "preference function," or at least a preference partial ordering, and something that resembles an "inductive logic" (i.e., the Machine must be able to "learn from experience"). (The meaning of these conditions, for Automata models, is discussed in my paper "The Mental Life of Some Machines.") In addition, it seems natural to require that the Machine possess "pain sensors," i.e., sensory organs which normally signal damage to the Machine's body, or dangerous temperatures, pressures, etc., which transmit a special subset of the inputs, the subset referred to in (4). Finally, and with respect to the second question, we would want to require at least that the inputs in the distinguished subset have a high disvalue on the Machine's preference function or ordering (further conditions are discussed in "The Mental Life of Some Machines"). The purpose of condition (3) is to rule out such "organisms" (if they can count as such) as swarms of bees as single pain-feelers. The condition (1) is, obviously, redundant, and is only introduced for expository reasons. (It is, in fact, empty, since everything is a Probabilistic Automaton under *some* Description.)

I contend, in passing, that this hypothesis, in spite of its admitted vagueness, is far *less* vague than the "physical-chemical state" hypothesis is today, and far more susceptible to investigation of both a mathematical and an empirical kind. Indeed, to investigate this hypothesis is just to attempt to produce "mechanical" models of organisms – and isn't this, in a sense, just what psychology is about? The difficult step, of course, will be to pass from models of *specific* organisms to a *normal form* for the psychological description of organisms – for this is what is required to make (2) and (4) precise. But this too seems to be an inevitable part of the program of psychology.

I shall now compare the hypothesis just advanced with (a) the hypothesis that pain is a brain state, and (b) the hypothesis that pain is a behavior disposition.

Functional State versus Brain State

It may, perhaps, be asked if I am not somewhat unfair in taking the brain-state theorist to be talking about *physical-chemical* states of the brain.

But (a) these are the only sorts of states ever mentioned by brain-state theorists. (b) The brain-state theorist usually mentions (with a certain pride, slightly reminiscent of the Village Atheist) the incompatibility of his hypothesis with all forms of dualism and mentalism. This is natural if physical-chemical states of the brain are what is at issue. However, functional states of whole systems are something quite different. In particular, the functional-state hypothesis is *not* incompatible with dualism! Although it goes without saying that the hypothesis is "mechanistic" in its inspiration, it is a slightly remarkable fact that a system consisting of a body and a "soul," if such things there be, can perfectly well be a Probabilistic Automaton. (c) One argument advanced by Smart is that the brain-state theory assumes only "physical" properties, and Smart finds "non-physical" properties unintelligible. The Total States and the "inputs" defined above are, of course, neither mental nor physical *per se*, and I cannot imagine a functionalist advancing this argument. (d) If the brain-state theorist does mean (or at least allow) states other than physical-chemical states, then his hypothesis is completely empty, at least until he specifies *what* sort of "states" he *does* mean.

Taking the brain-state hypothesis in this way, then, what reasons are there to prefer the functional-state hypothesis over the brain-state hypothesis? Consider what the brain-state theorist has to do to make good his claims. He has to specify a physical-chemical state such that *any* organism (not just a mammal) is in pain if and only if (a) it possesses a brain of a suitable physical-chemical structure; and (b) its brain is in that physical-chemical state. This means that the physical-chemical state in question must be a possible state of a mammalian brain, a reptilian brain, a mollusc's brain (octopuses are mollusca, and certainly feel pain), etc. At the same time, it must *not* be a possible (physically possible) state of the brain of any physically possible creature that cannot feel pain. Even if such a state can be found, it must be nomologically certain that it will also be a state of the brain of any extraterrestrial life that may be found that will be capable of feeling pain before we can even entertain the supposition that it may *be* pain.

It is not altogether impossible that such a state will be found. Even though octopus and mammal are examples of parallel (rather than sequential) evolution, for example, virtually identical structures (physically speaking) have evolved in the eye of the octopus and in the eye of the mammal, notwithstanding the fact that this organ has evolved from different kinds of cells in the two cases. Thus it is at least possible that parallel evolution, all over the universe, might *always* lead to *one and the same* physical "correlate" of pain. But this is certainly an ambitious hypothesis.

Finally, the hypothesis becomes still more ambitious when we realize that the brain-state theorist is not just saying that *pain* is a brain state; he is, of course, concerned to maintain that *every* psychological state is a brain state. Thus if we can find even one psychological predicate which can clearly be applied to both a mammal and an octopus (say "hungry"), but whose physical-chemical "correlate" is different in the two cases, the brain-state theory has collapsed. It seems to me overwhelmingly probable that we can do this. Granted, in such a case the brain-state theorist can save himself by *ad hoc* assumptions (e.g., defining the disjunction of two states to be a single "physical-chemical state"), but this does not have to be taken seriously.

Turning now to the considerations *for* the functional-state theory, let us begin with the fact that we identify organisms as in pain, or hungry, or angry, or in heat, etc., on the basis of their *behavior*. But it is a truism that similarities in the behavior of two systems are at least a reason to suspect similarities in the functional organization of the two systems, and a much *weaker* reason to suspect similarities in the actual physical details. Moreover, we expect the various psychological states – at least the basic ones, such as hunger, thirst, aggression, etc. – to have more or less similar "transition probabilities" (within wide and ill-defined limits, to be sure) with each other and with behavior in the case of different species, because this is an artifact of the way in which we identify these states. Thus, we would not count an animal as *thirsty* if its "unsatiated" behavior did not seem to be directed toward drinking and was not followed by "satiation for liquid." Thus any animal that we count as capable of these various states will at least *seem* to have a certain rough kind of functional organization. And, as already remarked, if the program of finding psychological laws that are not species-specific – i.e., of finding a normal form for psychological theories of different species – ever succeeds, then it will bring in its wake a delineation of the kind of functional organization that is necessary and sufficient for a given psychological state, as well as a precise definition of the notion "psychological state." In contrast, the brain-state theorist has to hope for the eventual development of neurophysiological laws that are species-independent, which seems much less reasonable than the hope that psychological laws (of a sufficiently general kind) may be species-independent, or, still weaker, that a species-independent *form* can be found in which psychological laws can be written.

Functional State versus Behavior-disposition

The theory that being in pain is neither a brain state nor a functional state but a behavior disposition has one apparent advantage: it appears to agree with the way in which we verify that organisms are in pain. We do not in practice know anything about the brain state of an animal when we say that it is in pain; and we possess little if any knowledge of its functional organization, except in a crude intuitive way. In fact, however, this "advantage" is no advantage at all: for, although statements about how we verify that *x* is *A* may have a good deal to do with what the concept of being *A* comes to, they have precious little to do with what the property *A* is. To argue on the ground just mentioned that pain is neither a brain state nor a functional state is like arguing that heat is not mean molecular kinetic energy from the fact that ordinary people do not (they think) ascertain the mean molecular kinetic energy of something when they verify that it is hot or cold. It is not necessary that they should; what is necessary is that the marks that they take as indications of heat should in fact be explained by the mean molecular kinetic energy. And, similarly, it is necessary to our hypothesis that the marks that are taken as behavioral indications of pain should be explained by the fact that the organism is in a functional state of the appropriate kind, but not that speakers should *know* that this is so.

The difficulties with "behavior disposition" accounts are so well known that I shall do little more than recall them here. The difficulty – it appears to be more than a "difficulty," in fact – of specifying the required behavior disposition except as "the disposition of X to behave as if X were in *pain*," is the chief one, of course. In contrast, we *can* specify the functional state with

which we propose to identify pain, at least roughly, without using the notion of pain. Namely, the functional state we have in mind is the state of receiving sensory inputs which play a certain role in the Functional Organization of the organism. This role is characterized, at least partially, by the fact that the sense organs responsible for the inputs in question are organs whose function is to detect damage to the body, or dangerous extremes of temperature, pressure, etc., and by the fact that the "inputs" themselves, whatever their physical realization, represent a condition that the organism assigns a high disvalue to. As I stressed in "The Mental Life of Some Machines," this does *not* mean that the Machine will always *avoid* being in the condition in question ("pain"); it only means that the condition will be avoided unless not avoiding it is necessary to the attainment of some more highly valued goal. Since the behavior of the Machine (in this case, an organism) will depend not merely on the sensory inputs, but also on the Total State (i.e., on other values, beliefs, etc.), it seems hopeless to make any general statement about how an organism in such a condition *must* behave; but this does not mean that we must abandon hope of characterizing the condition. Indeed, we have just characterized it.[4]

Not only does the behavior-disposition theory seem hopelessly vague; if the "behavior" referred to is peripheral behavior, and the relevant stimuli are peripheral stimuli (e.g., we do not say anything about what the organism will do if its brain is operated upon), then the theory seems clearly false. For example, two animals with all motor nerves cut will have the same actual and potential "behavior" (viz., none to speak of); but if one has cut pain fibers and the other has uncut pain fibers, then one will feel pain and the other won't. Again, if one person has cut pain fibers, and another suppresses all pain responses deliberately due to some strong compulsion, then the actual and potential peripheral behavior may be the same, but one will feel pain and the other won't. (Some philosophers maintain that this last case is conceptually impossible, but the only evidence for this appears to be that *they* can't, or don't want to, conceive of it.[5]) If, instead of pain, we take some sensation the "bodily expression" of which is easier to suppress – say, a slight coolness in one's left little finger – the case becomes even clearer.

Finally, even if there *were* some behavior disposition invariantly correlated with pain (species-independently!), and specifiable without using the term 'pain,' it would still be more plausible to identify being in pain with some state whose presence *explains* this behavior disposition – the brain state or functional state – than with the behavior disposition itself. Such considerations of plausibility may be somewhat subjective; but if other things *were* equal (of course, they aren't) why shouldn't we allow considerations of plausibility to play the deciding role?

Methodological Considerations

So far we have considered only what might be called the "empirical" reasons for saying that being in pain is a functional state, rather than a brain state or a behavior disposition; viz., that it seems more likely that the functional state we described is invariantly "correlated" with pain, species-independently, than that there is either a physical-chemical state of the brain (must an organism have a *brain* to feel pain? perhaps some ganglia will do) or a behavior disposition so correlated. If this is correct, then it follows that the identification we proposed is at least a candidate for consideration. What of methodological considerations?

The methodological considerations are roughly similar in all cases of reduction, so no surprises need be expected here. First, identification of psychological states with functional states means that the laws of psychology can be derived from statements of the form "such-and-such organisms have such-and-such Descriptions" together with the identification statements ("being in pain is such-and-such a functional state," etc.). Secondly, the presence of the functional state (i.e., of inputs which play the role we have described in the Functional Organization of the organism) is not merely "correlated with" but actually explains the pain behavior on the part of the organism. Thirdly, the identification serves to exclude questions which (if a naturalistic view is correct) represent an altogether wrong way of looking at the matter, e.g., "What *is* pain if it isn't either the brain state or the functional state?" and "What causes the pain to be always accompanied by this sort of functional state?" In short, the identification is to be tentatively accepted as a theory which leads to both fruitful predictions and to fruitful *questions*, and which serves to discourage fruitless and empirically senseless questions, where by 'empirically senseless' I mean "senseless" not merely from the standpoint of verification, but from the standpoint of what there in fact *is*.

Notes

1 I have discussed these and related topics in the following papers: "Minds and Machines," in *Dimensions of Mind*, ed. Sidney Hook (New York, 1960), pp. 148–79; "Brains and Behavior," in *Analytical Philosophy*, 2nd series, ed. Ronald Butler (Oxford, 1965), pp. 1–20; and "The Mental Life of Some Machines," in *Intentionality, Minds, and Perception*, ed. Hector-Neri Castañeda (Detroit, 1967), pp. 177–200.

2 In this paper I wish to avoid the vexed question of the relation between *pains* and *pain states*. I only remark in passing that one common argument *against* identification of these two – viz., that a pain can be in one's arm but a state (of the organism) cannot be in one's arm – is easily seen to be fallacious.

3 There are some well-known remarks by Alonzo Church on this topic. Those remarks do not bear (as might at first be supposed) on the identification of concepts with synonymy-classes as such, but rather support the view that (in formal semantics) it is necessary to retain Frege's distinction between the normal and the "oblique" use of expressions. That is, even if we say that the concept of temperature *is* the synonymy-class of the word 'temperature,' we must not thereby be led into the

error of supposing that 'the concept of temperature' is synonymous with 'the synonymy-class of the word "temperature"' – for then 'the concept of temperature' and 'der Begriff der Temperatur' would not be synonymous, which they are. Rather, we must say that 'the concept of temperature' *refers to* the synonymy-class of the word 'temperature' (on this particular reconstruction); but that class is *identified* not as "the synonymy class to which such-and-such a word belongs," but in another way (e.g., as the synonymy-class whose members have such-and-such a characteristic use).

4 In "The Mental Life of Some Machines" a further, and somewhat independent, characteristic of the pain inputs is discussed in terms of Automata models – namely the spontaneity of the inclination to withdraw the injured part, etc. This raises the question, which is discussed in that paper, of giving a functional analysis of the notion of a spontaneous inclination. Of course, still further characteristics come readily to mind – for example, that feelings of pain are (or seem to be) *located* in the parts of the body.

5 Cf. the discussion of "super-spartans" in "Brains and Behavior."

24

Mental Events

Donald Davidson

Mental events such as perceivings, remember-ings, decisions, and actions resist capture in the nomological net of physical theory. How can this fact be reconciled with the causal role of mental events in the physical world? Reconciling freedom with causal determinism is a special case of the problem if we suppose that causal determinism entails capture in, and freedom requires escape from, the nomological net. But the broader issue can remain alive even for someone who believes a correct analysis of free action reveals no conflict with determinism. *Autonomy* (freedom, self-rule) may or may not clash with determinism; *anomaly* (failure to fall under a law) is, it would seem, another matter.

I start from the assumption that both the causal dependence, and the anomalousness, of mental events are undeniable facts. My aim is therefore to explain, in the face of apparent difficulties, how this can be. I am in sympathy with Kant when he says,

> it is as impossible for the subtlest philosophy as for the commonest reasoning to argue free-dom away. Philosophy must therefore assume that no true contradiction will be found be-tween freedom and natural necessity in the same human actions, for it cannot give up the idea of nature any more than that of freedom. Hence even if we should never be able to

Previously published in *Experience and Theory*, ed. I. Foster and W. Swanson (University of Massachu-setts Press, Amherst, 1970).

conceive how freedom is possible, at least this apparent contradiction must be convincingly eradicated. For if the thought of freedom contradicts itself or nature . . . it would have to be surrendered in competition with natural necessity.[1]

Generalize human actions to mental events, sub-stitute anomaly for freedom, and this is a descrip-tion of my problem. And of course the connection is closer, since Kant believed freedom entails anomaly.

Now let me try to formulate a little more care-fully the "apparent contradiction" about mental events that I want to discuss and finally dis-sipate. It may be seen as stemming from three principles.

The first principle asserts that at least some mental events interact causally with physical events. (We could call this the Principle of Causal Interaction.) Thus for example if someone sank the *Bismarck*, then various mental events such as perceivings, notings, calculations, judgments, decisions, intentional actions and changes of belief played a causal role in the sinking of the *Bismarck*. In particular, I would urge that the fact that someone sank the *Bismarck* entails that he moved his body in a way that was caused by mental events of certain sorts, and that this bodily movement in turn caused the *Bismarck* to sink.[2] Perception illustrates how causality may run from the physical to the mental: if a man perceives that a ship is approaching, then a ship approaching must have caused him to come to believe that a ship is approaching. (Nothing depends on accepting these as examples of causal interaction.)

Though perception and action provide the most obvious cases where mental and physical events interact causally, I think reasons could be given for the view that all mental events ultimately, perhaps through causal relations with other mental events, have causal intercourse with physical events. But if there are mental events that have no physical events as causes or effects, the argument will not touch them.

The second principle is that where there is causality, there must be a law: events related as cause and effect fall under strict deterministic laws. (We may term this the Principle of the Nomological Character of Causality.) This principle, like the first, will be treated here as an assumption, though I shall say something by way of interpretation.[3]

The third principle is that there are no strict deterministic laws on the basis of which mental events can be predicted and explained (the Anomalism of the Mental).

The paradox I wish to discuss arises for someone who is inclined to accept these three assumptions or principles, and who thinks they are inconsistent with one another. The inconsistency is not, of course, formal unless more premises are added. Nevertheless it is natural to reason that the first two principles, that of causal interaction, and that of the nomological character of causality, together imply that at least some mental events can be predicted and explained on the basis of laws, while the principle of the anomalism of the mental denies this. Many philosophers have accepted, with or without argument, the view that the three principles do lead to a contradiction. It seems to me, however, that all three principles are true, so that what must be done is to explain away the appearance of contradiction; essentially the Kantian line.

The rest of this paper falls into three parts. The first part describes a version of the identity theory of the mental and the physical that shows how the three principles may be reconciled. The second part argues that there cannot be strict psychophysical laws; this is not quite the principle of the anomalism of the mental, but on reasonable assumptions entails it. The last part tries to show that from the fact that there can be no strict psychophysical laws, and our other two principles, we can infer the truth of a version of

the identity theory, that is, a theory that identifies at least some mental events with physical events. It is clear that this "proof" of the identity theory will be at best conditional, since two of its premises are unsupported, and the argument for the third may be found less than conclusive. But even someone unpersuaded of the truth of the premises may be interested to learn how they may be reconciled and that they serve to establish a version of the identity theory of the mental. Finally, if the argument is a good one, it should lay to rest the view, common to many friends and some foes of identity theories, that support for such theories can come only from the discovery of psycho-physical laws.

I

The three principles will be shown consistent with one another by describing a view of the mental and the physical that contains no inner contradiction and that entails the three principles. According to this view, mental events are identical with physical events. Events are taken to be unrepeatable, dated individuals such as the particular eruption of a volcano, the (first) birth or death of a person, the playing of the 1968 World Series, or the historic utterance of the words, "You may fire when ready, Gridley." We can easily frame identity statements about individual events; examples (true or false) might be:

> The death of Scott = the death of the author of *Waverley*;
> The assassination of the Archduke Ferdinand = the event that started the First World War;
> The eruption of Vesuvius in AD 79 = the cause of the destruction of Pompeii.

The theory under discussion is silent about processes, states, and attributes if these differ from individual events.

What does it mean to say that an event is mental or physical? One natural answer is that an event is physical if it is describable in a purely physical vocabulary, mental if describable in mental terms. But if this is taken to suggest that an event is physical, say, if some physical predicate is true of it, then there is the following difficulty. Assume that the predicate 'x took place at Noosa Heads' belongs to the physical vocabulary; then so also must the predicate 'x did not take place at Noosa Heads' belong to the physical vocabulary. But the predicate 'x did or did not take place at Noosa Heads' is true of every event, whether mental or physical.[4] We might rule out predicates that are tautologically true of every event, but this will not help since every event is truly describable either by 'x took place at Noosa Heads' or by 'x did not take place at Noosa Heads.' A different approach is needed.[5]

We may call those verbs mental that express propositional attitudes like believing, intending, desiring, hoping, knowing, perceiving, noticing, remembering, and so on. Such verbs are characterized by the fact that they sometimes feature in sentences with subjects that refer to persons, and are completed by embedded sentences in which the usual rules of substitution appear to break down. This criterion is not precise, since I do not want to include these verbs when they occur in contexts that are fully extensional ('He knows Paris,' 'He perceives the moon' may be cases), nor exclude them whenever they are not followed by embedded sentences. An alternative characterization of the desired class of mental verbs might be that they are psychological verbs as used when they create apparently nonextensional contexts.

Let us call a description of the form 'the event that is M' or an open sentence of the form 'event x is M' a *mental description* or a *mental open sentence* if and only if the expression that replaces 'M' contains at least one mental verb essentially. (Essentially, so as to rule out cases where the description or open sentence is logically equivalent to one not containing mental vocabulary.) Now we may say that an event is mental if and only if it has a mental description, or (the description operator not being primitive) if there is a mental open sentence true of that event alone. Physical events are those picked out by descriptions or open sentences that contain only the physical vocabulary essentially. It is less important to characterize a physical vocabulary because relative to the mental it is, so to speak, recessive in determining whether a description is mental or physical. (There will be some comments presently on the nature of a physical vocabulary, but these comments will fall far short of providing a criterion.)

On the proposed test of the mental, the distinguishing feature of the mental is not that it is private, subjective, or immaterial, but that it exhibits what Brentano called intentionality. Thus intentional actions are clearly included in the realm of the mental along with thoughts, hopes, and regrets (or the events tied to these). What may seem doubtful is whether the criterion will include events that have often been considered paradigmatic of the mental. Is it obvious, for example, that feeling a pain or seeing an afterimage will count as mental? Sentences that report such events seem free from taint of nonextensionality, and the same should be true of reports of raw feels, sense data, and other uninterpreted sensations, if there are any.

However, the criterion actually covers not only the havings of pains and afterimages, but much more besides. Take some event one would intuitively accept as physical, let's say the collision of two stars in distant space. There must be a purely physical predicate 'Px' true of this collision, and of others, but true of only this one at the time it occurred. This particular time, though, may be pinpointed as the same time that Jones notices that a pencil starts to roll across his desk. The distant stellar collision is thus *the* event x such that Px and x is simultaneous with Jones' noticing that a pencil starts to roll across his desk. The collision has now been picked out by a mental description and must be counted as a mental event.

This strategy will probably work to show every event to be mental; we have obviously failed to capture the intuitive concept of the mental. It would be instructive to try to mend this trouble, but it is not necessary for present purposes. We can afford Spinozistic extravagance with the mental since accidental inclusions can only strengthen the hypothesis that all mental events are identical with physical events. What would matter would be failure to include bona fide mental events, but of this there seems to be no danger.

I want to describe, and presently to argue for, a version of the identity theory that denies that there can be strict laws connecting the mental and the physical. The very possibility of such a theory is easily obscured by the way in which identity theories are commonly defended and attacked. Charles Taylor, for example, agrees with protagonists of identity theories that the sole "ground" for accepting such theories is the supposition that correlations or laws can be established linking events described as mental with events described as physical. He says, "It is easy to see why this is so: unless a given mental event is invariably accompanied by a given, say, brain process, there is no ground for even mooting a general identity between the two."[6] Taylor goes on (correctly, I think) to allow that there may be identity without correlating laws, but my present interest is in noticing the invitation to confusion in the statement just quoted. What can "a given mental event" mean here? Not a particular, dated, event, for it would not make sense to speak of an individual event being "invariably accompanied" by another. Taylor is evidently thinking of events of a given *kind*. But if the only identities are of kinds of events, the identity theory presupposes correlating laws.

One finds the same tendency to build laws into the statement of the identity theory in these typical remarks:

> When I say that a sensation is a brain process or that lightning is an electrical discharge, I am using 'is' in the sense of strict identity . . . there are not two things: a flash of lightning and an electrical discharge. There is one thing, a flash of lightning, which is described scientifically as an electrical discharge to the earth from a cloud of ionized water molecules.[7]

The last sentence of this quotation is perhaps to be understood as saying that for every lightning flash there exists an electrical discharge to the earth from a cloud of ionized water molecules with which it is identical. Here we have an honest ontology of individual events and can make literal sense of identity. We can also see how there could be identities without correlating laws. It is possible, however, to have an ontology of events with the conditions of individuation specified in such a way that any identity implies a correlating law. Kim, for example, suggests that Fa and Gb "describe or refer to the same event" if and only if $a = b$ and the property of being F = the property of being G. The identity of the properties in turn entails that (x) (F$x \leftrightarrow$ Gx).[8] No wonder Kim says:

> If pain is identical with brain state B, there must be a concomitance between occurrences of pain and occurrences of brain state B. . . . Thus, a necessary condition of the pain–brain state B identity is that the two expressions 'being in pain' and 'being in brain state B' have the same extension. . . . There is no conceivable observation that would confirm

or refute the identity but not the associated correlation.[9]

It may make the situation clearer to give a fourfold classification of theories of the relation between mental and physical events that emphasizes the independence of claims about laws and claims of identity. On the one hand there are those who assert, and those who deny, the existence of psychophysical laws; on the other hand there are those who say mental events are identical with physical and those who deny this. Theories are thus divided into four sorts: *nomological monism*, which affirms that there are correlating laws and that the events correlated are one (materialists belong in this category); *nomological dualism*, which comprises various forms of parallelism, interactionism, and epiphenomenalism; *anomalous dualism*, which combines ontological dualism with the general failure of laws correlating the mental and the physical (Cartesianism). And finally there is *anomalous monism*, which classifies the position I wish to occupy.[10]

Anomalous monism resembles materialism in its claim that all events are physical, but rejects the thesis, usually considered essential to materialism, that mental phenomena can be given purely physical explanations. Anomalous monism shows an ontological bias only in that it allows the possibility that not all events are mental, while insisting that all events are physical. Such a bland monism, unbuttressed by correlating laws or conceptual economies, does not seem to merit the term "reductionism"; in any case it is not apt to inspire the nothing-but reflex ("Conceiving the *Art of the Fugue* was nothing but a complex neural event," and so forth).

Although the position I describe denies there are psychophysical laws, it is consistent with the view that mental characteristics are in some sense dependent, or supervenient, on physical characteristics. Such supervenience might be taken to mean that there cannot be two events alike in all physical respects but differing in some mental respect, or that an object cannot alter in some mental respect without altering in some physical respect. Dependence or supervenience of this kind does not entail reducibility through law or definition: if it did, we could reduce moral properties to descriptive, and this there is good reason to *believe* cannot be done; and we might be able to reduce truth in a formal system to syntactical properties, and this we *know* cannot in general be done.

Donald Davidson

This last example is in useful analogy with the sort of lawless monism under consideration. Think of the physical vocabulary as the entire vocabulary of some language L with resources adequate to express a certain amount of mathematics, and its own syntax. L′ is L augmented with the truth predicate 'true-in-L,' which is "mental." In L (and hence L′) it is possible to pick out, with a definite description or open sentence, each sentence in the extension of the truth predicate, but if L is consistent there exists no predicate of syntax (of the "physical" vocabulary), no matter how complex, that applies to all and only the true sentences of L. There can be no "psychophysical law" in the form of a biconditional, '(x) (x is true-in-L if and only if x is φ)' where 'φ' is replaced by a "physical" predicate (a predicate of L). Similarly, we can pick out each mental event using the physical vocabulary alone, but no purely physical predicate, no matter how complex, has, as a matter of law, the same extension as a mental predicate.

It should now be evident how anomalous monism reconciles the three original principles. Causality and identity are relations between individual events no matter how described. But laws are linguistic; and so events can instantiate laws, and hence be explained or predicted in the light of laws, only as those events are described in one or another way. The principle of causal interaction deals with events in extension and is therefore blind to the mental–physical dichotomy. The principle of the anomalism of the mental concerns events described as mental, for events are mental only as described. The principle of the nomological character of causality must be read carefully: it says that when events are related as cause and effect, they have descriptions that instantiate a law. It does not say that every true singular statement of causality instantiates a law.[11]

II

The analogy just bruited, between the place of the mental amid the physical, and the place of the semantical in a world of syntax, should not be strained. Tarski proved that a consistent language cannot (under some natural assumptions) contain an open sentence 'Fx' true of all and only the true sentences of that language. If our analogy were pressed, then we would expect a proof that there can be no physical open sentence 'Px' true of all and only the events having some mental property. In fact, however, nothing I can say about the irreducibility of the mental deserves to be called a proof; and the kind of irreducibility is different. For if anomalous monism is correct, not only can every mental event be uniquely singled out using only physical concepts, but since the number of events that falls under each mental predicate may, for all we know, be finite, there may well exist a physical open sentence coextensive with each mental predicate, though to construct it might involve the tedium of a lengthy and uninstructive alternation. Indeed, even if finitude is not assumed, there seems no compelling reason to deny that there could be coextensive predicates, one mental and one physical.

The thesis is rather that the mental is nomologically irreducible: there may be *true* general statements relating the mental and the physical, statements that have the logical form of a law; but they are not *lawlike* (in a strong sense to be described). If by absurdly remote chance we were to stumble on a nonstochastic true psychophysical generalization, we would have no reason to believe it more than roughly true.

Do we, by declaring that there are no (strict) psychophysical laws, poach on the empirical preserves of science – a form of *hubris* against which philosophers are often warned? Of course, to judge a statement lawlike or illegal is not to decide its truth outright; relative to the acceptance of a general statement on the basis of instances, ruling it lawlike must be a priori. But such relative apriorism does not in itself justify philosophy, for in general the grounds for deciding to trust a statement on the basis of its instances will in turn be governed by theoretical and empirical concerns not to be distinguished from those of science. If the case of supposed laws linking the mental and the physical is different, it can only be because to allow the possibility of such laws would amount to changing the subject. By changing the subject I mean here: deciding not to accept the criterion of the mental in terms of the vocabulary of the propositional attitudes. This short answer cannot prevent further ramifications of the problem, however, for there is no clear line between changing the subject and changing what one says on an old subject, which is to admit, in the present context at least, that there is no clear line between philosophy and science. Where there are no fixed boundaries only the timid never risk trespass.

It will sharpen our appreciation of the anomological character of mental–physical generalizations to consider a related matter, the failure of definitional behaviorism. Why are we willing (as I assume we are) to abandon the attempt to give explicit definitions of mental concepts in terms of behavioral ones? Not, surely, just because all actual tries are conspicuously inadequate. Rather it is because we are persuaded, as we are in the case of so many other forms of definitional reductionism (naturalism in ethics, instrumentalism and operationalism in the sciences, the causal theory of meaning, phenomenalism, and so on – the catalogue of philosophy's defeats), that there is system in the failures. Suppose we try to say, not using any mental concepts, what it is for a man to believe there is life on Mars. One line we could take is this: when a certain sound is produced in the man's presence ("Is there life on Mars?") he produces another ("Yes"). But of course this shows he believes there is life on Mars only if he understands English, his production of the sound was intentional, and was a response to the sounds as meaning something in English; and so on. For each discovered deficiency, we add a new proviso. Yet no matter how we patch and fit the nonmental conditions, we always find the need for an additional condition (provided he *notices, understands,* etc.) that is mental in character.[12]

A striking feature of attempts at definitional reduction is how little seems to hinge on the question of synonymy between definiens and definiendum. Of course, by imagining counterexamples we do discredit claims of synonymy. But the pattern of failure prompts a stronger conclusion: if we were to find an open sentence couched in behavioral terms and exactly coextensive with some mental predicate, nothing could reasonably persuade us that we had found it. We know too much about thought and behavior to trust exact and universal statements linking them. Beliefs and desires issue in behavior only as modified and mediated by further beliefs and desires, attitudes and attendings, without limit. Clearly this holism of the mental realm is a clue both to the autonomy and to the anomalous character of the mental.

These remarks apropos definitional behaviorism provide at best hints of why we should not expect nomological connections between the mental and the physical. The central case invites further consideration.

Lawlike statements are general statements that support counterfactual and subjunctive claims, and are supported by their instances. There is (in my view) no nonquestion-begging criterion of the lawlike, which is not to say there are no reasons in particular cases for a judgment. Lawlikeness is a matter of degree, which is not to deny that there may be cases beyond debate. And within limits set by the conditions of communication, there is room for much variation between individuals in the pattern of statements to which various degrees of nomologicality are assigned. In all these respects, nomologicality is much like analyticity, as one might expect since both are linked to meaning.

'All emeralds are green' is lawlike in that its instances confirm it, but 'all emeralds are grue' is not, for 'grue' means 'observed before time t and green, otherwise blue,' and if our observations were all made before t and uniformly revealed green emeralds, this would not be a reason to expect other emeralds to be blue. Nelson Goodman has suggested that this shows that some predicates, 'grue' for example, are unsuited to laws (and thus a criterion of suitable predicates could lead to a criterion of the lawlike). But it seems to me the anomalous character of 'All emeralds are grue' shows only that the predicates 'is an emerald' and 'is grue' are not suited to one another: grueness is not an inductive property of emeralds. Grueness *is* however an inductive property of entities of other sorts, for instance of emerires. (Something is an emerire if it is examined before t and is an emerald, and otherwise is a sapphire.) Not only is 'All emerires are grue' entailed by the conjunction of the lawlike statements 'All emeralds are green' and 'All sapphires are blue,' but there is no reason, as far as I can see, to reject the deliverance of intuition, that it is itself lawlike.[13] Nomological statements bring together predicates that we know a priori are made for each other – know, that is, independently of knowing whether the evidence supports a connection between them. 'Blue,' 'red,' and 'green' are made for emeralds, sapphires, and roses; 'grue,' 'bleen,' and 'gred' are made for sapphalds, emerires, and emeroses.

The direction in which the discussion seems headed is this: mental and physical predicates are not made for one another. In point of lawlikeness, psychophysical statements are more like 'All emeralds are grue' than like 'All emeralds are green.'

Before this claim is plausible, it must be seriously modified. The fact that emeralds examined before t are grue not only is no reason to believe all emeralds are grue; it is not even a reason (if we know the time) to believe *any* unobserved emeralds are grue. But if an event of a certain mental sort has usually been accompanied by an event of a certain physical sort, this often is a good reason to expect other cases to follow suit roughly in proportion. The generalizations that embody such practical wisdom are assumed to be only roughly true, or they are explicitly stated in probabilistic terms, or they are insulated from counterexample by generous escape clauses. Their importance lies mainly in the support they lend singular causal claims and related explanations of particular events. The support derives from the fact that such a generalization, however crude and vague, may provide good reason to believe that underlying the particular case there is a regularity that could be formulated sharply and without caveat.

In our daily traffic with events and actions that must be foreseen or understood, we perforce make use of the sketchy summary generalization, for we do not know a more accurate law, or if we do, we lack a description of the particular events in which we are interested that would show the relevance of the law. But there is an important distinction to be made within the category of the rude rule of thumb. On the one hand, there are generalizations whose positive instances give us reason to believe the generalization itself could be improved by adding further provisos and conditions stated in the same general vocabulary as the original generalization. Such a generalization points to the form and vocabulary of the finished law: we may say that it is a *homonomic* generalization. On the other hand there are generalizations which when instantiated may give us reason to believe there is a precise law at work, but one that can be stated only by shifting to a different vocabulary. We may call such generalizations *heteronomic*.

I suppose most of our practical lore (and science) is heteronomic. This is because a law can hope to be precise, explicit, and as exceptionless as possible only if it draws its concepts from a comprehensive closed theory. This ideal theory may or may not be deterministic, but it is if any true theory is. Within the physical sciences we do find homonomic generalizations, generalizations such that if the evidence supports them, we then have reason to believe they may be sharpened indefinitely by drawing upon further

physical concepts: there is a theoretical asymptote of perfect coherence with all the evidence, perfect predictability (under the terms of the system), total explanation (again under the terms of the system). Or perhaps the ultimate theory is probabilistic, and the asymptote is less than perfection; but in that case there will be no better to be had.

Confidence that a statement is homonomic, correctible within its own conceptual domain, demands that it draw its concepts from a theory with strong constitutive elements. Here is the simplest possible illustration; if the lesson carries, it will be obvious that the simplification could be mended.

The measurement of length, weight, temperature, or time depends (among many other things, of course) on the existence in each case of a two-place relation that is transitive and asymmetric: warmer than, later than, heavier than, and so forth. Let us take the relation *longer than* as our example. The law or postulate of transitivity is this:

(L) $L(x,y)$ and $L(y,z) \rightarrow L(x,z)$

Unless this law (or some sophisticated variant) holds, we cannot easily make sense of the concept of length. There will be no way of assigning numbers to register even so much as ranking in length, let alone the more powerful demands of measurement on a ratio scale. And this remark goes not only for any three items directly involved in an intransitivity: it is easy to show (given a few more assumptions essential to measurement of length) that there is no consistent assignment of a ranking to any item unless (L) holds in full generality.

Clearly (L) alone cannot exhaust the import of 'longer than' – otherwise it would not differ from 'warmer than' or 'later than'. We must suppose there is some empirical content, however difficult to formulate in the available vocabulary, that distinguishes 'longer than' from the other two-place transitive predicates of measurement and on the basis of which we may assert that one thing is longer than another. Imagine this empirical content to be partly given by the predicate '$O(x,y)$'. So we have this 'meaning postulate':

(M) $O(x,y) \rightarrow L(x,y)$

that partly interprets (L). But now (L) and (M) together yield an empirical theory of great strength, for together they entail that there do not exist three objects a, b, and c such that $O(a,b)$, $O(b,c)$, and $O(c,a)$. Yet what is to prevent this happening if '$O(x,y)$' is a predicate we can ever, with confidence, apply? Suppose we *think* we observe an intransitive triad; what do we say? We could count (L) false, but then we would have no application for the concept of length. We could say (M) gives a wrong test for length; but then it is unclear what we thought was the *content* of the idea of one thing being longer than another. Or we could say that the objects under observation are not, as the theory requires, *rigid* objects. It is a mistake to think we are forced to accept some one of these answers. Concepts such as that of length are sustained in equilibrium by a number of conceptual pressures, and theories of fundamental measurement are distorted if we force the decision, among such principles as (L) and (M): analytic or synthetic. It is better to say the whole set of axioms, laws, or postulates for the measurement of length is partly constitutive of the idea of a system of macroscopic, rigid, physical objects. I suggest that the existence of lawlike statements in physical science depends upon the existence of constitutive (or synthetic a priori) laws like those of the measurement of length within the same conceptual domain.

Just as we cannot intelligibly assign a length to any object unless a comprehensive theory holds of objects of that sort, we cannot intelligibly attribute any propositional attitude to an agent except within the framework of a viable theory of his beliefs, desires, intentions, and decisions.

There is no assigning beliefs to a person one by one on the basis of his verbal behavior, his choices, or other local signs no matter how plain and evident, for we make sense of particular beliefs only as they cohere with other beliefs, with preferences, with intentions, hopes, fears, expectations, and the rest. It is not merely, as with the measurement of length, that each case tests a theory and depends upon it, but that the content of a propositional attitude derives from its place in the pattern.

Crediting people with a large degree of consistency cannot be counted mere charity: it is unavoidable if we are to be in a position to accuse them meaningfully of error and some degree of irrationality. Global confusion, like universal mistake, is unthinkable, not because imagination boggles, but because too much confusion leaves nothing to be confused about and massive error

erodes the background of true belief against which alone failure can be construed. To appreciate the limits to the kind and amount of blunder and bad thinking we can intelligibly pin on others is to see once more the inseparability of the question what concepts a person commands and the question what he does with those concepts in the way of belief, desire, and intention. To the extent that we fail to discover a coherent and plausible pattern in the attitudes and actions of others we simply forego the chance of treating them as persons.

The problem is not bypassed but given center stage by appeal to explicit speech behavior. For we could not begin to decode a man's sayings if we could not make out his attitudes towards his sentences, such as holding, wishing, or wanting them to be true. Beginning from these attitudes, we must work out a theory of what he means, thus simultaneously giving content to his attitudes and to his words. In our need to make him make sense, we will try for a theory that finds him consistent, a believer of truths, and a lover of the good (all by our own lights, it goes without saying). Life being what it is, there will be no simple theory that fully meets these demands. Many theories will effect a more or less acceptable compromise, and between these theories there may be no objective grounds for choice.

The heteronomic character of general statements linking the mental and the physical traces back to this central role of translation in the description of all propositional attitudes, and to the indeterminacy of translation.[14] There are no strict psychophysical laws because of the disparate commitments of the mental and physical schemes. It is a feature of physical reality that physical change can be explained by laws that connect it with other changes and conditions physically described. It is a feature of the mental that the attribution of mental phenomena must be responsible to the background of reasons, beliefs, and intentions of the individual. There cannot be tight connections between the realms if each is to retain allegiance to its proper source of evidence. The nomological irreducibility of the mental does not derive merely from the seamless nature of the world of thought, preference and intention, for such interdependence is common to physical theory, and is compatible with there being a single right way of interpreting a man's attitudes without relativization to a scheme of translation. Nor is the irreducibility due simply to the possibility of many equally eligible schemes, for this is compatible with an arbitrary choice of one scheme relative to which assignments of mental traits are made. The point is rather that when we use the concepts of belief, desire and the rest, we must stand prepared, as the evidence accumulates, to adjust our theory in the light of considerations of overall cogency: the constitutive ideal of rationality partly controls each phase in the evolution of what must be an evolving theory. An arbitrary choice of translation scheme would preclude such opportunistic tempering of theory; put differently, a right arbitrary choice of a translation manual would be of a manual acceptable in the light of all possible evidence, and this is a choice we cannot make. We must conclude, I think, that nomological slack between the mental and the physical is essential as long as we conceive of man as a rational animal.

III

The gist of the foregoing discussion, as well as its conclusion, will be familiar. That there is a categorial difference between the mental and the physical is a commonplace. It may seem odd that I say nothing of the supposed privacy of the mental, or the special authority an agent has with respect to his own propositional attitudes, but this appearance of novelty would fade if we were to investigate in more detail the grounds for accepting a scheme of translation. The step from the categorial difference between the mental and the physical to the impossibility of strict laws relating them is less common, but certainly not new. If there is a surprise, then, it will be to find the lawlessness of the mental serving to help establish the identity of the mental with that paradigm of the lawlike, the physical.

The reasoning is this. We are assuming, under the Principle of the Causal Dependence of the Mental, that some mental events at least are causes or effects of physical events; the argument applies only to these. A second Principle (of the Nomological Character of Causality) says that each true singular causal statement is backed by a strict law connecting events of kinds to which the events mentioned as cause and effect belong. Where there are rough, but homonomic, laws, there are laws drawing on concepts from the same conceptual domain and upon which there is no improving in point of precision and com-

prehensiveness. We urged in the last section that such laws occur in the physical sciences. Physical theory promises to provide a comprehensive closed system guaranteed to yield a standardized, unique description of every physical event couched in a vocabulary amenable to law.

It is not plausible that mental concepts alone can provide such a framework, simply because the mental does not, by our first principle, constitute a closed system. Too much happens to affect the mental that is not itself a systematic part of the mental. But if we combine this observation with the conclusion that no psychophysical statement is, or can be built into, a strict law, we have the Principle of the Anomalism of the Mental: there are no strict laws at all on the basis of which we can predict and explain mental phenomena.

The demonstration of identity follows easily. Suppose m, a mental event, caused p, a physical event; then under some description m and p instantiate a strict law. This law can only be physical, according to the previous paragraph. But if m falls under a physical law, it has a physical description; which is to say it is a physical event. An analogous argument works when a physical event causes a mental event. So every mental event that is causally related to a physical event is a physical event. In order to establish anomalous monism in full generality it would be sufficient to show that every mental event is cause or effect of some physical event; I shall not attempt this.

If one event causes another, there is a strict law which those events instantiate when properly described. But it is possible (and typical) to know of the singular causal relation without knowing the law or the relevant descriptions. Knowledge requires reasons, but these are available in the form of rough heteronomic generalizations, which are lawlike in that instances make it reasonable to expect other instances to follow suit without being lawlike in the sense of being indefinitely refinable. Applying these facts to knowledge of identities, we see that it is possible to know that a mental event is identical with some physical event without knowing which one (in the sense of being able to give it a unique physical description that brings it under a relevant law). Even if someone knew the entire physical history of the world, and every mental event were identical with a physical, it would not follow that he could predict or explain a single mental event (so described, of course).

Two features of mental events in their relation to the physical – causal dependence and nomological independence – combine, then, to dissolve what has often seemed a paradox, the efficacy of thought and purpose in the material world, and their freedom from law. When we portray events as perceivings, rememberings, decisions and actions, we necessarily locate them amid physical happenings through the relation of cause and effect; but that same mode of portrayal insulates mental events, as long as we do not change the idiom, from the strict laws that can in principle be called upon to explain and predict physical phenomena.

Mental events as a class cannot be explained by physical science; particular mental events can when we know particular identities. But the explanations of mental events in which we are typically interested relate them to other mental events and conditions. We explain a man's free actions, for example, by appeal to his desires, habits, knowledge and perceptions. Such accounts of intentional behavior operate in a conceptual framework removed from the direct reach of physical law by describing both cause and effect, reason and action, as aspects of a portrait of a human agent. The anomalism of the mental is thus a necessary condition for viewing action as autonomous. I conclude with a second passage from Kant:

> It is an indispensable problem of speculative philosophy to show that its illusion respecting the contradiction rests on this, that we think of man in a different sense and relation when we call him free, and when we regard him as subject to the laws of nature. . . . It must therefore show that not only can both of these very well co-exist, but that both must be thought *as necessarily united* in the same subject. . . .[15]

Notes

I was helped and influenced by Daniel Bennett, Sue Larson, and Richard Rorty, who are not responsible for the result. My research was supported by the National Science Foundation and the Center for Advanced Study in the Behavioral Sciences.

1 *Fundamental Principles of the Metaphysics of Morals*, trans. T. K. Abbott (London, 1909), pp. 75–6.

2 These claims are defended in my "Actions, Reasons and Causes," *Journal of Philosophy* 60 (1963), pp. 685–700 and in "Agency," a paper forthcoming in the proceedings of the November, 1968, colloquium on Agent, Action, and Reason at the University of Western Ontario, London, Canada.

3 In "Causal Relations," *Journal of Philosophy* 64 (1967), pp. 691–703, I elaborate on the view of causality assumed here. The stipulation that the laws be deterministic is stronger than required by the reasoning, and will be relaxed.

4 The point depends on assuming that mental events may intelligibly be said to have a location; but it is an assumption that must be true if an identity theory is, and here I am not trying to prove the theory but to formulate it.

5 I am indebted to Lee Bowie for emphasizing this difficulty.

6 Charles Taylor, "Mind–Body Identity, a Side Issue?," *Philosophical Review* 76 (1967), p. 202.

7 J. J. C. Smart, "Sensations and Brain Processes," *Philosophical Review* 68 (1959), pp. 141–56. The quoted passages are on pp. 163–5 of the reprinted version in *The Philosophy of Mind*, ed. V. C. Chappell (Englewood Cliffs, NJ, 1962). For another example, see David K. Lewis, "An Argument for the Identity Theory," *Journal of Philosophy* 63 (1966), pp. 17–25. Here the assumption is made explicit when Lewis takes events as universals (p. 17, nn. 1 and 2). I do not suggest that Smart and Lewis are confused, only that their way of stating the identity theory tends to obscure the distinction between particular events and kinds of events on which the formulation of my theory depends.

8 Jaegwon Kim, "On the Psycho-Physical Identity Theory," *American Philosophical Quarterly* 3 (1966), p. 231.

9 Ibid., pp. 227–8. Richard Brandt and Jaegwon Kim propose roughly the same criterion in "The Logic of the Identity Theory," *Journal of Philosophy* 64 (1967), pp. 515–37. They remark that on their conception of event identity, the identity theory "makes a stronger claim than merely that there is a pervasive phenomenal-physical correlation" (p. 518). I do not discuss the stronger claim.

10 Anomalous monism is more or less explicitly recognized as a possible position by Herbert Feigl, "The 'Mental' and the 'Physical,'" in *Concepts, Theories and the Mind–Body Problem*, vol. II, *Minnesota Studies in the Philosophy of Science* (Minneapolis, 1958); Sydney Shoemaker, "Ziff's Other Minds," *Journal of Philosophy* 62 (1965), p. 589; David Randall Luce, "Mind–Body Identity and Psycho-Physical Correlation," *Philosophical Studies* 17 (1966), pp. 1–7; Charles Taylor, "Mind–Body Identity",

p. 207. Something like my position is tentatively accepted by Thomas Nagel, "Physicalism," *Philosophical Review* 74 (1965), pp. 339–56, and briefly endorsed by P. F. Strawson in *Freedom and the Will*, ed. D. F. Pears (London, 1963), pp. 63–7.

11 The point that substitutivity of identity fails in the context of explanation is made in connection with the present subject by Norman Malcolm, "Scientific Materialism and the Identity Theory," *Dialogue* 3 (1964–5), pp. 123–4. See also my "Actions, Reasons and Causes," *Journal of Philosophy* 60 (1963), pp. 696–9 and "The Individuation of Events" in *Essays in Honor of Carl G. Hempel*, ed. N. Rescher, et al. (Dordrecht, 1969).

12 The theme is developed in Roderick Chisholm, *Perceiving* (Ithaca, NY, 1957), ch. 11.

13 This view is accepted by Richard C. Jeffrey, "Goodman's Query," *Journal of Philosophy* 63 (1966), p. 286ff., John R. Wallace, "Goodman, Logic, Induction," same journal and issue, p. 318, and John M. Vickers, "Characteristics of Projectible Predicates," *Journal of Philosophy* 64 (1967), p. 285. On pp. 328–9 and 286–7 of these journal issues respectively Goodman disputes the lawlikeness of statements like "All emerires are grue." I cannot see, however, that he meets the point of my "Emeroses by Other Names," *Journal of Philosophy* 63 (1966), pp. 778–80.

14 The influence of W. V. Quine's doctrine of the indeterminacy of translation, as in ch. 2 of *Word and Object* (Cambridge, MA, 1960), is, I hope, obvious. In §45 Quine develops the connection between translation and the propositional attitudes, and remarks that "Brentano's thesis of the irreducibility of intentional idioms is of a piece with the thesis of indeterminacy of translation" (p. 221).

15 Kant, *Fundamental Principles*, p. 76.

25

What Is It Like To Be a Bat?

Thomas Nagel

Consciousness is what makes the mind–body problem really intractable. Perhaps that is why current discussions of the problem give it little attention or get it obviously wrong. The recent wave of reductionist euphoria has produced several analyses of mental phenomena and mental concepts designed to explain the possibility of some variety of materialism, psychophysical identification, or reduction.[1] But the problems dealt with are those common to this type of reduction and other types, and what makes the mind–body problem unique, and unlike the water–H_2O problem or the Turing machine–IBM machine problem or the lightning–electrical discharge problem or the gene–DNA problem or the oak tree–hydrocarbon problem, is ignored.

Every reductionist has his favorite analogy from modern science. It is most unlikely that any of these unrelated examples of successful reduction will shed light on the relation of mind to brain. But philosophers share the general human weakness for explanations of what is incomprehensible in terms suited for what is familiar and well understood, though entirely different. This has led to the acceptance of implausible accounts of the mental largely because they would permit familiar kinds of reduction. I shall try to explain why the usual examples do not help us to understand the relation between mind and body – why,

indeed, we have at present no conception of what an explanation of the physical nature of a mental phenomenon would be. Without consciousness the mind–body problem would be much less interesting. With consciousness it seems hopeless. The most important and characteristic feature of conscious mental phenomena is very poorly understood. Most reductionist theories do not even try to explain it. And careful examination will show that no currently available concept of reduction is applicable to it. Perhaps a new theoretical form can be devised for the purpose, but such a solution, if it exists, lies in the distant intellectual future.

Conscious experience is a widespread phenomenon. It occurs at many levels of animal life, though we cannot be sure of its presence in the simpler organisms, and it is very difficult to say in general what provides evidence of it. (Some extremists have been prepared to deny it even of mammals other than man.) No doubt it occurs in countless forms totally unimaginable to us, on other planets in other solar systems throughout the universe. But no matter how the form may vary, the fact that an organism has conscious experience *at all* means, basically, that there is something it is like to *be* that organism. There may be further implications about the form of the experience; there may even (though I doubt it) be implications about the behavior of the organism. But fundamentally an organism has conscious mental states if and only if there is something that it is like to *be* that organism – something it is like *for* the organism.

We may call this the subjective character of experience. It is not captured by any of the familiar, recently devised reductive analyses of the mental, for all of them are logically compatible with its absence. It is not analyzable in terms of any explanatory system of functional states, or intentional states, since these could be ascribed to robots or automata that behaved like people though they experienced nothing.[2] It is not analyzable in terms of the causal role of experiences in relation to typical human behavior – for similar reasons.[3] I do not deny that conscious mental states and events cause behavior, nor that they may be given functional characterizations. I deny only that this kind of thing exhausts their analysis. Any reductionist program has to be based on an analysis of what is to be reduced. If the analysis leaves something out, the problem will be falsely posed. It is useless to base the defense of materialism on any analysis of mental phenomena that fails to deal explicitly with their subjective character. For there is no reason to suppose that a reduction which seems plausible when no attempt is made to account for consciousness can be extended to include consciousness. Without some idea, therefore, of what the subjective character of experience is, we cannot know what is required of a physicalist theory.

While an account of the physical basis of mind must explain many things, this appears to be the most difficult. It is impossible to exclude the phenomenological features of experience from a reduction in the same way that one excludes the phenomenal features of an ordinary substance from a physical or chemical reduction of it – namely, by explaining them as effects on the minds of human observers.[4] If physicalism is to be defended, the phenomenological features must themselves be given a physical account. But when we examine their subjective character it seems that such a result is impossible. The reason is that every subjective phenomenon is essentially connected with a single point of view, and it seems inevitable that an objective, physical theory will abandon that point of view.

Let me first try to state the issue somewhat more fully than by referring to the relation between the subjective and the objective, or between the *pour-soi* and the *en-soi*. This is far from easy. Facts about what it is like to be an X are very peculiar, so peculiar that some may be inclined to doubt their reality, or the significance of claims about them. To illustrate the connection between

subjectivity and a point of view, and to make evident the importance of subjective features, it will help to explore the matter in relation to an example that brings out clearly the divergence between the two types of conception, subjective and objective.

I assume we all believe that bats have experience. After all, they are mammals, and there is no more doubt that they have experience than that mice or pigeons or whales have experience. I have chosen bats instead of wasps or flounders because if one travels too far down the phylogenetic tree, people gradually shed their faith that there is experience there at all. Bats, although more closely related to us than those other species, nevertheless present a range of activity and a sensory apparatus so different from ours that the problem I want to pose is exceptionally vivid (though it certainly could be raised with other species). Even without the benefit of philosophical reflection, anyone who has spent some time in an enclosed space with an excited bat knows what it is to encounter a fundamentally *alien* form of life.

I have said that the essence of the belief that bats have experience is that there is something that it is like to be a bat. Now we know that most bats (the microchiroptera, to be precise) perceive the external world primarily by sonar, or echolocation, detecting the reflections, from objects within range, of their own rapid, subtly modulated, high-frequency shrieks. Their brains are designed to correlate the outgoing impulses with the subsequent echoes, and the information thus acquired enables bats to make precise discriminations of distance, size, shape, motion, and texture comparable to those we make by vision. But bat sonar, though clearly a form of perception, is not similar in its operation to any sense that we possess, and there is no reason to suppose that it is subjectively like anything we can experience or imagine. This appears to create difficulties for the notion of what it is like to be a bat. We must consider whether any method will permit us to extrapolate to the inner life of the bat from our own case,[5] and if not, what alternative methods there may be for understanding the notion.

Our own experience provides the basic material for our imagination, whose range is therefore limited. It will not help to try to imagine that one has webbing on one's arms, which enables one to fly around at dusk and dawn catching insects in one's mouth; that one has very poor vision, and perceives the surrounding world by a system of reflected high-frequency sound signals; and that one spends the day hanging upside down by one's feet in an attic. In so far as I can imagine this (which is not very far), it tells me only what it would be like for *me* to behave as a bat behaves. But that is not the question. I want to know what it is like for a *bat* to be a bat. Yet if I try to imagine this, I am restricted to the resources of my own mind, and those resources are inadequate to the task. I cannot perform it either by imagining additions to my present experience, or by imagining segments gradually subtracted from it, or by imagining some combination of additions, subtractions, and modifications.

To the extent that I could look and behave like a wasp or a bat without changing my fundamental structure, my experiences would not be anything like the experiences of those animals. On the other hand, it is doubtful that any meaning can be attached to the supposition that I should possess the internal neurophysiological constitution of a bat. Even if I could by gradual degrees be transformed into a bat, nothing in my present constitution enables me to imagine what the experiences of such a future stage of myself thus metamorphosed would be like. The best evidence would come from the experiences of bats, if we only knew what they were like.

So if extrapolation from our own case is involved in the idea of what it is like to be a bat, the extrapolation must be incompletable. We cannot form more than a schematic conception of what it *is* like. For example, we may ascribe general *types* of experience on the basis of the animal's structure and behavior. Thus we describe bat sonar as a form of three-dimensional forward perception; we believe that bats feel some versions of pain, fear, hunger, and lust, and that they have other, more familiar types of perception besides sonar. But we believe that these experiences also have in each case a specific subjective character, which it is beyond our ability to conceive. And if there is conscious life elsewhere in the universe, it is likely that some of it will not be describable even in the most general experiential terms available to us.[6] (The problem is not confined to exotic cases, however, for it exists between one person and another. The subjective character of the experience of a person deaf and blind from birth is not accessible to me, for example, nor presumably is mine to him. This

does not prevent us each from believing that the other's experience has such a subjective character.)

If anyone is inclined to deny that we can believe in the existence of facts like this whose exact nature we cannot possibly conceive, he should reflect that in contemplating the bats we are in much the same position that intelligent bats or Martians[7] would occupy if they tried to form a conception of what it was like to be us. The structure of their own minds might make it impossible for them to succeed, but we know they would be wrong to conclude that there is not anything precise that it is like to be us: that only certain general types of mental state could be ascribed to us (perhaps perception and appetite would be concepts common to us both; perhaps not). We know they would be wrong to draw such a skeptical conclusion because we know what it is like to be us. And we know that while it includes an enormous amount of variation and complexity, and while we do not possess the vocabulary to describe it adequately, its subjective character is highly specific, and in some respects describable in terms that can be understood only by creatures like us. The fact that we cannot expect ever to accommodate in our language a detailed description of Martian or bat phenomenology should not lead us to dismiss as meaningless the claim that bats and Martians have experiences fully comparable in richness of detail to our own. It would be fine if someone were to develop concepts and a theory that enabled us to think about those things; but such an understanding may be permanently denied to us by the limits of our nature. And to deny the reality or logical significance of what we can never describe or understand is the crudest form of cognitive dissonance.

This brings us to the edge of a topic that requires much more discussion than I can give it here: namely, the relation between facts on the one hand and conceptual schemes or systems of representation on the other. My realism about the subjective domain in all its forms implies a belief in the existence of facts beyond the reach of human concepts. Certainly it is possible for a human being to believe that there are facts which humans never *will* possess the requisite concepts to represent or comprehend. Indeed, it would be foolish to doubt this, given the finiteness of humanity's expectations. After all, there would have been transfinite numbers even if everyone had been wiped out by the Black Death before

Cantor discovered them. But one might also believe that there are facts which *could* not ever be represented or comprehended by human beings, even if the species lasted forever – simply because our structure does not permit us to operate with concepts of the requisite type. This impossibility might even be observed by other beings, but it is not clear that the existence of such beings, or the possibility of their existence, is a precondition of the significance of the hypothesis that there are humanly inaccessible facts. (After all, the nature of beings with access to humanly inaccessible facts is presumably itself a humanly inaccessible fact.) Reflection on what it is like to be a bat seems to lead us, therefore, to the conclusion that there are facts that do not consist in the truth of propositions expressible in a human language. We can be compelled to recognize the existence of such facts without being able to state or comprehend them.

I shall not pursue this subject, however. Its bearing on the topic before us (namely, the mind–body problem) is that it enables us to make a general observation about the subjective character of experience. Whatever may be the status of facts about what it is like to be a human being, or a bat, or a Martian, these appear to be facts that embody a particular point of view.

I am not adverting here to the alleged privacy of experience to its possessor. The point of view in question is not one accessible only to a single individual. Rather it is a *type*. It is often possible to take up a point of view other than one's own, so the comprehension of such facts is not limited to one's own case. There is a sense in which phenomenological facts are perfectly objective: one person can know or say of another what the quality of the other's experience is. They are subjective, however, in the sense that even this objective ascription of experience is possible only for someone sufficiently similar to the object of ascription to be able to adopt his point of view – to understand the ascription in the first person as well as in the third, so to speak. The more different from oneself the other experiencer is, the less success one can expect with this enterprise. In our own case we occupy the relevant point of view, but we will have as much difficulty understanding our own experience properly if we approach it from another point of view as we would if we tried to understand the experience of another species without taking up *its* point of view.[8]

This bears directly on the mind–body problem. For if the facts of experience – facts about what it is like *for* the experiencing organism – are accessible only from one point of view, then it is a mystery how the true character of experiences could be revealed in the physical operation of that organism. The latter is a domain of objective facts *par excellence* – the kind that can be observed and understood from many points of view and by individuals with differing perceptual systems. There are no comparable imaginative obstacles to the acquisition of knowledge about bat neurophysiology by human scientists, and intelligent bats or Martians might learn more about the human brain than we ever will.

This is not by itself an argument against reduction. A Martian scientist with no understanding of visual perception could understand the rainbow, or lightning, or clouds as physical phenomena, though he would never be able to understand the human concepts of rainbow, lightning, or cloud, or the place these things occupy in our phenomenal world. The objective nature of the things picked out by these concepts could be apprehended by him because, although the concepts themselves are connected with a particular point of view and a particular visual phenomenology, the things apprehended from that point of view are not: they are observable from the point of view but external to it; hence they can be comprehended from other points of view also, either by the same organisms or by others. Lightning has an objective character that is not exhausted by its visual appearance, and this can be investigated by a Martian without vision. To be precise, it has a *more* objective character than is revealed in its visual appearance. In speaking of the move from subjective to objective characterization, I wish to remain noncommittal about the existence of an end point, the completely objective intrinsic nature of the thing, which one might or might not be able to reach. It may be more accurate to think of objectivity as a direction in which the understanding can travel. And in understanding a phenomenon like lightning, it is legitimate to go as far away as one can from a strictly human viewpoint.[9]

In the case of experience, on the other hand, the connection with a particular point of view seems much closer. It is difficult to understand what could be meant by the *objective* character of an experience, apart from the particular point of view from which its subject apprehends it. After all, what would be left of what it was like to be a bat if one removed the viewpoint of the bat? But if experience does not have, in addition to its subjective character, an objective nature that can be apprehended from many different points of view, then how can it be supposed that a Martian investigating my brain might be observing physical processes which were my mental processes (as he might observe physical processes which were bolts of lightning), only from a different point of view? How, for that matter, could a human physiologist observe them from another point of view?[10]

We appear to be faced with a general difficulty about psychophysical reduction. In other areas the process of reduction is a move in the direction of greater objectivity, toward a more accurate view of the real nature of things. This is accomplished by reducing our dependence on individual or species-specific points of view toward the object of investigation. We describe it not in terms of the impressions it makes on our senses, but in terms of its more general effects and of properties detectable by means other than the human senses. The less it depends on a specifically human viewpoint, the more objective is our description. It is possible to follow this path because although the concepts and ideas we employ in thinking about the external world are initially applied from a point of view that involves our perceptual apparatus, they are used by us to refer to things beyond themselves – toward which we *have* the phenomenal point of view. Therefore we can abandon it in favor of another, and still be thinking about the same things.

Experience itself, however, does not seem to fit the pattern. The idea of moving from appearance to reality seems to make no sense here. What is the analogue in this case to pursuing a more objective understanding of the same phenomena by abandoning the initial subjective viewpoint toward them in favor of another that is more objective but concerns the same thing? Certainly it *appears* unlikely that we will get closer to the real nature of human experience by leaving behind the particularity of our human point of view and striving for a description in terms accessible to beings that could not imagine what it was like to be us. If the subjective character of experience is fully comprehensible only from one point of view, then any shift to greater objectivity – that is, less attachment to a specific viewpoint

– does not take us nearer to the real nature of the phenomenon: it takes us farther away from it.

In a sense, the seeds of this objection to the reducibility of experience are already detectable in successful cases of reduction; for in discovering sound to be, in reality, a wave phenomenon in air or other media, we leave behind one viewpoint to take up another, and the auditory, human or animal viewpoint that we leave behind remains unreduced. Members of radically different species may both understand the same physical events in objective terms, and this does not require that they understand the phenomenal forms in which those events appear to the senses of members of the other species. Thus it is a condition of their referring to a common reality that their more particular viewpoints are not part of the common reality that they both apprehend. The reduction can succeed only if the species-specific viewpoint is omitted from what is to be reduced.

But while we are right to leave this point of view aside in seeking a fuller understanding of the external world, we cannot ignore it permanently, since it is the essence of the internal world, and not merely a point of view on it. Most of the neobehaviorism of recent philosophical psychology results from the effort to substitute an objective concept of mind for the real thing, in order to have nothing left over which cannot be reduced. If we acknowledge that a physical theory of mind must account for the subjective character of experience, we must admit that no presently available conception gives us a clue how this could be done. The problem is unique. If mental processes are indeed physical processes, then there is something it is like, intrinsically,[11] to undergo certain physical processes. What it is for such a thing to be the case remains a mystery.

What moral should be drawn from these reflections, and what should be done next? It would be a mistake to conclude that physicalism must be false. Nothing is proved by the inadequacy of physicalist hypotheses that assume a faulty objective analysis of mind. It would be truer to say that physicalism is a position we cannot understand because we do not at present have any conception of how it might be true. Perhaps it will be thought unreasonable to require such a conception as a condition of understanding. After all, it might be said, the meaning of physicalism is clear enough: mental states are states of the body; mental events are physical events.

We do not know *which* physical states and events they are, but that should not prevent us from understanding the hypothesis. What could be clearer than the words "is" and "are"?

But I believe it is precisely this apparent clarity of the word "is" that is deceptive. Usually, when we are told that X is Y we know *how* it is supposed to be true, but that depends on a conceptual or theoretical background and is not conveyed by the "is" alone. We know how both "X" and "Y" refer, and the kinds of things to which they refer, and we have a rough idea how the two referential paths might converge on a single thing, be it an object, a person, a process, an event, or whatever. But when the two terms of the identification are very disparate it may not be so clear how it could be true. We may not have even a rough idea of how the two referential paths could converge, or what kind of things they might converge on, and a theoretical framework may have to be supplied to enable us to understand this. Without the framework, an air of mysticism surrounds the identification.

This explains the magical flavor of popular presentations of fundamental scientific discoveries, given out as propositions to which one must subscribe without really understanding them. For example, people are now told at an early age that all matter is really energy. But despite the fact that they know what "is" means, most of them never form a conception of what makes this claim true, because they lack the theoretical background.

At the present time the status of physicalism is similar to that which the hypothesis that matter is energy would have had if uttered by a pre-Socratic philosopher. We do not have the beginnings of a conception of how it might be true. In order to understand the hypothesis that a mental event is a physical event, we require more than an understanding of the word "is." The idea of how a mental and a physical term might refer to the same thing is lacking, and the usual analogies with theoretical identification in other fields fail to supply it. They fail because if we construe the reference of mental terms to physical events on the usual model, we either get a reappearance of separate subjective events as the effects through which mental reference to physical events is secured, or else we get a false account of how mental terms refer (for example, a causal behaviorist one).

Strangely enough, we may have evidence for the truth of something we cannot really understand.

Suppose a caterpillar is locked in a sterile safe by someone unfamiliar with insect metamorphosis, and weeks later the safe is reopened, revealing a butterfly. If the person knows that the safe has been shut the whole time, he has reason to believe that the butterfly is or was once the caterpillar, without having any idea in what sense this might be so. (One possibility is that the caterpillar contained a tiny winged parasite that devoured it and grew into the butterfly.)

It is conceivable that we are in such a position with regard to physicalism. Donald Davidson has argued that if mental events have physical causes and effects, they must have physical descriptions. He holds that we have reason to believe this even though we do not – and in fact *could not* – have a general psychophysical theory.[12] His argument applies to intentional mental events, but I think we also have some reason to believe that sensations are physical processes, without being in a position to understand how. Davidson's position is that certain physical events have irreducibly mental properties, and perhaps some view describable in this way is correct. But nothing of which we can now form a conception corresponds to it; nor have we any idea what a theory would be like that enabled us to conceive of it.[13]

Very little work has been done on the basic question (from which mention of the brain can be entirely omitted) whether any sense can be made of experiences' having an objective character at all. Does it make sense, in other words, to ask what my experiences are *really* like, as opposed to how they appear to me? We cannot genuinely understand the hypothesis that their nature is captured in a physical description unless we understand the more fundamental idea that they *have* an objective nature (or that objective processes can have a subjective nature).[14]

I should like to close with a speculative proposal. It may be possible to approach the gap between subjective and objective from another direction. Setting aside temporarily the relation between the mind and the brain, we can pursue a more objective understanding of the mental in its own right. At present we are completely unequipped to think about the subjective character of experience without relying on the imagination – without taking up the point of view of the experiential subject. This should be regarded as a challenge to form new concepts and devise a new method – an objective phenomenology not dependent on empathy or the imagination. Though presumably it would not capture everything, its goal would be to describe, at least in part, the subjective character of experiences in a form comprehensible to beings incapable of having those experiences.

We would have to develop such a phenomenology to describe the sonar experiences of bats; but it would also be possible to begin with humans. One might try, for example, to develop concepts that could be used to explain to a person blind from birth what it was like to see. One would reach a blank wall eventually, but it should be possible to devise a method of expressing in objective terms much more than we can at present, and with much greater precision. The loose intermodal analogies – for example, "Red is like the sound of a trumpet" – which crop up in discussions of this subject are of little use. That should be clear to anyone who has both heard a trumpet and seen red. But structural features of perception might be more accessible to objective description, even though something would be left out. And concepts alternative to those we learn in the first person may enable us to arrive at a kind of understanding even of our own experience which is denied us by the very ease of description and lack of distance that subjective concepts afford.

Apart from its own interest, a phenomenology that is in this sense objective may permit questions about the physical[15] basis of experience to assume a more intelligible form. Aspects of subjective experience that admitted this kind of objective description might be better candidates for objective explanations of a more familiar sort. But whether or not this guess is correct, it seems unlikely that any physical theory of mind can be contemplated until more thought has been given to the general problem of subjective and objective. Otherwise we cannot even pose the mind–body problem without sidestepping it.

Notes

1 Examples are J. J. C. Smart, *Philosophy and Scientific Realism* (London, 1963); David K. Lewis, "An Argument for the Identity Theory," *Journal of Philosophy* 63 (1966), reprinted with addenda in David M. Rosenthal, *Materialism & the Mind–Body Problem* (Englewood Cliffs, NJ, 1971); Hilary Putnam, "Psychological Predicates," in W. H. Capitan and D. D. Merrill, *Art, Mind, and Religion* (Pittsburgh, 1967), reprinted in Rosenthal, *Materialism & the Mind–Body Problem*, as "The Nature of Mental States"; D. M. Armstrong, *A Materialist Theory of the Mind* (London, 1968); D. C. Dennett, *Content and Consciousness* (London, 1969). I have expressed earlier doubts in "Armstrong on the Mind," *Philosophical Review* 79 (1970), pp. 394–403; "Brain Bisection and the Unity of Consciousness," *Synthèse* 22 (1971); and a review of Dennett, *Journal of Philosophy* 69 (1972). See also Saul Kripke, "Naming and Necessity," in D. Davidson and G. Harman, *Semantics of Natural Language* (Dordrecht, 1972), esp. pp. 334–42; and M. T. Thornton, "Ostensive Terms and Materialism," *The Monist* 56 (1972).

2 Perhaps there could not actually be such robots. Perhaps anything complex enough to behave like a person would have experiences. But that, if true, is a fact which cannot be discovered merely by analyzing the concept of experience.

3 It is not equivalent to that about which we are incorrigible, both because we are not incorrigible about experience and because experience is present in animals lacking language and thought, who have no beliefs at all about their experiences.

4 Cf. Richard Rorty, "Mind–Body Identity, Privacy, and Categories," *Review of Metaphysics* 19 (1965), esp. pp. 37–8.

5 By "our own case" I do not mean just "my own case," but rather the mentalistic ideas that we apply unproblematically to ourselves and other human beings.

6 Therefore the analogical form of the English expression "what it is *like*" is misleading. It does not mean "what (in our experience) it *resembles*," but rather "how it is for the subject himself."

7 Any intelligent extraterrestrial beings totally different from us.

8 It may be easier than I suppose to transcend inter-species barriers with the aid of the imagination. For example, blind people are able to detect objects near them by a form of sonar, using vocal clicks or taps of a cane. Perhaps if one knew what that was like, one could by extension imagine roughly what it was like to possess the much more refined sonar of a bat. The distance between oneself and other persons and other species can fall anywhere on a continuum. Even for other persons the understanding of what it is like to be them is only partial, and when one moves to species very different from oneself, a lesser degree of partial understanding may still be available. The imagination is remarkably flexible. My point, however, is not that we cannot *know* what it is like to be a

bat. I am not raising that epistemological problem. My point is rather that even to form a *conception* of what it is like to be a bat (and a fortiori to know what it is like to be a bat) one must take up the bat's point of view. If one can take it up roughly, or partially, then one's conception will also be rough or partial. Or so it seems in our present state of understanding.

9   The problem I am going to raise can therefore be posed even if the distinction between more sub-jective and more objective descriptions or view-points can itself be made only within a larger human point of view. I do not accept this kind of conceptual relativism, but it need not be refuted to make the point that psychophysical reduction cannot be accommodated by the subjective-to-objective model familiar from other cases.

10 The problem is not just that when I look at the "Mona Lisa," my visual experience has a certain quality, no trace of which is to be found by some-one looking into my brain. For even if he did observe there a tiny image of the "Mona Lisa," he could have no reason to identify it with the experience.

11 The relation would therefore not be a contingent one, like that of a cause and its distinct effect. It would be necessarily true that a certain physical state felt a certain way. Saul Kripke ("Naming and Necessity") argues that causal behaviorist and related analyses of the mental fail because they construe, e.g., "pain" as a merely contingent name of pains. The subjective character of an experi-ence ("its immediate phenomenological quality" Kripke calls it (p. 340)) is the essential property left out by such analyses, and the one in virtue of which it is, necessarily, the experience it is. My view is closely related to his. Like Kripke, I find the hypothesis that a certain brain state should *necessarily* have a certain subjective character in-comprehensible without further explanation. No such explanation emerges from theories which view the mind–brain relation as contingent, but perhaps there are other alternatives, not yet discovered.

A theory that explained how the mind–brain relation was necessary would still leave us with Kripke's problem of explaining why it neverthe-less appears contingent. That difficulty seems to me surmountable, in the following way. We may imagine something by representing it to ourselves either perceptually, sympathetically, or symbolically. I shall not try to say how symbolic imagination works, but part of what happens in the other two cases is this. To imagine something perceptually, we put ourselves in a conscious state resembling the state we would be in if we perceived it. To imagine something sympathetically, we put our-selves in a conscious state resembling the thing

itself. (This method can be used only to imagine mental events and states – our own or another's.) When we try to imagine a mental state occurring without its associated brain state, we first sym-pathetically imagine the occurrence of the mental state: that is, we put ourselves into a state that resembles it mentally. At the same time, we at-tempt to perceptually imagine the non-occurrence of the associated physical state, by putting our-selves into another state unconnected with the first: one resembling that which we would be in if we perceived the non-occurrence of the physical state. Where the imagination of physical features is perceptual and the imagination of mental fea-tures is sympathetic, it appears to us that we can imagine any experience occurring without its asso-ciated brain state, and vice versa. The relation between them will appear contingent even if it is necessary, because of the independence of the disparate types of imagination.

(Solipsism, incidentally, results if one misinter-prets sympathetic imagination as if it worked like perceptual imagination: it then seems impossible to imagine any experience that is not one's own.)

12 See "Mental Events" in L. Foster and J. W. Swanson, *Experience and Theory* (Amherst, MA, 1970); though I don't understand the argument against psychophysical laws.

13 Similar remarks apply to my paper "Physicalism," *Philosophical Review* 74 (1965), pp. 339–56, re-printed with postscript in John O'Connor, *Modern Materialism* (New York, 1969).

14 This question also lies at the heart of the problem of other minds, whose close connection with the mind–body problem is often overlooked. If one understood how subjective experience would have an objective nature, one would understand the existence of subjects other than oneself.

15 I have not defined the term "physical." Obviously it does not apply just to what can be described by the concepts of contemporary physics, since we expect further developments. Some may think there is nothing to prevent mental phenomena from eventually being recognized as physical in their own right. But whatever else may be said of the physical, it has to be objective. So if our idea of the physical ever expands to include mental phe-nomena, it will have to assign them an objective character – whether or not this is done by analyzing them in terms of other phenomena already re-garded as physical. It seems to me more likely, however, that mental–physical relations will even-tually be expressed in a theory whose fundamental terms cannot be placed clearly in either category.

I have read versions of this paper to a number of audiences, and am indebted to many people for their comments.

26

Mad Pain and Martian Pain

David Lewis

I

There might be a strange man who sometimes feels pain, just as we do, but whose pain differs greatly from ours in its causes and effects. Our pain is typically caused by cuts, burns, pressure, and the like; his is caused by moderate exercise on an empty stomach. Our pain is generally distracting; his turns his mind to mathematics, facilitating concentration on that but distracting him from anything else. Intense pain has no tendency whatever to cause him to groan or writhe, but does cause him to cross his legs and snap his fingers. He is not in the least motivated to prevent pain or to get rid of it. In short, he feels pain but his pain does not at all occupy the typical causal role of pain. He would doubtless seem to us to be some sort of madman, and that is what I shall call him, though of course the sort of madness I have imagined may bear little resemblance to the real thing.

I said there might be such a madman. I don't know how to prove that something is possible, but my opinion that this is a possible case seems pretty firm. If I want a credible theory of mind, I need a theory that does not deny the possibility of mad pain. I needn't mind conceding that perhaps the madman is not in pain in *quite* the

Previously published in *Readings in the Philosophy of Psychology*, vol. 1, ed. Ned Block (Harvard University Press, Cambridge, Mass., 1980).

same sense that the rest of us are, but there had better be some straightforward sense in which he and we are both in pain.

Also, there might be a Martian who sometimes feels pain, just as we do, but whose pain differs greatly from ours in its physical realization. His hydraulic mind contains nothing like our neurons. Rather, there are varying amounts of fluid in many inflatable cavities, and the inflation of any one of these cavities opens some valves and closes others. His mental plumbing pervades most of his body – in fact, all but the heat exchanger inside his head. When you pinch his skin you cause no firing of C-fibers – he has none – but, rather, you cause the inflation of many smallish cavities in his feet. When these cavities are inflated, he is in pain. And the effects of his pain are fitting: his thought and activity are disrupted, he groans and writhes, he is strongly motivated to stop you from pinching him and to see to it that you never do again. In short, he feels pain but lacks the bodily states that either are pain or else accompany it in us.

There might be such a Martian; this opinion too seems pretty firm. A credible theory of mind had better not deny the possibility of Martian pain. I needn't mind conceding that perhaps the Martian is not in pain in *quite* the same sense that we Earthlings are, but there had better be some straightforward sense in which he and we are both in pain.

II

A credible theory of mind needs to make a place both for mad pain and for Martian pain. Prima facie, it seems hard for a materialist theory to pass this twofold test. As philosophers, we would like to characterize pain a priori. (We might settle for less, but let's start by asking for all we want.) As materialists, we want to characterize pain as a physical phenomenon. We can speak of the place of pain in the causal network from stimuli to inner states to behavior. And we can speak of the physical processes that go on when there is pain and that take their place in that causal network. We seem to have no other resources but these. But the lesson of mad pain is that pain is associated only contingently with its causal role, while the lesson of Martian pain is that pain is connected only contingently with its physical realization. How can we characterize pain a priori in terms of causal role and physical realization, and yet respect both kinds of contingency?

A simple identity theory straightforwardly solves the problem of mad pain. It goes just as straightforwardly wrong about Martian pain. A simple behaviorism or functionalism goes the other way: right about the Martian, wrong about the madman. The theories that fail our twofold test so decisively are altogether too simple. (Perhaps they are too simple ever to have had adherents.) It seems that a theory that can pass our test will have to be a mixed theory. It will have to be able to tell us that the madman and the Martian are both in pain, but for different reasons: the madman because he is in the right physical state, the Martian because he is in a state rightly situated in the causal network.

Certainly we can cook up a mixed theory. Here's an easy recipe: First, find a theory to take care of the common man and the madman, disregarding the Martian – presumably an identity theory. Second, find a theory to take care of the common man and the Martian, disregarding the madman – presumably some sort of behaviorism or functionalism. Then disjoin the two: say that to be in pain is to be in pain either according to the first theory or according to the second. Alternatively, claim ambiguity: say that to be in pain in one sense is to be in pain according to the first theory, to be in pain in another sense is to be in pain according to the second theory.

This strategy seems desperate. One wonders why we should have a disjunctive or ambiguous concept of pain, if common men who suffer pain are always in pain according to both disjuncts or both disambiguations. It detracts from the credibility of a theory that it posits a useless complexity in our concept of pain – useless in application to the common man, at least, and therefore useless almost always.

I don't object to the strategy of claiming ambiguity. As you'll see, I shall defend a version of it. But it's not plausible to cook up an ambiguity *ad hoc* to account for the compossibility of mad pain and Martian pain. It would be better to find a widespread sort of ambiguity, a sort we would believe in no matter what we thought about pain, and show that it will solve our problem. That is my plan.

III

A dozen years or so ago, D. M. Armstrong and I (independently) proposed a materialist theory of mind that joins claims of type-type psychophysical identity with a behaviorist or functionalist way of characterizing mental states such as pain.[1] I believe our theory passes the twofold test. Positing no ambiguity without independent reason, it provides natural senses in which both madman and Martian are in pain. It wriggles through between Scylla and Charybdis.

Our view is that the concept of pain, or indeed of any other experience or mental state, is the concept of a state that occupies a certain causal role, a state with certain typical causes and effects. It is the concept of a state apt for being caused by certain stimuli and apt for causing certain behavior. Or, better, of a state apt for being caused in certain ways by stimuli plus other mental states and apt for combining with certain other mental states to jointly cause certain behavior. It is the concept of a member of a system of states that together more or less realize the pattern of causal generalizations set forth in commonsense psychology. (That system may be characterized as a whole and its members characterized afterward by reference to their place in it.)

If the concept of pain is the concept of a state that occupies a certain causal role, then whatever state does occupy that role is pain. If the state of having neurons hooked up in a certain way and firing in a certain pattern is the state properly apt for causing and being caused, as we materialists think, then that neural state is pain. But the concept of pain is not the concept of that neural state. ("The concept of . . ." is an intensional functor.) The concept of pain, unlike the concept of that neural state which in fact is pain, would have applied to some different state if the relevant causal relations had been different. Pain might have not been pain. The occupant of the role might have not occupied it. Some other state might have occupied it instead. Something that is not pain might have been pain.

This is not to say, of course, that it might have been that pain was not pain and nonpain was pain; that is, that it might have been that the occupant of the role did not occupy it and some nonoccupant did. Compare: "The winner might have lost" (true) versus "It might have been that the winner lost" (false). No wording is entirely unambiguous, but I trust my meaning is clear.

In short, the concept of pain as Armstrong and I understand it is a *nonrigid* concept. Likewise the word "pain" is a nonrigid designator. It is a contingent matter what state the concept and the word apply to. It depends on what causes what. The same goes for the rest of our concepts and ordinary names of mental states.

Some need hear no more. The notion that mental concepts and names are nonrigid, wherefore what *is* pain might not have been, seems to them just self-evidently false.[2] I cannot tell why they think so. Bracketing my own theoretical commitments, I think I would have no opinion one way or the other. It's not that I don't care about shaping theory to respect naive opinion as well as can be, but in this case I have no naive opinion to respect. If I am not speaking to your condition, so be it.

If pain is identical to a certain neural state, the identity is contingent. Whether it holds is one of the things that varies from one possible world to another. But take care. I do not say that here we have two states, pain and some neural state, that are contingently identical, identical at this world but different at another. Since I'm serious about the identity, we have not two states but one. This one state, this neural state which is pain, is not contingently identical to itself. It does not differ from itself at any world. Nothing does.[3] What's true is, rather, that the concept and name of pain contingently apply to some neural state at this world, but do not apply to it at another. Similarly, it is a contingent truth that Bruce is our cat, but it's wrong to say

that Bruce and our cat are contingently identical. Our cat Bruce is necessarily self-identical. What is contingent is that the nonrigid concept of being our cat applies to Bruce rather than to some other cat, or none.

IV

Nonrigidity might begin at home. All actualities are possibilities, so the variety of possibilities includes the variety of actualities. Though some possibilities are thoroughly otherworldly, others may be found on planets within range of our telescopes. One such planet is Mars.

If a nonrigid concept or name applies to different states in different possible cases, it should be no surprise if it also applies to different states in different actual cases. Nonrigidity is to logical space as other relativities are to ordinary space. If the word "pain" designates one state at our actual world and another at a possible world where our counterparts have a different internal structure, then also it may designate one state on Earth and another on Mars. Or, better, since Martians may come here and we may go to Mars, it may designate one state for Earthlings and another for Martians.

We may say that some state *occupies a causal role for a population*. We may say this whether the population is situated entirely at our actual world, or partly at our actual world and partly at other worlds, or entirely at other worlds. If the concept of pain is the concept of a state that occupies that role, then we may say that a state *is pain for a population*. Then we may say that a certain pattern of firing of neurons is pain for the population of actual Earthlings and some but not all of our otherworldly counterparts, whereas the inflation of certain cavities in the feet is pain for the population of actual Martians and some of their otherworldly counterparts. Human pain is the state that occupies the role of pain for humans. Martian pain is the state that occupies the same role for Martians.

A state occupies a causal role for a population, and the concept of occupant of that role applies to it, if and only if, with few exceptions, whenever a member of that population is in that state, his being in that state has the sort of causes and effects given by the role.

The thing to say about Martian pain is that the Martian is in pain because he is in a state that occupies the causal role of pain for Martians, whereas we are in pain because we are in a state that occupies the role of pain for us.

V

Now, what of the madman? He is in pain, but he is not in a state that occupies the causal role of pain for him. He is in a state that occupies that role for most of us, but he is an exception. The causal role of a pattern of firing of neurons depends on one's circuit diagram, and he is hooked up wrong.

His state does not occupy the role of pain for a population comprising himself and his fellow madmen. But it does occupy that role for a more salient population – mankind at large. He is a man, albeit an exceptional one, and a member of that larger population.

We have allowed for exceptions. I spoke of the definitive syndrome of *typical* causes and effects. Armstrong spoke of a state *apt for* having certain causes and effects; that does not mean that it has them invariably. Again, I spoke of a system of states that *comes near to* realizing commonsense psychology. A state may therefore occupy a role for mankind even if it does not at all occupy that role for some mad minority of mankind.

The thing to say about mad pain is that the madman is in pain because he is in the state that occupies the causal role of pain for the population comprising all mankind. He is an exceptional member of that population. The state that occupies the role for the population does not occupy it for him.

VI

We may say that X is in pain *simpliciter* if and only if X is in the state that occupies the causal role of pain for the *appropriate* population. But what is the appropriate population? Perhaps (1) it should be *us*; after all, it's our concept and our word. On the other hand, if it's X we're talking about, perhaps (2) it should be a population that X himself belongs to, and (3) it should preferably be one in which X is not exceptional. Either way, (4) an appropriate population should be a natural kind – a species, perhaps.

If X is you or I – human and unexceptional – all four considerations pull together. The appropriate population consists of mankind as it actually is, extending into other worlds only to an extent that does not make the actual majority exceptional.

Since the four criteria agree in the case of the common man, which is the case we usually have in mind, there is no reason why we should have made up our minds about their relative importance in cases of conflict. It should be no surprise if ambiguity and uncertainty arise in such cases. Still, some cases do seem reasonably clear.

If X is our Martian, we are inclined to say that he is in pain when the cavities in his feet are inflated; and so says the theory, provided that criterion (1) is outweighed by the other three, so that the appropriate population is taken to be the species of Martians to which X belongs.

If X is our madman, we are inclined to say that he is in pain when he is in the state that occupies the role of pain for the rest of us; and so says the theory, provided that criterion (3) is outweighed by the other three, so that the appropriate population is taken to be mankind.

We might also consider the case of a mad Martian, related to other Martians as the madman is to the rest of us. If X is a mad Martian, I would be inclined to say that he is in pain when the cavities in his feet are inflated; and so says our theory, provided that criteria (2) and (4) together outweigh either (1) or (3) by itself.

Other cases are less clear-cut. Since the balance is less definitely in favor of one population or another, we may perceive the relativity to population by feeling genuinely undecided. Suppose the state that plays the role of pain for us plays instead the role of thirst for a certain small subpopulation of mankind, and vice versa. When one of them has the state that is pain for us and thirst for him, there may be genuine and irresolvable indecision about whether to call him pained or thirsty – that is, whether to think of him as a madman or as a Martian. Criterion (1) suggests calling his state pain and regarding him as an exception; criteria (2) and (3) suggest shifting to a subpopulation and calling his state thirst. Criterion (4) could go either way, since mankind and the exceptional subpopulation may both be natural kinds. (Perhaps it is relevant to ask whether membership in the subpopulation is hereditary.)

The interchange of pain and thirst parallels the traditional problem of inverted spectra. I have suggested that there is no determinate fact of the matter about whether the victim of interchange undergoes pain or thirst. I think this conclusion accords well with the fact that there seems to be no persuasive solution one way or the other to the old problem of inverted spectra. I would say that there is a good sense in which the alleged victim of inverted spectra sees red when he looks at grass: he is in a state that occupies the role of seeing red for mankind in general. And there is an equally good sense in which he sees green: he is in a state that occupies the role of seeing green for him, and for a small subpopulation of which he is an unexceptional member and which has some claim to be regarded as a natural kind. You are right to say either, though not in the same breath. Need more be said?

To sum up. Armstrong and I claim to give a schema that, if filled in, would characterize pain and other states a priori. If the causal facts are right, then also we characterize pain as a physical phenomenon. By allowing for exceptional members of a population, we associate pain only contingently with its causal role. Therefore we do not deny the possibility of mad pain, provided there is not too much of it. By allowing for variation from one population to another (actual or merely possible) we associate pain only contingently with its physical realization. Therefore we do not deny the possibility of Martian pain. If different ways of filling in the relativity to population may be said to yield different senses of the word "pain," then we plead ambiguity. The madman is in pain in one sense, or relative to one population. The Martian is in pain in another sense, or relative to another population. (So is the mad Martian.)

But we do not posit ambiguity *ad hoc*. The requisite flexibility is explained simply by supposing that we have not bothered to make up our minds about semantic niceties that would make no difference to any commonplace case. The ambiguity that arises in cases of inverted spectra and the like is simply one instance of a commonplace kind of ambiguity – a kind that may arise whenever we have tacit relativity and criteria of selection that sometimes fail to choose a definite *relatum*. It is the same kind of ambiguity that arises if someone speaks of relevant studies without making clear whether he means relevance to current affairs, to spiritual well-being, to understanding, or what.

VII

We have a place for commonplace pain, mad pain, Martian pain, and even mad Martian pain. But one case remains problematic. What about pain in a being who is mad, alien, and unique? Have we made a place for that? It seems not. Since he is mad, we may suppose that his alleged state of pain does not occupy the proper causal role for him. Since he is alien, we may also suppose that it does not occupy the proper role for us. And since he is unique, it does not occupy the proper role for others of his species. What is left?

(One thing that might be left is the population consisting of him and his unactualized counterparts at other worlds. If he went mad as a result of some improbable accident, perhaps we can say that he is in pain because he is in the state that occupies the role for most of his alternative possible selves; the state that would have occupied the role for him if he had developed in a more probable way. To make the problem as hard as possible, I must suppose that this solution is unavailable. He did *not* narrowly escape being so constituted that his present state would have occupied the role of pain.)

I think we cannot and need not solve this problem. Our only recourse is to deny that the case is possible. To stipulate that the being in this example is in pain was illegitimate. That seems credible enough. Admittedly, I might have thought offhand that the case was possible. No wonder; it merely combines elements of other cases that are possible. But I am willing to change my mind. Unlike my opinions about the possibility of mad pain and Martian pain, my naive opinions about this case are not firm enough to carry much weight.

VIII

Finally, I would like to try to preempt an objection. I can hear it said that I have been strangely silent about the very center of my topic. *What is it like* to be the madman, the Martian, the mad Martian, the victim of interchange of pain and thirst, or the being who is mad, alien, and unique? What is the *phenomenal character* of his state? If it *feels* to him like pain, then it *is* pain, whatever its causal role or physical nature. If not, it isn't. It's that simple!

Yes. It would indeed be a mistake to consider whether a state is pain while ignoring what it is

David Lewis

like to have it. Fortunately, I have not made that mistake. Indeed, it is an impossible mistake to make. It is like the impossible mistake of considering whether a number is composite while ignoring the question of what factors it has.

Pain is a feeling.[4] Surely that is uncontroversial. To have pain and to feel pain are one and the same. For a state to be pain and for it to feel painful are likewise one and the same. A theory of what it is for a state to be pain is inescapably

a theory of what it is like to be in that state, of how that state feels, of the phenomenal character of that state. Far from ignoring questions of how states feel in the odd cases we have been considering, I have been discussing nothing else! Only if you believe on independent grounds that considerations of causal role and physical realization have no bearing on whether a state is pain should you say that they have no bearing on how that state feels.

Notes

This paper was presented at a conference on mind–body identity held at Rice University in April 1978. I am grateful to many friends, and especially to Patricia Kitcher, for valuable discussions of the topic.

1 D. M. Armstrong, *A Materialist Theory of the Mind* (London: Routledge, 1968); "The Nature of Mind," in C. V. Borst (ed.) *The Mind/Brain Identity Theory* (London: Macmillan, 1970), pp. 67–97; "The Causal Theory of the Mind," *Neue Heft für Philosophie*, no. 11 (Vendenhoek & Ruprecht, 1977), pp. 82–95; David Lewis, "An Argument for the Identity Theory," *Journal of Philosophy* 63 (1966), pp. 17–25, reprinted with additions in *Materialism and the Mind–Body Problem*, ed. David M. Rosenthal (Englewood Cliffs, NJ: Prentice-Hall, 1971), pp. 162–71; "Review of *Art, Mind, and Religion*," *Journal of Philosophy* 66 (1969), pp. 22–7, particularly pp. 23–5; "Psychophysical and Theoretical Identifications," *Australasian Journal of Philosophy* 50 (1972), pp. 249–

58; "Radical Interpretation," *Synthèse* 23 (1974), pp. 331–44.

2 For instance, see Saul A. Kripke, "Naming and Necessity," in *Semantics of Natural Language*, ed. Gilbert Harman and Donald Davidson (Dordrecht: Reidel, 1972), pp. 253–355, 763–9, particularly pp. 335–6. Note that the sort of identity theory that Kripke opposes by argument, rather than by appeal to self-evidence, is not the sort that Armstrong and I propose.

3 The closest we can come is to have something at one world with twin counterparts at another. See my "Counterpart Theory and Quantified Modal Logic," *Journal of Philosophy* 65 (1968), pp. 113–26. That possibility is irrelevant to the present case.

4 Occurrent pain, that is. Maybe a disposition that sometimes but not always causes occurrent pain might also be called "pain."

27

Can Computers Think?

John Searle

I have provided at least the outlines of a solution to the so-called 'mind–body problem'. Though we do not know in detail how the brain functions, we do know enough to have an idea of the general relationships between brain processes and mental processes. Mental processes are caused by the behaviour of elements of the brain. At the same time, they are realised in the structure that is made up of those elements. I think this answer is consistent with the standard biological approaches to biological phenomena. Indeed, it is a kind of commonsense answer to the question, given what we know about how the world works. However, it is very much a minority point of view. The prevailing view in philosophy, psychology, and artificial intelligence is one which emphasises the analogies between the functioning of the human brain and the functioning of digital computers. According to the most extreme version of this view, the brain is just a digital computer and the mind is just a computer program. One could summarise this view – I call it 'strong artificial intelligence', or 'strong AI' – by saying that the mind is to the brain, as the program is to the computer hardware.

This view has the consequence that there is nothing essentially biological about the human mind. The brain just happens to be one of an indefinitely large number of different kinds of

Reprinted by permission of the publisher from *Minds, Brains, and Science*, by John Searle (Harvard University Press, Cambridge, Mass.). Copyright © 1984 by J. R. Searle.

hardware computers that could sustain the programs which make up human intelligence. On this view, any physical system whatever that had the right program with the right inputs and outputs would have a mind in exactly the same sense that you and I have minds. So, for example, if you made a computer out of old beer cans powered by windmills; if it had the right program, it would have to have a mind. And the point is not that for all we know it might have thoughts and feelings, but rather that it must have thoughts and feelings, because that is all there is to having thoughts and feelings: implementing the right program.

Most people who hold this view think we have not yet designed programs which are minds. But there is pretty much general agreement among them that it's only a matter of time until computer scientists and workers in artificial intelligence design the appropriate hardware and programs which will be the equivalent of human brains and minds. These will be artificial brains and minds which are in every way the equivalent of human brains and minds.

Many people outside of the field of artificial intelligence are quite amazed to discover that anybody could believe such a view as this. So, before criticising it, let me give you a few examples of the things that people in this field have actually said. Herbert Simon of Carnegie–Mellon University says that we already have machines that can literally think. There is no question of waiting for some future machine, because existing digital computers already have thoughts in exactly the same sense that you and I do. Well, fancy that! Philosophers have been worried for centuries about whether or not a machine could think, and now we discover that they already have such machines at Carnegie–Mellon. Simon's colleague Alan Newell claims that we have now discovered (and notice that Newell says 'discovered' and not 'hypothesised' or 'considered the possibility', but we have *discovered*) that intelligence is just a matter of physical symbol manipulation; it has no essential connection with any specific kind of biological or physical wetware or hardware. Rather, any system whatever that is capable of manipulating physical symbols in the right way is capable of intelligence in the same literal sense as human intelligence of human beings. Both Simon and Newell, to their credit, emphasise that there is nothing metaphorical about these claims; they mean them quite literally. Freeman Dyson is quoted as having said that computers have an advantage over the rest of us when it comes to evolution. Since consciousness is just a matter of formal processes, in computers these formal processes can go on in substances that are much better able to survive in a universe that is cooling off than beings like ourselves made of our wet and messy materials. Marvin Minsky of MIT says that the next generation of computers will be so intelligent that we will 'be lucky if they are willing to keep us around the house as household pets'. My all-time favourite in the literature of exaggerated claims on behalf of the digital computer is from John McCarthy, the inventor of the term 'artificial intelligence'. McCarthy says even 'machines as simple as thermostats can be said to have beliefs'. And indeed, according to him, almost any machine capable of problem-solving can be said to have beliefs. I admire McCarthy's courage. I once asked him: 'What beliefs does your thermostat have?' And he said: 'My thermostat has three beliefs – it's too hot in here, it's too cold in here, and it's just right in here.' As a philosopher, I like all these claims for a simple reason. Unlike most philosophical theses, they are reasonably clear, and they admit of a simple and decisive refutation. It is this refutation that I am going to undertake in this chapter.

The nature of the refutation has nothing whatever to do with any particular stage of computer technology. It is important to emphasise this point because the temptation is always to think that the solution to our problems must wait on some as yet uncreated technological wonder. But in fact, the nature of the refutation is completely independent of any state of technology. It has to do with the very definition of a digital computer, with what a digital computer is.

It is essential to our conception of a digital computer that its operations can be specified purely formally; that is, we specify the steps in the operation of the computer in terms of abstract symbols – sequences of zeroes and ones printed on a tape, for example. A typical computer 'rule' will determine that when a machine is in a certain state and it has a certain symbol on its tape, then it will perform a certain operation such as erasing the symbol or printing another symbol and then enter another state such as moving the tape one square to the left. But the symbols have no meaning; they have no semantic content; they are not about anything. They have to be specified purely in terms of their formal or syntactical structure. The zeroes and ones, for example, are just numerals; they don't even stand for numbers. Indeed, it is this feature of digital computers that makes them so powerful. One and the same type of hardware, if it is appropriately designed, can be used to run an indefinite range of different programs. And one and the same program can be run on an indefinite range of different types of hardwares.

But this feature of programs, that they are defined purely formally or syntactically, is fatal to the view that mental processes and program processes are identical. And the reason can be stated quite simply. There is more to having a mind than having formal or syntactical processes. Our internal mental states, by definition, have certain sorts of contents. If I am thinking about Kansas City or wishing that I had a cold beer to drink or wondering if there will be a fall in interest rates, in each case my mental state has a certain mental content in addition to whatever formal features it might have. That is, even if my thoughts occur to me in strings of symbols, there must be more to the thought than the abstract strings, because strings by themselves can't have any meaning. If my thoughts are to be *about* anything, then the strings must have a *meaning* which makes the thoughts about those things. In a word, the mind has more than a syntax, it has a semantics. The reason that no computer program can ever be a mind is simply that a computer program is only syntactical, and minds are more than syntactical. Minds are semantical, in the sense that they have more than a formal structure, they have a content.

To illustrate this point I have designed a certain thought-experiment. Imagine that a bunch of computer programmers have written a program that will enable a computer to simulate the understanding of Chinese. So, for example, if the computer is given a question in Chinese, it will match the question against its memory, or data base, and produce appropriate answers to the questions in Chinese. Suppose for the sake of argument that the computer's answers are as good as those of a native Chinese speaker. Now then, does the computer, on the basis of this, understand Chinese, does it literally understand Chinese, in the way that Chinese speakers understand Chinese? Well, imagine that you are locked in a room, and in this room are several baskets full of Chinese symbols. Imagine that you (like me) do not understand a word of Chinese, but that you are given a rule book in English for manipulating these Chinese symbols. The rules specify the manipulations of the symbols purely formally, in terms of their syntax, not their semantics. So the rule might say: 'Take a squiggle-squiggle sign out of basket number one and put it next to a squoggle-squoggle sign from basket number two.' Now suppose that some other Chinese symbols are passed into the room, and that you are given further rules for passing back Chinese symbols out of the room. Suppose that unknown to you the symbols passed into the room are called 'questions' by the people outside the room, and the symbols you pass back out of the room are called 'answers to the questions'. Suppose, furthermore, that the programmers are so good at designing the programs and that you are so good at manipulating the symbols, that very soon your answers are indistinguishable from those of a native Chinese speaker. There you are locked in your room shuffling your Chinese symbols and passing out Chinese symbols in response to incoming Chinese symbols. On the basis of the situation as I have described it, there is no way you could learn any Chinese simply by manipulating these formal symbols.

Now the point of the story is simply this: by virtue of implementing a formal computer program from the point of view of an outside observer, you behave exactly as if you understood Chinese, but all the same you don't understand a word of Chinese. But if going through the appropriate computer program for understanding Chinese is not enough to give *you* an understanding of Chinese, then it is not enough to give *any other digital computer* an understanding of Chinese. And again, the reason for this can be stated quite simply. If you don't understand Chinese, then no other computer could understand Chinese because no digital computer, just by virtue of running a program, has anything that you don't have. All that the computer has, as you have, is a formal program for manipulating uninterpreted Chinese symbols. To repeat, a computer has a syntax, but no semantics. The whole point of the parable of the Chinese room is to remind us of a fact that we knew all along. Understanding a language, or indeed, having mental states at all, involves more than just having a bunch of formal symbols. It involves having an interpretation, or a meaning attached to those symbols. And a digital computer, as defined, cannot have more than just formal symbols because the operation of the computer, as I said earlier, is defined in terms of its ability to implement programs. And these programs are purely formally specifiable – that is, they have no semantic content.

We can see the force of this argument if we contrast what it is like to be asked and to answer questions in English, and to be asked and to answer questions in some language where we have no knowledge of any of the meanings of the words. Imagine that in the Chinese room you are also given questions in English about such things as your age or your life history, and that you answer these questions. What is the difference between the Chinese case and the English case? Well again, if like me you understand no Chinese and you do understand English, then the difference is obvious. You understand the questions in English because they are expressed in symbols whose meanings are known to you. Similarly, when you give the answers in English you are producing symbols which are meaningful to you. But in the case of the Chinese, you have none of that. In the case of the Chinese, you simply manipulate formal symbols according to a computer program, and you attach no meaning to any of the elements.

Various replies have been suggested to this argument by workers in artificial intelligence and in psychology, as well as philosophy. They all have something in common; they are all inadequate. And there is an obvious reason why they have to be inadequate, since the argument rests on a very simple logical truth, namely, syntax alone is not sufficient for semantics, and digital computers insofar as they are computers have, by definition, a syntax alone.

I want to make this clear by considering a couple of the arguments that are often presented against me.

Some people attempt to answer the Chinese room example by saying that the whole system understands Chinese. The idea here is that though I, the person in the room manipulating the symbols do not understand Chinese, I am just the central processing unit of the computer system. They argue that it is the whole system, including the room, the baskets full of symbols and the ledgers containing the programs and perhaps other items as well, taken as a totality, that understands Chinese. But this is subject to exactly the same objection I made before. There is no way that the system can get from the syntax to the semantics. I, as the central processing unit have no way of figuring out what any of these symbols means; but then neither does the whole system.

Another common response is to imagine that we put the Chinese understanding program inside a robot. If the robot moved around and interacted causally with the world, wouldn't that be enough to guarantee that it understood Chinese? Once again the inexorability of the semantics–syntax distinction overcomes this manoeuvre. As long as we suppose that the robot has only a computer for a brain then, even though it might behave exactly as if it understood Chinese, it would still have no way of getting from the syntax to the semantics of Chinese. You can see this if you imagine that I am the computer. Inside a room in the robot's skull I shuffle symbols without knowing that some of them come in to me from television cameras attached to the robot's head and others go out to move the robot's arms and legs. As long as all I have is a formal computer program, I have no way of attaching any meaning to any of the symbols. And the fact that the robot is engaged in causal interactions with the outside world won't help me to attach any meaning to the symbols unless I have some way of finding out about that fact. Suppose the robot picks up a hamburger and this triggers the symbol for hamburger to come into the room. As long as all I have is the symbol with no knowledge of its causes or how it got there, I have no way of knowing what it means. The causal interactions between the robot and the rest of the world are irrelevant unless those causal interactions are represented in some mind or other. But there is

no way they can be if all that the so-called mind consists of is a set of purely formal, syntactical operations.

It is important to see exactly what is claimed and what is not claimed by my argument. Suppose we ask the question that I mentioned at the beginning: 'Could a machine think?' Well, in one sense, of course, we are all machines. We can construe the stuff inside our heads as a meat machine. And of course, we can all think. So, in one sense of 'machine', namely that sense in which a machine is just a physical system which is capable of performing certain kinds of operations, in that sense, we are all machines, and we can think. So, trivially, there are machines that can think. But that wasn't the question that bothered us. So let's try a different formulation of it. Could an artefact think? Could a man-made machine think? Well, once again, it depends on the kind of artefact. Suppose we designed a machine that was molecule-for-molecule indistinguishable from a human being. Well then, if you can duplicate the causes, you can presumably duplicate the effects. So once again, the answer to that question is, in principle at least, trivially yes. If you could build a machine that had the same structure as a human being, then presumably that machine would be able to think. Indeed, it would be a surrogate human being. Well, let's try again.

The question isn't: 'Can a machine think?' or: 'Can an artefact think?' The question is: 'Can a digital computer think?' But once again we have to be very careful in how we interpret the question. From a mathematical point of view, anything whatever can be described *as if* it were a digital computer. And that's because it can be described as instantiating or implementing a computer program. In an utterly trivial sense, the pen that is on the desk in front of me can be described as a digital computer. It just happens to have a very boring computer program. The program says: 'Stay there.' Now since in this sense, anything whatever is a digital computer, because anything whatever can be described as implementing a computer program, then once again, our question gets a trivial answer. Of course our brains are digital computers, since they implement any number of computer programs. And of course our brains can think. So once again, there is a trivial answer to the question. But that wasn't really the question we were trying to ask. The question we wanted to ask is this: 'Can a digital computer, as defined, think?' That is to say: 'Is instantiating or implementing the right computer program with the right inputs and outputs, sufficient for, or constitutive of, thinking?' And to this question, unlike its predecessors, the answer is clearly 'no'. And it is 'no' for the reason that we have spelled out, namely, the computer program is defined purely syntactically. But thinking is more than just a matter of manipulating meaningless symbols, it involves meaningful semantic contents. These semantic contents are what we mean by 'meaning'.

It is important to emphasise again that we are not talking about a particular stage of computer technology. The argument has nothing to do with the forthcoming, amazing advances in computer science. It has nothing to do with the distinction between serial and parallel processes, or with the size of programs, or the speed of computer operations, or with computers that can interact causally with their environment, or even with the invention of robots. Technological progress is always grossly exaggerated, but even subtracting the exaggeration, the development of computers has been quite remarkable, and we can reasonably expect that even more remarkable progress will be made in the future. No doubt we will be much better able to simulate human behaviour on computers than we can at present, and certainly much better than we have been able to in the past. The point I am making is that if we are talking about having mental states, having a mind, all of these simulations are simply irrelevant. It doesn't matter how good the technology is, or how rapid the calculations made by the computer are. If it really is a computer, its operations have to be defined syntactically, whereas consciousness, thoughts, feelings, emotions, and all the rest of it involve more than a syntax. Those features, by definition, the computer is unable to *duplicate* however powerful may be its ability to *simulate*. The key distinction here is between duplication and simulation. And no simulation by itself ever constitutes duplication.

What I have done so far is give a basis to the sense that those citations I began this talk with are really as preposterous as they seem. There is a puzzling question in this discussion though, and that is: 'Why would anybody ever have thought that computers could think or have feelings and emotions and all the rest of it?' After all, we can do computer simulations of any process whatever that can be given a formal description. So, we can do a computer simulation of the flow of

money in the British economy, or the pattern of power distribution in the Labour Party. We can do computer simulation of rain storms in the home counties, or warehouse fires in East London. Now, in each of these cases, nobody supposes that the computer simulation is actually the real thing; no one supposes that a computer simulation of a storm will leave us all wet, or a computer simulation of a fire is likely to burn the house down. Why on earth would anyone in his right mind suppose a computer simulation of mental processes actually had mental processes? I don't really know the answer to that, since the idea seems to me, to put it frankly, quite crazy from the start. But I can make a couple of speculations.

First of all, where the mind is concerned, a lot of people are still tempted to some sort of behaviourism. They think if a system behaves as if it understood Chinese, then it really must understand Chinese. But we have already refuted this form of behaviourism with the Chinese room argument. Another assumption made by many people is that the mind is not a part of the biological world, it is not a part of the world of nature. The strong artificial intelligence view relies on that in its conception that the mind is purely formal; that somehow or other, it cannot be treated as a concrete product of biological processes like any other biological product. There is in these discussions, in short, a kind of residual dualism. AI partisans believe that the mind is more than a part of the natural biological world; they believe that the mind is purely formally specifiable. The paradox of this is that the AI literature is filled with fulminations against some view called 'dualism', but in fact, the whole thesis of strong AI rests on a kind of dualism. It rests on a rejection of the idea that the mind is just a natural biological phenomenon in the world like any other.

I want to conclude this chapter by putting together the thesis of my last chapter and the thesis of this one. Both of these theses can be stated very simply. And indeed, I am going to state them with perhaps excessive crudeness. But if we put them together I think we get a quite powerful conception of the relations of minds, brains and computers. And the argument has a very simple logical structure, so you can see whether it is valid or invalid. The first premise is:

(1) *Brains cause minds.*

Now, of course, that is really too crude. What we mean by that is that mental processes that we consider to constitute a mind are caused, entirely caused, by processes going on inside the brain. But let's be crude, let's just abbreviate that as three words – brains cause minds. And that is just a fact about how the world works. Now let's write proposition number two:

(2) *Syntax is not sufficient for semantics.*

That proposition is a conceptual truth. It just articulates our distinction between the notion of what is purely formal and what has content. Now, to these two propositions – that brains cause minds and that syntax is not sufficient for semantics – let's add a third and a fourth:

(3) *Computer programs are entirely defined by their formal, or syntactical, structure.*

That proposition, I take it, is true by definition; it is part of what we mean by the notion of a computer program.

(4) *Minds have mental contents; specifically, they have semantic contents.*

And that, I take it, is just an obvious fact about how our minds work. My thoughts, and beliefs, and desires are about something, or they refer to something, or they concern states of affairs in the world; and they do that because their content directs them at these states of affairs in the world. Now, from these four premises, we can draw our first conclusion; and it follows obviously from premises 2, 3 and 4:

Conclusion 1. *No computer program by itself is sufficient to give a system a mind. Programs, in short, are not minds, and they are not by themselves sufficient for having minds.*

Now, that is a very powerful conclusion, because it means that the project of trying to create minds solely by designing programs is doomed from the start. And it is important to re-emphasise that this has nothing to do with any particular state of technology or any particular state of the complexity of the program. This is a purely formal, or logical, result from a set of axioms which are agreed to by all (or nearly all) of the disputants concerned. That is, even most of the hardcore enthusiasts for artificial intelligence agree that in fact, as a matter of biology, brain processes cause mental states, and they agree that programs are defined purely formally. But if you put these conclusions together with certain other things that we know, then it follows immediately that the project of strong AI is incapable of fulfilment.

However, once we have got these axioms, let's see what else we can derive. Here is a second conclusion:

Conclusion 2. *The way that brain functions cause minds cannot be solely in virtue of running a computer program.*

And this second conclusion follows from conjoining the first premise together with our first conclusion. That is, from the fact that brains cause minds and that programs are not enough to do the job, it follows that the way that brains cause minds can't be solely by running a computer program. Now that also I think is an important result, because it has the consequence that the brain is not, or at least is not just, a digital computer. We saw earlier that anything can trivially be described as if it were a digital computer, and brains are no exception. But the importance of this conclusion is that the computational properties of the brain are simply not enough to explain its functioning to produce mental states. And indeed, that ought to seem a commonsense scientific conclusion to us anyway because all it does is remind us of the fact that brains are biological engines; their biology matters. It is not, as several people in artificial intelligence have claimed, just an irrelevant fact about the mind that it happens to be realised in human brains.

Now, from our first premise, we can also derive a third conclusion:

Conclusion 3. *Anything else that caused minds would have to have causal powers at least equivalent to those of the brain.*

And this third conclusion is a trivial consequence of our first premise. It is a bit like saying that if my petrol engine drives my car at seventy-five miles an hour, then any diesel engine that was capable of doing that would have to have a power output at least equivalent to that of my petrol engine. Of course, some other system might cause mental processes using entirely different chemical or biochemical features from those the brain in fact uses. It might turn out that there are beings on other planets, or in other solar systems, that have mental states and use an entirely different biochemistry from ours. Suppose that Martians arrived on earth and we concluded that they had mental states. But suppose that when their heads were opened up, it was discovered that all they had inside was green slime. Well still, the green slime, if it functioned to produce consciousness and all the rest of their mental life, would have to have causal powers equal to those of the human brain. But now, from our first conclusion, that programs are not enough, and our third conclusion, that any other system would have to have causal powers equal to the brain, conclusion four follows immediately:

Conclusion 4. *For any artefact that we might build which had mental states equivalent to human mental states, the implementation of a computer program would not by itself be sufficient. Rather the artefact would have to have powers equivalent to the powers of the human brain.*

The upshot of this discussion I believe is to remind us of something that we have known all along: namely, mental states are biological phenomena. Consciousness, intentionality, subjectivity and mental causation are all a part of our biological life history, along with growth, reproduction, the secretion of bile, and digestion.

Further reading in philosophy of mind

Block, Ned (ed.) *Readings in the Philosophy of Psychology*, 2 vols. Cambridge, MA: Harvard University Press, 1980.

Chalmers, David, *The Conscious Mind*, New York: Oxford University Press, 1996.

Dennett, Daniel, *The Intentional Stance*, Cambridge, MA: MIT Press, 1987.

Dretske, Fred, *Knowledge and the Flow of Information*, Cambridge, MA: MIT Press, 1981.

Fodor, Jerry, *The Language of Thought*, Cambridge, MA: Harvard University Press, 1979.

—— *Psychosemantics*, Cambridge, MA: MIT Press, 1987.

Kim, Jaegwon, *Supervenience and Mind*, Cambridge: Cambridge University Press, 1993.

Kripke, Saul, *Wittgenstein on Rules and Private Language*, Cambridge, MA: Harvard University Press, 1982.

Millikan, Ruth Garrett, *Language, Thought, and Other Biological Categories*, Cambridge, MA: MIT Press, 1984.

Ryle, Gilbert, *The Concept of Mind*, New York: Barnes & Noble, 1949.

Searle, John, *Intentionality*, Cambridge: Cambridge University Press, 1983.

—— *Minds, Brains, and Science*, Cambridge, MA: Harvard University Press, 1984.

PART V

Freedom and Personal Identity

28

The Conceivability of Mechanism

Norman Malcolm

1.   By "mechanism" I am going to understand
a special application of physical determinism –
namely, to all organisms with neurological systems,
including human beings. The version of mechanism I wish to study assumes a neurophysiological
theory which is adequate to explain and predict all
movements of human bodies except those caused
by outside forces. The human body is assumed
to be as complete a causal system as is a gasoline
engine. Neurological states and processes are conceived to be correlated by general laws with the
mechanisms that produce movements. Chemical
and electrical changes in the nervous tissue of
the body are assumed to cause muscle contractions, which in turn cause movements such as
blinking, breathing, and puckering of the lips,
as well as movements of fingers, limbs, and head.
Such movements are sometimes produced by
forces (pushes and pulls) applied externally to
the body. If someone forced my arm up over my
head, the theory could not explain that movement of my arm. But it could explain any movement not due to an external push or pull. It
could explain, and predict, the movements that
occur when a person signals a taxi, plays chess,
writes an essay, or walks to the store.[1]

It is assumed that the neurophysiological system
of the human body is subject to various kinds of
stimulation. Changes of temperature or pressure
in the environment; sounds, odors; the ingestion

of foods and liquids: all these will have an effect
on the nerve pulses that turn on the movement-
producing mechanisms of the body.

2.   The neurophysiological theory we are envis-
aging would, as said, be rich enough to provide
systematic causal explanations of all bodily movements not due to external physical causes. These
explanations should be understood as stating
sufficient conditions of movement and not merely
necessary conditions. They would employ laws
that connect neurophysiological states or processes
with movements. The laws would be universal
propositions of the following form: whenever an
organism of structure S is in state q it will emit
movement m. Having ascertained that a given
organism is of structure S and is in state q, one
could deduce the occurrence of movement m.

It should be emphasized that this theory
makes no provision for desires, aims, goals, purposes, motives, or intentions. In explaining such
an occurrence as a man's walking across a room,
it will be a matter of indifference to the theory
whether the man's purpose, intention, or desire
was to open a window, or even whether his walking across the room was intentional. This aspect
of the theory can be indicated by saying that it
is a "nonpurposive" system of explanation.

The viewpoint of mechanism thus assumes a
theory that would provide systematic, complete,
nonpurposive, causal explanations of all human
movements not produced by external forces. Such
a theory does not at present exist. But nowadays
it is ever more widely held that in the not far

distant future there will be such a theory – and that it will be true. I will raise the question of whether this is conceivable. The subject belongs to an age-old controversy. It would be unrealistic for me to hope to make any noteworthy contribution to its solution. But the problem itself is one of great human interest and worthy of repeated study.

3. To appreciate the significance of mechanism, one must be aware of the extent to which a comprehensive neurophysiological theory of human behavior would diverge from those everyday explanations of behavior with which all of us are familiar. These explanations refer to purposes, desires, goals, intentions. "He is running to catch the bus." "He is climbing the ladder in order to inspect the roof." "He is stopping at this store because he wants some cigars." Our daily discourse is filled with explanations of behavior in terms of the agent's purposes or intentions. The behavior is claimed to occur in order that some state of affairs should be brought about or avoided – that the bus should be caught, the roof inspected, cigars purchased. Let us say that these are "purposive" explanations.

We can note several differences between these common purposive explanations and the imagined neurophysiological explanations. First, the latter were conceived by us to be systematic – that is, to belong to a comprehensive theory – whereas the familiar purposive explanations are not organized into a theory. Second, the neurophysiological explanations do not employ the concept of purpose or intention. Third, the neurophysiological explanations embody contingent laws, but purposive explanations do not.

Let us dwell on this third point. A neurophysiological explanation of some behavior that has occurred is assumed to have the following form:

Whenever an organism of structure S is in neurophysiological state q it will emit movement m.
Organism O of structure S was in neurophysiological state q.
Therefore, O emitted m.[2]

The general form of purposive explanation is the following:

Whenever an organism O has goal G and believes that behavior B is required to bring about G, O will emit B.

O had G and believed B was required of G. Therefore, O emitted B.

Let us compare the first premise of a neurophysiological explanation with the first premise of a purposive explanation. The first premise of a neurophysiological explanation is a contingent proposition, but the first premise of a purposive explanation is not a contingent proposition. This difference will appear more clearly if we consider how, in both cases, the first premise would have to be qualified in order to be actually true. In both cases a *ceteris paribus* clause must be added to the first premise, or at least be implicitly understood. (It will be more perspicuous to translate "*ceteris paribus*" as "provided there are no countervailing factors" rather than as "other things being equal.")

Let us consider what "*ceteris paribus*" will mean in concrete terms. Suppose a man climbed a ladder leading to a roof. An explanation is desired. The fact is that the wind blew his hat onto the roof and he wants it back. The explanation would be spelled out in detail as follows:

If a man wants to retrieve his hat and believes this requires him to climb a ladder, he will do so provided there are no countervailing factors.
This man wanted to retrieve his hat and believed that this required him to climb a ladder, and there were no countervailing factors.
Therefore, he climbed a ladder.

What sorts of things might be included under "countervailing factors" in such a case? The unavailability of a ladder, the fear of climbing one, the belief that someone would remove the ladder while he was on the roof, and so on. (The man's failure to climb a ladder would *not* be a countervailing factor.)

An important point emerging here is that the addition of the *ceteris paribus* clause to the first premise turns this premise into an a priori proposition. If there were no countervailing factors whatever (if the man knew a ladder was available, had no fear of ladders or high places, no belief that he might be marooned on the roof, and so on); if there were no hindrances or hazards, real or imagined, physical or psychological; then if the man did not climb a ladder it would not be true that he *wanted* his hat back, or *intended* to get it back.[3]

In his important recent book, *The Explanation of Behaviour*, Charles Taylor puts the point as follows:

> This is part of what we mean by "intending X," that, in the absence of interfering factors, it is followed by doing X. I could not be said to intend X if, even with no obstacles or other countervailing factors, I still didn't do it.[4]

This feature of the meaning of "intend" also holds true of "want," "purpose," and "goal."

Thus the universal premise of a purposive explanation is an a priori principle, not a contingent law. Some philosophers have made this a basis for saying that a purposive explanation is not a causal explanation.[5] But this is a stipulation (perhaps a useful one), rather than a description of how the word "cause" is actually used in ordinary language.

Let us consider the effect of adding a *ceteris paribus* clause to the universal premise of a neural explanation of behavior. Would a premise of this form be true a priori? Certainly not. Suppose it were believed that whenever a human being is in neural state q his right hand will move up above his head, provided there are no countervailing factors. What could be countervailing factors? That the subject's right arm is broken or that it is tied to his side, and so on. But the exclusion of such countervailing factors would have no tendency to make the premise true a priori. There is no connection of meaning, explicit or implicit, between the description of any neural state and the description of any movement of the hand. No matter how many countervailing factors are excluded, the proposition will not lose the character of a contingent law (unless, of course, we count the failure of the hand to move as itself a countervailing factor, in which case the premise becomes a tautology).

4. Making explicit the *ceteris paribus* conditions points up the different logical natures of the universal premises of the two kinds of explanation. Premises of the one sort express contingent correlations between neurological processes and behavior. Premises of the other sort express a priori connections between intentions (purposes, desires, goals) and behavior.

This difference is of the utmost importance. Some students of behavior have believed that purposive explanations of behavior will be found to be less basic than the explanations that will arise from a future neurophysiological theory. They think that the principles of purposive explanation will turn out to be dependent on the neurophysiological laws. On this view our ordinary explanations of behavior will often be true: but the neural explanations will also be true – and they will be *more fundamental*. Thus we could, theoretically, *by-pass* explanations of behavior in terms of purpose, and the day might come when they simply fall into disuse.

I wish to show that neurophysiological laws could not be more basic than purposive principles. I shall understand the statement that a law L_2 is "more basic" than a law L_1 to mean that L_1 is dependent on L_2 but L_2 is not dependent on L_1. To give an example, let us suppose there is a uniform connection between food abstinence and hunger: that is, going without food for n hours always results in hunger. This is L_1. Another law L_2 is discovered – namely, a uniform connection between a certain chemical condition of body tissue (called "cell-starvation") and hunger. Whenever cell-starvation occurs, hunger results. It is also discovered that L_2 is more basic than L_1. This would amount to the following fact: food abstinence for n hours will not result in hunger *unless* cell-starvation occurs; and if the latter occurs, hunger will result *regardless of whether* food abstinence occurs. Thus the L_1 regularity is contingently dependent on the L_2 regularity, and the converse is not true. Our knowledge of this dependency would reveal to us the conditions under which the L_1 regularity would no longer hold.

Our comparison of the differing logical natures of purposive principles and neurophysiological laws enables us to see that the former cannot be dependent on the latter. The a priori connection between intention or purpose and behavior cannot fail to hold. It cannot be contingently dependent on any contingent regularity. The neurophysiological explanations of behavior could not, in the sense explained, turn out to be more basic than our everyday purposive explanations.[6]

5. There is a second important consequence of the logical difference between neurophysiological laws and purposive principles. Someone might suppose that although purposive explanations cannot be dependent on nonpurposive explanations, they would be refuted by the verification

of a comprehensive neurophysiological theory of behavior. I think this view is correct: but it is necessary to understand what it *cannot* mean. It cannot mean that the principles (the universal premises) of purposive explanations would be proved false. They cannot be proved false. It could not fail to be true that if a person wanted X and believed Y was necessary for X, and there were absolutely no countervailing factors, he would do Y.[7] This purposive principle is true a priori, not because of its form but because of its meaning – that is, because of the connection of meaning between the words "He wanted X and he realized that Y was necessary for X" and the words "He did Y." The purposive principle is not a law of nature but a conceptual truth. It cannot be confirmed or refuted by experience. Since the verification of a neurophysiological theory could never *disprove* any purposive principles, the only possible outcome of such verification, logically speaking, would be to prove that the purposive principles have no application to the world. I shall return to this point later.

6. We must come to closer grips with the exact logical relationship between neural and purposive explanations of behavior. Can explanations of both types be true of the same bit of behavior on one and the same occasion? Is there any rivalry between them? Some philosophers would say not. They would say that, for one thing, the two kinds of explanation explain different things. Purposive explanations explain actions. Neurophysiological explanations explain movements. Both explain behavior: but we can say this only because we use the latter word ambiguously to cover both actions and movements. For a second point, it may be held that the two kinds of explanation belong to different "bodies of discourse" or to different "language games." They employ different concepts and assumptions. One kind of explanation relates behavior to causal laws and to concepts of biochemistry and physiology, to nerve pulses and chemical reactions. The other kind of explanation relates behavior to the desires, intentions, goals, and reasons of persons. The two forms of explanation can co-exist, because they are irrelevant to one another.[8]

It is true that the two kinds of explanation employ different concepts and, in a sense, explain different things: but are they really independent of one another? Take the example of the man climbing a ladder in order to retrieve his hat from the roof. This explanation relates his climbing to his intention. A neurophysiological explanation of his climbing would say nothing about his intention but would connect his movements on the ladder with chemical changes in body tissue or with the firing of neurons. Do the two accounts interfere with one another?

7. I believe there *would* be a collision between the two accounts if they were offered as explanations of one and the same occurrence of a man's climbing a ladder. We will recall that the envisaged neurophysiological theory was supposed to provide *sufficient* causal explanations of behavior. Thus the movements of the man on the ladder would be *completely* accounted for in terms of electrical, chemical, and mechanical processes in his body. This would surely imply that his desire or intention to retrieve his hat had nothing to do with his movement up the ladder. It would imply that on this same occasion he would have moved up the ladder in exactly this way even if he had had no intention to retrieve his hat, or even no intention to climb the ladder. To mention his intention or purpose would be no explanation, nor even part of an explanation, of his movements on the ladder. Given the antecedent neurological states of his bodily system together with general laws correlating those states with the contractions of muscles and movements of limbs, he would have moved as he did regardless of his desire or intention. If every movement of his was completely accounted for by his antecedent neurophysiological states (his "programming"), then it was not true that those movements occurred *because* he wanted or intended to get his hat.

8. I will briefly consider three possible objections to my claim that if mechanism were true the man would have moved up the ladder as he did even if he had not had any intention to climb the ladder. The first objection comes from a philosopher who espouses the currently popular psychophysical identity thesis. He holds that there is a neural condition that causes the man's movements up the ladder, and he further holds that the man's intention to climb the ladder (or, possibly, his having the intention) is contingently identical with the neural condition that causes the movements. Thus, if the man had not intended to climb the ladder, the cause of his movements would not have existed, and so those movements

would not have occurred. My reply would be that the view that there may be a contingent identity (and not merely an extensional equivalence) between an intention (or the having of the intention) and a neural condition is not a meaningful hypothesis. One version of the identity thesis is that A's intention to climb the ladder is contingently identical with some process in A's brain. Verifying this identity would require the meaningless step of trying to discover whether A's intention is located in his brain. One could give meaning to the notion of the location of A's intention in his brain by stipulating that it has the same location as does the correlated neural process. But the identity that arose from this stipulation would not be contingent.[9] Another version of the identity thesis is that the event of Smith's having the intention I is identical with the event of Smith's being in neural condition N. This version avoids the above "location problem"; but it must take on the task (which seems hopeless) of explaining how the property "having intention I" and the property "being in neural condition N" could be contingently identical and not merely co-extensive.[10]

The second objection comes from an epiphenomenalist. He holds that the neurophysiological condition that contingently causes the behavior on the ladder also contingently causes the intention to climb the ladder, but that the intention stands in no causal relation to the behavior. If the intention had not existed, the cause of it and of the behavior would not have existed, and so the behavior would not have occurred. A decisive objection to epiphenomenalism is that, according to it, the relation between intention and behavior would be purely contingent. It would be conceivable that the neurophysiological condition that always causes ladder-climbing movements should also always cause the intention to not climb up a ladder. Epiphenomenalism would permit it to be universally true that whenever any person intended to not do any action, he did it, and that whenever any person intended to do any action, he did not do it. This is a conceptual absurdity.

The third objection springs from a philosopher who combines mechanism with logical behaviorism. He holds that some condition of the neurophysiological system causes the preparatory movements, gestures, and utterances that are expressions of the man's intention to climb the ladder; and it also causes his movements up the

ladder. The component of logical behaviorism in his overall view is this: he holds that the man's having the intention to climb the ladder is simply a logical construction out of the occurrence of the expressions of intention and also the occurrence of the ladder-climbing movements. Having the intention is nothing other than the expressive behavior plus the subsequent climbing behavior. Having the intention is defined in terms of behavior-events that are contingently caused by a neurophysiological condition. The supposition that the man did not have the intention to climb the ladder would be identical with the supposition that either the expressive behavior or the climbing behavior, or both, did not occur. If either one did not occur, then neither occurred, since by hypothesis both of them have the same cause. Thus it would be false that the man would have moved up the ladder as he did even if he had not had an intention to climb the ladder.

I think that this third position gives an unsatisfactory account of the nature of intention. Actually climbing the ladder is not a necessary condition *simpliciter* for the existence of the intention to climb the ladder. It is a necessary condition *provided* there are no countervailing factors. But there is no definite number of countervailing factors, and so they cannot be exhaustively enumerated. In addition, some of them will themselves involve the concepts of desire, belief, or purpose. For example: a man intends to climb the ladder, but also he does not want to look ridiculous; as he is just about to start climbing he is struck by the thought that he will look ridiculous; so he does not climb the ladder, although he had intended to. An adequate logical behaviorism would have to analyze away not only the initial reference to intention, but also the reference to desire, belief, purpose, and all other psychological concepts, that would occur in the listing of possible countervailing factors. There is no reason for thinking that such a program of analysis could be carried out.

Thus a mechanist can hope to avoid the consequence that the man would have moved up the ladder as he did even if he had not had the intention of climbing the ladder, by combining his mechanist doctrine with the psychophysical identity thesis, or with epiphenomenalism, or with logical behaviorism. But these supplementary positions are so objectionable or implausible that the mechanist is not really saved from the above consequence.

9. Let us remember that the postulated neurophysiological theory is comprehensive. It is assumed to provide complete causal explanations for all bodily movements that are not produced by external physical forces. It is a closed system in the sense that it does not admit, as antecedent conditions, anything other than neurophysiological states and processes. Desires and intentions have no place in it.

If the neurophysiological theory were true, then in no cases would desires, intentions, purposes be necessary conditions of any human movements. It would never be true that a man would *not* have moved as he did if he had *not* had such and such an intention. Nor would it ever be true that a certain movement of his was due to, or brought about by, or caused by his having a certain intention or purpose. Purposive explanations of human bodily movements would *never* be true. Desires and intentions would not be even potential causes of human movements in the actual world (as contrasted with some possible world in which the neurophysiological theory did not hold true).

It might be thought that there could be two different systems of causal explanations of human movements, a purposive system and a neurophysiological system. The antecedent conditions in the one system would be the desires and intentions of human beings; in the other they would be the neurophysiological states and processes of those same human beings. Each system would provide adequate causal explanations of the same movements.

Generally speaking, it is possible for there to be a plurality of simultaneous sufficient causal conditions of an event. But if we bear in mind the comprehensive aspect of the neurophysiological theory – that is, the fact that it provides sufficient causal conditions for all movements – we shall see that desires and intentions could not be causes of movements. It has often been noted that to say *B causes C* does not mean merely that whenever *B* occurs, *C* occurs. Causation also has subjunctive and counterfactual implications: if *B* *were to* occur, *C* *would* occur; and if *B* had *not* occurred, *C* would *not* have occurred. But the neurophysiological theory would provide sufficient causal conditions for every human movement, and so there would be no cases at all in which a certain movement would not have occurred if the person had not had this desire or intention. Since the counterfactual would be false in all cases, desires and intentions would not be causes

of human movements. They would not ever be sufficient causal conditions nor would they ever be necessary causal conditions.

10. Let us tackle this immensely important point from a different angle. Many descriptions of behavior ascribe actions to persons: they say that someone *did* something – for example, "He signed the check," "You lifted the table," "She broke the vase." Two things are implied by an ascription of an "action" to a person:[11] first, that a certain state of affairs came into existence (his signature's being present on the check, the table's being lifted, the vase's being broken); second, that the person intended that this state of affairs should occur. If subsequently we learn that not both conditions were satisfied, either we qualify the ascription of action or reject it entirely. If the mentioned state of affairs did not come into existence (for example, the vase was not broken), then the ascription of action ("She broke the vase") must be withdrawn. If it did come into existence but without the person's intention, then the ascription of action to the person must be diminished by some such qualification as "unintentionally" or "accidentally" or "by mistake" or "inadvertently," it being a matter of the circumstances which qualification is more appropriate. A qualified ascription of action still implies that the person played some part in bringing about the state of affairs – for example, her hand struck the vase. If she played no part at all, then it cannot rightly be said, even with qualification, that she broke the vase.

Suppose a man intends to open the door in front of him. He turns the knob and the door opens. Since turning the knob is what normally causes the door to open, we should think it right to say that *he* opened the door. Then we learn that there is an electric mechanism concealed in the door which caused the door to open at the moment he turned the knob, and furthermore that there is no causal connection between the turning of the knob and the operation of the mechanism. So his act of turning the knob had nothing to do with the opening of the door. We can no longer say that *he* opened the door: nothing he did had any causal influence on that result. We might put the matter in this way: because of the operation of the electric mechanism he had no opportunity to open the door.

The man of our example could say that at least he turned the knob. He would have to surrender this claim, however, if it came to light that still another electrical mechanism caused the knob to turn when it did, independently of the motion of his hand. The man could assert that, in any case, he moved his hand. But now the neurophysiological theory enters the scene, providing a complete causal explanation of the motion of his hand, without regard to his intention.

The problem of what to say becomes acute. Should we deny that he moved his hand? Should we admit that he moved his hand, but with some qualification? Or should we say, without qualification, that he moved his hand?

11. There is an important similarity between our three examples and an important difference. The similarity is that in all three cases a mechanism produced the intended states of affairs, and nothing the agent did had any influence on the operation of the mechanism. But there is a difference between the cases. In each of the first two, we can specify something the man did (an action) which would normally cause the intended result to occur, but which did not have that effect on this occasion. The action in the first case was turning the knob, and in the second it was gripping the knob and making a turning motion of the hand. In each of these cases there was an action, the causal efficacy of which was nullified by the operation of a mechanism. Consequently, we can rightly say that the man's action *failed* to make a contribution to the intended occurrence, and so we can deny that *he* opened the door or turned the knob.

In the third case is there something the man did which normally causes that movement of the hand? What was it? When I move my hand in the normal way is there something else *I do* that causes my hand to move? No. Various events take place in my body (for example, nerve pulses) but they cannot be said to be *actions* of mine. They are not things I do.

But in this third case the man *intended* to make a turning motion of his hand. Is this a basis for a similarity between the third case and the first two? Can we say that one's intention to move one's hand is normally a cause of the motion of one's hand, but that in our third case the causal efficacy of the intention was nullified by the operation of the neurophysiological mechanism?

On the question of whether intentions are causes of actions, Taylor says something that is both interesting and puzzling. He declares that

to call something an action, in an unqualified sense "means not just that the man who displayed this behaviour had framed the relevant intention or had this purpose, but also that *his intending it brought it about*."[12] Now to say that *A* "brings about" *B* is to use the language of causation. "Brings about" is indeed a synonym for "causes."

12. Is there any sense at all in which a man's intention to do something can be a cause of his doing it? In dealing with this point I shall use the word "cause" in its widest sense, according to which anything that explains, or partly explains, the occurrence of some behavior is the cause, or part of the cause, of the behavior. To learn that a man intended to climb a ladder would not, in many cases, explain why he climbed it. It would not explain what he climbed it for, what his reason or purpose was in climbing it, whereas to say what his purpose was would, in our broad sense, give the cause or part of the cause of his climbing it.

In considering intention as a cause of behavior *X*, it is important to distinguish between the intention to do *X* (let us call this *simple intention*) and in the intention to do something else *Y* in or by doing *X* (let us call this *further intention*). To say that a man intended to climb a ladder would not usually give a cause of his climbing it; but stating his purpose in climbing it would usually be giving the (or a) cause of the action. It is a natural use of language to ask, "What caused you to climb the ladder?"; and it is an appropriate answer to say, "I wanted to get my hat." (*Question*: "Good heavens, what caused you to vote a straight Republican ticket?" *Answer*: "I wanted to restore the two-party system.") Our use of the language of causation is not restricted to the cases in which cause and effect are assumed to be contingently related.

13. Can the simple intention to do *X* ever be a cause of the doing of *X*? Can it ever be said that a person's intention to climb a ladder caused him to climb it, or brought about his action of climbing it? It is certainly true that whether a man does or does not intend to do *X* will make a difference in whether he will do *X*. This fact comes out strongly if we are concerned to predict whether he will do *X*; obviously, it would be important to find out whether he intends to do it. Does not this imply that his intention has "an effect on his behavior"?[13]

Commonly, we think of dispositions as causes of behavior. If with the same provocation one man loses his temper and another does not, this difference in their reactions might be explained by the fact that the one man, but not the other, is of an irritable disposition. If dispositions are causes, we can hardly deny the same role to intentions. Both are useful in predicting behavior. If I am trying to estimate the likelihood that this man is going to do so-and-so, the information that he has a disposition to do it in circumstances like these will be an affirmative consideration. I am entitled to give equal or possibly greater weight to the information that he intends to do it.

Not only do simple intentions have weight in predicting actions, but also they figure in the explanation of actions that have already occurred. If a man who has just been released from prison promptly climbs a flagpole, I may want an explanation of that occurrence. If I learn that he had previously made up his mind to do it, but had been prevented by his imprisonment, I have received a partial explanation of why he is climbing the flagpole, even if I do not yet know his further intention, if any, in climbing it. In general, if I am surprised at an action, it will help me to understand its occurrence if I find out that the agent had previously decided to do it but was prevented by an obstacle which has just been removed.

14.   The simple intentions so far considered were formed in advance of the corresponding action. But many simple intentions are not formed in advance of the corresponding action. Driving a car, one suddenly (and intentionally) presses the brake pedal: but there was no time before this action occurred when one intended to do it. The intention existed only at the time of the action, or only *in* the action. Let us call this a merely concurrent simple intention. Can an intention of this kind be a causal factor in the corresponding action?

Here we have to remember that if the driver did not press the brake intentionally, his pressing of the brake was not unqualified action. The presence of simple intention in the action (that is, its being intentional) is an analytically necessary condition for its being unqualified action. This condition is not a cause but a defining condition of unqualified action. If this condition were not fulfilled, one would have to use some mitigating

phrase – for example, that the driver pressed the brake by mistake. Thus, a simple intention that is merely concurrent cannot be a cause of the corresponding action.

15.   Can we not avoid committing ourselves to the assumption that the pressing of the driver's foot on the brake was either intentional or not intentional? Can we not think of it, in a neutral way, as merely behavior? Yes, we can. But it *was* either intentional or not intentional. If the latter, then there was no simple intention to figure as a cause of the behavior. If the former, then the behavior was action, and the driver's merely concurrent simple intention was a defining condition and not a cause of the behavior. The "neutral way" of thinking about the behavior would be merely incomplete. It would be owing to ignorance and not to the existence of a third alternative. It is impossible, by the definition of "action," that the behavior of pressing the brake should be an action and yet not be intentional. Thus it is impossible that a merely concurrent simple intention should have caused the behavior of pressing the brake, whether the behavior was or was not action.

To summarize this discussion of intentions as causes: we need to distinguish between simple intentions and further intentions. If an agent does X with the further intention Y, then it is proper to speak of this further intention as the (or a) cause of the doing of X. Simple intentions may be divided into those that are formed prior to the corresponding actions, and those that are merely concurrent with the actions. By virtue of being previously formed, a simple intention can be a cause of action. But in so far as it is merely concurrent, a simple intention cannot be a cause of the corresponding action.

16.   Let us try now to appraise Taylor's view as to the causal role of intention in behavior. He holds that it would not be true, without qualification, that one person stabbed another unless his intention to stab him "brought about" the stabbing (*Explanation of Behaviour*, p. 33). The example was meant to be of a previously formed intention – for Taylor speaks of the agent's *deciding* to stab someone. But a majority of actions do not embody intentions formed in advance. They embody merely concurrent intentions. The latter cannot be said to cause (bring about) the corresponding actions. Possibly because he has fixed

his attention too narrowly on cases of decision, Taylor errs in holding that, in general, the concept of action requires that the agent's intention should have brought about the behavior. When the action is merely intentional (without previous intention) the agent's intention cannot be said to bring about his behavior. In such cases his intention gives his behavior the character of *action*, but it does this by virtue of being a defining condition of action, not by virtue of being a cause of either behavior or action.

17. Our reflections on the relationship of intention to behavior arose from a consideration of three examples of supposed action – opening a door, turning a knob, making a turning motion of the hand. In the first two cases we imagined mechanisms that produced the intended results independently of the agent's intervention. Consequently, we had to deny that *he* opened the door or turned the knob. Then we imagined a neurophysiological cause of the motion of his hand, and we asked whether this would imply, in turn, that *he* did not move his hand.

Is the movement of his hand independent of his "intervention" by virtue of being independent of his intention? We saw previously (section 8) that a comprehensive neurophysiological theory would leave no room for desires and intentions as causal factors. Consequently, neither the man's previously formed simple intention to move his hand nor his further intention (to open the door) could be causes of the movement of his hand.

18. We noticed before that it is true a priori that if a man wants Y, or has Y as a goal, and believes that X is required for Y, then in the absence of countervailing factors he will do X. It is also true a priori that if a man forms the intention (for example, decides) to do X, then in the absence of countervailing factors he will do X. These a priori principles of action are assumed in our everyday explanations of behavior.

We saw that mechanistic explanations could not be more basic than are explanations in terms of intentions or purposes.

We saw that the verification of mechanistic laws could not disprove the a priori principles of action.

Yet a mechanistic explanation of behavior rules out any explanation of it in terms of the agent's intentions. If a comprehensive neurophysiological theory is true, then people's intentions never are causal factors in behavior.

19. Thus if mechanism is true, the a priori principles of action do not apply to the world. This would have to mean one or the other of two alternatives. The first would be that people do not have intentions, purposes, or desires, or that they do not have beliefs as to what behavior is required for the fulfillment of their desires and purposes. The second alternative would be that although they have intentions, beliefs, and so forth, there always are countervailing factors – that is, factors that interfere with the operation of intentions, desires, and decisions.

The second alternative cannot be taken seriously. If a man wants to be on the opposite bank of a river and believes that swimming it is the only thing that will get him there, he will swim it unless there are countervailing factors, such as an inability to swim or a fear of drowning or a strong dislike of getting wet. In this sense it is not true that countervailing factors are present *whenever* someone has a goal. There are not *always* obstacles to the fulfillment of any purpose or desire.

It might be objected that mechanistic causation itself is a universal countervailing factor. Now if this were so it would imply that purposes, intentions, and desires never have any effect on behavior. But it is not a coherent position to hold that some creatures have purposes and so forth, yet that these have no effect on their behavior. Purposes and intentions are, in concept, so closely tied to behavioral effects that the total absence of behavioral effects would mean the total absence of purposes and intentions. Thus the only position open to the exponent of mechanism is the first alternative – namely, that people do not have intentions, purposes, or beliefs.

What I have called "a principle of action" is a conditional proposition, having an antecedent and a consequent. The whole conditional is true a priori, and therefore if the antecedent holds in a particular case, the consequent must also hold in that case. To say that the antecedent holds in a particular case means that it is true of some person (or animal). It means that the person has some desire or intention, and also has the requisite belief. If this were so, and if there were no countervailing factors, it would follow that the person would act in an appropriate manner. His intention or desire would, in our broad sense, be a cause of his action – that is, it would be a factor in the explanation of the occurrence of the action.

But this is incompatible with mechanism. A mechanist must hold, therefore, that the principles of action have no application to reality, in the sense that no one has intentions or desires or beliefs.

Some philosophers would regard this result as an adequate refutation of mechanism. But others would not. They would say that the confirmation of a comprehensive neurophysiological theory of behavior is a logical possibility, and therefore it is logically possible that there are no desires, intentions, and so forth, and that to deny these logical possibilities is to be dogmatic and antiscientific. I will avoid adopting this "dogmatic" and "antiscientific" position, and will formulate a criticism of mechanism from a more "internal" point of view.

20. I wish to make a closer approach to the question of the conceivability of mechanism. We have seen that mechanism is incompatible with purposive behavior, but we have not yet established that it is incompatible with the existence of merely intentional behavior. A man can do something intentionally but with no further intention: his behavior is intentional but not purposive. One possibility is that this behavior should embody a merely concurrent simple intention. Since such intentions are not causes of the behavior to which they belong, their existence does not appear to conflict with mechanistic causation. Mechanism's incompatibility with purposive behavior has not yet shown it to be incompatible with intentional behavior as such.

But could it be true that sometimes people acted intentionally although it was never true that they acted for any purpose? Could they do things intentionally but never with any further intention?

If some intentional actions are purposeless, it does not follow that all of them could be purposeless. And I do not think this is really a possibility. I will not attempt to deal with every kind of action. But consider that subclass of actions that are activities. Any physical activity is analyzable into components. If a man is painting a wall, he is grasping a brush, dipping the brush into the paint, moving his arm back and forth. He does these things in painting. They are parts of his activity of painting. If someone is rocking in a chair, he is pushing against the floor with his feet, and pressing his back against the back of the chair. These are subordinate activities in the activity of rocking. If the one who is painting is asked why he is dipping the brush into the paint, he can answer, "I am painting this wall." This is an explanation of what he is doing in dipping the brush, and also of what he is dipping it *for*. It is a purposive explanation. A person can put paint on a wall, or rock in a chair, or pace back and forth, without having any purpose in doing so. Still these activities could be intentional, although not for any purpose.

Whether intentional or not, these activities would be analyzable into component parts. If the activity is intentional, then at least some of its components will be intentional. If none of them were, the whole to which they belong would not be intentional. A man could not be intentionally putting paint on a wall if he did not intentionally have hold of a brush. Now this is not strictly true since he might not be aware that he was holding a *brush*, rather than a roller or a cloth. But there will have to be *some* description of what he is holding according to which it is true that he is intentionally holding it and intentionally dipping it in the paint.

Thus an intentional activity must have intentional components. The components will be purposive in relation to the whole activity. If X is an intentional component of Y, one can say with equal truth that in X-ing one is Y-ing, or that one is X-ing in order to Y. In moving the pencil on the paper one is drawing a figure: but also one is moving the pencil in order to draw a figure.

I conclude that if there could be no purposive behavior, there could be no intentional activities. Strictly speaking, this does not prove that there could be no intentional action, since many actions are not activities (for example, catching a ball or winning a race, as contrasted with playing ball or running in a race). But many of the actions that are not activities are stages in, or terminations of, activities and could not exist if the activities did not. Although I do not know how to prove the point for all cases, it seems to me highly plausible that if there could be no intentional activities there could be no intentional behavior of any sort – so plausible that I will assume it to be so. A life that was totally devoid of activities certainly could not be a human life. My conclusion is that since mechanism is incompatible with purposive behavior, it is incompatible with intentional activities, and consequently is incompatible with *all* intentional behavior.

21. The long-deferred question of whether the man of our example moved his hand on the doorknob will be answered as follows. The action of moving his hand cannot be rightly ascribed to him. It should not even be ascribed to him with some qualification such as "unintentionally" or "accidentally," for the use of these qualifications implies that there are cases in which it is right to say of a man that he did something "intentionally" or "purposely." But mechanism rules this out. On the other hand, to say "He did not move his hand" would be misleading, not only for the reason just stated, but also for the further reason that this statement would normally carry the implication that his hand did not move – which is false. Neither the sentence "He moved his hand" nor the sentence "He did not move his hand" would be appropriate. We would, of course, say "He moved his hand" if we understood this as merely equivalent to "His hand moved." (It is interesting that we do use these two sentences interchangeably when we are observing someone whom we know to be asleep or unconscious: we are equally ready to say either "He moved his hand" or "His hand moved.") But if we came to believe in mechanism we should, in consistency, give up the ascribing of action, even in a qualified way.

22. We can now proceed directly to the question of whether mechanism is conceivable. Sometimes when philosophers ask whether a proposition is conceivable, they mean to be asking whether it is self-contradictory. Nothing in our examination has indicated that mechanism is a self-contradictory theory, and I am sure it is not. Logically speaking, the earth and the whole universe might have been inhabited solely by organisms of such a nature that all of their movements could have been completely explained in terms of the neuro-physiological theory we have envisaged. We can conceive that the world might have been such that mechanism was true. In this sense mechanism is conceivable.

But there is a respect in which mechanism is not conceivable. This is a consequence of the fact that mechanism is incompatible with the existence of any intentional behavior. The speech of human beings is, for the most part, intentional behavior. In particular, stating, asserting, or saying that so-and-so is true requires the intentional uttering of some sentence. If mechanism is true, therefore, no one can state or assert anything. In a sense, no one can *say* anything. Specifically, no one can assert or state that mechanism is true. If anyone were to assert this, the occurrence of his intentional "speech act" would imply that mechanism is false.

Thus there is a logical absurdity in asserting that mechanism is true. It is not that the doctrine of mechanism is self-contradictory. The absurdity lies in the human act of asserting the doctrine. The occurrence of this act of assertion is inconsistent with the content of the assertion. The mere proposition that mechanism is true is not self-contradictory. But the conjunctive proposition, "Mechanism is true and someone asserts it to be true," *is* self-contradictory. Thus anyone's assertion that mechanism is true is necessarily false. The assertion implies its own falsity by virtue of providing a counterexample to what is asserted.

23. A proponent of mechanism might claim that since the absurdity we have been describing is a mere "pragmatic paradox" and not a self-contradiction in the doctrine of mechanism, it does not provide a sense in which mechanism is inconceivable. He may say that the paradox is similar to the paradox of a man's asserting that he himself is unconscious. There is an inconsistency between this man's act of stating he is unconscious and what he states. His act of stating it implies that what he states is false. But this paradox does not establish that a man cannot be unconscious, or that we cannot conceive that a man should be unconscious.

Now there is some similarity between the paradox of stating that oneself is unconscious and the paradox of stating that mechanism is true. But there is an important difference. *I* cannot state, without absurdity, that *I* am unconscious. But anyone else can, without absurdity, state that I am unconscious. There is only one person (myself) whose act of stating this proposition is inconsistent with the proposition. But an assertion of mechanism by any person whomsoever is inconsistent with mechanism. That I am unconscious is not (in consistency) statable by me. The unstatability is relative to only one person. But the unstatability of mechanism is absolute.

Furthermore, no one can consistently assert that although mechanism is unstatable it may be true. For this assertion, too, would require an intentional utterance (speech act) and so would be incompatible with mechanism.

We have elucidated a sense in which mechanism can properly be said to be inconceivable. The sense is that no one can consistently assert (or state, or say) that mechanism is, or may be, true.

If someone were to insist on asserting that mechanism is or may be true, his only recourse (if he were to be consistent) would be to adopt a form of solipsism. He could claim that mechanism is true for other organisms but not for himself. In this way he would free his assertion of inconsistency, but at the cost of accepting the embarrassments and logical difficulties of solipsism. He would also be repudiating the scientific respectability of mechanism by denying the universality of the envisaged neurophysiological laws.

24. Our criticism that mechanism is not a consistently statable doctrine is, of course, purely logical in nature. It consists in deducing a consequence of mechanism. Now one may feel that this consequence cannot refute mechanism or jeopardize its status as a scientific theory. It would seem to be up to science alone to determine whether or not there is a comprehensive neurophysiological theory to explain all bodily movements in accordance with universal laws. If scientific investigation should confirm such a theory, then so be it! To confirm it would be to confirm its consequences. If confirming the theory were to prove that people do not have desires, purposes, or goals, then this result would have to be swallowed, no matter how upsetting it would be not only to our ordinary beliefs but also to our ordinary concepts.

Almost anyone will feel some persuasiveness in this viewpoint. Determinism is a painful problem because it creates a severe tension between two viewpoints, each of which is strongly attractive: one is that the concepts of purpose, intention, and desire, of our ordinary language, cannot be rendered void by scientific advance; the other is that those concepts cannot prescribe limits to what it is possible for empirical science to achieve.

Let us see what would be the effect on our thinking of a scientific confirmation of mechanism. Suppose I am playing catch with a small boy. The ball escapes his grasp and he runs after it. Any observer would agree that the boy is running after the ball. This description implies that the purpose of the boy's running is to get the ball, or that he is running because he wants to capture the ball.

Now suppose a neurological technician could explain and predict every movement of the boy's limbs without regard to the whereabouts of the ball, solely in terms of the changing states of the boy's neurophysiological system. Or, what is worse, suppose the technician could control the boy's movements by altering the states of his central nervous system at will – that is, by "programming." We can imagine that it should be impossible for us to tell in a given instance, by observation of the boy's outward behavior and circumstances, whether the boy's limbs were responding to programming or whether he was running in order to retrieve the ball. And suppose that in many instances when we thought the behavior was intentional, it was subsequently proved to us that exactly the same inner physiological processes occurred as on those occasions when the technician controlled the boy's movements. We can also suppose that the neurologist's predictions of behavior would be both more reliable and more accurate than are the predictions based on purposive assumptions.

If such demonstrations occurred on a massive scale, we should be learning that the principles of purposive explanation have a far narrower application than we had thought. On more and more occasions we (that is, each one of us) would be forced to regard other human beings as mechanisms. The ultimate outcome of this development would be that we should cease to think of the behavior of others as being influenced by desires and intentions.

25. Having become believers in mechanistic explanations of the behavior of others, could each of us also come to believe that mechanistic causation is the true doctrine for his own case? Not if we realized what this would imply, for each of us would see that he could not include himself within the scope of the doctrine. Saying or doing something *for a reason* (in the sense of grounds as well as in the sense of purpose) implies that the saying or doing is intentional. Since mechanism is incompatible with the intentionality of behavior, my acceptance of mechanism as true for myself would imply that I am incapable of saying or doing anything for a reason. There could be *a* reason (that is, a cause) but there could not be such a thing as *my* reason. There could not, for example, be such a thing as my reason for stating that mechanism is true. Thus my assertion of mechanism would involve a second

paradox. Not only would the assertion be inconsistent, in the sense previously explained, but also it would imply that I am incapable of having rational grounds for asserting anything, including mechanism.

Once again we see that mechanism engenders a form of solipsism. In asserting mechanism I must deny its application to my own case; for otherwise my assertion would imply that I could not be asserting mechanism on rational grounds.

26. Some philosophers hold that if mechanism is true then a radical revision of our concepts is required. We need to junk all such terms as "intentionally," "unintentionally," "purposely," "by mistake," "deliberately," "accidentally," and so on. The classifying of utterances such as "asserting," "repeating," "quoting," "mimicking," "translating," and so forth, would have to be abandoned. We should need an entirely new repertoire of descriptions of a sort that would be compatible with the viewpoint of mechanism.

I think these philosophers have not grasped the full severity of the predicament. If mechanism is true, not only should we give up speaking of "asserting," but also of "describing" or even of "speaking." It would not even be right to say that a person *meant* something by the noise that came from him. No marks or sounds would mean anything. There could not be *language*.

A proponent of mechanism should not think that at present we are using the wrong concepts and that a revision is called for. If he is right, we do not use concepts at all. There is nothing to revise – and nothing to say. The motto of a mechanist ought to be: One cannot speak, therefore one must be silent.

27. To conclude: We have uncovered two respects in which mechanism is not a conceivable doctrine. The first is that the occurrence of an act of asserting mechanism is inconsistent with mechanism's being true. The second is that the asserting of mechanism implies that the one who makes the assertion cannot be making it on rational grounds.

In order to avoid these paradoxes, one must deny that mechanism is universally true. One can hold that it is true for others but not for oneself. It is highly ironical that the affirmation of mechanism requires one to affirm its metaphysical and methodological opposite – solipsism.

The inconceivability of mechanism, in the two respects we have elucidated, does not establish that mechanism is false. It would seem, logically speaking, that a comprehensive neurophysiological theory of human behavior ought to be confirmable by scientific investigation. Yet the assertion that this confirmation had been achieved would involve the two paradoxes we have elucidated. Mechanism thus presents a harsh, and perhaps insoluble, antinomy to human thought.

Concluding unscientific postscript: I must confess that I am not entirely convinced of the correctness of the position I have taken in respect of the crux of this paper – namely, the problem of whether it is possible for there to be both a complete neurophysiological explanation and also a complete purposive explanation of one and the same sequence of movements. I do not believe I have really proved this to be impossible. On the other hand, it is true that for me (and for others, too) a sequence of sounds tends to lose the aspect of speech (language) when we conceive of those sounds as being caused neurophysiologically (especially if we imagine a technician to be controlling the production of the sounds). Likewise, a sequence of movements loses the aspect of action. Is this tendency due to some false picture or to some misleading analogy? Possibly so; but also possibly not. Perhaps the publication of the present paper will be justified if it provokes a truly convincing defense of the compatibility of the two forms of explanation.[14]

Notes

1 If you said "Get up!" and I got up, the theory would explain my movements in terms of neurophysiological events produced by the impact of sound waves on my auditory organs.

2 A neurophysiological *prediction* would be of the same form, with these differences: the second premise would say that O is or will be in state *q* (instead of *was*), and the conclusion would say that O *will* emit m (instead of *emitted*).

3 The correct diagnosis of such a failure will not be evident in all cases. Suppose a youth wants to be a trapeze performer in a circus, and he believes this requires daily exercise on the parallel bars. But he is lazy and frequently fails to exercise. Doesn't

he really have the goal he professes to have: is it just talk? Or doesn't he really believe in the necessity of the daily exercise? Or is it that he has the goal and the belief and his laziness is a genuine countervailing factor? One might have to know him very well in order to give the right answer. In some cases there might be no definite right answer.

4   Charles Taylor, *The Explanation of Behaviour* (New York, 1964), p. 33.

5   E.g., Taylor says that the agent's intention is not a "causal antecedent" of his behavior, for intention and behavior "are not contingently connected in the normal way" (ibid.).

6   Taylor puts the point as follows:

Because explanation by intentions or purposes is like explanation by an "antecedent" which is non-contingently linked with its consequent, i.e., because the fact that the behaviour follows from the intention other things being equal is not a contingent fact, we cannot account for this fact by more basic laws. For to explain a fact by more basic laws is to give the regularities on which this fact causally depends. But not being contingent, the dependence of behaviour on intention is not contingent on anything, and hence not on any such regularities. (ibid., p. 44)

7   This is true if we use "wants X" to mean "is aiming at X." But sometimes we may mean no more than "would like to have X," which may represent a mere wish.

8   The following remarks by A. I. Melden present both of these points:

Where we are concerned with causal explanations, with events of which the happenings in question are effects in accordance with some law of causality, to that extent we are not concerned with human actions at all but, at best, with bodily movements or happenings; and where we are concerned with explanations of human action, there causal factors and causal laws in the sense in which, for example, these terms are employed in the biological sciences are wholly irrelevant to the understanding we seek. The reason is simple, namely, the radically different logical characteristics of the two bodies of discourse we employ in these distinct cases – the different concepts which are applicable to these different orders of inquiry. (A. I. Melden, *Free Action* (New York, 1961), p. 184)

9   This point is argued in my "Scientific Materialism and the Identity Theory," *Dialogue* 3 (1964); also in my forthcoming monograph, *Problems of Mind*, sec. 18, to be published in the Harper Guide to Philosophy, edited by Arthur Danto.

10 For an exposition of this problem see Jaegwon Kim's "On the Psycho-Physical Identity Theory," *American Philosophical Quarterly* 3 (1966).

11 I am following Charles Taylor here: *Explanation of Behaviour*, pp. 27–32.

12 Taylor, *Explanation of Behaviour*, p. 33 (my italics). Taylor says that an intention is *not* "a causal antecedent" of the intended behavior, for the reason that the intention and the behavior are not *contingently connected*. I think he may be fairly represented as holding that an intention does *cause* the intended behavior, although not in the sense of "cause" in which cause and effect are contingently correlated.

13 Taylor's phrase, *Explanation of Behaviour*, p. 34. In my review of Taylor's book ("Explaining Behavior," *Philosophical Review* 76 (1967), pp. 97–104), I say that Taylor is wrong in holding that a simple intention *brings about* the corresponding behavior. But now I am holding that he is partly right and partly wrong: right about previously formed simple intentions, wrong about merely concurrent simple intentions.

14 A number of people have read various versions of this paper and I have profited from their criticisms. I am especially indebted to Elizabeth Anscombe, Keith Donnellan, Philippa Foot, G. H. von Wright, and Ann Wilbur. They are not responsible for the mistakes I have retained.

29

Freedom and Resentment

P. F. Strawson

I

Some philosophers say they do not know what the thesis of determinism is. Others say, or imply, that they do know what it is. Of these, some – the pessimists perhaps – hold that if the thesis is true, then the concepts of moral obligation and responsibility really have no application, and the practices of punishing and blaming, of expressing moral condemnation and approval, are really unjustified. Others – the optimists perhaps – hold that these concepts and practices in no way lose their *raison d'être* if the thesis of determinism is true. Some hold even that the justification of these concepts and practices requires the truth of the thesis. There is another opinion which is less frequently voiced: the opinion, it might be said, of the genuine moral sceptic. This is that the notions of moral guilt, of blame, of moral responsibility are inherently confused and that we can see this to be so if we consider the consequences either of the truth of determinism or of its falsity. The holders of this opinion agree with the pessimists that these notions lack application if determinism is true, and add simply that they also lack it if determinism is false. If I am asked which of these parties I belong to, I must say it is the first of all, the party of those who do not know what the thesis of determinism is. But this does not stop me from having some

sympathy with the others, and a wish to reconcile them. Should not ignorance, rationally, inhibit such sympathies? Well, of course, though darkling, one has some inkling – some notion of what sort of thing is being talked about. This lecture is intended as a move towards reconciliation; so is likely to seem wrongheaded to everyone.

But can there be any possibility of reconciliation between such clearly opposed positions as those of pessimists and optimists about determinism? Well, there might be a formal withdrawal on one side in return for a substantial concession on the other. Thus, suppose the optimist's position were put like this: (1) the facts as we know them do not show determinism to be false; (2) the facts as we know them supply an adequate basis for the concepts and practices which the pessimist feels to be imperilled by the possibility of determinism's truth. Now it might be that the optimist is right in this, but is apt to give an inadequate account of the facts as we know them, and of how they constitute an adequate basis for the problematic concepts and practices; that the reasons he gives for the adequacy of the basis are themselves inadequate and leave out something vital. It might be that the pessimist is rightly anxious to get this vital thing back and, in the grip of his anxiety, feels he has to go beyond the facts as we know them; feels that the vital thing can be secure only if, beyond the facts as we know them, there is the further fact that determinism is false. Might *he* not be brought to make a formal withdrawal in return for a vital concession?

Originally published in *Proceedings of the British Academy* 48 (1962).

II

Let me enlarge very briefly on this, by way of preliminary only. Some optimists about determinism point to the efficacy of the practices of punishment, and of moral condemnation and approval, in regulating behaviour in socially desirable ways.[1] In the fact of their efficacy, they suggest, is an adequate basis for these practices; and this fact certainly does not show determinism to be false. To this the pessimists reply, all in a rush, that *just* punishment and *moral* condemnation imply moral guilt and guilt implies moral responsibility and moral responsibility implies freedom and freedom implies the falsity of determinism. And to this the optimists are wont to reply in turn that it is true that these practices require freedom in a sense, and the existence of freedom in this sense is one of the facts as we know them. But what 'freedom' means here is nothing but the absence of certain conditions the presence of which would make moral condemnation or punishment inappropriate. They have in mind conditions like compulsion by another, or innate incapacity, or insanity, or other less extreme forms of psychological disorder, or the existence of circumstances in which the making of any other choice would be morally inadmissible or would be too much to expect of any man. To this list they are constrained to add other factors which, without exactly being limitations of freedom, may also make moral condemnation or punishment inappropriate or mitigate their force: as some forms of ignorance, mistake, or accident. And the general reason why moral condemnation or punishment are inappropriate when these factors or conditions are present is held to be that the practices in question will be generally efficacious means of regulating behaviour in desirable ways only in cases where these factors are *not* present. Now the pessimist admits that the facts as we know them include the existence of freedom, the occurrence of cases of free action, in the negative sense which the optimist concedes; and admits, or rather insists, that the existence of freedom in this sense is compatible with the truth of determinism. Then what does the pessimist find missing? When he tries to answer this question, his language is apt to alternate between the very familiar and the very unfamiliar.[2] Thus he may say, familiarly enough, that the man who is the subject of justified punishment, blame or moral condemnation must really *deserve* it; and then

add, perhaps, that, in the case at least where he is blamed for a positive act rather than an omission, the condition of his really deserving blame is something that goes beyond the negative freedoms that the optimist concedes. It is, say, a genuinely free identification of the will with the act. And this is the condition that is incompatible with the truth of determinism.

The conventional, but conciliatory, optimist need not give up yet. He may say: Well, people often decide to do things, really intend to do what they do, know just what they're doing in doing it; the reasons they think they have for doing what they do, often really are their reasons and not their rationalizations. These facts, too, are included in the facts as we know them. If this is what you mean by freedom – by the identification of the will with the act – then freedom may again be conceded. But again the concession is compatible with the truth of the determinist thesis. For it would not follow from that thesis that nobody decides to do anything; that nobody ever does anything intentionally; that it is false that people sometimes know perfectly well what they are doing. I tried to define freedom negatively. You want to give it a more positive look. But it comes to the same thing. Nobody denies freedom in this sense, or these senses, and nobody claims that the existence of freedom in these senses shows determinism to be false.

But it is here that the lacuna in the optimistic story can be made to show. For the pessimist may be supposed to ask: But *why* does freedom in this sense justify blame, etc.? You turn towards me first the negative, and then the positive, faces of a freedom which nobody challenges. But the only reason you have given for the practices of moral condemnation and punishment in cases where this freedom is present is the efficacy of these practices in regulating behaviour in socially desirable ways. But this is not a sufficient basis, it is not even the right *sort* of basis, for these practices as we understand them.

Now my optimist, being the sort of man he is, is not likely to invoke an intuition of fittingness at this point. So he really has no more to say. And my pessimist, being the sort of man he is, has only one more thing to say; and that is that the admissibility of these practices, as we understand them, demands another kind of freedom, the kind that in turn demands the falsity of the thesis of determinism. But might we not induce the pessimist to give up saying this by giving the optimist something more to say?

III

I have mentioned punishing and moral condemnation and approval; and it is in connection with these practices or attitudes that the issue between optimists and pessimists – or, if one is a pessimist, the issue between determinists and libertarians – is felt to be particularly important. But it is not of these practices and attitudes that I propose, at first, to speak. These practices or attitudes permit, where they do not imply, a certain detachment from the actions or agents which are their objects. I want to speak, at least at first, of something else: of the non-detached attitudes and reactions of people directly involved in transactions with each other; of the attitudes and reactions of offended parties and beneficiaries; of such things as gratitude, resentment, forgiveness, love, and hurt feelings. Perhaps something like the issue between optimists and pessimists arises in this neighbouring field too; and since this field is less crowded with disputants, the issue might here be easier to settle; and if it is settled here, then it might become easier to settle it in the disputant-crowded field.

What I have to say consists largely of commonplaces. So my language, like that of commonplaces generally, will be quite unscientific and imprecise. The central commonplace that I want to insist on is the very great importance that we attach to the attitudes and intentions towards us of other human beings, and the great extent to which our personal feelings and reactions depend upon, or involve, our beliefs about these attitudes and intentions. I can give no simple description of the field of phenomena at the centre of which stands this commonplace truth; for the field is too complex. Much imaginative literature is devoted to exploring its complexities; and we have a large vocabulary for the purpose. There are simplifying styles of handling it in a general way. Thus we may, like La Rochefoucauld, put self-love or self-esteem or vanity at the centre of the picture and point out how it may be caressed by the esteem, or wounded by the indifference or contempt, of others. We might speak, in another jargon, of the need for love, and the loss of security which results from its withdrawal; or, in another, of human self-respect and its connec-

tion with the recognition of the individual's dignity. These simplifications are of use to me only if they help to emphasize how much we actually mind, how much it matters to us, whether the actions of other people – and particularly of *some* other people – reflect attitudes towards us of goodwill, affection, or esteem on the one hand or contempt, indifference, or malevolence on the other. If someone treads on my hand accidentally, while trying to help me, the pain may be no less acute than if he treads on it in contemptuous disregard of my existence or with a malevolent wish to injure me. But I shall generally feel in the second case a kind and degree of resentment that I shall not feel in the first. If someone's actions help me to some benefit I desire, then I am benefited in any case; but if he intended them so to benefit me because of his general goodwill towards me, I shall reasonably feel a gratitude which I should not feel at all if the benefit was an incidental consequence, unintended or even regretted by him, of some plan of action with a different aim.

These examples are of actions which confer benefits or inflict injuries over and above any conferred or inflicted by the mere manifestation of attitude and intention themselves. We should consider also in how much of our behaviour the benefit or injury resides mainly or entirely in the manifestation of attitude itself. So it is with good manners, and much of what we call kindness, on the one hand; with deliberate rudeness, studied indifference, or insult on the other.

Besides resentment and gratitude, I mentioned just now forgiveness. This is a rather unfashionable subject in moral philosophy at present; but to be forgiven is something we sometimes ask, and forgiving is something we sometimes say we do. To ask to be forgiven is in part to acknowledge that the attitude displayed in our actions was such as might properly be resented and in part to repudiate that attitude for the future (or at least for the immediate future); and to forgive is to accept the repudiation and to forswear the resentment.

We should think of the many different kinds of relationship which we can have with other people – as sharers of a common interest; as members of the same family; as colleagues; as friends; as lovers; as chance parties to an enormous range of transactions and encounters. Then we should think, in each of these connections in turn, and in others, of the kind of importance we attach to the attitudes and intentions towards us of those who stand in these relationships to us, and of the kinds of *reactive* attitudes and feelings to which we ourselves are prone. In general, we demand some degree of goodwill or regard on the part of those who stand in these relationships to us, though the forms we require it to take vary widely in different connections. The range and intensity of our *reactive* attitudes towards goodwill, its absence or its opposite vary no less widely. I have mentioned, specifically, resentment and gratitude; and they are a usefully opposed pair. But, of course, there is a whole continuum of reactive attitude and feeling stretching on both sides of these and – the most comfortable area – in between them.

The object of these commonplaces is to try to keep before our minds something it is easy to forget when we are engaged in philosophy, especially in our cool, contemporary style, viz. what it is actually like to be involved in ordinary inter-personal relationships, ranging from the most intimate to the most casual.

IV

It is one thing to ask about the general causes of these reactive attitudes I have alluded to; it is another to ask about the variations to which they are subject, the particular conditions in which they do or do not seem natural or reasonable or appropriate; and it is a third thing to ask what it would be like, what it *is* like, not to suffer them. I am not much concerned with the first question; but I am with the second; and perhaps even more with the third.

Let us consider, then, occasions for resentment: situations in which one person is offended or injured by the action of another and in which – in the absence of special considerations – the offended person might naturally or normally be expected to feel resentment. Then let us consider what sorts of special considerations might be expected to modify or mollify this feeling or remove it altogether. It needs no saying now how multifarious these considerations are. But, for my purpose, I think they can be roughly divided into two kinds. To the first group belong all those which might give occasion for the employment of such expressions as 'He didn't mean to', 'He hadn't realized', 'He didn't know'; and also all those which might give occasion for

the use of the phrase 'He couldn't help it', when this is supported by such phrases as 'He was pushed', 'He had to do it', 'It was the only way', 'They left him no alternative', etc. Obviously these various pleas, and the kinds of situations in which they would be appropriate, differ from each other in striking and important ways. But for my present purpose they have something still more important in common. None of them invites us to suspend towards the agent, either at the time of his action or in general, our ordinary reactive attitudes. They do not invite us to view the *agent* as one in respect of whom these attitudes are in any way inappropriate. They invite us to view the *injury* as one in respect of which a particular one of these attitudes is inappropriate. They do not invite us to see the *agent* as other than a fully responsible agent. They invite us to see the *injury* as one for which he was not fully, or at all, responsible. They do not suggest that the agent is in any way an inappropriate object of that kind of demand for goodwill or regard which is reflected in our ordinary reactive attitudes. They suggest instead that the fact of injury was not in this case incompatible with that demand's being fulfilled, that the fact of injury was quite consistent with the agent's attitude and intentions being just what we demand they should be.[3] The agent was just ignorant of the injury he was causing, or had lost his balance through being pushed or had reluctantly to cause the injury for reasons which acceptably override his reluctance. The offering of such pleas by the agent and their acceptance by the sufferer is something in no way opposed to, or outside the context of, ordinary inter-personal relationships and the manifestation of ordinary reactive attitudes. Since things go wrong and situations are complicated, it is an essential and integral element in the transactions which are the life of these relationships.

The second group of considerations is very different. I shall take them in two subgroups of which the first is far less important than the second. In connection with the first subgroup we may think of such statements as 'He wasn't himself', 'He has been under very great strain recently', 'He was acting under post-hypnotic suggestion'; in connection with the second, we may think of 'He's only a child', 'He's a hopeless schizophrenic', 'His mind has been systematically perverted', 'That's purely compulsive behaviour on his part'. Such pleas as these do, as pleas of my first general group do not, invite us to suspend our ordinary reactive attitudes towards the agent, either at the time of his action or all the time. They do not invite us to see the agent's action in a way consistent with the full retention of ordinary inter-personal attitudes and merely inconsistent with one particular attitude. They invite us to view the agent himself in a different light from the light in which we should normally view one who has acted as he has acted. I shall not linger over the first subgroup of cases. Though they perhaps raise, in the short term, questions akin to those raised, in the long term, by the second subgroup, we may dismiss them without considering those questions by taking that admirably suggestive phrase, 'He wasn't himself', with the seriousness that – for all its being logically comic – it deserves. We shall not feel resentment against the man he is for the action done by the man he is not; or at least we shall feel less. We normally have to deal with him under normal stresses; so we shall not feel towards him, when he acts as he does under abnormal stresses, as we should have felt towards him had he acted as he did under normal stresses.

The second and more important subgroup of cases allows that the circumstances were normal, but presents the agent as psychologically abnormal – or as morally undeveloped. The agent was himself; but he is warped or deranged, neurotic or just a child. When we see someone in such a light as this, all our reactive attitudes tend to be profoundly modified. I must deal here in crude dichotomies and ignore the ever-interesting and ever-illuminating varieties of case. What I want to contrast is the attitude (or range of attitudes) of involvement or participation in a human relationship, on the one hand, and what might be called the objective attitude (or range of attitudes) to another human being, on the other. Even in the same situation, I must add, they are not altogether *exclusive* of each other; but they are, profoundly, *opposed* to each other. To adopt the objective attitude to another human being is to see him, perhaps, as an object of social policy; as a subject for what, in a wide range of sense, might be called treatment; as something certainly to be taken account, perhaps precautionary account, of; to be managed or handled or cured or trained; perhaps simply to be avoided, though *this* gerundive is not peculiar to cases of objectivity of attitude. The objective attitude may be emotionally toned in many ways, but not in all

ways: it may include repulsion or fear, it may include pity or even love, though not all kinds of love. But it cannot include the range of reactive feelings and attitudes which belong to involvement or participation with others in inter-personal human relationships; it cannot include resentment, gratitude, forgiveness, anger, or the sort of love which two adults can sometimes be said to feel reciprocally, for each other. If your attitude towards someone is wholly objective, then though you may fight him, you cannot quarrel with him, and though you may talk to him, even negotiate with him, you cannot reason with him. You can at most pretend to quarrel, or to reason, with him.

Seeing someone, then, as warped or deranged or compulsive in behaviour or peculiarly unfortunate in his formative circumstances – seeing someone so tends, at least to some extent, to set him apart from normal participant reactive attitudes on the part of one who so sees him, tends to promote, at least in the civilized, objective attitudes. But there is something curious to add to this. The objective attitude is not only something we naturally tend to fall into in cases like these, where participant attitudes are partially or wholly inhibited by abnormalities or by immaturity. It is also something which is available as a resource in other cases too. We look with an objective eye on the compulsive behaviour of the neurotic or the tiresome behaviour of a very young child, thinking in terms of treatment or training. But we *can* sometimes look with something like the same eye on the behaviour of the normal and the mature. We *have* this resource and can sometimes use it: as a refuge, say, from the strains of involvement; or as an aid to policy; or simply out of intellectual curiosity. Being human, we cannot, in the normal case, do this for long, or altogether. If the strains of involvement, say, continue to be too great, then we have to do something else – like severing a relationship. But what is above all interesting is the tension there is, in us, between the participant attitude and the objective attitude. One is tempted to say: between our humanity and our intelligence. But to say this would be to distort both notions.

What I have called the participant reactive attitudes are essentially natural human reactions to the good or ill will or indifference of others towards us, as displayed in *their* attitudes and actions. The question we have to ask is: What effect would, or should, the acceptance of the

P. F. Strawson

truth of a general thesis of determinism have upon these reactive attitudes? More specifically, would, or should, the acceptance of the truth of the thesis lead to the decay or the repudiation of all such attitudes? Would, or should, it mean the end of gratitude, resentment, and forgiveness; of all reciprocated adult loves; of all the essentially *personal* antagonisms?

But how can I answer, or even pose, this question without knowing *exactly* what the thesis of determinism is? Well, there is one thing we do know: that if there is a coherent thesis of determinism, then there must be a sense of 'determined' such that, if that thesis is true, then all behaviour whatever is determined in that sense. Remembering this, we can consider at least what possibilities lie formally open; and then perhaps we shall see that the question can be answered *without* knowing exactly what the thesis of determinism is. We can consider what possibilities lie open because we have already before us an account of the ways in which particular reactive attitudes, or reactive attitudes in general, may be, and, sometimes, we judge, should be, inhibited. Thus I considered earlier a group of considerations which tend to inhibit, and, we judge, should inhibit, resentment, in particular cases of an agent causing an injury, without inhibiting reactive attitudes in general towards that agent. Obviously this group of considerations cannot strictly bear upon our question; for that question concerns reactive attitudes in general. But resentment has a particular interest; so it is worth adding that it has never been claimed as a consequence of the truth of determinism that one or another of *these* considerations was operative in every case of an injury being caused by an agent; that it would follow from the truth of determinism that anyone who caused an injury *either* was quite simply ignorant of causing it *or* had acceptably overriding reasons for acquiescing reluctantly in causing it *or* . . . , etc. The prevalence of this happy state of affairs would not be a consequence of the reign of universal determinism, but of the reign of universal goodwill. We cannot, then, find here the possibility of an affirmative answer to our question, even for the particular case of resentment.

Next, I remarked that the participant attitude, and the personal reactive attitudes in general, tend to give place, and it is judged by the civilized should give place, to objective attitudes, just in so far as the agent is seen as excluded from

ordinary adult human relationships by deep-rooted psychological abnormality – or simply by being a child. But it cannot be a consequence of any thesis which is not itself self-contradictory that abnormality is the universal condition.

Now this dismissal might seem altogether too facile; and so, in a sense, it is. But whatever is too quickly dismissed in this dismissal is allowed for in the only possible form of affirmative answer that remains. We can sometimes, and in part, I have remarked, look on the normal (those we rate as 'normal') in the objective way in which we have learned to look on certain classified cases of abnormality. And our question reduces to this: could, or should, the acceptance of the determinist thesis lead us always to look on everyone exclusively in this way? For this is the only condition worth considering under which the acceptance of determinism could lead to the decay or repudiation of participant reactive attitudes.

It does not seem to be self-contradictory to suppose that this might happen. So I suppose we must say that it is not absolutely inconceivable that it should happen. But I am strongly inclined to think that it is, for us as we are, practically inconceivable. The human commitment to participation in ordinary inter-personal relationships is, I think, too thoroughgoing and deeply rooted for us to take seriously the thought that a general theoretical conviction might so change our world that, in it, there were no longer any such things as inter-personal relationships as we normally understand them; and being involved in inter-personal relationships as we normally understand them precisely is being exposed to the range of reactive attitudes and feelings that is in question.

This, then, is a part of the reply to our question. A sustained objectivity of inter-personal attitude, and the human isolation which that would entail, does not seem to be something of which human beings would be capable, even if some general truth were a theoretical ground for it. But this is not all. There is a further point, implicit in the foregoing, which must be made explicit. Exceptionally, I have said, we can have direct dealings with human beings without any degree of personal involvement, treating them simply as creatures to be handled in our own interests, or our side's, or society's – or even theirs. In the extreme case of the mentally deranged, it is easy to see the connection between the possibility of a wholly objective attitude and the impossibility of what we understand by ordinary inter-personal relationships. Given this latter impossibility, no other civilized attitude is available than that of viewing the deranged person simply as something to be understood and controlled in the most desirable fashion. To view him as outside the reach of personal relationships is already, for the civilized, to view him in this way. For reasons of policy or self-protection we may have occasion, perhaps temporary, to adopt a fundamentally similar attitude to a 'normal' human being; to concentrate, that is, on understanding 'how he works', with a view to determining our policy accordingly or to finding in that very understanding a relief from the strains of involvement. Now it is certainly true that in the case of the abnormal, though not in the case of the normal, our adoption of the objective attitude is a consequence of our viewing the agent as *incapacitated* in some or all respects for ordinary inter-personal relationships. He is thus incapacitated, perhaps, by the fact that his picture of reality is pure fantasy, that he does not, in a sense, live in the real world at all; or by the fact that his behaviour is, in part, an unrealistic acting out of unconscious purposes; or by the fact that he is an idiot, or a moral idiot. But there is something else which, *because* this is true, is equally certainly *not* true. And that is that there is a sense of 'determined' such that (1) if determinism is true, all behaviour is determined in this sense, and (2) determinism might be true, i.e. it is not inconsistent with the facts as we know them to suppose that all behaviour might be determined in this sense, and (3) our adoption of the objective attitude towards the abnormal is the result of a prior embracing of the belief that the behaviour, or the relevant stretch of behaviour, of the human being in question *is* determined in this sense. Neither in the case of the normal, then, nor in the case of the abnormal is it true that, when we adopt an objective attitude, we do so *because* we hold such a belief. So my answer has two parts. The first is that we cannot, as we are, seriously envisage ourselves adopting a thoroughgoing objectivity of attitude to others as a result of theoretical conviction of the truth of determinism; and the second is that when we do in fact adopt such an attitude in a particular case, our doing so is not the consequence of a theoretical conviction which might be expressed as 'Determinism in this case', but is a consequence of our abandoning, for different reasons

in different cases, the ordinary inter-personal attitudes.

It might be said that all this leaves the real question unanswered, and that we cannot hope to answer it without knowing exactly what the thesis of determinism is. For the real question is not a question about what we actually do, or why we do it. It is not even a question about what we would *in fact* do if a certain theoretical conviction gained general acceptance. It is a question about what it would be *rational* to do if determinism were true, a question about the rational justification of ordinary inter-personal attitudes in general. To this I shall reply, first, that such a question could seem real only to one who had utterly failed to grasp the purport of the preceding answer, the fact of our natural human commitment to ordinary inter-personal attitudes. This commitment is part of the general framework of human life, not something that can come up for review as particular cases can come up for review within this general framework. And I shall reply, second, that if we could imagine what we cannot have, viz. a choice in this matter, then we could choose rationally only in the light of an assessment of the gains and losses to human life, its enrichment or impoverishment; and the truth or falsity of a general thesis of determinism would not bear on the rationality of *this* choice.[4]

V

The point of this discussion of the reactive attitudes in their relation – or lack of it – to the thesis of determinism was to bring us, if possible, nearer to a position of compromise in a more usual area of debate. We are not now to discuss reactive attitudes which are essentially those of offended parties or beneficiaries. We are to discuss reactive attitudes which are essentially not those, or only incidentally are those, of offended parties or beneficiaries, but are nevertheless, I shall claim, kindred attitudes to those I have discussed. I put resentment in the centre of the previous discussion. I shall put moral indignation – or, more weakly, moral disapprobation – in the centre of this one.

The reactive attitudes I have so far discussed are essentially reactions to the quality of others' wills towards us, as manifested in their behaviour: to their good or ill will or indifference or lack of concern. Thus resentment, or what I have called resentment, is a reaction to injury or indifference. The reactive attitudes I have now to discuss might be described as the sympathetic or vicarious or impersonal or disinterested or generalized analogues of the reactive attitudes I have already discussed. They are reactions to the qualities of others' wills, not towards ourselves, but towards others. Because of this impersonal or vicarious character, we give them different names. Thus one who experiences the vicarious analogue of resentment is said to be indignant or disapproving, or morally indignant or disapproving. What we have here is, as it were, resentment on behalf of another, where one's own interest and dignity are not involved; and it is this impersonal or vicarious character of the attitude, added to its others, which entitle it to the qualification 'moral'. Both my description of, and my name for, these attitudes are, in one important respect, a little misleading. It is not that these attitudes are essentially vicarious – one can feel indignation on one's own account – but that they are essentially capable of being vicarious. But I shall retain the name for the sake of its suggestiveness; and I hope that what is misleading about it will be corrected in what follows.

The personal reactive attitudes rest on, and reflect, an expectation of, and demand for, the manifestation of a certain degree of goodwill or regard on the part of other human beings towards ourselves; or at least on the expectation of, and demand for, an absence of the manifestation of active ill will or indifferent disregard. (What will, in particular cases, *count* as manifestations of good or ill will or disregard will vary in accordance with the particular relationship in which we stand to another human being.) The generalized or vicarious analogues of the personal reactive attitudes rest on, and reflect, exactly the same expectation or demand in a generalized form; they rest on, or reflect, that is, the demand for the manifestation of a reasonable degree of goodwill or regard, on the part of others, not simply towards oneself, but towards all those on whose behalf moral indignation may be felt, i.e., as we now think, towards all men. The generalized and non-generalized forms of demand, and the vicarious and personal reactive attitudes which rest upon, and reflect, them are connected not merely logically. They are connected humanly; and not merely with each other. They are connected also with yet another set of attitudes which I must mention now in order to complete the picture.

I have considered from two points of view the demands we make on others and our reactions to their possibly injurious actions. These were the points of view of one whose interest was directly involved (who suffers, say, the injury) and of others whose interest was not directly involved (who do not themselves suffer the injury). Thus I have spoken of personal reactive attitudes in the first connection and of their vicarious analogues in the second. But the picture is not complete unless we consider also the correlates of these attitudes on the part of those on whom the demands are made, on the part of the agents. Just as there are personal and vicarious reactive attitudes associated with demands on others for oneself and demands on others for others, so there are self-reactive attitudes associated with demands on oneself for others. And here we have to mention such phenomena as feeling bound or obliged (the 'sense of obligation'); feeling compunction; feeling guilty or remorseful or at least responsible; and the more complicated phenomenon of shame.

All these three types of attitude are humanly connected. One who manifested the personal reactive attitudes in a high degree but showed no inclination at all to their vicarious analogues would appear as an abnormal case of moral egocentricity, as a kind of moral solipsist. Let him be supposed fully to acknowledge the claims to regard that others had on him, to be susceptible of the whole range of self-reactive attitudes. He would then see himself as unique both as one (*the* one) who had a general claim on human regard and as one (*the* one) on whom human beings in general had such a claim. This would be a kind of moral solipsism. But it is barely more than a conceptual possibility; if it is that. In general, though within varying limits, we demand of others for others, as well as of ourselves for others, something of the regard which we demand of others for ourselves. Can we imagine, besides that of the moral solipsist, any other case of one or two of these three types of attitude being fully developed, but quite unaccompanied by any trace, however slight, of the remaining two or one? If we can, then we imagine something far below or far above the level of our common humanity – a moral idiot or a saint. For all these types of attitude alike have common roots in our human nature and our membership of human communities.

Now, as of the personal reactive attitudes, so of their vicarious analogues, we must ask in what ways, and by what considerations, they tend to be inhibited. Both types of attitude involve, or express, a certain sort of demand for inter-personal regard. The fact of injury constitutes a prima facie appearance of this demand's being flouted or unfulfilled. We saw, in the case of resentment, how one class of considerations may show this appearance to be mere appearance, and hence inhibit resentment, *without* inhibiting, or displacing, the sort of demand of which resentment can be an expression, without in any way tending to make us suspend our ordinary inter-personal attitudes to the agent. Considerations of this class operate in just the same way, for just the same reasons, in connection with moral disapprobation or indignation; they inhibit indignation without in any way inhibiting the sort of demand on the agent of which indignation can be an expression, the range of attitudes towards him to which it belongs. But in this connection we may express the facts with a new emphasis. We may say, stressing the moral, the generalized aspect of the demand, considerations of this group have no tendency to make us see the agent as other than a morally responsible agent; they simply make us see the injury as one for which he was not morally responsible. The offering and acceptance of such exculpatory pleas as are here in question in no way detracts in our eyes from the agent's status as a term of moral relationships. On the contrary, since things go wrong and situations are complicated, it is an essential part of the life of such relationships.

But suppose we see the agent in a different light: as one whose picture of the world is an insane delusion; or as one whose behaviour, or a part of whose behaviour, is unintelligible to us, perhaps even to him, in terms of conscious purposes, and intelligible only in terms of unconscious purposes; or even, perhaps, as one wholly impervious to the self-reactive attitudes I spoke of, wholly lacking, as we say, in moral sense. Seeing an agent in such a light as this tends, I said, to inhibit resentment in a wholly different way. It tends to inhibit resentment because it tends to inhibit ordinary inter-personal attitudes in general, and the kind of demand and expectation which those attitudes involve; and tends to promote instead the purely objective view of the agent as one posing problems simply of intellectual understanding, management, treatment, and control. Again the parallel holds for those generalized or moral attitudes towards the agent which

we are now concerned with. The same abnormal light which shows the agent to us as one in respect of whom the personal attitudes, the personal demand, are to be suspended, shows him to us also as one in respect of whom the impersonal attitudes, the generalized demand, are to be suspended. Only, abstracting now from direct personal interest, we may express the facts with a new emphasis. We may say: to the extent to which the agent is seen in this light, he is not seen as one on whom demands and expectations lie in that particular way in which we think of them as lying when we speak of moral obligation; he is not, to that extent, seen as a morally responsible agent, as a term of moral relationships, as a member of the moral community.

I remarked also that the suspension of ordinary inter-personal attitudes and the cultivation of a purely objective view is sometimes possible even when we have no such reasons for it as I have just mentioned. Is this possible also in the case of the moral reactive attitudes? I think so; and perhaps it is easier. But the motives for a total suspension of moral reactive attitudes are fewer, and perhaps weaker: fewer, because only where there is antecedent personal involvement can there be the motive of seeking refuge from the strains of such involvement; perhaps weaker, because the tension between objectivity of view and the moral reactive attitudes is perhaps less than the tension between objectivity of view and the personal reactive attitudes, so that we can in the case of the moral reactive attitudes more easily secure the speculative or political gains of objectivity of view by a kind of setting on one side, rather than a total suspension, of those attitudes.

These last remarks are uncertain; but also, for the present purpose, unimportant. What concerns us now is to inquire, as previously in connection with the personal reactive attitudes, what relevance any general thesis of determinism might have to their vicarious analogues. The answers once more are parallel; though I shall take them in a slightly different order. First, we must note, as before, that when the suspension of such an attitude or such attitudes occurs in a particular case, it is *never* the consequence of the belief that the piece of behaviour in question was determined in a sense such that all behaviour *might be*, and, if determinism is true, all behaviour *is*, determined in that sense. For it is not a consequence of any general thesis of determinism which might be true that nobody knows what

P. F. Strawson

he's doing or that everybody's behaviour is unintelligible in terms of conscious purposes or that everybody lives in a world of delusion or that nobody has a moral sense, i.e. is susceptible of self-reactive attitudes, etc. In fact no such sense of 'determined' as would be required for a general thesis of determinism is ever relevant to our actual suspensions of moral reactive attitudes. Second, suppose it granted, as I have already argued, that we cannot take seriously the thought that theoretical conviction of such a general thesis would lead to the total decay of the personal reactive attitudes. Can we then take seriously the thought that such a conviction – a conviction, after all, that many have held or said they held – would nevertheless lead to the total decay or repudiation of the vicarious analogues of these attitudes? I think that the change in our social world which would leave us exposed to the personal reactive attitudes but not at all to their vicarious analogues, the generalization of abnormal egocentricity which this would entail, is perhaps even harder for us to envisage as a real possibility than the decay of both kinds of attitude together. Though there are some necessary and some contingent differences between the ways and cases in which these two kinds of attitudes operate or are inhibited in their operation, yet, as general human capacities or pronenesses, they stand or lapse together. Finally, to the further question whether it would not be *rational*, given a general theoretical conviction of the truth of determinism, so to change our world that in it all these attitudes were wholly suspended, I must answer, as before, that one who presses this question has wholly failed to grasp the import of the preceding answer, the nature of the human commitment that is here involved: it is *useless* to ask whether it would not be rational for us to do what it is not in our nature to (be able to) do. To this I must add, as before, that if there were, say, for a moment open to us the possibility of such a godlike choice, the rationality of making or refusing it would be determined by quite other considerations than the truth or falsity of the general theoretical doctrine in question. The latter would be simply irrelevant; and this becomes ironically clear when we remember that for those convinced that the truth of determinism nevertheless really would make the one choice rational, there has always been the insuperable difficulty of explaining in intelligible terms how its falsity would make the opposite choice rational.

I am aware that in presenting the argument as I have done, neglecting the ever-interesting varieties of case, I have presented nothing more than a schema, using sometimes a crude opposition of phrase where we have a great intricacy of phenomena. In particular the simple opposition of objective attitudes on the one hand and the various contrasted attitudes which I have opposed to them must seem as grossly crude as it is central. Let me pause to mitigate this crudity a little, and also to strengthen one of my central contentions, by mentioning some things which straddle these contrasted kinds of attitude. Thus parents and others concerned with the care and upbringing of young children cannot have to their charges either kind of attitude in a pure or unqualified form. They are dealing with creatures who are potentially and increasingly capable both of holding, and being objects of, the full range of human and moral attitudes, but are not yet truly capable of either. The treatment of such creatures must therefore represent a kind of compromise, constantly shifting in one direction, between objectivity of attitude and developed human attitudes. Rehearsals insensibly modulate towards true performances. The punishment of a child is both like and unlike the punishment of an adult. Suppose we try to relate this progressive emergence of the child as a responsible being, as an object of non-objective attitudes, to that sense of 'determined' in which, if determinism is a possibly true thesis, all behaviour *may* be determined, and in which, if it is a true thesis, all behaviour *is* determined. What bearing *could* such a sense of 'determined' have upon the progressive modification of attitudes towards the child? Would it not be grotesque to think of the development of the child as a progressive or patchy emergence from an area in which its behaviour is in this sense determined into an area in which it isn't? Whatever sense of 'determined' is required for stating the thesis of determinism, it can scarcely be such as to allow of compromise, borderlinestyle answers to the question, 'Is this bit of behaviour determined or isn't it?' But in this matter of young children, it is essentially a borderline, penumbral area that we move in. Again, consider – a very different matter – the strain in the attitude of a psychoanalyst to his patient. *His* objectivity of attitude, *his* suspension of ordinary moral reactive attitudes, is profoundly modified by the fact that the aim of the enterprise is to make such suspension unnecessary or less necessary. Here we may and do naturally speak of restoring the agent's freedom. But here the restoring of freedom means bringing it about that the agent's behaviour shall be intelligible in terms of conscious purposes rather than in terms only of unconscious purposes. *This* is the object of the enterprise; and it is in so far as *this* object is attained that the suspension, or half-suspension, of ordinary moral attitudes is deemed no longer necessary or appropriate. And in this we see once again the *irrelevance* of that concept of 'being determined' which must be the central concept of determinism. For we cannot both agree that this object is attainable and that its attainment has this consequence and yet hold (1) that neurotic behaviour is determined in a sense in which, it may be, all behaviour is determined, and (2) that it is because neurotic behaviour is determined in this sense that objective attitudes are deemed appropriate to neurotic behaviour. Not, at least, without accusing ourselves of incoherence in our attitude to psychoanalytic treatment.

VI

And now we can try to fill in the lacuna which the pessimist finds in the optimist's account of the concept of moral responsibility, and of the bases of moral condemnation and punishment; and to fill it in from the facts as we know them. For, as I have already remarked, when the pessimist himself seeks to fill it in, he rushes beyond the facts as we know them and proclaims that it cannot be filled in at all unless determinism is false.

Yet a partial sense of the facts as we know them is certainly present to the pessimist's mind. When his opponent, the optimist, undertakes to show that the truth of determinism would not shake the foundations of the concept of moral responsibility and of the practices of moral condemnation and punishment, he typically refers, in a more or less elaborated way, to the efficacy of these practices in regulating behaviour in socially desirable ways. These practices are represented solely as instruments of policy, as methods of individual treatment and social control. The pessimist recoils from this picture; and in his recoil there is, typically, an element of emotional shock. He is apt to say, among much else, that the humanity of the offender himself is offended by *this* picture of his condemnation and punishment.

The reasons for this recoil – the explanation of the sense of an emotional, as well as a conceptual, shock – we have already before us. The picture painted by the optimists is painted in a style appropriate to a situation envisaged as wholly dominated by objectivity of attitude. The only operative notions invoked in this picture are such as those of policy, treatment, control. But a thoroughgoing objectivity of attitude, excluding as it does the moral reactive attitudes, excludes at the same time essential elements in the concepts of *moral* condemnation and *moral* responsibility. This is the reason for the conceptual shock. The deeper emotional shock is a reaction, not simply to an inadequate conceptual analysis, but to the suggestion of a change in our world. I have remarked that it is possible to cultivate an exclusive objectivity of attitude in some cases, and for some reasons, where the object of the attitude is not set aside from developed inter-personal and moral attitudes by immaturity or abnormality. And the suggestion which seems to be contained in the optimist's account is that such an attitude should be universally adopted to all offenders. This is shocking enough in the pessimist's eyes. But, sharpened by shock, his eyes see further. It would be hard to make *this* division in our natures. If to all offenders, then to all mankind. Moreover, to whom could this recommendation be, in any real sense, addressed? Only to the powerful, the authorities. So abysses seem to open.[5]

But we will confine our attention to the case of the offenders. The concepts we are concerned with are those of responsibility and guilt, qualified as 'moral', on the one hand – together with that of membership of a moral community; of demand, indignation, disapprobation and condemnation, qualified as 'moral', on the other hand – together with that of punishment. Indignation, disapprobation, like resentment, tend to inhibit or at least to limit our goodwill towards the object of these attitudes, tend to promote an at least partial and temporary withdrawal of goodwill; they do so in proportion as they are strong; and their strength is in general proportioned to what is felt to be the magnitude of the injury and to the degree to which the agent's will is identified with, or indifferent to, it. (These, of course, are not contingent connections.) But these attitudes of disapprobation and indignation are precisely the correlates of the moral demand in the case where the demand is felt to be disregarded. The making of the demand *is* the proneness to such attitudes. The holding of them does not, as the holding of objective attitudes does, involve as a part of itself viewing their object other than as a member of the moral community. The partial withdrawal of goodwill which *these* attitudes entail, the modification *they* entail of the general demand that another should, if possible, be spared suffering, is, rather, the consequence of *continuing* to view him as a member of the moral community; only as one who has offended against its demands. So the preparedness to acquiesce in that infliction of suffering on the offender which is an essential part of punishment is all of a piece with this whole range of attitudes of which I have been speaking. It is not only moral reactive attitudes towards the offender which are in question here. We must mention also the self-reactive attitudes of offenders themselves. Just as the other-reactive attitudes are associated with a readiness to acquiesce in the infliction of suffering on an offender, within the 'institution' of punishment, so the self-reactive attitudes are associated with a readiness on the part of the offender to acquiesce in such infliction *without* developing the reactions (e.g. of resentment) which he would normally develop to the infliction of injury upon him; i.e. with a readiness, as we say, to accept punishment[6] as 'his due' or as 'just'.

I am not in the least suggesting that these readinesses to acquiesce, either on the part of the offender himself or on the part of others, are always or commonly accompanied or preceded by indignant boilings or remorseful pangs; only that we have here a continuum of attitudes and feelings to which these readinesses to acquiesce themselves belong. Nor am I in the least suggesting that it belongs to this continuum of attitudes that we should be ready to acquiesce in the infliction of injury on offenders in a fashion which we saw to be quite indiscriminate or in accordance with procedures which we knew to be wholly useless. On the contrary, savage or civilized, we have some belief in the utility of practices of condemnation and punishment. But the social utility of these practices, on which the optimist lays such exclusive stress, is not what is now in question. What is in question is the pessimist's justified sense that to speak in terms of social utility alone is to leave out something vital in our conception of these practices. The vital thing can be restored by attending to that complicated web of attitudes and feelings which form an essential part of the moral life as we know it,

and which are quite opposed to objectivity of attitude. Only by attending to this range of attitudes can we recover from the facts as we know them a sense of what we mean, i.e. of *all* we mean, when, speaking the language of morals, we speak of desert, responsibility, guilt, condemnation, and justice. But we *do* recover it from the facts as we know them. We do not have to go beyond them. Because the optimist neglects or misconstrues these attitudes, the pessimist rightly claims to find a lacuna in his account. We can fill the lacuna for him. But in return we must demand of the pessimist a surrender of his metaphysics.

Optimist and pessimist misconstrue the facts in very different styles. But in a profound sense there is something in common to their misunderstandings. Both seek, in different ways, to over-intellectualize the facts. Inside the general structure or web of human attitudes and feelings of which I have been speaking, there is endless room for modification, redirection, criticism, and justification. But questions of justification are internal to the structure or relate to modifications internal to it. The existence of the general framework of attitudes itself is something we are given with the fact of human society. As a whole, it neither calls for, nor permits, an external 'rational' justification. Pessimist and optimist alike show themselves, in different ways, unable to accept this.[7] The optimist's style of over-intellectualizing the facts is that of a characteristically incomplete empiricism, a one-eyed utilitarianism. He seeks to find an adequate basis for certain social practices in calculated consequences, and loses sight (perhaps wishes to lose sight) of the human attitudes of which these practices are, in part, the expression. The pessimist does not lose sight of these attitudes, but is unable to accept the fact that it is just these attitudes themselves which fill the gap in the optimist's account. Because of this, he thinks the gap can be filled only if some general metaphysical proposition is repeatedly verified, verified in all cases where it is appropriate to attribute moral responsibility. This proposition he finds it as difficult to state coherently and with intelligible relevance as its determinist contradictory. Even when a formula has been found ('contra-causal freedom' or something of the kind) there still seems to remain a gap between its applicability in particular cases and its supposed moral consequences. Sometimes he plugs this gap with an intuition of fittingness – a pitiful intellectualist trinket for a philosopher to wear as a charm against the recognition of his own humanity.

Even the moral sceptic is not immune from his own form of the wish to over-intellectualize such notions as those of moral responsibility, guilt, and blame. He sees that the optimist's account is inadequate and the pessimist's libertarian alternative inane; and finds no resource except to declare that the notions in question are inherently confused, that 'blame is metaphysical'. But the metaphysics was in the eye of the metaphysician. It is a pity that talk of the moral sentiments has fallen out of favour. The phrase would be quite a good name for that network of human attitudes in acknowledging the character and place of which we find, I suggest, the only possibility of reconciling these disputants to each other and the facts.

There are, at present, factors which add, in a slightly paradoxical way, to the difficulty of making this acknowledgement. These human attitudes themselves, in their development and in the variety of their manifestations, have to an increasing extent become objects of study in the social and psychological sciences; and this growth of human self-consciousness, which we might expect to reduce the difficulty of acceptance, in fact increases it in several ways. One factor of comparatively minor importance is an increased historical and anthropological awareness of the great variety of forms which these human attitudes may take at different times and in different cultures. This makes one rightly chary of claiming as essential features of the concept of morality in general, forms of these attitudes which may have a local and temporary prominence. No doubt to some extent my own descriptions of human attitudes have reflected local and temporary features of our own culture. But an awareness of variety of forms should not prevent us from acknowledging also that in the absence of *any* forms of these attitudes it is doubtful whether we should have anything that *we* could find intelligible as a system of human relationships, as human society. A quite different factor of greater importance is that psychological studies have made us rightly mistrustful of many particular manifestations of

the attitudes I have spoken of. They are a prime realm of self-deception, of the ambiguous and the shady, of guilt-transference, unconscious sadism and the rest. But it is an exaggerated horror, itself suspect, which would make us unable to acknowledge the facts because of the seamy side of the facts. Finally, perhaps the most important factor of all is the prestige of these theoretical studies themselves. That prestige is great, and is apt to make us forget that in philosophy, though it also is a theoretical study, we have to take account of the facts in *all* their bearings; we are not to suppose that we are required, or permitted, as philosophers, to regard ourselves, as human beings, as detached from the attitudes which, as scientists, we study with detachment. This is in no way to deny the possibility and desirability of redirection and modification of our human attitudes in the light of these studies. But we may reasonably think it unlikely that our progressively greater understanding of certain aspects of ourselves will lead to the total disappearance of those aspects. Perhaps it is not inconceivable that it should; and perhaps, then, the dreams of some philosophers will be realized.

If we sufficiently, that is *radically*, modify the view of the optimist, his view is the right one. It is far from wrong to emphasize the efficacy of all those practices which express or manifest our moral attitudes, in regulating behaviour in ways considered desirable; or to add that when certain of our beliefs about the efficacy of some of these practices turn out to be false, then we may have good reason for dropping or modifying those practices. What *is* wrong is to forget that these practices, and their reception, the reactions to them, really *are* expressions of our moral attitudes and not merely devices we calculatingly employ for regulative purposes. Our practices do not merely exploit our natures, they express them. Indeed the very understanding of the kind of efficacy these expressions of our attitudes have turns on our remembering this. When we do remember this, and modify the optimist's position accordingly, we simultaneously correct its conceptual deficiencies and ward off the dangers it seems to entail, without recourse to the obscure and panicky metaphysics of libertarianism.

Notes

1 Cf. P. H. Nowell-Smith, 'Freewill and Moral Responsibility', *Mind* 57 (1948).

2 As Nowell-Smith pointed out in a later article: 'Determinists and Libertarians', *Mind* 63 (1954).

3 Perhaps not in every case *just* what we demand they should be, but in any case *not* just what we demand they should not be. For my present purpose these differences do not matter.

4 The question, then, of the connection between rationality and the adoption of the objective attitude to others is misposed when it is made to seem dependent on the issue of determinism. But there is another question which should be raised, if only to distinguish it from the misposed question. Quite apart from the issue of determinism might it not be said that we should be nearer to being purely rational creatures in proportion as our relation to others was in fact dominated by the objective attitude? I think this might be said; only it would have to be added, once more, that if such a choice were possible, it would not necessarily be rational to choose to be more purely rational than we are.

5 See J. D. Mabbott's 'Freewill and Punishment', published in *Contemporary British Philosophy*, 3rd ser. (London: Allen & Unwin, 1956).

6 Of course not *any* punishment for *anything* deemed an offence.

7 Compare the question of the justification of induction. The human commitment to inductive belief-formation is original, natural, non-rational (not *ir*rational), in no way something we choose or could give up. Yet rational criticism and reflection can refine standards and their application, supply 'rules for judging of cause and effect'. Even since the facts were made clear by Hume, people have been resisting acceptance of them.

30

Human Freedom and the Self

Roderick Chisholm

A staff moves a stone, and is moved by a hand, which is moved by a man.

(Aristotle, *Physics*, 256a)

1. The metaphysical problem of human freedom might be summarized in the following way: Human beings are responsible agents; but this fact appears to conflict with a deterministic view of human action (the view that every event that is involved in an act is caused by some other event); and it *also* appears to conflict with an indeterministic view of human action (the view that the act, or some event that is essential to the act, is not caused at all.) To solve the problem, I believe, we must make somewhat far-reaching assumptions about the self or the agent – about the man who performs the act.

Perhaps it is needless to remark that, in all likelihood, it is impossible to say anything significant about this ancient problem that has not been said before.[1]

2. Let us consider some deed, or misdeed, that may be attributed to a responsible agent: one man, say, shot another. If the man *was* responsible for what he did, then, I would urge, what was to happen at the time of the shooting was something that was entirely up to the man himself. There was a moment at which it was true, both

Originally the Lindley Lecture, University of Kansas, 1964. Reprinted from *On Metaphysics* (University of Minnesota Press, 1989).

that he could have fired the shot and also that he could have refrained from firing it. And if this is so, then, even though he did fire it, he could have done something else instead. (He didn't find himself firing the shot 'against his will', as we say.) I think we can say, more generally, then, that if a man is responsible for a certain event or a certain state of affairs (in our example, the shooting of another man), then that event or state of affairs was brought about by some act of his, and the act was something that was in his power either to perform or not to perform.

But now if the act which he *did* perform was an act that was also in his power *not* to perform, then it could not have been caused or determined by any event that was not itself within his power either to bring about or not to bring about. For example, if what we say he did was really something that was brought about by a second man, one who forced his hand upon the trigger, say, or who, by means of hypnosis, compelled him to perform the act, then since the act was caused by the *second* man it was nothing that was within the power of the *first* man to prevent. And precisely the same thing is true, I think, if instead of referring to a second man who compelled the first one, we speak instead of the *desires* and *beliefs* which the first man happens to have had. For if what we say he did was really something that was brought about by his own beliefs and desires, if these beliefs and desires in the particular situation in which he happened to have found himself caused him to do just what it was that we say he did do, then since *they* caused it, *he* was unable to do anything other than just what it was that he did do. It makes no difference whether the cause of the deed was internal or external; if the cause was some state or event for which the man himself was not responsible, then he was not responsible for what we have been mistakenly calling his act. If a flood caused the poorly constructed dam to break, then, given the flood and the constitution of the dam, the break, we may say, *had* to occur and nothing could have happened in its place. And if the flood of desire caused the weak-willed man to give in, then he, too, had to do just what it was that he did do and he was no more responsible than was the dam for the results that followed. (It is true, of course, that if the man is responsible for the beliefs and desires that he happens to have, then he may also be responsible for the things they lead him to do. But the question now becomes: *is* he responsible for the beliefs and desires he happens to have? If he is, then there was a time when they were within his power either to acquire or not to acquire, and we are left, therefore, with our general point.)

One may object: But surely if there were such a thing as a man who is really *good*, then he would be responsible for things that he would do; yet, he would be unable to do anything other than just what it is that he does do, since, being good, he will always choose to do what is best. The answer, I think, is suggested by a comment that Thomas Reid makes on an ancient author. The author had said of Cato, 'He was good because he could not be otherwise', and Reid observes: 'This saying, if understood literally and strictly, is not the praise of Cato, but of his constitution, which was no more the work of Cato than his existence'.[2] If Cato was himself responsible for the good things that he did, then Cato, as Reid suggests, was such that, although he had the power to do what was not good, he exercised his power only for that which was good.

All of this, if it is true, may give a certain amount of comfort to those who are tender-minded. But we should remind them that it also conflicts with a familiar view about the nature of God – with the view that St. Thomas Aquinas expresses by saying that 'every movement both of the will and of nature proceeds from God as the Prime Mover'.[3] If the act of the sinner *did* proceed from God as the Prime Mover, then God was in the position of the second agent we just discussed – the man who forced the trigger

finger, or the hypnotist – and the sinner, so-called, was *not* responsible for what he did. (This may be a bold assertion, in view of the history of western theology, but I must say that I have never encountered a single good reason for denying it.)

There is one standard objection to all of this and we should consider it briefly.

3. The objection takes the form of a stratagem – one designed to show that determinism (and divine providence) is consistent with human responsibility. The stratagem is one that was used by Jonathan Edwards and by many philosophers in the present century, most notably, G. E. Moore.[4]

One proceeds as follows: The expression

(a) He could have done otherwise,

it is argued, means no more nor less than

(b) If he had chosen to do otherwise, then he would have done otherwise.

(In place of 'chosen', one might say 'tried', 'set out', 'decided', 'undertaken', or 'willed'.) The truth of statement (b), it is then pointed out, is consistent with determinism (and with divine providence); for even if all of the man's actions were causally determined, the man could still be such that, *if* he had chosen otherwise, then he would have done otherwise. What the murderer saw, let us suppose, along with his beliefs and desires, *caused* him to fire the shot; yet he was such that *if*, just then, he had chosen or decided *not* to fire the shot, then he would not have fired it. All of this is certainly possible. Similarly, we could say, of the dam, that the flood caused it to break and also that the dam was such that, *if* there had been no flood or any similar pressure, then the dam would have remained intact. And therefore, the argument proceeds, if (b) is consistent with determinism, and if (a) and (b) say the same thing, then (a) is also consistent with determinism; hence we can say that the agent *could* have done otherwise even though he was caused to do what he did do; and therefore determinism and moral responsibility are compatible.

Is the argument sound? The conclusion follows from the premises, but the catch, I think, lies in the first premiss – the one saying that statement (a) tells us no more nor less than what statement

(b) tells us. For (b), it would seem, could be true while (a) is false. That is to say, our man might be such that, if he had chosen to do otherwise, then he would have done otherwise, and yet *also* such that he could not have done otherwise. Suppose, after all, that our murderer could not have *chosen*, or could not have *decided*, to do otherwise. Then the fact that he happens also to be a man such that, if he had chosen not to shoot he would not have shot, would make no difference. For if he could *not* have chosen *not* to shoot, then he could not have done anything other than just what it was that he did do. In a word: from our statement (b) above ('If he had chosen to do otherwise, then he would have done otherwise'), we cannot make an inference to (a) above ('He could have done otherwise') unless we can *also* assert:

(c) He could have chosen to do otherwise.

And therefore, if we must reject this third statement (c), then, even though we may be justified in asserting (b), we are not justified in asserting (a). If the man could not have chosen to do otherwise, then he would not have done otherwise – *even if* he was such that, if he *had* chosen to do otherwise, then he would have done otherwise.

The stratagem in question, then, seems to me not to work, and I would say, therefore, that the ascription of responsibility conflicts with a deterministic view of action.

4. Perhaps there is less need to argue that the ascription of responsibility also conflicts with an indeterministic view of action – with the view that the act, or some event that is essential to the act, is not caused at all. If the act – the firing of the shot – was not caused at all, if it was fortuitous or capricious, happening so to speak out of the blue, then, presumably, no one – and nothing – was responsible for the act. Our conception of action, therefore, should be neither deterministic nor indeterministic. Is there any other possibility?

5. We must not say that every event involved in the act is caused by some other event; and we must not say that the act is something that is not caused at all. The possibility that remains, therefore, is this: We should say that at least one of the events that are involved in the act is caused, not by any other events, but by some-

thing else instead. And this something else can only be the agent – the man. If there is an event that is caused, not by other events, but by the man, then there are some events involved in the act that are not caused by other events. But if the event in question is caused by the man then it *is* caused and we are not committed to saying that there is something involved in the act that is not caused at all.

But this, of course, is a large consequence, implying something of considerable importance about the nature of the agent or the man.

6. If we consider only inanimate natural objects, we may say that causation, if it occurs, is a relation between *events* or *states of affairs*. The dam's breaking was an event that was caused by a set of other events – the dam being weak, the flood being strong, and so on. But if a man is responsible for a particular deed, then, if what I have said is true, there is some event, or set of events, that is caused, *not* by other events or states of affairs, but by the agent, whatever he may be.

I shall borrow a pair of medieval terms, using them, perhaps, in a way that is slightly different from that for which they were originally intended. I shall say that when one event or state of affairs (or set of events or states of affairs) causes some other event or state of affairs, then we have an instance of *transeunt* causation. And I shall say that when an *agent*, as distinguished from an event, causes an event or state of affairs, then we have an instance of *immanent* causation.

The nature of what is intended by the expression 'immanent causation' may be illustrated by this sentence from Aristotle's *Physics*: "Thus, a staff moves a stone, and is moved by a hand, which is moved by a man" (VII, 5, 256a). If the man was responsible, then we have in this illustration a number of instances of causation – most of them transeunt but at least one of them immanent. What the staff did to the stone was an instance of transeunt causation, and thus we may describe it as a relation between events: "the motion of the staff caused the motion of the stone." And similarly for what the hand did to the staff: "the motion of the hand caused the motion of the staff." And, as we know from physiology, there are still other events which caused the motion of the hand. Hence we need not introduce the agent at this particular point, as Aristotle does – we *need* not, though we *may*. We *may* say that the hand was moved by the man, but we may *also* say that the motion of the hand was caused by the motion of certain muscles; and we may say that the motion of the muscles was caused by certain events that took place within the brain. But some event, and presumably one of those that took place within the brain, was caused by the agent and not by any other events.

There are, of course, objections to this way of putting the matter; I shall consider the two that seem to me to be most important.

7.   One may object, firstly: "If the *man* does anything, then, as Aristotle's remark suggests, what he does is to move the *hand*. But he certainly does not *do* anything to his brain – he may not even know that he *has* a brain. And if he doesn't do anything to the brain, and if the motion of the hand was caused by something that happened within the brain, then there is no point in appealing to 'immanent causation' as being something incompatible with 'transeunt causation' – for the whole thing, after all, is a matter of causal relations among events or states of affairs."

The answer to this objection, I think, is this: It is true that the agent does not *do* anything with his brain, or to his brain, in the sense in which he *does* something with his hand and does something to the staff. But from this it does not follow that the agent was not the immanent cause of something that happened within his brain.

We should note a useful distinction that has been proposed by Professor A. I. Melden – namely, the distinction between 'making something A happen' and 'doing A'.[5] If I reach for the staff and pick it up, then one of the things that I *do* is just that – reach for the staff and pick it up. And if it is something that I do, then there is a very clear sense in which it may be said to be something that I know that I do. If you ask me, "Are you doing something, or trying to do something, with the staff?", I will have no difficulty in finding an answer. But in doing something with the staff, I also make various things happen which are not in this same sense things that I do: I will make various air-particles move; I will free a number of blades of grass from the pressure that had been upon them; and I may cause a shadow to move from one place to another. If these are merely things that I make happen, as distinguished from things that I do, then I may know nothing whatever about them; I may not have the slightest idea that, in moving the staff, I am bringing about any such thing as

the motion of air-particles, shadows, and blades of grass.

We may say, in answer to the first objection, therefore, that it is true that our agent does nothing to his brain or with his brain; but from this it does not follow that the agent is not the immanent cause of some event within his brain; for the brain event may be something which, like the motion of the air-particles, he made happen in picking up the staff. The only difference between the two cases is this: in each case, he made something happen when he picked up the staff; but in the one case – the motion of the air particles or of the shadows – it was the motion of the staff that caused the event to happen; and in the other case – the event that took place in the brain – it was this event that caused the motion of the staff.

The point is, in a word, that whenever a man does something A, then (by 'immanent causation') he makes a certain cerebral event happen, and this cerebral event (by 'transeunt causation') makes A happen.

8.   The second objection is more difficult and concerns the very concept of 'immanent causation', or causation by an agent, as this concept is to be interpreted here. The concept is subject to a difficulty which has long been associated with that of the prime mover removed. We have said that there must be some event A, presumably some cerebral event, which is caused not by another event, but by the agent. Since A was not caused by any other event, then the agent himself cannot be said to have undergone any change or produced any other event (such as 'an act of will' or the like) which brought A about. But if, when the agent made A happen, there was no event involved other than A itself, no event which could be described as *making* A happen, what did the agent's causation consist of? What, for example, is the difference between A's just happening, and the agent's *causing* A to happen? We cannot attribute the difference to any event that took place within the agent. And so far as the event A itself is concerned, there would seem to be no discernible difference. Thus Aristotle said that the activity of the prime mover is nothing in addition to the motion that it produces, and Suarez said that 'the action is in reality nothing but the effect as it flows from the agent'.[6] Must we conclude, then, that there is no more to the man's action in causing event A

than there is to the event A's happening by itself? Here we would seem to have a distinction without a difference – in which case we have failed to find a *via media* between a deterministic and an indeterministic view of action.

The only answer, I think, can be this: that the difference between the man's causing A, on the one hand, and the event A just happening, on the other, lies in the fact that, in the first case but not the second, the event A *was* caused and was caused by the man. There was a brain event A; the agent did, in fact, cause the brain event; but there was nothing that he did to cause it.

This answer may not entirely satisfy and it will be likely to provoke the following question: 'But what are you really *adding* to the assertion that A happened when you utter the words "The agent *caused* A to happen"?' As soon as we have put the question this way, we see, I think, that whatever difficulty we may have encountered is one that may be traced to the concept of causation generally – whether 'immanent' or 'transeunt'. The problem, in other words, is not a problem that is peculiar to our conception of human action. It is a problem that must be faced by anyone who makes use of the concept of causation at all; and therefore, I would say, it is a problem for everyone but the complete indeterminist.

For the problem, as we put it, referring just to 'immanent causation', or causation by an agent, was this: 'What is the difference between saying, of an event A, that A just happened and saying that someone caused A to happen?' The analogous problem, which holds for 'transeunt causation', or causation by an event, is this: 'What is the difference between saying, of two events A and B, that B happened and then A happened, and saying that B's happening was the *cause* of A's happening?' And the only answer that one can give is this – that in the one case the agent was the cause of A's happening and in the other case event B was the cause of A's happening. The nature of transeunt causation is no more clear than is that of immanent causation.

9. But we may plausibly say – and there is a respectable philosophical tradition to which we may appeal – that the notion of immanent causation; or causation by an agent, is in fact more clear than that of transeunt causation, or causation by an event, and that it is only by understanding our own causal efficacy, as agents, that we can grasp the concept of *cause* at all. Hume

may be said to have shown that we do not derive the concept of *cause* from what we perceive of external things. How, then, do we derive it? The most plausible suggestion, it seems to me, is that of Reid, once again: namely that 'the conception of an efficient cause may very probably be derived from the experience we have had . . . of our own power to produce certain effects'.[7] If we did not understand the concept of immanent causation, we would not understand that of transeunt causation.

10. It may have been noted that I have avoided the term 'free will' in all of this. For even if there is such a faculty as 'the will', which somehow sets our acts agoing, the question of freedom, as John Locke said, is not the question "*whether the will be free*"; it is the question "*whether a man be free.*"[8] For if there is a 'will', as a moving faculty, the question is whether the man is free to will to do these things that he does will to do – and also whether he is free *not* to will any of those things that he does will to do, and, again, whether he is free to will any of those things that he does not will to do. Jonathan Edwards tried to restrict himself to the question – "Is the man free to do what it is that he wills?" – but the answer to this question will not tell us whether the man is responsible for what it is that he *does* will to do. Using still another pair of medieval terms, we may say that the metaphysical problem of freedom does not concern the *actus imperatus*; it does not concern the question whether we are free to accomplish whatever it is that we will or set out to do; it concerns the *actus elicitus*, the question whether we are free to will or to set out to do those things that we do will or set out to do.

11. If we are responsible, and if what I have been trying to say is true, then we have a prerogative which some would attribute only to God: each of us, when we act, is a prime mover unmoved. In doing what we do, we cause certain events to happen, and nothing – or no one – causes us to cause those events to happen.

12. If we are thus prime movers unmoved and if our actions, or those for which we are responsible, are not causally determined, then they are not causally determined by our *desires*. And this means that the relation between what we want or what we desire, on the one hand, and what it is

that we do, on the other, is not as simple as most philosophers would have it.

We may distinguish between what we might call the 'Hobbist approach' and what we might call the 'Kantian approach' to this question. The Hobbist approach is the one that is generally accepted at the present time, but the Kantian approach, I believe, is the one that is true. According to Hobbism, if we *know*, of some man, what his beliefs and desires happen to be and how strong they are, if we know what he feels certain of, what he desires more than anything else, and if we know the state of his body and what stimuli he is being subjected to, then we may *deduce*, logically, just what it is that he will do – or, more accurately, just what it is that he will try, set out, or undertake to do. Thus Professor Melden has said that "the connection between wanting and doing is logical."[9] But according to the Kantian approach to our problem, and this is the one that I would take, there is no such logical connection between wanting and doing, nor need there even be a causal connection. No set of statements about a man's desires, beliefs, and stimulus situation at any time implies any statement telling us what the man will try, set out, or undertake to do at that time. As Reid put it, though we may 'reason from men's motives to their actions and, in many cases, with great probability', we can never do so 'with absolute certainty'.[10]

This means that, in one very strict sense of the terms, there can be no science of man. If we think of science as a matter of finding out what laws happen to hold, and if the statement of a law tells us what kinds of events are caused by what other kinds of events, then there will be human actions which we cannot explain by subsuming them under any laws. We cannot say, "It is causally necessary that, given such and such desires and beliefs, and being subject to such and such stimuli, the agent will do so and so." For at times the agent, if he chooses, may rise above his desires and do something else instead.

But all of this is consistent with saying that, perhaps more often than not, our desires do exist under conditions such that those conditions necessitate us to act. And we may also say, with Leibniz, that at other times our desires may 'incline without necessitating'.

13. Leibniz's phrase presents us with our final philosophical problem. What does it mean to say

that a desire, or a motive, might "incline without necessitating"? There is a temptation, certainly, to say that "to incline" means to cause and that "not to necessitate" means not to cause, but obviously we cannot have it both ways.

Nor will Leibniz's own solution do. In his letter to Coste, he puts the problem as follows: "When a choice is proposed, for example to go out or not to go out, it is a question whether, with all the circumstances, internal and external, motives, perceptions, dispositions, impressions, passions, inclinations taken together, I am still in a contingent state, or whether I am necessitated to make the choice, for example, to go out; that is to say, whether this proposition true and determined in fact, *In all these circumstances taken together I shall choose to go out*, is contingent or necessary."[11] Leibniz's answer might be put us follows: in one sense of the terms "necessary" and "contingent", the proposition "In all these circumstances taken together I shall choose to go out," may be said to be contingent and not necessary, and in another sense of these terms, it may be said to be necessary and not contingent. But the sense in which the proposition may be said to be contingent, according to Leibniz, is only this: there is no logical contradiction involved in denying the proposition. And the sense in which it may be said to be necessary is this: since "nothing ever occurs without cause or determining reason," the proposition is causally necessary. "Whenever all the circumstances taken together are such that the balance of deliberation is heavier on one side than on the other, it is certain and infallible that that is the side that is going to win out." But if what we have been saying is true, the proposition "In all these circumstances taken together I shall choose to go out" may be causally as well as logically contingent. Hence we must find another interpretation for Leibniz's statement that our motives and desires may incline us, or influence us, to choose without thereby necessitating us to choose.

Let us consider a public official who has some moral scruples but who also, as one says, could be had. Because of the scruples that he does have, he would never take any positive steps to receive a bribe – he would not actively solicit one. But his morality has its limits and he is also such that, if we were to confront him with a *fait accompli* or to let him see what is about to happen ($10,000 in cash is being deposited behind the garage), then he would succumb and be unable to resist. The general situation is a familiar one and this is one reason that people pray to be delivered from temptation. (It also justifies Kant's remark: "And how many there are who may have led a long blameless life, who are only *fortunate* in having escaped so many temptations."[12] Our relation to the misdeed that we contemplate may not be a matter simply of being able to bring it about or not to bring it about. As St. Anselm noted, there are at least four possibilities. We may illustrate them by reference to our public official and the event which is his receiving the bribe, in the following way: (i) he may be able to bring the event about himself (*facere esse*), in which case he would actively cause himself to receive the bribe; (ii) he may be able to refrain from bringing it about himself (*non facere esse*), in which case he would not himself do anything to insure that he receive the bribe; (iii) he may be able to do something to prevent the event from occurring (*facere non esse*), in which case he would make sure that the $10,000 was *not* left behind the garage; or (iv) he may be unable to do anything to prevent the event from occurring (*non facere non esse*), in which case, though he may not solicit the bribe, he would allow himself to keep it.[13] We have envisaged our official as a man who can resist the temptation to (i) but cannot resist the temptation to

(iv): he can refrain from bringing the event about himself, but he cannot bring himself to do anything to prevent it.

Let us think of 'inclination without necessitation', then, in such terms as these. First we may contrast the two propositions:

1 He can resist the temptation to do something in order to make A happen;
2 He can resist the temptation to allow A to happen (i.e. to do nothing to prevent A from happening).

We may suppose that the man has some desire to have A happen and thus has a motive for making A happen. His motive for making A happen, I suggest, is one that *necessitates* provided that, because of the motive, (1) is false; he cannot resist the temptation to do something in order to make A happen. His motive for making A happen is one that *inclines* provided that, because of the motive, (2) is false; like our public official, he cannot bring himself to do anything to prevent A from happening. And therefore we can say that this motive for making A happen is one that *inclines but does not necessitate* provided that, because of the motive, (1) is true and (2) is false; he can resist the temptation to make it happen but he cannot resist the temptation to allow it to happen.

Notes

1 The general position to be presented here is suggested in the following writings, among others: Aristotle, *Eudemian Ethics*, Book II, ch. 6; *Nicomachean Ethics*, Book III, chs. 1–5; Thomas Reid, *Essays on the Active Powers of Man*; C. A. Campbell, "Is 'Free Will' a Pseudo-Problem?" *Mind* NS 60 (1951), pp. 441–65; Roderick M. Chisholm, "Responsibility and Avoidability," and Richard Taylor, "Determination and the Theory of Agency," in *Determinism and Freedom, in the Age of Modern Science*, ed. Sidney Hook (New York: New York University Press, 1958).

2 Thomas Reid, *Essays on the Active Powers of Man*, Essay IV, ch. 4 (*Works*, p. 600).

3 *Summa Theologia*, First Part of the Second Part, Question VI ("On the Voluntary and Involuntary").

4 Jonathan Edwards, *Freedom of the Will* (New Haven, CT: Yale University Press, 1957); G. E. Moore, *Ethics* (New York: H. Holt (Home University Library), 1912), ch. 6.

5 A. I. Melden, *Free Action*, Oxford: Blackwell, 1961, especially ch. 3. Prof. Melden's own views, however, are quite the contrary of those proposed here.

6 Aristotle, *Physics*, Book III, ch. 3; Suarez. *Disputationes Metaphysicae*, Disputation 18, sec. 10.

7 Reid, *Essays on the Active Powers of Man*, *Works*, p. 524.

8 *Essay Concerning Human Understanding*, Book II, ch. 21.

9 Melden, *Free Action*, p. 166.

10 Reid, *Essays on the Active Powers of Man*, *Works*, pp. 608, 612.

11 "Lettre à Mr. Coste de la Nécessité et de la Contingence" (1707), in Johanne E. Erdmann (ed.) *Opera Philosophica* (Berlin: Sumptibus G. Eichleri, 1840), pp. 447–9.

12 In the preface to the *Metaphysical Elements of Ethics*, in T. K. Abbot (ed.) *Kant's Critique of Practical Reason and Other Works on the Theory of Ethics* (London: Longmans Green, 1959), p. 303.

13 Cf. D. P. Henry, "Saint Anselm's De 'Grammatico'," *Philosophical Quarterly* 10 (1960), pp. 115–26. St. Anselm noted that (i) and (iii), respectively, may be thought of as forming the upper left and the upper right corners of a square of opposition, and (ii) and (iv) the lower right and the lower left.

31

The Self and the Future

Bernard Williams

Suppose that there were some process to which two persons, A and B, could be subjected as a result of which they might be said – question-beggingly – to have *exchanged bodies*. That is to say – less question-beggingly – there is a certain human body which is such that when previously we were confronted with it, we were confronted with person A, certain utterances coming from it were expressive of memories of the past experiences of A, certain movements of it partly constituted the actions of A and were taken as expressive of the character of A, and so forth; but now, after the process is completed, utterances coming from this body are expressive of what seem to be just those memories which previously we identified as memories of the past experiences of B, its movements partly constitute actions expressive of the character of B, and so forth; and conversely with the other body.

There are certain important philosophical limitations on how such imaginary cases are to be constructed, and how they are to be taken when constructed in various ways. I shall mention two principal limitations, not in order to pursue them further here, but precisely in order to get them out of the way.

There are certain limitations, particularly with regard to character and mannerisms, to our ability to imagine such cases even in the most restricted sense of our being disposed to take the later

Originally published in *Philosophical Review* 79 (1970). Copyright 1970 Cornell University. Reprinted by permission of the publisher.

performances of that body which was previously A's as expressive of B's character; if the previous A and B were extremely unlike one another both physically and psychologically, and if, say, in addition, they were of different sex, there might be grave difficulties in reading B's dispositions in any possible performances of A's body. Let us forget this, and for the present purpose just take A and B as being sufficiently alike (however alike that has to be) for the difficulty not to arise; after the experiment, persons familiar with A and B are just *overwhelmingly struck* by the B-ish character of the doings associated with what was previously A's body, and conversely. Thus the feat of imagining an exchange of bodies is supposed possible in the most restricted sense. But now there is a further limitation which has to be overcome if the feat is to be not merely possible in the most restricted sense but also is to have an outcome which, on serious reflection, we are prepared to describe as A and B having changed bodies – that is, an outcome where, confronted with what was previously A's body, we are prepared seriously to say that we are now confronted with B.

It would seem a necessary condition of so doing that the utterances coming from that body be taken as genuinely expressive of memories of B's past. But memory is a causal notion; and as we actually use it, it seems a necessary condition of x's present knowledge of x's earlier experiences constituting memory of those experiences that the causal chain linking the experiences and the knowledge should not run outside x's body.

Hence if utterances coming from a given body are to be taken as expressive of memories of the experiences of B, there should be some suitable causal link between the appropriate state of that body and the original happening of those experiences to B. One radical way of securing that condition in the imagined exchange case is to suppose, with Shoemaker,[1] that the brains of A and of B are transposed. We may not need so radical a condition. Thus suppose it were possible to extract information from a man's brain and store it in a device while his brain was repaired, or even renewed, the information then being replaced: it would seem exaggerated to insist that the resultant man could not possibly have the memories he had before the operation. With regard to our knowledge of our own past, we draw distinctions between merely recalling, being reminded, and learning again, and those distinctions correspond (roughly) to distinctions between no new input, partial new input, and total new input with regard to the information in question; and it seems clear that the information-parking case just imagined would not count as new input in the sense necessary and sufficient for 'learning again'. Hence we can imagine the case we are concerned with in terms of information extracted into such devices from A's and B's brains and replaced in the other brain; this is the sort of model which, I think not unfairly for the present argument, I shall have in mind.

We imagine the following. The process considered above exists; two persons can enter some machine, let us say, and emerge changed in the appropriate ways. If A and B are the persons who enter, let us call the persons who emerge the *A-body-person* and the *B-body-person*: the A-body-person is that person (whoever it is) with whom I am confronted when, after the experiment, I am confronted with that body which previously was A's body – that is to say, that person who would naturally be taken for A by someone who just saw this person, was familiar with A's appearance before the experiment, and did not know about the happening of the experiment. A non-question-begging description of the experiment will leave it open which (if either) of the persons A and B the A-body-person is; the description of the experiment as 'persons changing bodies' of course implies that the A-body-person is actually B.

We take two persons A and B who are going to have the process carried out on them. (We can suppose, rather hazily, that they are willing for this to happen; to investigate at all closely at this stage why they might be willing or unwilling, what they would fear, and so forth, would anticipate some later issues.) We further announce that one of the two resultant persons, the A-body-person and the B-body-person, is going after the experiment to be given $100,000, while the other is going to be tortured. We then ask each of A and B to choose which treatment should be dealt out to which of the persons who will emerge from the experiment, the choice to be made (if it can be) on selfish grounds.

Suppose that A chooses that the B-body-person should get the pleasant treatment and the A-body-person the unpleasant treatment; and B chooses conversely (this might indicate that they thought that 'changing bodies' was indeed a good description of the outcome). The experimenter cannot act in accordance with both these sets of preferences, those expressed by A and those expressed by B. Hence there is one clear sense in which A and B cannot both get what they want: namely, that if the experimenter, before the experiment, announces to A and B that he intends to carry out the alternative (for example), of treating the B-body-person unpleasantly and the A-body-person pleasantly – then A can say rightly, 'That's not the outcome I chose to happen', and B can say rightly, 'That's just the outcome I chose to happen'. So, evidently, A and B before the experiment can each come to know either that the outcome he chose will be that which will happen, or that the one he chose will not happen, and in that sense they can get or fail to get what they wanted. But is it also true that when the experimenter proceeds after the experiment to act in accordance with one of the preferences and not the other, *then* one of A and B will have got what he wanted, and the other not?

There seems very good ground for saying so. For suppose the experimenter, having elicited A's and B's preference, says nothing to A and B about what he will do; conducts the experiment; and then, for example, gives the unpleasant treatment to the B-body-person and the pleasant treatment to the A-body-person. Then the B-body-person will not only complain of the unpleasant treatment as such, but will complain (since he has A's memories) that that was not the outcome he chose, since he chose that the B-body-person should be well treated; and since A made his choice in selfish spirit, he may add that he precisely chose in that way because he did not want the unpleasant things to happen to *him*. The A-body-person meanwhile will express satisfaction both at the receipt of the $100,000, and also at the fact that the experimenter has chosen to act in the way that he, B, so wisely chose. These facts make a strong case for saying that the experimenter has brought it about that B did in the outcome get what he wanted and A did not. It is therefore a strong case for saying that the B-body-person really is A, and the A-body-person really is B; and therefore for saying that the process of the experiment really is that of changing bodies. For the same reasons it would seem that A and B in our example really did choose wisely, and that it was A's bad luck that the choice he correctly made was not carried out, B's good luck that the choice he correctly made was carried out. This seems to show that to care about what happens to me in the future is not necessarily to care about what happens to *this* body (the one I now have); and this in turn might be taken to show that in some sense of Descartes's obscure phrase, I and my body are 'really distinct' (though, of course, nothing in these considerations could support the idea that I could exist without a body at all).

These suggestions seem to be reinforced if we consider the cases where A and B make other choices with regard to the experiment. Suppose that A chooses that the A-body-person should get the money, and the B-body-person get the pain, and B chooses conversely. Here again there can be no outcome which matches the expressed preferences of both of them: they cannot both get what they want. The experimenter announces, before the experiment, that the A-body-person will in fact get the money, and the B-body-person will get the pain. So A at this stage gets what he wants (the announced outcome matches his expressed preference). After the experiment, the distribution is carried out as announced. Both the A-body-person and the B-body-person will have to agree that what is happening is in accordance with the preference that A originally expressed. The B-body-person will naturally express this acknowledgement (since he has A's memories) by saying that this is the distribution he chose; he will recall, among other things, the experimenter announcing this outcome, his approving it as what he chose, and so forth. However, he (the B-body-person) certainly does not like

what is now happening to him, and would much prefer to be receiving what the A-body-person is receiving – namely, $100,000. The A-body-person will on the other hand recall choosing an outcome other than this one, but will reckon it good luck that the experimenter did not do what he recalls choosing. It looks, then, as though the A-body-person has got what he wanted, but not what he chose, while the B-body-person has got what he chose, but not what he wanted. So once more it looks as though they are, respectively, B and A; and that in this case the original choices of both A and B were unwise.

Suppose, lastly, that in the original choice A takes the line of the first case and B of the second: that is, A chooses that the B-body-person should get the money and the A-body-person the pain, and B chooses exactly the same thing. In this case, the experimenter would seem to be in the happy situation of giving both persons what they want – or at least, like God, what they have chosen. In this case, the B-body-person likes what he is receiving, recalls choosing it, and congratulates himself on the wisdom of (as he puts it) his choice; while the A-body-person does not like what he is receiving, recalls choosing it, and is forced to acknowledge that (as he puts it) his choice was unwise. So once more we seem to get results to support the suggestions drawn from the first case.

Let us now consider the question, not of A and B choosing certain outcomes to take place after the experiment, but of their willingness to engage in the experiment at all. If they were initially inclined to accept the description of the experiment as 'changing bodies' then one thing that would interest them would be the character of the other person's body. In this respect also what would happen after the experiment would seem to suggest that 'changing bodies' was a good description of the experiment. If A and B agreed to the experiment, being each not displeased with the appearance, physique, and so forth of the other person's body; after the experiment the B-body-person might well be found saying such things as: 'When I agreed to this experiment, I thought that B's face was quite attractive, but now I look at it in the mirror, I am not so sure'; or the A-body-person might say 'When I agreed to this experiment I did not know that A had a wooden leg; but now, after it is over, I find that I have this wooden leg, and I want the experiment reversed.' It is possible that he might say further that he finds the leg very uncomfortable, and that the B-body-person should say, for instance, that he recalls that he found it very uncomfortable at first, but one gets used to it: but perhaps one would need to know more than at least I do about the physiology of habituation to artificial limbs to know whether the A-body-person would find the leg uncomfortable: that body, after all, has had the leg on it for some time. But apart from this sort of detail, the general line of the outcome regarded from this point of view seems to confirm our previous conclusions about the experiment.

Now let us suppose that when the experiment is proposed (in non-question-begging terms) A and B think rather of their psychological advantages and disadvantages. A's thoughts turn primarily to certain sorts of anxiety to which he is very prone, while B is concerned with the frightful memories he has of past experiences which still distress him. They each hope that the experiment will in some way result in their being able to get away from these things. They may even have been impressed by philosophical arguments to the effect that bodily continuity is at least a necessary condition of personal identity: A, for example, reasons that, granted the experiment comes off, then the person who is bodily continuous with him will not have this anxiety, and while the other person will no doubt have some anxiety – perhaps in some sense his anxiety – at least that person will not be he. The experiment is performed and the experimenter (to whom A and B previously revealed privately their several difficulties and hopes) asks the A-body-person whether he has got rid of his anxiety. This person presumably replies that he does not know what the man is talking about; he never had such anxiety, but he did have some very disagreeable memories, and recalls engaging in the experiment to get rid of them, and is disappointed to discover that he still has them. The B-body-person will react in a similar way to questions about his painful memories, pointing out that he still has his anxiety. These results seem to confirm still further the description of the experiment as 'changing bodies'. And all the results suggest that the only rational thing to do, confronted with such an experiment, would be to identify oneself with one's memories, and so forth, and not with one's body. The philosophical arguments designed to show that bodily continuity was at least a necessary condition of personal identity would seem to be just mistaken.

Let us now consider something apparently different. Someone in whose power I am tells me that I am going to be tortured tomorrow. I am frightened, and look forward to tomorrow in great apprehension. He adds that when the time comes, I shall not remember being told that this was going to happen to me, since shortly before the torture something else will be done to me which will make me forget the announcement. This certainly will not cheer me up, since I know perfectly well that I can forget things, and that there is such a thing as indeed being tortured unexpectedly because I had forgotten or been made to forget a prediction of the torture: that will still be a torture which, so long as I do know about the prediction, I look forward to in fear. He then adds that my forgetting the announcement will be only part of a larger process: when the moment of torture comes, I shall not remember any of the things I am now in a position to remember. This does not cheer me up, either, since I can readily conceive of being involved in an accident, for instance, as a result of which I wake up in a completely amnesiac state and also in great pain; that could certainly happen to me, I should not like it to happen to me, nor to know that it was going to happen to me. He now further adds that at the moment of torture I shall not only not remember the things I am now in a position to remember, but will have a different set of impressions of my past, quite different from the memories I now have. I do not think that this would cheer me up, either. For I can at least conceive the possibility, if not the concrete reality, of going completely mad, and thinking perhaps that I am George IV or somebody; and being told that something like that was going to happen to me would have no tendency to reduce the terror of being told authoritatively that I was going to be tortured, but would merely compound the horror. Nor do I see why I should be put into any better frame of mind by the person in charge adding lastly that the impressions of my past with which I shall be equipped on the eve of torture will exactly fit the past of another person now living, and that indeed I shall acquire these impressions by (for instance) information now in his brain being copied into mine. Fear, surely, would still be the proper reaction: and not because one did not know what was going to happen, but because in one vital respect at least one did know what was going to happen – torture, which one can indeed expect to happen to oneself, and to be preceded by certain mental derangements as well.

If this is right, the whole question seems now to be totally mysterious. For what we have just been through is of course merely one side, differently represented, of the transaction which we considered before; and it represents it as a perfectly hateful prospect, while the previous considerations represented it as something one should rationally, perhaps even cheerfully, choose out of the options there presented. It is differently presented, of course, and in two notable respects; but when we look at these two differences of presentation, can we really convince ourselves that the second presentation is wrong or misleading, thus leaving the road open to the first version which at the time seemed so convincing? Surely not.

The first difference is that in the second version the torture is throughout represented as going to happen to *me*: 'you', the man in charge persistently says. Thus he is not very neutral. But should he have been neutral? Or, to put it another way, does his use of the second person have a merely emotional and rhetorical effect on me, making me afraid when further reflection would have shown that I had no reason to be? It is certainly not obviously so. The problem just is that through every step of his predictions I seem to be able to follow him successfully. And if I reflect on whether what he has said gives me grounds for fearing that I shall be tortured, I could consider that behind my fears lies some principle such as this: that my undergoing physical pain in the future is not excluded by any psychological state I may be in at the time, with the platitudinous exception of those psychological states which in themselves exclude experiencing pain, notably (if it is a psychological state) unconsciousness. In particular, what impressions I have about the past will not have any effect on whether I undergo the pain or not. This principle seems sound enough.

It is an important fact that not everything I would, as things are, regard as an evil would be something that I should rationally fear as an evil if it were predicted that it would happen to me in the future and also predicted that I should undergo significant psychological changes in the meantime. For the fact that I regard that happening, things being as they are, as an evil can be dependent on factors of belief or character which might themselves be modified by the psychological changes in question. Thus if I am

appallingly subject to acrophobia, and am told that I shall find myself on top of a steep mountain in the near future, I shall to that extent be afraid; but if I am told that I shall be psychologically changed in the meantime in such a way as to rid me of my acrophobia (and as with the other prediction, I believe it), then I have no reason to be afraid of the predicted happening, or at least not the same reason. Again, I might look forward to meeting a certain person again with either alarm or excitement because of my memories of our past relations. In some part, these memories operate in connexion with my emotion, not only on the present time, but projectively forward: for it is to a meeting itself affected by the presence of those memories that I look forward. If I am convinced that when the time comes I shall not have those memories, then I shall not have just the same reasons as before for looking forward to that meeting with the one emotion or the other. (Spiritualism, incidentally, appears to involve the belief that I have just the same reasons for a given attitude toward encountering people again after I am dead, as I did before: with the one modification that I can be sure it will all be very nice.)

Physical pain, however, the example which for simplicity (and not for any obsessional reason) I have taken, is absolutely minimally dependent on character or belief. No amount of change in my character or my beliefs would seem to affect substantially the nastiness of tortures applied to me; correspondingly, no degree of predicted change in my character and beliefs can unseat the fear of torture which, together with those changes, is predicted for me.

I am not at all suggesting that the *only* basis, or indeed the only rational basis, for fear in the face of these various predictions is how things will be relative to my psychological state in the eventual outcome. I am merely pointing out that this is one component; it is not the only one. For certainly one will fear and otherwise reject the changes themselves, or in very many cases one would. Thus one of the old paradoxes of hedonistic utilitarianism; if one had assurances that undergoing certain operations and being attached to a machine would provide one for the rest of one's existence with an unending sequence of delicious and varied experiences, one might very well reject the option, and react with fear if someone proposed to apply it compulsorily; and that fear and horror would seem appropriate reactions in the second case may help to discredit the interpretation (if anyone has the nerve to propose it) that one's reason for rejecting the option voluntarily would be a consciousness of duties to others which one in one's hedonic state would leave undone. The prospect of contented madness or vegetableness is found by many (not perhaps by all) appalling in ways which are obviously not a function of how things would then be for them, for things would then be for them not appalling. In the case we are at present discussing, these sorts of considerations seem merely to make it clearer that the predictions of the man in charge provide a double ground of horror: at the prospect of torture, and at the prospect of the change in character and in impressions of the past that will precede it. And certainly, to repeat what has already been said, the prospect of the second certainly seems to provide no ground for rejecting or not fearing the prospect of the first.

I said that there were two notable differences between the second presentation of our situation and the first. The first difference, which we have just said something about, was that the man predicted the torture for *me*, a psychologically very changed 'me'. We have yet to find a reason for saying that he should not have done this, or that I really should be unable to follow him if he does; I seem to be able to follow him only too well. The second difference is that in this presentation he does not mention the other man, except in the somewhat incidental role of being the provenance of the impressions of the past I end up with. He does not mention him at all as someone who will end up with impressions of the past derived from me (and, incidentally, with $100,000 as well – a consideration which, in the frame of mind appropriate to this version, will merely make me jealous).

But why *should* he mention this man and what is going to happen to him? My selfish concern is to be told what is going to happen to me, and now I know: torture, preceded by changes of character, brain operations, changes in impressions of the past. The knowledge that one other person, or none, or many will be similarly mistreated may affect me in other ways, of sympathy, greater horror at the power of this tyrant, and so forth; but surely it cannot affect my expectations of torture? But – someone will say – this is to leave out exactly the feature which, as the first presentation of the case showed, makes all the dif-

ference: for it is to leave out the person who, as the first presentation showed, will be you. It is to leave out not merely a feature which should fundamentally affect your fears, it is to leave out the very person for whom you are fearful. So of course, the objector will say, this makes all the difference.

But can it? Consider the following series of cases. In each case we are to suppose that after what is described, A is, as before, to be tortured; we are also to suppose the person A is informed beforehand that just these things followed by the torture will happen to him:

(i)   A is subjected to an operation which produces total amnesia;
(ii) amnesia is produced in A, and other interference leads to certain changes in his character;
(iii) changes in his character are produced, and at the same time certain illusory 'memory' beliefs are induced in him: these are of a quite fictitious kind and do not fit the life of any actual person;
(iv) the same as (iii), except that both the character traits and the 'memory' impressions are designed to be appropriate to another actual person, B;
(v)   the same as (iv), except that the result is produced by putting the information into A from the brain of B, by a method which leaves B the same as he was before;
(vi) the same happens to A as in (v), but B is not left the same, since a similar operation is conducted in the reverse direction.

I take it that no one is going to dispute that A has reasons, and fairly straightforward reasons, for fear of pain when the prospect is that of situation (i); there seems no conceivable reason why this should not extend to situation (ii), and the situation (iii) can surely introduce no difference of principle – it just seems a situation which for more than one reason we should have grounds for fearing, as suggested above. Situation (iv) at least introduces the person B, who was the focus of the objection we are now discussing. But it does not seem to introduce him in any way which makes a material difference; if I can expect pain through a transformation which involves new 'memory'-impressions, it would seem a purely external fact, relative to that, that the 'memory'-impressions had a model. Nor, in (iv), do we satisfy a causal condition which I mentioned at the beginning for the 'memories' actually being memories; though notice that if the job were done thoroughly, I might well be able to elicit from the A-body-person the kinds of remarks about his previous expectations of the experiment – remarks appropriate to the original B – which so impressed us in the first version of the story. I shall have a similar assurance of this being so in situation (v), where, moreover, a plausible application of the causal condition is available.

But two things are to be noticed about this situation. First, if we concentrate on A and the A-body-person, we do not seem to have added anything which from the point of view of his fears makes any material difference; just as, in the move from (iii) to (iv), it made no relevant difference that the new 'memory'-impressions which precede the pain had, as it happened, a model, so in the move from (iv) to (v) all we have added is that they have a model which is also their cause: and it is still difficult to see why that, to him looking forward, could possibly make the difference between expecting pain and not expecting pain. To illustrate that point from the case of character: if A is capable of expecting pain, he is capable of expecting pain preceded by a change in his dispositions – and to that expectation it can make no difference, whether that change in his dispositions is modelled on, or indeed indirectly caused by, the dispositions of some other person. If his fears can, as it were, reach through the change, it seems a mere trimming how the change is in fact induced. The second point about situation (v) is that if the crucial question for A's fears with regard to what befalls the A-body-person is whether the A-body-person is or is not the person B,[2] then that condition has not yet been satisfied in situation (v): for there we have an undisputed B in addition to the A-body-person, and certainly those two are not the same person.

But in situation (vi), we seemed to think, that is finally what he is. But if A's original fears could reach through the expected changes in (v), as they did in (iv) and (iii), then certainly they can reach through in (vi). Indeed, from the point of view of A's expectations and fears, there is less difference between (vi) and (v) than there is between (v) and (iv) or between (iv) and (iii). In those transitions, there were at least differences – though we could not see that they were really relevant differences – in the content or cause of

what happened to him; in the present case there is absolutely no difference at all in what happens to him, the only difference being in what happens to someone else. If he can fear pain when (v) is predicted, why should be cease to when (vi) is?

I can see only one way of relevantly laying great weight on the transition from (v) to (vi); and this involves a considerable difficulty. This is to deny that, as I put it, the transition from (v) to (vi) involves merely the addition of something happening to *somebody else*; what rather it does, it will be said, is to involve the reintroduction of A himself, as the B-body-person; since he has reappeared in this form, it is for this person, and not for the unfortunate A-body-person, that A will have his expectations. This is to reassert, in effect, the viewpoint emphasized in our first presentation of the experiment. But this surely has the consequence that A should not have fears for the A-body-person who appeared in situation (v). For by the present argument, the A-body-person in (vi) is not A; the B-body-person is. But the A-body-person in (v) is, in character, history, everything, exactly the same as the A-body-person in (vi); so if the latter is not A, then neither is the former. (It is this point, no doubt, that encourages one to speak of the difference that goes with (vi) as being, on the present view, the *reintroduction* of A.) But no one else in (v) has any better claim to be A. So in (v), it seems, A just does not exist. This would certainly explain why A should have no fears for the state of things in (v) – though he might well have fears for the path to it. But it rather looked earlier as though he could well have fears for the state of things in (v). Let us grant, however, that that was an illusion, and that A really does not exist in (v); then does he exist in (iv), (iii), (ii), or (i)? It seems very difficult to deny it for (i) and (ii); are we perhaps to draw the line between (iii) and (iv)?

Here someone will say: you must not insist on drawing a line – borderline cases are borderline cases, and you must not push our concepts beyond their limits. But this well-known piece of advice, sensible as it is in many cases, seems in the present case to involve an extraordinary difficulty. It may intellectually comfort observers of A's situation; but what is A supposed to make of it? To be told that a future situation is a borderline one for its being myself that is hurt, that it is conceptually undecidable whether it will be me or not, is something which, it seems, I can do nothing with; because, in particular, it seems to have no comprehensible representation in my expectations and the emotions that go with them.

If I expect that a certain situation, S, will come about in the future, there is of course a wide range of emotions and concerns, directed on S, which I may experience now in relation to my expectation. Unless I am exceptionally egoistic, it is not a condition on my being concerned in relation to this expectation, that I myself will be involved in S – where my being 'involved' in S means that I figure in S as someone doing something at that time or having something done to me, or, again, that S will have consequences affecting me at that or some subsequent time. There are some emotions, however, which I will feel only if I will be involved in S, and fear is an obvious example.

Now the description of S under which it figures in my expectations will necessarily be, in various ways, indeterminate; and one way in which it may be indeterminate is that it leaves open whether I shall be involved in S or not. Thus I may have good reason to expect that one of us five is going to get hurt, but no reason to expect it to be me rather than one of the others. My present emotions will be correspondingly affected by this indeterminacy. Thus, sticking to the egoistic concern involved in fear, I shall presumably be somewhat more cheerful than if I knew it was going to be me, somewhat less cheerful than if I had been left out altogether. Fear will be mixed with, and qualified by, apprehension; and so forth. These emotions revolve around the thought of the eventual determination of the indeterminacy; moments of straight fear focus on its really turning out to be me, of hope on its turning out not to be me. All the emotions are related to the coming about of what I expect: and what I expect in such a case just cannot come about save by coming about in one of the ways or another.

There are other ways in which indeterminate expectations can be related to fear. Thus I may expect (perhaps neurotically) that something nasty is going to happen to me, indeed expect that when it happens it will take some determinate form, but have no range, or no closed range, of candidates for the determinate form to rehearse in my present thought. Different from this would be the fear of something radically indeterminate – the fear (one might say) of a nameless horror. If somebody had such a fear, one could even say

that he had, in a sense, a perfectly determinate expectation: if what he expects indeed comes about, there will be nothing more determinate to be said about it after the event than was said in the expectation. Both these cases of course are cases of *fear* because one thing that is fixed amid the indeterminacy is the belief that it is me to whom the things will happen.

Central to the expectation of S is the thought of what it will be like when it happens – thought which may be indeterminate, range over alternatives, and so forth. When S involves me, there can be the possibility of a special form of such thought: the thought of how it will be for me, the imaginative projection of myself as participant in S.[3] I do not have to think about S in this way, when it involves me; but I may be able to. (It might be suggested that this possibility was even mirrored in the language, in the distinction between 'expecting to be hurt' and 'expecting that I shall be hurt'; but I am very doubtful about this point, which is in any case of no importance.)

Suppose now that there is an S with regard to which it is for conceptual reasons undecidable whether it involves me or not, as is proposed for the experimental situation by the line we are discussing. It is important that the expectation of S is not *indeterminate* in any of the ways we have just been considering. It is not like the nameless horror, since the fixed point of that case was that it was going to happen to the subject, and that made his state unequivocally fear. Nor is it like the expectation of the man who expects one of the five to be hurt; his fear was indeed equivocal, but its focus, and that of the expectation, was that when S came about, it would certainly come about in one way or the other. In the present case, fear (of the torture, that is to say, not of the initial experiment) seems neither appropriate, nor inappropriate, nor appropriately equivocal. Relatedly, the subject has an incurable difficulty about how he may think about S. If he engages in projective imaginative thinking (about how it will be for him), he implicitly answers the necessarily unanswerable question; if he thinks that he cannot engage in such thinking, it looks very much as if he also answers it, though in the opposite direction. Perhaps he must just refrain from such thinking; but is he just refraining from it, if it is incurably undecidable whether he can or cannot engage in it?

It may be said that all that these considerations can show is that fear, at any rate, does not get its proper footing in this case; but that there could be some other, more ambivalent, form of concern which would indeed be appropriate to this particular expectation, the expectation of the conceptually undecidable situation. There are, perhaps, analogous feelings that actually occur in actual situations. Thus material objects do occasionally undergo puzzling transformations which leave a conceptual shadow over their identity. Suppose I were sentimentally attached to an object to which this sort of thing then happened; it might be that I could neither feel about it quite as I did originally, nor be totally indifferent to it, but would have some other and rather ambivalent feeling towards it. Similarly, it may be said, toward the prospective sufferer of pain, my identity relations with whom are conceptually shadowed, I can feel neither as I would if he were certainly me, nor as I would if he were certainly not, but rather some such ambivalent concern.

But this analogy does little to remove the most baffling aspect of the present case – an aspect which has already turned up in what was said about the subject's difficulty in thinking either projectively or non-projectively about the situation. For to regard the prospective pain-sufferer *just* like the transmogrified object of sentiment, and to conceive of my ambivalent distress about his future pain as just like ambivalent distress about some future damage to such an object, is of course to leave him and me clearly distinct from one another, and thus to displace the conceptual shadow from its proper place. I have to get nearer to him than that. But is there any nearer that I can get to him without expecting his pain? If there is, the analogy has not shown us it. We can certainly not get nearer by expecting, as it were, *ambivalent* pain; there is no place at all for that. There seems to be an obstinate bafflement to mirroring in my expectations a situation in which it is conceptually undecidable whether I occur.

The bafflement seems, moreover, to turn to plain absurdity if we move from conceptual undecidability to its close friend and neighbour, conventionalist decision. This comes out if we consider another description, overtly conventionalist, of the series of cases which occasioned the present discussion. This description would reject a point I relied on in an earlier argument – namely, that if we deny that the A-body-person in (vi) is A (because the B-body-person is), then we must deny that the A-body-person in (v) is

A, since they are exactly similar. 'No', it may be said, 'this is just to assume that we say the same in different sorts of situation. No doubt when we have the very good candidate for being A – namely, the B-body-person – we call him A; but this does not mean that we should not call the A-body-person A in that other situation when we have no better candidate around. Different situations call for different descriptions.' This line of talk is the sort of thing indeed appropriate to lawyers deciding the ownership of some property which has undergone some bewildering set of transformations; they just have to decide, and in each situation, let us suppose, it has got to go to somebody, on as reasonable grounds as the facts and the law admit. But as a line to deal with a person's fears or expectations about his own future, it seems to have no sense at all. If A's fears can extend to what will happen to the A-body-person in (v), I do not see how they can be rationally diverted from the fate of the exactly similar person in (vi) by his being told that someone would have a reason in the latter situation which he would not have in the former for deciding to call another person A.

Thus, to sum up, it looks as though there are two presentations of the imagined experiment and the choice associated with it, each of which carries conviction, and which lead to contrary conclusions. The idea, moreover, that the situation after the experiment is conceptually undecidable in the relevant respect seems not to assist, but rather to increase, the puzzlement; while the idea (so often appealed to in these matters) that it is conventionally decidable is even worse. Following from all that, I am not in the least clear which option it would be wise to take if one were presented with them before the experiment. I find that rather disturbing.

Whatever the puzzlement, there is one feature of the arguments which have led to it which is worth picking out, since it runs counter to something which is, I think, often rather vaguely supposed. It is often recognised that there are 'first-personal' and 'third-personal' aspects of questions about persons, and that there are difficulties about the relations between them. It is also recognised that 'mentalistic' considerations (as we may vaguely call them) and considerations of bodily continuity are involved in questions of personal identity (which is not to say that there are mentalistic and bodily criteria of personal identity). It is tempting to think that the two distinctions run in parallel: roughly, that a first-person approach concentrates attention on mentalistic considerations, while a third-personal approach emphasises considerations of bodily continuity. The present discussion is an illustration of exactly the opposite. The first argument, which led to the 'mentalistic' conclusion that A and B would change bodies and that each person should identify himself with the destination of his memories and character, was an argument entirely conducted in third-personal terms. The second argument, which suggested the bodily continuity identification, concerned itself with the first-personal issue of what A could expect. That this is so seems to me (though I will not discuss it further here) of some significance.

I will end by suggesting one rather shaky way in which one might approach a resolution of the problem, using only the limited materials already available.

The apparently decisive arguments of the first presentation, which suggested that A should identify himself with the B-body-person, turned on the extreme neatness of the situation in satisfying, if any could, the description of 'changing bodies'. But this neatness is basically artificial; it is the product of the will of the experimenter to produce a situation which would naturally elicit, with minimum hesitation, that description. By the sorts of methods he employed, he could easily have left off earlier or gone on further.

He could have stopped at situation (v), leaving B as he was; or he could have gone on and produced two persons each with A-like character and memories, as well as one or two with B-like characteristics. If he had done either of those, we should have been in yet greater difficulty about what to say; he just chose to make it as easy as possible for us to find something to say. Now if we had some model of ghostly persons in bodies, which were in some sense actually moved around by certain procedures, we could regard the neat experiment just as the *effective* experiment: the one method that really did result in the ghostly persons' changing places without being destroyed, dispersed, or whatever. But we cannot seriously use such a model. The experimenter has not in the sense of that model *induced* a change of bodies; he has rather produced the one situation out of a range of equally possible situations which we should be most disposed to call a change of bodies. As against this, the principle that one's fears can extend to future pain whatever psychological changes precede it seems positively straightforward. Perhaps, indeed, it is not; but we need to be shown what is wrong with it. Until we are shown what is wrong with it, we should perhaps decide that if we were the person A then, if we were to decide selfishly, we should pass the pain to the B-body-person. It would be risky: that there is room for the notion of a *risk* here is itself a major feature of the problem.

Notes

1 S. Shoemaker, *Self-Knowledge and Self-Identity* (Ithaca, NY: Cornell University Press, 1963), pp. 23ff.
2 This of course does not have to be the crucial question, but it seems one fair way of taking up the present objection.
3 For a more detailed treatment of issues related to this, see 'Imagination and the Self', in *Problems of the Self* (Cambridge: Cambridge University Press, 1973), pp. 38ff.

32

Actions, Reasons, and Causes

Donald Davidson

What is the relation between a reason and an action when the reason explains the action by giving the agent's reason for doing what he did? We may call such explanations *rationalizations*, and say that the reason *rationalizes* the action.

In this paper I want to defend the ancient – and commonsense – position that rationalization is a species of causal explanation. The defence no doubt requires some redeployment, but it does not seem necessary to abandon the position, as has been urged by many recent writers.[1]

I

A reason rationalizes an action only if it leads us to see something the agent saw, or thought he saw, in his action – some feature, consequence, or aspect of the action the agent wanted, desired, prized, held dear, thought dutiful, beneficial, obligatory, or agreeable. We cannot explain why someone did what he did simply by saying the particular action appealed to him; we must indicate what it was about the action that appealed. Whenever someone does something for a reason, therefore, he can be characterized as (a) having some sort of pro attitude toward actions of a certain kind, and (b) believing (or knowing, perceiving, noticing, remembering) that his action is of that kind. Under (a) are to be included desires, wantings, urges, promptings, and a great variety

Originally published in *Journal of Philosophy* 60/23 (November 7, 1963).

of moral views, aesthetic principles, economic prejudices, social conventions, and public and private goals and values in so far as these can be interpreted as attitudes of an agent directed toward actions of a certain kind. The word 'attitude' does yeoman service here, for it must cover not only permanent character traits that show themselves in a lifetime of behaviour, like love of children or a taste for loud company, but also the most passing fancy that prompts a unique action, like a sudden desire to touch a woman's elbow. In general, pro attitudes must not be taken for convictions, however temporary, that every action of a certain kind ought to be performed, is worth performing, or is, all things considered, desirable. On the contrary, a man may all his life have a yen, say, to drink a can of paint, without ever, even at the moment he yields, believing it would be worth doing.

Giving the reason why an agent did something is often a matter of naming the pro attitude (a) or the related belief (b) or both; let me call this pair the *primary reason* why the agent performed the action. Now it is possible both to reformulate the claim that rationalizations are causal explanations and to give structure to the argument by stating two theses about primary reasons:

1 In order to understand how a reason of any kind rationalizes an action it is necessary and sufficient that we see, at least in essential outline, how to construct a primary reason.
2 The primary reason for an action is its cause.

I shall argue for these points in turn.

II

I flip the switch, turn on the light, and illumin-ate the room. Unbeknownst to me I also alert a prowler to the fact that I am home. Here I need not have done four things, but only one, of which four descriptions have been given.[2] I flipped the switch because I wanted to turn on the light and by saying I wanted to turn on the light I explain (give my reason for, rationalize) the flipping. But I do not, by giving this reason, rationalize my alerting of the prowler nor my illuminating of the room. Since reasons may rationalize what someone does when it is described in one way and not when it is described in another, we cannot treat what was done simply as a term in sentences like 'My reason for flipping the switch was that I wanted to turn on the light'; other-wise we would be forced to conclude, from the fact that flipping the switch was identical with alerting the prowler, that my reason for alerting the prowler was that I wanted to turn on the light. Let us mark this quasi-intensional[3] character of action descriptions in rationalizations by stat-ing a bit more precisely a necessary condition for primary reasons:

C1. *R* is a primary reason why an agent per-formed the action *A* under the description *d* only if *R* consists of a pro attitude of the agent towards actions with a certain prop-erty, and a belief of the agent that *A*, under the description *d*, has that property.

How can my wanting to turn on the light be (part of) a primary reason, since it appears to lack the required element of generality? We may be taken in by the verbal parallel between 'I turned on the light' and 'I wanted to turn on the light'. The first clearly refers to a particular event, so we conclude that the second has this same event as its object. Of course it is obvious that the event of my turning on the light can't be referred to in the same way by both sentences since the existence of the event is required by the truth of 'I turned on the light' but not by the truth of 'I wanted to turn on the light'. If the reference were the same in both cases, the second sentence would entail the first; but in fact the sentences are logically independent. What is less obvious, at least until we attend to it, is that the event whose occurrence makes 'I turned on the light' true cannot be called the object,

however intentional, of 'I wanted to turn on the light'. If I turned on the light, then I must have done it at a precise moment, in a particular way – every detail is fixed. But it makes no sense to demand that my want be directed to an action performed at any one moment or done in some unique manner. Any one of an indefinitely large number of actions would satisfy the want and can be considered equally eligible as its object. Wants and desires often are trained on physical objects. However, 'I want that gold watch in the window' is not a primary reason and explains why I went into the store only because it sug-gests a primary reason – for example, that I wanted to buy the watch.

Because 'I wanted to turn on the light' and 'I turned on the light' are logically independent, the first can be used to give a reason why the second is true. Such a reason gives minimal information: it implies that the action was intentional, and wanting tends to exclude some other pro attitudes, such as a sense of duty or obligation. But the exclusion depends very much on the action and the context of explanation. Wanting seems pallid beside lusting, but it would be odd to deny that someone who lusted after a woman or a cup of coffee wanted her or it. It is not unnatural, in fact, to treat wanting as a genus including all pro attitudes as species. When we do this and when we know some action is intentional, it is easy to answer the question, 'Why did you do it?' with, 'For no reason', meaning not that there is no reason but that there is no *further* reason, no reason that cannot be inferred from the fact that the action was done intentionally; no reason, in other words, besides wanting to do it. This last point is not essential to the present argument, but it is of interest because it defends the pos-sibility of defining an intentional action as one done for a reason.

A primary reason consists of a belief and an attitude, but it is generally otiose to mention both. If you tell me you are easing the jib because you think that will stop the main from backing, I don't need to be told that you want to stop the main from backing; and if you say you are biting your thumb at me because you want to insult me, there is no point in adding that you think that by biting your thumb at me you will insult me. Similarly, many explanations of ac-tions in terms of reasons that are not primary do not require mention of the primary reason to complete the story. If I say I am pulling weeds because I want a beautiful lawn, it would be fatuous to eke out the account with, 'And so I see something desirable in any action that does, or has a good chance of, making the lawn beautiful'. Why insist that there is any *step*, logical or psychological, in the transfer of desire from an end that is not an action to the actions one conceives as means? It serves the argument as well that the desired end explains the action only if what are believed by the agent to be means are desired.

Fortunately, it is not necessary to classify and analyse the many varieties of emotions, sentiments, moods, motives, passions, and hungers whose mention may answer the question, 'Why did you do it?' in order to see how, when such mention rationalizes the action, a primary reason is involved. Claustrophobia gives a man's reason for leaving a cocktail party because we know people want to avoid, escape from, be safe from, put distance between themselves and what they fear. Jealousy is the motive in a poisoning because, among other things, the poisoner believes his action will harm his rival, remove the cause of his agony, or redress an injustice, and these are the sorts of things a jealous man wants to do. When we learn that a man cheated his son out of greed, we do not necessarily know what the primary reason was, but we know there was one, and its general nature. Ryle analyses 'he boasted from vanity' into 'he boasted on meeting the stranger and his doing so satisfies the law-like proposition that whenever he finds a chance of securing the admiration and envy of others, he does whatever he thinks will produce this admiration and envy'.[4] This analysis is often, and perhaps justly, criticized on the ground that a man may boast from vanity just once. But if Ryle's boaster did what he did from vanity, then something entailed by Ryle's analysis is true: the boaster wanted to secure the admiration and envy of others, and he believed that his action would produce this admiration and envy; true or false, Ryle's analysis does not dispense with primary reasons, but depends upon them.

To know a primary reason why someone acted as he did is to know an intention with which the action was done. If I turn left at the fork because I want to get to Katmandu, my intention in turning left is to get to Katmandu. But to know the intention is not necessarily to know the primary reason in full detail. If James goes to church with the intention of pleasing his mother,

then he must have some pro attitude toward pleasing his mother, but it needs more information to tell whether his reason is that he enjoys pleasing his mother, or thinks it right, his duty, or an obligation. The expression 'the intention with which James went to church' has the outward form of a description, but in fact it is syncategorematic and cannot be taken to refer to an entity, state, disposition, or event. Its function in context is to generate new descriptions of actions in terms of their reasons; thus 'James went to church with the intention of pleasing his mother' yields a new, and fuller, description of the action described in 'James went to church'. Essentially the same process goes on when I answer the question, 'Why are you bobbing around that way?' with, 'I'm knitting, weaving, exercising, sculling, cuddling, training fleas'.

Straight description of an intended result often explains an action better than stating that the result was intended or desired. 'It will soothe your nerves' explains why I pour you a shot as efficiently as 'I want to do something to soothe your nerves', since the first in the context of explanation implies the second; but the first does better, because, if it is true, the facts will justify my choice of action. Because justifying and explaining an action so often go hand in hand, we frequently indicate the primary reason for an action by making a claim which, if true, would also verify, vindicate, or support the relevant belief or attitude of the agent. 'I knew I ought to return it', 'The paper said it was going to snow', 'You stepped on *my* toes', all, in appropriate reason-giving contexts, perform this familiar dual function.

The justifying role of a reason, given this interpretation, depends upon the explanatory role, but the converse does not hold. Your stepping on my toes neither explains nor justifies my stepping on your toes unless I believe you stepped on my toes, but the belief alone, true or false, explains my action.

III

In the light of a primary reason, an action is revealed as coherent with certain traits, long- or short-termed, characteristic or not, of the agent, and the agent is shown in his role of Rational Animal. Corresponding to the belief and attitude of a primary reason for an action, we can always construct (with a little ingenuity) the premises of a syllogism from which it follows that the action has some (as Anscombe calls it) 'desirability characteristic'.[5] Thus there is a certain irreducible – though somewhat anaemic – sense in which every rationalization justifies: from the agent's point of view there was, when he acted, something to be said for the action.

Noting that nonteleological causal explanations do not display the element of justification provided by reasons, some philosophers have concluded that the concept of cause that applies elsewhere cannot apply to the relation between reasons and actions, and that the pattern of justification provides, in the case of reasons, the required explanation. But suppose we grant that reasons alone justify actions in the course of explaining them; it does not follow that the explanation is not also – and necessarily – causal. Indeed our first condition for primary reasons (C1) is designed to help set rationalizations apart from other sorts of explanation. If rationalization is, as I want to argue, a species of causal explanation, then justification, in the sense given by C1, is at least one differentiating property. How about the other claim: that justifying is a kind of explaining, so that the ordinary notion of cause need not be brought in? Here it is necessary to decide what is being included under justification. It could be taken to cover only what is called for by C1: that the agent have certain beliefs and attitudes in the light of which the action is reasonable. But then something essential has certainly been left out, for a person can have a reason for an action, and perform the action, and yet this reason not be the reason why he did it. Central to the relation between a reason and an action it explains is the idea that the agent performed the action *because* he had the reason. Of course, we can include this idea too in justification; but then the notion of justification becomes as dark as the notion of reason until we can account for the force of that 'because'.

When we ask why someone acted as he did, we want to be provided with an interpretation. His behaviour seems strange, alien, outré, pointless, out of character, disconnected; or perhaps we cannot even recognize an action in it. When we learn his reason, we have an interpretation, a new description of what he did, which fits it into a familiar picture. The picture includes some of the agent's beliefs and attitudes; perhaps also goals, ends, principles, general character traits, virtues or

vices. Beyond this, the redescription of an action afforded by a reason may place the action in a wider social, economic, linguistic, or evaluative context. To learn, through learning the reason, that the agent conceived his action as a lie, a repayment of a debt, an insult, the fulfilment of an avuncular obligation, or a knight's gambit is to grasp the point of the action in its setting of rules, practices, conventions, and expectations.

Remarks like these, inspired by the later Wittgenstein, have been elaborated with subtlety and insight by a number of philosophers. And there is no denying that this is true: when we explain an action, by giving the reason, we do redescribe the action; redescribing the action gives the action a place in a pattern, and in this way the action is explained. Here it is tempting to draw two conclusions that do not follow. First, we can't infer, from the fact that giving reasons merely redescribes the action and that causes are separate from effects, that therefore reasons are not causes. Reasons, being beliefs and attitudes, are certainly not identical with actions; but, more important, events are often redescribed in terms of their causes. (Suppose someone was injured. We could redescribe this event 'in terms of a cause' by saying he was burned.) Second, it is an error to think that, because placing the action in a larger pattern explains it, therefore we now understand the sort of explanation involved. Talk of patterns and contexts does not answer the question of how reasons explain actions, since the relevant pattern or context contains both reason and action. One way we can explain an event is by placing it in the context of its cause; cause and effect form the sort of pattern that explains the effect, in a sense of 'explain' that we understand as well as any. If reason and action illustrate a different pattern of explanation, that pattern must be identified.

Let me urge the point in connection with an example of Melden's. A man driving an automobile raises his arm in order to signal. His intention, to signal, explains his action, raising his arm, by redescribing it as signalling. What is the pattern that explains the action? Is it the familiar pattern of an action done for a reason? Then it does indeed explain the action, but only because it assumes the relation of reason and action that we want to analyse. Or is the pattern rather this: the man is driving, he is approaching a turn; he knows he ought to signal; he knows how to signal, by raising his arm. And now, in this context, he

Donald Davidson

raises his arm. Perhaps, as Melden suggests, if all this happens, he does signal. And the explanation would then be this; if, under these conditions, a man raises his arm, then he signals. The difficulty is, of course, that this explanation does not touch the question of why he raised his arm. He had a reason to raise his arm, but this has not been shown to be the reason why he did it. If the description 'signalling' explains his action by giving his reason, then the signalling must be intentional; but, on the account just given, it may not be.

If, as Melden claims, causal explanations are 'wholly irrelevant to the understanding we seek' of human action then we are without an analysis of the 'because' in 'He did it because . . .', where we go on to name a reason.[6] Hampshire remarks, of the relation between reasons and action, 'In philosophy one ought surely to find this . . . connection altogether mysterious'. Hampshire rejects Aristotle's attempt to solve the mystery by introducing the concept of wanting as a causal factor, on the grounds that the resulting theory is too clear and definite to fit all cases and that, 'There is still no compelling ground for insisting that the word "want" *must* enter into every full statement of reasons for acting'. I agree that the concept of wanting is too narrow, but I have argued that, at least in a vast number of typical cases, some pro attitude must be assumed to be present if a statement of an agent's reasons in acting is to be intelligible. Hampshire does not see how Aristotle's scheme can be appraised as true or false, 'for it is not clear what could be the basis of assessment, or what kind of evidence could be decisive'.[7] But I would urge that, failing a satisfactory alternative, the best argument for a scheme like Aristotle's is that it alone promises to give an account of the 'mysterious connection' between reasons and actions.

IV

In order to turn the first 'and' to 'because' in 'He exercised *and* he wanted to reduce and thought exercise would do it', we must, as the basic move,[8] augment condition C1 with:

C2. A primary reason for an action is its cause.

The considerations in favour of C2 are by now, I hope, obvious; in the remainder of this paper I wish to defend C2 against various lines of attack and, in the process, to clarify the notion of causal explanation involved.

A. The first line of attack is this. Primary reasons consist of attitudes and beliefs, which are states or dispositions, not events; therefore they cannot be causes.

It is easy to reply that states, dispositions, and conditions are frequently named as the causes of events: the bridge collapsed because of a structural defect; the plane crashed on takeoff because the air temperature was abnormally high; the plate broke because it had a crack. This reply does not, however, meet a closely related point. Mention of a causal condition for an event gives a cause only on the assumption that there was also a preceding event. But what is the preceding event that causes an action?

In many cases it is not difficult at all to find events very closely associated with the primary reason. States and dispositions are not events, but the onslaught of a state or disposition is. A desire to hurt your feelings may spring up at the moment you anger me; I may start wanting to eat a melon just when I see one; and beliefs may begin at the moment we notice, perceive, learn, or remember something. Those who have argued that there are no mental events to qualify as causes of actions have often missed the obvious because they have insisted that a mental event be observed or noticed (rather than an observing or a noticing) or that it be like a stab, a qualm, a prick or a quiver, a mysterious prod of conscience or act of the will. Melden, in discussing the driver who signals a turn by raising his arm, challenges those who want to explain actions causally to identify 'an event which is common and peculiar to all such cases' (p. 87), perhaps a motive or an intention, anyway 'some particular feeling or experience' (p. 95). But of course there is a mental event; at some moment the driver noticed (or thought he noticed) his turn coming up, and that is the moment he signalled. During any continuing activity, like driving, or elaborate performance, like swimming the Hellespont, there are more or less fixed purposes, standards, desires, and habits that give direction and form to the entire enterprise, and there is the continuing input of information about what we are doing, about changes in the environment, in terms of which we regulate and adjust our actions. To dignify a driver's awareness that his turn has come by calling it an experience, or even a feeling, is no doubt exaggerated, but whether it deserves a name or not, it had better be the reason why he raises his arm. In this case, and typically, there may not be anything we would call a motive, but if we mention such a general purpose as wanting to get to one's destination safely, it is clear that the motive is not an event. The intention with which the driver raises his arm is also not an event, for it is no thing at all, neither event, attitude, disposition, nor object. Finally, Melden asks the causal theorist to find an event that is common and peculiar to all cases where a man intentionally raises his arm, and this, it must be admitted, cannot be produced. But then neither can a common and unique cause of bridge failures, plane crashes, or plate breakings be produced.

The signalling driver can answer the question, 'Why did you raise your arm when you did?', and from the answer we learn the event that caused the action. But can an actor always answer such a question? Sometimes the answer will mention a mental event that does not give a reason: 'Finally I made up my mind.' However, there also seem to be cases of intentional action where we cannot explain at all why we acted when we did. In such cases, explanation in terms of primary reasons parallels the explanation of the collapse of the bridge from a structural defect: we are ignorant of the event or sequence of events that led up to (caused) the collapse, but we are sure there was such an event or sequence of events.

B. According to Melden, a cause must be 'logically distinct from the alleged effect';[9] but a reason for an action is not logically distinct from the action; therefore, reasons are not causes of actions.[10]

One possible form of this argument has already been suggested. Since a reason makes an action intelligible by redescribing it, we do not have two events, but only one under different descriptions. Causal relations, however, demand distinct events.

Someone might be tempted into the mistake of thinking that my flipping of the switch caused my turning on of the light (in fact it caused the light to go on). But it does not follow that it is a mistake to take, 'My reason for flipping the switch was that I wanted to turn on the light' as entailing, in part, 'I flipped the switch, and this action is further describable as having been caused by wanting to turn on the light'. To describe an event in terms of its cause is not to confuse the event with its cause, nor does explanation by redescription exclude causal explanation.

The example serves also to refute the claim that we cannot describe the action without using words that link it to the alleged cause. Here the action is to be explained under the description: 'my flipping the switch', and the alleged cause is 'my wanting to turn on the light'. What relevant logical relation is supposed to hold between these phrases? It seems more plausible to urge a logical link between 'my turning on the light' and 'my wanting to turn on the light', but even here the link turns out, on inspection, to be grammatical rather than logical.

In any case there is something very odd in the idea that causal relations are empirical rather than logical. What can this mean? Surely not that every true causal statement is empirical. For suppose 'A caused B' is true. Then the cause of $B = A$; so substituting, we have 'The cause of B caused B', which is analytic. The truth of a causal statement depends on *what* events are described; its status as analytic or synthetic depends on *how* the events are described. Still, it may be maintained that a reason rationalizes an action only when the descriptions are appropriately fixed, and the appropriate descriptions are not logically independent.

Suppose that to say a man wanted to turn on the light *meant* that he would perform any action he believed would accomplish his end. Then the statement of his primary reason for flipping the switch would entail that he flipped the switch – 'straightway he acts', as Aristotle says. In this case there would certainly be a logical connection between reason and action, the same sort of connection as that between, 'It's water-soluble and was placed in water' and 'It dissolved'. Since the implication runs from description of cause to description of effect but not conversely, naming the cause still gives information. And, though the point is often overlooked, 'Placing it in water caused it to dissolve' does not entail 'It's water-soluble'; so the latter has additional explanatory force. Nevertheless, the explanation would be far more interesting if, in place of solubility, with its obvious definitional connection with the event to be explained, we could refer to some property, say a particular crystalline structure, whose connection with dissolution in water was known only through experiment. Now it is clear why primary reasons like desires and wants do not explain actions in the relatively trivial way solubility explains dissolvings. Solubility, we are assuming, is a pure disposition property: it is defined in terms of a single test. But desires cannot be defined in terms of the actions they may rationalize, even though the relation between desire and action is not simply empirical; there are other, equally essential criteria for desires – their expression in feelings and in actions that they do not rationalize, for example. The person who has a desire (or want or belief) does not normally need criteria at all – he generally knows, even in the absence of any clues available to others, what he wants, desires, and believes. These logical features of primary reasons show that it is not just lack of ingenuity that keeps us from defining them as dispositions to act for these reasons.

C. According to Hume, 'we may define a cause to be an object, followed by another, and where all the objects similar to the first are followed by objects similar to the second'. But, Hart and Honoré claim, 'The statement that one person did something because, for example, another threatened him, carries no implication or covert assertion that if the circumstances were repeated the same action would follow'.[11] Hart and Honoré allow that Hume is right in saying that ordinary singular causal statements imply generalizations, but wrong for this very reason in supposing that motives and desires are ordinary causes of actions. In brief, laws are involved essentially in ordinary causal explanations, but not in rationalizations.

It is common to try to meet this argument by suggesting that we do have rough laws connecting reasons and actions, and these can, in theory, be improved. True, threatened people do not always respond in the same way; but we may distinguish between threats and also between agents, in terms of their beliefs and attitudes.

The suggestion is delusive, however, because generalizations connecting reasons and actions are not – and cannot be sharpened into – the kind of law on the basis of which accurate predictions can reliably be made. If we reflect on the way in which reasons determine choice, decision, and behaviour, it is easy to see why this is so. What emerges, in the *ex post facto* atmosphere of explanation and justification, as *the* reason frequently was, to the agent at the time of action, one consideration among many, *a* reason. Any serious theory for predicting action on the basis of reasons must find a way of evaluating the relative force

of various desires and beliefs in the matrix of decision; it cannot take as its starting point the refinement of what is to be expected from a single desire. The practical syllogism exhausts its role in displaying an action as falling under one reason; so it cannot be subtilized into a reconstruction of practical reasoning, which involves the weighing of competing reasons. The practical syllogism provides a model neither for a predictive science of action nor for a normative account of evaluative reasoning.

Ignorance of competent predictive laws does not inhibit valid causal explanation, or few causal explanations could be made. I am certain the window broke because it was struck by a rock – I saw it all happen; but I am not (is anyone?) in command of laws on the basis of which I can predict what blows will break which windows. A generalization like, 'Windows are fragile, and fragile things tend to break when struck hard enough, other conditions being right' is not a predictive law in the rough – the predictive law, if we had it, would be quantitative and would use very different concepts. The generalization, like our generalizations about behaviour, serves a different function: it provides evidence for the existence of a causal law covering the case at hand.[12]

We are usually far more certain of a singular causal connection than we are of any causal law governing the case; does this show that Hume was wrong in claiming that singular causal statements entail laws? Not necessarily, for Hume's claim, as quoted above, is ambiguous. It may mean that '*A* caused *B*' entails some particular law involving the predicates used in the descriptions '*A*' and '*B*', or it may mean that '*A* caused *B*' entails that there exists a causal law instantiated by some true descriptions of *A* and *B*.[13] Obviously, both versions of Hume's doctrine give a sense to the claim that singular causal statements entail laws, and both sustain the view that causal explanations 'involve laws'. But the second version is far weaker, in that no particular law is entailed by a singular causal claim, and a singular causal claim can be defended, if it needs defence, without defending any law. Only the second version of Hume's doctrine can be made to fit with most causal explanations; it suits rationalizations equally well.

The most primitive explanation of an event gives its cause; more elaborate explanations may tell more of the story, or defend the singular causal claim by producing a relevant law or by giving reasons for believing such exists. But it is an error to think no explanation has been given until a law has been produced. Linked with these errors is the idea that singular causal statements necessarily indicate, by the concepts they employ, the concepts that will occur in the entailed law. Suppose a hurricane, which is reported on page 5 of Tuesday's *Times*, causes a catastrophe, which is reported on page 13 of Wednesday's *Tribune*. Then the event reported on page 5 of Tuesday's *Times* caused the event reported on page 13 of Wednesday's *Tribune*. Should we look for a law relating events of these *kinds*? It is only slightly less ridiculous to look for a law relating hurricanes and catastrophes. The laws needed to predict the catastrophe with precision would, of course, have no use for concepts like hurricane and catastrophe. The trouble with predicting the weather is that the descriptions under which events interest us – 'a cool, cloudy day with rain in the afternoon' – have only remote connections with the concepts employed by the more precise known laws.

The laws whose existence is required if reasons are causes of actions do not, we may be sure, deal in the concepts in which rationalizations must deal. If the causes of a class of events (actions) fall in a certain class (reasons) and there is a law to back each singular causal statement, it does not follow that there is any law connecting events classified as reasons with events classified as actions – the classifications may even be neurological, chemical, or physical.

D.   It is said that the kind of knowledge one has of one's own reasons in acting is not compatible with the existence of a causal relation between reasons and actions: a person knows his own intentions in acting infallibly, without induction or observation, and no ordinary causal relation can be known in this way. No doubt our knowledge of our own intentions in acting will show many of the oddities peculiar to first-person knowledge of one's own pains, beliefs, desires, and so on; the only question is whether these oddities prove that reasons do not cause, in any ordinary sense at least, the actions that they rationalize.

You may easily be wrong about the truth of a statement of the form 'I am poisoning Charles because I want to save him pain', because you may be wrong about whether you are poisoning Charles – you may yourself be drinking the poisoned cup by mistake. But it also seems that you may err about your reasons, particularly when

you have two reasons for an action, one of which pleases you and one which does not. For example, you do want to save Charles pain; you also want him out of the way. You may be wrong about which motive made you do it.

The fact that you may be wrong does not show that in general it makes sense to ask you how you know what your reasons were or to ask for your evidence. Though you may, on rare occasions, accept public or private evidence as showing you are wrong about your reasons, you usually have no evidence and make no observations. Then your knowledge of your own reasons for your actions is not generally inductive, for where there is induction, there is evidence. Does this show the knowledge is not causal? I cannot see that it does.

Causal laws differ from true but nonlawlike generalizations in that their instances confirm them; induction is, therefore, certainly a good way to learn the truth of a law. It does not follow that it is the only way to learn the truth of a law. In any case, in order to know that a singular causal statement is true, it is not necessary to know the truth of a law; it is necessary only to know that some law covering the events at hand exists. And it is far from evident that induction, and induction alone, yields the knowledge that a causal law satisfying certain conditions exists. Or, to put it differently, one case is often enough, as Hume admitted, to persuade us that a law exists, and this amounts to saying that we are persuaded without direct inductive evidence, that a causal relation exists.

E.   Finally I should like to say something about a certain uneasiness some philosophers feel in speaking of causes of actions at all. Melden, for example, says that actions are often identical with bodily movements, and that bodily movements have causes; yet he denies that the causes are causes of the actions. This is, I think, a contradiction. He is led to it by the following sort of consideration: 'It is futile to attempt to explain conduct through the causal efficacy of desire – all *that* can explain is further happenings, not actions performed by agents. The agent confronting the causal nexus in which such happenings occur is a helpless victim of all that occurs in and to him'.[14] Unless I am mistaken, this argument, if it were valid, would show that actions cannot have causes at all. I shall not point out the obvious difficulties in removing actions from the realm of causality entirely. But perhaps it is worth trying to uncover the source of the trouble. Why on earth should a cause turn an action into a mere happening and a person into a helpless victim? Is it because we tend to assume, at least in the arena of action, that a cause demands a causer, agency an agent? So we press the question; if my action is caused, what caused it? If I did, then there is the absurdity of infinite regress; if I did not, I am a victim. But of course the alternatives are not exhaustive. Some causes have no agents. Among these agentless causes are the states and changes of state in persons which, because they are reasons as well as causes, constitute certain events free and intentional actions.

Notes

1 Some examples: Gilbert Ryle, *The Concept of Mind*, G. E. M. Anscombe, *Intention*, Stuart Hampshire, *Thought and Action*, H. L. A. Hart and A. M. Honoré, *Causation in the Law*, William Dray, *Laws and Explanation in History*, and most of the books in the series edited by R. F. Holland, *Studies in Philosophical Psychology*, including Anthony Kenny, *Action, Emotion and Will*, and A. I. Melden, *Free Action*.

2 We might not call my unintentional alerting of the prowler an action, but it should not be inferred from this that alerting the prowler is therefore something different from flipping the switch, say just its consequence. Actions, performances, and events not involving intention are alike in that they are often referred to or defined partly in terms of some terminal stage, outcome, or consequence.

The word 'action' does not very often occur in ordinary speech, and when it does it is usually reserved for fairly portentous occasions. I follow a useful philosophical practice in calling anything an agent does intentionally an action, including intentional omissions. What is really needed is some suitably generic term to bridge the following gap: suppose '*A*' is a description of an action, '*B*' is a description of something done voluntarily, though not intentionally, and '*C*' is a description of something done involuntarily and unintentionally; finally, suppose $A = B = C$. Then *A*, *B*, and *C* are the same – what? 'Action', 'event', 'thing done', each have, at least in some contexts, a strange ring when coupled with the wrong sort of description. Only the question, 'Why did you (he) do *A*?' has the true generality required. Obviously, the problem is greatly aggravated if we assume, as Melden does, that an action ('raising one's arm') can be identical with a bodily movement ('one's arm going up').

3 'Quasi-intentional' because, besides its intentional aspect, the description of the action must also refer in rationalizations; otherwise it could be true that an action was done for a certain reason and yet the action not have been performed. Compare 'the author of *Waverley*' in 'George IV knew the author of Waverley wrote *Waverley*'. This semant-

ical feature of action descriptions is discussed further in Essays 3 and 6 [of *Essays on Actions and Events*].

4 *The Concept of Mind* (New York: Barnes & Noble (University Paperbacks), 1949. Published by special arrangement with Hutchinson, London), p. 89.

5 Anscombe denies that the practical syllogism is deductive. This she does partly because she thinks of the practical syllogism, as Aristotle does, as corresponding to a piece of practical reasoning (whereas for me it is only part of the analysis of the concept of a reason with which someone acted), and therefore she is bound, again following Aristotle, to think of the conclusion of a practical syllogism as corresponding to a judgement, not merely that the action has a desirable characteristic, but that the action is desirable (reasonable, worth doing, etc.). Practical reasoning is discussed further in Essay 2 [of *Essays on Actions and Events*].

6 *Free Action* (London: Routledge and Kegan Paul, 1961), p. 184.

7 *Thought and Action* (London: Chatto and Windus), pp. 166, 168, 167, respectively.

8 I say 'as the basic move' to cancel any suggestion that C1 and C2 are jointly *sufficient* to define the relation of reasons to the actions they explain. For discussion of this point, see the Introduction and Essay 4 [of *Essays on Actions and Events*].

9 *Free Action*, p. 52.

10 This argument can be found in one or more versions, in Kenny, Hampshire, and Melden, as well as in P. Winch, *The Idea of a Social Science*, and R. S. Peters, *The Concept of Motivation*. In one of its forms, the argument was of course inspired by Ryle's treatment of motives in *The Concept of Mind*.

11 *Causation in the Law* (Oxford: Clarendon Press, 1959), p. 52.

12 Essays 11, 12, and 13 [in *Essays on Actions and Events*] discuss the issues of this paragraph and the one before it.

13 We could roughly characterize the analysis of singular causal statements hinted at here as follows: '*A* caused *B*' is true if and only if there are

descriptions of A and B such that the sentence obtained by putting these descriptions for 'A' and 'B' in 'A caused B' follows from a true causal law. This analysis is saved from triviality by the fact that not all true generalizations are causal laws; causal laws are distinguished (though of course

this is no analysis) by the fact that they are inductively confirmed by their instances and by the fact that they support counterfactual and subjunctive singular causal statements. There is more on causality in Essay 7 [of *Essays*].

14   *Free Action*, pp. 128–9.

Further reading in freedom and personal identity

Dennett, Daniel, *Elbow Room*, Cambridge, MA: MIT Press, 1984.

Kane, Robert, *The Significance of Free Will*, New York: Oxford University Press, 1996.

Parfit, Derek, *Reasons and Persons*, Oxford: Clarendon Press, 1984.

Perry, John, *Personal Identity*, Berkeley: University of California Press, 1975.

Shoemaker, Sydney and Swinburne, Richard, *Personal Identity* (Great Debates in Philosophy), Oxford: Blackwell Publishers, 1984.

Strawson, P. F., *Freedom and Resentment*, London: Methuen, 1974.

Watson, Gary, *Free Will*, Oxford: Oxford University Press, 1982.

Williams, Bernard, *Problems of the Self*, Cambridge: Cambridge University Press, 1973.

PART VI

Ethics

33

The Subject-matter of Ethics

G. E. Moore

1. It is very easy to point out some among our every-day judgments, with the truth of which Ethics is undoubtedly concerned. Whenever we say, 'So and so is a good man,' or 'That fellow is a villain'; whenever we ask, 'What ought I to do?' or 'Is it wrong for me to do like this?'; whenever we hazard such remarks as 'Temperance is a virtue and drunkenness a vice' – it is undoubtedly the business of Ethics to discuss such questions and such statements; to argue what is the true answer when we ask what it is right to do, and to give reasons for thinking that our statements about the character of persons or the morality of actions are true or false. In the vast majority of cases, where we make statements involving any of the terms 'virtue,' 'vice,' 'duty,' 'right,' 'ought,' 'good,' 'bad,' we are making ethical judgments; and if we wish to discuss their truth, we shall be discussing a point of Ethics.

So much as this is not disputed; but it falls very far short of defining the province of Ethics. That province may indeed be defined as the whole truth about that which is at the same time common to all such judgments and peculiar to them. But we have still to ask the question: What is it that is thus common and peculiar? And this is a question to which very different answers have been given by ethical philosophers of acknowledged reputation, and none of them, perhaps, completely satisfactory.

Originally published in *Principia Ethica* (Cambridge University Press, Cambridge, 1903).

2. If we take such examples as those given above, we shall not be far wrong in saying that they are all of them concerned with the question of 'conduct' – with the question, what, in the conduct of us, human beings, is good, and what is bad, what is right, and what is wrong. For when we say that a man is good, we commonly mean that he acts rightly; when we say that drunkenness is a vice, we commonly mean that to get drunk is a wrong or wicked action. And this discussion of human conduct is, in fact, that with which the name 'Ethics' is most intimately associated. It is so associated by derivation; and conduct is undoubtedly by far the commonest and most generally interesting object of ethical judgments.

Accordingly, we find that many ethical philosophers are disposed to accept as an adequate definition of 'Ethics' the statement that it deals with the question what is good or bad in human conduct. They hold that its enquiries are properly confined to 'conduct' or to 'practice'; they hold that the name 'practical philosophy' covers all the matter with which it has to do. Now, without discussing the proper meaning of the word (for verbal questions are properly left to the writers of dictionaries and other persons interested in literature; philosophy, as we shall see, has no concern with them), I may say that I intend to use 'Ethics' to cover more than this – a usage, for which there is, I think, quite sufficient authority. I am using it to cover an enquiry for which, at all events, there is no other word: the general enquiry into what is good.

345

Ethics is undoubtedly concerned with the question what good conduct is; but, being concerned with this, it obviously does not start at the beginning, unless it is prepared to tell us what is good as well as what is conduct. For 'good conduct' is a complex notion: all conduct is not good; for some is certainly bad and some may be indifferent. And on the other hand, other things, beside conduct, may be good; and if they are so, then, 'good' denotes some property, that is common to them and conduct; and if we examine good conduct alone of all good things, then we shall be in danger of mistaking for this property, some property which is not shared by those other things: and thus we shall have made a mistake about Ethics even in this limited sense; for we shall not know what good conduct really is. This is a mistake which many writers have actually made, from limiting their enquiry to conduct. And hence I shall try to avoid it by considering first what is good in general; hoping, that if we can arrive at any certainty about this, it will be much easier to settle the question of good conduct: for we all know pretty well what 'conduct' is. This, then, is our first question: What is good? and What is bad? and to the discussion of this question (or these questions) I give the name of Ethics, since that science must, at all events, include it.

3.   But this is a question which may have many meanings. If, for example, each of us were to say 'I am doing good now' or 'I had a good dinner yesterday,' these statements would each of them be some sort of answer to our question, although perhaps a false one. So, too, when A asks B what school he ought to send his son to, B's answer will certainly be an ethical judgment. And similarly all distribution of praise or blame to any personage or thing that has existed, now exists, or will exist, does give some answer to the question 'What is good?' In all such cases some particular thing is judged to be good or bad: the question 'What?' is answered by 'This.' But this is not the sense in which a scientific Ethics asks the question. Not one, of all the many million answers of this kind, which must be true, can form a part of an ethical system; although that science must contain reasons and principles sufficient for deciding on the truth of all of them. There are far too many persons, things and events in the world, past, present, or to come, for a discussion of their individual merits to be embraced

in any science. Ethics, therefore, does not deal at all with facts of this nature, facts that are unique, individual, absolutely particular; facts with which such studies as history, geography, astronomy, are compelled, in part at least, to deal. And, for this reason, it is not the business of the ethical philosopher to give personal advice or exhortation.

4.   But there is another meaning which may be given to the question 'What is good?' 'Books are good' would be an answer to it, though an answer obviously false; for some books are very bad indeed. And ethical judgments of this kind do indeed belong to Ethics; though I shall not deal with many of them. Such is the judgment 'Pleasure is good' – a judgment, of which Ethics should discuss the truth, although it is not nearly as important as that other judgment, with which we shall be much occupied presently – 'Pleasure *alone* is good.' It is judgments of this sort, which are made in such books on Ethics as contain a list of 'virtues' – in Aristotle's 'Ethics' for example. But it is judgments of precisely the same kind, which form the substance of what is commonly supposed to be a study different from Ethics, and one much less respectable – the study of Casuistry. We may be told that Casuistry differs from Ethics, in that it is much more detailed and particular, Ethics much more general. But it is most important to notice that Casuistry does not deal with anything that is absolutely particular – particular in the only sense in which a perfectly precise line can be drawn between it and what is general. It is not particular in the sense just noticed, the sense in which this book is a particular book, and A's friend's advice particular advice. Casuistry may indeed be *more* particular and Ethics *more* general; but that means that they differ only in degree and not in kind. And this is universally true of 'particular' and 'general,' when used in this common, but inaccurate, sense. So far as Ethics allows itself to give lists of virtues or even to name constituents of the Ideal, it is indistinguishable from Casuistry. Both alike deal with what is general, in the sense in which physics and chemistry deal with what is general. Just as chemistry aims at discovering what are the properties of oxygen, *wherever it occurs*, and not only of this or that particular specimen of oxygen; so Casuistry aims at discovering what actions are good, *whenever they occur*. In this respect Ethics and Casuistry alike are to be classed with such sciences as physics, chemistry

and physiology, in their absolute distinction from those of which history and geography are instances. And it is to be noted that, owing to their detailed nature, casuistical investigations are actually nearer to physics and to chemistry than are the investigations usually assigned to Ethics. For just as physics cannot rest content with the discovery that light is propagated by waves of ether, but must go on to discover the particular nature of the ether-waves corresponding to each several colour; so Casuistry, not content with the general law that charity is a virtue, must attempt to discover the relative merits of every different form of charity. Casuistry forms, therefore, part of the ideal of ethical science: Ethics cannot be complete without it. The defects of Casuistry are not defects of principle; no objection can be taken to its aim and object. It has failed only because it is far too difficult a subject to be treated adequately in our present state of knowledge. The casuist has been unable to distinguish, in the cases which he treats, those elements upon which their value depends. Hence he often thinks two cases to be alike in respect of value, when in reality they are alike only in some other respect. It is to mistakes of this kind that the pernicious influence of such investigations has been due. For Casuistry is the goal of ethical investigation. It cannot be safely attempted at the beginning of our studies, but only at the end.

5.   But our question 'What is good?' may have still another meaning. We may, in the third place, mean to ask, not what thing or things are good, but how 'good' is to be defined. This is an enquiry which belongs only to Ethics, not to Casuistry; and this is the enquiry which will occupy us first.

It is an enquiry to which most special attention should be directed; since this question, how 'good' is to be defined, is the most fundamental question in all Ethics. That which is meant by 'good' is, in fact, except its converse 'bad,' the *only* simple object of thought which is peculiar to Ethics. Its definition is, therefore, the most essential point in the definition of Ethics; and moreover a mistake with regard to it entails a far larger number of erroneous ethical judgments than any other. Unless this first question be fully understood, and its true answer clearly recognised, the rest of Ethics is as good as useless from the point of view of systematic knowledge. True ethical judgments, of the two kinds last

dealt with, may indeed be made by those who do not know the answer to this question as well as by those who do; and it goes without saying that the two classes of people may lead equally good lives. But it is extremely unlikely that the *most general* ethical judgments will be equally valid, in the absence of a true answer to this question: I shall presently try to shew that the gravest errors have been largely due to beliefs in a false answer. And, in any case, it is impossible that, till the answer to this question be known, any one should know *what is the evidence* for any ethical judgment whatsoever. But the main object of Ethics, as a systematic science, is to give correct *reasons* for thinking that this or that is good; and, unless this question be answered, such reasons cannot be given. Even, therefore, apart from the fact that a false answer leads to false conclusions, the present enquiry is a most necessary and important part of the science of Ethics.

6.   What, then, is good? How is good to be defined? Now, it may be thought that this is a verbal question. A definition does indeed often mean the expressing of one word's meaning in other words. But this is not the sort of definition I am asking for. Such a definition can never be of ultimate importance in any study except lexicography. If I wanted that kind of definition I should have to consider in the first place how people generally used the word 'good'; but my business is not with its proper usage, as established by custom. I should, indeed, be foolish, if I tried to use it for something which it did not usually denote: if, for instance, I were to announce that, whenever I used the word 'good,' I must be understood to be thinking of that object which is usually denoted by the word 'table.' I shall, therefore, use the word in the sense in which I think it is ordinarily used; but at the same time I am not anxious to discuss whether I am right in thinking that it is so used. My business is solely with that object or idea, which I hold, rightly or wrongly, that the word is generally used to stand for. What I want to discover is the nature of that object or idea, and about this I am extremely anxious to arrive at an agreement.

But, if we understand the question in this sense, my answer to it may seem a very disappointing one. If I am asked 'What is good?' my answer is that good is good, and that is the end of the matter. Or if I am asked 'How is good to be defined?' my answer is that it cannot be defined, and that is all I have to say about it. But disappointing as these answers may appear, they are of the very last importance. To readers who are familiar with philosophic terminology, I can express their importance by saying that they amount to this: That propositions about the good are all of them synthetic and never analytic; and that is plainly no trivial matter. And the same thing may be expressed more popularly, by saying that, if I am right, then nobody can foist upon us such an axiom as that 'Pleasure is the only good' or that 'The good is the desired' on the pretence that this is 'the very meaning of the word.'

7. Let us, then, consider this position. My point is that 'good' is a simple notion, just as 'yellow' is a simple notion; that, just as you cannot, by any manner of means, explain to any one who does not already know it, what yellow is, so you cannot explain what good is. Definitions of the kind that I was asking for, definitions which describe the real nature of the object or notion denoted by a word, and which do not merely tell us what the word is used to mean, are only possible when the object or notion in question is something complex. You can give a definition of a horse, because a horse has many different properties and qualities, all of which you can enumerate. But when you have enumerated them all, when you have reduced a horse to his simplest terms, then you can no longer define those terms. They are simply something which you think of or perceive, and to any one who cannot think of or perceive them, you can never, by any definition, make their nature known. It may perhaps be objected to this that we are able to describe to others, objects which they have never seen or thought of. We can, for instance, make a man understand what a chimaera is, although he has never heard of one or seen one. You can tell him that it is an animal with a lioness's head and body, with a goat's head growing from the middle of its back, and with a snake in place of a tail. But here the object which you are describing is a complex object; it is entirely composed of parts, with which we are all perfectly familiar – a snake, a goat, a lioness; and we know, too, the manner in which those parts are to be put together, because we know what is meant by the middle of a lioness's back, and where her tail is wont to grow. And so it is with all objects, not previously known, which we are able to define: they are all complex; all composed of parts, which may themselves, in the first instance, be capable of similar definition, but which must in the end be reducible to simplest parts, which can no longer be defined. But yellow and good, we say, are not complex: they are notions of that simple kind, out of which definitions are composed and with which the power of further defining ceases.

8. When we say, as Webster says, 'The definition of horse is "A hoofed quadruped of the genus Equus,"' we may, in fact, mean three different things. (1) We may mean merely: 'When I say "horse," you are to understand that I am talking about a hoofed quadruped of the genus Equus.' This might be called the arbitrary verbal definition: and I do not mean that good is indefinable in that sense. (2) We may mean, as Webster ought to mean: 'When most English people say "horse," they mean a hoofed quadruped of the genus Equus.' This may be called the verbal definition proper, and I do not say that good is indefinable in this sense either; for it is certainly possible to discover how people use a word: otherwise, we could never have known that 'good' may be translated by 'gut' in German and by 'bon' in French. But (3) we may, when we define horse, mean something much more important. We may mean that a certain object, which we all of us know, is composed in a certain manner: that it has four legs, a head, a heart, a liver, etc., etc., all of them arranged in definite relations to one another. It is in this sense that I deny good to be definable. I say that it is not composed of any parts, which we can substitute for it in our minds when we are thinking of it. We might think just as clearly and correctly about a horse, if we thought of all its parts and their arrangement instead of thinking of the whole: we could, I say, think how a horse differed from a donkey just as well, just as truly, in this way, as now we do, only not so easily; but there is nothing whatsoever which we could so substitute for good; and that is what I mean, when I say that good is indefinable.

9. But I am afraid I have still not removed the chief difficulty which may prevent acceptance of the proposition that good is indefinable. I do not mean to say that *the* good, that which is good, is thus indefinable; if I did think so, I should not be writing on Ethics, for my main object is to help towards discovering that definition. It is

just because I think there will be less risk of error in our search for a definition of 'the good,' that I am now insisting that *good* is indefinable. I must try to explain the difference between these two. I suppose it may be granted that 'good' is an adjective. Well 'the good,' 'that which is good,' must therefore be the substantive to which the adjective 'good' will apply: it must be the whole of that to which the adjective will apply, and the adjective must *always* truly apply to it. But if it is that to which the adjective will apply, it must be something different from that adjective itself; and the whole of that something different, whatever it is, will be our definition of *the* good. Now it may be that this something will have other adjectives, beside 'good,' that will apply to it. It may be full of pleasure, for example; it may be intelligent: and if these two adjectives are really part of its definition, then it will certainly be true, that pleasure and intelligence are good. And many people appear to think that, if we say 'Pleasure and intelligence are good,' or if we say 'Only pleasure and intelligence are good,' we are defining 'good.' Well, I cannot deny that propositions of this nature may sometimes be called definitions; I do not know well enough how the word is generally used to decide upon this point. I only wish it to be understood that that is not what I mean when I say there is no possible definition of good, and that I shall not mean this if I use the word again. I do most fully believe that some true proposition of the form 'Intelligence is good and intelligence alone is good' can be found; if none could be found, our definition of *the* good would be impossible. As it is, I believe *the* good to be definable; and yet I still say that good itself is indefinable.

10. 'Good,' then, if we mean by it that quality which we assert to belong to a thing, when we say that the thing is good, is incapable of any definition, in the most important sense of that word. The most important sense of 'definition' is that in which a definition states what are the parts which invariably compose a certain whole; and in this sense 'good' has no definition because it is simple and has no parts. It is one of those innumerable objects of thought which are themselves incapable of definition, because they are the ultimate terms by reference to which whatever *is* capable of definition must be defined. That there must be an indefinite number of such terms is obvious, on reflection; since we cannot define

anything except by an analysis, which, when carried as far as it will go, refers us to something, which is simply different from anything else, and which by that ultimate difference explains the peculiarity of the whole which we are defining: for every whole contains some parts which are common to other wholes also. There is, therefore, no intrinsic difficulty in the contention that 'good' denotes a simple and indefinable quality. There are many other instances of such qualities.

Consider yellow, for example. We may try to define it, by describing its physical equivalent; we may state what kind of light-vibrations must stimulate the normal eye, in order that we may perceive it. But a moment's reflection is sufficient to shew that those light-vibrations are not themselves what we mean by yellow. *They* are not what we perceive. Indeed we should never have been able to discover their existence, unless we had first been struck by the patent difference of quality between the different colours. The most we can be entitled to say of those vibrations is that they are what corresponds in space to the yellow which we actually perceive.

Yet a mistake of this simple kind has commonly been made about 'good.' It may be true that all things which are good are *also* something else, just as it is true that all things which are yellow produce a certain kind of vibration in the light. And it is a fact, that Ethics aims at discovering what are those other properties belonging to all things which are good. But far too many philosophers have thought that when they named those other properties they were actually defining good; that these properties, in fact, were simply not 'other,' but absolutely and entirely the same with goodness. This view I propose to call the 'naturalistic fallacy' and of it I shall now endeavour to dispose.

11. Let us consider what it is such philosophers say. And first it is to be noticed that they do not agree among themselves. They not only say that they are right as to what good is, but they endeavour to prove that other people who say that it is something else, are wrong. One, for instance, will affirm that good is pleasure, another, perhaps, that good is that which is desired; and each of these will argue eagerly to prove that the other is wrong. But how is that possible? One of them says that good is nothing but the object of desire, and at the same time tries to prove that it is not pleasure. But

G. E. Moore

from his first assertion, that good just means the object of desire, one of two things must follow as regards his proof:

(1) He may be trying to prove that the object of desire is not pleasure. But, if this be all, where is his Ethics? The position he is maintaining is merely a psychological one. Desire is something which occurs in our minds, and pleasure is something else which so occurs; and our would-be ethical philosopher is merely holding that the latter is not the object of the former. But what has that to do with the question in dispute? His opponent held the ethical proposition that pleasure was the good, and although he should prove a million times over the psychological proposition that pleasure is not the object of desire, he is no nearer proving his opponent to be wrong. The position is like this. One man says a triangle is a circle: another replies 'A triangle is a straight line, and I will prove to you that I am right: *for*' (this is the only argument) 'a straight line is not a circle.' 'That is quite true,' the other may reply; 'but nevertheless a triangle is a circle, and you have said nothing whatever to prove the contrary. What is proved is that one of us is wrong, for we agree that a triangle cannot be both a straight line and a circle: but which is wrong, there can be no earthly means of proving, since you define triangle as straight line and I define it as circle.' – Well, that is one alternative which any naturalistic Ethics has to face; if good is *defined* as something else, it is then impossible either to prove that any other definition is wrong or even to deny such definition.

(2) The other alternative will scarcely be more welcome. It is that the discussion is after all a verbal one. When A says 'Good means pleasant' and B says 'Good means desired,' they may merely wish to assert that most people have used the word for what is pleasant and for what is desired respectively. And this is quite an interesting subject for discussion: only it is not a whit more an ethical discussion than the last was. Nor do I think that any exponent of naturalistic Ethics would be willing to allow that this was all he meant. They are all so anxious to persuade us that what they call the good is what we really ought to do. 'Do, pray, act so, because the word "good" is generally used to denote actions of this nature': such, on this view, would be the substance of their teaching. And in so far as they tell us how we ought to act, their teaching is truly ethical, as they mean it to be. But how perfectly

absurd is the reason they would give for it! 'You are to do this, because most people use a certain word to denote conduct such as this.' 'You are to say the thing which is not, because most people call it lying.' That is an argument just as good! – My dear sirs, what we want to know from you as ethical teachers, is not how people use a word; it is not even, what kind of actions they approve, which the use of this word 'good' may certainly imply: what we want to know is simply what *is* good. We may indeed agree that what most people do think good, is actually so; we shall at all events be glad to know their opinions: but when we say their opinions about what *is* good, we do mean what we say; we do not care whether they call that thing which they mean 'horse' or 'table' or 'chair,' 'gut' or 'bon' or 'ἀγαθός'; we want to know what it is that they so call. When they say 'Pleasure is good,' we cannot believe that they merely mean 'Pleasure is pleasure' and nothing more than that.

12. Suppose a man says 'I am pleased'; and suppose that is not a lie or a mistake but the truth. Well, if it is true, what does that mean? It means that his mind, a certain definite mind, distinguished by certain definite marks from all others, has at this moment a certain definite feeling called pleasure. 'Pleased' *means* nothing but having pleasure, and though we may be more pleased or less pleased, and even, we may admit for the present, have one or another kind of pleasure; yet in so far as it is pleasure we have, whether there be more or less of it, and whether it be of one kind or another, what we have is one definite thing, absolutely indefinable, some one thing that is the same in all the various degrees and in all the various kinds of it that there may be. We may be able to say how it is related to other things: that, for example, it is in the mind, that it causes desire, that we are conscious of it, etc., etc. We can, I say, describe its relations to other things, but define it we can *not*. And if anybody tried to define pleasure for us as being any other natural object; if anybody were to say, for instance, that pleasure *means* the sensation of red, and were to proceed to deduce from that that pleasure is a colour, we should be entitled to laugh at him and to distrust his future statements about pleasure. Well, that would be the same fallacy which I have called the naturalistic fallacy. That 'pleased' does not mean 'having the sensation of red,' or anything else

whatever, does not prevent us from understanding what it does mean. It is enough for us to know that 'pleased' does mean 'having the sensation of pleasure,' and though pleasure is absolutely indefinable, though pleasure is pleasure and nothing else whatever, yet we feel no difficulty in saying that we are pleased. The reason is, of course, that when I say 'I am pleased,' I do *not* mean that 'I' am the same thing as 'having pleasure.' And similarly no difficulty need be found in my saying that 'pleasure is good' and yet not meaning that 'pleasure' is the same thing as 'good,' that pleasure *means* good, and that good *means* pleasure. If I were to imagine that when I said 'I am pleased,' I meant that I was exactly the same thing as 'pleased,' I should not indeed call that a naturalistic fallacy, although it would be the same fallacy as I have called naturalistic with reference to Ethics. The reason of this is obvious enough. When a man confuses two natural objects with one another, defining the one by the other, if for instance, he confuses himself, who is one natural object, with 'pleased' or with 'pleasure' which are others, then there is no reason to call the fallacy naturalistic. But if he confuses 'good,' which is not in the same sense a natural object, with any natural object whatever, then there is a reason for calling that a naturalistic fallacy; its being made with regard to 'good' marks it as something quite specific, and this specific mistake deserves a name because it is so common. As for the reasons why good is not to be considered a natural object, they may be reserved for discussion in another place. But, for the present, it is sufficient to notice this: Even if it were a natural object, that would not alter the nature of the fallacy nor diminish its importance one whit. All that I have said about it would remain quite equally true: only the name which I have called it would not be so appropriate as I think it is. And I do not care about the name: what I do care about is the fallacy. It does not matter what we call it, provided we recognise it when we meet with it. It is to be met with in almost every book on Ethics; and yet it is not recognised: and that is why it is necessary to multiply illustrations of it, and convenient to give it a name. It is a very simple fallacy indeed. When we say that an orange is yellow, we do not think our statement binds us to hold that 'orange' means nothing else than 'yellow,' or that nothing can be yellow but an orange. Supposing the orange is also sweet! Does that bind us to say that

'sweet' is exactly the same thing as 'yellow,' that 'sweet' must be defined as 'yellow'? And supposing it be recognised that 'yellow' just means 'yellow' and nothing else whatever, does that make it any more difficult to hold that oranges are yellow? Most certainly it does not: on the contrary, it would be absolutely meaningless to say that oranges were yellow, unless yellow did in the end mean just 'yellow' and nothing else whatever – unless it was absolutely indefinable. We should not get any very clear notion about things, which are yellow – we should not get very far with our science, if we were bound to hold that everything which was yellow, *meant* exactly the same thing as yellow. We should find we had to hold that an orange was exactly the same thing as a stool, a piece of paper, a lemon, anything you like. We could prove any number of absurdities; but should we be the nearer to the truth? Why, then, should it be different with 'good'? Why, if good is good and indefinable, should I be held to deny that pleasure is good? Is there any difficulty in holding both to be true at once? On the contrary, there is no meaning in saying that pleasure is good, unless good is something different from pleasure. It is absolutely useless, so far as Ethics is concerned, to prove, as Mr Spencer tries to do, that increase of pleasure coincides with increase of life, unless good *means* something different from either life or pleasure. He might just as well try to prove that an orange is yellow by shewing that it always is wrapped up in paper.

13. In fact, if it is not the case that 'good' denotes something simple and indefinable, only two alternatives are possible: either it is a complex, a given whole, about the correct analysis of which there may be disagreement; or else it means nothing at all, and there is no such subject as Ethics. In general, however, ethical philosophers have attempted to define good, without recognising what such an attempt must mean. They actually use arguments which involve one or both of the absurdities considered in §11. We are, therefore, justified in concluding that the attempt to define good is chiefly due to want of clearness as to the possible nature of definition. There are, in fact, only two serious alternatives to be considered, in order to establish the conclusion that 'good' does denote a simple and indefinable notion. It might possibly denote a complex, as 'horse' does; or it might have no meaning at all. Neither of these

G. E. Moore

possibilities has, however, been clearly conceived and seriously maintained, as such, by those who presume to define good; and both may be dismissed by a simple appeal to facts.

(1) The hypothesis that disagreement about the meaning of good is disagreement with regard to the correct analysis of a given whole, may be most plainly seen to be incorrect by consideration of the fact that, whatever definition be offered, it may be always asked, with significance, of the complex so defined, whether it is itself good. To take, for instance, one of the more plausible, because one of the more complicated, of such proposed definitions, it may easily be thought, at first sight, that to be good may mean to be that which we desire to desire. Thus if we apply this definition to a particular instance and say 'When we think that A is good, we are thinking that A is one of the things which we desire to desire,' our proposition may seem quite plausible. But, if we carry the investigation further, and ask ourselves 'Is it good to desire to desire A?' it is apparent, on a little reflection, that this question is itself as intelligible, as the original question 'Is A good?' – that we are, in fact, now asking for exactly the same information about the desire to desire A, for which we formerly asked with regard to A itself. But it is also apparent that the meaning of this second question cannot be correctly analysed into 'Is the desire to desire A one of the things which we desire to desire?': we have not before our minds anything so complicated as the question 'Do we desire to desire to desire to desire A?' Moreover any one can easily convince himself by inspection that the predicate of this proposition – 'good' – is positively different from the notion of 'desiring to desire' which enters into its subject: 'That we should desire to desire A is good' is *not* merely equivalent to 'That A should be good is good.' It may indeed be true that what we desire to desire is always also good; perhaps, even the converse may be true: but it is very doubtful whether this is the case, and the mere fact that we understand very well what is meant by doubting it, shews clearly that we have two different notions before our minds.

(2) And the same consideration is sufficient to dismiss the hypothesis that 'good' has no meaning whatsoever. It is very natural to make the mistake of supposing that what is universally true is of such a nature that its negation would be self-contradictory: the importance which has been assigned to analytic propositions in the history of philosophy shews how easy such a mistake is. And thus it is very easy to conclude that what seems to be a universal ethical principle is in fact an identical proposition; that, if, for example, whatever is called 'good' seems to be pleasant, the proposition 'Pleasure is the good' does not assert a connection between two different notions, but involves only one, that of pleasure, which is easily recognised as a distinct entity. But whoever will attentively consider with himself what is actually before his mind when he asks the question 'Is pleasure (or whatever it may be) after all good?' can easily satisfy himself that he is not merely wondering whether pleasure is pleasant. And if he will try this experiment with each suggested definition in succession, he may become expert enough to recognise that in every case he has before his mind a unique object, with regard to the connection of which with any other object, a distinct question may be asked. Everyone does in fact understand the question 'Is this good?' When he thinks of it, his state of mind is different from what it would be, were he asked 'Is this pleasant, or desired, or approved?' It has a distinct meaning for him, even though he may not recognise in what respect it is distinct. Whenever he thinks of 'intrinsic value,' or 'intrinsic worth,' or says that a thing 'ought to exist,' he has before his mind the unique object – the unique property of things – which I mean by 'good.' Everybody is constantly aware of this notion, although he may never become aware at all that it is different from other notions of which he is also aware. But, for correct ethical reasoning, it is extremely important that he should become aware of this fact; and, as soon as the nature of the problem is clearly understood, there should be little difficulty in advancing so far in analysis.

14. 'Good,' then, is indefinable; and yet, so far as I know, there is only one ethical writer, Prof. Henry Sidgwick, who has clearly recognised and stated this fact. We shall see, indeed, how far many of the most reputed ethical systems fall short of drawing the conclusions which follow from such a recognition. At present I will only quote one instance, which will serve to illustrate the meaning and importance of this principle that 'good' is indefinable, or, as Prof. Sidgwick says, an 'unanalysable notion.' It is an instance to which Prof. Sidgwick himself refers in a note on the passage, in which he argues that 'ought' is unanalysable.[1]

'Bentham,' says Sidgwick, 'explains that his fundamental principle "states the greatest happiness of all those whose interest is in question as being the right and proper end of human action"'; and yet 'his language in other passages of the same chapter would seem to imply' that he *means* by the word 'right' 'conducive to the general happiness.' Prof. Sidgwick sees that, if you take these two statements together, you get the absurd result that 'greatest happiness is the end of human action, which is conducive to the general happiness'; and so absurd does it seem to him to call this result, as Bentham calls it, 'the fundamental principle of a moral system,' that he suggests that Bentham cannot have meant it. Yet Prof. Sidgwick himself states elsewhere[2] that Psychological Hedonism is 'not seldom confounded with Egoistic Hedonism'; and that confusion, as we shall see, rests chiefly on that same fallacy, the naturalistic fallacy, which is implied in Bentham's statements. Prof. Sidgwick admits therefore that this fallacy is sometimes committed, absurd as it is; and I am inclined to think that Bentham may really have been one of those who committed it. Mill, as we shall see, certainly did commit it. In any case, whether Bentham committed it or not, his doctrine, as above quoted, will serve as a very good illustration of this fallacy, and of the importance of the contrary proposition that good is indefinable.

Let us consider this doctrine. Bentham seems to imply, so Prof. Sidgwick says, that the word 'right' *means* 'conducive to general happiness.' Now this, by itself, need not necessarily involve the naturalistic fallacy. For the word 'right' is very commonly appropriated to actions which lead to the attainment of what is good; which are regarded as *means* to the ideal and not as ends-in-themselves. This use of 'right,' as denoting what is good as a means, whether or not it be also good as an end, is indeed the use to which I shall confine the word. Had Bentham been using 'right' in this sense, it might be perfectly consistent for him to *define* right as 'conducive to the general happiness,' *provided only* (and notice this proviso) he had already proved, or laid down as an axiom, that general happiness was *the* good, or (what is equivalent to this) that general happiness alone was good. For in that case he would have already defined *the* good as general happiness (a position perfectly consistent, as we have seen, with the contention that 'good' is indefinable), and, since right was to be defined as

'conducive to *the* good,' it would actually *mean* 'conducive to general happiness.' But this method of escape from the charge of having committed the naturalistic fallacy has been closed by Bentham himself. For his fundamental principle is, we see, that the greatest happiness of all concerned is the *right* and proper *end* of human action. He applies the word 'right,' therefore, to the end, as such, not only to the means which are conducive to it; and, that being so, right can no longer be defined as 'conducive to the general happiness,' without involving the fallacy in question. For now it is obvious that the definition of right as conducive to general happiness can be used by him in support of the fundamental principle that general happiness is the right end; instead of being itself derived from that principle. If right, by definition, means conducive to general happiness, then it is obvious that general happiness is the right end. It is not necessary now first to prove or assert that general happiness is the right end, before right is defined as conducive to general happiness – a perfectly valid procedure; but on the contrary the definition of right as conducive to general happiness proves general happiness to be the right end – a perfectly invalid procedure, since in this case the statement that 'general happiness is the right end of human action' is not an ethical principle at all, but either, as we have seen, a proposition about the meaning of words, or else a proposition about the *nature* of general happiness, not about its rightness or goodness.

Now, I do not wish the importance I assign to this fallacy to be misunderstood. The discovery of it does not at all refute Bentham's contention that greatest happiness is the proper end of human action, if that be understood as an ethical proposition, as he undoubtedly intended it. That principle may be true all the same; we shall consider whether it is so in succeeding chapters. Bentham might have maintained it, as Prof. Sidgwick does, even if the fallacy had been pointed out to him. What I am maintaining is that the *reasons* which he actually gives for his ethical proposition are fallacious ones so far as they consist in a definition of right. What I suggest is that he did not perceive them to be fallacious; that, if he had done so, he would have been led to seek for other reasons in support of his Utilitarianism; and that, had he sought for other reasons, he *might* have found none which he thought to be sufficient. In that case he would have changed his whole system – a most important consequence. It is undoubtedly also possible that he would have thought other reasons to be sufficient, and in that case his ethical system, in its main results, would still have stood. But, even in this latter case, his use of the fallacy would be a serious objection to him as an ethical philosopher. For it is the business of Ethics, I must insist, not only to obtain true results, but also to find valid reasons for them. The direct object of Ethics is knowledge and not practice; and any one who uses the naturalistic fallacy has certainly not fulfilled this first object, however correct his practical principles may be.

My objections to Naturalism are then, in the first place, that it offers no reason at all, far less any valid reason, for any ethical principle whatever; and in this it already fails to satisfy the requirements of Ethics, as a scientific study. But in the second place I contend that, though it gives a reason for no ethical principle, it is a *cause* of the acceptance of false principles – it deludes the mind into accepting ethical principles which are false; and in this it is contrary to every aim of Ethics. It is easy to see that if we start with a definition of right conduct as conduct conducive to general happiness; then, knowing that right conduct is universally conduct conducive to the good, we very easily arrive at the result that the good is general happiness. If, on the other hand, we once recognise that we must start our Ethics without a definition, we shall be much more apt to look about us, before we adopt any ethical principle whatever; and the more we look about us, the less likely are we to adpot a false one. It may be replied to this: Yes, but we shall look about us just as much, before we settle on our definition, and are therefore just as likely to be right. But I will try to shew that this is not the case. If we start with the conviction that a definition of good can be found, we start with the conviction that good *can mean* nothing else than some one property of things; and our only business will then be to discover what that property is. But if we recognise that, so far as the meaning of good goes, anything whatever may be good, we start with a much more open mind. Moreover, apart from the fact that, when we think we have a definition, we cannot logically defend our ethical principles in any way whatever, we shall also be much less apt to defend them well, even if illogically. For we shall start with the conviction that good must mean so and so, and shall therefore be inclined either to misunderstand our opponent's arguments or to cut them short with the reply, 'This is not an open question: the very meaning of the word decides it; no one can think otherwise except through confusion.'

15.   Our first conclusion as to the subject-matter of Ethics is, then, that there is a simple, indefinable, unanalysable object of thought by reference to which it must be defined.

Notes

1   *Methods of Ethics*, Bk. 1, ch. III, §1 (6th edn.).
2   *Methods of Ethics*, Bk. 1, ch. IV, §1.

34

The Emotive Meaning of Ethical Terms

C. L. Stevenson

I

Ethical questions first arise in the form "Is so and so good?", or "Is this alternative better than that?" These questions are difficult partly because we don't quite know what we are seeking. We are asking, "Is there a needle in that haystack?" without even knowing just what a needle is. So the first thing to do is to examine the questions themselves. We must try to make them clearer, either by defining the terms in which they are expressed, or by any other method that is available.

The present paper is concerned wholly with this preliminary step of making ethical questions clear. In order to help answer the question "Is X good?" we must *substitute* for it a question which is free from ambiguity and confusion.

It is obvious that in substituting a clearer question we must not introduce some utterly different kind of question. It won't do (to take an extreme instance of a prevalent fallacy) to substitute for "Is X good?" the question "Is X pink with yellow trimmings?" and then point out how easy the question really is. This would beg the original question, not help answer it. On the other hand, we must not expect the substituted question to be strictly "identical" with the original one. The original question may embody hypostatization, anthropomorphism, vagueness, and all the other ills to which our ordinary discourse is subject. If

Originally published in *Mind* 46 (1937). Reprinted by permission of Oxford University Press, Oxford.

our substituted question is to be clearer, it must remove these ills. The questions will be identical only in the sense that a child is identical with the man he later becomes. Hence we must not demand that the substitution strike us, on immediate introspection, as making no change in meaning.

Just how, then, must the substituted question be related to the original? Let us assume (inaccurately) that it must result from replacing "good" by some set of terms which define it. The question then resolves itself to this: How must the defined meaning of "good" be related to its original meaning?

I answer that it must be *relevant*. A defined meaning will be called "relevant" to the original meaning under these circumstances: Those who have understood the definition must be able to say all that they then want to say by using the term in the defined way. They must never have occasion to use the term in the old, unclear sense. (If a person did have to go on using the word in the old sense, then to this extent his meaning would not be clarified, and the philosophical task would not be completed.) It frequently happens that a word is used so confusedly and ambiguously that we must give it *several* defined meanings, rather than one. In this case only the whole set of defined meanings will be called "relevant," and any one of them will be called "partially relevant". This is not a rigorous treatment of *relevance*, by any means; but it will serve for the present purposes.

Let us now turn to our particular task – that of giving a relevant definition of "good". Let us first examine some of the ways in which others have attempted to do this.

The word "good" has often been defined in terms of *approval*, or similar psychological attitudes. We may take as typical examples: "good" means *desired by me* (Hobbes); and "good" means *approved by most people* (Hume, in effect). It will be convenient to refer to definitions of this sort as "interest theories", following Mr. R. B. Perry, although neither "interest" nor "theory" is used in the most usual way.

Are definitions of this sort relevant?

It is idle to deny their *partial* relevance. The most superficial inquiry will reveal that "good" is exceedingly ambiguous. To maintain that "good" is *never* used in Hobbes's sense, and never in Hume's, is only to manifest an insensitivity to the complexities of language. We must recognize, perhaps, not only these senses, but a variety of similar ones, differing both with regard to the kind of interest in question, and with regard to the people who are said to have the interest.

But this is a minor matter. The essential question is not whether interest theories are *partially* relevant, but whether they are *wholly* relevant. This is the only point for intelligent dispute. Briefly: Granted that some senses of "good" may relevantly be defined in terms of interest, is there some *other* sense which is *not* relevantly so defined? We must give this question careful attention. For it is quite possible that when philosophers (and many others) have found the question "Is X good?" so difficult, they have been grasping for this *other* sense of "good", and not any sense relevantly defined in terms of interest. If we insist on defining "good" in terms of interest, and answer the question when thus interpreted, we may be begging *their* question entirely. Of course this *other* sense of "good" may not exist, or it may be a complete confusion; but that is what we must discover.

Now many have maintained that interest theories are *far* from being completely relevant. They have argued that such theories neglect the very sense of "good" which is most vital. And certainly, their arguments are not without plausibility.

Only . . . what *is* this "vital" sense of "good"? The answers have been so vague, and so beset with difficulties, that one can scarcely determine.

There are certain requirements, however, with which this "vital" sense has been expected to comply – requirements which appeal strongly to our common sense. It will be helpful to summar-

ize these, showing how they exclude the interest theories:

In the first place, we must be able sensibly to *disagree* about whether something is "good". This condition rules out Hobbes's definition. For consider the following argument: "This is good." "That isn't so; it's not good." As translated by Hobbes, this becomes: "I desire this." "That isn't so, for *I* don't." The speakers are not contradicting one another, and think they are, only because of an elementary confusion in the use of pronouns. The definition, "good" means *desired by my community*, is also excluded, for how could people from different communities disagree?[1]

In the second place, "goodness" must have, so to speak, a magnetism. A person who recognizes X to be "good" must *ipso facto* acquire a stronger tendency to act in its favour than he otherwise would have had. This rules out the Humian type of definition. For according to Hume, to recognize that something is "good" is simply to recognize that the majority approve of it. Clearly, a man may see that the majority approve of X without having, himself, a stronger tendency to favour it. This requirement excludes any attempt to define "good" in terms of the interest of people *other* than the speaker.[2]

In the third place, the "goodness" of anything must not be verifiable solely by use of the scientific method. "Ethics must not be psychology." This restriction rules out all of the traditional interest theories, without exception. It is so sweeping a restriction that we must examine its plausibility. What are the methodological implications of interest theories which are here rejected?

According to Hobbes's definition, a person can prove his ethical judgments, with finality, by showing that he is not making an introspective error about his desires. According to Hume's definition, one may prove ethical judgments (roughly speaking) by taking a vote. *This* use of the empirical method, at any rate, seems highly remote from what we usually accept as proof, and reflects on the complete relevance of the definitions which imply it.

But aren't there more complicated interest theories which are immune from such methodological implications? No, for the same factors appear; they are only put off for a while. Consider, for example, the definition: "X is good" means *most people would approve of X if they knew its nature and consequences*. How, according to this definition, could we prove that a certain X was good?

We should first have to find out, empirically, just what X was like, and what its consequences would be. To this extent the empirical method, as required by the definition, seems beyond intelligent objection. But what remains? We should next have to discover whether most people would approve of the sort of thing we had discovered X to be. This couldn't be determined by popular vote – but only because it would be too difficult to explain to the voters, beforehand, what the nature and consequences of X really were. Apart from this, voting would be a pertinent method. We are again reduced to counting noses, as a *perfectly final* appeal.

Now we need not scorn voting entirely. A man who rejected interest theories as irrelevant might readily make the following statement: "If I believed that X would be approved by the majority, when they knew all about it, I should be strongly *led* to say that X was good." But he would continue: "*Need* I say that X was good, under the circumstances? Wouldn't my acceptance of the alleged 'final proof' result simply from my being democratic? What about the more aristocratic people? They would simply say that the approval of most people, even when they knew all about the object of their approval, simply had nothing to do with the goodness of anything, and they would probably add a few remarks about the low state of people's interests." It would indeed seem, from these considerations, that the definition we have been considering has presupposed democratic ideals from the start; it has dressed up democratic propaganda in the guise of a definition.

The omnipotence of the empirical method, as implied by interest theories and others, may be shown unacceptable in a somewhat different way. Mr. G. E. Moore's familiar objection about the open question is chiefly pertinent in this regard. No matter what set of scientifically knowable properties a thing may have (says Moore, in effect), you will find, on careful introspection, that it is an open question to ask whether anything having these properties is *good*. It is difficult to believe that this recurrent question is a totally confused one, or that it seems open only because of the ambiguity of "good". Rather, we must be using some sense of "good" which is not definable, relevantly, in terms of anything scientifically knowable. That is, the scientific method is not sufficient for ethics.[3]

These, then, are the requirements with which the "vital" sense of "good" is expected to comply:

(1) goodness must be a topic for intelligent disagreement; (2) it must be "magnetic"; and (3) it must not be discoverable solely through the scientific method.

II

Let us now turn to my own analysis of ethical judgments. First let me present my position dogmatically, showing to what extent I vary from tradition.

I believe that the three requirements, given above, are perfectly sensible; that there is some *one* sense of "good" which satisfies all three requirements; and that no traditional interest theory satisfies them all. But this does not imply that "good" must be explained in terms of a Platonic Idea, or of a Categorical Imperative, or of an unique, unanalyzable property. On the contrary, the three requirements can be met by a *kind* of interest theory. *But we must give up a presupposition which all the traditional interest theories have made.*

Traditional interest theories hold that ethical statements are *descriptive* of the existing state of interests – that they simply *give information* about interests. (More accurately, ethical judgments are said to describe what the state of interests is, was, or will be, or to indicate what the state of interests *would* be under specified circumstances.) It is this emphasis on description, on information, which leads to their incomplete relevance. Doubtless there is always *some* element of description in ethical judgments, but this is by no means all. Their major use is not to indicate facts, but to *create an influence*. Instead of merely describing people's interests, they *change* or *intensify* them. They *recommend* an interest in an object, rather than state that the interest already exists.

For instance: When you tell a man that he oughtn't to steal, your object isn't merely to let him know that people disapprove of stealing. You are attempting, rather, to get *him* to disapprove of it. Your ethical judgment has a quasi-imperative force which, operating through suggestion, and intensified by your tone of voice, readily permits you to begin to *influence*, to *modify*, his interests. If in the end you do not succeed in getting *him* to disapprove of stealing, you will feel that you've failed to convince him that stealing is wrong. You will continue to feel this, even though he fully acknowledges that you disapprove of it, and that almost everyone else does. When you point out to him the consequences of his actions – consequences which you suspect he already disapproves of – these *reasons* which support your ethical judgment are simply a means of facilitating your influence. If you think you can change his interests by making vivid to him how others will disapprove of him, you will do so; otherwise not. So the consideration about other people's interest is just an additional means you may employ, in order to move him, and is not a part of the ethical judgment itself. Your ethical judgment doesn't merely describe interests to him, it directs his very interests. The difference between the traditional interest theories and my view is like the difference between describing a desert and irrigating it.

Another example: A munition maker declares that war is a good thing. If he merely meant that he approved of it, he would not have to insist so strongly, nor grow so excited in his argument. People would be quite easily convinced that he approved of it. If he merely meant that most people approved of war, or that most people would approve of it if they knew the consequences, he would have to yield his point if it were proved that this wasn't so. But he wouldn't do this, nor does consistency require it. He is not *describing* the state of people's approval; he is trying to *change* it by his influence. If he found that few people approved of war, he might insist all the more strongly that it was good, for there would be more changing to be done.

This example illustrates how "good" may be used for what most of us would call bad purposes. Such cases are as pertinent as any others. I am not indicating the *good* way of using "good". I am not influencing people, but am describing the way this influence sometimes goes on. If the reader wishes to say that the munition maker's influence is bad – that is, if the reader wishes to awaken people's disapproval of the man, and to make him disapprove of his own actions – I should at another time be willing to join in this undertaking. But this is not the present concern. I am not using ethical terms, but am indicating how they *are* used. The munition maker, in his use of "good", illustrates the persuasive character of the word just as well as does the unselfish man who, eager to encourage in each of us a desire for the happiness of all, contends that the supreme good is peace.

Thus ethical terms are *instruments* used in the complicated interplay and readjustment of human interests. This can be seen plainly from more general observations. People from widely separated communities have different moral attitudes. Why? To a great extent because they have been subject to different social influences. Now clearly this influence doesn't operate through sticks and stones alone; words play a great part. People praise one another, to encourage certain inclinations, and blame one another, to discourage others. Those of forceful personalities issue commands which weaker people, for complicated instinctive reasons, find it difficult to disobey, quite apart from fears of consequences. Further influence is brought to bear by writers and orators. Thus social influence is exerted, to an enormous extent, by means that have nothing to do with physical force or material reward. The ethical terms facilitate such influence. Being suited for use in *suggestion*, they are a means by which men's attitudes may be led this way or that. The reason, then, that we find a greater similarity in the moral attitudes of one community than in those of different communities is largely this: ethical judgments propagate themselves. One man says "This is good"; this may influence the approval of another person, who then makes the same ethical judgment, which in turn influences another person, and so on. In the end, by a process of mutual influence, people take up more or less the same attitudes. Between people of widely separated communities, of course, the influence is less strong; hence different communities have different attitudes.

These remarks will serve to give a general idea of my point of view. We must now go into more detail. There are several questions which must be answered: How does an ethical sentence acquire its power of influencing people – why is it suited to suggestion? Again, what has this influence to do with the *meaning* of ethical terms? And finally, do these considerations really lead us to a sense of "good" which meets the requirements mentioned in the preceding section?

Let us deal first with the question about *meaning*. This is far from an easy question, so we must enter into a preliminary inquiry about meaning in general. Although a seeming digression, this will prove indispensable.

III

Broadly speaking, there are two different *purposes* which lead us to use language. On the one hand we use words (as in science) to record, clarify, and communicate *beliefs*. On the other hand we use words to give vent to our feelings (interjections), or to create moods (poetry), or to incite people to actions or attitudes (oratory).

The first use of words I shall call "descriptive"; the second, "dynamic". Note that the distinction depends solely upon the *purpose* of the *speaker*.

When a person says "Hydrogen is the lightest known gas", his purpose *may* be simply to lead the hearer to believe this, or to believe that the speaker believes it. In that case the words are used descriptively. When a person cuts himself and says "Damn", his purpose is not ordinarily to record, clarify, or communicate any belief. The word is used dynamically. The two ways of using words, however, are by no means mutually exclusive. This is obvious from the fact that our purposes are often complex. Thus when one says "I want you to close the door", part of his purpose, ordinarily, is to lead the hearer to believe that he has this want. To that extent the words are used descriptively. But the major part of one's purpose is to lead the hearer to *satisfy* the want. To that extent the words are used dynamically.

It very frequently happens that the same sentence may have a dynamic use on one occasion, and may not have a dynamic use on another; and that it may have different dynamic uses on different occasions. For instance: A man says to a visiting neighbour, "I am loaded down with work". His purpose may be to let the neighbour know how life is going with him. This would *not* be a dynamic use of words. He may make the remark, however, in order to drop a hint. This *would* be dynamic usage (as well as descriptive). Again, he may make the remark to arouse the neighbour's sympathy. This would be a *different* dynamic usage from that of hinting.

Or again, when we say to a man, "Of course you won't make those mistakes any more", we *may* simply be making a prediction. But we are more likely to be using "suggestion", in order to encourage him and hence *keep* him from making mistakes. The first use would be descriptive; the second, mainly dynamic.

From these examples it will be clear that we can't determine whether words are used dynamically or not, merely by reading the dictionary – even assuming that everyone is faithful to dictionary meanings. Indeed, to know whether a person is using a word dynamically, we must note his tone of voice, his gestures, the general circumstances under which he is speaking, and so on.

We must now proceed to an important question: What has the dynamic use of words to do with their *meaning*? One thing is clear – we must not define "meaning" in a way that would make meaning vary with dynamic usage. If we did, we should have no use for the term. All that we could say about such "meaning" would be that it is very complicated, and subject to constant change. So we must certainly distinguish between the dynamic use of words and their meaning.

It doesn't follow, however, that we must define "meaning" in some non-psychological fashion. We must simply restrict the psychological field. Instead of identifying meaning with *all* the psychological causes and effects that attend a word's utterance, we must identify it with those that it has a *tendency* (causal property, dispositional property) to be connected with. The tendency must be of a particular kind, moreover. It must exist for all who speak the language; it must be persistent; and must be realizable more or less independently of determinate circumstances attending the word's utterance. There will be further restrictions dealing with the interrelation of words in different contexts. Moreover, we must include, under the psychological responses which the words tend to produce, not only immediately introspectable experiences, but *dispositions* to react in a given way with appropriate stimuli. I hope to go into these matters in a subsequent paper. Suffice it now to say that I think "meaning" may be thus defined in a way to include "propositional" meaning as an important kind. Now a word may *tend* to have causal relations which in fact it sometimes doesn't; and it may sometimes have causal relations which it *doesn't* tend to have. And since the tendency of words which constitutes their meaning must be of a particular kind, and may include, as responses, dispositions to reactions, of which any of *several* immediate experiences may be a sign, then there is nothing surprising in the fact that words have a permanent meaning, in spite of the fact that the immediately introspectable experiences which attend their usage are so highly varied.

When "meaning" is defined in this way, meaning will not include dynamic use. For although words are sometimes accompanied by dynamic purposes, they do not *tend* to be accompanied by them in the way above mentioned. E.g., there is no tendency realizable independently of the determinate circumstances under which the words are uttered.

There will be a kind of meaning, however, in the sense above defined, which has an intimate relation to dynamic usage. I refer to "emotive" meaning (in a sense roughly like that employed by Ogden and Richards).[4] The emotive meaning of a word is a tendency of a word, arising through the history of its usage, to produce (result from) *affective* responses in people. It is the immediate aura of feeling which hovers about a word. Such tendencies to produce affective responses cling to words very tenaciously. It would be difficult, for instance, to express merriment by using the interjection "alas". Because of the persistence of such affective tendencies (among other reasons) it becomes feasible to classify them as "meanings".

Just *what* is the relation between emotive meaning and the dynamic use of words? Let us take an example. Suppose that a man is talking with a group of people which includes Miss Jones, aged 59. He refers to her, without thinking, as an "old maid". Now even if his purposes are perfectly innocent – even if he is using the words purely descriptively – Miss Jones won't think so. She will think he is encouraging the others to have contempt for her, and will draw in her skirts, defensively. The man might have done better if instead of saying "old maid" he had said "elderly spinster". The latter words could have been put to the same descriptive use, and would not so readily have caused suspicions about the dynamic use.

"Old maid" and "elderly spinster" differ, to be sure, only in emotive meaning. From the example it will be clear that certain words, because of their emotive meaning, are suited to a certain kind of dynamic use – so well suited, in fact, that the hearer is likely to be misled when we use them in any other way. The more pronounced a word's emotive meaning is, the less likely people are to use it purely descriptively. Some words are suited to encourage people, some to discourage them, some to quiet them, and so on.

Even in these cases, of course, the dynamic purposes are not to be identified with any sort of meaning; for the emotive meaning accompanies a word much more persistently than do the dynamic purposes. But there is an important contingent relation between emotive meaning and dynamic purpose: the former assists the latter.

Hence if we define emotively laden terms in a way that neglects their emotive meaning, we are likely to be confusing. *We lead people to think that the terms defined are used dynamically less often than they are.*

IV

Let us now apply these remarks in defining "good". This word may be used morally or non-morally. I shall deal with the non-moral usage almost entirely, but only because it is simpler. The main points of the analysis will apply equally well to either usage.

As a preliminary definition, let us take an inaccurate approximation. It may be more misleading than helpful, but will do to begin with. Roughly, then, the sentence "X is good" means *We like X.* ("We" includes the hearer or hearers.)

At first glance this definition sounds absurd. If used, we should expect to find the following sort of conversation: A. "This is good." B. "But I *don't* like it. What led you to believe that I did?" The unnaturalness of B's reply, judged by ordinary word-usage, would seem to cast doubt on the relevance of my definition.

B's unnaturalness, however, lies simply in this: he is assuming that "We like it" (as would occur implicitly in the use of "good") is being used descriptively. This won't do. When "We like it" is to take the place of "This is good", the former sentence must be used not purely descriptively, but dynamically. More specifically, it must be used to promote a very subtle (and for the non-moral sense in question, a very easily resisted) kind of *suggestion*. To the extent that "we" refers to the hearer, it must have the dynamic use, essential to suggestion, of leading the hearer to *make* true what is said, rather than merely to believe it. And to the extent that "we" refers to the speaker, the sentence must have not only the descriptive use of indicating belief about the speaker's interest, but the quasi-interjectory, dynamic function of giving direct expression to the interest. (This immediate expression of feelings assists in the process of suggestion. It is difficult to disapprove in the face of another's enthusiasm.)

For an example of a case where "We like this" is used in the dynamic way that "This is good" is used, consider the case of a mother who says to her several children, "One thing is certain, *we all like to be neat*". If she really believed this, she wouldn't bother to say so. But she is not using the words descriptively. She is *encouraging* the children to like neatness. By telling them that they like neatness, she will lead them to *make* her statement true, so to speak. If, instead of saying "We all like to be neat" in this way, she had said "It's a good thing to be neat", the effect would have been approximately the same.

But these remarks are still misleading. Even when "We like it" is used for suggestion, it isn't quite like "This is good". The latter is more subtle. With such a sentence as "This is a good book", for example, it would be practically impossible to use instead "We like this book". When the latter is used, it must be accompanied by so exaggerated an intonation, to prevent its becoming confused with a descriptive statement, that the force of suggestion becomes stronger, and ludicrously more overt, than when "good" is used.

The definition is inadequate, further, in that the definiens has been restricted to dynamic usage. Having said that dynamic usage was different from meaning, I should not have to mention it in giving the *meaning* of "good".

It is in connection with this last point that we must return to emotive meaning. The word "good" has a pleasing emotive meaning which fits it especially for the dynamic use of suggesting favourable interest. But the sentence "We like it" has no such emotive meaning. Hence my definition has neglected emotive meaning entirely. Now to neglect emotive meaning is likely to lead to endless confusions, as we shall presently see; so I have sought to make up for the inadequacy of the definition by letting the restriction about dynamic usage take the place of emotive meaning. What I should do, of course, is to find a definiens whose emotive meaning, like that of "good", simply does *lead* to dynamic usage.

Why didn't I do this? I answer that it isn't possible, if the definition is to afford us increased clarity. No two words, in the first place, have quite the same emotive meaning. The most we can hope for is a rough approximation. But if we seek for such an approximation for "good", we shall find nothing more than synonyms, such as "desirable" or "valuable"; and these are profitless because they do not clear up the connection between "good" and favourable interest. If we reject such synonyms, in favour of non-ethical

terms, we shall be highly misleading. For instance: "This is good" has something like the meaning of "I *do* like this; do so as well". But this is certainly not accurate. For the imperative makes an appeal to the conscious efforts of the hearer. Of course he can't like something just by trying. He must be led to like it through suggestion. Hence an ethical sentence differs from an imperative in that it enables one to make changes in a much more subtle, less fully conscious way. Note that the ethical sentence centres the hearer's attention not on his interests, but on the object of interest, and thereby facilitates suggestion. Because of its subtlety, moreover, an ethical sentence readily permits counter-suggestion, and leads to the give and take situation which is so characteristic of arguments about values.

Strictly speaking, then, it is impossible to define "good" in terms of favourable interest if emotive meaning is not to be distorted. Yet it is possible to say that "this is good" is *about* the favourable interest of the speaker and the hearer or hearers, and that it has a pleasing emotive meaning which fits the words for use in suggestion. This is a rough description of meaning, not a definition. But it serves the same clarifying function that a definition ordinarily does; and that, after all, is enough.

A word must be added about the moral use of "good". This differs from the above in that it is about a different kind of interest. Instead of being about what the hearer and speaker *like*, it is about a stronger sort of approval. When a person *likes* something, he is pleased when it prospers, and disappointed when it doesn't. When a person *morally approves* of something, he experiences a rich feeling of security when it prospers, and is indignant, or "shocked" when it doesn't. These are rough and inaccurate examples of the many factors which one would have to mention in distinguishing the two kinds of interest. In the moral usage, as well as in the non-moral, "good" has an emotive meaning which adapts it to suggestion.

And now, are these considerations of any importance? Why do I stress emotive meanings in this fashion? Does the omission of them really lead people into errors? I think, indeed, that the errors resulting from such omissions are enormous. In order to see this, however, we must return to the restrictions, mentioned in section I, with which the "vital" sense of "good" has been expected to comply.

V

The first restriction, it will be remembered, had to do with disagreement. Now there is clearly some sense in which people disagree on ethical points; but we must not rashly assume that all disagreement is modelled after the sort that occurs in the natural sciences. We must distinguish between "disagreement in belief" (typical of the sciences) and "disagreement in interest". Disagreement in belief occurs when A believes *p* and B disbelieves it. Disagreement in interest occurs when A has a favourable interest in X, when B has an unfavourable one in it, and when neither is content to let the other's interest remain unchanged.

Let me give an example of disagreement in interest. A. "Let's go to a cinema to-night." B. "I don't want to do that. Let's go to the symphony." A continues to insist on the cinema, B on the symphony. This is disagreement in a perfectly conventional sense. They can't agree on where they want to go, and each is trying to redirect the other's interest. (Note that imperatives are used in the example.)

It is disagreement in *interest* which takes place in ethics. When C says "This is good", and D says "No, it's bad", we have a case of suggestion and counter-suggestion. Each man is trying to redirect the other's interest. There obviously need be no domineering, since each may be willing to give ear to the other's influence; but each is trying to move the other none the less. It is in this sense that they disagree. Those who argue that certain interest theories make no provision for disagreement have been misled, I believe, simply because the traditional theories, in leaving out emotive meaning, give the impression that ethical judgments are used descriptively only; and of course when judgments are used purely descriptively, the only disagreement that can arise is disagreement in *belief*. Such disagreement may be disagreement in belief *about* interests; but this is not the same as disagreement *in* interest. My definition doesn't provide for disagreement in belief about interests, any more than does Hobbes's; but that is no matter, for there is no reason to believe, at least on common-sense grounds, that this kind of disagreement exists. There is only disagreement *in* interest. (We shall see in a moment that disagreement in interest does not remove ethics from sober argument

— that this kind of disagreement may often be resolved through empirical means.)

The second restriction, about "magnetism", or the connection between goodness and actions, requires only a word. This rules out *only* those interest theories which do *not* include the interest of the speaker, in defining "good". My account does include the speaker's interest; hence is immune.

The third restriction, about the empirical method, may be met in a way that springs naturally from the above account of disagreement. Let us put the question in this way: When two people disagree over an ethical matter, can they completely resolve the disagreement through empirical considerations, assuming that each applies the empirical method exhaustively, consistently, and without error?

I answer that sometimes they can, and sometimes they cannot; and that at any rate, even when they can, the relation between empirical knowledge and ethical judgments is quite different from the one which traditional interest theories seem to imply.

This can best be seen from an analogy. Let's return to the example where A and B couldn't agree on a cinema or a symphony. The example differed from an ethical argument in that imperatives were used, rather than ethical judgments; but was analogous to the extent that each person was endeavouring to modify the other's interest. Now how would these people argue the case, assuming that they were too intelligent just to shout at one another?

Clearly, they would give "reasons" to support their imperatives. A might say, "But you know, Garbo is at the Bijou". His hope is that B, who admires Garbo, will acquire a desire to go to the cinema when he knows what play will be there. B may counter, "But Toscanini is guest conductor to-night, in an all-Beethoven programme". And so on. Each supports his imperative (*"Let's* do so and so") by reasons which may be empirically established.

To generalize from this: disagreement in interest may be rooted in disagreement in belief. That is to say, people who disagree in interest would often cease to do so if they knew the precise nature and consequences of the object of their interest. To this extent disagreement in interest may be resolved by securing agreement in belief, which in turn may be secured empirically.

This generalization holds for ethics. If A and B, instead of using imperatives, had said, respectively, "It would be *better* to go to the cinema", and "It would be better to go to the symphony", the reasons which they would advance would be roughly the same. They would each give a more thorough account of the object of interest, with the purpose of completing the re-direction of interest which was begun by the suggestive force of the ethical sentence. On the whole, of course, the suggestive force of the ethical statement merely exerts enough pressure to start such trains of reasons, since the reasons are much more essential in resolving disagreement in interest than the persuasive effect of the ethical judgment itself.

Thus the empirical method is relevant to ethics simply because our knowledge of the world is a determining factor to our interests. But note that empirical facts are not inductive grounds from which the ethical judgment problematically follows. (This is what traditional interest theories imply.) If someone said "Close the door", and added the reason "We'll catch cold", the latter would scarcely be called an inductive ground of the former. Now imperatives are related to the reasons which support them in the same way that ethical judgments are related to reasons.

Is the empirical method *sufficient* for attaining ethical agreement? Clearly not. For empirical knowledge resolves disagreement in interest only to the extent that such disagreement is rooted in disagreement in belief. Not all disagreement in interest is of this sort. For instance: A is of a sympathetic nature, and B isn't. They are arguing about whether a public dole would be good. Suppose that they discovered all the consequences of the dole. Isn't it possible, even so, that A will say that it's good, and B that it's bad? The disagreement in interest may arise not from limited factual knowledge, but simply from A's sympathy and B's coldness. Or again, suppose, in the above argument, that A was poor and unemployed, and that B was rich. Here again the disagreement might not be due to different factual knowledge. It would be due to the different social positions of the men, together with their predominant self-interest.

When ethical disagreement is not rooted in disagreement in belief, is there *any* method by which it may be settled? If one means by

"method" a *rational* method, then there is no method. But in any case there is a "way". Let's consider the above example, again, where disagreement was due to A's sympathy and B's coldness. Must they end by saying, "Well, it's just a matter of our having different temperaments"? Not necessarily. A, for instance, may try to *change* the temperament of his opponent. He may pour out his enthusiasms in such a moving way – present the sufferings of the poor with such appeal – that he will lead his opponent to see life through different eyes. He may build up, by the contagion of his feelings, an influence which will modify B's temperament, and create in him a sympathy for the poor which didn't previously exist. This is often the only way to obtain ethical agreement, if there is any way at all. It is persuasive, not empirical or rational; but that is no reason for neglecting it. There is no reason to scorn it, either, for it is only by such means that our personalities are able to grow, through our contact with others.

The point I wish to stress, however, is simply that the empirical method is instrumental to ethical agreement only to the extent that disagreement in interest is rooted in disagreement in belief. There is little reason to believe that all disagreement is of this sort. Hence the empirical method is not sufficient for ethics. In any case, ethics is not psychology, since psychology doesn't endeavour to *direct* our interests; it discovers facts about the ways in which interests are or can be directed, but that's quite another matter.

To summarize this section: my analysis of ethical judgments meets the three requirements for the "vital" sense of "good" that were mentioned in section I. The traditional interest theories fail to meet these requirements simply because they neglect emotive meaning. This neglect leads them to neglect dynamic usage, and the sort of disagreement that results from such usage, together with the method of resolving the disagreement. I may add that my analysis answers Moore's objection about the open question. Whatever scientifically knowable properties a thing may have, it *is* always open to question whether a thing having these (enumerated) qualities is good. For to ask whether it is good is to ask for *influence*. And whatever I may know about an object, I can still ask, quite pertinently, to be influenced with regard to my interest in it.

C. L. Stevenson

VI

And now, have I really pointed out the "vital" sense of "good"?

I suppose that many will still say "No", claiming that I have simply failed to set down *enough* requirements which this sense must meet, and that my analysis, like all others given in terms of interest, is a way of begging the issue. They will say: "When we ask 'Is X good?' we don't want mere influence, mere advice. We decidedly don't want to be influenced through persuasion, nor are we fully content when the influence is supported by a wide scientific knowledge of X. The answer to our question will, of course, modify our interests. But this is only because an unique sort of *truth* will be revealed to us – a truth which must be apprehended a priori. We want our interests to be guided by this truth, and by nothing else. To substitute for such a truth mere emotive meaning and suggestion is to conceal from us the very object of our search."

I can only answer that I do not understand. What is this truth to be *about*? For I recollect no Platonic Idea, nor do I know what to *try* to recollect. I find no indefinable property, nor do I know what to look for. And the "self-evident" deliverances of reason, which so many philosophers have claimed, seem, on examination, to be deliverances of their respective reasons only (if of anyone's) and not of mine.

I strongly suspect, indeed, that any sense of "good" which is expected both to unite itself in synthetic a priori fashion with other concepts, and to influence interests as well, is really a great confusion. I extract from this meaning the power of influence alone, which I find the only intelligible part. If the rest is confusion, however, then it certainly deserves more than the shrug of one's shoulders. What I should like to do is to *account* for the confusion – to examine the psychological needs which have given rise to it, and to show how these needs may be satisfied in another way. This is *the* problem, if confusion is to be stopped at its source. But it is an enormous problem, and my reflections on it, which are at present worked out only roughly, must be reserved until some later time.

I may add that if "X is good" is essentially a vehicle for suggestion, it is scarcely a statement which philosophers, any more than many other men, are called upon to make. To the extent that ethics predicates the ethical terms of anything, rather than explains their meaning, it ceases to be a reflective study. Ethical statements are social instruments. They are used in a co-operative enterprise in which we are mutually adjusting ourselves to the interests of others. Philosophers have a part in this, as do all men, but not the major part.

Notes

1 See G. E. Moore's *Philosophical Studies* (London: Routledge and Kegan Paul, 1922), pp. 332–4.
2 See G. C. Field's *Moral Theory*, 2nd edn., rev. (London: Methuen, 1932), pp. 52, 56–7.
3 See G. E. Moore's *Principia Ethica* (Cambridge: Cambridge University Press, 1903), ch. I. I am simply trying to preserve the spirit of Moore's objection, and not the exact form of it.
4 See *The Meaning of Meaning*, by C. K. Ogden and I. A. Richards (London: Routledge and Kegan Paul, 1926). On p. 125, 2nd edition, there is a passage on ethics which was the source of the ideas embodied in this paper.

35

Justice as Fairness

John Rawls

1. It might seem at first sight that the concepts of justice and fairness are the same, and that there is no reason to distinguish them, or to say that one is more fundamental than the other. I think that this impression is mistaken. In this paper I wish to show that the fundamental idea in the concept of justice is fairness; and I wish to offer an analysis of the concept of justice from this point of view. To bring out the force of this claim, and the analysis based upon it, I shall then argue that it is this aspect of justice for which utilitarianism, in its classical form, is unable to account, but which is expressed, even if misleadingly, by the idea of the social contract.

To start with I shall develop a particular conception of justice by stating and commenting upon two principles which specify it, and by considering the circumstances and conditions under which they may be thought to arise. The principles defining this conception, and the conception itself, are, of course, familiar. It may be possible, however, by using the notion of fairness as a framework, to assemble and to look at them in a new way. Before stating this conception, however, the following preliminary matters should be kept in mind.

Throughout I consider justice only as a virtue of social institutions, or what I shall call practices.[1] The principles of justice are regarded as formulating restrictions as to how practices may

Originally published in *Philosophical Review* 67 (1958). Copyright 1958 Cornell University. Reprinted by permission of the publisher.

define positions and offices, and assign thereto powers and liabilities, rights and duties. Justice as a virtue of particular actions or of persons I do not take up at all. It is important to distinguish these various subjects of justice, since the meaning of the concept varies according to whether it is applied to practices, particular actions, or persons. These meanings are, indeed, connected, but they are not identical. I shall confine my discussion to the sense of justice as applied to practices, since this sense is the basic one. Once it is understood, the other senses should go quite easily.

Justice is to be understood in its customary sense as representing but *one* of the many virtues of social institutions, for these may be antiquated, inefficient, degrading, or any number of other things, without being unjust. Justice is not to be confused with an all-inclusive vision of a good society; it is only one part of any such conception. It is important, for example, to distinguish that sense of equality which is an aspect of the concept of justice from that sense of equality which belongs to a more comprehensive social ideal. There may well be inequalities which one concedes are just, or at least not unjust, but which, nevertheless, one wishes, on other grounds, to do away with. I shall focus attention, then, on the usual sense of justice in which it is essentially the elimination of arbitrary distinctions and the establishment, within the structure of a practice, of a proper balance between competing claims.

Finally, there is no need to consider the principles discussed below as *the* principles of justice.

For the moment it is sufficient that they are typical of a family of principles normally associated with the concept of justice. The way in which the principles of this family resemble one another, as shown by the background against which they may be thought to arise, will be made clear by the whole of the subsequent argument.

2. The conception of justice which I want to develop may be stated in the form of two principles as follows: first, each person participating in a practice, or affected by it, has an equal right to the most extensive liberty compatible with a like liberty for all; and second, inequalities are arbitrary unless it is reasonable to expect that they will work out for everyone's advantage, and provided the positions and offices to which they attach, or from which they may be gained, are open to all. These principles express justice as a complex of three ideas: liberty, equality, and reward for services contributing to the common good.[2]

The term "person" is to be construed variously depending on the circumstances. On some occasions it will mean human individuals, but in others it may refer to nations, provinces, business firms, churches, teams, and so on. The principles of justice apply in all these instances, although there is a certain logical priority to the case of human individuals. As I shall use the term "person," it will be ambiguous in the manner indicated.

The first principle holds, of course, only if other things are equal: that is, while there must always be a justification for departing from the initial position of equal liberty (which is defined by the pattern of rights and duties, powers and liabilities, established by a practice), and the burden of proof is placed on him who would depart from it, nevertheless, there can be, and often there is, a justification for doing so. Now, that similar particular cases, as defined by a practice, should be treated similarly as they arise, is part of the very concept of a practice; it is involved in the notion of an activity in accordance with rules.[3] The first principle expresses an analogous conception, but as applied to the structure of practices themselves. It holds, for example, that there is a presumption against the distinctions and classifications made by legal systems and other practices to the extent that they infringe on the original and equal liberty of the persons participating in them. The second principle defines how this presumption may be rebutted.

It might be argued at this point that justice requires only an equal liberty. If, however, a greater liberty were possible for all without loss or conflict, then it would be irrational to settle on a lesser liberty. There is no reason for circumscribing rights unless their exercise would be incompatible, or would render the practice defining them less effective. Therefore no serious distortion of the concept of justice is likely to follow from including within it the concept of the greatest equal liberty.

The second principle defines what sorts of inequalities are permissible; it specifies how the presumption laid down by the first principle may be put aside. Now by inequalities it is best to understand not *any* differences between offices and positions, but differences in the benefits and burdens attached to them either directly or indirectly, such as prestige and wealth, or liability to taxation and compulsory services. Players in a game do not protest against there being different positions, such as batter, pitcher, catcher, and the like, nor to there being various privileges and powers as specified by the rules; nor do the citizens of a country object to there being the different offices of government such as president, senator, governor, judge, and so on, each with their special rights and duties. It is not differences of this kind that are normally thought of as inequalities, but differences in the resulting distribution established by a practice, or made possible by it, of the things men strive to attain or avoid. Thus they may complain about the pattern of honors and rewards set up by a practice (e.g., the privileges and salaries of government officials) or they may object to the distribution of power and wealth which results from the various ways in which men avail themselves of the opportunities allowed by it (e.g., the concentration of wealth which may develop in a free price system allowing large entrepreneurial or speculative gains).

It should be noted that the second principle holds that an inequality is allowed only if there is reason to believe that the practice with the inequality, or resulting in it, will work for the advantage of *every* party engaging in it. Here it is important to stress that *every* party must gain from the inequality. Since the principle applies to practices, it implies that the representative man in every office or position defined by a practice, when he views it as a going concern, must find it reasonable to prefer his condition and prospects with the inequality to what they would be under the practice without it. The principle excludes, therefore, the justification of inequalities on the grounds that the disadvantages of those in one position are outweighed by the greater advantages of those in another position. This rather simple restriction is the main modification I wish to make in the utilitarian principle as usually understood. When coupled with the notion of a practice, it is a restriction of consequence,[4] and one which some utilitarians, e.g., Hume and Mill, have used in their discussions of justice without realizing apparently its significance, or at least without calling attention to it.[5] Why it is a significant modification of principle, changing one's conception of justice entirely, the whole of my argument will show.

Further, it is also necessary that the various offices to which special benefits or burdens attach are open to all. It may be, for example, to the common advantage, as just defined, to attach special benefits to certain offices. Perhaps by doing so the requisite talent can be attracted to them and encouraged to give its best efforts. But any offices having special benefits must be won in a fair competition in which contestants are judged on their merits. If some offices were not open, those excluded would normally be justified in feeling unjustly treated, even if they benefited from the greater efforts of those who were allowed to compete for them. Now if one can assume that offices are open, it is necessary only to consider the design of practices themselves and how they jointly, as a system, work together. It will be a mistake to focus attention on the varying relative positions of particular persons, who may be known to us by their proper names, and to require that each such change, as a once for all transaction viewed in isolation, must be in itself just. It is the system of practices which is to be judged, and judged from a general point of view: unless one is prepared to criticize it from the standpoint of a representative man holding some particular office, one has no complaint against it.

3. Given these principles one might try to derive them from a priori principles of reason, or claim that they were known by intuition. These are familiar enough steps and, at least in the case of the first principle, might be made with some success. Usually, however, such arguments, made at this point, are unconvincing. They are not likely to lead to an understanding of the basis of the principles of justice, not at least as principles of justice. I wish, therefore, to look at the principles in a different way.

Imagine a society of persons amongst whom a certain system of practices is *already* well established. Now suppose that by and large they are mutually self-interested; their allegiance to their established practices is normally founded on the prospect of self-advantage. One need not assume that, in all senses of the term "person," the persons in this society are mutually self-interested. If the characterization as mutually self-interested applies when the line of division is the family, it may still be true that members of families are bound by ties of sentiment and affection and willingly acknowledge duties in contradiction to self-interest. Mutual self-interestedness in the relations between families, nations, churches, and the like, is commonly associated with intense loyalty and devotion on the part of individual members. Therefore, one can form a more realistic conception of this society if one thinks of it as consisting of mutually self-interested families, or some other association. Further, it is not necessary to suppose that these persons are mutually self-interested under all circumstances, but only in the usual situations in which they participate in their common practices.

Now suppose also that these persons are rational: they know their own interests more or less accurately; they are capable of tracing out the likely consequences of adopting one practice rather than another; they are capable of adhering to a course of action once they have decided upon it; they can resist present temptations and the enticements of immediate gain; and the bare knowledge or perception of the difference between their condition and that of others is not, within certain limits and in itself, a source of great dissatisfaction. Only the last point adds anything to the usual definition of rationality. This definition should allow, I think, for the idea that a rational man would not be greatly downcast from knowing, or seeing, that others are in a better position than himself, unless he thought their being so was the result of injustice, or the consequence of letting chance work itself out for no useful common purpose, and so on. So if these persons strike us as unpleasantly egoistic, they are at least free in some degree from the fault of envy.[6]

Finally, assume that these persons have roughly similar needs and interests, or needs and interests in various ways complementary, so that fruitful cooperation amongst them is possible; and suppose that they are sufficiently equal in power and ability to guarantee that in normal circumstances none is able to dominate the others. This condition (as well as the others) may seem excessively vague; but in view of the conception of justice to which the argument leads, there seems no reason for making it more exact here.

Since these persons are conceived as engaging in their common practices, which are already established, there is no question of our supposing them to come together to deliberate as to how they will set these practices up for the first time. Yet we can imagine that from time to time they discuss with one another whether any of them has a legitimate complaint against their established institutions. Such discussions are perfectly natural in any normal society. Now suppose that they have settled on doing this in the following way. They first try to arrive at the principles by which complaints, and so practices themselves, are to be judged. Their procedure for this is to let each person propose the principles upon which he wishes his complaints to be tried with the understanding that, if acknowledged, the complaints of others will be similarly tried, and that no complaints will be heard at all until everyone is roughly of one mind as to how complaints are to be judged. They each understand further that the principles proposed and acknowledged on this occasion are binding on future occasions. Thus each will be wary of proposing a principle which would give him a peculiar advantage, in his present circumstances, supposing it to be accepted. Each person knows that he will be bound by it in future circumstances the peculiarities of which cannot be known, and which might well be such that the principle is then to his disadvantage. The idea is that everyone should be required to make *in advance* a firm commitment, which others also may reasonably be expected to make, and that no one be given the opportunity to tailor the canons of a legitimate complaint to fit his own special condition, and then to discard them when they no longer suit his purpose. Hence each person will propose principles of a general kind which will, to a large degree, gain their sense from the various applications to be made of them, the particular circumstances of which being as yet unknown. These principles will express the conditions in accordance with which each is the least unwilling to have his interests limited in the design of practices, given the competing interests of the others, on the supposition that the interests of others will be limited likewise. The restrictions which would so arise might be thought of as those a person would keep in mind if he were designing a practice in which his enemy were to assign him his place.

The two main parts of this conjectural account have a definite significance. The character and respective situations of the parties reflect the typical circumstances in which questions of justice arise. The procedure whereby principles are proposed and acknowledged represents constraints, analogous to those of having a morality, whereby rational and mutually self-interested persons are brought to act reasonably. Thus the first part reflects the fact that questions of justice arise when conflicting claims are made upon the design of a practice and where it is taken for granted that each person will insist, as far as possible, on what he considers his rights. It is typical of cases of justice to involve persons who are pressing on one another their claims, between which a fair balance or equilibrium must be found. On the other hand, as expressed by the second part, having a morality must at least imply the acknowledgment of principles as impartially applying to one's own conduct as well as to another's, and moreover principles which may constitute a constraint, or limitation, upon the pursuit of one's own interests. There are, of course, other aspects of having a morality: the acknowledgment of moral principles must show itself in accepting a reference to them as reasons for limiting one's claims, in acknowledging the burden of providing a special explanation, or excuse, when one acts contrary to them, or else in showing shame and remorse and a desire to make amends, and so on. It is sufficient to remark here that having a morality is analogous to having made a firm commitment in advance; for one must acknowledge the principles of morality even when to one's disadvantage.[7] A man whose moral judgments always coincided with his interests could be suspected of having no morality at all.

Thus the two parts of the foregoing account are intended to mirror the kinds of circumstances in which questions of justice arise and the constraints which having a morality would impose upon persons so situated. In this way one can see how the acceptance of the principles of justice might come about, for given all these conditions as described, it would be natural if the two principles of justice were to be acknowledged.

Since there is no way for anyone to win special advantages for himself, each might consider it reasonable to acknowledge equality as an initial principle. There is, however, no reason why they should regard this position as final; for if there are inequalities which satisfy the second principle, the immediate gain which equality would allow can be considered as intelligently invested in view of its future return. If, as is quite likely, these inequalities work as incentives to draw out better efforts, the members of this society may look upon them as concessions to human nature: they, like us, may think that people ideally should want to serve one another. But as they are mutually self-interested, their acceptance of these inequalities is merely the acceptance of the relations in which they actually stand, and a recognition of the motives which lead them to engage in their common practices. *They* have no title to complain of one another. And so provided that the conditions of the principle are met, there is no reason why they should not allow such inequalities. Indeed, it would be short-sighted of them to do so, and could result, in most cases, only from their being dejected by the bare knowledge, or perception, that others are better situated. Each person will, however, insist on an advantage to himself, and so on a common advantage, for none is willing to sacrifice anything for the others.

These remarks are not offered as a proof that persons so conceived and circumstanced would settle on the two principles, but only to show that these principles could have such a background, and so can be viewed as those principles which mutually self-interested and rational persons, when similarly situated and required to make in advance a firm commitment, could acknowledge as restrictions governing the assignment of rights and duties in their common practices, and thereby accept as limiting their rights against one another. The principles of justice may, then, be regarded as those principles which arise when the constraints of having a morality are imposed upon parties in the typical circumstances of justice.

4.   These ideas are, of course, connected with a familiar way of thinking about justice which goes back at least to the Greek Sophists, and which regards the acceptance of the principles of justice as a compromise between persons of roughly equal power who would enforce their will on each other if they could, but who, in view of the equality of forces amongst them and for the sake of their own peace and security, acknowledge certain forms of conduct insofar as prudence seems to require. Justice is thought of as a pact between rational egoists the stability of which is dependent on a balance of power and a similarity of circumstances.[8] While the previous account is connected with this tradition, and with its most recent variant, the theory of games,[9] it differs from it in several important respects which, to forestall misinterpretations, I will set out here.

First, I wish to use the previous conjectural account of the background of justice as a way of analyzing the concept. I do not want, therefore, to be interpreted as assuming a general theory of human motivation: when I suppose that the parties are mutually self-interested, and are not willing to have their (substantial) interests sacrificed to others, I am referring to their conduct and motives as they are taken for granted in cases where questions of justice ordinarily arise. Justice is the virtue of practices where there are assumed to be competing interests and conflicting claims, and where it is supposed that persons will press their rights on each other. That persons are mutually self-interested in certain situations and for certain purposes is what gives rise to the question of justice in practices covering those circumstances. Amongst an association of saints, if such a community could really exist, the disputes about justice could hardly occur; for they would all work selflessly together for one end, the glory of God as defined by their common religion, and reference to this end would settle every question of right. The justice of practices does not come up until there are several different parties (whether we think of these as individuals, associations, or nations and so on, is irrelevant) who do press their claims on one another, and who do regard themselves as representatives of interests which deserve to be considered. Thus the previous account involves no general theory of human motivation. Its intent is simply to incorporate into the conception of justice the relations of men to one another which set the stage for questions of justice. It makes no difference how wide or general these relations are, as this matter does not bear on the analysis of the concept.

Again, in contrast to the various conceptions of the social contract, the several parties do not establish any particular society or practice; they do not covenant to obey a particular sovereign body or to accept a given constitution.[10] Nor do they, as in the theory of games (in certain respects a marvelously sophisticated development of this tradition), decide on individual strategies adjusted to their respective circumstances in the game. What the parties do is to *jointly* acknowledge certain *principles* of appraisal relating to their common *practices* either as already established or merely proposed. They accede to standards of judgment, not to a given practice; they do not make any specific agreement, or bargain, or adopt a particular strategy. The subject of their acknowledgment is, therefore, very general indeed; it is simply the acknowledgment of certain principles of judgment, fulfilling certain general conditions, to be used in criticizing the arrangement of their common affairs. The relations of mutual self-interest between the parties who are similarly circumstanced mirror the conditions under which questions of justice arise, and the procedure by which the principles of judgment are proposed and acknowledged reflects the constraints of having a morality. Each aspect, then, of the preceding hypothetical account serves the purpose of bringing out a feature of the notion of justice. One could, if one liked, view the principles of justice as the "solution" of this highest order "game" of adopting, subject to the procedure described, principles of argument for all coming particular "games" whose peculiarities one can in no way foresee. But this comparison, while no doubt helpful, must not obscure the fact that this highest order "game" is of a special sort.[11] Its significance is that its various pieces represent aspects of the concept of justice.

Finally, I do not, of course, conceive the several parties as necessarily coming together to establish their common practices for the first time. Some institutions may, indeed, be set up *de novo*; but I have framed the preceding account so that it will apply when the full complement of social institutions already exists and represents the result of a long period of development. Nor is the account in any way fictitious. In any society where people reflect on their institutions they will have an idea of what principles of justice would be acknowledged under the conditions described, and there will be occasions when questions of justice are actually discussed in this way. Therefore if their practices do not accord with these principles, this will affect the quality of their social relations. For in this case there will be some recognized situations wherein the parties are mutu-

ally aware that one of them is being forced to accept what the other would concede is unjust. The foregoing analysis may then be thought of as representing the actual quality of relations between persons as defined by practices accepted as just. In such practices the parties will acknowledge the principles on which it is constructed, and the general recognition of this fact shows itself in the absence of resentment and in the sense of being justly treated. Thus one common objection to the theory of the social contract, its apparently historical and fictitious character, is avoided.

5.   That the principles of justice may be regarded as arising in the manner described illustrates an important fact about them. Not only does it bring out the idea that justice is a primitive moral notion in that it arises once the concept of morality is imposed on mutually self-interested agents similarly circumstanced, but it emphasizes that, fundamental to justice, is the concept of fairness which relates to right dealing between persons who are cooperating with or competing against one another, as when one speaks of fair games, fair competition, and fair bargains. The question of fairness arises when free persons, who have no authority over one another, are engaging in a joint activity and amongst themselves settling or acknowledging the rules which define it and which determine the respective shares in its benefits and burdens. A practice will strike the parties as fair if none feels that, by participating in it, they or any of the others are taken advantage of, or forced to give in to claims which they do not regard as legitimate. This implies that each has a conception of legitimate claims which he thinks it reasonable for others as well as himself to acknowledge. If one thinks of the principles of justice as arising in the manner described, then they do define this sort of conception. A practice is just or fair, then, when it satisfies the principles which those who participate in it could propose to one another for mutual acceptance under the afore-mentioned circumstances. Persons engaged in a just, or fair, practice can face one another openly and support their respective positions, should they appear questionable, by reference to principles which it is reasonable to expect each to accept.

It is this notion of the possibility of mutual acknowledgement of principles by free persons who have no authority over one another which makes the concept of fairness fundamental to justice. Only if such acknowledgment is possible can there be true community between persons in their common practices; otherwise their relations will appear to them as founded to some extent on force. If, in ordinary speech, fairness applies more particularly to practices in which there is a choice whether to engage or not (e.g., in games, business competition), and justice to practices in which there is no choice (e.g., in slavery), the element of necessity does not render the conception of mutual acknowledgment inapplicable, although it may make it much more urgent to change unjust than unfair institutions. For one activity in which one can always engage is that of proposing and acknowledging principles to one another supposing each to be similarly circumstanced; and to judge practices by the principles so arrived at is to apply the standard of fairness to them.

Now if the participants in a practice accept its rules as fair, and so have no complaint to lodge against it, there arises a prima-facie duty (and a corresponding prima-facie right) of the parties to each other to act in accordance with the practice when it falls upon them to comply. When any number of persons engage in a practice, or conduct a joint undertaking according to rules, and thus restrict their liberty, those who have submitted to these restrictions when required have the right to a similar acquiescence on the part of those who have benefited by their submission. These conditions will obtain if a practice is correctly acknowledged to be fair, for in this case all who participate in it will benefit from it. The rights and duties so arising are special rights and duties in that they depend on previous actions voluntarily undertaken, in this case on the parties having engaged in a common practice and knowingly accepted its benefits.[12] It is not, however, an obligation which presupposes a deliberate performative act in the sense of a promise, or contract, and the like.[13] An unfortunate mistake of proponents of the idea of the social contract was to suppose that political obligation does require some such act, or at least to use language which suggests it. It is sufficient that one has knowingly participated in and accepted the benefits of a practice acknowledged to be fair. This prima-facie obligation may, of course, be overridden: it may happen, when it comes one's turn to follow a rule, that other considerations will justify not doing so. But one cannot, in general, be released

from this obligation by denying the justice of the practice only when it falls on one to obey. If a person rejects a practice, he should, so far as possible, declare his intention in advance, and avoid participating in it or enjoying its benefits.

This duty I have called that of fair play, but it should be admitted that to refer to it in this way is, perhaps, to extend the ordinary notion of fairness. Usually acting unfairly is not so much the breaking of any particular rule, even if the infraction is difficult to detect (cheating), but taking advantage of loop-holes or ambiguities in rules, availing oneself of unexpected or special circumstances which make it impossible to enforce them, insisting that rules be enforced to one's advantage when they should be suspended, and more generally, acting contrary to the intention of a practice. It is for this reason that one speaks of the sense of fair play: acting fairly requires more than simply being able to follow rules; what is fair must often be felt, or perceived, one wants to say. It is not, however, an unnatural extension of the duty of fair play to have it include the obligation which participants who have knowingly accepted the benefits of their common practice owe to each other to act in accordance with it when their performance falls due; for it is usually considered unfair if someone accepts the benefits of a practice but refuses to do his part in maintaining it. Thus one might say of the tax-dodger that he violates the duty of fair play: he accepts the benefits of government but will not do his part in releasing resources to it; and members of labor unions often say that fellow workers who refuse to join are being unfair: they refer to them as "free riders," as persons who enjoy what are the supposed benefits of unionism, higher wages, shorter hours, job security, and the like, but who refuse to share in its burdens in the form of paying dues, and so on.

The duty of fair play stands beside other prima-facie duties such as fidelity and gratitude as a basic moral notion; yet it is not to be confused with them.[14] These duties are all clearly distinct, as would be obvious from their definitions. As with any moral duty, that of fair play implies a constraint on self-interest in particular cases; on occasion it enjoins conduct which a rational egoist strictly defined would not decide upon. So while justice does not require of anyone that he sacrifice his interests in that *general position* and procedure whereby the principles of justice are proposed and acknowledged, it may happen that in particular situations, arising in the context of engaging in a practice, the duty of fair play will often cross his interests in the sense that he will be required to forego particular advantages which the peculiarities of his circumstances might permit him to take. There is, of course, nothing surprising in this. It is simply the consequence of the firm commitment which the parties may be supposed to have made, or which they would make, in the general position, together with the fact that they have participated in and accepted the benefits of a practice which they regard as fair.

Now the acknowledgment of this constraint in particular cases, which is manifested in acting fairly or wishing to make amends, feeling ashamed, and the like, when one has evaded it, is one of the forms of conduct by which participants in a common practice exhibit their recognition of each other as persons with similar interests and capacities. In the same way that, failing a special explanation, the criterion for the recognition of suffering is helping one who suffers, acknowledging the duty of fair play is a necessary part of the criterion for recognizing another as a person with similar interests and feelings as oneself.[15] A person who never under any circumstances showed a wish to help others in pain would show, at the same time, that he did not recognize that they were in pain; nor could he have any feelings of affection or friendship for anyone; for having these feelings implies, failing special circumstances, that he comes to their aid when they are suffering. Recognition that another is a person in pain shows itself in sympathetic action; this primitive natural response of compassion is one of those responses upon which the various forms of moral conduct are built.

Similarly, the acceptance of the duty of fair play by participants in a common practice is a reflection in each person of the recognition of the aspirations and interests of the others to be realized by their joint activity. Failing a special explanation, their acceptance of it is a necessary part of the criterion for their recognizing one another as persons with similar interests and capacities, as the conception of their relations in the general position supposes them to be. Otherwise they would show no recognition of one another as persons with similar capacities and interests, and indeed, in some cases perhaps hypothetical, they would not recognize one another as persons at all, but as complicated objects involved in a complicated activity. To recognize another as a person one must respond to him and act towards him in certain ways; and these ways are intimately connected with the various prima-facie duties. Acknowledging these duties in *some* degree, and so having the elements of morality, is not a matter of choice, or of intuiting moral qualities, or a matter of the expression of feelings or attitudes (the three interpretations between which philosophical opinion frequently oscillates); it is simply the possession of one of the forms of conduct in which the recognition of others as persons is manifested.

These remarks are unhappily obscure. Their main purpose here, however, is to forestall, together with the remarks in Section 4, the misinterpretation that, on the view presented, the acceptance of justice and the acknowledgment of the duty of fair play depends in everyday life solely on there being a *de facto* balance of forces between the parties. It would indeed be foolish to underestimate the importance of such a balance in securing justice; but it is not the only basis thereof. The recognition of one another as persons with similar interests and capacities engaged in a common practice must, failing a special explanation, show itself in the acceptance of the principles of justice and the acknowledgement of the duty of fair play.

The conception at which we have arrived, then, is that the principles of justice may be thought of as arising once the constraints of having a morality are imposed upon rational and mutually self-interested parties who are related and situated in a special way. A practice is just if it is in accordance with the principles which all who participate in it might reasonably be expected to propose or to acknowledge before one another when they are similarly circumstanced and required to make a firm commitment in advance without knowledge of what will be their peculiar condition, and thus when it meets standards which the parties could accept as fair should occasion arise for them to debate its merits. Regarding the participants themselves, once persons knowingly engage in a practice which they acknowledge to be fair and accept the benefits of doing so, they are bound by the duty of fair play to follow the rules when it comes their turn to do so, and this implies a limitation on their pursuit of self-interest in particular cases.

Now one consequence of this conception is that, where it applies, there is no moral value in the satisfaction of a claim incompatible with it.

Such a claim violates the conditions of reciprocity and community amongst persons, and he who presses it, not being willing to acknowledge it when pressed by another, has no grounds for complaint when it is denied; whereas he against whom it is pressed can complain. As it cannot be mutually acknowledged it is a resort to coercion; granting the claim is possible only if one party can compel acceptance of what the other will not admit. But it makes no sense to concede claims the denial of which cannot be complained of in preference to claims the denial of which can be objected to. Thus in deciding on the justice of a practice it is not enough to ascertain that it answers to wants and interests in the fullest and most effective manner. For if any of these conflict with justice, they should not be counted, as their satisfaction is no reason at all for having a practice. It would be irrelevant to say, even if true, that it resulted in the greatest satisfaction of desire. In tallying up the merits of a practice one must toss out the satisfaction of interests the claims of which are incompatible with the principles of justice.

6. The discussion so far has been excessively abstract. While this is perhaps unavoidable, I should now like to bring out some of the features of the conception of justice as fairness by comparing it with the conception of justice in classical utilitarianism as represented by Bentham and Sidgwick, and its counterpart in welfare economics. This conception assimilates justice to benevolence and the latter in turn to the most efficient design of institutions to promote the general welfare. Justice is a kind of efficiency.[16]

Now it is said occasionally that this form of utilitarianism puts no restrictions on what might be a just assignment of rights and duties in that there might be circumstances which, on utilitarian grounds, would justify institutions highly offensive to our ordinary sense of justice. But the classical utilitarian conception is not totally unprepared for this objection. Beginning with the notion that the general happiness can be represented by a social utility function consisting of a sum of individual utility functions with identical weights (this being the meaning of the maxim that each counts for one and no more than one),[17] it is commonly assumed that the utility functions of individuals are similar in all essential respects. Differences between individuals are ascribed to accidents of education and upbringing, and they

should not be taken into account. This assumption, coupled with that of diminishing marginal utility, results in a prima-facie case for equality, e.g., of equality in the distribution of income during any given period of time, laying aside indirect effects on the future. But even if utilitarianism is interpreted as having such restrictions built into the utility function, and even if it is supposed that these restrictions have in practice much the same result as the application of the principles of justice (and appear, perhaps, to be ways of expressing these principles in the language of mathematics and psychology), the fundamental idea is very different from the conception of justice as fairness. For one thing, that the principles of justice should be accepted is interpreted as the contingent result of a higher order administrative decision. The form of this decision is regarded as being similar to that of an entrepreneur deciding how much to produce of this or that commodity in view of its marginal revenue, or to that of someone distributing goods to needy persons according to the relative urgency of their wants. The choice between practices is thought of as being made on the basis of the allocation of benefits and burdens to individuals (these being measured by the present capitalized value of their utility over the full period of the practice's existence), which results from the distribution of rights and duties established by a practice.

Moreover, the individuals receiving these benefits are not conceived as being related in any way: they represent so many different directions in which limited resources may be allocated. The value of assigning resources to one direction rather than another depends solely on the preferences and interests of individuals as individuals. The satisfaction of desire has its value irrespective of the moral relations between persons, say as members of a joint undertaking, and of the claims which, in the name of these interests, they are prepared to make on one another;[18] and it is this value which is to be taken into account by the (ideal) legislator who is conceived as adjusting the rules of the system from the center so as to maximize the value of the social utility function.

It is thought that the principles of justice will not be violated by a legal system so conceived provided these executive decisions are correctly made. In this fact the principles of justice are said to have their derivation and explanation; they simply express the most important general features of social institutions in which the administrative problem is solved in the best way. These principles have, indeed, a special urgency because, given the facts of human nature, so much depends on them; and this explains the peculiar quality of the moral feelings associated with justice.[19] This assimilation of justice to a higher order executive decision, certainly a striking conception, is central to classical utilitarianism; and it also brings out its profound individualism, in one sense of this ambiguous word. It regards persons as so many *separate* directions in which benefits and burdens may be assigned; and the value of the satisfaction or dissatisfaction of desire is not thought to depend in any way on the moral relations in which individuals stand, or on the kinds of claims which they are willing, in the pursuit of their interests, to press on each other.

7. Many social decisions are, of course, of an administrative nature. Certainly this is so when it is a matter of social utility in what one may call its ordinary sense: that is, when it is a question of the efficient design of social institutions for the use of common means to achieve common ends. In this case either the benefits and burdens may be assumed to be impartially distributed, or the question of distribution is misplaced, as in the instance of maintaining public order and security or national defense. But as an interpretation of the basis of the principles of justice, classical utilitarianism is mistaken. It *permits* one to argue, for example, that slavery is unjust on the grounds that the advantages to the slaveholder as slaveholder do not counterbalance the disadvantages to the slave and to society at large burdened by a comparatively inefficient system of labor. Now the conception of justice as fairness, when applied to the practice of slavery with its offices of slaveholder and slave, would not allow one to consider the advantages of the slaveholder in the first place. As that office is not in accordance with principles which could be mutually acknowledged, the gains accruing to the slaveholder, assuming them to exist, cannot be counted as in *any* way mitigating the injustice of the practice. The question whether these gains outweigh the disadvantages to the slave and to society cannot arise, since in considering the justice of slavery these gains have no weight at all which requires that they be overridden. Where the conception of justice as fairness applies, slavery is *always* unjust.

I am not, of course, suggesting the absurdity that the classical utilitarians approved of slavery. I am only rejecting a type of argument which their view allows them to use in support of their disapproval of it. The conception of justice as derivative from efficiency implies that judging the justice of a practice is always, in principle at least, a matter of weighing up advantages and disadvantages, each having an intrinsic value or disvalue as the satisfaction of interests, irrespective of whether or not these interests necessarily involve acquiescence in principles which could not be mutually acknowledged. Utilitarianism cannot account for the fact that slavery is always unjust, nor for the fact that it would be recognized as irrelevant in defeating the accusation of injustice for one person to say to another, engaged with him in a common practice and debating its merits, that nevertheless it allowed of the greatest satisfaction of desire. The charge of injustice cannot be rebutted in this way. If justice were derivative from a higher order executive efficiency, this would not be so.

But now, even if it is taken as established that, so far as the ordinary conception of justice goes, slavery is always unjust (that is, slavery by definition violates commonly recognized principles of justice), the classical utilitarian would surely reply that these principles, as other moral principles subordinate to that of utility, are only generally correct. It is simply for the most part true that slavery is less efficient than other institutions; and while common sense may define the concept of justice so that slavery is unjust, nevertheless, where slavery would lead to the greatest satisfaction of desire, it is not wrong. Indeed, it is then right, and for the very same reason that justice, as ordinarily understood, is usually right. If, as ordinarily understood, slavery is always unjust, to this extent the utilitarian conception of justice might be admitted to differ from that of common moral opinion. Still the utilitarian would want to hold that, as a matter of moral principle, his view is correct in giving no special weight to considerations of justice beyond that allowed for by the general presumption of effectiveness. And this, he claims, is as it should be. The everyday opinion is morally in error, although, indeed, it is a useful error, since it protects rules of generally high utility.

The question, then, relates not simply to the analysis of the concept of justice as common sense defines it, but the analysis of it in the wider sense as to how much weight considerations of justice, as defined, are to have when laid against other kinds of moral considerations. Here again I wish to argue that reasons of justice have a *special* weight for which only the conception of justice as fairness can account. Moreover, it belongs to the concept of justice that they do have this special weight. While Mill recognized that this was so, he thought that it could be accounted for by the special urgency of the moral feelings which naturally support principles of such high utility. But it is a mistake to resort to the urgency of feeling; as with the appeal to intuition, it manifests a failure to pursue the question far enough. The special weight of considerations of justice can be explained from the conception of justice as fairness. It is only necessary to elaborate a bit what has already been said as follows.

If one examines the circumstances in which a certain tolerance of slavery is justified, or perhaps better, excused, it turns out that these are of a rather special sort. Perhaps slavery exists as an inheritance from the past and it proves necessary to dismantle it piece by piece; at times slavery may conceivably be an advance on previous institutions. Now while there may be some excuse for slavery in special conditions, it is never an excuse for it that it is sufficiently advantageous to the slaveholder to outweigh the disadvantages to the slave and to society. A person who argues in this way is not perhaps making a wildly irrelevant remark; but he is guilty of a moral fallacy. There is disorder in his conception of the ranking of moral principles. For the slaveholder, by his own admission, has no moral title to the advantages which he receives as a slaveholder. He is no more prepared than the slave to acknowledge the principle upon which is founded the respective positions in which they both stand. Since slavery does not accord with principles which they could mutually acknowledge, they each may be supposed to agree that it is unjust: it grants claims which it ought not to grant and in doing so denies claims which it ought not to deny. Amongst persons in a general position who are debating the form of their common practices, it cannot, therefore, be offered as a reason for a practice that, in conceding these very claims that ought to be denied, it nevertheless meets existing interests more effectively. By their very nature the satisfaction of these claims is without weight and cannot enter into any tabulation of advantages and disadvantages.

Furthermore, it follows from the concept of morality that, to the extent that the slaveholder recognizes his position vis-à-vis the slave to be unjust, he would not choose to press his claims. His not wanting to receive his special advantages is one of the ways in which he shows that he thinks slavery is unjust. It would be fallacious for the legislator to suppose, then, that it is a ground for having a practice that it brings advantages greater than disadvantages, if those for whom the practice is designed, and to whom the advantages flow, acknowledge that they have no moral title to them and do not wish to receive them.

For these reasons the principles of justice have a special weight; and with respect to the principle of the greatest satisfaction of desire, as cited in the general position amongst those discussing the merits of their common practices, the principles of justice have an absolute weight. In this sense they are not contingent; and this is why their force is greater than can be accounted for by the general presumption (assuming that there is one) of the effectiveness, in the utilitarian sense, of practices which in fact satisfy them.

If one wants to continue using the concepts of classical utilitarianism, one will have to say, to meet this criticism, that at least the individual or social utility functions must be so defined that no value is given to the satisfaction of interests the representative claims of which violate the principles of justice. In this way it is no doubt possible to include these principles within the form of the utilitarian conception; but to do so is, of course, to change its inspiration altogether as a moral conception. For it is to incorporate within it principles which cannot be understood on the basis of a higher order executive decision aiming at the greatest satisfaction of desire.

It is worth remarking, perhaps, that this criticism of utilitarianism does not depend on whether or not the two assumptions, that of individuals having similar utility functions and that of diminishing marginal utility, are interpreted as psychological propositions to be supported or refuted by experience, or as moral and political principles expressed in a somewhat technical language. There are, certainly, several advantages in taking them in the latter fashion.[20] For one thing, one might say that this is what Bentham and others really meant by them, as least as shown by how they were used in arguments for social reform. More importantly, one could hold that the best way to defend the classical utilitarian view is to interpret these assumptions as moral and political principles. It is doubtful whether, taken as psychological propositions, they are true of men in general as we know them under normal conditions. On the other hand, utilitarians would not have wanted to propose them merely as practical working principles of legislation, or as expedient maxims to guide reform, given the egalitarian sentiments of modern society.[21] When pressed they might well have invoked the idea of a more or less equal capacity of men in relevant respects if given an equal chance in a just society. But if the argument above regarding slavery is correct, then granting these assumptions as moral and political principles makes no difference. To view individuals as equally fruitful lines for the allocation of benefits, even as a matter of moral principle, still leaves the mistaken notion that the satisfaction of desire has value in itself irrespective of the relations between persons as members of a common practice, and irrespective of the claims upon one another which the satisfaction of interests represents. To see the error of this idea one must give up the conception of justice as an executive decision altogether and refer to the notion of justice as fairness: that participants in a common practice be regarded as having an original and equal liberty and that their common practices be considered unjust unless they accord with principles which persons so circumstanced and related could freely acknowledge before one another, and so could accept as fair. Once the emphasis is put upon the concept of the mutual recognition of principles by participants in a common practice the rules of which are to define their several relations and give form to their claims on one another, then it is clear that the granting of a claim the principle of which could not be acknowledged by each in the general position (that is, in the position in which the parties propose and acknowledge principles before one another) is not a reason for adopting a practice. Viewed in this way, the background of the claim is seen to exclude it from consideration; that it can represent a value in itself arises from the conception of individuals as separate lines for the assignment of benefits, as isolated persons who stand as claimants on an administrative or benevolent largesse. Occasionally persons do so stand to one another; but this is not the general case, nor, more importantly, is it the case when it is a matter of the justice of practices

themselves in which participants stand in various relations to be appraised in accordance with standards which they may be expected to acknowledge before one another. Thus however mistaken the notion of the social contract may be as history, and however far it may overreach itself as a general theory of social and political obligation, it does express, suitably interpreted, an essential part of the concept of justice.[22]

8. By way of conclusion I should like to make two remarks: first, the original modification of the utilitarian principle (that it require of practices that the offices and positions defined by them be equal unless it is reasonable to suppose that the representative man in *every* office would find the inequality to his advantage), slight as it may appear at first sight, actually has a different conception of justice standing behind it. I have tried to show how this is so by developing the concept of justice as fairness and by indicating how this notion involves the mutual acceptance, from a general position, of the principles on which a practice is founded, and how this in turn requires the exclusion from consideration of claims violating the principles of justice. Thus the slight alteration of principle reveals another family of notions, another way of looking at the concept of justice.

Second, I should like to remark also that I have been dealing with the *concept* of justice. I have tried to set out the kinds of principles upon which judgments concerning the justice of practices may be said to stand. The analysis will be successful to the degree that it expresses the principles involved in these judgments when made by competent persons upon deliberation and reflection.[23] Now every people may be supposed to have the concept of justice, since in the life of every society there must be at least some relations in which the parties consider themselves to be circumstanced and related as the concept of justice as fairness requires. Societies will differ from one another not in having or in failing to have this notion but in the range of cases to which they apply it and in the emphasis which they give to it as compared with other moral concepts.

A firm grasp of the concept of justice itself is necessary if these variations, and the reasons for them, are to be understood. No study of the development of moral ideas and of the differences between them is more sound than the analysis of the fundamental moral concepts upon which it must depend. I have tried, therefore, to give an analysis of the concept of justice which should apply generally, however large a part the concept may have in a given morality, and which can be used in explaining the course of men's thoughts about justice and its relations to other

moral concepts. How it is to be used for this purpose is a large topic which I cannot, of course, take up here. I mention it only to emphasize that I have been dealing with the concept of justice itself and to indicate what use I consider such an analysis to have.

Notes

An abbreviated version of this paper (less than one-half the length) was presented in a symposium with the same title at the American Philosophical Association, Eastern Division, December 28, 1957, and appeared in the *Journal of Philosophy* 54, pp. 653–62.

1 I use the word "practice" throughout as a sort of technical term meaning any form of activity specified by a system of rules which defines offices, roles, moves, penalties, defenses, and so on, and which gives the activity its structure. As examples one may think of games and rituals, trials and parliaments, markets and systems of property. I have attempted a partial analysis of the notion of a practice in a paper "Two Concepts of Rules," *Philosophical Review* 64 (1955), pp. 3–32.

2 These principles are, of course, well known in one form or another and appear in many analyses of justice even where the writers differ widely on other matters. Thus if the principle of equal liberty is commonly associated with Kant (see *The Philosophy of Law*, trans. W. Hastie (Edinburgh, 1887), pp. 56f.), it may be claimed that it can also be found in J. S. Mill's *On Liberty* and elsewhere, and in many other liberal writers. Recently H. L. A. Hart has argued for something like it in his paper "Are There Any Natural Rights?," *Philosophical Review* 64 (1955), pp. 175–91. The injustice of inequalities which are not won in return for a contribution to the common advantage is, of course, widespread in political writings of all sorts. The conception of justice here discussed is distinctive, if at all, only in selecting these two principles in this form; but for another similar analysis, see the discussion by W. D. Lamont, *The Principles of Moral Judgment* (Oxford, 1946), ch. v.

3 This point was made by Sidgwick, *Methods of Ethics*, 6th edn. (London, 1901), Bk. III, ch. v, sec. i. It has recently been emphasized by Sir Isaiah Berlin in a symposium, "Equality," *Proceedings of the Aristotelian Society*, NS 56 (1955–6), pp. 305f.

4 In the paper referred to above, footnote 2, I have tried to show the importance of taking practices as the proper subject of the utilitarian principle. The criticisms of so-called "restricted utilitarianism" by J. J. C. Smart, "Extreme and Restricted Utilitarianism," *Philosophical Quarterly* 6 (1956), pp. 344–54, and by H. J. McCloskey, "An Examination of

Restricted Utilitarianism," *Philosophical Review* 66 (1957), pp. 466–85, do not affect my argument. These papers are concerned with the very general proposition, which is attributed (with what justice I shall not consider) to S. E. Toulmin and P. H. Nowell-Smith (and in the case of the latter paper, also, apparently, to me); namely, the proposition that particular moral actions are justified by appealing to moral rules, and moral rules in turn by reference to utility. But clearly I meant to defend no such view. My discussion of the concept of rules as maxims is an explicit rejection of it. What I did argue was that, in the *logically special* case of practices (although actually quite a common case) where the rules have special features and are not moral rules at all but legal rules or rules of games and the like (except, perhaps, in the case of promises), there is a peculiar force to the distinction between justifying particular actions and justifying the system of rules themselves. Even then I claimed only that restricting the utilitarian principle to practices as defined strengthened it. I did not argue for the position that this amendment alone is sufficient for a complete defense of utilitarianism as a general theory of morals. In this paper I take up the question as to how the utilitarian principle itself must be modified, but here, too, the subject of inquiry is not all of morality at once, but a limited topic, the concept of justice.

5 It might seem as if J. S. Mill, in paragraph 36 of chapter v of *Utilitarianism*, expressed the utilitarian principle in this modified form, but in the remaining two paragraphs of the chapter, and elsewhere, he would appear not to grasp the significance of the change. Hume often emphasizes that *every* man must benefit. For example, in discussing the utility of general rules, he holds that they are requisite to the "well-being of every individual"; from a stable system of property "every individual person must find himself a gainer in balancing the account...." "Every member of society is sensible of this interest; everyone expresses this sense to his fellows along with the resolution he has taken of squaring his actions by it, on the conditions that others will do the same" (*A Treatise of Human Nature*, Bk. III, Pt. II, sec. ii, paragraph 22).

6 It is not possible to discuss here this addition to the usual conception of rationality. If it seems peculiar, it may be worth remarking that it is analogous to the modification of the utilitarian principle which the argument as a whole is designed to explain and justify. In the same way that the satisfaction of interests, the representative claims of which violate the principles of justice, is not a reason for having a practice (see section 7), unfounded envy, within limits, need not to be taken into account.

7 The idea that accepting a principle as a moral principle implies that one generally acts on it, failing a special explanation, has been stressed by R. M. Hare, *The Language of Morals* (Oxford, 1952). His formulation of it needs to be modified, however, along the lines suggested by P. L. Gardiner, "On Assenting to a Moral Principle," *Proceedings of the Aristotelian Society*, NS 55 (1955), pp. 23–44. See also C. K. Grant, "Akrasia and the Criteria of Assent to Practical Principles," *Mind* 65 (1956), pp. 400–7, where the complexity of the criteria for assent is discussed.

8 Perhaps the best known statement of this conception is that given by Glaucon at the beginning of Book II of Plato's *Republic*. Presumably it was, in various forms, a common view among the Sophists; but that Plato gives a fair representation of it is doubtful. See K. R. Popper, *The Open Society and Its Enemies*, rev. edn. (Princeton, 1950), pp. 112–18. Certainly Plato usually attributes to it a quality of manic egoism which one feels must be an exaggeration; on the other hand, see the Melian Debate in Thucydides, *The Peloponnesian War*, Bk. V, ch. VII, although it is impossible to say to what extent the views expressed there reveal any current philosophical opinion. Also in this tradition are the remarks of Epicurus on justice in *Principal Doctrines*, XXXI–XXXVIII. In modern times elements of the conception appear in a more sophisticated form in Hobbes, *The Leviathan* and in Hume, *A Treatise of Human Nature*, Bk. III, Pt. II, as well as in the writings of the school of natural law such as Pufendorf's *De jure naturae et gentium*. Hobbes and Hume are especially instructive. For Hobbes's argument see Howard Warrender's *The Political Philosophy of Hobbes* (Oxford, 1957). W. J. Baumol's *Welfare Economics and the Theory of the State* (London, 1952), is valuable in showing the wide applicability of Hobbes's fundamental idea (interpreting his natural law as principles of prudence), although in this book it is traced back only to Hume's *Treatise*.

9 See J. von Neumann and O. Morgenstern, *The Theory of Games and Economic Behavior*, 2nd edn. (Princeton, 1947). For a comprehensive and not too technical discussion of the developments since, see R. Duncan Luce and Howard Raiffa, *Games and Decisions: Introduction and Critical Survey* (New York, 1957). Chs. VI and XIV discuss the developments most obviously related to the analysis of justice.

10 For a general survey see J. W. Gough, *The Social Contract*, 2nd edn. (Oxford, 1957), and Otto von Gierke, *The Development of Political Theory*, trans. B. Freyd (London, 1939), Pt. II, ch. II.

11 The difficulty one gets into by a mechanical application of the theory of games to moral philosophy can be brought out by considering among several possible examples, R. B. Braithwaite's study, *Theory of Games as a Tool for the Moral Philosopher* (Cambridge, 1955). On the analysis there given, it turns out that the fair division of playing time between Matthew and Luke depends on their preferences, and these in turn are connected with the instruments they wish to play. Since Matthew has a threat advantage over Luke, arising purely from the fact that Matthew, the trumpeter, prefers both of them playing at once to neither of them playing, whereas Luke, the pianist, prefers silence to cacophony, Matthew is allotted 26 evenings of play to Luke's 17. If the situation were reversed, the threat advantage would be with Luke. See pp. 36f. But now we have only to suppose that Matthew is a jazz enthusiast who plays the drums, and Luke a violinist who plays sonatas, in which case it will be fair, on this analysis, for Matthew to play whenever and as often as he likes, assuming, of course, as it is plausible to assume, that he does not care whether Luke plays or not. Certainly something has gone wrong. To each according to his threat advantage is hardly the principle of fairness. What is lacking is the concept of morality, and it must be brought into the conjectural account in some way or other. In the text this is done by the form of the procedure whereby principles are proposed and acknowledged (section 3). If one starts directly with the particular case as known, and if one accepts as given and definitive the preferences and relative positions of the parties, whatever they are, it is impossible to give an analysis of the moral concept of fairness. Braithwaite's use of the theory of games, insofar as it is intended to analyze the concept of fairness, is, I think, mistaken. This is not, of course, to criticize in any way the theory of games as a mathematical theory, to which Braithwaite's book certainly contributes, nor as an analysis of how rational (and amoral) egoists might behave (and so as an analysis of how people sometimes actually do behave). But it is to say that if the theory of games is to be used to analyze moral concepts, its formal structure must be interpreted in a special and general manner as indicated in the text. Once we do this, though, we are in touch again with a much older tradition.

12 For the definition of this prima-facie duty, and the idea that it is a special duty, I am indebted to H. L. A. Hart. See his paper "Are There Any Natural Rights?," *Philosophical Review* 64 (1955), pp. 185f.

13 The sense of "performative" here is to be derived from J. L. Austin's paper in the symposium, "Other Minds," *Proceedings of the Aristotelian Society*, suppl. vol. (1946), pp. 170–4.

14 This, however, commonly happens. Hobbes, for example, when invoking the notion of a "tacit covenant," appeals not to the natural law that promises should be kept but to his fourth law of nature, that of gratitude. On Hobbes's shift from fidelity to gratitude, see Warrender, *Political Philosophy of Hobbes*, pp. 51–2, 233–7. While it is not a serious criticism of Hobbes, it would have improved his argument had he appealed to the duty of fair play. On his premises he is perfectly entitled to do so. Similarly Sidgwick thought that a principle of justice, such as every man ought to receive adequate requital for his labor, is like gratitude universalized. See *Methods of Ethics*, Bk. III, ch. v, sec. 5. There is a gap in the stock of moral concepts used by philosophers into which the concept of the duty of fair play fits quite naturally.

15 I am using the concept of criterion here in what I take to be Wittgenstein's sense. See *Philosophical Investigations* (Oxford, 1953); and Norman Malcolm's review, "Wittgenstein's *Philosophical Investigations*," *Philosophical Review* 63 (1954), pp. 543–7. That the response of compassion, under appropriate circumstances, is part of the criterion for whether or not a person understands what "pain" means, is, I think, in the *Philosophical Investigations*. The view in the text is simply an extension of this idea. I cannot, however, attempt to justify it here. Similar thoughts are to be found, I think, in Max Scheler, *The Nature of Sympathy*, trans. Peter Heath (New Haven, CT, 1954). His way of writing is often so obscure that I cannot be certain.

16 While this assimilation is implicit in Bentham's and Sidgwick's moral theory, explicit statements of it as applied to justice are relatively rare. One clear instance in *The Principles of Morals and Legislation* occurs in chapter x, footnote 2 to section xl: "justice, in the only sense in which it has a meaning, is an imaginary personage, feigned for the convenience of discourse, whose dictates are the dictates of utility, applied to certain particular cases. Justice, then, is nothing more than an imaginary instrument, employed to forward on certain occasions, and by certain means, the purposes of benevolence. The dictates of justice are nothing more than a part of the dictates of benevolence, which, on certain occasions, are applied to certain

subjects." Likewise in *The Limits of Jurisprudence Defined*, ed. C. W. Everett (New York, 1945), pp. 117f., Bentham criticizes Grotius for denying that justice derives from utility; and in *The Theory of Legislation*, ed. C. K. Ogden (London, 1931), p. 3, he says that he uses the words "just" and "unjust" along with other words "simply as collective terms including the ideas of certain pains or pleasures." That Sidgwick's conception of justice is similar to Bentham's is admittedly not evident from his discussion of justice in Book III, ch. v of *Methods of Ethics*. But it follows, I think, from the moral theory he accepts. Hence C. D. Broad's criticisms of Sidgwick in the matter of distributive justice in *Five Types of Ethical Theory* (London, 1930), pp. 249–53, do not rest on a misinterpretation.

17 This maxim is attributed to Bentham by J. S. Mill in *Utilitarianism*, ch. v, paragraph 36. I have not found it in Bentham's writings, nor seen such a reference. Similarly James Bonar, *Philosophy and Political Economy* (London, 1893), p. 234n. But it accords perfectly with Bentham's ideas. See the hitherto unpublished manuscript in David Baumgardt, *Bentham and the Ethics of Today* (Princeton, 1952), Appendix IV. For example, "the total value of the stock of pleasure belonging to the whole community is to be obtained by multiplying the number expressing the value of it as respecting any one person, by the number expressing the multitude of such individuals" (p. 556).

18 An idea essential to the classical utilitarian conception of justice. Bentham is firm in his statement of it: "It is only upon that principle [the principle of asceticism], and not from the principle of utility, that the most abominable pleasure which the vilest of malefactors ever reaped from his crime would be reprobated, if it stood alone. The case is, that it never does stand alone; but is necessarily followed by such a quantity of pain (or, what comes to the same thing, such a chance for a certain quantity of pain) that the pleasure in comparison of it, is as nothing: and this is the true and sole, but perfectly sufficient, reason for making it a ground for punishment" (*The Principles of Morals and Legislation*, ch. II, sec. iv. See also ch. x, sec. x, footnote 1). The same point is made in *The Limits of Jurisprudence Defined*, pp. 115f. Although much recent welfare economics, as found in such important works as I. M. D. Little, *A Critique of Welfare Economics*, 2nd edn. (Oxford, 1957) and K. J. Arrow, *Social Choice and Individual Values* (New York, 1951), dispenses with the idea of cardinal utility, and uses instead the theory of ordinal utility as stated by J. R. Hicks, *Value and Capital*, 2nd edn. (Oxford, 1946), Pt. I, it assumes with utilitarianism that individual preferences have value as such, and so accepts the idea being criticized here. I hasten to add, however,

that this is no objection to it as a means of analyzing economic policy, and for that purpose it may, indeed, be a necessary simplifying assumption. Nevertheless it is an assumption which cannot be made in so far as one is trying to analyze moral concepts, especially the concept of justice, as economists would, I think, agree. Justice is usually regarded as a separate and distinct part of any comprehensive criterion of economic policy. See, for example, Tibor Scitovsky, *Welfare and Competition* (London, 1952), pp. 56–69, and Little, *Critique of Welfare Economics*, ch. VII.

19 See J. S. Mill's argument in *Utilitarianism*, ch. v, paras. 16–25.

20 See D. G. Ritchie, *Natural Rights* (London, 1894), pp. 95ff., 249ff. Lionel Robbins has insisted on this point on several occasions. See *An Essay on the Nature and Significance of Economic Science*, 2nd edn. (London, 1935), pp. 134–43, "Interpersonal Comparisons of Utility: A Comment," *Economic Journal* 48 (1938), pp. 635–41, and more recently, "Robertson on Utility and Scope," *Economica*, NS 20 (1953), pp. 108f.

21 As Sir Henry Maine suggested Bentham may have regarded them. See *The Early History of Institutions* (London, 1875), pp. 398ff.

22 Thus Kant was not far wrong when he interpreted the original contract merely as an "Idea of Reason"; yet he still thought of it as a *general* criterion of right and as providing a general theory of political obligation. See the second part of the essay, "On the Saying 'That may be right in theory but has no value in practice'" (1793), in *Kant's Principles of Politics*, trans. W. Hastie (Edinburgh, 1891). I have drawn on the contractarian tradition not for a general theory of political obligation but to clarify the concept of justice.

23 For a further discussion of the idea expressed here, see my paper, "Outline of a Decision Procedure for Ethics," in the *Philosophical Review* 60 (1951), pp. 177–97. For an analysis, similar in many respects but using the notion of the ideal observer instead of that of the considered judgment of a competent person, see Roderick Firth, "Ethical Absolutism and the Ideal Observer," *Philosophy and Phenomenological Research* 12 (1952), pp. 317–45. While the similarities between these two discussions are more important than the differences, an analysis based on the notion of a considered judgment of a competent person, as it is based on a kind of judgment, may prove more helpful in understanding the features of moral judgment than an analysis based on the notion of an ideal observer, although this remains to be shown. A man who rejects the conditions imposed on a considered judgment of a competent person could no longer profess to *judge* at all. This seems more fundamental than his rejecting the conditions of observation, for these do not seem to apply, in an ordinary sense, to making a moral judgment.

36

Modern Moral Philosophy

G. E. M. Anscombe

I will begin by stating three theses which I present in this paper. The first is that it is not profitable for us at present to do moral philosophy; that should be laid aside at any rate until we have an adequate philosophy of psychology, in which we are conspicuously lacking. The second is that the concepts of obligation, and duty – *moral* obligation and *moral* duty, that is to say – and of what is *morally* right and wrong, and of the *moral* sense of "ought," ought to be jettisoned if this is psychologically possible; because they are survivals, or derivatives from survivals, from an earlier conception of ethics which no longer generally survives, and are only harmful without it. My third thesis is that the differences between the well-known English writers on moral philosophy from Sidgwick to the present day are of little importance.

Anyone who has read Aristotle's *Ethics* and has also read modern moral philosophy must have been struck by the great contrasts between them. The concepts which are prominent among the moderns seem to be lacking, or at any rate buried or far in the background, in Aristotle. Most noticeably, the term "moral" itself, which we have by direct inheritance from Aristotle, just doesn't seem to fit, in its modern sense, into an account of Aristotelian ethics. Aristotle distinguishes virtues as moral and intellectual. Have some of what he calls "intellectual" virtues what *we* should call a "moral" aspect? It would seem

Originally published in *Philosophy* 33 (1958) (Cambridge University Press, Cambridge, 1958).

so; the criterion is presumably that a failure in an "intellectual" virtue – like that of having good judgment in calculating how to bring about something useful, say in municipal government – may be *blameworthy*. But – it may reasonably be asked – cannot *any* failure be made a matter of blame or reproach? Any derogatory criticism, say of the workmanship of a product or the design of a machine, can be called blame or reproach. So we want to put in the word "morally" again: sometimes such a failure may be *morally* blameworthy, sometimes not. Now has Aristotle got this idea of *moral* blame, as opposed to any other? If he has, why isn't it more central? There are some mistakes, he says, which are causes, not of involuntariness in actions, but of scoundrelism, and for which a man is blamed. Does this mean that there is a *moral* obligation not to make certain intellectual mistakes? Why doesn't he discuss obligation in general, and this obligation in particular? If someone professes to be expounding Aristotle and talks in a modern fashion about "moral" such-and-such, he must be very imperceptive if he does not constantly feel like someone whose jaws have somehow got out of alignment: the teeth don't come together in a proper bite.

We cannot, then, look to Aristotle for any elucidation of the modern way of talking about "moral" goodness, obligation, etc. And all the best-known writers on ethics in modern times, from Butler to Mill, appear to me to have faults as thinkers on the subject which make it impossible to hope for any direct light on it from them. I will state these objections with the brevity which their character makes possible.

Butler exalts conscience, but appears ignorant that a man's conscience may tell him to do the vilest things.

Hume defines "truth" in such a way as to exclude ethical judgments from it, and professes that he has proved that they are so excluded. He also implicitly defines "passion" in such a way that aiming at anything is having a passion. His objection to passing from "is" to "ought" would apply equally to passing from "is" to "owes" or from "is" to "needs." (However, because of the historical situation, he has a point here, which I shall return to.)

Kant introduces the idea of "legislating for oneself," which is as absurd as if in these days, when majority votes command great respect, one were to call each reflective decision a man made a *vote* resulting in a majority, which as a matter of proportion is overwhelming, for it is always 1–0. The concept of legislation requires superior power in the legislator. His own rigoristic convictions on the subject of lying were so intense that it never occurred to him that a lie could be relevantly described as anything but just a lie (e.g. as "a lie in such-and-such circumstances"). His rule about universalizable maxims is useless without stipulations as to what shall count as a relevant description of an action with a view to constructing a maxim about it.

Bentham and Mill do not notice the difficulty of the concept "pleasure." They are often said to have gone wrong through committing the "naturalistic fallacy"; but this charge does not impress me, because I do not find accounts of it coherent. But the other point – about pleasure – seems to me a fatal objection from the very outset. The ancients found this concept pretty baffling. It reduced Aristotle to sheer babble about "the bloom on the cheek of youth" because, for good reasons, he wanted to make it out both identical with and different from the pleasurable activity. Generations of modern philosophers found this concept quite unperplexing, and it reappeared in the literature as a problematic one only a year or two ago when Ryle wrote about it. The reason is simple: since Locke, pleasure was taken to be some sort of internal impression. But it was superficial, if that was the right account of it, to make it the point of actions. One might adapt something Wittgenstein said about "meaning" and say "Pleasure cannot be an internal impression,

for no internal impression could have the consequences of pleasure."

Mill also, like Kant, fails to realize the necessity for stipulation as to relevant descriptions, if his theory is to have content. It did not occur to him that acts of murder and theft could be otherwise described. He holds that where a proposed action is of such a kind as to fall under some one principle established on grounds of utility, one must go by that; where it falls under none or several, the several suggesting contrary views of the action, the thing to do is to calculate particular consequences. But pretty well any action can be so described as to make it fall under a variety of principles of utility (as I shall say for short) if it falls under any.

I will now return to Hume. The features of Hume's philosophy which I have mentioned, like many other features of it, would incline me to think that Hume was a mere – brilliant – sophist; and his procedures are certainly sophistical. But I am forced, not to reverse, but to add to, this judgment by a peculiarity of Hume's philosophizing: namely that although he reaches his conclusions – with which he is in love – by sophistical methods, his considerations constantly open up very deep and important problems. It is often the case that in the act of exhibiting the sophistry one finds oneself noticing matters which deserve a lot of exploring: the obvious stands in need of investigation as a result of the points that Hume pretends to have made. In this, he is unlike, say, Butler. It was already well known that conscience could dictate vile actions; for Butler to have written disregarding this does not open up any new topics for us. But with Hume it is otherwise: hence he is a very profound and great philosopher, in spite of his sophistry. For example:

Suppose that I say to my grocer "Truth consists in *either* relations of ideas, as that $20s. = £1$, *or* matters of fact, as that I ordered potatoes, you supplied them, and you sent me a bill. So it doesn't apply to such a proposition as that I *owe* you such-and-such a sum."

Now if one makes this comparison, it comes to light that the relation of the facts mentioned to the description "X owes Y so much money" is an interesting one, which I will call that of being "brute relative to" that description. Further, the "brute" facts mentioned here themselves have descriptions relatively to which *other* facts are "brute" – as, e.g., *he had potatoes carted to my house* and *they were left there* are brute facts relative to "he supplied me with potatoes." And the fact *X owes Y money* is in turn "brute" relative to other descriptions – e.g. "X is solvent." Now the relation of "relative bruteness" is a complicated one. To mention a few points: if xyz is a set of facts brute relative to a description A, then xyz is a set out of a range some set among which holds if A holds; but the holding of some set among these does not necessarily entail A, because exceptional circumstances can always make a difference; and what are exceptional circumstances relatively to A can generally only be explained by giving a few diverse examples, and *no* theoretically adequate provision can be made for exceptional circumstances, since a further special context can theoretically always be imagined that would reinterpret any special context. Further, though in normal circumstances, xyz would be a justification for A, that is not to say that A just comes to the same as "xyz"; and also there is apt to be an institutional context which gives its point to the description A, of which institution A is of course not itself a description. (E.g. the statement that I give someone a shilling is not a description of the institution of money or of the currency of this country.) Thus, though it would be ludicrous to pretend that there can be no such thing as a transition from, e.g., "is" to "owes," the character of the transition is in fact rather interesting and comes to light as a result of reflecting on Hume's arguments.[1]

That I owe the grocer such-and-such a sum would be one of a set of facts which would be "brute" in relation to the description "I am a bilker." "Bilking" is of course a species of "dishonesty" or "injustice." (Naturally the consideration will not have any effect on my actions unless I want to commit or avoid acts of injustice.)

So far, in spite of their strong associations, I conceive "bilking," "injustice" and "dishonesty" in a merely "factual" way. That I can do this for "bilking" is obvious enough; "justice" I have no idea how to define, except that its sphere is that of actions which relate to someone else, but "injustice," its defect, can for the moment be offered as a generic name covering various species. E.g.: "bilking," "theft" (which is relative to whatever property institutions exist), "slander," "adultery," "punishment of the innocent."

In present-day philosophy an explanation is required how an unjust man is a bad man, or an unjust action a bad one; to give such an explanation belongs to ethics; but it cannot even be begun until we are equipped with a sound philosophy of psychology. For the proof that an unjust man is a bad man would require a positive account of justice as a "virtue." This part of the subject-matter of ethics is, however, completely closed to us until we have an account of what *type of characteristic* a virtue is – a problem, not of ethics, but of conceptual analysis – and how it relates to the actions in which it is instanced: a matter which I think Aristotle did not succeed in really making clear. For this we certainly need an account at least of what a human action is at all, and how its description as "doing such-and-such" is affected by its motive and by the intention or intentions in it; and for this an account of such concepts is required.

The terms "should" or "ought" or "needs" relate to good and bad: e.g. machinery needs oil, or should or ought to be oiled, in that running without oil is bad for it, or it runs badly without oil. According to this conception, of course, "should" and "ought" are not used in a special "moral" sense when one says that a man should not bilk. (In Aristotle's sense of the term "moral" ($\dot{\eta}\theta\iota\kappa\acute{o}s$), they are being used in connection with a *moral* subject-matter: namely that of human passions and [non-technical] actions.) But they have now acquired a special so-called "moral" sense – i.e. a sense in which they imply some absolute verdict (like one of guilty/not guilty on a man) on what is described in the "ought" sentences used in certain types of context: not merely the contexts that *Aristotle* would call "moral" – passions and actions – but also some of the contexts that he would call "intellectual."

The ordinary (and quite indispensable) terms "should," "needs," "ought," "must" acquired this special sense by being equated in the relevant contexts with "is obliged," or "is bound," or "is required to," in the sense in which one can be obliged or bound by law or something can be required by law.

How did this come about? The answer is in history: between Aristotle and us came Christianity, with its *law* conception of ethics. For Christianity derived its ethical notions from the Torah. (One might be inclined to think that a law conception of ethics could arise only among people who accepted an allegedly divine positive law; that this is not so is shown by the example of the Stoics, who also thought that whatever was involved in conformity to human virtues was required by divine law.)

In consequence of the dominance of Christianity for many centuries, the concepts of being bound, permitted, or excused became deeply embedded in our language and thought. The Greek word ἁμαρτάνειν, the aptest to be turned to that use, acquired the sense "sin," from having meant "mistake," "missing the mark," "going wrong." The Latin *peccatum* which roughly corresponded to ἁμάρτημα was even apter for the sense "sin," because it was already associated with *culpa* – "guilt" – a juridical notion. The blanket term "illicit," "unlawful," meaning much the same as our blanket term "wrong," explains itself. It is interesting that Aristotle did not have such a blanket term. He has blanket terms for wicked-ness – "villain," "scoundrel"; but of course a man is not a villain or a scoundrel by the perform-ance of one bad action, or a few bad actions. And he has terms like "disgraceful," "impious"; and specific terms signifying defect of the relev-ant virtue, like "unjust"; but no term corres-ponding to "illicit." The extension of this term (i.e. the range of its application) could be indic-ated in his terminology only by a quite lengthy sentence: that is "illicit" which, whether it is a thought or a consented-to passion or an action or an omission in thought or action, is some-thing contrary to one of the virtues the lack of which shows a man to be bad *qua* man. That formulation would yield a concept coextensive with the concept "illicit."

To have a *law* conception of ethics is to hold that what is needed for conformity with the virtues failure in which is the mark of being bad *qua* man (and not merely, say, *qua* craftsman or logician) – that what is needed for *this*, is re-quired by divine law. Naturally it is not possible to have such a conception unless you believe in God as a law-giver; like Jews, Stoics, and Chris-tians. But if such a conception is dominant for many centuries, and then is given up, it is a natural result that the concepts of "obligation," of being bound or required as by a law, should remain though they had lost their root; and if the word "ought" has become invested in certain contexts with the sense of "obligation," it too will remain to be spoken with a special emphasis and a special feeling in these contexts.

It is as if the notion "criminal" were to re-main when criminal law and criminal courts had been abolished and forgotten. A Hume discover-ing this situation might conclude that there was a special sentiment, expressed by "criminal," which alone gave the word its sense. So Hume discovered the situation in which the notion "ob-ligation" survived, and the notion "ought" was invested with that peculiar force having which it is said to be used in a "moral" sense, but in which the belief in divine law had long since been abandoned: for it was substantially given up among Protestants at the time of the Reforma-tion.[2] The situation, if I am right, was the inter-esting one of the survival of a concept outside the framework of thought that made it a really intelligible one.

When Hume produced his famous remarks about the transition from "is" to "ought," he was, then, bringing together several quite differ-ent points. One I have tried to bring out by my remarks on the transition from "is" to "owes" and on the relative "bruteness" of facts. It would be possible to bring out a different point by enquiring about the transition from "is" to "needs"; from the characteristics of an organism to the environment that it needs, for example. To say that it needs that environment is not to say, e.g., that you want it to have that environ-ment, but that it won't flourish unless it has it. Certainly, it all depends whether you *want* it to flourish! as Hume would say. But what "all de-pends" on whether you want it to flourish is whether the fact that it needs that environment, or won't flourish without it, has the slightest influence on your actions. Now *that* such-and-such "ought" to be or "is needed" is supposed to have an influence on your actions: from which it seemed natural to infer that to judge that it "ought to be" was in fact to grant what you judged "ought to be" influence on your actions. And no amount of truth as to what *is* the case could possibly have a logical claim to have influ-ence on your actions. (It is not judgment as such that sets us in motion; but our judgment on how to get or do something we *want*.) Hence it *must* be impossible to infer "needs" or "ought to be" from "is." But in the case of a plant, let us say, the inference from "is" to "needs" is certainly not in the least dubious. It is interesting and worth examining; but not at all fishy. Its interest is similar to the interest of the relation between brute and less brute facts: these relations have been very little considered. And while you can contrast "what it needs" with "what it's got" – like contrasting *de facto* and *de jure* – that does not make its needing this environment less of a "truth."

Certainly in the case of what the plant needs, the thought of a need will only affect action if you want the plant to flourish. Here, then, there is no necessary connection between what you can judge the plant "needs" and what you want. But there is some sort of necessary connection between what you think *you* need, and what you want. The connection is a complicated one; it is possible *not* to want something that you judge you need. But, e.g., it is not possible never to want *anything* that you judge you need. This, however, is not a fact about the meaning of the word "to need," but about the phenomenon of *wanting*. Hume's reasoning, we might say, in effect, leads one to think it must be about the word "to need," or "to be good for."

Thus we find two problems already wrapped up in the remark about a transition from "is" to "ought"; now supposing that we had clarified the "relative bruteness" of facts on the one hand, and the notions involved in "needing," and "flourishing" on the other – there would *still* remain a third point. For, following Hume, someone might say: Perhaps you have made out your point about a transition from "is" to "owes" and from "is" to "needs": but only at the cost of showing "owes" and "needs" sentences to express a *kind* of truths, a *kind* of facts. And it remains impossible to infer "*morally ought*" from "is" sentences.

This comment, it seems to me, would be correct. This word "ought," having become a word of mere mesmeric force, could not, in the character of having that force, be inferred from anything whatever. It may be objected that it could be inferred from other "morally ought" sentences: but that cannot be true. The appearance that this is so is produced by the fact that we say "All men are ϕ" and "Socrates is a man" implies "Socrates is ϕ" But here "ϕ" is a dummy predicate. We mean that if you substitute a real predicate for "ϕ" the implication is valid. A real predicate is required; not just a word containing no intelligible thought: a word retaining the suggestion of force, and apt to have a strong psychological effect, but which no longer signifies a real concept at all.

For its suggestion is one of a *verdict* on my action, according as it agrees or disagrees with the description in the "ought" sentence. And where one does not think there is a judge or a law, the notion of a verdict may retain its psychological effect, but not its meaning. Now imagine that just this word "verdict" *were* so used – with a characteristically solemn emphasis – as to retain its atmosphere but not its meaning, and someone were to say: "For a *verdict*, after all, you need a law and a judge." The reply might be made: "Not at all, for if there were a law and a judge who gave a verdict, the question for us would be whether accepting that verdict is something that there is a *Verdict* on." This is an analogue of an argument which is so frequently referred to as decisive: If someone does have a divine law conception of ethics, all the same, he has to agree that he has to have a judgment that he *ought* (morally ought) to obey the divine law; so his ethic is in exactly the same position as any other: he merely has a "practical major premise":[3] "Divine law ought to be obeyed" where someone else has, e.g., "The greatest happiness principle ought to be employed in all decisions."

I should judge that Hume and our present-day ethicists had done a considerable service by showing that no content could be found in the notion "morally ought"; if it were not that the latter philosophers try to find an alternative (very fishy) content and to retain the psychological force of the term. It would be most reasonable to drop it. It has no reasonable sense outside a law conception of ethics; they are not going to maintain such a conception; and you can do ethics without it, as is shown by the example of Aristotle. It would be a great improvement if, instead of "morally wrong," one always named a genus such as "untruthful," "unchaste," "unjust." We should no longer ask whether doing something was "wrong," passing directly from some description of an action to this notion; we should ask whether, e.g., it was unjust; and the answer would sometimes be clear at once.

I now come to the epoch in modern English moral philosophy marked by Sidgwick. There is a startling change that seems to have taken place between Mill and Moore. Mill assumes, as we saw, that there is no question of calculating the particular consequences of an action such as murder or theft; and we saw too that his position was stupid, because it is not at all clear how an action *can* fall under just one principle of utility. In Moore and in subsequent academic moralists of England we find it taken to be pretty obvious that "the right action" is the action which produces the best possible consequences (reckoning among consequences the intrinsic values ascribed to certain kinds of act by some "Objectivists"[4]). Now it follows from this that a man does well, subjectively speaking, if he acts for the best in the particular circumstances according to his judgment of the total consequences of this particular action. I say that this follows, not that any philosopher has said precisely that. For discussion of these questions can of course get extremely complicated: e.g. it can be doubted whether "such-and-such is the right action" is a satisfactory formulation, on the grounds that things have to exist to have predicates – so perhaps the best formulation is "I am obliged"; or again, a philosopher may deny that "right" is a "descriptive" term, and then take a roundabout route through linguistic analysis to reach a view which comes to the same thing as "the right action is the one productive of the best consequences" (e.g. the view that you frame your "principles" to effect the end you choose to pursue, the connexion between "choice" and "best" being supposedly such that choosing reflectively means that you choose how to act so as to produce the best consequences); further, the roles of what are called "moral principles" and of the "motive of duty" have to be described; the differences between "good" and "morally good" and "right" need to be explored, the special characteristics of "ought" sentences investigated. Such discussions generate an appearance of significant diversity of views where what is really significant is an overall similarity. The overall similarity is made clear if you consider that every one of the best-known English academic moral philosophers has put out a philosophy according to which, e.g., it is not possible to hold that it cannot be right to kill the innocent as a means to any end whatsoever and that someone who thinks otherwise is in error. (I have to mention both points; because Mr Hare, for example, while teaching a philosophy which would encourage a person to judge that killing the innocent would be what he "ought" to choose for overriding purposes, would also teach, I think, that if a man chooses to make avoiding killing the innocent for any purpose his "supreme practical principle," he cannot be impugned for error: that just is his "principle." But with that qualification, I think it can be seen that the point I have mentioned holds good of every single English academic moral philosopher since Sidgwick.) Now this is a significant thing: for it means that all these philosophies are quite incompatible with the Hebrew-Christian ethic. For it has been characteristic of that ethic to teach that there are certain things forbidden whatever *consequences* threaten, such as: choosing to kill the innocent for any purpose, however good; vicarious punishment; treachery (by which I mean obtaining a man's confidence in a grave matter by promises of trustworthy friendship and then betraying him to his enemies); idolatry; sodomy; adultery; making a false profession of faith. The prohibition of certain things simply in virtue of their description as such-and-such identifiable kinds of action, regardless of any further consequences, is certainly not the whole of the Hebrew-Christian ethic; but it is a noteworthy feature of it; and if every academic philosopher since Sidgwick has written in such a way as to exclude this ethic, it would argue a certain provinciality of mind not to see this incompatibility as the most important fact about these philosophers, and the differences between them as somewhat trifling by comparison.

It is noticeable that none of these philosophers displays any consciousness that there is such an ethic, which he is contradicting: it is pretty well taken for obvious among them all that a prohibition such as that on murder does not operate in face of some consequences. But of course the strictness of the prohibition has as its point *that you are not to be tempted by fear or hope of consequences.*

If you notice the transition from Mill to Moore, you will suspect that it was made somewhere by someone; Sidgwick will come to mind as a likely name; and you will in fact find it going on, almost casually, in him. He is rather a dull author; and the important things in him occur in asides and footnotes and small bits of argument which are not concerned with his grand classification of the "methods of ethics." A divine law theory of ethics is reduced to an insignificant variety by a footnote telling us that "the best theologians" (God knows whom he meant) tell us that God is to be obeyed in his capacity of a *moral* being. ἡ φορτικός ὁ ἔπαινος; one seems to hear Aristotle saying: "Isn't the praise vulgar?"[5] – But Sidgwick *is* vulgar in that kind of way: he thinks, for example, that humility consists in underestimating your own merits – i.e. in a species of untruthfulness; and that the ground for having laws against blasphemy was that it was offensive to believers; and that to go accurately into the virtue of purity is to offend against its canons, a thing he reproves "medieval theologians" for not realizing.

From the point of view of the present enquiry, the most important thing about Sidgwick was his definition of intention. He defines intention in such a way that one must be said to intend any foreseen consequences of one's voluntary action. This definition is obviously incorrect, and I dare say that no one would be found to defend it now. He uses it to put forward an ethical thesis which would now be accepted by many people: the thesis that it does not make any difference to a man's responsibility for something that he foresaw, that he felt no desire for it, either as an end or as a means to an end. Using the language of intention more correctly, and avoiding Sidgwick's faulty conception, we may state the thesis thus: it does not make any difference to a man's responsibility for an effect of his action which he can foresee, that he does not intend it. Now this sounds rather edifying; it is I think quite characteristic of very bad degenerations of thought on such questions that they sound edifying. We can see what it amounts to by considering an example. Let us suppose that a man has a responsibility for the maintenance of some child. Therefore deliberately to withdraw support from it is a bad sort of thing for him to do. It would be bad for him to withdraw its maintenance because he didn't want to maintain it any longer; *and* also bad for him to withdraw it because by doing so he would, let us say, compel someone else to do something. (We may suppose for the sake of argument that compelling that person to do that thing is in itself quite admirable.) But now he has to choose between doing something disgraceful and going to prison; if he goes to prison, it will follow that he withdraws support from the child. By Sidgwick's doctrine, there is no difference in his responsibility for ceasing to maintain the child, between the case where he does it for its own sake or as a means to some other purpose, and when it happens as a foreseen and unavoidable consequence of his going to prison rather than do something disgraceful. It follows that he must weigh up the relative badness of withdrawing support from the child and of doing the disgraceful thing; and it may easily be that the disgraceful thing is in fact a less vicious action than intentionally withdrawing support from the child would be; if then the fact that withdrawing support from the child is a side effect of his going to prison does not make any difference to his responsibility, this

consideration will incline him to do the disgraceful thing; which can still be pretty bad. And of course, once he has started to look at the matter in this light, the only reasonable thing for him to consider will be the consequences and not the intrinsic badness of this or that action. So that, given that he judges reasonably that no *great* harm will come of it, he can do a much more disgraceful thing than deliberately withdrawing support from the child. And if his calculations turn out in fact wrong, it will appear that he was not responsible for the consequences, because he did not foresee them. For in fact Sidgwick's thesis leads to its being quite impossible to estimate the badness of an action except in the light of *expected* consequences. But if so, then *you* must estimate the badness in the light of the consequences *you* expect; and so it will follow that you can exculpate yourself from the *actual* consequences of the most disgraceful actions, so long as you can make out a case for not having foreseen them. Whereas I should contend that a man is responsible for the bad consequences of his bad actions, but gets no credit for the good ones; and contrariwise is not responsible for the bad consequences of good actions.

The denial of *any* distinction between foreseen and intended consequences, as far as responsibility is concerned, was not made by Sidgwick in developing any one "method of ethics"; he made this important move on behalf of everybody and just on its own account; and I think it plausible to suggest that *this* move on the part of Sidgwick explains the difference between old-fashioned Utilitarianism and the *consequentialism*, as I name it, which marks him and every English academic moral philosopher since him. By it, the kind of consideration which would formerly have been regarded as a temptation, the kind of consideration urged upon men by wives and flattering friends, was given a status by moral philosophers in their theories.

It is a necessary feature of consequentialism that it is a shallow philosophy. For there are always borderline cases in ethics. Now if you are either an Aristotelian, or a believer in divine law, you will deal with a borderline case by considering whether doing such-and-such in such-and-such circumstances is, say, murder, or is an act of injustice; and according as you decide it is or it isn't, you judge it to be a thing to do or not. This would be the method of casuistry; and while it may lead you to stretch a point on the circumference, it will not permit you to destroy the centre. But if you are a consequentialist, the question "What is it right to do in such-and-such circumstances?" is a stupid one to raise. The casuist raises such a question only to ask "Would it be *permissible* to do so-and-so?" or "Would it be permissible *not* to do so-and-so?" Only if it would *not* be permissible *not* to do so-and-so could he say "*This* would be *the* thing to do."[6] Otherwise, though he may speak *against* some action, he cannot prescribe any – for in an *actual* case, the circumstances (beyond the ones imagined) might suggest all sorts of possibilities, and you can't know in advance what the possibilities are going to be. Now the consequentialist has no footing on which to say "This would be permissible, this not"; because by his own hypothesis, it is the consequences that are to decide, and he has no business to pretend that he can lay it down what possible twists a man could give doing this or that; the most he can say is: a man must not *bring about* this or that; he has no right to say he will, in an actual case, bring about such-and-such unless he does so-and-so. Further, the consequentialist, in order to be imagining borderline cases at all, has of course to assume some sort of law or standard according to which this is a borderline case. Where then does he get the standard from? In practice the answer invariably is: from the standards current in his society or his circle. And it has in fact been the mark of all these philosophers that they have been extremely conventional; they have nothing in them by which to revolt against the conventional standards of their sort of people; it is impossible that they should be profound. But the chance that a whole range of conventional standards will be decent is small. Finally, the point of considering hypothetical situations, perhaps very improbable ones, *seems* to be to elicit from yourself or someone else a hypothetical decision to do something of a bad kind. I don't doubt this has the effect of predisposing people – who will never get into the situations for which they have made hypothetical choices – to consent to similar bad actions, or to praise and flatter those who do them, so long as their crowd does so too, when the desperate circumstances imagined don't hold at all.

Those who recognize the origins of the notions of "obligation" and of the emphatic, "moral," *ought*, in the divine law conception of ethics, but who reject the notion of a divine legislator, sometimes look about for the possibility of retaining a law conception without a divine legislator. This search, I think, has some interest in it. Perhaps the first thing that suggests itself is the "norms" of a society. But just as one cannot be impressed by Butler when one reflects what conscience can tell people to do, so, I think, one cannot be impressed by this idea if one reflects what the "norms" of a society can be like. That legislation can be "for oneself" I reject as absurd; whatever you do "for yourself" may be admirable; but is not legislating. Once one sees this, one may say: I have to frame my own rules, and these are the best I can frame, and I shall go by them until I know something better: as a man might say "I shall go by the customs of my ancestors." Whether this leads to good or evil will depend on the *content* of the rules or of the customs of one's ancestors. If one is lucky it will lead to good. Such an attitude would be hopeful in this at any rate: it seems to have in it some Socratic doubt where, from having to fall back on such expedients, it should be clear that Socratic doubt is good; in fact rather generally it must be good for anyone to think "Perhaps in some way I can't see, I may be on a bad path, perhaps I am hopelessly wrong in some essential way." The search for "norms" might lead someone to look for laws of nature, as if the universe were a legislator; but in the present day this is not likely to lead to good results: it might lead one to eat the weaker according to the laws of nature, but would hardly lead anyone nowadays to notions of justice; the pre-Socratic feeling about justice as comparable to the balance or harmony which kept things going is very remote to us.

There is another possibility here: "obligation" may be contractual. Just as we look at the law to find out what a man subject to it is required by it to do, so we look at a contract to find out what the man who has made it is required by it to do. Thinkers, admittedly remote from us, might have the idea of a *foedus rerum*, of the universe not as a legislator but as the embodiment of a contract. Then if you could find out what the contract was, you would learn your obligations under it. Now, you cannot be under a law unless it has been promulgated to you; and the thinkers, who believed in "natural divine law" held that it was promulgated to every grown man in his knowledge of good and evil. Similarly you cannot be in a contract without having contracted, i.e. given signs of entering upon the contract.

Just possibly, it might be argued that the use of language which one makes in the ordinary conduct of life amounts in some sense to giving the signs of entering into various contracts. If anyone had this theory, we should want to see it worked out. I suspect that it would be largely formal; it might be possible to construct a system embodying the law (whose status might be compared to that of "laws" of logic): "what's sauce for the goose is sauce for the gander," but hardly one descending to such particularities as the prohibition on murder or sodomy. Also, while it is clear that you can be subject to a law that you do not acknowledge and have not thought of as law, it does not seem reasonable to say that you can enter upon a contract without knowing that you are doing so; such ignorance is usually held to be destructive of the nature of a contract.

It might remain to look for "norms" in human virtues: just as *man* has so many teeth, which is certainly not the average number of teeth men have, but is the number of teeth for the species, so perhaps the species *man*, regarded not just biologically, but from the point of view of the activity of thought and choice in regard to the various departments of life – powers and faculties and use of things needed – "has" such-and-such virtues: and this "man" with the complete set of virtues is the "norm," as "man" with, e.g., a complete set of teeth is a norm. But in *this* sense "norm" has ceased to be roughly equivalent to "law." In *this* sense the notion of a "norm" brings us nearer to an Aristotelian than a law conception of ethics. There is, I think, no harm in that; but if someone looked in this direction to give "norm" a sense, then he ought to recognize what has happened to the notion "norm," which he wanted to mean "law – without bringing God in" – it has ceased to mean "law" at all; and so the notions of "moral obligation," "the moral ought," and "duty" are best put on the Index, if he can manage it.

But meanwhile – is it not clear that there are several concepts that need investigating simply as part of the philosophy of psychology and – as I should recommend – *banishing ethics totally* from our minds? Namely – to begin with: "action," "intention," "pleasure," "wanting." More will probably turn up if we start with these. Eventually it might be possible to advance to considering the concept "virtue"; with which, I suppose, we should be beginning some sort of a study of ethics.

I will end by describing the advantages of using the word "ought" in a non-emphatic fashion, and not in a special "moral" sense; of discarding the term "wrong" in a "moral" sense, and using such notions as "unjust."

It is possible, if one is allowed to proceed just by giving example, to distinguish between the intrinsically unjust, and what is unjust given the circumstances. To arrange to get a man judicially punished for something which it can be clearly seen he has not done is intrinsically unjust. This might be done, of course, and often has been done, in all sorts of ways; by suborning false witnesses, by a rule of law by which something is "deemed" to be the case which is admittedly not the case as a matter of fact, and by open insolence on the part of the judges and powerful people when they more or less openly say: "A fig for the fact that you did not do it; we mean to sentence you for it all the same." What is unjust given, e.g., normal circumstances is to deprive people of their ostensible property without legal procedure, not to pay debts, not to keep contracts, and a host of other things of the kind. Now, the circumstances can clearly make a great deal of difference in estimating the justice or injustice of such procedures as these; and these circumstances may *sometimes* include expected consequences; for example, a man's claim to a bit of property can become a nullity when its seizure and use can avert some obvious disaster: as, e.g., if you could use a machine of his to produce an explosion in which it would be destroyed, but by means of which you could divert a flood or make a gap which a fire could not jump. Now this certainly does not mean that what would ordinarily be an act of injustice, but is not intrinsically unjust, can always be rendered just by a reasonable calculation of better consequences; far from it; but the problems that would be raised in an attempt to draw a boundary line (or boundary area) here are obviously complicated. And while there are certainly some general remarks which ought to be made here, and some boundaries that can be drawn, the decision on particular cases would for the most part be determined κατὰ τὸν ὀρθὸν λόγον "according to what's reasonable." E.g. that *such-and-such* a delay of payment of a *such-and-such* debt to a person *so* circumstanced, on the part of a person *so* circumstanced, would or would not be unjust, is really only to be decided "according to what's reasonable"; and for this there can *in principle*

G. E. M. Anscombe

be no canon other than giving a few examples. That is to say, while it is because of a big gap in philosophy that we can give no general account of the concept of virtue and of the concept of justice, but have to proceed, using the concepts, only by giving examples; still there is an area where it is not because of any gap, but is in principle the case, that there is no account except by way of examples: and that is where the canon is "what's reasonable"; which of course is *not* a canon.

That is all I wish to say about what is just in some circumstances, unjust in others; and about the way in which expected consequences can play a part in determining what is just. Returning to my example of the intrinsically unjust: if a procedure *is* one of judicially punishing a man for what he is clearly understood not to have done, there can be absolutely no argument about the description of this as unjust. No circumstances, and no expected consequences, which do *not* modify the description of the procedure as one of judicially punishing a man for what he is known not to have done can modify the description of it as unjust. Someone who attempted to dispute this would only be pretending not to know what "unjust" means: for this is a paradigm case of injustice.

And here we see the superiority or the term "unjust" over the terms "morally right" and "morally wrong." For in the context of English moral philosophy since Sidgwick it appears legitimate to discuss whether it *might* be "morally right" in some circumstances to adopt that procedure; but it cannot be argued that the procedure would in any circumstances be just.

Now I am not able to do the philosophy involved – and I think that no one in the present situation of English philosophy *can* do the philosophy involved – but it is clear that a good man is a just man; and a just man is a man who habitually refuses to commit or participate in any unjust actions for fear of any consequences, or to obtain any advantage, for himself or anyone else. Perhaps no one will disagree. But, it will be said, what *is* unjust is sometimes determined by expected consequences; and certainly that is true. But there are cases where it is not: now if someone says, "I agree, but all this wants a lot of explaining," then he is right, and, what is more, the situation at present is that we can't do the explaining; we lack the philosophic equipment. But if someone really thinks, *in advance,*[7]

that it is open to question whether such an action as procuring the judicial execution of the innocent should be quite excluded from consideration – I do not want to argue with him; he shows a corrupt mind.

In such cases our moral philosophers seek to impose a dilemma upon us. "If we have a case where the term 'unjust' applies purely in virtue of a factual description, can't one raise the question whether one sometimes conceivably ought to do injustice? If 'what is unjust' is determined by consideration of whether it is *right* to do so-and-so in such-and-such circumstances, then the question whether it is 'right' to commit injustice can't arise, just because 'wrong' has been built into the definition of injustice. But if we have a case where the description 'unjust' applies purely in virtue of the facts, without bringing 'wrong' in, then the question can arise whether one 'ought' perhaps to commit an injustice, whether it might not be 'right' to? And of course 'ought' and 'right' are being used in their *moral* senses here. Now either you must decide what is 'morally right' in the light of certain *other* 'principles,' or you make a 'principle' about *this* and decide that an injustice is never 'right'; but even if you do the latter you are going beyond the facts; you are making a decision that you will not, or that it is wrong to, commit injustice. But in either case, *if* the term 'unjust' is determined simply by the facts, it is not the term 'unjust' that determines that the term 'wrong' applies, but a decision that injustice is *wrong*, together with the diagnosis of the 'factual' description as entailing injustice. But the man who makes an absolute decision that injustice is 'wrong' has no footing on which to criticize someone who does *not* make that decision as judging falsely."

In this argument "wrong" of course is explained as meaning "morally wrong," and all the atmosphere of the term is retained while its substance is guaranteed quite null. Now let us remember that "morally wrong" is the term which is the heir of the notion "illicit," or "what there is an obligation *not* to do"; which belongs in a divine law theory or ethics. Here it really does add something to the description "unjust" to say there is an obligation not to do it; for what obliges is the divine law – as rules oblige in a game. So if the divine law obliges not to commit injustice by forbidding injustice, it really does add something to the description "unjust" to say there is an obligation not to do it. And it is because "morally wrong" is the heir of this concept, but an heir that is cut off from the family of concepts from which it sprang, that "morally wrong" *both* goes beyond the mere factual description "unjust" *and* seems to have no discernible content except a certain compelling force, which I should call purely psychological. And such is the force of the term that philosophers actually suppose that the divine law notion can be dismissed as making no essential difference even if it is held – *because* they think that a "practical principle" running "I *ought* (i.e. am morally obliged) to obey divine laws" is required for the man who believes in divine laws. But actually this notion of obligation is a notion which only operates in the context of law. And I should be inclined to congratulate the present-day moral philosophers on depriving "morally ought" of its now delusive appearance of content, if only they did not manifest a detestable desire to retain the atmosphere of the term.

It may be possible, if we are resolute, to discard the notion "morally ought," and simply return to the ordinary "ought", which, we ought to notice, is such an extremely frequent term of human language that it is difficult to imagine getting on without it. Now if we do return to it, can't it reasonably be asked whether one might ever need to commit injustice, or whether it won't be the best thing to do? Of course it can. And the answers will be various. One man – a philosopher – may say that since justice is a virtue, and injustice a vice, and virtues and vices are built up by the performances of the action in which they are instanced, an act of injustice will tend to make a man bad; and essentially the flourishing of a man *qua* man consists in his being good (e.g. in virtues); but for any X to which such terms apply, X needs what makes it flourish, so a man needs, or ought to perform, only virtuous actions; and even if, as it must be admitted may happen, he flourishes less, or not at all, in inessentials, by avoiding injustice, his life is spoiled in essentials by not avoiding injustice – so he still needs to perform only just actions. That is roughly how Plato and Aristotle talk; but it can be seen that philosophically there is a huge gap, at present unfillable as far as we are concerned, which needs to be filled by an account of human nature, human action, the type of characteristic a virtue is, and above all of human "flourishing." And it is the last concept that appears the most doubtful. For it is a

bit much to swallow that a man in pain and hunger and poor and friendless is "flourishing," as Aristotle himself admitted. Further, someone might say that one at least needed to stay alive to "flourish." Another man unimpressed by all that will say in a hard case "What we need is such-and-such, which we won't get without doing this (which is unjust) – so this is what we ought to do." Another man, who does not follow the rather elaborate reasoning of the philosophers, simply says "I know it is in any case a disgraceful thing to say that one had better commit this unjust action." The man who believes in divine laws will say perhaps "It is forbidden, and however it looks, it cannot be to anyone's profit to commit injustice"; he like the Greek philosophers can think in terms of "flourishing." If he is a Stoic, he is apt to have a decidedly strained notion of what "flourishing consists" in; if he is a Jew or Christian, he need not have any very distinct notion: the way it will profit him to abstain from injustice is something that he leaves it to God to determine, himself only saying "It can't do me any good to go against his law." (But he also hopes for a great reward in a new life later on, e.g. at the coming of Messiah; but in this he is relying on special promises.)

It is left to modern moral philosophy – the moral philosophy of all the well-known English ethicists since Sidgwick – to construct systems according to which the man who says "We need such-and-such, and will only get it this way" *may* be a virtuous character: that is to say, it is left open to debate whether such a procedure as the judicial punishment of the innocent may not in some circumstances be the "right" one to adopt; and though the present Oxford moral philosophers would accord a man *permission* to "make it his principle" not to do such a thing, they teach a philosophy according to which the particular consequences of such an action *could* "morally" be taken into account by a man who was debating what to do; and if they were such as to conflict with his "ends," it might be a step in his moral education to frame a moral principle under which he "managed" (to use Mr Nowell-Smith's phrase[8]) to bring the action; or it might be a new "decision of principle," making which was an advance in the formation of his moral thinking (to adopt Mr Hare's conception), to decide: in such-and-such circumstances one ought to procure the judicial condemnation of the innocent. And that is my complaint.

G. E. M. Anscombe

Notes

1   The above two paragraphs are an abstract of a paper "On Brute Facts" [*Analysis* 18/3 (1958)].
2   They did not deny the existence of divine law; but their most characteristic doctrine was that it was given, not to be obeyed, but to show man's incapacity to obey it, even by grace; and this applied not merely to the ramified prescriptions of the Torah, but to the requirements of "natural divine law." Cf. in this connection the decree of Trent against the teaching that Christ was only to be trusted in as mediator, not obeyed as legislator.
3   As it is absurdly called. Since major premise = premise containing the term which is predicate in the conclusion, it is a solecism to speak of it in the connection with practical reasoning.
4   Oxford Objectivists of course distinguish between "consequences" and "intrinsic values" and so produce a misleading appearance of not being "consequentialists." But they do not hold – and Ross explicitly denies – that the gravity of, e.g., procuring the condemnation of the innocent is such that it cannot be outweighed by, e.g., national interest. Hence their distinction is of no importance.
5   *Nicomachean Ethics* 1178b16.
6   Necessarily a rare case: for the positive precepts, e.g. "Honour your parents," hardly ever prescribe, and seldom even necessitate, any particular action.
7   If he thinks it in the concrete situation, he is of course merely a normally tempted human being. In discussion when this paper was read, as was perhaps to be expected, this case was produced: a government is required to have an innocent man tried, sentenced and executed under threat of a "hydrogen bomb war." It would seem strange to me to have much hope of so averting a war threatened by such men as made this demand. But the most important thing about the way in which cases like this are invented in discussions, is the assumption that only two courses are open: here, compliance and open defiance. No one can say in advance of such a situation what the possibilities are going to be – e.g. that there is none of stalling by a feigned willingness to comply, accompanied by a skilfully arranged "escape" of the victim.
8   *Ethics* (Harmondsworth: Penguin Books, 1954), p. 308.

37

Morality as a System of Hypothetical Imperatives

Philippa Foot

There are many difficulties and obscurities in
Kant's moral philosophy, and few contemporary
moralists will try to defend it all; many, for
instance, agree in rejecting Kant's derivation of
duties from the mere form of law expressed in
terms of a universally legislative will. Nevertheless, it is generally supposed, even by those who
would not dream of calling themselves his followers, that Kant established one thing beyond
doubt – namely, the necessity of distinguishing
moral judgments from hypothetical imperatives.
That moral judgments cannot be hypothetical
imperatives has come to seem an unquestionable
truth. It will be argued here that it is not.

In discussing so thoroughly Kantian a notion
as that of the hypothetical imperative, one naturally begins by asking what Kant himself meant
by a hypothetical imperative, and it may be useful to say a little about the idea of an imperative
as this appears in Kant's works. In writing about
imperatives Kant seems to be thinking at least
as much of statements about what ought to be or
should be done, as of injunctions expressed in
the imperative mood. He even describes as an
imperative the assertion that it would be "good
to do or refrain from doing something"[1] and
explains that for a will that "does not always do
something simply because it is presented to it
as a good thing to do" this has the force of a
command of reason. We may therefore think of

Originally published in *Philosophical Review* 81
(1972). Copyright 1972 Cornell University. Reprinted
by permission of the publisher.

Kant's imperatives as statements to the effect
that something ought to be done or that it would
be good to do it.

The distinction between hypothetical imperatives and categorical imperatives, which plays so
important a part in Kant's ethics, appears in
characteristic form in the following passages from
the *Foundations of the Metaphysics of Morals*:

> All imperatives command either hypothetic-
> ally or categorically. The former present the
> practical necessity of a possible action as a
> means to achieving something else which one
> desires (or which one may possibly desire).
> The categorical imperative would be one which
> presented an action as of itself objectively
> necessary, without regard to any other end.[2]

> If the action is good only as a means to
> something else, the imperative is hypothet-
> ical; but if it is thought of as good in itself,
> and hence as necessary in a will which of
> itself conforms to reason as the principle of
> this will, the imperative is categorical.[3]

The hypothetical imperative, as Kant defines
it, "says only that the action is good to some
purpose" and the purpose, he explains, may be
possible or actual. Among imperatives related to
actual purposes Kant mentions rules of prudence,
since he believes that all men necessarily desire
their own happiness. Without committing ourselves to this view it will be useful to follow Kant
in classing together as "hypothetical imperatives"
those telling a man what he ought to do because

(or if) he wants something and those telling him what he ought to do on grounds of self-interest. Common opinion agrees with Kant in insisting that a moral man must accept a rule of duty whatever his interests or desires.[4]

Having given a rough description of the class of Kantian hypothetical imperatives it may be useful to point to the heterogeneity within it. Sometimes what a man should do depends on his passing inclination, as when he wants his coffee hot and should warm the jug. Sometimes it depends on some long-term project, when the feelings and inclinations of the moment are irrelevant. If one wants to be a respectable philosopher one should get up in the mornings and do some work, though just at that moment when one should do it the thought of being a respectable philosopher leaves one cold. It is true nevertheless to say of one, at that moment, that one wants to be a respectable philosopher,[5] and this can be the foundation of a desire-dependent hypothetical imperative. The term "desire" as used in the original account of the hypothetical imperative was meant as a grammatically convenient substitute for "want," and was not meant to carry any implication of inclination rather than long-term aim or project. Even the word "project," taken strictly, introduces undesirable restrictions. If someone is devoted to his famliy or his country or to any cause, there are certain things he wants, which may then be the basis of hypothetical imperatives, without either inclinations or projects being quite what is in question. Hypothetical imperatives should already be appearing as extremely diverse; a further important distinction is between those that concern an individual and those that concern a group. The desires on which a hypothetical imperative is dependent may be those of one man, or may be taken for granted as belonging to a number of people, engaged in some common project or sharing common aims.

Is Kant right to say that moral judgments are categorical, not hypothetical, imperatives? It may seem that he is, for we find in our language two different uses of words such as "should" and "ought," apparently corresponding to Kant's hypothetical and categorical imperatives, and we find moral judgments on the "categorical" side. Suppose, for instance, we have advised a traveler that he should take a certain train, believing him to be journeying to his home. If we find that he has decided to go elsewhere, we will most likely have to take back what we said: the "should" will now be unsupported and in need of support. Similarly, we must be prepared to withdraw our statement about what he should do if we find that the right relation does not hold between the action and the end – that it is either no way of getting what he wants (or doing what he wants to do) or not the most eligible among possible means. The use of "should" and "ought" in moral contexts is, however, quite different. When we say that a man should do something and intend a moral judgment we do not have to back up what we say by considerations about his interests or his desires; if no such connection can be found the "should" need not be withdrawn. It follows that the agent cannot rebut an assertion about what, morally speaking, he should do by showing that the action is not ancillary to his interests or desires. Without such a connection the "should" does not stand unsupported and in need of support; the support that *it* requires is of another kind.[6]

There is, then, one clear difference between moral judgments and the class of "hypothetical imperatives" so far discussed. In the latter "should" is used "hypothetically," in the sense defined, and if Kant were merely drawing attention to this piece of linguistic usage his point would be easily proved. But obviously Kant meant more than this; in describing moral judgments as non-hypothetical – that is, categorical imperatives – he is ascribing to them a special dignity and necessity which this usage cannot give. Modern philosophers follow Kant in talking, for example, about the "unconditional requirement" expressed in moral judgments. These tell us what we have to do whatever our interests or desires, and by their inescapability they are distinguished from hypothetical imperatives.

The problem is to find proof for this further feature of moral judgments. If anyone fails to see the gap that has to be filled it will be useful to point out to him that we find "should" used non-hypothetically in some non-moral statements to which no one attributes the special dignity and necessity conveyed by the description "categorical imperative." For instance, we find this non-hypothetical use of "should" in sentences enunciating rules of etiquette, as, for example, that an invitation in the third person should be answered in the third person, where the rule does not *fail to apply* to someone who has his own good reasons for ignoring this piece of nonsense, or who simply does not care about what, from the point of view of etiquette, he should do. Similarly, there is a non-hypothetical use of "should" in contexts where something like a club rule is in question. The club secretary who has told a member that he should not bring ladies into the smoking room does not say, "Sorry, I was mistaken" when informed that this member is resigning tomorrow and cares nothing about his reputation in the club. Lacking a connection with the agent's desires or interests, this "should" does not stand "unsupported and in need of support"; it requires only the backing of the rule. The use of "should" is therefore "non-hypothetical" in the sense defined.

It follows that if a hypothetical use of "should" gives a hypothetical imperative, and a non-hypothetical use of "should" a categorical imperative, then "should" statements based on rules of etiquette, or rules of a club, are categorical imperatives. Since this would not be accepted by defenders of the categorical imperative in ethics, who would insist that these other "should" statements give hypothetical imperatives, they must be using this expression in some other sense. We must therefore ask what they mean when they say that "You should answer . . . in the third person" is a hypothetical imperative. Very roughly the idea seems to be that one may reasonably ask why anyone should bother about what should$_e$ (should from the point of view of etiquette) be done, and that such considerations deserve no notice unless reason is shown. So although people give as their reason for doing something the fact that it is required by etiquette, we do not take this consideration as *in itself giving us reason to act*. Considerations of etiquette do not have any automatic reason-giving force, and a man might be right if he denied that he had reason to do "what's done."

This seems to take us to the heart of the matter, for, by contrast, it is supposed that moral considerations necessarily give reasons for acting to any man. The difficulty is, of course, to defend this proposition which is more often repeated than explained. Unless it is said, implausibly, that all "should" or "ought" statements give reasons for acting, which leaves the old problem of assigning a special categorical status to moral judgment, we must be told what it is that makes the moral "should" relevantly different from the "shoulds" appearing in normative statements of other kinds.[7] Attempts have sometimes been made to show that some kind of irrationality is involved

in ignoring the "should" of morality: in saying "Immoral – so what?" as one says "Not *comme il faut* – so what?" But as far as I can see these have all rested on some illegitimate assumption, as, for instance, of thinking that the amoral man, who agrees that some piece of conduct is immoral but takes no notice of that, is inconsistently disregarding a rule of conduct that he has accepted; or again of thinking it inconsistent to desire that others will not do to one what one proposes to do to them. The fact is that the man who rejects morality because he sees no reason to obey its rules can be convicted of villainy but not of inconsistency. Nor will his action necessarily be irrational. Irrational actions are those in which a man in some way defeats his own purposes, doing what is calculated to be disadvantageous or to frustrate his ends. Immorality does not *necessarily* involve any such thing.

It is obvious that the normative character of moral judgment does not guarantee its reason-giving force. Moral judgments are normative, but so are judgments of manners, statements of club rules, and many others. Why should the first provide reasons for acting as the others do not? In every case it is because there is a background of teaching that the non-hypothetical "should" can be used. The behavior is required, not simply recommended, but the question remains as to why we should do what we are required to do. It is true that moral rules are often enforced much more strictly than the rules of etiquette, and our reluctance to press the non-hypothetical "should" of etiquette may be one reason why we think of the rules of etiquette as hypothetical imperatives. But are we then to say that there is nothing behind the idea that moral judgments are categorical imperatives but the relative stringency of our moral teaching? I believe that this may have more to do with the matter than the defenders of the categorical imperative would like to admit. For if we look at the kind of thing that is said in its defense we may find ourselves puzzled about what the words can even mean unless we connect them with the feelings that this stringent teaching implants. People talk, for instance, about the "binding force" of morality, but it is not clear what this means if not that we *feel* ourselves unable to escape. Indeed the "inescapability" of moral requirements is often cited when they are being contrasted with hypothetical imperatives. No one, it is said, escapes the requirements of ethics by having or not having particular interests or desires. Taken in one way this only reiterates the contrast between the "should" of morality and the hypothetical "should," and once more places morality alongside of etiquette. Both are inescapable in that behavior does not cease to offend against either morality or etiquette because the agent is indifferent to their purposes and to the disapproval he will incur by flouting them. But morality is supposed to be inescapable in some special way and this may turn out to be merely the reflection of the way morality is taught. Of course, we must try other ways of expressing the fugitive thought. It may be said, for instance, that moral judgments have a kind of necessity since they tell us what we "must do" or "have to do" whatever our interests and desires. The sense of this is, again, obscure. Sometimes when we use such expressions we are referring to physical or mental compulsion. (A man has to go along if he is pulled by strong men, and he has to give in if tortured beyond endurance.) But it is only in the absence of such conditions that moral judgments apply. Another and more common sense of the words is found in sentences such as "I caught a bad cold and had to stay in bed" where a penalty for acting otherwise is in the offing. The necessity of acting morally is not, however, supposed to depend on such penalties. Another range of examples, not necessarily having to do with penalties, is found where there is an unquestioned acceptance of some project or role, as when a nurse tells us that she has to make her rounds at a certain time, or we say that we have to run for a certain train.[8] But these too are irrelevant in the present context, since the acceptance condition can always be revoked.

No doubt it will be suggested that it is in some other sense of the words "have to" or "must" that one has to or must do what morality demands. But why should one insist that there must be such a sense when it proves so difficult to say what it is? Suppose that what we take for a puzzling thought were really no thought at all but only the reflection of our *feelings* about morality? Perhaps it makes no sense to say that we "have to" submit to the moral law, or that morality is "inescapable" in some special way. For just as one may feel as if one is falling without believing that one is moving downward, so one may feel as if one has to do what is morally required without believing oneself to be under physical or psychological compulsion, or about

to incur a penalty if one does not comply. No one thinks that if the word "falling" is used in a statement reporting one's sensations it must be used in a special sense. But this kind of mistake may be involved in looking for the special sense in which one "has to" do what morality demands. There is no difficulty about the idea that we feel we *have to* behave morally, and given the psychological conditions of the learning of moral behavior it is natural that we should have such feelings. What we cannot do is quote them in support of the doctrine of the categorical imperative. It seems, then, that in so far as it is backed up by statements to the effect that the moral *is* inescapable, or that we *do* have to do what is morally required of us, it is uncertain whether the doctrine of the categorical imperative even makes sense.

The conclusion we should draw is that moral judgments have no better claim to be categorical imperatives than do statements about matters of etiquette. People may indeed follow either morality or etiquette without asking why they should do so, but equally well they may not. They may ask for reasons and may reasonably refuse to follow either if reasons are not to be found.

It will be said that this way of viewing moral considerations must be totally destructive of morality, because no one could ever act morally unless he accepted such considerations as in themselves sufficient reason for action. Actions that are truly moral must be done "for their own sake," "because they are right," and not for some ulterior purpose. This argument we must examine with care, for the doctrine of the categorical imperative has owed much to its persuasion.

Is there anything to be said for the thesis that a truly moral man acts "out of respect for the moral law" or that he does what is morally right because it is morally right? That such propositions are not prima-facie absurd depends on the fact that moral judgment concerns itself with a man's reasons for acting as well as with what he does. Law and etiquette require only that certain things are done or left undone, but no one is counted as charitable if he gives alms "for the praise of men," and one who is honest only because it pays him to be honest does not have the virtue of honesty. This kind of consideration was crucial in shaping Kant's moral philosophy. He many times contrasts acting out of respect for the moral law with acting from an ulterior motive, and what is more from one that is self-interested. In the early *Lectures on Ethics* he gave the principle of truth-telling under a system of hypothetical imperatives as that of not lying *if it harms one* to lie. In the *Metaphysics of Morals* he says that ethics cannot start from the ends which a man may propose to himself, since these are all "selfish."[9] In the *Critique of Practical Reason* he argues explicitly that when acting not out of respect for the moral law but "on a material maxim" men do what they do for the sake of pleasure or happiness.

> All material practical principles are, as such, of one and the same kind and belong under the general principle of self love or one's own happiness.[10]

Kant, in fact, was a psychological hedonist in respect of all actions except those done for the sake of the moral law, and this faulty theory of human nature was one of the things preventing him from seeing that moral virtue might be compatible with the rejection of the categorical imperative.

If we put this theory of human action aside, and allow as ends the things that seem to be ends, the picture changes. It will surely be allowed that quite apart from thoughts of duty a man may care about the suffering of others, having a sense of identification with them, and wanting to help if he can. Of course he must want not the reputation of charity, nor even a gratifying role helping others, but, quite simply, their good. If this is what he does care about, then he will be attached to the end proper to the virtue of charity and a comparison with someone acting from an ulterior motive (even a respectable ulterior motive) is out of place. Nor will the conformity of his action to the rule of charity be merely contingent. Honest action may happen to further a man's career; charitable actions do not *happen* to further the good of others.

Can a man accepting only hypothetical imperatives possess other virtues besides that of charity? Could he be just or honest? This problem is more complex because there is no one end related to such virtues as the good of others is related to charity. But what reason could there be for refusing to call a man a just man if he acted justly because he loved truth and liberty, and wanted every man to be treated with a certain minimum respect? And why should the truly honest man not follow honesty for the sake of the good that honest dealing brings to men? Of course, the usual difficulties can be raised about the rare case in which no good is foreseen from an individual act of honesty. But it is not evident that a man's desires could not give him reason to act honestly even here. He wants to live openly and in good faith with his neighbors; it is not all the same to him to lie and conceal.

If one wants to know whether there could be a truly moral man who accepted moral principles as hypothetical rules of conduct, as many people accept rules of etiquette as hypothetical rules of conduct, one must consider the right kind of example. A man who demanded that morality should be brought under the heading of self-interest would not be a good candidate, nor would anyone who was ready to be charitable or honest only so long as he felt inclined. A cause such as justice makes strenuous demands, but this is not peculiar to morality, and men are prepared to toil to achieve many ends not endorsed by morality. That they are prepared to fight so hard for moral ends – for example, for liberty and justice – depends on the fact that these are the kinds of ends that arouse devotion. To sacrifice a great deal for the sake of etiquette one would need to be under the spell of the emphatic "ought$_e$." One could hardly be devoted to behaving *comme il faut*.

In spite of all that has been urged in favor of the hypothetical imperative in ethics, I am sure that many people will be unconvinced and will argue that one element essential to moral virtue is still missing. This missing feature is the recognition of a *duty* to adopt those ends which we have attributed to the moral man. We have said that he *does* care about others, and about causes such as liberty and justice; that it is on this account that he will accept a system of morality. But what if he never cared about such things, or what if he ceased to care? Is it not the case that he *ought* to care? This is exactly what Kant would say, for though at times he sounds as if he thought that morality is not concerned with ends, at others he insists that the adoption of ends such as the happiness of others is itself dictated by morality.[11] How is this proposition to be regarded by one who rejects all talk about the binding force of the moral law? He will agree that a moral man has moral ends and cannot be indifferent to matters such as suffering and injustice. Further, he will recognize in the statement that one *ought* to care about these things a correct application of the non-hypothetical moral "ought" by which society is apt to voice its demands. He will not, however, take the fact that he ought to have certain ends as in itself reason to adopt them. If he himself is a moral man then he cares about such things, but not "because he ought." If he is an amoral man he may deny that he has any reason to trouble his head over this or any other moral demand. Of course he may be mistaken, and his life as well as others' lives may be most sadly spoiled by his selfishness. But this is not what is urged by those who think they can close the matter by an emphatic use of "ought." My argument is that they are relying on an illusion, as if trying to give the moral "ought" a magic force.[12]

This conclusion may, as I said, appear dangerous and subversive of morality. We are apt to panic at the thought that we ourselves, or other people, might stop caring about the things we do care about, and we feel that the categorical imperative gives us some control over the situation. But it is interesting that the people of Leningrad were not similarly struck by the thought that only the *contingent* fact that other citizens shared their loyalty and devotion to the city stood between them and the Germans during the terrible years of the siege. Perhaps we should be less troubled than we are by fear of defection from the moral cause; perhaps we should even have less reason to fear it if people thought of themselves as volunteers banded together to fight for liberty and justice and against inhumanity and oppression. It is often felt, even if obscurely, that there is an element of deception in the official line about morality. And while some have been persuaded by talk about the authority of the moral law, others have turned away with a sense of distrust.

Notes

1 *Foundations of the Metaphysics of Morals*, sec. II, trans. L. W. Beck (Indianapolis and New York: Bobbs-Merrill, 1969).
2 Ibid.
3 Ibid.
4 According to the position sketched here we have three forms of the hypothetical imperative: "If you want *x* you should do *y*," "Because you want *x* you should do *y*," and "Because *x* is in your interest you should do *y*." For Kant the third would automatically be covered by the second.
5 To say that at that moment one wants to be a respectable philosopher would be another matter. Such a statement requires a special connection between the desire and the moment.
6 I am here going back on something I said in an earlier article ("Moral Beliefs," *Proceedings of the Aristotelian Society* 59, 1958–9) where I thought it necessary to show that virtue must benefit the agent. I believe the rest of the article can stand.
7 To say that moral considerations are *called* reasons is blatantly to ignore the problem.
8 I am grateful to Rogers Albritton for drawing my attention to this interesting use of expressions such as "have to" or "must."
9 Pt. II, Introduction, sec. II.
10 Immanuel Kant, *Critique of Practical Reason*, trans. L. W. Beck (Chicago: University of Chicago Press, 1949), p. 133.
11 See, e.g., *The Metaphysics of Morals*, Pt. II, sec. 30.
12 See G. E. M. Anscombe, "Modern Moral Philosophy," *Philosophy* 33 (1958). My view is different from Miss Anscombe's, but I have learned from her.

So many people have made useful comments on drafts of this article that I despair of thanking them all. Derek Parfit's help has been sustained and invaluable, and special thanks are also due to Barry Stroud.

An earlier version of this paper was read at the Center for Philosophical Exchange, Brockport, NY, and published in *Philosophical Exchange* (Summer 1971).

Further reading in ethics

Broad, C. D., *Five Types of Ethical Theory*, Totowa, NJ: Littlefield, Adams, 1965.

Darwall, Stephen, Gibbard, Allan, and Railton, Peter (eds.) *Moral Theory and Practice*, Oxford: Oxford University Press, 1997.

Foot, Philippa (ed.) *Theories of Ethics*, New York: Oxford University Press, 1967.

Goodin, Robert, and Pettit, Philip (eds.) *A Companion to Contemporary Political Philosophy*, Malden, MA: Blackwell Publishers, 1993.

Hare, R. M., *The Language of Morals*, Oxford: Oxford University Press, 1952; reprinted 1964, 1991.

Rawls, John, *A Theory of Justice*, rev. edn., Cambridge, MA: Harvard University Press, 1999.

Singer, Peter (ed.) *A Companion to Ethics*, Malden, MA: Blackwell Publishers, 1991.

Smart, J. J. C. and Williams, Bernard, *Utilitarianism: For and Against*, Cambridge: Cambridge University Press, 1973.

Stevenson, C. L., *Ethics and Language*, New Haven, CT: Yale University Press, 1944.

PART VII

Methodology

38

The Notion of Analysis in Moore's Philosophy

C. H. Langford

Any examination of Professor Moore's philosophical position would be incomplete without a discussion of his notion of analysis, since, as is well known, this notion plays a decisive role in determining the character of his views. Like other philosophers, Moore has of course used analysis for the purpose of answering philosophical questions and clarifying philosophical ideas. But a man may employ the method of analysis without recognizing that he is doing so, and we must, in any case, distinguish between giving analyses of philosophical ideas and making use of the notion of analysis. When, for example, Moore somewhere tentatively suggests that an action is right if and only if it will be productive of at least as great a balance of good over evil as any other action open to an agent on a given occasion, he is merely suggesting an analysis of right conduct; but when he tells us that the notion of the good is unanalyzable, or again that perceptual judgments are analyzable, he is making use of the notion of analysis.[1]

Perhaps the most important use which Moore makes of this notion is in his defense of the doctrine of common sense, where he is concerned to refute certain opposing views.[2] There is, for example, the view that the common notion of time is self-contradictory, in such a way that no

temporal judgment except a negative one can be wholly true, since nothing can literally happen before, or simultaneously with, or after anything else. Moore holds, if I have understood him correctly, that any argument to the effect that time is unreal must involve some analysis of the notion of time, and that the conclusion of such an argument will itself show this analysis to be incorrect. Possibly some people who have tried to show that time is unreal, by arguing that the notion of time itself entails a contradiction, have been unaware that they were making use of an analysis of this notion; possibly others have been aware of this and have held that the analysis employed was plainly a correct one; but however that may be, it follows from the doctrine of common sense that the conclusion of such an argument must be taken to refute its premises, and one of these premises will be that such and such is a correct analysis of the notion of time.

A somewhat similar example is to be found in another startling view, which has been advanced by some philosophers, to the effect that human beings never do actually see physical things, such as tables, chairs, and trees, despite the fact that they constantly suppose themselves to do so. What people actually see, according to this view, are various sensible appearances; and they systematically confuse these appearances with physical objects. Any one who advances an argument purporting to establish such a view, however, must tell us what it means to see a physical object, must give an analysis of that common notion. Moore would say, I believe, that from the mere fact that, were this proposed analysis correct, nobody could ever have seen a physical thing, it follows that the analysis is actually incorrect. Finally, Professor Moore has said many times over that he can on occasion know a given proposition to be true without at the same time knowing how to give an analysis of that proposition in certain respects. In enunciating this doctrine he is, of course, making use of the notion of analysis.[3]

It is indeed possible to deny that analysis can be a significant philosophical or logical procedure. This is possible, in particular, on the ground of the so-called paradox of analysis, which may be formulated as follows. Let us call what is to be analyzed the analysandum, and let us call that which does the analyzing the analysans. The analysis then states an appropriate relation of equivalence between the analysandum and the analysans. And the paradox of analysis is to the effect that, if the verbal expression representing the analysandum has the same meaning as the verbal expression representing the analysans, the analysis states a bare identity and is trivial; but if the two verbal expressions do not have the same meaning, the analysis is incorrect. One is tempted to say that there must be some appropriate sense of "meaning" in which the two verbal expressions do have the same meaning and some other appropriate sense in which they do not. A view answering to this requirement will be discussed below. But it is possible to argue that having the same meaning does not entail triviality, owing to important grammatical differences between the verbal expressions involved, and a view to this effect will also be considered.

So far as I know, Professor Moore has not attempted to apply his method of analysis to the notion of analysis itself. He has made remarks concerning this notion which serve to clarify it in certain respects, especially in his discussion of indefinability in *Principia Ethica*,[4] but he had not, I believe, attempted to examine systematically the question what relation it is that must hold between an analysandum and an analysans is order that the latter should correctly analyze the former. On his own view, it is not necessary that he should do this. But the important part played by the notion of analysis in his philosophical position makes it nevertheless desirable. I am therefore going to proceed in the following way. I am going to present two views of the nature of analysis, to be called the first and the second view, in the order of their presentation. I am going to do this in connection with a series of examples, some of which are designed merely for illustrative purposes and others of which have a degree of intrinsic importance. The purpose of this procedure is twofold. I want first of all to induce Professor Moore to state more explicitly his own position regarding the nature of analysis, and I want also to ask, in the case of each of the two views, whether the analysis of the notion of analysis suggested tends to support those doctrines in the expression of which Professor Moore makes use of this notion. Any analysis of the notion of analysis must of course be self-applicable, and the question whether a given view adequately characterizes itself will be an important question concerning its correctness.

We may first direct attention to a remarkable and important characteristic of language. There are, in the English language, sentences which have never been used, and some of these will be uttered and immediately understood tomorrow for the first time. There are, similarly, descriptive phrases, such as "the tallest mountain in the state of Virginia," which we understand without instruction and which we ourselves employ without hesitation on the first occasion of their use. If it were not for this property of language, we should find it impossible either to convey new information or to record new observations. A language in which the meaning of each sentence had to be independently specified would be a mere collection of idioms, and any assertion that was intelligible would be trite. There are, indeed, in any natural language sentences whose meanings have to be independently specified. "It looks like rain" is such an English sentence, unless we use it in reference to a waterfall or to rain that is actually falling. It is not, of course, that the sentence "It looks like rain" cannot be used to express many different judgments; on different occasions of its use, this sentence, like a standard one, will express judgments varying in their indexical elements, such as time, place, and the like; but it differs in principle from a standard sentence in that its meaning cannot be derived from the meanings of its component parts. There are also English sentences which are quasi-idiomatic in character. Why, for example, should we be told, "All that glitters is not gold," which ought to mean, according to standard grammatical principles, that all things that glitter are not gold, but actually means, according to idiomatic usage, that some things that glitter are not gold? Why, again, is the assertion "It has not stopped raining" false if made on a sunny day? And why is it that the statement "I haven't seen him recently" does not entail "I haven't seen him sober recently"? Such sentences would be misinterpreted by a foreigner who was making use of his dictionary and grammar book.

The distinction between a phrase or sentence which can be understood on the first occasion of its use and one which cannot has long been employed by linguists to distinguish a standard expression from an idiom. I am going to borrow this term "idiom" for my present purposes, and I am going to proceed immediately to misuse it in two ways. First, an idiomatic expression looks as if it had a grammatical form. This is a pointless restriction for my purposes, and I propose to call a single word an idiom if only it is such as could not be understood on the first occasion of its use and is not an abbreviation or a contraction of a verbal expression which could be. In the second place, I am not going to be at all careful to refer only to verbal expressions as idioms. A verbal expression is idiomatic in virtue of an idea which it expresses, and I am going to say that an idea is idiomatic if it has been formed, not with the aid of grammar, but by cognitive contact with objects to which it applies, or, in other words, if it has been ostensively defined.

Charles Peirce has called a concept a conscious habit. In so doing, he presumably meant to hold that a concept was the power to recognize objects as being or not being of a certain sort, and that this power was developed through experience of objects of the kind in question as well as of other objects. Such a characterization seems unobjectionable, and indeed instructive, when applied to ostensively defined ideas or idioms; but it does not apply to an idea like that expressed by "the tallest mountain in Virginia." This latter may be thought of as a resultant or function of several conscious habits, but it is not itself a habit in any sense at all. Let us consider, however, an idea which is idiomatic and which therefore might properly be called a conscious habit. When we ask in English, "Does A know the meaning of the word chair?" we commonly intend to ask, "Does A know that the word chair means such-and-such?" Yet one might play upon an ambiguity here and reply, "Yes, A knows the meaning of the word chair, because he knows the meaning of the word *Stuhl* and these are the

same, although he speaks no English." But if A had been deaf and dumb from birth and had yet had good vision and the like, might he not in this sense know the meaning of the word chair? In other words, might he not know what a chair *is*? I suppose that to know what a chair *is* is to know how to recognize chairs, how to discriminate them from other objects and from one another, in short, to know how to form the class of chairs. We may therefore say that A knows what a chair is if he has formed a certain conscious habit of recognition.

The first view that I am going to suggest concerning the nature of analysis can now be adumbrated. Suppose that we have before us an analysis of a single idiomatic idea. Then, in passing from the analysandum to the analysans, we shall observe that there is, in some sense or other, a decrease in idiomatic content. The analysans will be more articulate than the analysandum; it will be a grammatical function of more than one idea. One who uses the verbal expression representing the analysandum will mention objects of a certain class; one who uses the verbal expression representing the analysans will mention these same objects, but will mention them descriptively by reference to other kinds of objects. The two verbal expressions will therefore not be synonymous; but the analysandum and the analysans will be cognitively equivalent in some appropriate sense.

Suppose that we are trying to teach a child by an ostensive procedure what a square object is, or, in other words, that we are trying to teach him how to form the class of square objects. We may present to him a great variety of things, some of which we designate as square and others as not square, in the hope that he will catch on and be able to proceed on his own initiative. It is, I imagine, possible to develop a high degree of discrimination by such a procedure, and we may suppose this to have been accomplished. Then, on each occasion on which the child recognizes an object as being square, there will be something else that is true: it will always also be true that the object in question has *four* sides. But we must not hastily conclude that he will recognize or be able to recognize this fact. For to recognize that a square has four sides requires knowing what the number four *is*, and this is tantamount to knowing how to form the class of quadruples. In order that a child should know what the number four is, it is necessary that he should be able to know such things as: the sides of a square, the legs of a dog, the wheels of an automobile, and the noises *one, two, three, four,* are alike in being quadruples. It would hardly be plausible to maintain that the ability to effect such comparisons is involved in the ability to discriminate objects which are square from those which are not. Yet that an object have four sides will be a necessary condition that it be recognized as being square. And we may therefore conclude that a fact can be causally effective in recognition even though it is not itself recognized.

Perhaps the simplicity of this example makes it less suitable for illustrative purposes than a somewhat more complicated example. The reader will know how to recognize a cubical object, such as a die, a cube of sugar, or a cubical container. Let him then answer immediately the question: How many edges has a cube? In order to recognize an object as being a cube, it is not necessary to form the class of its edges and compare this class in respect of number with other classes; it is not necessary to know, for example, that the edges of a cube are, in a certain respect, apostolic, that a cube is related to the Apostles in that both they and its edges are twelve. And if a person does not happen to know how many edges a cube has, but proceeds to find out by counting, then having twelve edges can be no part of his notion of what a cube is, since, if it were, he would then not know what it was the edges of which he was counting. Such a person will recognize an object as being cubical, however, only if it has twelve edges in point of fact. I am trying to maintain that the property of being a cube is not a truth-function or any other logical function of the property of having twelve edges.

Before we go on to examine further examples of analysis, I think I had better clear up three points which, if left in abeyance, would very likely cause confusion. I have spoken above as if, given an idiom to be analyzed, an appropriate analysans would be a function exclusively of other idioms. But in fact I wish to allow the analysans to be a function of the analysandum as well. This is because I wish to say that when we point out that being a cube entails having twelve edges, we have given an analysis of this notion, in the sense that we have explicated it in a certain respect, and yet, of course, having twelve edges cannot stand to being a cube in the relation of analysans to analysandum as explained above. I

am therefore going to make use of the triviality that P implies Q if and only if P is equivalent to $P \& Q$ in order to be able to say that "X is a cube if and only if X is a cube with twelve edges" is an analysis of the notion of being a cube. When the analysans is not a function of the analysandum, we may say that the analysis *removes* an idiom, and when it is a function of the analysandum, we may say that the analysis *mitigates* an idiom. This way of putting the matter is of course formally arbitrary and without theoretical significance; it serves merely to enable us to maintain a more uniform terminology than would otherwise be possible. To be sure, the purpose of an analysis is often that of superseding an idiom by a merely verbal definition in terms of the analysans, and this cannot be accomplished if the analysans is a function of the analysandum. A moralist, for example, may wish to give an analysis of the notion of telling a lie; he may say: "A man is telling a lie if and only if he is asserting a proposition with a view to inducing a hearer to judge that he, the speaker, believes the proposition when in fact he does not believe it or positively disbelieves it." Having given this analysis, however, the moralist may thereupon lose interest in the analysandum and propose to use the words "telling a lie" as short for the verbal expression representing the analysans, although it will not have been a verbal definition that was initially in question, as can be seen from the fact that a common notion controlled the choice of the analysans. Perhaps one reason why we so frequently speak of giving a definition of a common idea, rather than of giving an analysis of it, is that we so often wish to allow the analysans to supersede the analysandum in this way. It must be recognized, however, that this is possible only when an analysis removes an idiom, and not merely mitigates one.

A question also arises concerning the proper way in which to formulate an analysis on the present view. I propose often to use the causal mode of speech: "Anything that was a cube would be a cube with twelve edges and conversely." This serves to obviate the plainly false presumption that the equivalence in question is merely material; and I think that the causal mode is not incompatible with a stronger relation, that "would be" is not incompatible with "would necessarily be." Moreover, although anything that was a cube with twelve edges would necessarily be a cube, I am not at all sure that the converse relation is anything stronger than a causal one. For the most obvious objection to such a view does not appear to be conclusive. It is, namely, that when a property P causally entails a property Q, we know very well what an object would be like which had P but not Q, whereas the notion of finding a cube without twelve edges is not an intelligible expectation. But the view is that the causal connection in question determines our conscious habits of recognition, and it is not to be expected that we should be able to frame an idea contrary to a principle which governs the process of conceiving itself. This is all very feeble, and I shall not refer to it again; but it forms part of my excuses for adopting the causal mode of speech.

Finally, I have allowed myself throughout a certain falsifying idealization, in that I have not taken account of the phenomenon of vagueness, but have spoken as if the several ideas which occur in an analysis were quite precise. This is of course not the case; indeed, when it is the purpose of an analysis to issue in a definition, the motive is usually that of supplanting a relatively vague idea by a more precise one. Consider a layman's notion of an isosceles triangle. He will perhaps be able to classify triangles as isosceles or not isosceles with considerable facility; but we may suppose that when he is presented with an equilateral triangle, he is simply baffled and does not know what to say. This will reveal a point of vagueness in his idea, and I think we must allow that "having at least two equal sides" and "having exactly two equal sides" are both correct analyses of this vague idea.[5] It actually often happens that the question whether an analysis is or is not strictly correct is unimportant. Consider, for example, the definition of a lie just given, as a proposition knowingly so expressed as to induce a hearer to judge that the speaker believes the proposition when in fact he does not believe it or positively disbelieves it. One might object that this allows a speaker to be lying and at the same time speaking the truth, if only he is himself in ignorance of the fact; or one might object that a man must positively disbelieve what he asserts in order to be lying. But so soon as all the different things that might be meant can be clearly set out, what is actually meant on a given occasion becomes irrelevant. This circumstance has, I believe, caused some people to fail to see the importance of analysis. It is true that no mathematician cares much nowadays about New-

ton's notion of an integral, because more powerful ideas are available. But one who is interested in the foundations of mathematics will be very much interested in the common notion of a natural number, because no satisfactory analysis of this idea exists. Or consider the important class of causal propositions. The statement "Everyone who has attempted to swim this stream has succeeded, but if I had tried I should have failed" is self-consistent, because the first clause expresses a merely factual universal; whereas "Any good swimmer who had tried to swim this stream would have succeeded, but had I been a good swimmer and had I tried I should have failed" is self-contradictory, because this statement is causal throughout. Some logicians arbitrarily construe causal propositions merely as universals of fact, and thereupon translate them into a truth-function formalism. Contrary to all appearances, they may be right; but until some one produces a convincing analysis of these propositions, we shall simply not know what our logic is adequate to.

I want to consider one further simple example of analysis, before going on to a more substantial illustration. In some boxes of children's colored crayons, there is no crayon which is labeled Orange, but instead there is a crayon called Red-Yellow. I suppose that the manufacturers have here provided us with an analysis of a common idiom, which we might express on the present view by saying: "Anything that was orange would be intermediate in color between red and yellow, and conversely." Possibly the converse is dogmatic, but part of the example will survive even if it is disallowed. We may suppose a person who has lived always in a world plentifully supplied with objects orange in color, but who has never seen anything either red or yellow. He will be unable to understand the analysis here suggested, and this will not be due merely to a defect in vocabulary. Yet such a person would not recognize an object as being orange in color unless it was a fact, which he would be unable to recognize, that the object in question possessed a color which was intermediate between red and yellow. We may suppose, further, a second person, who has seen all his life things that were red and yellow, but has never observed anything orange in color. Will it be possible to define for him the term orange so that he will be able to recognize objects to which the term is applicable when they are presented to him? It is to be emphasized that there is no requirement that he be able to imagine beforehand what an object orange in color would be like; people with poor visual imagery cannot do this whatever their experiences of color may have been. The requirement is merely that he be able to distinguish objects as answering or not answering to the definition; and we may suppose this to be possible, as it appears to be. Then there is a sense in which the expressions "being orange" and "being intermediate in color between red and yellow" do not have the same meaning, and there is another sense in which these expressions do have the same meaning. They have the same meaning in the sense that they mean the same things and yet, as Moore has on occasion put the matter, it is no accident that they do, as it would be if the terms red and round happened to apply to exactly the same objects. The sense in question is therefore stronger than that of having the same denotation and is yet not so strong that the two verbal expressions can be said to be synonymous.

It seems desirable not to confine attention to trivial instances of analysis, but to consider examples which have a degree of intrinsic importance as well. It is difficult to find illustrations of this kind which can be presented briefly, but perhaps the example I have chosen will not prove too tiresome.

Let us consider the notion of a command, and that of an imperative sentence which is employed in giving a command. It is sometimes stated in textbooks on logic that to give a command is not to express anything true or false, that imperative sentences do not express propositions. In contrast to such a view, I am going to try to show that giving a command involves expressing a proposition, or, in other words, that the sense of an imperative sentence is indistinguishable from that of the corresponding indicative sentence. If this can be shown, then, according to the theory of analysis we are considering, the idiomatic content of the notion of giving a command will have been mitigated.[6]

Everyone will recognize that there is a loose sense of "meaning" in which an imperative sentence and the indicative sentence corresponding to it do not have the same meaning. This is the sense in which the question "Is it raining?" and the assertion "It is raining" do not have the same meaning. If I use the first of these sentences, that means that I want to know whether or not it is raining, whereas if I use the second, that means that I think it is. But of course neither of the sentences states anything about one who uses it, and a speaker who does so is not talking about himself. Nevertheless, when in ordinary circumstances I use the indicative sentence "It is raining," I intend one to whom I am speaking to judge from my linguistic behavior that I believe what I say and am not considering it as a question or as an hypothesis. We may call what a man does not state, but intends his linguistic behavior to signify, his pragmatical meaning, and we may distinguish this from the sense of his words, which is the proposition expressed by them.[7] Although the distinction here in question is a familiar one, and has often been drawn,[8] I want to cite an example which is due to A. M. MacIver and which is worth repeating on its own account.[9] Suppose someone to remark: "He thinks that he has been to Grantchester but he has not." The person referred to may entertain this proposition as an hypothesis. But suppose he actually asserts the proposition: "I think that I have been to Grantchester but I have not." This sounds self-contradictory, and the reason is that he will actually be saying that he thinks he has been to Grantchester, whereas the but-clause in the indicative mood will signify or mean pragmatically that he does not think so.[10]

Consider, then, a command of the form "John, close the door," and suppose this command actually to be given on a certain occasion. Suppose, further, that on the same occasion some one remarks: "He will close the door." When we consider what observations would determine whether or not this command was obeyed and what observations would determine whether or not the corresponding prediction was true, we see that these are indistinguishable, and that in fact the two sentences have the same sense, or express the same idea, namely, that of John's closing the door. To be sure, if John did not close the door, we should say that the person who made the prediction had been in error, but should not say this of the person who gave the command. That, however, is because the indicative mood signifies that the speaker believes what he expresses, whereas the imperative mood does not, and we must distinguish between error, which pertains to beliefs, and falsehood, which pertains to propositions. Now the sense of an indicative sentence is a proposition, and therefore the sense of an imperative sentence is a proposition. Hence, to give a command is to express a proposition.

It may be plausibly argued on the present view that most English-speaking people do not know what a proposition is. And this does not mean merely that they use no word which is synonymous with the word proposition. It means also that they have never compared objects with one another in respect of the fact that they are propositions and have never distinguished such objects from others. Of course English-speaking people know very well what an assertion is and what a command is; they know also what it is to express hope or fear, as in "I hope that you will have lunch with me" or "I am afraid that it will rain"; and all these require the use of propositions. But on the present view it does not follow that because making an assertion, giving a command, and expressing a hope, all involve the use of propositions, one who knows what assertions, commands, and hopes are knows also what a proposition is. It follows only that anything which did not involve the use of a proposition would not be recognized as an assertion, a command, or the expression of a hope.[11]

The foregoing interpretation of the nature of analysis probably cannot be true. Yet it quite possibly correctly characterizes a good many examples of analysis which might be cited; and I want to ask how this interpretation bears upon Moore's doctrine about analysis in its relation to judgments of common sense. According to the doctrine in question, common-sense judgments are never systematically in error, but only inadvertently so. We may on occasion judge an object to have a certain color when in fact it does not have that color; there are ways of checking such errors and explaining how they arise. But we must not allow the paradoxes of perception to lead us to the view that we are in error all day long in supposing objects to have this or that color, or indeed any color at all. We may construe common-sense judgments in surprising ways, but our interpretations must show how these judgments can be true, not that they cannot be true. A phenomenalist interpretation of judgments of perception, for example, might seem surprising to a common-sense person, just as the definition of a cardinal number as a class of similar classes might seem surprising to a working mathematician, but this would not show these proposed analyses to be incorrect. On the view of analysis we are considering, this is understandable; for it is not held that the analysandum and the analysans must be identical in a correct

analysis, but only that they must be equivalent in the sense of having the same truth-conditions. The view has it that there are two species of entailing, one synthetic and the other analytic. In either case, if P entails Q, the truth-conditions of Q will be among those of P; but if the relation is synthetic, the observations involved in verifying Q will not be among those involved in verifying P. In certifying in the ordinary way that an object is a cube, we do not certify anything from which it can be shown by formal deduction that the object in question has twelve edges. In other words, "X is not a cube or X has twelve edges" is not a truth-value tautology.

We come now to examples of analysis which apparently do not conform to the foregoing theory. And we may, as before, consider a trivial example to begin with. It will be admitted that since an elephant is an animal, a grey elephant is a grey animal. But it will hardly be admitted that, since an elephant is an animal, a small elephant is a small animal. This very mild paradox, which could hardly puzzle anyone, arises in the following way. Consider how we may proceed to verify a statement of the form "X is a grey animal": we may first observe that X is grey and then observe that X is an animal. But the sentence "X is a small animal" has the same grammatical form, and we are therefore tempted to suppose that the verification of the proposition expressed will be similar: that we may first observe that X is small and then observe that X is an animal; whereas the actual procedure is of course to observe that X is an animal and is also smaller than animals generally are. It is a requirement of good syntax that propositions whose verifications are not analogous should not be symbolized by analogous sentences, because it is with the aid of grammatical analogies that we are able to understand new sentences.

Now if the two verbal expressions "X is a small Y" and "X is a Y and is smaller than most Y's" really are synonymous, as they appear to be, and if we have here given an analysis, then the proposition "Anything that was a small Y would be a Y smaller than most Y's and conversely" cannot express that analysis; for since, by hypothesis, the two verbal expressions are synonymous, this proposition will be indistinguishable from "Anything that was a small Y would be a small Y and conversely," which is certainly not an analysis. Nor can we express the analysis by saying that the expression "X is a small Y" means that X is a Y which is smaller than most Y's, because this again will be indistinguishable from saying that the expression "X is a small Y" means that X is a small Y. We shall apparently have to put the analysis in the form: "X is a small Y" means what is meant by "X is a Y and is smaller than most Y's." Both the analysandum and the analysans will then be verbal expressions, not concepts or propositions as before, and the analysis will be to the effect that the two verbal expressions are synonymous. This might be called a logical analysis, because it construes the meaning of a sentence as identical with that of the conjunction of two other sentences. And note that a statement of the form "Either X is not a small Y or X is smaller than most Y's" will be a truth-value tautology even though it is not explicitly so represented.

We may consider next an almost equally simple example, which nevertheless has been of some importance historically. In regard to A-propositions of the traditional logic, English-speaking people commonly speak Aristotelian, and not Boolean. That is to say, an English-speaking person who wishes to tell the truth does not make a statement of the form "All A's are B's" unless he is convinced that there are A's. If this were not so, then to the question "Are all your brothers older than you?" the answer "Yes, I have no brothers" would sound normal, as it would to one who spoke Boolean. Consider, moreover, how we go about verifying such a proposition. Suppose that you are looking into a room in such way that you cannot see the whole room, but can see a number of people seated there and cannot see anyone who is standing or otherwise disposed. Even if it is in fact the case that you are seeing all the people in the room, you will not be seeing that you are seeing them all, and you will not be prepared to assert "Everyone in that room is seated"; it will still be necessary to make sure that there is no one there whom you are not seeing and who is not seated. We can easily convince ourselves from such examples that a sentence of the form "All A's are B's" means what is meant by "There are A's and there are no A's that are not B's." This is typical of many instances of logical analysis, and the point about it is that the two sentences involved seem to have precisely the same meaning; in verifying a statement of the form "All A's are B's" we seem always to verify both that A's exist and that A's which are not B's do not exist.

The view which these examples suggest is that an analysis is a translation, although not of course just any translation, but one satisfying a further requirement. This further requirement concerns the adequacy of the analysans in contrast to the analysandum as an expression of what is meant; and I think we may still maintain that it is sufficient to have the analysans less idiomatic than the analysandum, but this time in a grammatical sense, and not in the sense in which an idea may be said to be idiomatic when it is ostensively defined. There is, for example, a pretty clear sense in which "There are A's and no A's are not B's" is less idiomatic than "All A's are B's." One who had never heard a sentence of the form "All A's are B's" could not understand such a sentence; but one who had learned the meaning of "and" from other contexts could construct the meaning of a sentence of the form "There are A's and no A's are not B's" out of the meanings of its component parts.

This view of analysis is, I believe, one which has been suggested on occasion by Professor Moore. And since it seems on the face of it less favorable to his doctrine about analysis in its relation to judgments of common sense than the other view here presented, we must ask how the distinction between knowing a statement to be true and knowing an analysis of that statement may be justified, even if all analysis is, as we are now supposing, logical analysis, the difficulty being that if the analysandum and the analysans have the same meaning, the analysis will apparently be trivial.

It is to be noted that to say we know the meaning of a sentence or other verbal expression is to say something about a power or capacity, and not something about an actual process of knowing. To know the meaning of a sentence is to know how to use that sentence whenever an occasion for its use arises, and it need not be immediately obvious that two verbal expressions have the same meaning if it is true that they do have. Although it is correct to say that we know what a sentence means if we know what states of affairs would answer to its meaning and what ones would not, it is incorrect to say that we fully realize what a sentence means when we observe that some given state of affairs does answer to its meaning. If, for example, upon finding yourself in a certain room, you make the judgment "All books in this room are on that shelf," and if you observe that there are some thirty books on the shelf and none anywhere else, you will have observed one particular sufficient condition of the truth of what you judge; but you will not have observed thereby that, had there been just three books on the shelf, your judgment might have been equally true. If, on the other hand, you had seen a half-dozen books lying on a table in the room, you would have observed a particular sufficient condition of the falsity of your judgment, but you would not have observed in so doing that, had the room been wholly devoid of books, your judgment would have been equally false. The meaning of a sentence is revealed discursively in a variety of situations, and it is for this reason that a good notation with a standard syntax is all but indispensable for logical purposes.

Let us consider an example of two notational conventions where one notation is less idiomatic than the other in a certain respect. We find among natural languages two devices for indicating the roles ascribed to the several terms mentioned in a relational statement. Thus in English, in order to say that one person a sees another b, we mention a first to indicate that he plays the role of the observer and b second to indicate that he plays the role of the observed. We employ, that is to say, a convention concerning the order in which terms are to be mentioned. In an inflected language, on the other hand, such a convention is unnecessary, the roles of the several terms being distinguished by inflection of their names. And even in English "He saw me and him saw I" is intelligible and adequate, despite its want of grace and beauty. Thus, in effect, we write in English Sab to say that a and b stand in the relation of seeing with a as the observer and b the observed. Sometimes, however, we want to assign more than one role to a single term, as when we want to say that a sees himself, and then we write in effect Saa, mentioning a twice over to indicate that he plays both roles. But we might just as well follow the pattern of inflected languages and make use of subscripts attached to the names of the several terms. Thus we might write Sa_1b_2 to say that a sees b, Sa_2b_1 to say that b sees a, and Sa_1a_2 to say that a sees himself. It might seem, moreover, as if these two notational devices had the same power of expression; but this is not the case. For it happens not only that one and the same term may play more than one role in a relational complex, but also that one and the same role may be played by more than one term. Let Mab represent that relation which

holds between a and b in virtue of the fact that they are both members of the class of men. Then to write "Mab and Mba" is to say the same thing twice, because verifying that a and b are men is indistinguishable from verifying that b and a are men; to mention a term either in the first place or in the second is to ascribe to it the role of a co-member in the class of men. Or let Icd mean that c and d are intersecting lines. Then since no conceivable observation could certify either Icd or Idc without certifying both, these expressions are synonymous. This is a good example of a bad notation, because Icd and Idc look like Sab and Sba, which are importantly different in meaning. But just as we write Sa_1a_2 to indicate that one and the same term plays each of two roles, so we may write Ic_1d_1 to indicate that two terms play one and the same role. In a language employing order of mention, however, this property of relations must remain unsymbolized, simply because we cannot repeat a position as we can a subscript. Thus there will be a difference in meaning without a corresponding difference in notation, and that is characteristic of idiomatic expressions.

Considerations like these tend to show that logical analysis is not trivial, even though the analysandum and the analysans have precisely the same meaning. It seems clear also that the first view considered above, to the effect that all analysis pertains to ideas and not to verbal expressions, cannot be true; although it does not follow that there is no such thing as conceptual analysis in the sense there described. It may well be that both sorts of analysis occur, as they appear to do; indeed, I shall presently try to show that Moore is committed in *Principia Ethica* to exactly this view. But the question I am now concerned with is this. If all analysis is formal in the sense of the second view, what bearing does this have on Moore's doctrine about the relation of analysis to judgments of common sense? It follows, I think, that the analysans in a correct analysis must not be too Pickwickian, as some people have held the Frege–Russell definition of a cardinal number to be. That the analysandum and the analysans have the same meaning need not be at all obvious, but it cannot be just obvious that they do not. It follows, further, that analysis can do no more than clarify judgments of common sense by expressing them precisely; and it is therefore difficult to see how there can be any ideas which are peculiar to philosophy or to logic. For these reasons, I think that the distinction between knowing a statement to be true and knowing an analysis of that statement will be a more significant distinction if giving an analysis does not always consist in translating one verbal expression into another, but sometimes consists in passing from one idea or complex of ideas to another.

I want, finally, to examine what Professor Moore has to say about analysis in his discussion in *Principia Ethica*, and to suggest that what he there tells us implies a view to the effect that there are two kinds of analysis, one conceptual and the other formal, in the sense of the two views here considered.[12] He says, in the first place, that the notion of the good is indefinable, because it is simple, like the color yellow. And, clearly, being indefinable entails being unanalyzable, as he himself explicitly states.[13] He therefore commits himself to saying that the notion of the good is not a function of other ideas, and is thus formally unanalyzable in the sense of the second view described above. But he then goes on immediately to explain that, although the notion of the good cannot be defined, the good itself, which is what answers to this notion, in his opinion can be, and that if it cannot, his enterprise will be pointless. Such an assertion is puzzling when taken alone, but what he means seems reasonably clear from the context. He tells us that he hopes to find characteristics which belong to everything that is good, and even char-

acteristics which belong to an object if and only if it is good. Suppose, then, that pleasantness is a characteristic of such a sort that we can say: "Being intrinsically good implies being pleasant." This sounds like saying: "Being a cube implies having twelve edges" or "Being orange implies being intermediate in color between red and yellow." The implication in question could hardly be merely material because, if it were, although the proposition might be true in fact, we should have no way of knowing this, and Moore hopes to discover some propositions like this one to be true. On the other hand, the proposition could hardly be a truth-value tautology because, if it were, not only the good but the notion of the good would be analyzable. Yet, since the implication will not be merely material, we shall be able to say in some sense: "Anything that was intrinsically good would be pleasant." The only question remaining is whether this will be a synthetic a priori proposition or will be merely causal in the sense of a scientific law. From what Moore tells us concerning the intuitive character of facts about the good, as contrasted with the empirical character of facts about right conduct, I think we may conclude that the proposition will be a priori.[14] The reason why Moore is able to speak as if all analysis were formal, in the sense of the second view, is that he has spoken equivocally of defining an idea and defining an object, as if these were definable in the same sense.

Notes

1 *See Principia Ethica* (Cambridge: Cambridge University Press, 1903), p. 37, and *Philosophical Studies* (London: Kegan Paul, Trench, Trubner; New York: Harcourt Brace, 1922), pp. 220ff.

2 "A Defence of Common Sense," in *Contemporary British Philosophy*, 2nd series (London: George Allen & Unwin, 1924; 2nd edn., 1953), pp. 193–223, and see also "The Conception of Reality," reprinted in *Philosophical Studies*, pp. 197–219.

3 Thus: "I am not at all sceptical as to the *truth* of such propositions as 'The earth has existed for many years past', 'Many human bodies have each lived for many years upon it', i.e., propositions which assert the existence of material things: on the contrary, I hold that we all know, with certainty, many such propositions to be true. But I am very sceptical as to what, in certain respects, the correct *analysis* of such propositions is." ("A Defence of Common Sense," p. 216)

4 Sections 6–13 and *passim*.

5 We must guard against an error of conventionalism at this point, which consists in saying that the person in question has not made up his mind whether to call an equilateral triangle isosceles or not, as if it were a matter for decision in a particular case. It is the purpose of a general idea, to effect decisions beforehand, and anybody who clearly means "having at least two equal sides" or clearly means "having exactly two equal sides" has already determined the answer to the question whether or not an equilateral triangle is isosceles, even if he has never thought of such a triangle and never will. It is, moreover, not a significant procedure in classification to group objects together merely in virtue of the fact that they are to be designated by the same word, after the fashion of a pun.

6 Max Black has argued that to give a command is to express an ordinary contingent proposition, with

a view to showing that necessary propositions cannot be construed as imperatives. See *Analysis* 4 (1936–7), pp. 28–32, and a review in *The Journal of Symbolic Logic* 3 (1938), pp. 92–3.

7   This term has been used by Charles Morris in the same or a similar sense.

8   It has been drawn by Moore in his *Ethics* (London: Williams & Norgate; New York: H. Holt, 1912), p. 125.

9   See *Analysis* 5 (1937–8), pp. 43–50, and *The Journal of Symbolic Logic* 3 (1938), p. 158.

10 The course of Moore's argument in "A Defence of Common Sense" will be clearer if this distinction between formal and pragmatical contradiction is carefully observed. For in saying that certain philosophers contradict themselves when they assert, in effect, "There have been many other human beings beside myself, and none of them, including myself, has ever known of the existence of other human beings," Moore is not holding that a formal contradiction can be derived from the sense of these words, but only that the pragmatical meaning of such an assertion is incompatible with its literal meaning.

11 In a sentence such as "I hope that you will have lunch with me," it is the that-clause which expresses the hope and the whole sentence which states that what the that-clause expresses is a hope. Commands, also, are sometimes put in this form, as in "I command that you close the door," and confusion will arise if we fail to observe that the whole sentence in such a case does not express a command, but rather states that what the that-clause expresses is a command. It is true that there is a current dogma according to which that-clauses do not express propositions at all, but rather function as exhibits or names of themselves, just as in the question "How do you spell Ann Arbor?" mention is made of a word and not a city. The motive which gives rise to this curious view is as follows. If that-clauses express propositions, these propositions will almost always have non-extensional occurrences, and the desire is that all functions of propositions should be truth-functions. The view, however, is easily false and may be disregarded. Consider, for example, the statement "The ancients believed that the earth was flat but it was not," and note that the but-clause has an extensional occurrence, whereas the that-clause has a non-extensional occurrence. If, now, the that-clause is construed as not expressing a proposition, then up to the but-clause the earth has not been mentioned, and it becomes unintelligible what the "it" of the but-clause refers to and what it was that was not what. Let us speak more virtuously, according to the view in question, and give the that-clause a name; let us call it Henry. Then: "The ancients believed Henry but it wasn't."

12 See especially sections 6–10 of *Principia Ethica*.

13 Ibid., p. 17.

14 Ibid., pp. 142ff.

39

Reply to Langford

G. E. Moore

I cannot possibly do justice to Mr. Langford's essay. He seems to me to raise an immense number of very puzzling questions which deserve examination; but my time is very limited, and on many of those questions I do not at all know what to say. All I can try to do is "to state more explicitly my own position regarding the nature of analysis," which is what Mr. Langford (p. 404) says that he wanted to induce me to do; and even here I shall not be able to do more than to try to make clear some comparatively simple points.

I think that what Mr. Langford must primarily want is a statement as to how I myself have intended to use, and, so far as I know, actually used, the word "analysis." Other people may have used it in different senses, but I do not think he wants me to state my position with regard to what they may have meant by it. And as to how I have intended to use it (and, I believe, actually used it), I think I can say three fairly definite things.

(1) Let us, as Mr. Langford does, call that which is to be analysed the *analysandum*. He himself tries to explain to us what he calls two "different views as to the nature of analysis," but which, I think, might be called two different ways in which the word "analysis" might be

used. And he seems to say that, if the word is used in the first way, the *analysandum* will be an "idea" or a "concept" or a "proposition," whereas if it is used in the second way it will be a "verbal expression" (p. 409).

Now I think I can say quite definitely that I never intended to use the word in such a way that the *analysandum* would be a *verbal expression*. When I have talked of analysing anything, *what* I have talked of analysing has always been an idea or concept or proposition, and *not* a verbal expression; that is to say, if I talked of analysing a "proposition," I was always using "proposition" in such a sense that no verbal expression (no sentence, for instance) can be a "proposition," in that sense. There is, of course, a sense in which verbal expressions can be "analysed." To take an example from Mr. Langford: Consider the verbal expression "x is a small y." I should say that you could quite properly be said to be analysing this expression if you said of it: "It contains the letter 'x', the word 'is', the word 'a', the word 'small', and the letter 'y'; and it begins with 'x', 'is' comes next in it, then 'a', then 'small', and then 'y'." It seems to me that nothing but making some such statement as this could properly be called "giving an analysis of a verbal expression." And I, when I talked of "giving an analysis," have never meant anything at all like this.

(2) Mr. Langford seems to imply (p. 409) that he thinks that to make the statement: "'X is a small Y' means what is meant by 'X is a Y and is smaller than most Y's'," could be properly

called giving an analysis of the verbal expression 'X is a small Y'. I do not think it could. But I wish to make it plain that I never intended so to use the word "analysis," that by making a statement of this sort you would be *giving an analysis* at all. I think many philosophers (e.g., Mr. W. E. Johnson) have supposed that by making this statement you would be giving an analysis, not indeed of the verbal expression 'X is a small Y', but of the *concept* 'is a small Y'. And I may, perhaps (I do not know), sometimes have talked as if, by making a statement of this sort you were giving an analysis of some *concept* expressed by the verbal expression which appears between inverted commas: as if, e.g., by saying "'*x* is a brother' means the same as '*x* is male and is a sibling',," I were giving an analysis of the *concept* "being a brother." But, if I have done so, it was merely through a confusion, which I shared with others, as to what you are doing when you make such a statement: had I seen what you *are* doing, I should never have called making such a statement "giving an analysis." For what are you doing? You are merely asserting, with regard to two verbal expressions, that they have (to use an expression of Mr. W. E. Johnson's) *some* the same meaning, or, at best, that they each have only one meaning, and that the meaning they have is the same. You are not *mentioning* the meaning of either, or saying *what* the meaning of either is; but are merely making a statement, which could be completely understood by a person who had not the least idea what either expression meant. A man might point out to me two expressions in a language of which I was completely ignorant and tell me that they had the same meaning, without telling me *what* they meant. So far as he was merely telling me that they had the same meaning, I should completely understand what he told me – namely that those two expressions had the same meaning. What could be a clearer statement? I see the two expressions to which he points, in a book that he shows me, and I know what is meant by saying that two expressions have the same meaning. But if this were all he was doing, he would not have told me anything at all about any *concept* or *idea*, which either of the expressions expressed; and would therefore certainly *not* have been giving me an analysis of any *concept*, just as, also, he would certainly *not* have given me an analysis of any expression.

I certainly, therefore, never intended to use the word "analysis" in such a way that a statement

of this sort, which *merely* asserts that two expressions have the same meaning, would "give an analysis" at all.

(3) Another fairly definite thing which I can say about how I intended to use (and, I believe, used) the word "analysis," is that I certainly did not intend to use it in the *first* of the two ways described by Mr. Langford. Mr. Langford has convinced me of the three following propositions: (a) that a man may know that an object which he sees is a cube without knowing that it has twelve edges; (b) that a man may verify that an object which he sees is a cube, without verifying that it has twelve edges; and (c) that it is incorrect to say that the expression "*x* is a cube," when used as we actually use it, is synonymous with the expression "*x* is a cube with twelve edges," when used with its standard English meaning. And I think that I always intended so to use the word "analysis" that from any *one* of these three propositions by itself, it would *follow* that the concept "having twelve edges" did not "enter into the *analysis*" of the concept "cube." It seems to me quite evident that from the function "*x* is a cube," there follows "logically" (and not merely "causally," as Mr. Langford suggests) the function "*x* is a cube and has twelve edges," and vice versa. But, in spite of the fact that these two functions are logically equivalent, I should have taken any *one* of the propositions (a), (b), and (c) as entailing the conclusion that the concept "having twelve edges" did not enter into the analysis of the concept "cube." Perhaps, I can formulate three conditions, which were necessary, if one was to be said to be "giving an analysis" in my sense, as follows: If you are to "give an analysis" of a given *concept*, which is the *analysandum*, you must mention, as your *analysans*, a *concept* such that (a) nobody can know that the *analysandum* applies to an object without knowing that the *analysans* applies to it, (b) nobody can verify that the *analysandum* applies without verifying that the *analysans* applies, (c) any expression which expresses the *analysandum* must be synonymous with any expression which expresses the *analysans*.

Now it will be seen, that if I am right in these statements as to my intended and actual usage of the word "analysis," it follows that my usage was not the same as *either* of the two possible usages described by Mr. Langford. It was not the same as his first usage, because of the necessary conditions for "analysis" in my sense, stated above.

And it was not the same as his second usage, because in his second usage, as stated by him, the *analysandum* is a verbal expression, whereas, in my usage, the *analysandum must* be a concept, or idea, or proposition, and *not* a verbal expression. Mr. Langford calls his second usage a "formal" usage – a usage such that any analysis which is an analysis in that sense can be called a "formal" analysis; and in his concluding sentence he implies that I have spoken as if all analysis were formal. But, if I am right in what I said under (1) as to my usage, he is making a mistake in saying that I have implied this, provided that he himself is right in stating that it is a necessary condition for what he means by a formal analysis that the *analysandum* should be a verbal expression. But, if my sense of "analysis" is neither of those which Mr. Langford describes, what can it be? Is there a third alternative?

I will try to describe what I think my usage was. It must be emphasized, first of all, that, in my usage, both *analysandum* and *analysans* must be concepts or propositions, *not* mere verbal expressions. But, of course, in order to *give* an analysis, you must *use* verbal expressions. What will be the proper way of *expressing* what I should call an analysis? I can give several. Suppose I say: "The concept 'being a brother' is identical with the concept 'being a male sibling'." I should say that, in making this assertion, I am "giving an analysis" of the concept "being a brother;" and, if my assertion is true, then I am giving a *correct* analysis of this concept. But I might also give the same analysis of the same concept by saying: "The propositional function '*x* is a brother' is identical with the propositional function '*x* is a male sibling'." And I might also give the same analysis by saying: "To say that a person is a brother is the same thing as to say that that person is a male sibling." And one important thing to notice about these ways of expressing an analysis is that they all avoid the use of the word "means." It is, in my view, very important to avoid the use of this word, because by using it, you at once imply that the *analysandum* is a *verbal expression*, and therefore give a false impression as to what the assertion is that you really wish to make. I am afraid it is pretty certain that I have often, in giving analyses, used this word "means" and thus given a false impression; the fact being that for a long time I did not distinguish clearly between *defining* a word or other verbal expression, and *defining* a concept.

To define a concept is the same thing as to give an analysis of it; but to define a word is neither the same thing as to give an analysis of that word, nor the same thing as to give an analysis of any concept.

But, now, if we say, as I propose to, that to make any of the above three statements is to "give an analysis" of the concept "brother," we are obviously faced with the puzzle which Mr. Langford calls "the paradox of analysis." Suppose we use still another way, a fourth way, of expressing the very same statement which is expressed in those three ways I gave, and say: "To be a brother is the same thing as to be a male sibling." The paradox arises from the fact that, *if* this statement is true, then it seems as if it must be the case that you would be making exactly the same statement if you said: "To be a brother is the same thing as to be a brother." But it is obvious that these two statements are *not* the same; and obvious also that nobody would say that by asserting "To be a brother is to be a brother" you were giving an analysis of the concept "brother." It is these facts, I think, which drive Mr. Langford to say that, in what he calls a "formal" analysis, both *analysandum* and *analysans* must be mere verbal expressions and that what is stated in giving the analysis must be merely that two verbal expressions have the same meaning. But I think this solution of his is obviously wrong, because if *all* you were asserting was that the first verbal expression had the same meaning as the second, nobody would call the making of such an assertion the "giving an analysis" *either* of the first expression *or* of any concept. Now I own I am not at all clear as to what the solution of the puzzle is. An obvious suggestion to make is that, if you say "To be a brother is the same thing as to be a male sibling," you are making a statement *both* about the *concept* brother and *also* about the two verbal expressions used; which would explain why this statement is not the same statement as the statement "To be a brother is the same thing as to be a brother." But this suggestion would be compatible with its being the case that the assertion "To be a brother is the same thing as to be a male sibling" is merely a *conjunction* of the assertion "The verbal expression '*x* is a brother' has the same meaning as the expression '*x* is a male sibling'" with some other assertion which is merely an assertion about the *concept* "*x* is a brother" and not an assertion about any verbal expression. But I do not think this can possibly be the case: what would the second assertion in this supposed conjunction be? I think that, in order to explain the fact that, even if "To be a brother is the same thing as to be a male sibling" is true, yet nevertheless this statement is *not* the same as the statement "To be a brother is to be a brother," one *must* suppose that both statements are in *some* sense about the expressions used as well as about the concept of being a brother. But in *what* sense they are about the expressions used I cannot see clearly; and therefore I cannot give any clear solution to the puzzle. The two plain facts about the matter which it seems to me one must hold fast to are these: That if in making a given statement one is to be properly said to be "giving an analysis" of a *concept*, then (a) both *analysandum* and *analysans* must be *concepts*, and, if the analysis is a *correct* one, must, in some sense, be *the same concept*, and (b) that the *expression* used for the *analysandum* must be a different *expression* from that used for the *analysans*.

These are two plain facts about the way in which I intended to use (and, I think, used) the term analysis, and a third may be added: namely this: (c) that the *expression* used for the *analysandum* must not only be *different* from that used for the *analysans*, but that they must differ in this way, namely, that the expression used for the *analysans* must *explicitly mention* concepts which are not explicitly mentioned by the expression used for the *analysandum*. Thus the expression "*x* is a male sibling" *explicitly mentions* the concepts "male" and "sibling," whereas the expression "*x* is a brother" does not. It is true, of course, that the former expression not only *mentions* these concepts, but also mentions the *way in which they are combined* in the concept "brother," which is, in this case, the way of mere conjunction, but in other cases may be very different from mere conjunction. And that the *method of combination*

should be explicitly mentioned by the expression used for the *analysans* is, I think, also a necessary condition for the giving of an analysis. From these two conditions there follows, I think, that the expression used for the *analysans* must be "less idiomatic," in Mr. Langford's sense, than that used for the *analysandum*. And this condition, in accordance with his view (which I consider mistaken) that in what he calls a "formal" analysis both *analysandum* and *analysans* are merely verbal expressions, he expresses (wrongly, as I think), by saying (p. 410) that the *analysans* must be less idiomatic than the *analysandum*.

This is all that I can say about my use of the term "analysis." For a full discussion of the subject it would be necessary to raise the question why I say that the concept "*x* is a male sibling" is *identical* with the concept "*x* is a brother," but refuse to say that the concept "*x* is a cube with twelve edges" is *identical* with the concept "*x* is a cube," although I insist that these latter *are* "logically equivalent." To raise this question would be to raise the question how an "analytic" necessary connection is to be distinguished from a "synthetic" one – a subject upon which I am far from clear. It seems to me that there are ever so many different cases of necessary connection, and that the line between "analytic" and "synthetic" might be drawn in many different ways. As it is, I do not think that the two terms have any clear meaning. I do not know, at all clearly, *what* I mean by saying that "*x* is a brother" is *identical* with "*x* is a male sibling," and that "*x* is a cube" is *not identical* with "*x* is a cube with twelve edges." It is obvious, for instance, that, in a sense, the expression "*x* is a brother" is *not* synonymous with, has *not* the same meaning as, "*x* is a male sibling," since if you were to translate the French word *frère* by the expression "male sibling," your translation would be *incorrect*, whereas if you were to translate it by "brother," it would not.

40

The Elimination of Metaphysics

A. J. Ayer

The traditional disputes of philosophers are, for the most part, as unwarranted as they are unfruitful. The surest way to end them is to establish beyond question what should be the purpose and method of a philosophical enquiry. And this is by no means so difficult a task as the history of philosophy would lead one to suppose. For if there are any questions which science leaves it to philosophy to answer, a straightforward process of elimination must lead to their discovery.

We may begin by criticising the metaphysical thesis that philosophy affords us knowledge of a reality transcending the world of science and common sense. Later on, when we come to define metaphysics and account for its existence, we shall find that it is possible to be a metaphysician without believing in a transcendent reality; for we shall see that many metaphysical utterances are due to the commission of logical errors, rather than to a conscious desire on the part of their authors to go beyond the limits of experience. But it is convenient for us to take the case of those who believe that it is possible to have knowledge of a transcendent reality as a starting-point for our discussion. The arguments which we use to refute them will subsequently be found to apply to the whole of metaphysics.

One way of attacking a metaphysician who claimed to have knowledge of a reality which transcended the phenomenal world would be to

Previously published in *Language, Truth and Logic*, 2nd edn. (Victor Gollancz, London, 1946).

enquire from what premises his propositions were deduced. Must he not begin, as other men do, with the evidence of his senses? And if so, what valid process of reasoning can possibly lead him to the conception of a transcendent reality? Surely from empirical premises nothing whatsoever concerning the properties, or even the existence, of anything super-empirical can legitimately be inferred. But this objection would be met by a denial on the part of the metaphysician that his assertions were ultimately based on the evidence of his senses. He would say that he was endowed with a faculty of intellectual intuition which enabled him to know facts that could not be known through sense-experience. And even if it could be shown that he was relying on empirical premises, and that his venture into a non-empirical world was therefore logically unjustified, it would not follow that the assertions which he made concerning this non-empirical world could not be true. For the fact that a conclusion does not follow from its putative premise is not sufficient to show that it is false. Consequently one cannot overthrow a system of transcendent metaphysics merely by criticising the way in which it comes into being. What is required is rather a criticism of the nature of the actual statements which comprise it. And this is the line of argument which we shall, in fact, pursue. For we shall maintain that no statement which refers to a "reality" transcending the limits of all possible sense-experience can possibly have any literal significance; from which it must follow that the labours of those who have striven to describe such a reality have all been devoted to the production of nonsense.

It may be suggested that this is a proposition which has already been proved by Kant. But although Kant also condemned transcendent metaphysics, he did so on different grounds. For he said that the human understanding was so constituted that it lost itself in contradictions when it ventured out beyond the limits of possible experience and attempted to deal with things in themselves. And thus he made the impossibility of a transcendent metaphysic not, as we do, a matter of logic, but a matter of fact. He asserted, not that our minds could not conceivably have had the power of penetrating beyond the phenomenal world, but merely that they were in fact devoid of it. And this leads the critic to ask how, if it is possible to know only what lies within the bounds of sense-experience, the author can be justified in asserting that real things do exist beyond, and how he can tell what are the boundaries beyond which the human understanding may not venture, unless he succeeds in passing them himself. As Wittgenstein says, "in order to draw a limit to thinking, we should have to think both sides of this limit,"[1] a truth to which Bradley gives a special twist in maintaining that the man who is ready to prove that metaphysics is impossible is a brother metaphysician with a rival theory of his own.[2]

Whatever force these objections may have against the Kantian doctrine, they have none whatsoever against the thesis that I am about to set forth. It cannot here be said that the author is himself overstepping the barrier he maintains to be impassable. For the fruitlessness of attempting to transcend the limits of possible sense-experience will be deduced, not from a psychological hypothesis concerning the actual constitution of the human mind, but from the rule which determines the literal significance of language. Our charge against the metaphysician is not that he attempts to employ the understanding in a field where it cannot profitably venture, but that he produces sentences which fail to conform to the conditions under which alone a sentence can be literally significant. Nor are we ourselves obliged to talk nonsense in order to show that all sentences of a certain type are necessarily devoid of literal significance. We need only formulate the criterion which enables us to test whether a sentence expresses a genuine proposition about a matter of fact, and then point

out that the sentences under consideration fail to satisfy it. And this we shall now proceed to do. We shall first of all formulate the criterion in somewhat vague terms, and then give the explanations which are necessary to render it precise.

The criterion which we use to test the genuineness of apparent statements of fact is the criterion of verifiability. We say that a sentence is factually significant to any given person, if, and only if, he knows how to verify the proposition which it purports to express – that is, if he knows what observations would lead him, under certain conditions, to accept the proposition as being true, or reject it as being false. If, on the other hand, the putative proposition is of such a character that the assumption of its truth, or falsehood, is consistent with any assumption whatsoever concerning the nature of his future experience, then, as far as he is concerned, it is, if not a tautology, a mere pseudo-proposition. The sentence expressing it may be emotionally significant to him; but it is not literally significant. And with regard to questions the procedure is the same. We enquire in every case what observations would lead us to answer the question, one way or the other; and, if none can be discovered, we must conclude that the sentence under consideration does not, as far as we are concerned, express a genuine question, however strongly its grammatical appearance may suggest that it does.

As the adoption of this procedure is an essential factor in the argument of this book, it needs to be examined in detail.

In the first place, it is necessary to draw a distinction between practical verifiability, and verifiability in principle. Plainly we all understand, in many cases believe, propositions which we have not in fact taken steps to verify. Many of these are propositions which we could verify if we took enough trouble. But there remain a number of significant propositions, concerning matters of fact, which we could not verify even if we chose; simply because we lack the practical means of placing ourselves in the situation where the relevant observations could be made. A simple and familiar example of such a proposition is the proposition that there are mountains on the farther side of the moon.[3] No rocket has yet been invented which would enable me to go and look at the farther side of the moon, so that I am unable to decide the matter by actual observation. But I do know what observations would decide it for me, if, as is theoretically conceivable,

I were once in a position to make them. And therefore I say that the proposition is verifiable in principle, if not in practice, and is accordingly significant. On the other hand, such a metaphysical pseudo-proposition as "the Absolute enters into, but is itself incapable of, evolution and progress,"[4] is not even in principle verifiable. For one cannot conceive of an observation which would enable one to determine whether the Absolute did, or did not, enter into evolution and progress. Of course it is possible that the author of such a remark is using English words in a way in which they are not commonly used by English-speaking people, and that he does, in fact, intend to assert something which could be empirically verified. But until he makes us understand how the proposition that he wishes to express would be verified, he fails to communicate anything to us. And if he admits, as I think the author of the remark in question would have admitted, that his words were not intended to express either a tautology or a proposition which was capable, at least in principle, of being verified, then it follows that he has made an utterance which has no literal significance even for himself.

A further distinction which we must make is the distinction between the "strong" and the "weak" sense of the term "verifiable." A proposition is said to be verifiable, in the strong sense of the term, if, and only if, its truth could be conclusively established in experience. But it is verifiable, in the weak sense, if it is possible for experience to render it probable. In which sense are we using the term when we say that a putative proposition is genuine only if it is verifiable?

It seems to me that if we adopt conclusive verifiability as our criterion of significance, as some positivists have proposed,[5] our argument will prove too much. Consider, for example, the case of general propositions of law – such propositions, namely, as "arsenic is poisonous"; "all men are mortal"; "a body tends to expand when it is heated." It is of the very nature of these propositions that their truth cannot be established with certainty by any finite series of observations. But if it is recognised that such general propositions of law are designed to cover an infinite number of cases, then it must be admitted that they cannot, even in principle, be verified conclusively. And then, if we adopt conclusive verifiability as our criterion of significance, we are logically obliged to treat these general propositions

of law in the same fashion as we treat the statements of the metaphysician.

In face of this difficulty, some positivists[6] have adopted the heroic course of saying that these general propositions are indeed pieces of nonsense, albeit an essentially important type of nonsense. But here the introduction of the term "important" is simply an attempt to hedge. It serves only to mark the authors' recognition that their view is somewhat too paradoxical, without in any way removing the paradox. Besides, the difficulty is not confined to the case of general propositions of law, though it is there revealed most plainly. It is hardly less obvious in the case of propositions about the remote past. For it must surely be admitted that, however strong the evidence in favour of historical statements may be, their truth can never become more than highly probable. And to maintain that they also constituted an important, or unimportant, type of nonsense would be unplausible, to say the very least. Indeed, it will be our contention that no proposition, other than a tautology, can possibly be anything more than a probable hypothesis. And if this is correct, the principle that a sentence can be factually significant only if it expresses what is conclusively verifiable is self-stultifying as a criterion of significance. For it leads to the conclusion that it is impossible to make a significant statement of fact at all.

Nor can we accept the suggestion that a sentence should be allowed to be factually significant if, and only if, it expresses something which is definitely confutable by experience.[7] Those who adopt this course assume that, although no finite series of observations is ever sufficient to establish the truth of a hypothesis beyond all possibility of doubt, there are crucial cases in which a single observation, or series of observations, can definitely confute it. But, as we shall show later on, this assumption is false. A hypothesis cannot be conclusively confuted any more than it can be conclusively verified. For when we take the occurrence of certain observations as proof that a given hypothesis is false, we presuppose the existence of certain conditions. And though, in any given case, it may be extremely improbable that this assumption is false, it is not logically impossible. We shall see that there need be no self-contradiction in holding that some of the relevant circumstances are other than we have taken them to be, and consequently that the hypothesis has not really broken down. And if it is not the case that any hypothesis can be definitely confuted, we cannot hold that the genuineness of a proposition depends on the possibility of its definite confutation.

Accordingly, we fall back on the weaker sense of verification. We say that the question that must be asked about any putative statement of fact is not, Would any observations make its truth or falsehood logically certain? but simply, Would any observations be relevant to the determination of its truth or falsehood? And it is only if a negative answer is given to this second question that we conclude that the statement under consideration is nonsensical.

To make our position clearer, we may formulate it in another way. Let us call a proposition which records an actual or possible observation an experiential proposition. Then we may say that it is the mark of a genuine factual proposition, not that it should be equivalent to an experiential proposition, or any finite number of experiential propositions, but simply that some experiential propositions can be deduced from it in conjunction with certain other premises without being deducible from those other premises alone.[8]

This criterion seems liberal enough. In contrast to the principle of conclusive verifiability, it clearly does not deny significance to general propositions or to propositions about the past. Let us see what kinds of assertion it rules out.

A good example of the kind of utterance that is condemned by our criterion as being not even false but nonsensical would be the assertion that the world of sense-experience was altogether unreal. It must, of course, be admitted that our senses do sometimes deceive us. We may, as the result of having certain sensations, expect certain other sensations to be obtainable which are, in fact, not obtainable. But, in all such cases, it is further sense-experience that informs us of the mistakes that arise out of sense-experience. We say that the senses sometimes deceive us, just because the expectations to which our sense-experiences give rise do not always accord with what we subsequently experience. That is, we rely on our senses to substantiate or confute the judgements which are based on our sensations. And therefore the fact that our perceptual judgements are sometimes found to be erroneous has not the slightest tendency to show that the world of sense-experience is unreal. And, indeed, it is plain that no conceivable observation, or series of observations, could have any tendency to show that

the world revealed to us by sense-experience was unreal. Consequently, anyone who condemns the sensible world as a world of mere appearance, as opposed to reality, is saying something which, according to our criterion of significance, is literally nonsensical.

An example of a controversy which the application of our criterion obliges us to condemn as fictitious is provided by those who dispute concerning the number of substances that there are in the world. For it is admitted both by monists, who maintain that reality is one substance, and by pluralists, who maintain that reality is many, that it is impossible to imagine any empirical situation which would be relevant to the solution of their dispute. But if we are told that no possible observation could give any probability either to the assertion that reality was one substance or to the assertion that it was many, then we must conclude that neither assertion is significant. We shall see later on[9] that there are genuine logical and empirical questions involved in the dispute between monists and pluralists. But the metaphysical question concerning "substance" is ruled out by our criterion as spurious.

A similar treatment must be accorded to the controversy between realists and idealists, in its metaphysical aspect. A simple illustration, which I have made use of in a similar argument elsewhere,[10] will help to demonstrate this. Let us suppose that a picture is discovered and the suggestion made that it was painted by Goya. There is a definite procedure for dealing with such a question. The experts examine the picture to see in what way it resembles the accredited works of Goya, and to see if it bears any marks which are characteristic of a forgery; they look up contemporary records for evidence of the existence of such a picture, and so on. In the end, they may still disagree, but each one knows what empirical evidence would go to confirm or discredit his opinion. Suppose, now, that these men have studied philosophy, and some of them proceed to maintain that this picture is a set of ideas in the perceiver's mind, or in God's mind, others that it is objectively real. What possible experience could any of them have which would be relevant to the solution of this dispute one way or the other? In the ordinary sense of the term "real," in which it is opposed to "illusory," the reality of the picture is not in doubt. The disputants have satisfied themselves that the picture is real, in this sense, by obtaining a correlated series of sensations of sight and sensations of touch. Is there any similar process by which they could discover whether the picture was real, in the sense in which the term "real" is opposed to "ideal"? Clearly there is none. But, if that is so, the problem is fictitious according to our criterion. This does not mean that the realist–idealist controversy may be dismissed without further ado. For it can legitimately be regarded as a dispute concerning the analysis of existential propositions, and so as involving a logical problem which, as we shall see, can be definitively solved.[11] What we have just shown is that the question at issue between idealists and realists becomes fictitious when, as is often the case, it is given a metaphysical interpretation.

There is no need for us to give further examples of the operation of our criterion of significance. For our object is merely to show that philosophy, as a genuine branch of knowledge, must be distinguished from metaphysics. We are not now concerned with the historical question how much of what has traditionally passed for philosophy is actually metaphysical. We shall, however, point out later on that the majority of the "great philosophers" of the past were not essentially metaphysicians, and thus reassure those who would otherwise be prevented from adopting our criterion by considerations of piety.

As to the validity of the verification principle, in the form in which we have stated it, a demonstration will be given in the course of this book. For it will be shown that all propositions which have factual content are empirical hypotheses; and that the function of an empirical hypothesis is to provide a rule for the anticipation of experience.[12] And this means that every empirical hypothesis must be relevant to some actual, or possible, experience, so that a statement which is not relevant to any experience is not an empirical hypothesis, and accordingly has no factual content. But this is precisely what the principle of verifiability asserts.

It should be mentioned here that the fact that the utterances of the metaphysician are nonsensical does not follow simply from the fact that they are devoid of factual content. It follows from that fact, together with the fact that they are not a priori propositions. And in assuming that they are not a priori propositions, we are once again anticipating the conclusions of a later chapter in this book.[13] For it will be shown there that a priori propositions, which have always been

attractive to philosophers on account of their certainty, owe this certainty to the fact that they are tautologies. We may accordingly define a metaphysical sentence as a sentence which purports to express a genuine proposition, but does, in fact, express neither a tautology nor an empirical hypothesis. And as tautologies and empirical hypotheses form the entire class of significant propositions, we are justified in concluding that all metaphysical assertions are nonsensical. Our next task is to show how they come to be made.

The use of the term "substance," to which we have already referred, provides us with a good example of the way in which metaphysics mostly comes to be written. It happens to be the case that we cannot, in our language, refer to the sensible properties of a thing without introducing a word or phrase which appears to stand for the thing itself as opposed to anything which may be said about it. And, as a result of this, those who are infected by the primitive superstition that to every name a single real entity must correspond assume that it is necessary to distinguish logically between the thing itself and any, or all, of its sensible properties. And so they employ the term "substance" to refer to the thing itself. But from the fact that we happen to employ a single word to refer to a thing, and make that word the grammatical subject of the sentences in which we refer to the sensible appearances of the thing, it does not by any means follow that the thing itself is a "simple entity," or that it cannot be defined in terms of the totality of its appearances. It is true that in talking of "its" appearances we appear to distinguish the thing from the appearances, but that is simply an accident of linguistic usage. Logical analysis shows that what makes these "appearances" the "appearances of" the same thing is not their relationship to an entity other than themselves, but their relationship to one another. The metaphysician fails to see this because he is misled by a superficial grammatical feature of his language.

A simpler and clearer instance of the way in which a consideration of grammar leads to metaphysics is the case of the metaphysical concept of Being. The origin of our temptation to raise questions about Being, which no conceivable experience would enable us to answer, lies in the fact that, in our language, sentences which express existential propositions and sentences which express attributive propositions may be of the same grammatical form. For instance, the sentences

"Martyrs exist" and "Martyrs suffer" both consist of a noun followed by an intransitive verb, and the fact that they have grammatically the same appearance leads one to assume that they are of the same logical type. It is seen that in the proposition "Martyrs suffer," the members of a certain species are credited with a certain attribute, and it is sometimes assumed that the same thing is true of such a proposition as "Martyrs exist." If this were actually the case, it would, indeed, be as legitimate to speculate about the Being of martyrs as it is to speculate about their suffering. But, as Kant pointed out,[14] existence is not an attribute. For, when we ascribe an attribute to a thing, we covertly assert that it exists: so that if existence were itself an attribute, it would follow that all positive existential propositions were tautologies, and all negative existential propositions self-contradictory; and this is not the case.[15] So that those who raise questions about Being which are based on the assumption that existence is an attribute are guilty of following grammar beyond the boundaries of sense.

A similar mistake has been made in connection with such propositions as "Unicorns are fictitious." Here again the fact that there is a superficial grammatical resemblance between the English sentences "Dogs are faithful" and "Unicorns are fictitious," and between the corresponding sentences in other languages, creates the assumption that they are of the same logical type. Dogs must exist in order to have the property of being faithful, and so it is held that unless unicorns in some way existed they could not have the property of being fictitious. But, as it is plainly self-contradictory to say that fictitious objects exist, the device is adopted of saying that they are real in some non-empirical sense – that they have a mode of real being which is different from the mode of being of existent things. But since there is no way of testing whether an object is real in this sense, as there is for testing whether it is real in the ordinary sense, the assertion that fictitious objects have a special non-empirical mode of real being is devoid of all literal significance. It comes to be made as a result of the assumption that being fictitious is an attribute. And this is a fallacy of the same order as the fallacy of supposing that existence is an attribute, and it can be exposed in the same way.

In general, the postulation of real non-existent entities results from the superstition, just now referred to, that, to every word or phrase that can be the grammatical subject of a sentence, there must somewhere be a real entity corresponding. For as there is no place in the empirical world for many of these "entities," a special non-empirical world is invoked to house them. To this error must be attributed, not only the utterances of a Heidegger, who bases his metaphysics on the assumption that "Nothing" is a name which is used to denote something peculiarly mysterious,[16] but also the prevalence of such problems as those concerning the reality of propositions and universals whose senselessness, though less obvious, is no less complete.

These few examples afford a sufficient indication of the way in which most metaphysical assertions come to be formulated. They show how easy it is to write sentences which are literally nonsensical without seeing that they are nonsensical. And thus we see that the view that a number of the traditional "problems of philosophy" are metaphysical, and consequently fictitious, does not involve any incredible assumptions about the psychology of philosophers.

Among those who recognise that if philosophy is to be accounted a genuine branch of knowledge it must be defined in such a way as to distinguish it from metaphysics, it is fashionable to speak of the metaphysician as a kind of misplaced poet. As his statements have no literal meaning, they are not subject to any criteria of truth or falsehood: but they may still serve to express, or arouse, emotion, and thus be subject to ethical or æsthetic standards. And it is suggested that they may have considerable value, as means of moral inspiration, or even as works of art. In this way, an attempt is made to compensate the metaphysician for his extrusion from philosophy.[17]

I am afraid that this compensation is hardly in accordance with his deserts. The view that the metaphysician is to be reckoned among the poets appears to rest on the assumption that both talk nonsense. But this assumption is false. In the vast majority of cases the sentences which are produced by poets do have literal meaning. The difference between the man who uses language scientifically and the man who uses it emotively is not that the one produces sentences which are incapable of arousing emotion, and the other sentences which have no sense, but that the one is primarily concerned with the expression of true propositions, the other with the creation of a work of art. Thus, if a work of science contains true and important propositions, its value as a work of science will hardly be diminished by the fact that they are inelegantly expressed. And similarly, a work of art is not necessarily the worse for the fact that all the propositions comprising it are literally false. But to say that many literary works are largely composed of falsehoods, is not to say that they are composed of pseudo-propositions. It is, in fact, very rare for a literary artist to produce sentences which have no literal meaning. And where this does occur, the sentences are carefully chosen for their rhythm and balance. If the author writes nonsense, it is because he considers it most suitable for bringing about the effects for which his writing is designed.

The metaphysician, on the other hand, does not intend to write nonsense. He lapses into it through being deceived by grammar, or through committing errors of reasoning, such as that which leads to the view that the sensible world is unreal. But it is not the mark of a poet simply to make mistakes of this sort. There are some, indeed, who would see in the fact that the metaphysician's utterances are senseless a reason against the view that they have æsthetic value. And, without going so far as this, we may safely say that it does not constitute a reason for it.

It is true, however, that although the greater part of metaphysics is merely the embodiment of humdrum errors, there remain a number of metaphysical passages which are the work of genuine mystical feeling; and they may more plausibly be held to have moral or æsthetic value. But, as far as we are concerned, the distinction between the kind of metaphysics that is produced by a philosopher who has been duped by grammar, and the kind that is produced by a mystic who is trying to express the inexpressible, is of no great importance: what is important to us is to realise that even the utterances of the metaphysician who is attempting to expound a vision are literally senseless; so that henceforth we may pursue our philosophical researches with as little regard for them as for the more inglorious kind of metaphysics which comes from a failure to understand the workings of our language.

Notes

1   *Tractatus Logico-Philosophicus*, Preface.
2   F. H. Bradley, *Appearance and Reality*, 2nd edn. (Oxford: Clarendon Press, 1930), p. 1.
3   This example has been used by Professor Schlick to illustrate the same point.
4   A remark taken at random from *Appearance and Reality*, by Bradley.
5   E.g. M. Schlick, "Positivismus und Realismus," *Erkenntnis* 1 (1930). F. Waismann, "Logische Analyse des Warscheinlichkeitsbegriffs," *Erkenntnis* 1 (1930).
6   E.g. M. Schlick, "Die Kausalität in der gegenwärtigen Physik," *Naturwissenschaft* 19 (1931).
7   This has been proposed by Karl Popper in his *Logik der Forschung*.
8   This is an over-simplified statement, which is not literally correct. I give what I believe to be the correct formulation in the Introduction [of *Language, Truth and Logic*], p. 13.
9   In ch. VIII [of *Language, Truth and Logic*].
10 See "Demonstration of the Impossibility of Metaphysics," *Mind* 43 (1934), p. 339.
11 See ch. VIII [of *Language, Truth and Logic*].
12 See ch. V [of *Language, Truth and Logic*].
13 Ch. IV [of *Language, Truth and Logic*].
14 See *The Critique of Pure Reason*, "Transcendental Dialectic," Bk. II, ch. III, sec. 4.
15 This argument is well stated by John Wisdom, *Interpretation and Analysis* (London: Kegan Paul, Trench, Trubner, 1931), pp. 62, 63.
16 See *Was ist Metaphysik*, by Heidegger: criticised by Rudolf Carnap in his "Überwindung der Metaphysik durch logische Analyse der Sprache," *Erkenntnis* 2 (1932).
17 For a discussion of this point, see also C. A. Mace, "Representation and Expression," *Analysis* 1/3; and "Metaphysics and Emotive Language," *Analysis* 2/1 and 2.

41

Empiricism, Semantics, and Ontology

Rudolf Carnap

The Problem of Abstract Entities

Empiricists are in general rather suspicious with respect to any kind of abstract entities like properties, classes, relations, numbers, propositions, etc. They usually feel much more in sympathy with nominalists than with realists (in the medieval sense). As far as possible they try to avoid any reference to abstract entities and to restrict themselves to what is sometimes called a nominalistic language, i.e., one not containing such references. However, within certain scientific contexts it seems hardly possible to avoid them. In the case of mathematics, some empiricists try to find a way out by treating the whole of mathematics as a mere calculus, a formal system for which no interpretation is given or can be given. Accordingly, the mathematician is said to speak not about numbers, functions, and infinite classes, but merely about meaningless symbols and formulas manipulated according to given formal rules. In physics it is more difficult to shun the suspected entities, because the language of physics serves for the communication of reports and predictions and hence cannot be taken as a mere calculus. A physicist who is suspicious of abstract entities may perhaps try to declare a certain part of the language of physics as uninterpreted and uninterpretable, that part which refers to real numbers as space-time coordinates or as values

Originally published in *Revue Internationale de Philosophie* 4 (1950).

of physical magnitudes, to functions, limits, etc. More probably he will just speak about all these things like anybody else but with an uneasy conscience, like a man who in his everyday life does with qualms many things which are not in accord with the high moral principles he professes on Sundays. Recently the problem of abstract entities has arisen again in connection with semantics, the theory of meaning and truth. Some semanticists say that certain expressions designate certain entities, and among these designated entities they include not only concrete material things but also abstract entities, e.g., properties as designated by predicates and propositions as designated by sentences.[1] Others object strongly to this procedure as violating the basic principles of empiricism and leading back to a metaphysical ontology of the Platonic kind.

It is the purpose of this article to clarify this controversial issue. The nature and implications of the acceptance of a language referring to abstract entities will first be discussed in general; it will be shown that using such a language does not imply embracing a Platonic ontology but is perfectly compatible with empiricism and strictly scientific thinking. Then the special question of the role of abstract entities in semantics will be discussed. It is hoped that the clarification of the issue will be useful to those who would like to accept abstract entities in their work in mathematics, physics, semantics, or any other field; it may help them to overcome nominalistic scruples.

Frameworks of Entities

Are there properties, classes, numbers, propositions? In order to understand more clearly the nature of these and related problems, it is above all necessary to recognize a fundamental distinction between two kinds of questions concerning the existence or reality of entities. If someone wishes to speak in his language about a new kind of entities, he has to introduce a system of new ways of speaking, subject to new rules; we shall call this procedure the construction of a *framework* for the new entities in question. And now we must distinguish two kinds of questions of existence: first, questions of the existence of certain entities of the new kind *within the framework*; we call them *internal questions*; and second, questions concerning the existence or reality *of the framework itself*, called *external questions*. Internal questions and possible answers to them are formulated with the help of the new forms of expressions. The answers may be found either by purely logical methods or by empirical methods, depending upon whether the framework is a logical or a factual one. An external question is of a problematic character which is in need of closer examination.

The world of things. Let us consider as an example the simplest framework dealt with in the everyday language: the spatio-temporally ordered system of observable things and events. Once we have accepted this thing-language and thereby the framework of things, we can raise and answer internal questions, e.g., "Is there a white piece of paper on my desk?", "Did King Arthur actually live?", "Are unicorns and centaurs real or merely imaginary?", and the like. These questions are to be answered by empirical investigations. Results of observations are evaluated according to certain rules as confirming or disconfirming evidence for possible answers. (This evaluation is usually carried out, of course, as a matter of habit rather than a deliberate, rational procedure. But it is possible, in a rational reconstruction, to lay down explicit rules for the evaluation. This is one of the main tasks of a pure, as distinguished from a psychological epistemology.) The concept of reality occurring in these internal questions is an empirical, scientific, nonmetaphysical concept. To recognize something as a real thing or event means to succeed in incorporating it into the framework of things at a particular space-time position so that it fits together with the other things recognized as real, according to the rules of the framework.

From these questions we must distinguish the external question of the reality of the thing world itself. In contrast to the former questions, this question is raised neither by the man in the street nor by scientists, but only by philosophers. Realists give an affirmative answer, subjective idealists a negative one, and the controversy goes on for centuries without ever being solved. And it cannot be solved because it is framed in a wrong way. To be real in the scientific sense means to be an element of the framework; hence this concept cannot be meaningfully applied to the framework itself. Those who raise the question of the reality of the thing world itself have perhaps in mind not a theoretical question as their formulation seems to suggest, but rather a practical question, a matter of a practical decision concerning the structure of our language. We have to make the choice whether or not to accept and use the forms of expression for the framework in question.

In the case of this particular example, there is usually no deliberate choice because we all have accepted the thing-language early in our lives as a matter of course. Nevertheless, we may regard it as a matter of decision in this sense: we are free to choose to continue using the thing-language or not; in the latter case we could restrict ourselves to a language of sense-data and other "phenomenal" entities, or construct an alternative to the customary thing-language with another structure, or, finally, we could refrain from speaking. If someone decides to accept the thing-language, there is no objection against saying that he has accepted the world of things. But this must not be interpreted as if it meant his acceptance of a *belief* in the reality of the thing world; there is no such belief or assertion or assumption, because it is not a theoretical question. To accept the thing world means nothing more than to accept a certain form of language, in other words, to accept rules for forming statements and for testing, accepting, or rejecting them. Thus the acceptance of the thing-language leads, on the basis of observations made, also to the acceptance, belief, and assertion of certain statements. But the thesis of the reality of the thing world cannot be among these statements, because it cannot be formulated in the thing-language or, it seems, in any other theoretical language.

The decision of accepting the thing-language, although itself not of a cognitive nature, will nevertheless usually be influenced by theoretical knowledge, just like any other deliberate decision concerning the acceptance of linguistic or other rules. The purposes for which the language is intended to be used, for instance, the purpose of communicating factual knowledge, will determine which factors are relevant for the decision. The efficiency, fruitfulness, and simplicity of the use of the thing-language may be among the decisive factors. And the questions concerning these qualities are indeed of a theoretical nature. But these questions cannot be identified with the question of realism. They are not yes–no questions but questions of degree. The thing-language in the customary form works indeed with a high degree of efficiency for most purposes of everyday life. This is a matter of fact, based upon the content of our experiences. However, it would be wrong to describe this situation by saying: "The fact of the efficiency of the thing-language is confirming evidence for the reality of the thing world"; we should rather say instead: "This fact makes it advisable to accept the thing-language".

The system of numbers. As an example of a framework which is of a logical rather than a factual nature let us take the system of natural numbers. This system is established by introducing into the language new expressions with suitable rules: (1) numerals like "five" and sentence forms like "there are five books on the table"; (2) The general term "number" for the new entities, and sentence forms like "five is a number"; (3) expressions for properties of numbers (e.g., "odd", "prime"), relations (e.g., "greater than"), and functions (e.g., "plus"), and sentence forms like "two plus three is five"; (4) numerical variables ("m", "n", etc.) and quantifiers for universal sentences ("for every n, . . .") and existential sentences ("there is an n such that . . .") with the customary deductive rules.

Here again there are internal questions, e.g., "Is there a prime number greater than hundred?" Here, however, the answers are found, not by empirical investigation based on observations, but by logical analysis based on the rules for the new expressions. Therefore the answers are here analytic, i.e., logically true.

What is now the nature of the philosophical question concerning the existence or reality of numbers? To begin with, there is the internal question which, together with the affirmative answer, can be formulated in the new terms, say, by "There are numbers" or, more explicitly, "There is an n such that n is a number". This statement follows from the analytic statement "five is a number" and is therefore itself analytic. Moreover, it is rather trivial (in contradistinction to a statement like "There is a prime number greater than a million", which is likewise analytic but far from trivial), because it does not say more than that the new system is not empty; but this is immediately seen from the rule which states that words like "five" are substitutable for the new variables. Therefore nobody who meant the question "Are there numbers?" in the internal sense would either assert or even seriously consider a negative answer. This makes it plausible to assume that those philosophers who treat the question of the existence of numbers as a serious philosophical problem and offer lengthy arguments on either side, do not have in mind the internal question. And, indeed, if we were to ask them: "Do you mean the question as to whether the system of numbers, *if* we were to accept it, would be found to be empty or not?", they would probably reply: "Not at all; we mean a question *prior* to the acceptance of the new framework." They might try to explain what they mean by saying that it is a question of the ontological status of numbers; the question whether or not numbers have a certain metaphysical characteristic called reality (but a kind of ideal reality, different from the material reality of the thing world) or subsistence or status of "independent entities". Unfortunately, these philosophers have so far not given a formulation of their question in terms of the common scientific language. Therefore our judgement must be that they have not succeeded in giving to the external question and to the possible answers any cognitive content. Unless and until they supply a clear cognitive interpretation, we are justified in our suspicion that their question is a pseudo-question, that is, one disguised in the form of a theoretical question while in fact it is non-theoretical; in the present case it is the practical problem whether or not to incorporate into the language the new linguistic forms which represent the framework of numbers.

The framework of propositions. New variables, "p", "q", etc., are introduced with a rule to the effect that any (declarative) sentence may be substituted for a variable of this kind; this includes, in addition to the sentences of the original thing

Rudolf Carnap

language, also all general sentences with variables of any kind which may have been introduced into the language. Further, the general term "proposition" is introduced. "p is a proposition" may be defined by "p or not p" (or by any other sentence form yielding only analytic sentences). Therefore, every sentence of the form ". . . is a proposition" (where any sentence may stand in the place of the dots) is analytic. This holds, for example, for the sentence:

(a) "Chicago is large is a proposition".

(We disregard here the fact that the rules of English grammar require not a sentence but a that-clause as the subject of another sentence; accordingly, instead of (a) we should have to say "That Chicago is large is a proposition".) Predicates may be admitted whose argument expressions are sentences; these predicates may be either extensional (e.g., the customary truth-functional connectives) or not (e.g., modal predicates like "possible", "necessary", etc.). With the help of the new variables, general sentences may be formed, e.g.

(b) "For every p, either p or not-p".
(c) "There is a p such that p is not necessary and not-p is not necessary".
(d) "There is a p such that p is a proposition".

(c) and (d) assert internal existence. The statement "There are propositions" may be meant in the sense of (d); in this case it is analytic (since it follows from (a)) and even trivial. If, however, the statement is meant in an external sense, then it is non-cognitive.

It is important to notice that the system of rules for the linguistic expressions of the propositional framework (of which only a few rules have here been briefly indicated) is sufficient for the introduction of the framework. Any further explanations as to the nature of the propositions (i.e., the elements of the framework indicated, the values of the variables "p", "q", etc.) are theoretically unnecessary because, if correct, they follow from the rules. For example, are propositions mental events (as in Russell's theory)? A look at the rules shows us that they are not, because otherwise existential statements would be of the form: "If the mental state of the person in question fulfils such and such conditions, then there is a p such that . . .". The fact that no references

to mental conditions occur in existential statements (like (c), (d), etc.) shows that propositions are not mental entities. Further, a statement of the existence of linguistic entities (e.g., expressions, classes of expressions, etc.) must contain a reference to a language. The fact that no such reference occurs in the existential statements here, shows that propositions are not linguistic entities. The fact that in these statements no reference to a subject (an observer or knower) occurs (nothing like: "There is a p which is necessary for Mr. X"), shows that the propositions (and their properties, like necessity, etc.) are not subjective. Although characterizations of these or similar kinds are, strictly speaking, unnecessary, they may nevertheless be practically useful. If they are given, they should be understood, not as ingredient parts of the system, but merely as marginal notes with the purpose of supplying to the reader helpful hints or convenient pictorial associations which may make his learning of the use of the expressions easier than the bare system of the rules would do. Such a characterization is analogous to an extra-systematic explanation which a physicist sometimes gives to the beginner. He might, for example, tell him to imagine the atoms of a gas as small balls rushing around with great speed, or the electromagnetic field and its oscillations as quasi-elastic tensions and vibrations in an ether. In fact, however, all that can accurately be said about atoms or the field is implicitly contained in the physical laws of the theories in question.[2]

The framework of thing properties. The thing-language contains words like "red", "hard", "stone", "house", etc., which are used for describing what things are like. Now we may introduce new variables, say "f", "g", etc., for which those words are substitutable and furthermore the general term "property". New rules are laid down which admit sentences like "Red is a property", "Red is a color", "These two pieces of paper have at least one color in common" (i.e., "There is an f such that f is a color, and . . ."). The last sentence is an internal assertion. It is of an empirical, factual nature. However, the external statement, the philosophical statement of the reality of properties – a special case of the thesis of the reality of universals – is devoid of cognitive content.

The frameworks of integers and rational numbers. Into a language containing the framework of natural numbers we may introduce first the (positive and negative) integers as relations among natural numbers and then the rational numbers as relations among integers. This involves introducing new types of variables, expressions substitutable for them and the general terms "integer" and "rational number".

The framework of real numbers. On the basis of the rational numbers, the real numbers may be introduced as classes of a special kind (segments) of rational numbers (according to the method developed by Dedekind and Frege). Here again a new type of variables is introduced, expressions substitutable for them (e.g., "$\sqrt{2}$"), and the general term "real number".

The framework of a spatio-temporal coordinate system for physics. The new entities are the space-time points. Each is an ordered quadruple of four real numbers, called its coordinates, consisting of three spatial and one temporal coordinates. The physical state of a spatio-temporal point or region is described either with the help of qualitative predicates (e.g., "hot") or by ascribing numbers as values of a physical magnitude (e.g., mass, temperature, and the like). The step from the framework of things (which does not contain space-time points but only extended objects with spatial and temporal relations between them) to the physical coordinate system is again a matter of decision. Our choice of certain features, although itself not theoretical, is suggested by theoretical knowledge, either logical or factual. For example, the choice of real numbers rather than rational numbers or integers as coordinates is not much influenced by the facts of experience but mainly due to considerations of mathematical simplicity. The restriction to rational coordinates would not be in conflict with any experimental knowledge we have, because the result of any measurement is a rational number. However, it would prevent the use of ordinary geometry (which says, e.g., that the diagonal of a square with the side 1 has the irrational value $\sqrt{2}$) and thus lead to great complications. On the other hand, the decision to use three rather than two or four spatial coordinates is strongly suggested, but still not forced upon us, by the result of common observations. If certain events allegedly observed in spiritualistic séances, e.g., a ball moving out of a sealed box, were confirmed beyond any reasonable doubt, it might seem advisable to use four spatial coordinates. Internal questions are here, in general, empirical questions to be answered by empirical investigations. On the

other hand, the external questions of the reality of physical space and physical time are pseudo-questions. A question like "Are there (really) space-time points?" is ambiguous. It may be meant as an internal question; then the affirmative answer is, of course, analytic and trivial. Or it may be meant in the external sense: "Shall we introduce such and such forms into our language?"; in this case it is not a theoretical but a practical question, a matter of decision rather than assertion, and hence the proposed formulation would be misleading. Or finally, it may be meant in the following sense: "Are our experiences such that the use of the linguistic forms in question will be expedient and fruitful?" This is a theoretical question of a factual, empirical nature. But it concerns a matter of degree; therefore a formulation in the form "real or not?" would be inadequate.

What does Acceptance of a Framework Mean?

Let us now summarize the essential characteristics of situations involving the introduction of a new framework of entities, characteristics which are common to the various examples outlined above.

The acceptance of a framework of new entities is represented in the language by introduction of new forms of expressions to be used according to a new set of rules. There may be new names for particular entities of the kind in question; but some such names may already occur in the language before the introduction of the new framework. (Thus, for example, the thing-language contains certainly words of the type of "blue" and "house" before the framework of properties is introduced; and it may contain words like "ten" in sentences of the form "I have ten fingers" before the framework of numbers is introduced.) The latter fact shows that the occurrence of constants of the type in question – regarded as names of entities of the new kind after the new framework is introduced – is not a sure sign of the acceptance of the framework. Therefore the introduction of such constants is not to be regarded as an essential step in the introduction of the framework. The two essential steps are rather the following. First, the introduction of a general term, a predicate of higher level, for the new kind of entities, permitting us to say of any particular entity that it belongs to this kind (e.g.,

"Red is a *property*", "Five is a *number*"). Second, the introduction of variables of the new type. The new entities are values of these variables; the constants (and the closed compound expressions, if any) are substitutable for the variables.[3] With the help of the variables, general sentences concerning the new entities can be formulated.

After the new forms are introduced into the language, it is possible to formulate with their help internal questions and possible answers to them. A question of this kind may be either empirical or logical; accordingly a true answer is either factually true or analytic.

From the internal questions we must clearly distinguish external questions, i.e., philosophical questions concerning the existence or reality of the framework itself. Many philosophers regard a question of this kind as an ontological question which must be raised and answered *before* the introduction of the new language forms. The latter introduction, they believe, is legitimate only if it can be justified by an ontological insight supplying an affirmative answer to the question of reality. In contrast to this view, we take the position that the introduction of the new ways of speaking does not need any theoretical justification because it does not imply any assertion of reality. We may still speak (and have done so) of "the acceptance of the framework" or "the acceptance of the new entities" since this form of speech is customary; but one must keep in mind that these phrases do not mean for us anything more than acceptance of the new linguistic forms. Above all, they must not be interpreted as referring to an assumption, belief, or assertion of "the reality of the entities". There is no such assertion. An alleged statement of the reality of the framework of entities is a pseudo-statement without cognitive content. To be sure, we have to face at this point an important question; but it is a practical, not a theoretical question; it is the question of whether or not to accept the new linguistic forms. The acceptance cannot be judged as being either true or false because it is not an assertion. It can only be judged as being more or less expedient, fruitful, conducive to the aim for which the language is intended. Judgments of this kind supply the motivation for the decision of accepting or rejecting the framework.[4]

Thus it is clear that the acceptance of a framework must not be regarded as implying a metaphysical doctrine concerning the reality of the entities in question. It seems to me due to a neglect of this important distinction that some contemporary nominalists label the admission of variables of abstract types as "Platonism".[5] This is, to say the least, an extremely misleading terminology. It leads to the absurd consequence, that the position of everybody who accepts the language of physics with its real number variables (as a language of communication, not merely as a calculus) would be called Platonistic, even if he is a strict empiricist who rejects Platonic metaphysics.

A brief historical remark may here be inserted. The non-cognitive character of the questions which we have called here external questions was recognized and emphasized already by the Vienna Circle under the leadership of Moritz Schlick, the group from which the movement of logical empiricism originated. Influenced by ideas of Ludwig Wittgenstein, the Circle rejected both the thesis of the reality of the external world and the thesis of its irreality as pseudo-statements;[6] the same was the case for both the thesis of the reality of universals (abstract entities, in our present terminology) and the nominalistic thesis that they are not real and that their alleged names are not names of anything but merely *flatus vocis*. (It is obvious that the apparent negation of a pseudo-statement must also be a pseudo-statement.) It is therefore not correct to classify the members of the Vienna Circle as nominalists, as is sometimes done. However, if we look at the basic anti-metaphysical and pro-scientific attitude of most nominalists (and the same holds for many materialists and realists in the modern sense), disregarding their occasional pseudo-theoretical formulations, then it is, of course, true to say that the Vienna Circle was much closer to those philosophers than to their opponents.

Abstract Entities in Semantics

The problem of the legitimacy and the status of abstract entities has recently again led to controversial discussions in connection with semantics. In a semantical meaning analysis certain expressions in a language are often said to designate (or name or denote or signify or refer to) certain extra-linguistic entities.[7] As long as physical things or events (e.g., Chicago or Caesar's death) are taken as designata (entities designated), no serious doubts arise. But strong objections have been raised, especially by some empiricists, against abstract entities as designata, e.g., against semantical statements of the following kind:

1 "The word 'red' designates a property of things";
2 "The word 'color' designates a property of properties of things";
3 "The word 'five' designates a number";
4 "The word 'odd' designates a property of numbers";
5 "The sentence 'Chicago is large' designates a proposition."

Those who criticize these statements do not, of course, reject the use of the expressions in question, like "red" or "five"; nor would they deny that these expressions are meaningful. But to be meaningful, they would say, is not the same as having a meaning in the sense of an entity designated. They reject the belief, which they regard as implicitly presupposed by those semantical statements, that to each expression of the types in question (adjectives like "red", numerals like "five", etc.) there is a particular real entity to which the expression stands in the relation of designation. This belief is rejected as incompatible with the basic principles of empiricism or of scientific thinking. Derogatory labels like "Platonic realism", "hypostatization", or " 'Fido'-Fido principle" are attached to it. The latter is the name given by Gilbert Ryle[8] to the criticized belief, which, in his view, arises by a naive inference of analogy: just as there is an entity well known to me, viz. my dog Fido, which is designated by the name "Fido", thus there must be for every meaningful expression a particular entity to which it stands in the relation of designation or naming, i.e., the relation exemplified by "Fido"-Fido. The belief criticized is thus a case of hypostatization, i.e., of treating as names expressions which are not names. While "Fido" is a name, expressions like "red", "five", etc. are said not to be names, not to designate anything.

Our previous discussions concerning the acceptance of frameworks enables us now to clarify the situation with respect to abstract entities as designata. Let us take as an example the statement:

(a) " 'Five' designates a number."

The formulation of this statement presupposes that our language L contains the forms of expressions corresponding to what we have called the

framework of numbers, in particular, numerical variables and the general term "number". If L contains these forms, the following is an analytic statement in L:

(b) "Five is a number."

Further, to make the statement (a) possible, L must contain an expression like "designates" or "is a name of" for the semantical relation of designation. If suitable rules for this term are laid down, the following is likewise analytic:

(c) " 'Five' designates five."

(Generally speaking, any expression of the form " '...' designates ..." is an analytic statement provided the term "..." is a constant in an accepted framework. If the latter condition is not fulfilled, the expression is not a statement.) Since (a) follows from (c) and (b), (a) is likewise analytic.

Thus it is clear that *if* someone accepts the framework of numbers, then he must acknowledge (c) and (b) and hence (a) as true statements. Generally speaking, if someone accepts a framework of entities, then he is bound to admit its entities as possible designata. Thus the question of the admissibility of entities of a certain type or of abstract entities in general as designata is reduced to the question of the acceptability of those entities. Both the nominalistic critics, who refuse the status of designators or names to expressions like "red", "five", etc., because they deny the existence of abstract entities, and the skeptics, who express doubts concerning the existence and demand evidence for it, treat the question of existence as a theoretical question. They do, of course, not mean the internal question; the affirmative answer to *this* question is analytic and trivial and too obvious for doubt or denial, as we have seen. Their doubts refer rather to the framework itself; hence they mean the external question. They believe that only after making sure that there really are entities of the kinds in question are we justified in accepting the framework by incorporating the linguistic forms into our language. However, we have seen that the external question is not a theoretical question but rather the practical question whether or not to accept those linguistic forms. This acceptance is not in need of a theoretical justification (except with respect to expediency and fruitfulness), because it does not imply a belief or assertion. Ryle says that the "Fido"-Fido principle is "a grotesque theory". Grotesque or not, Ryle is wrong in calling it a theory. It is rather the practical decision to accept certain frameworks. Maybe Ryle is historically right with respect to those whom he mentions as previous representatives of the principle, viz. John Stuart Mill, Frege, and Russell. If these philosophers regarded the acceptance of a framework of entities as a theory, an assertion, they were victims of the same old, metaphysical confusion. But it is certainly wrong to regard *my* semantic method as involving a belief in the reality of abstract entities, since I reject a thesis of this kind as a metaphysical pseudo-statement.

The critics of the use of abstract entities in semantics overlook the fundamental difference between the acceptance of a framework of entities and an internal assertion, e.g., an assertion that there are elephants or electrons or prime numbers greater than a million. Whoever makes an internal assertion is certainly obliged to justify it by providing evidence, empirical evidence in the case of electrons, logical proof in the case of the prime numbers. The demand for a theoretical justification, correct in the case of internal assertions, is sometimes wrongly applied to the acceptance of a framework of entities. Thus, for example, Ernest Nagel[9] asks for "evidence relevant for affirming with warrant that there are such entities as infinitesimals or propositions". He characterizes the evidence required in these cases – in distinction to the empirical evidence in the case of electrons – as "in the broad sense logical and dialectical". Beyond this no hint is given as to what might be regarded as relevant evidence. Some nominalists regard the acceptance of abstract entities as a kind of superstition or myth, populating the world with fictitious or at least dubious entities, analogous to the belief in centaurs or demons. This shows again the confusion mentioned, because a superstition or myth is a false (or dubious) internal statement.

Let us take as example the natural numbers as cardinal numbers, i.e., in contexts like "Here are three books". The linguistic forms of the framework of numbers, including variables and the general term "number" are generally used in our common language of communication; and it is easy to formulate explicit rules for their use. Thus the logical characteristics of this framework are sufficiently clear (while many internal questions,

i.e., arithmetical questions, are, of course, still open). In spite of this, the controversy concerning the external question of the ontological reality of numbers continues. Suppose that one philosopher says: "I believe that there are numbers as real entities. This gives me the right to use the linguistic forms of the numerical framework and to make semantical statements about numbers as designata of numerals." His nominalistic opponent replies: "You are wrong; there are no numbers. The numerals may still be used as meaningful expressions. But they are not names, there are no entities designated by them. Therefore the word 'number' and numerical variables must not be used (unless a way were found to introduce them as merely abbreviating devices, a way of translating them into the nominalistic thing language)." I cannot think of any possible evidence that would be regarded as relevant by both philosophers, and therefore, if actually found, would decide the controversy or at least make one of the opposite theses more probable than the other. (To construe the numbers as classes or properties of the second level, according to the Frege–Russell method does, of course, not solve the controversy, because the first philosopher would affirm and the second deny the existence of classes or properties of the second level.) Therefore I feel compelled to regard the external question as a pseudo-question, until both parties to the controversy offer a common interpretation of the question as a cognitive question; this would involve an indication of possible evidence regarded as relevant by both sides.

There is a particular kind of misinterpretation of the acceptance of abstract entities in various fields of science and in semantics, that needs to be cleared up. Certain early British empiricists (e.g., Berkeley and Hume) denied the existence of abstract entities on the ground that immediate experience presents us only with particulars, not with universals, e.g., with this red patch, but not with Redness or Color-in-General; with this scalene triangle, but not with Scalene Triangularity or Triangularity-in-General. Only entities belonging to a type of which examples were to be found within immediate experience could be accepted as ultimate constituents of reality. Thus, according to this way of thinking, the existence of abstract entities could be asserted only if one could show either that some abstract entities fall within the given, or that abstract entities can be defined in terms of the types of entity which are given. Since these empiricists found no abstract entities within the realm of sense-data, they either denied their existence, or else made a futile attempt to define universals in terms of particulars. Some contemporary philosophers, especially English philosophers following Bertrand Russell, think in basically similar terms. They emphasize a distinction between the data (that which is immediately given in consciousness, e.g. sense-data, immediately past experiences, etc.) and the constructs based on the data. Existence or reality is ascribed only to the data; the constructs are not real entities; the corresponding linguistic expressions are merely ways of speech not actually designating anything (reminiscent of the nominalists' *flatus vocis*). We shall not criticize here this general conception. (As far as it is a principle of accepting certain entities and not accepting others, leaving aside any ontological, phenomenalistic and nominalistic pseudo-statements, there cannot be any theoretical objection to it.) But if this conception leads to the view that other philosophers or scientists who accept abstract entities thereby assert or imply their occurrence as immediate data, then such a view must be rejected as a misinterpretation. References to space-time points, the electromagnetic field, or electrons in physics, to real or complex numbers and their functions in mathematics, to the excitatory potential or unconscious complexes in psychology, to an inflationary trend in economics, and the like, do not imply the assertion that entities of these kinds occur as immediate data. And the same holds for references to abstract entities as designata in semantics. Some of the criticisms by English philosophers against such references give the impression that, probably due to the misinterpretation just indicated, they accuse the semanticist not so much of bad metaphysics (as some nominalists would do) but of bad psychology. The fact that they regard a semantical method involving abstract entities not merely as doubtful and perhaps wrong, but as manifestly absurd, preposterous and grotesque, and that they show a deep horror and indignation against this method, is perhaps to be explained by a misinterpretation of the kind described. In fact, of course, the semanticist does not in the least assert or imply that the abstract entities to which he refers can be experienced as immediately given either by sensation or by a kind of rational intuition. An assertion of this kind would indeed be very dubious psychology. The psychological question

as to which kinds of entities do and which do not occur as immediate data is entirely irrelevant for semantics, just as it is for physics, mathematics, economics, etc., with respect to the examples mentioned above.[10]

Conclusion

For those who want to develop or use semantical methods, the decisive question is not the alleged ontological question of the existence of abstract entities but rather the question whether the use of abstract linguistic forms or, in technical terms, the use of variables beyond those for things (or phenomenal data), is expedient and fruitful for the purposes for which semantical analyses are made, viz. the analysis, interpretation, clarification, or construction of languages of communication, especially languages of science. This question is here neither decided nor even discussed. It is not a question simply of yes or no, but a matter of degree. Among those philosophers who have carried out semantical analyses and thought about suitable tools for this work, beginning with Plato and Aristotle and, in a more technical way on the basis of modern logic, with C. S. Pierce and Frege, a great majority accepted abstract entities. This does, of course, not prove the case. After all, semantics in the technical sense is still in the initial phases of its development, and we must be prepared for possible fundamental changes in methods. Let us therefore admit that the nominalistic critics may possibly be right. But if so, they will have to offer better arguments than they did so far. Appeal to ontological insight will not carry much weight. The critics will have to show that it is possible to construct a semantical method which avoids all references to abstract entities and achieves by simpler means essentially the same results as the other methods.

The acceptance or rejection of abstract linguistic forms, just as the acceptance or rejection of any other linguistic forms in any branch of science, will finally be decided by their efficiency as instruments, the ratio of the results achieved to the amount and complexity of the efforts required. To decree dogmatic prohibitions of certain linguistic forms instead of testing them by their success or failure in practical use, is worse than futile; it is positively harmful because it may obstruct scientific progress. The history of science shows examples of such prohibitions based on prejudices deriving from religious, mythological, metaphysical, or other irrational sources, which slowed up the developments for shorter or longer periods of time. Let us learn from the lessons of history. Let us grant to those who work in any special field of investigation the freedom to use any form of expression which seems useful to them; the work in the field will sooner or later lead to the elimination of those forms which have no useful function. *Let us be cautious in making assertions and critical in examining them, but tolerant in permitting linguistic forms.*

Notes

1 The terms "sentence" and "statement" are here used synonymously for declarative (indicative, propositional) sentences.

2 In my book *Meaning and Necessity* (Chicago, 1947) I have developed a semantic method which takes propositions as entities designated by sentences (more specifically, as intensions of sentences). In order to facilitate the understanding of the systematic development, I added some informal, extra-systematic explanations concerning the nature of propositions. I said that the term "proposition" "is used neither for a linguistic expression nor for a subjective, mental occurrence, but rather for something objective that may or may not be exemplified in nature ... We apply the term 'proposition' to any entities of a certain logical type, namely, those that may be expressed by (declarative) sentences in a language" (p. 27). After some more detailed discussions concerning the relation between propositions and facts, and the nature of false propositions, I added: "It has been the purpose of the preceding remarks to facilitate the understanding of our conception of propositions. If, however, a reader should find these explanations more puzzling than clarifying, or even unacceptable, he may disregard them" (p. 31) (that is, disregard these extra-systematic explanations, not the whole theory of the propositions as intensions of sentences, as one reviewer understood). In spite of this warning, it seems that some of those readers who were puzzled by the explanations, did not disregard them but thought that by raising objections against them they could refute the theory. This is analogous to the procedure of some laymen who by (correctly) criticizing the other picture or other visualizations of physical theories, thought they had refuted those theories. Perhaps the discussions in the present paper will help in clarifying the role of the system of linguistic rules for the introduction of a framework of entities on the one hand, and that of extra-systematic explanations concerning the nature of the entities on the other.

3 W. V. Quine was the first to recognize the importance of the introduction of variables as indicating the acceptance of entities. "The ontology to which one's use of language commits him comprises simply the objects that he treats as falling ... within the range of values of his variables" ("Notes on Existence and Necessity", *Journal of Philosophy* 40 (1943), pp. 113–27, see p. 118; compare also his "Designation and Existence", *Journal of Philosophy* 36 (1939), pp. 701–9, and "On Universals", *Journal of Symbolic Logic* 12 (1947), pp. 74–84).

4 For a closely related point of view on these questions see the detailed discussions in Herbert Feigl, "Existential Hypotheses", *Philosophy of Science* 17 (1950), pp. 35–62.

5 Paul Bernays, "Sur le platonisme dans les mathématiques", *L'Enseignement mathématique* 34 (1935), pp. 52–69. W. V. Quine, see note 3 above, and a recent paper "On What There Is," *Review of Metaphysics* 2 (1948), pp. 21–38. Quine does not acknowledge the distinction which I emphasize above, because according to his general conception there are no sharp boundary lines between logical and factual truth, between questions of meaning and questions of fact, between the acceptance of a language structure and the acceptance of an assertion formulated in the language. This conception, which seems to deviate considerably from customary ways of thinking, will be explained in his forthcoming book, *Foundations of Logic*. When Quine in the article mentioned above classifies my logicistic conception of mathematics (derived from Frege and Russell) as "platonic realism" (p. 33), this is meant (according to a personal communication from him) not as ascribing to me agreement with Plato's metaphysical doctrine of universals, but merely as referring to the fact that I accept a language of mathematics containing variables of higher levels. With respect to the basic attitude to take in choosing a language form (an "ontology" in Quine's terminology, which seems to me misleading), there appears now to be agreement between us: "the obvious counsel is tolerance and an experimental spirit" ("On What There Is", p. 38).

6 See Carnap, *Scheinprobleme in der Philosophie; das Fremdpsychische und der Realismusstreit*, Berlin, 1928. Moritz Schlick, *Positivismus und Realismus*, reprinted in *Gesammelte Aufsätze*, Vienna, 1938.

7 *See Introduction to Semantics* (Cambridge, MA, 1942); *Meaning and Necessity* (Chicago, 1947). The distinction I have drawn in the latter book between

the method of the name-relation and the method of intension and extension is not essential for our present discussion. The term "designation" is here used in a neutral way; it may be understood as referring to the name-relation or to the intension-relation or to the extension-relation or to any similar relations used in other semantical methods.

8 G. Ryle, "Meaning and Necessity", *Philosophy* 24 (1949), pp. 69–76.

9 E. Nagel, Review of Carnap, *Meaning and Necessity, Journal of Philosophy* 45 (1948), pp. 467–72.

10 Wilfrid Sellars ("Acquaintance and Description Again", in *Journal of Philosophy* 46 (1949), pp. 496–504, see pp. 502f.) analyzes clearly the roots of the mistake "of taking the designation relation of semantic theory to be a reconstruction of *being present to an experience*".

42

A Plea for Excuses

J. L. Austin

The subject of this paper, *Excuses*, is one not to be treated, but only to be introduced, within such limits. It is, or might be, the name of a whole branch, even a ramiculated branch, of philosophy, or at least of one fashion of philosophy. I shall try, therefore, first to state *what* the subject is, *why* it is worth studying, and *how* it may be studied, all this at a regrettably lofty level: and then I shall illustrate, in more congenial but desultory detail, some of the methods to be used, together with their limitations, and some of the unexpected results to be expected and lessons to be learned. Much, of course, of the amusement, and of the instruction, comes in drawing the coverts of the microglot, in hounding down the minutiae, and to this I can do no more here than incite you. But I owe it to the subject to say, that it has long afforded me what philosophy is so often thought, and made, barren of – the fun of discovery, the pleasures of co-operation, and the satisfaction of reaching agreement.

What, then, is the subject? I am here using the word 'excuses' *for a title*, but it would be unwise to freeze too fast to this one noun and its partner verb: indeed for some time I used to use 'extenuation' instead. Still, on the whole 'excuses' is probably the most central and embracing term in the field, although this includes others of importance – 'plea', 'defence', 'justification', and

so on. When, then, do we 'excuse' conduct, our own or somebody else's? When are 'excuses' proffered?

In general, the situation is one where someone is *accused* of having done something, or (if that will keep it any cleaner) where someone is *said* to have done something which is bad, wrong, inept, unwelcome, or in some other of the numerous possible ways untoward. Thereupon he, or someone on his behalf, will try to defend his conduct or to get him out of it.

One way of going about this is to admit flatly that he, X, did do that very thing, A, but to argue that it was a good thing, or the right or sensible thing, or a permissible thing to do, either in general or at least in the special circumstances of the occasion. To take this line is to *justify* the action, to give reasons for doing it: not to say, to brazen it out, to glory in it, or the like.

A different way of going about it is to admit that it wasn't a good thing to have done, but to argue that it is not quite fair or correct to say *baldly* 'X did A'. We may say it isn't fair just to say X did it; perhaps he was under somebody's influence, or was nudged. Or, it isn't fair to say baldly he *did* A; it may have been partly accidental, or an unintentional slip. Or, it isn't fair to say he did simply A – he was really doing something quite different and A was only incidental, or he was looking as the whole thing quite differently. Naturally these arguments can be combined or overlap or run into each other.

In the one defence, briefly, we accept responsibility but deny that it was bad: in the other, we

Originally published in *Proceedings of the Aristotelian Society* 57 (1956–7). Reprinted by courtesy of the Editor of the Aristotelian Society: © 1956–1957.

admit that it was bad but don't accept full, or even any, responsibility.

By and large, justifications can be kept distinct from excuses, and I shall not be so anxious to talk about them because they have enjoyed more than their fair share of philosophical attention. But the two certainly can be confused, and can *seem* to go very near to each other, even if they do not perhaps actually do so. You dropped the tea-tray: Certainly, but an emotional storm was about to break out: or, Yes, but there was a wasp. In each case the defence, very soundly, insists on a fuller description of the event in its context; but the first is a justification, the second an excuse. Again, if the objection is to the use of such a dyslogistic verb as 'murdered', this may be on the ground that the killing was done in battle (justification) or on the ground that it was only accidental if reckless (excuse). It is arguable that we do not use the terms justification and excuse as carefully as we might; a miscellany of even less clear terms, such as 'extenuation', 'palliation', 'mitigation', hovers uneasily between partial justification and partial excuse; and when we plead, say, provocation, there is genuine uncertainty or ambiguity as to what we mean – is *he* partly responsible, because he roused a violent impulse or passion in me, so that it wasn't truly or merely me acting 'of my own accord' (excuse)? Or is it rather that, he having done me such injury, I was entitled to retaliate (justification)? Such doubts merely make it the more urgent to clear up the usage of these various terms. But that the defences I have for convenience labelled 'justification' and 'excuse' are in principle distinct can scarcely be doubted.

This then is the sort of situation we have to consider under 'excuses'. I will only further point out how very wide a field it covers. We have, of course, to bring in the opposite numbers of excuses – the expressions that *aggravate*, such as 'deliberately', 'on purpose', and so on, if only for the reason that an excuse often takes the form of a rebuttal of one of these. But we have also to bring in a large number of expressions which at first blush look not so much like excuses as like accusations – 'clumsiness', 'tactlessness', 'thoughtlessness', and the like. Because it has always to be remembered that few excuses get us out of it *completely*: the average excuse, in a poor situation, gets us only out of the fire into the frying pan – but still, of course, any frying pan in a fire. If I have broken your dish or your

romance, maybe the best defence I can find will be clumsiness.

Why, if this is what 'excuses' are, should we trouble to investigate them? It might be thought reason enough that their production has always bulked so large among human activities. But to moral philosophy in particular a study of them will contribute in special ways, both positively towards the development of a cautious, latter-day version of conduct, and negatively towards the correction of older and hastier theories.

In ethics we study, I suppose, the good and the bad, the right and the wrong, and this must be for the most part in some connexion with conduct or the doing of actions. Yet before we consider what actions are good or bad, right or wrong, it is proper to consider first what is meant by, and what not, and what is included under, and what not, the expression 'doing an action' or 'doing something'. These are expressions still too little examined on their own account and merits, just as the general notion of 'saying something' is still too lightly passed over in logic. There is indeed a vague and comforting idea in the background that, after all, in the last analysis, doing an action must come down to the making of physical movements with parts of the body; but this is about as true as that saying something must, in the last analysis, come down to making movements of the tongue.

The beginning of sense, not to say wisdom, is to realize that 'doing an action', as used in philosophy,[1] is a highly abstract expression – it is a stand-in used in the place of any (or almost any?) verb with a personal subject, in the same sort of way that 'thing' is a stand-in for any (or when we remember, almost any) noun substantive, and 'quality' a stand-in for the adjective. Nobody, to be sure, relies on such dummies quite implicitly quite indefinitely. Yet notoriously it is possible to arrive at, or to derive the idea for, an over-simplified metaphysics from the obsession with 'things' and their 'qualities'. In a similar way, less commonly recognized even in these semi-sophisticated times, we fall for the myth of the verb. We treat the expression 'doing an action' no longer as a stand-in for a verb with a personal subject, as which it has no doubt some uses, and might have more if the range of verbs were not left unspecified, but as a self-explanatory, ground-level description, one which brings adequately into the open the essential features of everything that comes, by simple inspection, under it. We

437

scarcely notice even the most patent exceptions or difficulties (is to think something, or to say something, or to try to do something, to do an action?), any more than we fret, in the *ivresse des grandes profondeurs*, as to whether flames are things or events. So we come easily to think of our behaviour over any time, and of a life as a whole, as consisting in doing now action A, next action B, then action C, and so on, just as elsewhere we come to think of the world as consisting of this, that and the other substance or material thing, each with its properties. All 'actions' are, as actions (meaning what?), equal, composing a quarrel with striking a match, winning a war with sneezing: worse still, we assimilate them one and all to the supposedly most obvious and easy cases, such as posting letters or moving fingers, just as we assimilate all 'things' to horses or beds.

If we are to continue to use this expression in sober philosophy, we need to ask such questions as: Is to sneeze to do an action? Or is to breathe, or to see, or to checkmate, or each one of countless others? In short, for what range of verbs, as used on what occasions, is 'doing an action' a stand-in? What have they in common, and what do those excluded severally lack? Again we need to ask how we decide what is the correct name for 'the' action that somebody did – and what, indeed, are the rules for the use of 'the' action, 'an' action, 'one' action, a 'part' or 'phase' of an action and the like. Further, we need to realize that even the 'simplest' named actions are not so simple – certainly are not the mere makings of physical movements, and to ask what more, then, comes in (intentions? conventions?) and what does not (motives?), and what is the detail of the complicated internal machinery we use in 'acting' – the receipt of intelligence, the appreciation of the situation, the invocation of principles, the planning, the control of execution and the rest.

In two main ways the study of excuses can throw light on these fundamental matters. First, to examine excuses is to examine cases where there has been some abnormality or failure: and as so often, the abnormal will throw light on the normal, will help us to penetrate the blinding veil of ease and obviousness that hides the mechanisms of the natural successful act. It rapidly becomes plain that the breakdowns signalized by the various excuses are of radically different kinds, affecting different parts or stages of the machinery, which the excuses consequently pick out and sort out for us. Further, it emerges that not *every* slip-up occurs in connexion with *every*thing that could be called an 'action', that not every excuse is apt with every verb – far indeed from it: and this provides us with one means of introducing some classification into the vast miscellany of 'actions'. If we classify them according to the particular selection of breakdowns to which each is liable, this should assign them their places in some family group or groups of actions, or in some model of the machinery of acting.

In this sort of way, the philosophical study of conduct can get off to a positive fresh start. But by the way, and more negatively, a number of traditional cruces or mistakes in this field can be resolved or removed. First among these comes the problem of Freedom. While it has been the tradition to present this as the 'positive' term requiring elucidation, there is little doubt that to say we acted 'freely' (in the philosopher's use, which is only faintly related to the everyday use) is to say only that we acted *not* un-freely, in one or another of the many heterogeneous ways of so acting (under duress, or what not). Like 'real', 'free' is only used to rule out the suggestion of some or all of its recognized antitheses. As 'truth' is not a name for a characteristic of assertions, so 'freedom' is not a name for a characteristic of actions, but the name of a dimension in which actions are assessed. In examining all the ways in which each action may not be 'free', i.e. the cases in which it will not do to say simply 'X did A', we may hope to dispose of the problem of Freedom. Aristotle has often been chidden for talking about excuses or pleas and overlooking 'the real problem': in my own case, it was when I began to see the injustice of this charge that I first became interested in excuses.

There is much to be said for the view that, philosophical tradition apart, Responsibility would be a better candidate for the role here assigned to Freedom. If ordinary language is to be our guide, it is to evade responsibility, or full responsibility, that we most often make excuses, and I have used the word myself in this way above. But in fact 'responsibility' too seems not really apt in all cases: I do not exactly evade responsibility when I plead clumsiness or tactlessness, nor, often, when I plead that I only did it unwillingly or reluctantly, and still less if I plead that I had in the circumstances no choice: here I was constrained and have an excuse (or justification), yet may accept responsibility. It may be, then, that at least two key terms, Freedom and Responsibility, are needed: the relation between them is not clear, and it may be hoped that the investigation of excuses will contribute towards its clarification.[2]

So much, then, for ways in which the study of excuses may throw light on ethics. But there are also reasons why it is an attractive subject methodologically, at least if we are to proceed from 'ordinary language', that is, by examining *what we should say when*, and so why and what we should mean by it. Perhaps this method, at least as *one* philosophical method, scarcely requires justification at present – too evidently, there is gold in them thar hills: more opportune would be a warning about the care and thoroughness needed if it is not to fall into disrepute. I will, however, justify it very briefly.

First, words are our tools, and, as a minimum, we should use clean tools: we should know what we mean and what we do not, and we must forearm ourselves against the traps that language sets us. Secondly, words are not (except in their own little corner) facts or things: we need therefore to prise them off the world, to hold them apart from and against it, so that we can realize their inadequacies and arbitrariness, and can relook at the world without blinkers. Thirdly, and more hopefully, our common stock of words embodies all the distinctions men have found worth drawing, and the connexions they have found worth marking, in the lifetimes of many generations: these surely are likely to be more numerous, more sound, since they have stood up to the long test of the survival of the fittest, and more subtle, at least in all ordinary and reasonably practical matters, than any that you or I are likely to think up in our armchairs of an afternoon – the most favoured alternative method.

In view of the prevalence of the slogan 'ordinary language', and of such names as 'linguistic' or 'analytic' philosophy or 'the analysis of language', one thing needs specially emphasizing to counter misunderstandings. When we examine what we should say when, what words we should use in what situations, we are looking again not *merely* at words (or 'meanings', whatever they may be) but also at the realities we use the words to talk about: we are using a sharpened awareness of words to sharpen our perception of, though not as the final arbiter of, the phenomena. For this reason I think it might be better to use, for this way of doing philosophy, some less misleading name than those given above – for instance, 'linguistic phenomenology', only that is rather a mouthful.

Using, then, such a method, it is plainly preferable to investigate a field where ordinary language is rich and subtle, as it is in the pressingly practical matter of Excuses, but certainly is not in the matter, say, of Time. At the same time we should prefer a field which is not too much trodden into bogs or tracks by traditional philosophy, for in that case even 'ordinary' language will often have become infected with the jargon of extinct theories, and our own prejudices too, as the upholders or imbibers of theoretical views, will be too readily, and often insensibly, engaged. Here too, Excuses form an admirable topic; we can discuss at least clumsiness, or absence of mind, or inconsiderateness, even spontaneousness, without remembering what Kant thought, and so progress by degrees even to discussing deliberation without for once remembering Aristotle or self-control without Plato. Granted that our subject is, as already claimed for it, neighbouring, analogous or germane in some way to some notorious centre of philosophical trouble, then; with these two further requirements satisfied, we should be certain of what we are after: a good site for *field work* in philosophy. Here at last we should be able to unfreeze, to loosen up and get going on agreeing about discoveries, however small, and on agreeing about how to reach agreement.[3] How much it is to be wished that similar field work will soon be undertaken in, say, aesthetics; if only we could forget for a while about the beautiful and get down instead to the dainty and the dumpy.

There are, I know, or are supposed to be, snags in 'linguistic' philosophy, which those not very familiar with it find, sometimes not without glee or relief, daunting. But with snags, as with nettles, the thing to do is to grasp them – and to climb above them. I will mention two in particular, over which the study of excuses may help to encourage us. The first is the snag of Loose (or Divergent or Alternative) Usage; and the second the crux of the Last Word. Do we all say the same, and only the same, things in the same situations? Don't usages differ? And, Why should what we all ordinarily say be the only or the best or final way of putting it? Why should it even be true?

Well, people's usages do vary, and we do talk loosely, and we do say different things apparently indifferently. But first, not nearly as much as one would think. When we come down to cases, it transpires in the very great majority that what we had thought was our wanting to say different things of and in *the same* situation was really not so – we had simply imagined the situation *slightly* differently: which is all too easy to do, because of course no situation (and we are dealing with *imagined* situations) is ever 'completely' described. The more we imagine the situation in detail, with a background of story – and it is worth employing the most idiosyncratic or, sometimes, boring means to stimulate and to discipline our wretched imaginations – the less we find we disagree about what we should say. Nevertheless, *sometimes* we do ultimately disagree: sometimes we must allow a usage to be, though appalling, yet actual; sometimes we should genuinely use either or both of two different descriptions. But why should this daunt us? All that is happening is entirely explicable. If our usages disagree, then you use 'X' where I use 'Y', or more probably (and more intriguingly) your conceptual system is different from mine, though very likely it is at least equally consistent and serviceable: in short, we can find *why* we disagree – you choose to classify in one way, I in another. If the usage is loose, we can understand the temptation that leads to it, and the distinctions that it blurs: if there are 'alternative' descriptions, then the situation can be described or can be 'structured' in two ways, or perhaps it is one where, for current purposes, the two alternatives come down to the same. A disagreement as to what we should say is not to be shied off, but to be pounced upon: for the explanation of it can hardly fail to be illuminating. If we light on an electron that rotates the wrong way, that is a discovery, a portent to be followed up, not a reason for chucking physics: and by the same token, a genuinely loose or eccentric talker is a rare specimen to be prized.

As practice in learning to handle this bogey, in learning the essential *rubrics*, we could scarcely hope for a more promising exercise than the study of excuses. Here, surely, is just the sort of situation where people will say 'almost anything', because they are so flurried, or so anxious to get off. 'It was a mistake', 'It was an accident' – how readily these can *appear* indifferent, and even be used together. Yet, a story or two, and everybody will not merely agree that they are completely different, but even discover

for himself what the difference is and what each means.[4]

Then, for the Last Word. Certainly ordinary language has no claim to be the last word, if there is such a thing. It embodies, indeed, something better than the metaphysics of the Stone Age, namely, as was said, the inherited experience and acumen of many generations of men. But then, that acumen has been concentrated primarily upon the practical business of life. If a distinction works well for practical purposes in ordinary life (no mean feat, for even ordinary life is full of hard cases), then there is sure to be something in it, it will not mark nothing: yet this is likely enough to be not the best way of arranging things if our interests are more extensive or intellectual than the ordinary. And again, that experience has been derived only from the sources available to ordinary men throughout most of civilized history: it has not been fed from the resources of the microscope and its successors. And it must be added too, that superstition and error and fantasy of all kinds do become incorporated in ordinary language and even sometimes stand up to the survival test (only, when they do, why should we not detect it?). Certainly, then, ordinary language is *not* the last word: in principle it can everywhere be supplemented and improved upon and superseded. Only remember, it *is* the *first* word.[5]

For this problem too the field of Excuses is a fruitful one. Here is matter both contentious and practically important for everybody, so that ordinary language is on its toes: yet also, on its back it has long had a bigger flea to bite it, in the shape of the Law, and both again have lately attracted the attentions of yet another, and at least a healthily growing, flea, in the shape of psychology. In the law a constant stream of actual cases, more novel and more tortuous than the mere imagination could contrive, are brought up *for decision* – that is, formulae for docketing them must somehow be found. Hence it is necessary first to be careful with, but also to be brutal with, to torture, to fake and to override, ordinary language: we cannot here evade or forget the whole affair. (In ordinary life we dismiss the puzzles that crop up about time, but we cannot do that indefinitely in physics.) Psychology likewise produces novel cases, but it also produces new methods for bringing phenomena under observation and study: moreover, unlike the law, it has an unbiased interest in the totality of them and is unpressed for decision. Hence its own special and constant need to supplement, to revise and to supersede the classifications of both ordinary life and the law. We have, then, ample material for practice in learning to handle the bogey of the Last Word, however it should be handled.

Suppose, then, that we set out to investigate excuses, what are the methods and resources initially available? Our object is to imagine the varieties of situation in which we make excuses, and to examine the expressions used in making them. If we have a lively imagination, together perhaps with an ample experience of dereliction, we shall go far, only we need system: I do not know how many of you keep a list of the kinds of fool you make of yourselves. It is advisable to use systematic aids, of which there would appear to be three at least. I list them here in order of availability to the layman.

First we may use the dictionary – quite a concise one will do, but the use must be *thorough*. Two methods suggest themselves, both a little tedious, but repaying. One is to read the book through, listing all the words that seem relevant; this does not take as long as many suppose. The other is to start with a widish selection of obviously relevant terms, and to consult the dictionary under each: it will be found that, in the explanations of the various meanings of each, a surprising number of other terms occur, which are germane though of course not often synonymous. We then look up each of *these*, bringing in more for our bag from the 'definitions' given in each case; and when we have continued for a little, it will generally be found that the family circle begins to close, until ultimately it is complete and we come only upon repetitions. This method has the advantage of grouping the terms into convenient clusters – but of course a good deal will depend upon the comprehensiveness of our initial selection.

Working the dictionary, it is interesting to find that a high percentage of the terms connected with excuses prove to be *adverbs*, a type of word which has not enjoyed so large a share of the philosophical limelight as the noun, substantive or adjective, and the verb: this is natural because, as was said, the tenor of so many excuses is that I did it but only *in a way*, not just flatly like that – i.e. the verb needs modifying. Besides adverbs, however, there are other words of all kinds, including numerous abstract nouns, 'misconception,' 'accident', 'purpose', and the like, and

a few verbs too, which often hold key positions for the grouping of excuses into classes at a high level ('couldn't help', 'didn't mean to', 'didn't realize', or again 'intend', and 'attempt'). In connexion with the nouns another neglected class of words is prominent, namely, prepositions. Not merely does it matter considerably which preposition, often of several, is being used with a given substantive, but further the prepositions deserve study on their own account. For the question suggests itself, Why are the nouns in one, group governed by 'under', in another by 'on', in yet another by 'by' or 'through' or 'from' or 'for' or 'with', and so on? It will be disappointing if there prove to be no good reasons for such groupings.

Our second source-book will naturally be the law. This will provide us with an immense miscellany of untoward cases, and also with a useful list of recognized pleas, together with a good deal of acute analysis of both. No one who tries this resource will long be in doubt, I think, that the common law, and in particular the law of tort, is the richest storehouse; crime and contract contribute some special additions of their own, but tort is altogether more comprehensive and more flexible. But even here, and still more with so old and hardened a branch of the law as crime, much caution is needed with the arguments of counsel and the dicta or decisions of judges: acute though these are, it has always to be remembered that, in legal cases –

1 there is the overriding requirement that a decision be reached, and a relatively black or white decision – guilty or not guilty – for the plaintiff or for the defendant;
2 there is the general requirement that the charge or action and the pleadings be brought under one or another of the heads and procedures that have come in the course of history to be accepted by the Courts. These, though fairly numerous, are still few and stereotyped in comparison with the accusations and defences of daily life. Moreover contentions of many kinds are beneath the law, as too trivial, or outside it, as too purely moral – for example, inconsiderateness;
3 there is the general requirement that we argue from and abide by precedents. The value of this in the law is unquestionable, but it can certainly lead to distortions of ordinary beliefs and expressions.

For such reasons as these, obviously closely connected and stemming from the nature and function of the law, practising lawyers and jurists are by no means so careful as they might be to give to our ordinary expressions their ordinary meanings and applications. There is special pleading and evasion, stretching and strait-jacketing, besides the invention of technical terms, or technical senses for common terms. Nevertheless, it is a perpetual and salutary surprise to discover how much is to be learned from the law; and it is to be added that if a distinction drawn is a sound one, even though not yet recognized in law, a lawyer can be relied upon to take note of it, for it may be dangerous not to – if he does not, his opponent may.

Finally, the third source-book is psychology, with which I include such studies as anthropology and animal behaviour. Here I speak with even more trepidation than about the Law. But this at least is clear, that some varieties of behaviour, some ways of acting or explanations of the doing of actions, are here noticed and classified which have not been observed or named by ordinary men and hallowed by ordinary language, though perhaps they often might have been so if they had been of more practical importance. There is real danger in contempt for the 'jargon' of psychology, at least when it sets out to supplement, and at least sometimes when it sets out to supplant, the language of ordinary life.

With these sources, and with the aid of the imagination, it will go hard if we cannot arrive at the meanings of large numbers of expressions and at the understanding and classification of large numbers of 'actions'. Then we shall comprehend clearly much that, before, we only made use of ad hoc. Definition, I would add, explanatory definition, should stand high among our aims: it is not enough to show how clever we are by showing how obscure everything is. Clarity, too, I know, has been said to be not enough: but perhaps it will be time to go into that when we are within measurable distance of achieving clarity on some matter.

So much for the cackle. It remains to make a few remarks, not, I am afraid, in any very coherent order, about the types of significant result to be obtained and the more general lessons to be learned from the study of Excuses.

1. *No modification without aberration.* When it is stated that X did A, there is a temptation to suppose that given some, indeed perhaps *any*, expression modifying the verb we shall be entitled to insert either it or its opposite or negation in our statement: that is, we shall be entitled to ask, typically, 'Did X do A Mly or not Mly?' (e.g. 'Did X murder Y voluntarily or involuntarily?'), and to answer one or the other. Or as a minimum it is supposed that if X did A there must be at least *one* modifying expression that we could, justifiably and informatively, insert with the verb. In the great majority of cases of the use of the great majority of verbs ('murder' perhaps is not one of the majority) such suppositions are quite unjustified. The natural economy of language dictates that for the *standard* case covered by any normal verb – not, perhaps, a verb of omen such as 'murder', but a verb like 'eat' or 'kick' or 'croquet' – no modifying expression is required or even permissible. Only if we do the action named in some *special* way or circumstances, different from those in which such an act is naturally done (and of course both the normal and the abnormal differ according to what verb in particular is in question) is a modifying expression called for, or even in order. I sit in my chair, in the usual way – I am not in a daze or influenced by threats or the like: here, it will not do to say either that I sat in it intentionally or that I did not sit in it intentionally,[6] nor yet that I sat in it automatically or from habit or what you will. It is bedtime, I am alone, I yawn: but I do not yawn involuntarily (or voluntarily!), nor yet deliberately. To yawn in any such peculiar way is just not to just yawn.

2. *Limitation of application.* Expressions modifying verbs, typically adverbs, have limited ranges of application. That is, given any adverb of excuse, such as 'unwittingly' or 'spontaneously' or 'impulsively', it will not be found that it makes good sense to attach it to any and every verb of 'action' in any and every context: indeed, it will often apply only to a comparatively narrow range of such verbs. Something in the lad's upturned face appealed to him, he threw a brick at it – 'spontaneously'? The interest then is to discover why some actions can be excused in a particular way but not others, particularly perhaps the latter.[7] This will largely elucidate the meaning of the excuse, and at the same time will illuminate the characteristics typical of the group of 'actions' it picks out: very often too it will throw light on some detail of the machinery of

'action' in general (see 4), or on our standards of acceptable conduct (see 5). It is specially important in the case of some of the terms most favoured by philosophers or jurists to realize that at least in ordinary speech (disregarding back-seepage of jargon) they are not used so universally or so dichotomistically. For example, take 'voluntarily' and 'involuntarily': we may join the army or make a gift voluntarily, we may hiccough or make a small gesture involuntarily, and the more we consider further actions which we might naturally be said to do in either of these ways, the more circumscribed and unlike each other do the two classes become, until we even doubt whether there is *any* verb with which both adverbs are equally in place. Perhaps there are some such; but at least sometimes when we may think we have found one it is an illusion, an apparent exception that really does prove the rule. I can perhaps 'break a cup' voluntarily, *if* that is done, say, as an act of self-impoverishment: and I can perhaps break another involuntarily, *if*, say, I make an involuntary movement which breaks it. Here, plainly, the two acts described each as 'breaking a cup' are really very different, and the one is similar to acts typical of the 'voluntary' class, the other to acts typical of the 'involuntary' class.

3. *The importance of negations and opposites.* 'Voluntarily' and 'involuntarily', then, are not opposed in the obvious sort of way that they are made to be in philosophy or jurisprudence. The 'opposite', or rather 'opposites', of 'voluntarily' might be 'under constraint' of some sort, duress or obligation or influence:[8] the opposite of 'involuntarily' might be 'deliberately' or 'on purpose' or the like. Such divergences in opposites indicate that 'voluntarily' and 'involuntarily', in spite of their apparent connexion, are fish from very different kettles. In general, it will pay us to take nothing for granted or as obvious about negations and opposites. It does not pay to assume that a word must have an opposite, or one opposite, whether it is a 'positive' word like 'wilfully' or a 'negative' word like 'inadvertently'. Rather, we should be asking ourselves such questions as why there is no use for the adverb 'advertently'. For above all it will not do to assume that the 'positive' word must be around to wear the trousers; commonly enough the 'negative' (looking) word marks the (positive) abnormality, while the 'positive' word, *if* it exists, merely serves to rule out the suggestion of that abnormality. It is natural

enough, in view of what was said in (1) above, for the 'positive' word not to be found at all in some cases. I do an act A_1 (say, crush a snail) *inadvertently* if, in the course of executing by means of movements of my bodily parts some other act A_2 (say, in walking down the public path) I fail to exercise such meticulous supervision over the courses of those movements as would have been needed to ensure that they did not bring about the untoward event (here, the impact on the snail).[9] By claiming that A_1 was inadvertent we place it, where we imply it belongs, on this special level, in a class of incidental happenings which must occur in the doing of any physical act. To lift the act out of this class, we need and possess the expression 'not . . . inadvertently': 'advertently', if used for this purpose, would suggest that, if the act was not done inadvertently, then it must have been done noticing what I was doing, which is far from necessarily the case (e.g. if I did it absent-mindedly), or at least that there is *something* in common to the ways of doing all acts not done inadvertently, which is not the case. Again, there is no use for 'advertently' at the *same* level as 'inadvertently': in passing the butter I do not knock over the cream-jug, though I do (inadvertently) knock over the teacup – yet I do not by-pass the cream-jug *advertently*: for at this level, below supervision in detail, *anything* that we do is, if you like, inadvertent, though we only call it so, and indeed only call it something we have done, if there is something untoward about it.

A further point of interest in studying so-called 'negative' terms is the manner of their formation. Why are the words in one group formed with un- or in-, those in another with -less ('aimless', 'reckless', 'heedless', &c.), and those in another with mis- ('mistake', 'misconception', 'misjudgement', &c.)? Why care*less*ly but *in*attentively? Perhaps care and attention, so often linked, are rather different. Here are remunerative exercises.

4. *The machinery of action.* Not merely do adverbial expressions pick out classes of actions, they also pick out the internal detail of the machinery of doing actions, or the departments into which the business of doing actions is organized. There is for example the stage at which we have actually to *carry out* some action upon which we embark – perhaps we have to make certain bodily movements or to make a speech.

J. L. Austin

In the course of actually *doing* these things (getting weaving) we have to pay (some) attention to what we are doing and to take (some) care to guard against (likely) dangers: we may need to use judgement or tact: we must exercise sufficient control over our bodily parts: and so on. Inattention, carelessness, errors of judgement, tactlessness, clumsiness, all these and others are ills (with attendant excuses) which affect one specific stage in the machinery of action, the *executive* stage, the stage where we *muff* it. But there are many other departments in the business too, each of which is to be traced and mapped through its cluster of appropriate verbs and adverbs. Obviously there are departments of intelligence and planning, of decision and resolve, and so on: but I shall mention one in particular, too often overlooked, where troubles and excuses abound. It happens to us, in military life, to be in receipt of excellent intelligence, to be also in self-conscious possession of excellent principles (the five golden rules for winning victories), and yet to hit upon a plan of action which leads to disaster. One way in which this can happen is through failure at the stage of *appreciation* of the situation, that is at the stage where we are required to cast our excellent intelligence into such a form, under such heads and with such weights attached, that our equally excellent principles can be brought to bear on it properly, in a way to yield the right answer.[10] So too in real, or rather civilian, life, in moral or practical affairs, we can know the facts and yet look at them mistakenly or perversely, or not fully realize or appreciate something, or even be under a total misconception. Many expressions of excuse indicate failure at this particularly tricky stage: even thoughtlessness, inconsiderateness, lack of imagination, are perhaps less matters of failure in intelligence or planning than might be supposed, and more matters of failure to appreciate the situation. A course of E. M. Forster and we see things differently: yet perhaps we know no more and are no cleverer.

5. *Standards of the unacceptable.* It is characteristic of excuses to be 'unacceptable': given, I suppose, almost any excuse, there will be cases of such a kind or of such gravity that 'we will not accept' it. It is interesting to detect the standards and codes we thus invoke. The extent of the supervision we exercise over the execution of any act can never be quite unlimited, and usually is expected to fall within fairly definite

limits ('due care and attention') in the case of acts of some general kind, though of course we set very different limits in different cases. We may plead that we trod on the snail inadvertently: but not on a baby – you ought to look where you are putting your great feet. Of course it *was* (*really*), if you like, inadvertence: but that word constitutes a plea, which is not going to be allowed, because of standards. And if you try it on, you will be subscribing to such dreadful standards that your last state will be worse than your first. Or again, we set different standards, and will accept different excuses, in the case of acts which are rule-governed, like spelling, and which we are expected absolutely to get right, from those we set and accept for less stereotyped actions: a wrong spelling may be a slip, but hardly an accident, a winged beater may be an accident, but hardly a slip.

6. *Combination, dissociation and complication.* A belief in opposites and dichotomies encourages, among other things, a blindness to the combinations and dissociations of adverbs that are possible, even to such obvious facts as that we can act at once on impulse and intentionally, or that we can do an action intentionally yet for all that not deliberately, still less on purpose. We walk along the cliff, and I feel a sudden impulse to push you over, which I promptly do: I acted on impulse, yet I certainly intended to push you over, and may even have devised a little ruse to achieve it: yet even then I did not act deliberately, for I did not (stop to) ask myself whether to do it or not.

It is worth bearing in mind, too, the general rule that we must not expect to find simple labels for complicated cases. If a mistake results in an accident, it will not do to ask whether 'it' was an accident or a mistake, or to demand some briefer description of 'it'. Here the natural economy of language operates: if the words already available for simple cases suffice in combination to describe a complicated case, there will be need for special reasons before a special new word is invented for the complication. Besides, however well-equipped our language, it can never be forearmed against all possible cases that may arise and call for description: fact is richer than diction.

7. *Regina* v. *Finney.* Often the complexity and difficulty of a case is considerable. I will quote the case of *Regina* v. *Finney.*[11]

Shrewsbury Assizes. 1874   12 Cox 625

Prisoner was indicted for the manslaughter of Thomas Watkins.

The Prisoner was an attendant at a lunatic asylum. Being in charge of a lunatic, who was bathing, he turned on hot water into the bath, and thereby scalded him to death. The facts appeared to be truly set forth in the statement of the prisoner made before the committing magistrate, as follows: 'I had bathed Watkins, and had loosed the bath out. *I intended putting in a clean bath*, and asked Watkins if he would get out. At this time *my attention was drawn* to the next bath by the new attendant, who was asking me a question; and *my attention was taken from the bath* where Watkins was. I put my hand down to turn water on in the bath where Thomas Watkins was. *I did not intend to turn the hot water*, and *I made a mistake in the tap. I did not know what I had done until* I heard Thomas Watkins shout out; and *I did not find my mistake out till* I saw the steam from the water. You cannot get water in this bath when they are drawing water at the other bath; but at other times it shoots out like a water gun when the other baths are not in use. . . .'

(It was proved that the lunatic had such possession of his faculties as would enable him to understand what was said to him, and to get out of the bath.)

A. Young (for Prisoner). The death *resulted from accident*. There was no such *culpable negligence* on the part of the prisoner as will support this indictment. A *culpable mistake*, or some degree of *culpable negligence*, causing death, will not support a charge of manslaughter; unless the *negligence* be so gross as to be *reckless*. (*R. v. Noakes.*)

Lush, J. To render a person liable for *neglect of duty* there must be such a degree of culpability as to amount to *gross negligence* on his part. If you accept the prisoner's own statement, you find no such amount of *negligence* as would come within this definition. It is not every little *trip or mistake* that will make a man so liable. It was the duty of the attendant not to let hot water into the bath while the patient was therein. According to the prisoner's own account, *he did not believe that* he was letting the hot water in while the deceased remained there. The lunatic was, we have heard, a man capable of getting out by

himself and of understanding what was said to him. He was told to get out. A new attendant who had come on this day, was at an adjoining bath and he *took off the prisoner's attention*. Now, if the prisoner, knowing that the man was in the bath, had turned on the tap, and turned on the hot instead of the cold water, I should have said there was gross negligence; for he ought to have looked to see. But from his own account he had told the deceased to get out, and *thought he had got out*. If you think that indicates gross *carelessness*, then you should find the prisoner guilty of manslaughter. But if you think it *inadvertence* not amounting to culpability – i.e., what is properly termed an *accident* – then the prisoner is not liable.

Verdict, Not guilty.

In this case there are two morals that I will point:

(i) Both counsel and judge make very free use of a large number of terms of excuse, using several as though they were, and even stating them to be, indifferent or equivalent when they are not, and presenting as alternatives those that are not.

(ii) It is constantly difficult to be sure *what* act it is that counsel or judge is suggesting might be qualified by what expression of excuse.

The learned judge's concluding direction is a paradigm of these faults.[12] Finney, by contrast, stands out as an evident master of the Queen's English. He is explicit as to each of his acts and states, mental and physical: he uses different, and the correct, adverbs in connexion with each: and he makes no attempt to boil down.

8. *Small distinctions, and big too.* It should go without saying that terms of excuse are not equivalent, and that it matters which we use: we need to distinguish inadvertence not merely from (save the mark) such things as mistake and accident, but from such nearer neighbours as, say, aberration and absence of mind. By imagining cases with vividness and fullness we should be able to decide in which precise terms to describe, say, Miss Plimsoll's action in writing, so carefully, 'DAIRY' on her fine new book: we should be able to distinguish between sheer, mere, pure, and simple mistake or inadvertence. Yet unfortunately,

at least when in the grip of thought, we fail not merely at these stiffer hurdles. We equate even – I have seen it done – 'inadvertently' with 'automatically': as though to say I trod on your toe inadvertently means to say I trod on it automatically. Or we collapse succumbing to temptation into losing control of ourselves – a bad patch, this, for telescoping.[13]

All this is not so much a *lesson* from the study of excuses as the very object of it.

9. *The exact phrase and its place in the sentence.* It is not enough, either, to attend simply to the 'key' word: notice must also be taken of the full and exact form of the expression used. In considering mistakes, we have to consider seriatim 'by mistake', 'owing to a mistake', 'mistakenly', 'it was a mistake to', 'to make a mistake in or over or about', 'to be mistaken about', and so on: in considering purpose, we have to consider 'on', 'with the', 'for the', &c., besides 'purposeful', 'purposeless', and the like. These varying expressions may function quite differently – and usually do, or why should we burden ourselves with more than one of them?

Care must be taken too to observe the precise position of an adverbial expression in the sentence. This should of course indicate what verb it is being used to modify: but more than that, the position can also affect the *sense* of the expression, i.e. the way in which it modifies that verb. Compare, for example:

a_1 He clumsily trod on the snail.
a_2 Clumsily he trod on the snail.
b_1 He trod clumsily on the snail.
b_2 He trod on the snail clumsily.

Here, in a_1 and a_2 we describe his treading on the creature at all as a piece of clumsiness, incidental, we imply, to his performance of some other action: but with b_1 and b_2 to tread on it is, very likely, his aim or policy, what we criticize is his execution of the feat.[14] Many adverbs, though far from all (not, for example, 'purposely') are used in these two typically different ways.

10. *The style of performance.* With some adverbs the distinction between the two senses referred to in the last paragraph is carried a stage further. 'He ate his soup deliberately' may mean, like 'He deliberately ate his soup', that his eating his soup was a deliberate act, one perhaps that he

thought would annoy somebody, as it would more commonly if he deliberately ate *my* soup, and which he decided to do: but it will often mean that he went through the performance of eating his soup in a noteworthy manner or *style* – pause after each mouthful, careful choice of point of entry for the spoon, sucking of moustaches, and so on. That is, it will mean that he ate *with* deliberation rather than *after* deliberation. The style of the performance, slow and unhurried, is understandably called 'deliberate' because each movement *has the typical look* of a deliberate act: but it is scarcely being said that the making of each motion *is* a deliberate act or that he is 'literally' deliberating. This case, then, is more extreme than that of 'clumsily', which does in both uses describe literally a manner of performing.

It is worth watching out for this secondary use when scrutinizing any particular adverbial expression: when it definitely does not exist, the reason is worth inquiring into. Sometimes it is very hard to be sure whether it does exist or does not: it does, one would think, with 'carelessly', it does not with 'inadvertently', but does it or does it not with 'absent-mindedly' or 'aimlessly'? In some cases a word akin to but distinct from the primary adverb is used for this special role of describing a style of performance: we use 'purposefully' in this way, but never 'purposely'.

11. *What modifies what?* The Judge in *Regina* v. *Finney* does not make clear what event is being excused in what way. 'If you think that indicates gross carelessness, then. . . . But if you think it inadvertence not amounting to culpability – i.e. what is properly called an accident – then. . . .' Apparently he means that Finney may have *turned on the hot tap* inadvertently:[15] does he mean also that the tap may have been turned accidentally, or rather that *Watkins may have been scalded* and killed accidentally? And was the carelessness in turning the tap or in thinking Watkins had got out? Many disputes as to what excuse we should properly use arise because we will not trouble to state explicitly *what* is being excused.

To do so is all the more vital because it is in principle always open to us, along various lines, to describe or refer to 'what I did' in so many different ways. This is altogether too large a theme to elaborate here. Apart from the more general and obvious problems of the use of 'tendentious' descriptive terms, there are many special problems in the particular case of 'actions'.

Should we say, are we saying, that he took her money, or that he robbed her? That he knocked a ball into a hole, or that he sank a putt? That he said 'Done', or that he accepted an offer? How far, that is, are motives, intentions and conventions to be part of the description of actions? And more especially here, what is *an* or *one* or *the* action? For we can generally split up what might be named as one action in several distinct ways, into different *stretches* or *phases* or *stages*. Stages have already been mentioned: we can dismantle the machinery of the act, and describe (and excuse) separately the intelligence, the appreciation, the planning, the decision, the execution and so forth. Phases are rather different: we can say that he painted a picture or fought a campaign, or else we can say that first he laid on this stroke of paint and then that, first he fought this action and then that. Stretches are different again: a single term descriptive of what he did may be made to cover either a smaller or a larger stretch of events, those excluded by the narrower description being then called 'consequences' or 'results' or 'effects' or the like of his act. So here we can describe Finney's act *either* as turning on the hot tap, which he did by mistake, with the result that Watkins was scalded, *or* as scalding Watkins, which he did *not* do by mistake.

It is very evident that the problems of excuses and those of the different descriptions of actions are throughout bound up with each other.

12. *Trailing clouds of etymology*. It is these considerations that bring us up so forcibly against some of the most difficult words in the whole story of Excuses, such words as 'result', 'effect', and 'consequence', or again as 'intention', 'purpose', and 'motive'. I will mention two points of method which are, experience has convinced me, indispensable aids at these levels.

One is that a word never – well, hardly ever – shakes off its etymology and its formation. In spite of all changes in and extensions of and additions to its meanings, and indeed rather pervading and governing these, there will still persist the old idea. In an *accident* something befalls: by *mistake* you take the wrong one: in *error* you stray: when you act *deliberately* you act after weighing it up (*not* after thinking out ways and means). It is worth asking ourselves whether we know the etymology of 'result' or of 'spontaneously', and worth remembering that 'unwillingly' and 'involuntarily' come from very different sources.

And the second point is connected with this. Going back into the history of a word, very often into Latin, we come back pretty commonly to pictures or *models* of how things happen or are done. These models may be fairly sophisticated and recent, as is perhaps the case with 'motive' or 'impulse', but one of the commonest and most primitive types of model is one which is apt to baffle us through its very naturalness and simplicity. We take *some very simple action*, like shoving a stone, usually as done by and viewed by oneself, and use *this*, with the features distinguishable in it, as our model in terms of which to talk about other actions and events: and we continue to do so, scarcely realizing it, even when these other actions are pretty remote and perhaps much more interesting to us in their own right than the acts originally used in constructing the model ever were, and even when the model is really distorting the facts rather than helping us to observe them. In primitive cases we may get to see clearly the differences between, say, 'results', 'effects', and 'consequences', and yet discover that these differences are no longer clear, and the terms themselves no longer of real service to us, in the more complicated cases where we had been bandying them about most freely. A model must be recognized for what it is. 'Causing', I suppose, was a notion taken from a man's own experience of doing simple actions, and by primitive man every event was construed in terms of this model: every event has a cause, that is, every event is an action done by somebody – if not by a man, then by a quasi-man, a spirit. When, later, events which are *not* actions are realized to be such, we still say that they must be 'caused', and the word snares us: we are struggling to ascribe to it a new, unanthropomorphic meaning, yet constantly, in searching for its analysis, we unearth and incorporate the lineaments of the ancient model. As happened even to Hume, and consequently to Kant. Examining such a word historically, we may well find that it has been extended to cases that have by now too tenuous a relation to the model case, that it is a source of confusion and superstition.

There is too another danger in words that invoke models, half-forgotten or not. It must be remembered that there is no necessity whatsoever that the various models used in creating our vocabulary, primitive or recent, should all fit together neatly as parts into one single, total model or scheme of, for instance, the doing of actions.

It is possible, and indeed highly likely, that our assortment of models will include some, or many, that are overlapping, conflicting, or more generally simply *disparate*.[16]

13.   In spite of the wide and acute observation of the phenomena of action embodied in ordinary speech, modern scientists have been able, it seems to me, to reveal its inadequacy at numerous points, if only because they have had access to more comprehensive data and have studied them with more catholic and dispassionate interest than the ordinary man, or even the lawyer, has had occasion to do. I will conclude with two examples.

Observation of animal behaviour shows that regularly, when an animal is embarked on some recognizable pattern of behaviour but meets in the course of it with an insuperable obstacle, it will betake itself to energetic, but quite unrelated, activity of some wild kind, such as standing on its head. This phenomenon is called 'displacement behaviour' and is well identifiable. If now, in the light of this, we look back at ordinary human life, we see that displacement behaviour bulks quite large in it: yet we have apparently no word, or at least no clear and simple word, for it. If, when thwarted, we stand on our heads or wiggle our toes, then we are not exactly *just* standing on our heads, don't you know, in the ordinary way, yet is there any convenient adverbial expression we can insert to do the trick? 'In desperation'?

Take, again, 'compulsive' behaviour, however exactly psychologists define it, compulsive washing for example. There are of course hints in ordinary speech that we do things in this way – 'just feel I have to', 'shouldn't feel comfortable unless I did', and the like: but there is no adverbial expression satisfactorily pre-empted for it, as 'compulsively' is. This is understandable enough, since compulsive behaviour, like displacement behaviour, is not in general going to be of great practical importance.

Here I leave and commend the subject to you.

Notes

1   This use has little to do with the more down-to-earth occurrences of 'action' in ordinary speech.

2   Another well-flogged horse in these same stakes is Blame. At least two things seem confused together under this term. Sometimes when I blame X for doing A, say for breaking the vase, it is a question simply or mainly of my disapproval of A, breaking the vase, which unquestionably X did: but sometimes it is, rather, a question simply or mainly of how far I think X responsible for A, which unquestionably was bad. Hence if somebody says he blames me for something, I may answer by giving a *justification*, so that he will cease to disapprove of what I did, or else by giving an *excuse*, so that he will cease to hold me, at least entirely and in every way, responsible for doing it.

3   All of which was seen and claimed by Socrates, when he first betook himself to the way of Words.

4   You have a donkey, so have I, and they graze in the same field. The day comes when I conceive a dislike for mine. I go to shoot it, draw a bead on it, fire: the brute falls in its tracks. I inspect the victim, and find to my horror that it is *your* donkey. I appear on your doorstep with the remains and say – what? 'I say, old sport, I'm awfully sorry, &c., I've shot your donkey *by accident*'? Or '*by mistake*'? Then again, I go to shoot my donkey as before, draw a bead on it, fire – but as I do so, the beasts move, and to my horror yours falls. Again the scene on the doorstep – what do I say? 'By mistake'? Or 'by accident'?

5   And forget, for once and for a while, that other curious question 'Is it true?' May we?

6   Caveat or hedge: of course we can say 'I did *not* sit in it "intentionally"' as a way simply of repudiating the suggestion that I sat in it intentionally.

7   For we are sometimes not so good at observing what we *can't* say as what we can, yet the first is pretty regularly the more revealing.

8   But remember, when I sign a cheque in the normal way, I do *not* do so *either* 'voluntarily' *or* 'under constraint'.

9   Or analogously: I do an act A_1 (say, divulge my age, or imply you are a liar), *inadvertently* if, in the course of executing by the use of some medium of communication some other act A_2 (say, reminiscing about my war service) I fail to exercise such meticulous supervision over the choice and arrangement of the signs as would have been needed to ensure that ... It is interesting to note how such adverbs lead parallel lives, one in connexion with physical actions ('doing') and the other in connexion with acts of communication ('saying'), or sometimes also in connexion with acts of 'thinking' ('inadvertently assumed').

10   We know all about how to do quadratics: we know all the needful facts about pipes, cisterns, hours and plumbers: yet we reach the answer '3¾ men'.

We have failed to cast our facts correctly into mathematical form.

11 A somewhat distressing favourite in the class that Hart used to conduct with me in the years soon after the war. The italics are mine.

12 Not but what he probably manages to convey his meaning somehow or other. Judges seem to acquire a knack of conveying meaning, and even carrying conviction, through the use of a pithy Anglo-Saxon which sometimes has literally no meaning at all. Wishing to distinguish the case of shooting at a post in the belief that it was an enemy, as *not* an 'attempt', from the case of picking an empty pocket in the belief that money was in it, which *is* an 'attempt', the judge explains that in shooting at the post 'the man is never on the thing at all'.

13 Plato, I suppose, and after him Aristotle, fastened this confusion upon us, as bad in its day and way as the later, grotesque, confusion of moral weakness with weakness of will. I am very partial to ice cream, and a bombe is served divided into segments corresponding one to one with the persons at High Table: I am tempted to help myself to two segments and do so, thus succumbing to temptation and even conceivably (but why necessarily?) going against my principles. But do I lose control of myself? Do I raven, do I snatch the morsels from the dish and wolf them down, impervious to the consternation of my colleagues? Not a bit of it. We often succumb to temptation with calm and even with finesse.

14 As a matter of fact, most of these examples *can* be understood the other way, especially if we allow ourselves inflexions of the voice, or commas, or contexts. a_2 might be a poetic inversion for b_2: b_1, perhaps with commas round the 'clumsily', might

be used for a_1: and so on. Still, the two senses are clearly enough distinguishable.

15 What Finney says is different: he says he 'made a mistake in the tap'. This is the basic use of 'mistake', where we simply, and not necessarily accountably, take the wrong one. Finney here attempts to account for his mistake, by saying that his attention was distracted. But suppose the order is 'Right turn' and I turn left: no doubt the sergeant will insinuate that my attention was distracted, or that I cannot distinguish my right from my left – but it was not and I can, this was a simple, pure mistake. As often happens. Neither I nor the sergeant will suggest that there was any accident, or any inadvertence either. If Finney had turned the hot tap inadvertently, then it would have been knocked, say, in reaching for the cold tap: a different story.

16 This is by way of a general warning in philosophy. It seems to be too readily assumed that if we can only discover the true meanings of each of a cluster of key terms, usually historic terms, that we use in some particular field (as, for example, 'right', 'good' and the rest in morals), then it must without question transpire that each will fit into place in some single, interlocking, consistent, conceptual scheme. Not only is there no reason to assume this, but all historical probability is against it, especially in the case of a language derived from such various civilizations as ours is. We may cheerfully use, and with weight, terms which are not so much head-on incompatible as simply disparate, which just do not fit in or even on. Just as we cheerfully subscribe to, or have the grace to be torn between, simply disparate ideals – why *must* there be a conceivable amalgam, the Good Life for Man?

43

Two Dogmas of Empiricism

W. V. Quine

Modern empiricism has been conditioned in large part by two dogmas. One is a belief in some fundamental cleavage between truths which are *analytic*, or grounded in meanings independently of matters of fact, and truths which are *synthetic*, or grounded in fact. The other dogma is *reductionism*: the belief that each meaningful statement is equivalent to some logical construct upon terms which refer to immediate experience. Both dogmas, I shall argue, are ill founded. One effect of abandoning them is, as we shall see, a blurring of the supposed boundary between speculative metaphysics and natural science. Another effect is a shift toward pragmatism.

1 Background for Analyticity

Kant's cleavage between analytic and synthetic truths was foreshadowed in Hume's distinction between relations of ideas and matters of fact, and in Leibniz's distinction between truths of reason and truths of fact. Leibniz spoke of the truths of reason as true in all possible worlds. Picturesqueness aside, this is to say that the truths of reason are those which could not possibly be false. In the same vein we hear analytic statements defined as statements whose denials are self-contradictory. But this definition has small explanatory value; for the notion of self-

Originally published in *Philosophical Review* 60 (1951). Copyright 1951 Cornell University. Reprinted by permission of the publisher.

contradictoriness, in the quite broad sense needed for this definition of analyticity, stands in exactly the same need of clarification as does the notion of analyticity itself.[1] The two notions are the two sides of a single dubious coin.

Kant conceived of an analytic statement as one that attributes to its subject no more than is already conceptually contained in the subject. This formulation has two shortcomings: it limits itself to statements of subject-predicate form, and it appeals to a notion of containment which is left at a metaphorical level. But Kant's intent, evident more from the use he makes of the notion of analyticity than from his definition of it, can be restated thus: a statement is analytic when it is true by virtue of meanings and independently of fact. Pursuing this line, let us examine the concept of *meaning* which is presupposed.

We must observe to begin with that meaning is not to be identified with naming, or reference. Consider Frege's example of 'Evening Star' and 'Morning Star'. Understood not merely as a recurrent evening apparition but as a body, the Evening Star is the planet Venus, and the Morning Star is the same. The two singular terms *name* the same thing. But the meanings must be treated as distinct, since the identity 'Evening Star = Morning Star' is a statement of fact established by astronomical observation. If 'Evening Star' and 'Morning Star' were alike in meaning, the identity 'Evening Star = Morning Star' would be analytic.

Again there is Russell's example of 'Scott' and 'the author of *Waverley*'. Analysis of the meanings of words was by no means sufficient to reveal to George IV that the person named by these two singular terms was one and the same.

The distinction between meaning and naming is no less important at the level of abstract terms. The terms '9' and 'the number of planets' name one and the same abstract entity but presumably must be regarded as unlike in meaning; for astronomical observation was needed, and not mere reflection on meanings, to determine the sameness of the entity in question.

Thus far we have been considering singular terms. With general terms, or predicates, the situation is somewhat different but parallel. Whereas a singular term purports to name an entity, abstract or concrete, a general term does not; but a general term is *true of* an entity, or of each of many, or of none. The class of all entities of which a general term is true is called the *extension* of the term. Now paralleling the contrast between the meaning of a singular term and the entity named, we must distinguish equally between the meaning of a general term and its extension. The general terms 'creature with a heart' and 'creature with a kidney', e.g., are perhaps alike in extension but unlike in meaning.

Confusion of meaning with extension, in the case of general terms, is less common than confusion of meaning with naming in the case of singular terms. It is indeed a commonplace in philosophy to oppose intension (or meaning) to extension, or, in a variant vocabulary, connotation to denotation.

The Aristotelian notion of essence was the forerunner, no doubt, of the modern notion of intension or meaning. For Aristotle it was essential in men to be rational, accidental to be two-legged. But there is an important difference between this attitude and the doctrine of meaning. From the latter point of view it may indeed be conceded (if only for the sake of argument) that rationality is involved in the meaning of the word 'man' while two-leggedness is not; but two-leggedness may at the same time be viewed as involved in the meaning of 'biped' while rationality is not. Thus from the point of view of the doctrine of meaning it makes no sense to say of the actual individual, who is at once a man and a biped, that his rationality is essential and his two-leggedness accidental or vice versa. Things had essences, for Aristotle, but only linguistic forms have meanings. Meaning is what essence becomes when it is divorced from the object of reference and wedded to the word.

For the theory of meaning the most conspicuous question is as to the nature of its objects: what sort of things are meanings? They are evidently intended to be ideas, somehow – mental ideas for some semanticists, Platonic ideas for others. Objects of either sort are so elusive, not to say debatable, that there seems little hope of erecting a fruitful science about them. It is not even clear, granted meanings, when we have two and when we have one; it is not clear when linguistic forms should be regarded as *synonymous*, or alike in meaning, and when they should not. If a standard of synonymy should be arrived at, we may reasonably expect that the appeal to meanings as entities will not have played a very useful part in the enterprise.

A felt need for meant entities may derive from an earlier failure to appreciate that meaning and reference are distinct. Once the theory of meaning is sharply separated from the theory of reference, it is a short step to recognizing as the business of the theory of meaning simply the synonymy of linguistic forms and the analyticity of statements; meanings themselves, as obscure intermediary entities, may well be abandoned.

The description of analyticity as truth by virtue of meanings started us off in pursuit of a concept of meaning. But now we have abandoned the thought of any special realm of entities called meanings. So the problem of analyticity confronts us anew.

Statements which are analytic by general philosophical acclaim are not, indeed, far to seek. They fall into two classes. Those of the first class, which may be called *logically true*, are typified by:

(1) No unmarried man is married.

The relevant feature of this example is that it is not merely true as it stands, but remains true under any and all reinterpretations of 'man' and 'married'. If we suppose a prior inventory of *logical* particles, comprising 'no', 'un-', 'not', 'if', 'then', 'and', etc., then in general a logical truth is a statement which is true and remains true under all reinterpretations of its components other than the logical particles.

But there is also a second class of analytic statements, typified by:

(2)   No bachelor is married.

The characteristic of such a statement is that it can be turned into a logical truth by putting synonyms for synonyms; thus (2) can be turned into (1) by putting 'unmarried man' for its synonym 'bachelor'. We still lack a proper characterization of this second class of analytic statements, and therewith of analyticity generally, inasmuch as we have had in the above description to lean on a notion of "synonymy" which is no less in need of clarification than analyticity itself.

In recent years Carnap has tended to explain analyticity by appeal to what he calls state-descriptions.[2] A state-description is any exhaustive assignment of truth values to the atomic, or noncompound, statements of the language. All other statements of the language are, Carnap assumes, built up of their component clauses by means of the familiar logical devices, in such a way that the truth value of any complex statement is fixed for each state-description by specifiable logical laws. A statement is then explained as analytic when it comes out true under every state-description. This account is an adaptation of Leibniz's "true in all possible worlds." But note that this version of analyticity serves its purpose only if the atomic statements of the language are, unlike 'John is a bachelor' and 'John is married', mutually independent. Otherwise there would be a state-description which assigned truth to 'John is a bachelor' and falsity to 'John is married', and consequently 'All bachelors are married' would turn out synthetic rather than analytic under the proposed criterion. Thus the criterion of analyticity in terms of state-descriptions serves only for languages devoid of extralogical synonym-pairs, such as 'bachelor' and 'unmarried man': synonym-pairs of the type which give rise to the "second class" of analytic statements. The criterion in terms of state-descriptions is a reconstruction at best of logical truth.

I do not mean to suggest that Carnap is under any illusions on this point. His simplified model language with its state-descriptions is aimed primarily not at the general problem of analyticity but at another purpose, the clarification of probability and induction. Our problem, however, is analyticity; and here the major difficulty lies not in the first class of analytic statements, the logical truths, but rather in the second class, which depends on the notion of synonymy.

2   Definition

There are those who find it soothing to say that the analytic statements of the second class reduce to those of the first class, the logical truths, by *definition*; 'bachelor', e.g., is *defined* as 'unmarried man'. But how do we find that 'bachelor' is defined as 'unmarried man'? Who defined it thus, and when? Are we to appeal to the nearest dictionary, and accept the lexicographer's formulation as law? Clearly this would be to put the cart before the horse. The lexicographer is an empirical scientist, whose business is the recording of antecedent facts; and if he glosses 'bachelor' as 'unmarried man' it is because of his belief that there is a relation of synonymy between these forms, implicit in general or preferred usage prior to his own work. The notion of synonymy presupposed here has still to be clarified, presumably in terms relating to linguistic behavior. Certainly the "definition" which is the lexicographer's report of an observed synonymy cannot be taken as the ground of the synonymy.

Definition is not, indeed, an activity exclusively of philologists. Philosophers and scientists frequently have occasion to "define" a recondite term by paraphrasing it into terms of a more familiar vocabulary. But ordinarily such a definition, like the philologist's, is pure lexicography, affirming a relationship of synonymy antecedent to the exposition in hand.

Just what it means to affirm synonymy, just what the interconnections may be which are necessary and sufficient in order that two linguistic forms be properly describable as synonymous, is far from clear; but, whatever these interconnections may be, ordinarily they are grounded in usage. Definitions reporting selected instances of synonymy come then as reports upon usage.

There is also, however, a variant type of definitional activity which does not limit itself to the reporting of pre-existing synonymies. I have in mind what Carnap calls *explication* – an activity to which philosophers are given, and scientists also in their more philosophical moments. In explication the purpose is not merely to paraphrase the definiendum into an outright synonym, but actually to improve upon the definiendum by refining or supplementing its meaning. But even explication, though not merely reporting a pre-existing synonymy between definiendum and definiens, does rest nevertheless on *other* pre-existing synonymies. The matter may be viewed as follows. Any word worth explicating has some contexts which, as wholes, are clear and precise enough to be useful; and the purpose of explication is to preserve the usage of these favored contexts while sharpening the usage of other contexts. In order that a given definition be suitable for purposes of explication, therefore, what is required is not that the definiendum in its antecedent usage be synonymous with the definiens, but just that each of these favored contexts of the definiendum, taken as a whole in its antecedent usage, be synonymous with the corresponding context of the definiens.

Two alternative definientia may be equally appropriate for the purposes of a given task of explication and yet not be synonymous with each other; for they may serve interchangeably within the favored contexts but diverge elsewhere. By cleaving to one of these definientia rather than the other, a definition of explicative kind generates, by fiat, a relationship of synonymy between definiendum and definiens which did not hold before. But such a definition still owes its explicative function, as seen, to pre-existing synonymies.

There does, however, remain still an extreme sort of definition which does not hark back to prior synonymies at all; viz., the explicitly conventional introduction of novel notations for purposes of sheer abbreviation. Here the definiendum becomes synonymous with the definiens simply because it has been created expressly for the purpose of being synonymous with the definiens. Here we have a really transparent case of synonymy created by definition; would that all species of synonymy were as intelligible. For the rest, definition rests on synonymy rather than explaining it.

The word 'definition' has come to have a dangerously reassuring sound, due no doubt to its frequent occurrence in logical and mathematical writings. We shall do well to digress now into a brief appraisal of the role of definition in formal work.

In logical and mathematical systems either of two mutually antagonistic types of economy may be striven for, and each has its peculiar practical utility. On the one hand we may seek economy of practical expression: ease and brevity in the statement of multifarious relationships. This sort of economy calls usually for distinctive concise notations for a wealth of concepts. Second, however, and oppositely, we may seek economy in

grammar and vocabulary; we may try to find a minimum of basic concepts such that, once a distinctive notation has been appropriated to each of them, it becomes possible to express any desired further concept by mere combination and iteration of our basic notations. This second sort of economy is impractical in one way, since a poverty in basic idioms tends to a necessary lengthening of discourse. But it is practical in another way: it greatly simplifies theoretical discourse *about* the language, through minimizing the terms and the forms of construction wherein the language consists.

Both sorts of economy, though prima facie incompatible, are valuable in their separate ways. The custom has consequently arisen of combining both sorts of economy by forging in effect two languages, the one a part of the other. The inclusive language, though redundant in grammar and vocabulary, is economical in message lengths, while the part, called *primitive notation*, is economical in grammar and vocabulary. Whole and part are correlated by rules of translation whereby each idiom not in primitive notation is equated to some complex built up of primitive notation. These rules of translation are the so-called *definitions* which appear in formalized systems. They are best viewed not as adjuncts to one language but as correlations between two languages, the one a part of the other.

But these correlations are not arbitrary. They are supposed to show how the primitive notations can accomplish all purposes, save brevity and convenience, of the redundant language. Hence the definiendum and its definiens may be expected, in each case, to be related in one or another of the three ways lately noted. The definiens may be a faithful paraphrase of the definiendum into the narrower notation, preserving a direct synonymy as of antecedent usage; or the definiens may, in the spirit of explication, improve upon the antecedent usage of the definiendum; or finally, the definiendum may be a newly created notation, newly endowed with meaning here and now.

In formal and informal work alike, thus, we find that definition – except in the extreme case of the explicitly conventional introduction of new notations – hinges on prior relationships of synonymy. Recognizing then that the notion of definition does not hold the key to synonymy and analyticity, let us look further into synonymy and say no more of definition.

3 Interchangeability

A natural suggestion, deserving close examination, is that the synonymy of two linguistic forms consists simply in their interchangeability in all contexts without change of truth value; interchangeability, in Leibniz's phrase, *salva veritate*. Note that synonyms so conceived need not even be free from vagueness, as long as the vaguenesses match.

But it is not quite true that the synonyms 'bachelor' and 'unmarried man' are everywhere interchangeable *salva veritate*. Truths which become false under substitution of 'unmarried man' for 'bachelor' are easily constructed with help of 'bachelor of arts' or 'bachelor's buttons'. Also with help of quotation, thus:

'Bachelor' has less than ten letters.

Such counterinstances can, however, perhaps be set aside by treating the phrases 'bachelor of arts' and 'bachelor's buttons' and the quotation "bachelor" each as a single indivisible word and then stipulating that the interchangeability *salva veritate* which is to be the touchstone of synonymy is not supposed to apply to fragmentary occurrences inside of a word. This account of synonymy, supposing it acceptable on other counts, has indeed the drawback of appealing to a prior conception of "word" which can be counted on to present difficulties of formulation in its turn. Nevertheless some progress might be claimed in having reduced the problem of synonymy to a problem of wordhood. Let us pursue this line a bit, taking "word" for granted.

The question remains whether interchangeability *salva veritate* (apart from occurrences within words) is a strong enough condition for synonymy, or whether, on the contrary, some nonsynonymous expressions might be thus interchangeable. Now let us be clear that we are not concerned here with synonymy in the sense of complete identity in psychological associations or poetic quality; indeed no two expressions are synonymous in such a sense. We are concerned only with what may be called *cognitive synonymy*. Just what this is cannot be said without successfully finishing the present study; but we know something about it from the need which arose for it in connection with analyticity in Section I. The sort of synonymy needed there was merely such that any analytic statement could be turned into a logical

truth by putting synonyms for synonyms. Turning the tables and assuming analyticity, indeed, we could explain cognitive synonymy of terms as follows (keeping to the familiar example): to say that 'bachelor' and 'unmarried man' are cognitively synonymous is to say no more nor less than that the statement:

(3)   All and only bachelors are unmarried men

is analytic.[3]

What we need is an account of cognitive synonymy not presupposing analyticity – if we are to explain analyticity conversely with help of cognitive synonymy as undertaken in Section I. And indeed such an independent account of cognitive synonymy is at present up for consideration, viz., interchangeability *salva veritate* everywhere except within words. The question before us, to resume the thread at last, is whether such interchangeability is a sufficient condition for cognitive synonymy. We can quickly assure ourselves that it is, by examples of the following sort. The statement:

(4)   Necessarily all and only bachelors are
      bachelors

is evidently true, even supposing 'necessarily' so narrowly construed as to be truly applicable only to analytic statements. Then, *if* 'bachelor' and 'unmarried man' are interchangeable *salva veritate*, the result

(5)   Necessarily, all and only bachelors are
      unmarried men

of putting 'unmarried man' for an occurrence of 'bachelor' in (4) must, like (4), be true. But to say that (5) is true is to say that (3) is analytic, and hence that 'bachelor' and 'unmarried man' are cognitively synonymous.

Let us see what there is about the above argument that gives it its air of hocus-pocus. The condition of interchangeability *salva veritate* varies in its force with variations in the richness of the language at hand. The above argument supposes we are working with a language rich enough to contain the adverb 'necessarily', this adverb being so construed as to yield truth when and only when applied to an analytic statement. But can we condone a language which contains such an adverb? Does the adverb really make sense? To suppose that it does is to suppose that we have already made satisfactory sense of 'analytic'. Then what are we so hard at work on right now?

Our argument is not flatly circular, but something like it. It has the form, figuratively speaking, of a closed curve in space.

Interchangeability *salva veritate* is meaningless until relativized to a language whose extent is specified in relevant respects. Suppose now we consider a language containing just the following materials. There is an indefinitely large stock of one- and many-place predicates, mostly having to do with extralogical subject matter. The rest of the language is logical. The atomic sentences consist each of a predicate followed by one or more variables; and the complex sentences are built up of atomic ones by truth functions and quantification. In effect such a language enjoys the benefits also of descriptions and class names and indeed singular terms generally, these being contextually definable in known ways.[4] Such a language can be adequate to classical mathematics and indeed to scientific discourse generally, except in so far as the latter involves debatable devices such as modal adverbs and contrary-to-fact conditionals. Now a language of this type is *extensional*, in this sense: any two predicates which *agree extensionally* (i.e., are true of the same objects) are interchangeable *salva veritate*.

In an extensional language, therefore, interchangeability *salva veritate* is no assurance of cognitive synonymy of the desired type. That 'bachelor' and 'unmarried man' are interchangeable *salva veritate* in an extensional language assures us of no more than that (3) is true. There is no assurance here that the extensional agreement of 'bachelor' and 'unmarried man' rests on meaning rather than merely on accidental matters of fact, as does extensional agreement of 'creature with a heart' and 'creature with a kidney'.

For most purposes extensional agreement is the nearest approximation to synonymy we need care about. But the fact remains that extensional agreement falls far short of cognitive synonymy of the type required for explaining analyticity in the manner of Section I. The type of cognitive synonymy required there is such as to equate the synonymy of 'bachelor' and 'unmarried man' with the analyticity of (3), not merely with the truth of (3).

So we must recognize that interchangeability *salva veritate*, if construed in relation to an extensional language, is not a sufficient condition of cognitive synonymy in the sense needed for deriving analyticity in the manner of Section I. If a language contains an intensional adverb 'necessarily' in the sense lately noted, or other particles to the same effect, then interchangeability *salva veritate* in such a language does afford a sufficient condition of cognitive synonymy; but such a language is intelligible only if the notion of analyticity is already clearly understood in advance.

The effort to explain cognitive synonymy first, for the sake of deriving analyticity from it afterward as in Section I, is perhaps the wrong approach. Instead we might try explaining analyticity somehow without appeal to cognitive synonymy. Afterward we could doubtless derive cognitive synonymy from analyticity satisfactorily enough if desired. We have seen that cognitive synonymy of 'bachelor' and 'unmarried man' can be explained as analyticity of (3). The same explanation works for any pair of one-place predicates, of course, and it can be extended in obvious fashion to many-place predicates. Other syntactical categories can also be accommodated in fairly parallel fashion. Singular terms may be said to be cognitively synonymous when the statement of identity formed by putting '=' between them is analytic. Statements may be said simply to be cognitively synonymous when their biconditional (the result of joining them by 'if and only if') is analytic.[5] If we care to lump all categories into a single formulation, at the expense of assuming again the notion of "word" which was appealed to early in this section, we can describe any two linguistic forms as cognitively synonymous when the two forms are interchangeable (apart from occurrences within "words") *salva* (no longer *veritate* but) *analyticitate*. Certain technical questions arise, indeed, over cases of ambiguity or homonymy; let us not pause for them, however, for we are already digressing. Let us rather turn our backs on the problem of synonymy and address ourselves anew to that of analyticity.

4 Semantical Rules

Analyticity at first seemed most naturally definable by appeal to a realm of meanings. On refinement, the appeal to meanings gave way to an appeal to synonymy or definition. But definition turned out to be a will-o'-the-wisp, and synonymy turned out to be best understood only by dint of a prior appeal to analyticity itself. So we are back at the problem of analyticity.

I do not know whether the statement 'Everything green is extended' is analytic. Now does my indecision over this example really betray an incomplete understanding, an incomplete grasp of the "meanings", of 'green' and 'extended'? I think not. The trouble is not with 'green' or 'extended', but with 'analytic'.

It is often hinted that the difficulty in separating analytic statements from synthetic ones in ordinary language is due to the vagueness of ordinary language and that the distinction is clear when we have a precise artificial language with explicit "semantical rules." This, however, as I shall now attempt to show, is a confusion.

The notion of analyticity about which we are worrying is a purported relation between statements and languages: a statement S is said to be *analytic for* a language L, and the problem is to make sense of this relation generally, i.e., for variable 'S' and 'L'. The point that I want to make is that the gravity of this problem is not perceptibly less for artificial languages than for natural ones. The problem of making sense of the idiom 'S is analytic for L', with variable 'S' and 'L', retains its stubbornness even if we limit the range of the variable 'L' to artificial languages. Let me now try to make this point evident.

For artificial languages and semantical rules we look naturally to the writings of Carnap. His semantical rules take various forms, and to make my point I shall have to distinguish certain of the forms. Let us suppose, to begin with, an artificial language L_0 whose semantical rules have the form explicitly of a specification, by recursion or otherwise, of all the analytic statements of L_0. The rules tell us that such and such statements, and only those, are the analytic statements of L_0. Now here the difficulty is simply that the rules contain the word 'analytic', which we do not understand! We understand what expressions the rules attribute analyticity to, but we do not understand what the rules attribute to those expressions. In short, before we can understand a rule which begins "A statement S is analytic for language L_0 if and only if . . . ," we must understand the general relative term 'analytic for'; we must understand 'S is analytic for L' where 'S' and 'L' are variables.

Alternatively we may, indeed, view the so-called rule as a conventional definition of a new simple symbol 'analytic-for-L_0', which might better be written untendentiously as 'K' so as not to seem to throw light on the interesting word 'analytic'. Obviously any number of classes K, M, N, etc. of statements of L_0 can be specified for various purposes or for no purpose; what does it mean to say that K, as against M, N, etc., is the class of the "analytic" statements of L_0?

By saying what statements are analytic for L_0 we explain 'analytic-for-L_0' but not 'analytic', not 'analytic for'. We do not begin to explain the idiom 'S is analytic for L' with variable 'S' and 'L', even though we be content to limit the range of 'L' to the realm of artificial languages.

Actually we do know enough about the intended significance of 'analytic' to know that analytic statements are supposed to be true. Let us then turn to a second form of semantical rule, which says not that such and such statements are analytic but simply that such and such statements are included among the truths. Such a rule is not subject to the criticism of containing the un-understood word 'analytic'; and we may grant for the sake of argument that there is no difficulty over the broader term 'true'. A semantical rule of this second type, a rule of truth, is not supposed to specify all the truths of the language; it merely stipulates, recursively or otherwise, a certain multitude of statements which, along with others unspecified, are to count as true. Such a rule may be conceded to be quite clear. Derivatively, afterward, analyticity can be demarcated thus: a statement is analytic if it is (not merely true but) true according to the semantical rule.

Still there is really no progress. Instead of appealing to an unexplained word 'analytic', we are now appealing to an unexplained phrase 'semantical rule'. Not every true statement which says that the statements of some class are true can count as a semantical rule – otherwise *all* truths would be "analytic" in the sense of being true according to semantical rules. Semantical rules are distinguishable, apparently, only by the fact of appearing on a page under the heading 'Semantical Rules'; and this heading is itself then meaningless.

We can say indeed that a statement is *analytic-for-L_0* if and only if it is true according to such and such specifically appended "semantical rules," but then we find ourselves back at essentially the same case which was originally discussed: "S is analytic-for-L_0 if and only if. . . ." Once we seek to explain 'S is analytic for L' generally for variable 'L' (even allowing limitation of 'L' to artificial languages), the explanation 'true according to the semantic rules of L' is unavailing; for the relative term 'semantical rule of' is as much in need of clarification, at least, as 'analytic for'.

It might conceivably be protested that an artificial language L (unlike a natural one) is a language in the ordinary sense *plus* a set of explicit semantical rules – the whole constituting, let us say, an ordered pair; and that the semantical rules of L then are specifiable simply as the second component of the pair L. But, by the same token and more simply, we might construe an artificial language L outright as an ordered pair whose second component is the class of its analytic statements; and then the analytic statements of L become specifiable simply as the statements in the second component of L. Or better still, we might just stop tugging at our bootstraps altogether.

Not all the explanations of analyticity known to Carnap and his readers have been covered explicitly in the above considerations, but the extension to other forms is not hard to see. Just one additional factor should be mentioned which sometimes enters: sometimes the semantical rules are in effect rules of translation into ordinary language, in which case the analytic statements of the artificial language are in effect recognized as such from the analyticity of their specified translations in ordinary language. Here certainly there can be no thought of an illumination of the problem of analyticity from the side of the artificial language.

From the point of view of the problem of analyticity the notion of an artificial language with semantical rules is a *feu follet par excellence*. Semantical rules determining the analytic statements of an artificial language are of interest only in so far as we already understand the notion of analyticity; they are of no help in gaining this understanding.

Appeal to hypothetical languages of an artificially simple kind could conceivably be useful in clarifying analyticity, if the mental or behavioral or cultural factors relevant to analyticity – whatever they may be – were somehow sketched into the simplified model. But a model which takes analyticity merely as in irreducible character is unlikely to throw light on the problem of explicating analyticity.

It is obvious that truth in general depends on both language and extralinguistic fact. The statement 'Brutus killed Caesar' would be false if the world had been different in certain ways, but it would also be false if the word 'killed' happened rather to have the sense of 'begat'. Hence the temptation to suppose in general that the truth of a statement is somehow analyzable into a linguistic component and a factual component. Given this supposition, it next seems reasonable that in some statements the factual component should be null; and these are the analytic statements. But, for all its a priori reasonableness, a boundary between analytic and synthetic statements simply has not been drawn. That there is such a distinction to be drawn at all is an unempirical dogma of empiricists, a metaphysical article of faith.

5 The Verification Theory and Reductionism

In the course of these somber reflections we have taken a dim view first of the notion of meaning, then of the notion of cognitive synonymy, and finally of the notion of analyticity. But what, it may be asked, of the verification theory of meaning? This phrase has established itself so firmly as a catchword of empiricism that we should be very unscientific indeed not to look beneath it for a possible key to the problem of meaning and the associated problems.

The verification theory of meaning, which has been conspicuous in the literature from Peirce onward, is that the meaning of a statement is the method of empirically confirming or infirming it. An analytic statement is that limiting case which is confirmed no matter what.

As urged in Section I, we can as well pass over the question of meanings as entities and move straight to sameness of meaning, or synonymy. Then what the verification theory says is that statements are synonymous if and only if they are alike in point of method of empirical confirmation or infirmation.

This is an account of cognitive synonymy not of linguistic forms generally, but of statements.[6] However, from the concept of synonymy of statements we could derive the concept of synonymy for other linguistic forms, by considerations somewhat similar to those at the end of Section III. Assuming the notion of "word", indeed, we could explain any two forms as synonymous when the putting of the one form for an occurrence of the other in any statement (apart from occurrences within "words") yields a synonymous statement. Finally, given the concept of synonymy thus for linguistic forms generally, we could define analyticity in terms of synonymy and logical truth as in Section I. For that matter, we could define analyticity more simply in terms of just synonymy of statements together with logical truth; it is not necessary to appeal to synonymy of linguistic forms other than statements. For a statement may be described as analytic simply when it is synonymous with a logically true statement.

So, if the verification theory can be accepted as an adequate account of statement synonymy, the notion of analyticity is saved after all. However, let us reflect. Statement synonymy is said to be likeness of method of empirical confirmation or infirmation. Just what are these methods which are to be compared for likeness? What, in other words, is the nature of the relationship between a statement and the experiences which contribute to or detract from its confirmation?

The most naive view of the relationship is that it is one of direct report. This is *radical reductionism*. Every meaningful statement is held to be translatable into a statement (true or false) about immediate experience. Radical reductionism, in one form or another, well antedates the verification theory of meaning explicitly so-called. Thus Locke and Hume held that every idea must either originate directly in sense experience or else be compounded of ideas thus originating; and taking a hint from Tooke[7] we might rephrase this doctrine in semantical jargon by saying that a term, to be significant at all, must be either a name of a sense datum or a compound of such names or an abbreviation of such a compound. So stated, the doctrine remains ambiguous as between sense data as sensory events and sense data as sensory qualities; and it remains vague as to the admissible ways of compounding. Moreover, the doctrine is unnecessarily and intolerably restrictive in the term-by-term critique which it imposes. More reasonably, and without yet exceeding the limits of what I have called radical reductionism, we may take full statements as our significant units – thus demanding that our statements as wholes be translatable into sense–datum language, but not that they be translatable term by term.

This emendation would unquestionably have been welcome to Locke and Hume and Tooke, but historically it had to await two intermediate developments. One of these developments was the increasing emphasis on verification or confirmation, which came with the explicitly so-called verification theory of meaning. The objects of verification or confirmation being statements, this emphasis gave the statement an ascendency over the word or term as unit of significant discourse. The other development, consequent upon the first, was Russell's discovery of the concept of incomplete symbols defined in use.

Radical reductionism, conceived now with statements as units, sets itself the task of specifying a sense–datum language and showing how to translate the rest of significant discourse, statement by statement, into it. Carnap embarked on this project in the *Aufbau*.[8]

The language which Carnap adopted as his starting point was not a sense–datum language in the narrowest conceivable sense, for it included also the notations of logic, up through higher set theory. In effect it included the whole language of pure mathematics. The ontology implicit in it (i.e., the range of values of its variables) embraced not only sensory events but classes, classes of classes, and so on. Empiricists there are who would boggle at such prodigality. Carnap's starting point is very parsimonious, however, in its extralogical or sensory part. In a series of constructions in which he exploits the resources of modern logic with much ingenuity, he succeeds in defining a wide array of important additional sensory concepts which, but for his constructions, one would not have dreamed were definable on so slender a basis. Carnap was the first empiricist who, not content with asserting the reducibility of science to terms of immediate experience, took serious steps toward carrying out the reduction.

Even supposing Carnap's starting point satisfactory, his constructions were, as he himself stressed, only a fragment of the full program. The construction of even the simplest statements about the physical world was left in a sketchy state. Carnap's suggestions on this subject were, despite their sketchiness, very suggestive. He explained spatiotemporal point-instants as quadruples of real numbers and envisaged assignment of sense qualities to point-instants according to certain canons. Roughly summarized, the plan was that qualities should be assigned to point-instants in such a way as to achieve the laziest world compatible with our experience. The principle of least action was to be our guide in constructing a world from experience.

Carnap did not seem to recognize, however, that his treatment of physical objects fell short of reduction not merely through sketchiness, but in principle. Statements of the form 'Quality q is at point-instant $x; y; z; t$' were, according to his canons, to be apportioned truth values in such a way as to maximize and minimize certain overall features, and with growth of experience the truth values were to be progressively revised in the same spirit. I think this is a good schematization (deliberately oversimplified, to be sure) of what science really does; but it provides no indication, not even the sketchiest, of how a statement of the form 'Quality q is at $x; y; z; t$' could ever be translated into Carnap's initial language of sense data and logic. The connective 'is at' remains an added undefined connective; the canons counsel us in its use but not in its elimination.

Carnap seems to have appreciated this point afterward; for in his later writings he abandoned all notion of the translatability of statements about the physical world into statements about immediate experience. Reductionism in its radical form has long since ceased to figure in Carnap's philosophy.

But the dogma of reductionism has, in a subtler and more tenuous form, continued to influence the thought of empiricists. The notion lingers that to each statement, or each synthetic statement, there is associated a unique range of possible sensory events such that the occurrence of any of them would add to the likelihood of truth of the statement, and that there is associated also another unique range of possible sensory events whose occurrence would detract from that likelihood. This notion is of course implicit in the verification theory of meaning.

The dogma of reductionism survives in the supposition that each statement, taken in isolation from its fellows, can admit of confirmation or infirmation at all. My countersuggestion, issuing essentially from Carnap's doctrine of the physical world in the *Aufbau*, is that our statements about the external world face the tribunal of sense experience not individually but only as a corporate body.

The dogma of reductionism, even in its attenuated form, is intimately connected with the other dogma: that there is a cleavage between the analytic and the synthetic. We have found ourselves led, indeed, from the latter problem to the former through the verification theory of meaning. More directly, the one dogma clearly supports the other in this way: as long as it is taken to be significant in general to speak of the confirmation and infirmation of a statement, it seems significant to speak also of a limiting kind of statement which is vacuously confirmed, *ipso facto*, come what may; and such a statement is analytic.

The two dogmas are, indeed, at root identical. We lately reflected that in general the truth of statements does obviously depend both upon language and upon extralinguistic fact; and we noted that this obvious circumstance carries in its train, not logically but all too naturally, a feeling that the truth of a statement is somehow analyzable into a linguistic component and a factual component. The factual component must, if we are empiricists, boil down to a range of confirmatory experiences. In the extreme case where the linguistic component is all that matters, a true statement is analytic. But I hope we are now impressed with how stubbornly the distinction between analytic and synthetic has resisted any straightforward drawing. I am impressed also, apart from prefabricated examples of black and white balls in an urn, with how baffling the problem has always been of arriving at any explicit theory of the empirical confirmation of a synthetic statement. My present suggestion is that it is nonsense, and the root of much nonsense, to speak of a linguistic component and a factual component in the truth of any individual statement. Taken collectively, science has its double dependence upon language and experience; but this duality is not significantly traceable into the statements of science taken one by one.

Russell's concept of definition in use was, as remarked, an advance over the impossible term-by-term empiricism of Locke and Hume. The statement, rather than the term, came with Russell to be recognized as the unit accountable to an empiricist critique. But what I am now urging is that even in taking the statement as unit we have drawn our grid too finely. The unit of empirical significance is the whole of science.

6   Empiricism without the Dogmas

The totality of our so-called knowledge or beliefs, from the most casual matters of geography and history to the profoundest laws of atomic physics of even of pure mathematics and logic, is a man-made fabric which impinges on experience only along the edges. Or, to change the figure, total science is like a field of force whose boundary conditions are experience. A conflict with experience at the periphery occasions readjustments in the interior of the field. Truth values have to be redistributed over some of our statements. Re-evaluation of some statements entails re-evaluation of others, because of their logical interconnections – the logical laws being in turn simply certain further statements of the system, certain further elements of the field. Having re-evaluated one statement we must re-evaluate some others, whether they be statements logically connected with the first or whether they be the statements of logical connections themselves. But the total field is so undetermined by its boundary conditions, experience, that there is much latitude of choice as to what statements to re-evaluate in the light of any single contrary experience. No particular experiences are linked with any particular statements in the interior of the field, except indirectly through considerations of equilibrium affecting the field as a whole.

If this view is right, it is misleading to speak of the empirical content of an individual statement – especially if it be a statement at all remote from the experiential periphery of the field. Furthermore it becomes folly to seek a boundary between synthetic statements, which hold contingently on experience, and analytic statements which hold come what may. Any statement can be held true come what may, if we make drastic enough adjustments elsewhere in the system. Even a statement very close to the periphery can be held true in the face of recalcitrant experience by pleading hallucination or by amending certain statements of the kind called logical laws. Conversely, by the same token, no statement is immune to revision. Revision even of the logical law of the excluded middle has been proposed as a means of simplifying quantum mechanics; and what difference is there in principle between such a shift and the shift whereby Kepler superseded Ptolemy, or Einstein Newton, or Darwin Aristotle?

For vividness I have been speaking in terms of varying distances from a sensory periphery. Let me try now to clarify this notion without metaphor. Certain statements, though *about* physical objects and not sense experience, seem peculiarly germane to sense experience – and in a selective way: some statements to some experiences, others to others. Such statements, especially germane to particular experiences, I picture as near the periphery. But in this relation of "germaneness" I envisage nothing more than a loose association reflecting the relative likelihood, in practice, of our choosing one statement rather than another for revision in the event of recalcitrant experience. For example, we can imagine recalcitrant experiences to which we would surely be inclined to accommodate our system by re-evaluating just the statement that there are brick houses on Elm Street, together with related statements on the same topic. We can imagine other recalcitrant experiences to which we would be inclined to accommodate our system by re-evaluating just the statement that there are no centaurs, along with kindred statements. A recalcitrant experience can, I have already urged, be accommodated by any of various alternative re-evaluations in various alternative quarters of the total system; but, in the cases which we are now imagining, our natural tendency to disturb the total system as little as possible would lead us to focus our revisions upon these specific statements concerning brick houses or centaurs. These statements are felt, therefore, to have a sharper empirical reference than highly theoretical statements of physics or logic or ontology. The latter statements may be thought of as relatively centrally located within the total network, meaning merely that little preferential connection with any particular sense data obtrudes itself.

As an empiricist I continue to think of the conceptual scheme of science as a tool, ultimately, for predicting future experience in the light of past experience. Physical objects are conceptually imported into the situation as convenient intermediaries – not by definition in terms of experience, but simply as irreducible posits comparable, epistemologically, to the gods of Homer. Let me interject that for my part I do, qua lay physicist, believe in physical objects and not in Homer's gods; and I consider it a scientific error to believe otherwise. But in point of epistemological footing the physical objects and the gods differ only in degree and not in kind. Both sorts of entities enter our conception only as cultural posits. The myth of physical objects is epistemologically superior to most in that it has proved more efficacious than other myths as a device for working a manageable structure into the flux of experience.

Imagine, for the sake of analogy, that we are given the rational numbers. We develop an algebraic theory for reasoning about them, but we find it inconveniently complex, because certain functions such as square root lack values for some arguments. Then it is discovered that the rules of our algebra can be much simplified by conceptually augmenting our ontology with some mythical entities, to be called irrational numbers. All we continue to be really interested in, first and last, are rational numbers; but we find that we can commonly get from one law about rational numbers to another much more quickly and simply by pretending that the irrational numbers are there too.

I think this a fair account of the introduction of irrational numbers and other extensions of the number system. The fact that the mythical status of irrational numbers eventually gave way to the Dedekind–Russell version of them as certain infinite classes of ratios is irrelevant to my analogy. That version is impossible anyway as long as reality is limited to the rational numbers and not extended to classes of them.

Now I suggest that experience is analogous to the rational numbers and that the physical objects, in analogy to the irrational numbers, are posits which serve merely to simplify our treatment of experience. The physical objects are no more reducible to experience than the irrational numbers to rational numbers, but their incorporation into the theory enables us to get more easily from one statement about experience to another.

The salient differences between the positing of physical objects and the positing of irrational numbers are, I think, just two. First, the factor of simplification is more overwhelming in the case of physical objects than in the numerical case. Second, the positing of physical objects is far more archaic, being indeed coeval, I expect, with language itself. For language is social and so depends for its development upon intersubjective reference.

Positing does not stop with macroscopic physical objects. Objects at the atomic level and beyond are posited to make the laws of macroscopic objects, and ultimately the laws of experience, simpler and more manageable; and we need not expect or demand full definition of atomic and subatomic entities in terms of macroscopic ones, any more than definition of macroscopic things in terms of sense data. Science is a continuation of common sense, and it continues the common-sense expedient of swelling ontology to simplify theory.

Physical objects, small and large, are not the only posits. Forces are another example; and indeed we are told nowadays that the boundary between energy and matter is obsolete. Moreover, the abstract entities which are the substance of mathematics – ultimately classes and classes of classes and so on up – are another posit in the same spirit. Epistemologically these are myths on the same footing with physical objects and gods, neither better nor worse except for differences in the degree to which they expedite our dealings with sense experiences.

The overall algebra of rational and irrational numbers is underdetermined by the algebra of rational numbers, but is smoother and more convenient; and it includes the algebra of rational numbers as a jagged or gerrymandered part. Total science, mathematical and natural and human, is similarly but more extremely underdetermined by experience. The edge of the system must be kept squared with experience; the rest, with all its elaborate myths or fictions, has as its objective the simplicity of laws.

Ontological questions, under this view, are on a par with questions of natural science. Consider the question whether to countenance classes as entities. This, as I have argued elsewhere,[9] is the question whether to quantify with respect to variables which take classes as values. Now Carnap has maintained[10] that this is a question not of matters of fact but of choosing a convenient language form, a convenient conceptual scheme or framework for science. With this I agree, but only on the proviso that the same be conceded regarding scientific hypotheses generally. Carnap has recognized[11] that he is able to preserve a double standard for ontological questions and scientific hypotheses only by assuming an absolute distinction between the analytic and the synthetic; and I need not say again that this is a distinction which I reject.

Some issues do, I grant, seem more a question of convenient conceptual scheme and others more a question of brute fact. The issue over there being classes seems more a question of convenient conceptual scheme; the issue over there being centaurs, or brick houses on Elm Street, seems more a question of fact. But I have been urging that this difference is only one of degree, and that it turns upon our vaguely pragmatic inclination to adjust one strand of the fabric of

W. V. Quine

science rather than another in accommodating some particular recalcitrant experience. Conservatism figures in such choices, and so does the quest for simplicity.

Carnap, Lewis, and others take a pragmatic stand on the question of choosing between language forms, scientific frameworks; but their pragmatism leaves off at the imagined boundary between the analytic and the synthetic. In repudiating such a boundary I espouse a more thorough pragmatism. Each man is given a scientific heritage plus a continuing barrage of sensory stimulation; and the considerations which guide him in warping his scientific heritage to fit his continuing sensory promptings are, where rational, pragmatic.

Notes

Much of this paper is devoted to a critique of analyticity which I have been urging orally and in correspondence for years past. My debt to the other participants in those discussions, notably Carnap, Church, Goodman, Tarski, and White, is large and indeterminate. White's excellent essay "The Analytic and the Synthetic: An Untenable Dualism," in *John Dewey: Philosopher of Science and Freedom* (New York, 1950), says much of what needed to be said on the topic; but in the present paper I touch on some further aspects of the problem. I am grateful to Dr. Donald L. Davidson for valuable criticism of the first draft.

1   See White, "The Analytic and the Synthetic," p. 324.
2   R. Carnap, *Meaning and Necessity* (Chicago, 1947), pp. 9ff.; *Logical Foundations of Probability* (Chicago, 1950), pp. 70ff.
3   This is cognitive synonymy in a primary, broad sense. Carnap (*Meaning and Necessity*, pp. 56ff.) and Lewis (*Analysis of Knowledge and Valuation* (La Salle, IL, 1946), pp. 83ff.) have suggested how, once this notion is at hand, a narrower sense of cognitive synonymy which is preferable for some purposes can in turn be derived. But this special ramification of concept-building lies aside from the present purposes and must not be confused with the broad sort of cognitive synonymy here concerned.
4   See, e.g., my *Mathematical Logic* (New York, 1940; Cambridge, MA, 1947), sec. 24, 26, 27; or *Methods of Logic* (New York, 1950), sec. 37ff.
5   The 'if and only if' itself is intended in the truth functional sense. See Carnap, *Meaning and Necessity*, p. 14.
6   The doctrine can indeed be formulated with terms rather than statements as the units. Thus C. I. Lewis describes the meaning of a term as "*a criterion in mind*, by reference to which one is able to apply or refuse to apply the expression in question in the case of presented, or imagined, things or situations" (*Analysis of Knowledge*, p. 133).
7   John Horne Tooke, *The Diversions of Purley* (London, 1776; Boston, 1806), I, ch. ii.
8   R. Carnap, *Der logische Aufbau der Welt* (Berlin, 1928).
9   E.g., in "Notes on Existence and Necessity," *Journal of Philosophy* 40 (1943), pp. 113–27.
10   Carnap, "Empiricism, Semantics, and Ontology," *Revue internationale de philosophie* 4 (1950), pp. 20–40.
11   Ibid., p. 32, footnote.

44

In Defense of a Dogma

H. P. Grice and P. F. Strawson

In his article "Two Dogmas of Empiricism,"[1] Professor Quine advances a number of criticisms of the supposed distinction between analytic and synthetic statements, and of other associated notions. It is, he says, a distinction which he rejects.[2] We wish to show that his criticisms of the distinction do not justify his rejection of it.

There are many ways in which a distinction can be criticized, and more than one in which it can be rejected. It can be criticized for not being a sharp distinction (for admitting of cases which do not fall clearly on either side of it); or on the ground that the terms in which it is customarily drawn are ambiguous (have more than one meaning); or on the ground that it is confused (the different meanings being habitually conflated). Such criticisms alone would scarcely amount to a rejection of the distinction. They would, rather, be a prelude to clarification. It is not this sort of criticism which Quine makes.

Again, a distinction can be criticized on the ground that it is not useful. It can be said to be useless for certain purposes, or useless altogether, and, perhaps, pedantic. One who criticizes in this way may indeed be said to reject a distinction, but in a sense which also requires him to acknowledge its existence. He simply declares he can get on without it. But Quine's rejection of the analytic–synthetic distinction appears to be more radical than this. He would certainly say

he could get on without the distinction, but not in a sense which would commit him to acknowledging its existence.

Or again, one could criticize the way or ways in which a distinction is customarily expounded or explained on the ground that these explanations did not make it really clear. And Quine certainly makes such criticisms in the case of the analytic–synthetic distinction.

But he does, or seems to do, a great deal more. He declares, or seems to declare, not merely that the distinction is useless or inadequately clarified, but also that it is altogether illusory, that the belief in its existence is a philosophical mistake. "That there is such a distinction to be drawn at all," he says, "is an unempirical dogma of empiricists, a metaphysical article of faith."[3] It is the existence of the distinction that he here calls in question; so his rejection of it would seem to amount to a denial of its existence.

Evidently such a position of extreme skepticism about a distinction is not in general justified merely by criticisms, however just in themselves, of philosophical attempts to clarify it. There are doubtless plenty of distinctions, drawn in philosophy and outside it, which still await adequate philosophical elucidation, but which few would want on this account to declare illusory. Quine's article, however, does not consist wholly, though it does consist largely, in criticizing attempts at elucidation. He does try also to diagnose the causes of the belief in the distinction, and he offers some positive doctrine, acceptance of which he represents as incompatible with this belief. If there is any general prior presumption in favor of the existence of the distinction, it seems that Quine's radical rejection of it must rest quite heavily on this part of his article, since the force of any such presumption is not even impaired by philosophical failures to clarify a distinction so supported.

Is there such a presumption in favor of the distinction's existence? Prima facie, it must be admitted that there is. An appeal to philosophical tradition is perhaps unimpressive and is certainly unnecessary. But it is worth pointing out that Quine's objection is not simply to the words "analytic" and "synthetic," but to a distinction which they are supposed to express, and which at different times philosophers have supposed themselves to be expressing by means of such pairs of words or phrases as "necessary" and "contingent," "a priori" and "empirical," "truth of reason" and "truth of fact"; so Quine is certainly at odds with a philosophical tradition which is long and not wholly disreputable. But there is no need to appeal only to tradition; for there is also present practice. We can appeal, that is, to the fact that those who use the terms "analytic" and "synthetic" do to a very considerable extent agree in the applications they make of them. They apply the term "analytic" to more or less the same cases, withhold it from more or less the same cases, and hesitate over more or less the same cases. This agreement extends not only to cases which they have been *taught* so to characterize, but to new cases. In short, "analytic" and "synthetic" have a more or less established philosophical *use*; and this seems to suggest that it is absurd, even senseless, to say that there is no such distinction. For, in general, if a pair of contrasting expressions are habitually and generally used in application to the same cases, *where these cases do not form a closed list*, this is a sufficient condition for saying that there are *kinds* of cases to which the expressions apply; and nothing more is needed for them to mark a distinction.

In view of the possibility of this kind of argument, one may begin to doubt whether Quine really holds the extreme thesis which his words encourage one to attribute to him. It is for this reason that we made the attribution tentative. For on at least one natural interpretation of this extreme thesis, when we say of something true that it is analytic and of another true thing that it is synthetic, it simply never is the case that we thereby mark a distinction between them. And

this view seems terribly difficult to reconcile with the fact of an established philosophical usage (i.e., of general agreement in application in an open class). For this reason, Quine's thesis might be better represented not as the thesis that there is *no difference at all* marked by the use of these expressions, but as the thesis that the nature of, and reasons for, the difference or differences are totally misunderstood by those who use the expressions, that the stories they tell themselves *about* the difference are full of illusion.

We think Quine might be prepared to accept this amendment. If so, it could, in the following way, be made the basis of something like an answer to the argument which prompted it. Philosophers are notoriously subject to illusion, and to mistaken theories. Suppose there were a particular mistaken theory about language or knowledge, such that, seen in the light of this theory, some statements (or propositions or sentences) appeared to have a characteristic which no statements really have, or even, perhaps, which it does not make sense to suppose that any statement has, and which no one who was not consciously or subconsciously influenced by this theory would ascribe to any statement. And suppose that there were other statements which, seen in this light, did not appear to have this characteristic, and others again which presented an uncertain appearance. Then philosophers who were under the influence of this theory would tend to mark the supposed presence or absence of this characteristic by a pair of contrasting expressions, say "analytic" and "synthetic." Now in these circumstances it still could not be said that there was no distinction at all being marked by the use of these expressions, for there would be at least the distinction we have just described (the distinction, namely, between those statements which appeared to have and those which appeared to lack a certain characteristic), and there might well be other assignable differences too, which would account for the difference in appearance; but it certainly could be said that *the* difference these philosophers supposed themselves to be marking by the use of the expressions simply did not exist, and perhaps also (supposing the characteristic in question to be one which it was absurd to ascribe to any statement) that these expressions, as so used, were senseless or without meaning. We should only have to suppose that such a mistaken theory was very plausible and attractive, in order to reconcile the fact of an established philosophical usage for a pair of contrasting terms with the claim that *the* distinction which the terms purported to mark did not exist at all, though not with the claim that there simply did not exist a difference of any kind between the classes of statements so characterized. We think that the former claim would probably be sufficient for Quine's purposes. But to establish such a claim on the sort of grounds we have indicated evidently requires a great deal more argument than is involved in showing that certain explanations of a term do not measure up to certain requirements of adequacy in philosophical clarification – and not only more argument, but argument of a very different kind. For it would surely be too harsh to maintain that the *general* presumption is that philosophical distinctions embody the kind of illusion we have described. On the whole, it seems that philosophers are prone to make too few distinctions rather than too many. It is their assimilations, rather than their distinctions, which tend to be spurious.

So far we have argued as if the prior presumption in favor of the existence of the distinction which Quine questions rested solely on the fact of an agreed *philosophical* usage for the terms "analytic" and "synthetic." A presumption with only this basis could no doubt be countered by a strategy such as we have just outlined. But, in fact, if we are to accept Quine's account of the matter, the presumption in question is not only so based. For among the notions which belong to the analyticity-group is one which Quine calls "cognitive synonymy," and in terms of which he allows that the notion of analyticity could at any rate be formally explained. Unfortunately, he adds, the notion of cognitive synonymy is just as unclarified as that of analyticity. To say that two expressions *x* and *y* are cognitively synonymous seems to correspond, at any rate roughly, to what we should ordinarily express by saying that *x* and *y* have the same meaning or that *x* means the same as *y*. If Quine is to be consistent in his adherence to the extreme thesis, then it appears that he must maintain not only that the distinction we suppose ourselves to be marking by the use of the terms "analytic" and "synthetic" does not exist, but also that the distinction we suppose ourselves to be marking by the use of the expressions "means the same as," "does not mean the same as" does not exist either. At least, he must maintain this insofar as the notion of *meaning the same as*, in its application to predicate-

expressions, is supposed to differ from and go beyond the notion of *being true of just the same objects as*. (This latter notion – which we might call that of "coextensionality" – he is prepared to allow to be intelligible, though, as he rightly says, it is not sufficient for the explanation of analyticity.) Now since he cannot claim this time that the pair of expressions in question (viz., "means the same," "does not mean the same") is the special property of philosophers, the strategy outlined above of countering the presumption in favor of their marking a genuine distinction is not available here (or is at least enormously less plausible). Yet the denial that the distinction (taken as different from the distinction between the coextensional and the non-coextensional) really exists, is extremely paradoxical. It involves saying, for example, that anyone who seriously remarks that "bachelor" means the same as "unmarried man" but that "creature with kidneys" does not mean the same as "creature with a heart" – supposing the last two expressions to be coextensional – *either* is not in fact drawing attention to any distinction at all between the relations between the members of each pair of expressions *or* is making a philosophical mistake about the nature of the distinction between them. In either case, what he says, taken as he intends it to be taken, is senseless or absurd. More generally, it involves saying that it is always senseless or absurd to make a statement of the form "Predicates *x* and *y* in fact apply to the same objects, but do not have the same meaning." But the paradox is more violent than this. For we frequently talk of the presence or absence of relations of synonymy between kinds of expressions – e.g., conjunctions, particles of many kinds, whole sentences – where there does not appear to be any obvious substitute for the ordinary notion of synonymy, in the way in which coextensionality is said to be a substitute for synonymy of predicates. Is all such talk meaningless? Is all talk of correct or incorrect *translation* of sentences of one language into sentences of another meaningless? It is hard to believe that it is. But if we do successfully make the effort to believe it, we have still harder renunciations before us. If talk of sentence-synonymy is meaningless, then it seems that talk of sentences having a meaning at all must be meaningless too. For if it made sense to talk of a sentence having a meaning, or meaning something, then presumably it would make sense to ask "What does it mean?" And if it made sense to ask "What does it mean?" of a sentence, then sentence-synonymy could be roughly defined as follows: Two sentences are synonymous if and only if any true answer to the question "What does it mean?" asked of one of them, is a true answer to the same question, asked of the other. We do not, of course, claim any clarifying power for this definition. We want only to point out that if we are to give up the notion of sentence-synonymy as senseless, we must give up the notion of sentence-significance (of a sentence having meaning) as senseless too. But then perhaps we might as well give up the notion of sense. It seems clear that we have here a typical example of a philosopher's paradox. Instead of examining the actual use that we make of the notion of *meaning the same*, the philosopher measures it by some perhaps inappropriate standard (in this case some standard of clarifiability), and because it falls short of this standard, or seems to do so, denies its reality, declares it illusory.

We have argued so far that there is a strong presumption in favor of the existence of the distinction, or distinctions, which Quine challenges – a presumption resting both on philosophical and on ordinary usage – and that this presumption is not in the least shaken by the fact, if it is a fact, that the distinctions in question have not been, in some sense, adequately clarified. It is perhaps time to look at what Quine's notion of adequate clarification is.

The main theme of his article can be roughly summarized as follows. There is a certain circle or family of expressions, of which "analytic" is one, such that if any one member of the circle could be taken to be satisfactorily understood or explained, then other members of the circle could be verbally, and hence satisfactorily, explained in terms of it. Other members of the family are: "self-contradictory" (in a broad sense), "necessary," "synonymous," "semantical rule," and perhaps (but again in a broad sense) "definition." The list could be added to. Unfortunately each member of the family is in as great need of explanation as any other. We give some sample quotations: "The notion of self-contradictoriness (in the required broad sense of inconsistency) stands in exactly the same need of clarification as does the notion of analyticity itself."[4] Again, Quine speaks of "a notion of synonymy which is in no less need of clarification than analyticity itself."[5] Again, of the adverb "necessarily," as a candidate for use in the explanation of synonymy, he

says, "Does the adverb *really make sense*? To suppose that it does is to suppose that we have already *made satisfactory sense* of 'analytic.'"[6] To make "satisfactory sense" of one of these expressions would seem to involve two things. (1) It would seem to involve providing an explanation which does not incorporate any expression belonging to the family-circle. (2) It would seem that the explanation provided must be of the same general character as those rejected explanations which do incorporate members of the family-circle (i.e., it must specify some feature common and peculiar to all cases to which, for example, the word "analytic" is to be applied; it must have the same general form as an explanation beginning, "a statement is analytic if and only if . . ."). It is true that Quine does not explicitly state the second requirement; but since he does not even consider the question whether any other kind of explanation would be relevant, it seems reasonable to attribute it to him. If we take these two conditions together, and generalize the result, it would seem that Quine requires of a satisfactory explanation of an expression that it should take the form of a pretty strict definition but should not make use of any member of a group of interdefinable terms to which the expression belongs. We may well begin to feel that a satisfactory explanation is hard to come by. The other element in Quine's position is one we have already commented on in general, before enquiring what (according to him) is to count as a satisfactory explanation. It is the step from "We have not made satisfactory sense (provided a satisfactory explanation) of *x*" to "*x* does not make sense."

It would seem fairly clearly unreasonable to insist *in general* that the availability of a satisfactory explanation in the sense sketched above is a necessary condition of an expression's making sense. It is perhaps dubious whether *any* such explanations can *ever* be given. (The hope that they can be is, or was, the hope of reductive analysis in general.) Even if such explanations can be given in some cases, it would be pretty generally agreed that there are other cases in which they cannot. One might think, for example, of the group of expressions which includes "morally wrong," "blameworthy," "breach of moral rules," etc.; or of the group which includes the propositional connectives and the words "true" and "false," "statement," "fact," "denial," "assertion." Few people would want to say that the expressions belonging to either of these groups were senseless on the ground that they have not been formally defined (or even on the ground that it was impossible formally to define them) except in terms of members of the same group. It might, however, be said that while the unavailability of a satisfactory explanation in the special sense described was not a *generally* sufficient reason for declaring that a given expression was senseless, it was a sufficient reason in the case of the expressions of the analyticity group. But anyone who said this would have to advance a reason for discriminating in this way against the expressions of this group. The only plausible reason for being harder on these expressions than on others is a refinement on a consideration which we have already had before us. It starts from the point that "analytic" and "synthetic" themselves are technical philosophical expressions. To the rejoinder that other expressions of the family concerned, such as "means the same as" or "is inconsistent with," or "self-contradictory," are not at all technical expressions, but are common property, the reply would doubtless be that, to qualify for inclusion in the family circle, these expressions have to be used in specially adjusted and precise senses (or pseudo-senses) which they do not ordinarily possess. It is the fact, then, that all the terms belonging to the circle are *either* technical terms *or* ordinary terms used in specially adjusted senses, that might be held to justify us in being particularly suspicious of the claims of members of the circle to have any sense at all, and hence to justify us in requiring them to pass a test for significance which would admittedly be too stringent if generally applied. This point has some force, though we doubt if the special adjustments spoken of are in every case as considerable as it suggests. (This seems particularly doubtful in the case of the word "inconsistent" – a perfectly good member of the nontechnician's meta-logical vocabulary.) But though the point has some force, it does not have whatever force would be required to justify us in insisting that the expressions concerned should pass exactly that test for significance which is in question. The fact, if it is a fact, that the expressions cannot be explained in precisely the way which Quine seems to require, does not mean that they cannot be explained at all. There is no need to try to pass them off as expressing innate ideas. They can be and are explained, though in other and less formal ways than that

which Quine considers. (And the fact that they are so explained fits with the facts, first, that there is a generally agreed philosophical use for them, and second, that this use is technical or specially adjusted.) To illustrate the point briefly for one member of the analyticity family. Let us suppose we are trying to explain to someone the notion of *logical impossibility* (a member of the family which Quine presumably regards as no clearer than any of the others) and we decide to do it by bringing out the contrast between logical and natural (or causal) impossibility. We might take as our examples the logical impossibility of a child of three's being an adult, and the natural impossibility of a child of three's understanding Russell's Theory of Types. We might instruct our pupil to imagine two conversations one of which begins by someone (X) making the claim:

(1) "My neighbor's three-year-old child understands Russell's Theory of Types,"

and the other of which begins by someone (Y) making the claim:

(1') "My neighbor's three-year-old child is an adult."

It would not be inappropriate to reply to X, taking the remark as a hyperbole:

(2) "You mean the child is a particularly bright lad."

If X were to say:

(3) "No, I mean what I say – he really does understand it,"

one might be inclined to reply:

(4) "I don't believe you – the thing's impossible."

But if the child were then produced, and did (as one knows he would not) expound the theory correctly, answer questions on it, criticize it, and so on, one would in the end be forced to acknowledge that the claim was literally true and that the child was a prodigy. Now consider one's reaction to Y's claim. To begin with, it might be somewhat similar to the previous case. One might say:

(2′) "You mean he's uncommonly sensible or very advanced for his age."

If Y replies:

(3′) "No, I mean what I say,"

we might reply:

(4′) "Perhaps you mean that he won't grow any more, or that he's a sort of freak, that he's already fully developed."

Y replies:

(5′) "No, he's not a freak, he's just an adult."

At this stage – or possibly if we are patient, a little later – we shall be inclined to say that we just don't understand what Y is saying, and to suspect that he just does not know the meaning of some of the words he is using. For unless he is prepared to admit that he is using words in a figurative or unusual sense, we shall say, not that we don't believe him, but that his words have *no* sense. And whatever kind of creature is ultimately produced for our inspection, it will not lead us to say that what Y said was literally true, but at most to say that we now see what he meant. As a summary of the difference between the two imaginary conversations, we might say that in both cases we would tend to begin by supposing that the other speaker was using words in a figurative or unusual or restricted way; but in the face of his repeated claim to be speaking literally, it would be appropriate in the first case to say that we did not believe him and in the second case to say that we did not understand him. If, like Pascal, we thought it prudent to prepare against very long chances, we should in the first case know what to prepare for; in the second, we should have no idea.

We give this as an example of just one type of informal explanation which we might have recourse to in the case of one notion of the analyticity group. (We do not wish to suggest it is the only type.) Further examples, with different though connected types of treatment, might be necessary to teach our pupil the use of the notion of logical impossibility in its application to more complicated cases – if indeed he did not pick it up from the one case. Now of course

this type of explanation does not yield a formal statement of necessary and sufficient conditions for the application of the notion concerned. So it does not fulfill one of the conditions which Quine seems to require of a satisfactory explanation. On the other hand, it does appear to fulfill the other. It breaks out of the family circle. The distinction in which we ultimately come to test is that between not believing something and not understanding something; or between incredulity yielding to conviction, and incomprehension yielding to comprehension. It would be rash to maintain that *this* distinction does not need clarification; but it would be absurd to maintain that it does not exist. In the face of the availability of this informal type of explanation for the notions of the analyticity group, the fact that they have not received another type of explanation (which it is dubious whether *any* expressions *ever* receive) seems a wholly inadequate ground for the conclusion that the notions are pseudo-notions, that the expressions which purport to express them have no sense. To say this is not to deny that it would be philosophically desirable, and a proper object of philosophical endeavor, to find a more illuminating general characterization of the notions of this group than any that has been so far given. But the question of how, if at all, this can be done is quite irrelevant to the question of whether or not the expressions which belong to the circle have an intelligible use and mark genuine distinctions.

So far we have tried to show that sections 1 to 4 of Quine's article – the burden of which is that the notions of the analyticity group have not been satisfactorily explained – do not establish the extreme thesis for which he appears to be arguing. It remains to be seen whether sections 5 and 6, in which diagnosis and positive theory are offered, are any more successful. But before we turn to them, there are two further points worth making which arise out of the first two sections.

(1) One concerns what Quine says about *definition* and *synonymy*. He remarks that definition does not, as some have supposed, "hold the key to synonymy and analyticity," since "definition – except in the extreme case of the explicitly conventional introduction of new notations – hinges on prior relations of synonymy."[7] But now consider what he says of these extreme cases. He says: "Here the definiendum becomes synonymous with the definiens simply because it has

been expressly created for the purpose of being synonymous with the definiens. Here we have a really transparent case of synonymy created by definition; would that all species of synonymy were as intelligible." Now if we are to take these words of Quine seriously, then his position *as a whole* is incoherent. It is like the position of a man to whom we are trying to explain, say, the idea of one thing fitting into another thing, or two things fitting together, and who says: "I can understand what it means to say that one thing fits into another, or that two things fit together, in the case where one was specially made to fit the other; but I cannot understand what it means to say this in any other case." Perhaps we should not take Quine's words here too seriously. But if not, then we have the right to ask him exactly what state of affairs he thinks *is* brought about by explicit definition, what relation between expressions *is* established by this procedure, and why he thinks it unintelligible to suggest that the same (or a closely analogous) state of affairs, or relation, should exist in the absence of this procedure. For our part, we should be inclined to take Quine's words (or some of them) seriously, and reverse his conclusions; and maintain that the notion of synonymy by explicit convention would be unintelligible if the notion of synonymy by usage were not presupposed. There cannot be law where there is no custom, or rules where there are not practices (though perhaps we can understand better what a practice is by looking at a rule).

(2) The second point arises out of a paragraph on page 32 of Quine's book [p. 456 of the present volume]. We quote:

I do not know whether the statement "Everything green is extended" is analytic. Now does my indecision over this example really betray an incomplete understanding, an incomplete grasp, of the "meanings" of "green" and "extended"? I think not. The trouble is not with "green" or "extended," but with "analytic."

If, as Quine says, the trouble is with "analytic," then the trouble should doubtless disappear when "analytic" is removed. So let us remove it, and replace it with a word which Quine himself has contrasted favorably with "analytic" in respect of perspicuity – the word "true." Does the indecision at once disappear? We think not. The indeci-

sion over "analytic" (and equally, in this case, the indecision over "true") arises, of course, from a further indecision: viz., that which we feel when confronted with such questions as "Should we count a *point* of green light as *extended* or not?" As is frequent enough in such cases, the hesitation arises from the fact that the boundaries of application of words are not determined by usage in all possible directions. But the example Quine has chosen is particularly unfortunate for his thesis, in that it is only too evident that our hesitations are not *here* attributable to obscurities in "analytic." It would be possible to choose other examples in which we should hesitate between "analytic" and "synthetic" and have few qualms about "true." But no more in these cases than in the sample case does the hesitation necessarily imply any obscurity in the notion of analyticity; since the hesitation would be sufficiently accounted for by the same or a similar kind of indeterminacy in the relations between the words occurring within the statement about which the question, whether it is analytic or synthetic, is raised.

Let us now consider briefly Quine's positive theory of the relations between the statements we accept as true or reject as false on the one hand and the "experiences" in the light of which we do this accepting and rejecting on the other. This theory is boldly sketched rather than precisely stated.[8] We shall merely extract from it two assertions, one of which Quine clearly takes to be incompatible with acceptance of the distinction between analytic and synthetic statements, and the other of which he regards as barring one way to an explanation of that distinction. We shall seek to show that the first assertion is not incompatible with acceptance of the distinction, but is, on the contrary, most intelligibly interpreted in a way quite consistent with it, and that the second assertion leaves the way open to just the kind of explanation which Quine thinks it precludes. The two assertions are the following:

(1) It is an illusion to suppose that there is any class of accepted statements the members of which are in principle "immune from revision" in the light of experience, i.e., any that we accept as true and must continue to accept as true whatever happens.

(2) It is an illusion to suppose that an individual statement, taken in isolation from its fellows, can admit of confirmation or disconfirmation

at all. There is no particular statement such that a particular experience or set of experiences decides once for all whether that statement is true or false, independently of our attitudes to all other statements.

The apparent connection between these two doctrines may be summed up as follows. Whatever our experience may be, it is in principle possible to hold on to, or reject, any particular statement we like, so long as we are prepared to make extensive enough revisions elsewhere in our system of beliefs. In practice our choices are governed largely by considerations of convenience: we wish our system to be as simple as possible, but we also wish disturbances to it, as it exists, to be as small as possible.

The apparent relevance of these doctrines to the analytic–synthetic distinction is obvious in the first case, less so in the second.

(1) Since it is an illusion to suppose that the characteristic of immunity in principle from revision, come what may, belongs, or could belong, to any statement, it is an illusion to suppose that there is a distinction to be drawn between statements which possess this characteristic and statements which lack it. Yet, Quine suggests, this is precisely the distinction which those who use the terms "analytic" and "synthetic" suppose themselves to be drawing. Quine's view would perhaps also be (though he does not explicitly say this in the article under consideration) that those who believe in the distinction are inclined at least sometimes to mistake the characteristic of strongly resisting revision (which belongs to beliefs very centrally situated in the system) for the mythical characteristic of total immunity from revision.

(2) The connection between the second doctrine and the analytic–synthetic distinction runs, according to Quine, through the verification theory of meaning. He says: "If the verification theory can be accepted as an adequate account of statement synonymy, the notion of analyticity is saved after all."[9] For, in the first place, two statements might be said to be synonymous if and only if any experiences which contribute to, or detract from, the confirmation of one contribute to, or detract from, the confirmation of the other, to the same degree; and, in the second place, synonymy could be used to explain analyticity. But, Quine seems to argue, acceptance of any such account of synonymy can only rest on the mistaken belief

that individual statements, taken in isolation from their fellows, can admit of confirmation or disconfirmation at all. As soon as we give up the idea of a set of experiential truth-conditions for each statement taken separately, we must give up the idea of explaining synonymy in terms of identity of such sets.

Now to show that the relations between these doctrines and the analytic–synthetic distinction are not as Quine supposes. Let us take the second doctrine first. It is easy to see that acceptance of the second doctrine would not compel one to abandon, but only to revise, the suggested explanation of synonymy. Quine does not deny that individual statements are regarded as confirmed or disconfirmed, are in fact rejected or accepted, in the light of experience. He denies only that these relations between single statements and experience hold independently of our attitudes to *other* statements. He means that experience can confirm or disconfirm an individual statement, only given certain assumptions about the truth or falsity of other statements. When we are faced with a "recalcitrant experience," he says, we always have a choice of what statements to amend. What we have to renounce is determined by what we are anxious to keep. This view, however, requires only a slight modification of the definition of statement-synonymy in terms of confirmation and disconfirmation. All we have to say now is that two statements are synonymous if and only if any experiences which, *on certain assumptions about the truth-values of other statements*, confirm or disconfirm one of the pair, also, *on the same assumptions*, confirm or disconfirm the other to the same degree. More generally, Quine wishes to substitute for what he conceives to be an oversimple picture of the confirmation-relations between particular statements and particular experiences, the idea of a looser relation which he calls "germaneness." But however loosely "germaneness" is to be understood, it would apparently continue to make sense to speak of two statements as standing in the same germaneness-relation to the same particular experiences. So Quine's views are not only consistent with, but even suggest, an amended account of statement-synonymy along these lines. We are not, of course, concerned to defend such an account, or even to state it with any precision. We are only concerned to show that acceptance of Quine's doctrine of empirical confirmation does not, as he says it does, entail giving up the attempt to define statement-synonymy in terms of confirmation.

Now for the doctrine that there is no statement which is in principle immune from revision, no statement which might not be given up in the face of experience. Acceptance of this doctrine is quite consistent with adherence to the distinction between analytic and synthetic statements. Only, the adherent of *this* distinction must also insist on another: on the distinction between that kind of giving up which consists in merely admitting falsity, and that kind of giving up which involves changing or dropping a concept or set of concepts. Any form of words at one time held to express something true may, no doubt, at another time, come to be held to express something false. But it is not only philosophers who would distinguish between the case where this happens as the result of a change of opinion solely as to matters of fact, and the case where this happens at least partly as a result of a shift in the sense of the words. Where such a shift in the sense of the words is a necessary condition of the change in truth-value, then the adherent of the distinction will say that the form of words in question changes from expressing an analytic statement to expressing a synthetic statement. We are not now concerned, or called upon, to elaborate an adequate theory of conceptual revision, any more than we were called upon, just now, to elaborate an adequate theory of synonymy. If we can make sense of the idea that the same form of words, taken in one way (or bearing one sense), may express something true, and taken in another way (or bearing another sense), may express something false, then we can make sense of the idea of conceptual revision. And if we can make sense of this idea, then we can perfectly well preserve the distinction between the analytic and the synthetic, while conceding to Quine the revisability-in-principle of everything we say. As for the idea that the same form of words, taken in different ways, may bear different senses and perhaps be used to say things with different truth-values, the onus of showing that this is somehow a mistaken or confused idea rests squarely on Quine. The point of substance (or one of them) that Quine is making, by this emphasis on revisability, is that there is no absolute necessity about the adoption or use of any conceptual scheme whatever, or, more narrowly

and in terms that he would reject, that there is no analytic proposition such that we *must* have linguistic forms bearing just the sense required to express that proposition. But it is one thing to admit this, and quite another thing to say that there are no necessities within any conceptual scheme we adopt or use, or, more narrowly again, that there are no linguistic forms which do express analytic propositions.

The adherent of the analytic–synthetic distinction may go further and admit that there may be cases (particularly perhaps in the field of science) where it would be pointless to press the question whether a change in the attributed truth-value of a statement represented a conceptual revision or not, and correspondingly pointless to press the analytic–synthetic distinction. We cannot quote such cases, but this inability may well be the result of ignorance of the sciences. In any case, the existence, if they do exist, of statements about which it is pointless to press the question whether they are analytic or synthetic, does not entail the nonexistence of statements which are clearly classifiable in one or other of these ways and of statements our hesitation over which has different sources, such as the possibility of alternative interpretations of the linguistic forms in which they are expressed.

This concludes our examination of Quine's article. It will be evident that our purpose has been wholly negative. We have aimed to show merely that Quine's case against the existence of the analytic–synthetic distinction is not made out. His article has two parts. In one of them, the notions of the analyticity group are criticized on the ground that they have not been adequately explained. In the other, a positive theory of truth is outlined, purporting to be incompatible with views to which believers in the analytic–synthetic distinction either must be, or are likely to be, committed. In fact, we have contended, no single point is established which those who accept the notions of the analyticity group would feel any strain in accommodating in their own system of beliefs. This is not to deny that many of the points raised are of the first importance in connection with the problem of giving a satisfactory general account of analyticity and related concepts. We are here only criticizing the contention that these points justify the rejection, as illusory, of the analytic–synthetic distinction and the notions which belong to the same family.

H. P. Grice and P. F. Strawson

Notes

1 W. V. Quine, *From a Logical Point of View* (Cambridge, MA, 1953), pp. 20–46 [pp. 450–62 in this volume]. References below are to page numbers in Quine's book, which are followed, in brackets, by page numbers in the article reprinted in this volume.

2 P. 46 [461].

3 P. 37 [457].

4 P. 20 [450].

5 P. 23 [452].

6 P. 30 [454–5], our [Grice and Strawson] italics.

7 P. 27 [453].

8 Cf. pp. 37–46 [457–62].

9 P. 38 [458].

45

Philosophy and the Scientific Image of Man

Wilfrid Sellars

The Philosophical Quest

The aim of philosophy, abstractly formulated, is to understand how things in the broadest possible sense of the term hang together in the broadest possible sense of the term. Under "things in the broadest possible sense" I include such radically different items as not only "cabbages and kings," but numbers and duties, possibilities and finger snaps, aesthetic experience and death. To achieve success in philosophy would be, to use a contemporary turn of phrase, to "know one's way around" with respect to all these things, not in that unreflective way in which the centipede of the story knew its way around before it faced the question, "how do I walk?" but in that reflective way which means that no intellectual holds are barred.

Knowing one's way around is, to use a current distinction, a form of "knowing *how*" as contrasted with "knowing *that*." There is all the difference in the world between knowing *how* to ride a bicycle and knowing *that* a steady pressure by the legs of a balanced person on the pedals would result in forward motion. Again, to use an example somewhat closer to our subject, there is all the difference in the world between knowing *that* each step of a given proof in mathematics follows from the preceding steps, and knowing

Previously published in *Frontiers of Science and Philosophy*, ed. Robert G. Colodny. © 1962 by the University of Pittsburgh Press. Reprinted by permission of the University of Pittsburgh Press.

how to find a proof. Sometimes being able to find a proof is a matter of being able to follow a set procedure; more often it is not. It can be argued that anything which can be properly called "knowing how to do something" presupposes a body of knowledge *that*; or, to put it differently, knowledge of truth or facts. If this were so, then the statement that "ducks know *how* to swim" would be as metaphorical as the statement that they know *that* water supports them. However this may be, knowing how to do something at the level of characteristically human activity presupposes a great deal of knowledge *that*, and it is obvious that the reflective knowing one's way around in the scheme of things, which is the aim of philosophy, presupposes a great deal of reflective knowledge of truths.

Now the subject-matter of this knowledge of truths which is presupposed by philosophical "know-how," falls, in a sense, completely within the scope of the special disciplines. Philosophy in an important sense has no special subject-matter which stands to it as other subject-matters stand to other special disciplines. If philosophers did have such a special subject-matter, they could turn it over to a new group of specialists, as they have turned other special subject-matters to non-philosophers over the past 2,500 years, first mathematics, more recently psychology and sociology, and, currently, certain aspects of theoretical linguistics. What is characteristic of philosophy is not a special subject-matter, but the aim of knowing one's way around with respect to the subject-matters of all the special disciplines.

Wilfrid Sellars

Now the special disciplines know their way around their subject-matters, and each learns to do so in the process of discovering truths about its own subject-matter. But each special discipline must also have a sense of how its bailiwick fits into the countryside as a whole. This sense, in many cases, amounts to a little more than the unreflective "knowing one's way around," which is a common possession of us all. Again, the specialist must have a sense of how not only his subject-matter but also the methods and principles of his thinking about it fit into the intellectual landscape. Thus, the historian reflects not only on historical events themselves, but on what it is to think historically. It is part of his business to reflect on his own thinking – its aims, its criteria, its pitfalls. In dealing with historical questions he must face and answer questions which are not, themselves, in a primary sense historical questions. But he deals with these questions as they arise in the attempt to answer specifically historical questions.

Reflection on any special discipline can soon lead one to the conclusion that the *ideal* practitioner of that discipline would see his special subject-matter and his thinking about it in the light of a reflective insight into the intellectual landscape as a whole. There is much truth in the Platonic conception that the special disciplines are perfected by philosophy, but the companion conception that the philosopher must know his way around in each discipline, as does the specialist, has been an ever more elusive ideal since the scientific revolution began. But if the philosopher cannot hope to know his way around in each discipline as does the specialist, there is a sense in which he can know his way around with respect to the subject-matter of that discipline, and must do so if he is to approximate to the philosophic aim.

The multiplication of sciences and disciplines is a familiar feature of the intellectual scene. Scarcely less familiar is the unification of this manifold which is taking place by the building of scientific bridges between them. I shall have something to say about this unification below. What is not so obvious to the layman is that the task of "seeing all things together" has itself been (paradoxically) broken down into specialities. And there *is* a place for specialization in philosophy. For just as one cannot come to know one's way around in the highway system as a whole without knowing one's way around in the parts, so

one can't hope to know one's way around in "things in general," without knowing one's way around in the major groupings of things.

It is, therefore, the "eye on the whole" which distinguishes the philosophical enterprise. Otherwise, there is little to distinguish the philosopher from the persistently reflective specialist; the philosopher of history from the persistently reflective historian. To the extent that a specialist is more concerned to reflect on how his work as a specialist joins up with other intellectual pursuits, than in asking and answering questions within his specialty, he is said, properly, to be philosophically-minded. And, indeed, one can "have one's eye on the whole" without staring at it all the time. The latter would be a fruitless enterprise. Furthermore, like other specialists, the philosopher who specializes may derive much of his sense of the whole from the prereflective orientation which is our common heritage. On the other hand, a philosopher could scarcely be said to have his eye on the whole in the relevant sense, unless he has reflected on the nature of philosophical thinking. It is this reflection on the place of philosophy itself in the scheme of things which is the distinctive trait of the philosopher as contrasted with the reflective specialist; and in the absence of this critical reflection on the philosophical enterprise, one is at best but a potential philosopher.

It has often been said in recent years that the aim of the philosopher is not to discover new truths, but to "analyze" what we already know. But while the term "analysis" was helpful in its implication that philosophy as such makes no *substantive* contribution to what we know, and is concerned in some way to improve the *manner* in which we know it, it is most misleading by its contrast to "synthesis." For by virtue of this contrast, these statements suggest that philosophy is evermore myopic, tracing parts within parts, losing each in turn from sight as new parts come into view. One is tempted, therefore, to contrast the analytic conception of philosophy as myopia with the synoptic vision of true philosophy. And it must be admitted that if the contrast between "analysis" and "synthesis" were the operative connotation in the metaphor, then a purely analytic philosophy would be a contradiction in terms. Even if we construe "analysis" on the analogy of making ever smaller scale maps of the same overall terrain, which does more justice to the synoptic element, the analogy disturbs because we would have to compare philosophy to the making of small scale maps from an original large scale map; and a smaller scale map in this sense is a triviality.

Even if the analogy is changed to that of bringing a picture into focus, which preserves the synoptic element and the theme of working within the framework of what is already known while adding a dimension of gain, the analogy is disturbing in two respects:

(a) It suggests that the special disciplines are confused; as though the scientist had to wait for the philosopher to clarify his subject-matter, bring it into focus. To account for the creative role of philosophy it is not necessary to say that the scientist doesn't know his way around in his own area. What we must rather say is that the specialist knows his way around in his own neighborhood, as his neighborhood, but doesn't know his way around in it in the same way *as a part of the landscape as a whole*.

(b) It implies that the essential change brought about by philosophy is the standing out of detail within a picture which is grasped as a whole from the start. But, of course, to the extent that there is *one* picture to be grasped reflectively as a whole, the unity of the reflective vision is a task rather than an initial datum.

The search for this unity at the reflective level is therefore more appropriately compared to the contemplation of a large and complex painting which is not seen as a unity without a prior exploration of its parts. The analogy, however, is not complete until we take into account a *second* way in which unity is lacking in the original datum of the contemporary philosopher. For he is confronted not by one picture, but, *in principle*, by *two* and, in fact, by *many*. The plurality I have in mind is not that which concerns the distinction between the fact-finding, the ethical, the aesthetic, the logical, the religious, and other aspects of experience, for these are but aspects of one complex picture which is to be grasped reflectively as a whole. As such, it constitutes one term of a crucial duality which confronts the contemporary philosopher at the very beginning of his enterprise. Here the most appropriate analogy is stereoscopic vision, where two differing perspectives on a landscape are fused into one coherent experience.

For the philosopher is confronted not by one complex many dimensional picture, the unity of which, such as it is, he must come to appreciate; but by *two* pictures of essentially the same order of complexity, each of which purports to be a complete picture of man-in-the-world, and which, after separate scrutiny, he must fuse into one vision. Let me refer to these two perspectives, respectively, as the *manifest* and the *scientific* images of man-in-the-world. And let me explain my terms. First, by calling them images I do not mean to deny to either or both of them the status of "reality." I am, to use Husserl's term, "bracketing" them, transforming them from ways of experiencing the world into objects of philosophical reflection and evaluation. The term "image" is usefully ambiguous; on the one hand it suggests the contrast between an object, e.g., a tree, and a projection of the object on a plane, or its shadow on a wall. In this sense, an image is as much an existent as the object imaged, though, of course, it has a dependent status.

In the other sense, an "image" is something imagined, and that which is imagined may well not exist, although the imagining of it does – in which case we can speak of the image as *merely* imaginary or unreal. But the imagined *can* exist; as when one imagines that someone is dancing in the next room, and someone is. This ambiguity enables me to imply that the philosopher is confronted by two projections of man-in-the-world on the human understanding. One of these projections I will call the manifest image, the other the scientific image. These images exist and are as much a part and parcel of the world as this platform or the Constitution of the United States. But in addition to being confronted by these images as existents, he is confronted by them as images in the sense of "things imagined" – or, as I had better say at once, *conceived*; for I am using "image" in this sense as a metaphor for conception, and it is familiar fact that not everything that can be conceived, in the ordinary sense, can be imagined. The philosopher, then, is confronted by two conceptions, equally public, equally nonarbitrary, of man-in-the-world, and he cannot shirk the attempt to see how they fall together in one stereoscopic view.

Before I begin to explain the contrast between "manifest" and "scientific," as I shall use these terms, let me make it clear that they are both "idealizations" in something like the sense in which a frictionless body or an ideal gas is an idealization. They are designed to illuminate the inner dynamics of the development of philosophical ideas, as scientific idealizations illuminate the development of physical systems. From a somewhat different point of view they can be compared to the "ideal types" of Max Weber's sociology. The story is complicated by the fact that each image has a history, and while the main outlines of what I shall call the manifest image took shape in the mists of prehistory, the scientific image, promissory notes apart, has taken shape before our very eyes.

The Manifest Image

The "manifest" image of man-in-the-world can be characterized in two ways, which are supplementary rather than alternative. It is, first, the framework in terms of which man came to be aware of himself as man-in-the-world. It is the framework in terms of which, to use an existentialist turn of phrase, man first encountered himself – which is, of course, when he came to be man. For it is no merely incidental feature of man that he has a conception of himself as man-in-the-world, just as it is obvious, on reflection, that if man had a radically different conception of himself he would be a radically different kind of man.

I have given this quasi-historical dimension of our construct pride of place, because I want to highlight from the very beginning what might be called the paradox of man's encounter with himself, the paradox consisting of the fact that man couldn't be man until he encountered himself. It is this paradox which supports the last stand of Special Creation. Its central theme is the idea that anything which can properly be called conceptual thinking can occur only within a framework of conceptual thinking in terms of which it can be criticized, supported, refuted, in short, evaluated. To be able to think is to be able to measure one's thoughts by standards of correctness, of relevance, of evidence. In this sense a diversified conceptual framework is a whole which, however sketchy, is prior to its parts, and cannot be construed as a coming together of parts which are already conceptual in character. The conclusion is difficult to avoid that the transition from preconceptual patterns of behavior to conceptual thinking was a holistic one, a jump to a level of awareness which is irreducibly new, a jump which was the coming into being of man.

There is a profound truth in this conception of a radical difference in level between man and his precursors. The attempt to understand this difference turns out to be part and parcel of the attempt to encompass in one view the two images of man-in-the-world which I have set out to describe. For, as we shall see, this difference in level appears as an irreducible discontinuity in the *manifest* image, but as, in a sense requiring careful analysis, a reducible difference in the *scientific* image.

I have characterized the manifest image of man-in-the-world as the framework in terms of which man encountered himself. And this, I believe, is a useful way of characterizing it. But it is also misleading, for it suggests that the contrast I am drawing between the manifest and the scientific images is that between a prescientific, uncritical, naive conception of man-in-the-world, and a reflected, disciplined, critical – in short a scientific conception. This is not at all what I have in mind. For what I mean by the manifest image is a refinement or sophistication of what might be called the "original" image; a refinement to a degree which makes it relevant to the contemporary intellectual scene. This refinement or sophistication can be construed under two headings: (a) empirical; (b) categorial.

By empirical refinement I mean the sort of refinement which operates within the broad framework of the image and, by approaching the world in terms of something like the canons of inductive inference defined by John Stuart Mill, supplemented by canons of statistical inference, adds to and subtracts from the contents of the world as experienced in terms of this framework and the correlations which are believed to obtain between them. Thus, the conceptual framework which I am calling the manifest image is, in an appropriate sense, itself a scientific image. It is not only disciplined and critical; it also makes use of those aspects of scientific method which might be lumped together under the heading "correlational induction." There is, however, one type of scientific reasoning which it by stipulation does *not* include, namely, that which involves the postulation of imperceptible entities, and principles pertaining to them, to explain the behavior of perceptible things.

This makes it clear that the concept of the manifest image of man-in-the-world is not that of an historical and bygone stage in the development of man's conception of the world and his place in it. For it is a familiar fact that correlational and postulational methods have gone hand in hand in the evolution of science, and, indeed, have been dialectically related; postulational hypotheses, presupposing correlations to be explained and suggesting possible correlations to be investigated. The notion of a purely correlational scientific view of things is both a historical and a methodological fiction. It involves abstracting correlational fruits from the conditions of their discovery, and the theories in terms of which they are explained. Yet it is a useful fiction (and hence no *mere* fiction), for it will enable us to define a way of looking at the world, which, though disciplined and, in a limited sense, scientific, contrasts sharply with an image of man-in-the-world which is implicit in and can be constructed from the postulational aspects of contemporary scientific theory. And, indeed, what I have referred to as the "scientific" image of man-in-the-world and contrasted with the "manifest" image, might better be called the "postulational" or "theoretical" image. But, I believe, it will not be too misleading if I continue, for the most part, to use the former term.

Now, the manifest image is important for our purposes, because it defines one of the poles to which philosophical reflection has been drawn. It is not only the great speculative systems of ancient and medieval philosophy which are built around the manifest image, but also many systems and quasi-systems in recent and contemporary thought, some of which seem at first sight to have little if anything in common with the great classical systems. That I include the major schools of contemporary Continental thought might be expected. That I lump in with these the trends of contemporary British and American philosophy which emphasize the analysis of "common sense" and "ordinary usage" may be somewhat more surprising. Yet this kinship is becoming increasingly apparent in recent years, and I believe that the distinctions I am drawing in these lectures will make possible an understanding and interpretation of this kinship. For all these philosophies can, I believe, be fruitfully construed as more or less adequate accounts of the manifest image of man-in-the-world, which accounts are then taken to be an adequate and full description in general terms of what man and the world really are.

Let me elaborate on this theme by introducing another construct which I shall call borrowing a term with a not unrelated meaning – the perennial philosophy of man-in-the-world. This construct, which is the "ideal type" around which philosophies in what might be called in a suitably broad sense the platonic tradition cluster, is simply the manifest image endorsed as real, and its outline taken to be the large scale map of reality to which science brings a needlepoint of detail and elaborate technique of map-reading.

It will probably have occurred to you by now that there are negative overtones to both constructs: the "manifest image" and the "perennial philosophy." And, in a certain sense, this is indeed the case. I *am* implying that the perennial philosophy is analogous to what one gets when one looks through a stereoscope with one eye dominating. The manifest image dominates and mislocates the scientific image. But if the perennial philosophy of man-in-the-world is in this sense distorted, an important consequence lurks in the offing. For I have also implied that man is *essentially* that being which conceives of itself *in terms of the image which the perennial philosophy refines and endorses.* I seem, therefore, to be saying that man's conception of himself in the world does not easily accommodate the scientific image; that there is a genuine tension between them; that man is not the sort of thing he conceives himself to be; that his existence is in some measure built around error. If this were what I wished to say, I would be in distinguished company. One thinks, for example, of Spinoza, who contrasted man as he falsely conceives himself to be with man as he discovers himself to be in the scientific enterprise. It might well be said that Spinoza drew a distinction between a "manifest" and a "scientific" image of man, rejecting the former as false and accepting the latter as true.

But if in Spinoza's account the scientific image, as he interprets it, dominates the stereoscopic view (the manifest image appearing as a tracery of explainable error), the very fact that I use the analogy of stereoscopic vision implies that as I see it the manifest image is not overwhelmed in the synthesis.

But before there can be any point to these comparisons, I must characterize these images in more detail, adding flesh and blood to the bare bones I have laid before you. I shall devote the remainder of this section to developing the manifest image. In the concluding section I shall characterize the scientific image, and attempt to describe certain key features of how the two images blend together in a true stereoscopic view.

I distinguished above between two dimensions of the refinement which turned the "original" image into the "manifest" image: the empirical and the categorial. Nothing has been said so far about the categorial. Yet it is here that the most important things are to be said. It is in this connection that I will be able to describe the general structure of the manifest image.

A fundamental question with respect to any conceptual framework is, "Of what sort are the basic objects of the framework?" This question involves, on the one hand, the contrast between an object and what can be true of it in the way of properties, relations, and activities; and, on the other, a contrast between the basic objects of the framework and the various kinds of groups they can compose. The basic objects of a framework need not be things in the restricted sense of perceptible physical objects. Thus, the basic objects of current theoretical physics are notoriously imperceptible and unimaginable. Their "basic-ness" consists in the fact that they are not properties or groupings of anything more basic (at least until further notice). The questions, "Are the basic objects of the framework of physical theory *thing-like*? and if so, to what extent?" are meaningful ones.

Now to ask, "What are the basic objects of a (given) framework?" is to ask not for a *list*, but a *classification*. And the classification will be more or less "abstract" depending on what the purpose of the inquiry is. The philosopher is interested in a classification which is abstract enough to provide a synoptic view of the contents of the framework, but which falls short of simply referring to them as objects or entities. Thus we are approaching an answer to the question, "what are the basic objects of the manifest image?" when we say that it includes persons, animals, lower forms of life, and "merely material" things, like rivers and stones. The list is not intended to be complete, although it is intended to echo the lower stages of the "great chain of being" of the platonic tradition.

The first point I wish to make is that there is an important sense in which the primary objects of the manifest image are *persons*. And to understand how this is so, is to understand central, and indeed, crucial themes in the history of philosophy. Perhaps the best way to make the point is to refer back to the construct which we called the "original" image of man-in-the-world, and characterize it as a framework in which *all* the "objects" are persons. From this point of view, the refinement of the "original" image into the manifest image, is the gradual "de-personalization" of objects other than persons. That something like this has occurred with the advance of civilization is a familiar fact. Even persons, it is said (mistakenly, I believe), are being "de-personalized" by the advance of the scientific point of view.

The point I now wish to make is that although this gradual de-personalization of the original image is a familiar idea, it is radically misunderstood, if it is assimilated to the gradual abandonment of a superstitious belief. A primitive man did not *believe* that the tree in front of him was a person, in the sense that he thought of it both as a tree *and* as a person, as I might think that this brick in front of me is a doorstop. If this were so, then when he abandoned the idea that trees were persons, his concept of a tree could remain unchanged, although his beliefs about trees would be changed. The truth is, rather, that *originally* to be a tree was *a way of being a person*, as, to use a close analogy, to be a woman is a way of being a person, or to be a triangle is a way of being a plane figure. That a woman is a person is not something that one can be said to *believe*; though there is enough historical bounce to this example to make it worthwhile to use the different example, that one cannot be said to believe that a triangle is a plane figure. When primitive man ceased to think of what we called trees as persons, the change was more radical than a change in belief; it was a change in category.

Now, the human mind is not limited in its categories to what it has been able to refine out of the world view of primitive man, anymore than the limits of what we can conceive are set by what we can imagine. The categories of theoretical physics are not essences distilled from the framework of perceptive experience, yet, if the human mind can conceive of *new* categories, it can also refine the old; and it is just as important not to overestimate the rule of creativity in the development of the framework in terms of which you and I experience the world, as it is not to underestimate its role in the scientific enterprise.

I indicated above that in the construct which I have called, the "original" image of man-in-the-world, all "objects" are persons, and all kinds of objects, ways of being persons. This means that the sort of things that are said of objects in this framework are the sort of things that are said of persons. And let me make it clear that by "person" I do not mean "spirit" or "mind." The idea that a man is a team of two things, a mind *and* a body, is one for which many reasons of different kinds and weights have been given in the course of human intellectual development. But it is obvious, on reflection, that whatever philosophers have made of the idea of a *mind*, the pre-philosophical conception of a *spirit*, where it is found, is that of a ghostly *person*, something closely analogous to flesh and blood persons which "inhabits" them, or is otherwise intimately connected with them. It is, therefore, a development *within the framework of persons*, and it would be incorrect to construe the manifest image in such a way that persons are composite objects. On the other hand, if it is to do its work, the manifest framework must be such as to make meaningful the assertion that what we ordinarily call persons are composites of a person proper and a body – and, by doing so, make meaningful the contrary view that although man has many different types of ability, ranging from those he has in common with the lowest of things, to his ability to engage in scientific and philosophical reflections, he nevertheless is one object and not a team. For we shall see that the essential dualism in the manifest image is not that between mind and body as substances, but between two radically different ways in which the human individual is related to the world. Yet it must be admitted that most of the philosophical theories which are dominated by the manifest image are dualistic in the substantive sense. There are many factors which account for this, most of which fall outside the scope of this essay. Of the factors which concern us, one is a matter of the influence of the developing scientific image of man, and will be discussed in the following section. The other arises in the attempt to make sense of the manifest image in its own terms.

Now to understand the manifest image as a refinement or de-personalization of the "original" image, we must remind ourselves of the range of activities which are characteristic of persons. For when I say that the objects of the manifest image are primarily persons, I am implying that what the objects of this framework, primarily *are* and *do*, is what persons are and do. Thus persons are "impetuous" or "set in their ways." They apply old policies or adopt new ones. They do things from habit or ponder alternatives. They are immature or have an established character. For my present purposes the most important contrasts are those between actions which are expressions of character and actions which are *not* expressions of character, on the one hand, and

between habitual actions and deliberate actions, on the other. The first point that I want to make is that only a being capable of deliberation can properly be said to act, either impulsively or from habit. For in the full and non-metaphorical sense an action is the sort of thing that can be done deliberately. We speak of actions as *becoming* habitual, and this is no accident. It is important to realize that the use of the term "habit," in speaking of an earthworm as acquiring the habit of turning to the right in a T-maze, is a metaphorical extension of the term. There is nothing dangerous in the metaphor until the mistake is made of assuming that the habits of persons are the same sort of thing as the (metaphorical) "habits" of earthworms and white rats.

Again, when we say that something a person did was an expression of his character, we mean that it is "in character" – that it was to be expected. We do not mean that it was a matter of *habit*. To be *habitual* is to be "in character," but the converse is not true. To say of an action that it is "in character," that it was to be expected, is to say that it was predictable – *not*, however, predictable "no holds barred," but predictable with respect to evidence pertaining to what the person in question has done in the past, and the circumstances as he saw them in which he did it. Thus, a person can not, *logically* can not, *begin* by acting "in character," anymore than he can *begin* by acting from habit.

It is particularly important to see that while to be "in character" is to be predictable, the converse is not true. It does not follow from the fact that a piece of human behavior is predictable, that it is an expression of character. Thus the behavior of a burnt child with respect to the fire is predictable, but not an expression of character. If we use the phrase, "the nature of a person" to sum up the predictabilities *no holds barred* pertaining to that person, then we must be careful not to equate the *nature* of a person with his *character*, although his character will be a "part" of his nature in the broad sense. Thus, if everything a person did were predictable (in principle), given sufficient knowledge about the person and the circumstances in which he was placed, and was, therefore, an "expression of his nature," it would not follow that everything the person did was an expression of his *character*. Obviously, to say of a person that everything that he does is an expression of his character is to say that his life is simply a carrying out of formed habits and policies. Such a person is a type only approximated in real life. Not even a mature person always acts in character. And as we have seen, it cannot possibly be true that he has always acted in character. Yet, if determinism is true, everything he has done has been an expression of his "nature."

I am now in a position to explain what I mean when I say that the primary objects of the manifest image are persons. I mean that it is the modification of an image in which *all* the objects are capable of *the full range* of personal activity, the modification consisting of a gradual pruning of the implications of saying with respect to what *we* would call an inanimate object, that it *did* something. Thus, in the original image to say of the wind that it blew down one's house would imply that the wind *either* decided to do so with an end in view, and might, perhaps, have been persuaded not to do it, *or* that it acted thoughtlessly (either from habit or impulse) or, perhaps, inadvertently, in which case other appropriate action on one's part might have awakened it to the enormity of what it was about to do.

In the early stages of the development of the manifest image the wind was no longer conceived as acting deliberately, with an end in view; but rather from habit or impulse. Nature became the locus of "truncated persons"; that which things could be expected to do, its habits; that which exhibits no order, its impulses. Inanimate things no longer "did" things in the sense in which persons do them – not, however, because a *new* category of impersonal things and impersonal processes has been achieved, but because the category of *person* is now applied to these things in a pruned or truncated form. It is a striking exaggeration to say of a person that he is a "mere creature of habit and impulse," but in the early stages of the development of manifest image, the world includes truncated persons which *are* mere creatures of habit, acting out routines, broken by impulses, in a life which never rises above what ours is like in our most unreflective moments. Finally, the sense in which the wind "did" things was pruned, save for poetic and expressive purposes – and, one is tempted to add, for philosophical purposes – of implications pertaining to "knowing what one is doing" and "knowing what the circumstances are."

Just as it is important not to confuse between the "character" and the "nature" of a person (that is to say, between an action's being predictable with respect to evidence pertaining to prior action, and its being predictable no holds barred) so it is important not to confuse between an action's being *predictable* and its being *caused*. These terms are often treated as synonyms, but only confusion can arise from doing so. Thus, in the "original" image one person causes another person to do something he otherwise would not have done. But most of the things people do are not things they are *caused* to do, even if what they do is highly predictable. For example: when a person has well-established habits, what he does in certain circumstances is highly predictable, but it is not for that reason *caused*. Thus, the category of causation (as contrasted with the more inclusive category of predictability) betrays its origin in the "original" image. When all things were persons it was certainly not a framework conception that everything a person did was caused; nor, of course, was it a framework principle that everything a person did was predictable. To the extent that relationships between the truncated "persons" of the manifest framework were analogous to the causal relationships between persons, the category itself continued to be used, although pruned of its implications with respect to plans, purposes, and policies. The most obvious analogue at the inanimate level of causation in the original sense is one billiard ball causing another to change its course, but it is important to note that no one who distinguishes between causation and predictability would ask, "What *caused* the billiard ball on a smooth table to continue in a straight line?" The distinctive trait of the scientific revolution was the conviction that all events are *predictable* from relevant information about the context in which they occur, not that they are all, in any ordinary sense, *caused*.

Classical Philosophy and the Manifest Image

I have characterized the concept of the manifest image as one of the poles toward which philosophical thinking is drawn. This commits me, of course, to the idea that the manifest image is not a mere external standard, by relation to which one interested in the development of philosophy classifies philosophical positions, but has in its own way an objective existence in philosophical thinking itself, and, indeed, in human thought generally. And it can influence philosophical thinking only by having an existence which transcends in some way the individual thought of individual thinkers. I shall be picking up this theme shortly, and shall ask how an image of the world, which, after all, is a way of thinking *can* transcend the individual thinker which it influences. (The general lines of the answer must be obvious, but it has implications which have not always been drawn.) The point I wish to make now is that since this image has a being which transcends the individual thinker, *there is truth and error with respect to it, even though the image itself might have to be rejected in the last analysis as false.*

Thus, whether or not the world as we encounter it in perception and self-awareness is ultimately real, it is surely incorrect, for example, to say as some philosophers have said that the physical objects of the encountered world are "complexes of sensations" or, equally, to say that apples "aren't *really* colored," or that mental states are "behavioral dispositions," or that one cannot intend to do something without knowing that one intends to do it, or that to say that something is good is to say that one likes it, etc. For there is a correct and an incorrect way to describe this objective image which we have of the world in which we live, and it is possible to evaluate the correctness or incorrectness of such a description. I have already claimed that much of academic philosophy can be interpreted as an attempt by individual thinkers to delineate the manifest image (not recognized, needless to say, as such), an image which is both immanent in and transcendent of their thinking. In this respect, a philosophy can be evaluated as perceptive or imperceptive, mistaken or correct, even though one is prepared to say that the image they delineate is but one way in which reality appears to the human mind. And it is, indeed, a task of the first importance to delineate this image, particularly in so far as it concerns man himself. For, as was pointed out before, man is what he is because he thinks of himself in terms of this image, and the latter must be understood before it is proper to ask, "To what extent does manifest man survive in the synoptic view which does equal justice to the scientific image which now confronts us?"

I think it correct to say that the so-called "analytic" tradition in recent British and American philosophy, particularly under the influence of the later Wittgenstein, has done increasing justice to the manifest image, and has increasingly succeeded in isolating it in something like

its pure form, and has made clear the folly of attempting to replace it *piecemeal* by fragments of the scientific image. By doing so it has made apparent and has come to realize its continuity with the perennial tradition.

Now one of the most interesting features of the perennial philosophy is its attempt to understand the status in the individual thinker of the framework of ideas in terms of which he grasps himself as a person in the world. How do individuals come to be able to think in terms of this complex conceptual framework? How do they come to have this image? Two things are to be noticed here: (1) The manifest image does not present conceptual thinking as a complex of items which, considered in themselves and apart from these relations, are not conceptual in character. (The most plausible candidates are images, but all attempts to construe thoughts as complex patterns of images have failed, and, as we now know, were bound to fail.) (2) Whatever the ultimate constituents of conceptual thinking, the process itself as it occurs in the individual mind must echo, more or less adequately, the intelligible structure of the world.

There was, of course, a strong temptation not only to think of the constituents of thinking as qualitatively similar to the constituents of the world, but also to think of the world as causing these constituents to occur in patterns which echo the patterns of events. The attempt by precursors of scientific psychology to understand the genesis of conceptual thinking in the individual in terms of an "association" of elemental processes which were not themselves conceptual, by a direct action of the physical environment on the individual – the paradigm case being the burnt child fearing the fire – was a premature attempt to construct a scientific image of man.

The perennial tradition had no sympathy with such attempts. It recognized (a) that association of *thoughts* is not association of images, and, as presupposing a framework of conceptual thinking cannot account for it; (b) that the direct action of perceptible nature, *as perceptible*, on the *individual* can account for associative connection, *but not the rational connections of conceptual thinking.*

Yet, somehow the world *is* the cause of the individual's image of the world, and, as is well-known, for centuries the dominant conception of the perennial tradition was that of a direct causal influence of the world as intelligible on the

Wilfrid Sellars

individual mind. This theme, initiated by Plato, can be traced through western thought to the present day. In the Platonic tradition this mode of causation is attributed to a being which is analogous, to a greater or lesser degree, to a person. Even the Aristotelian distinguishes between the way in which sensations make available the intelligible structure of things to man, from the way in which contingencies of perceptual experience establish expectations and permit a nonrational accommodation of animals to their environment. And there is, as we know today, a sound score to the idea that while reality is the "cause" of the human conceptual thinking which represents it, this causal role cannot be equated with a conditioning of the individual by his environment in a way which could in principle occur without the mediation of the family and the community. The Robinson Crusoe conception of the world as generating conceptual thinking directly in the individual is too simple a model. The perennial tradition long limited itself to accounting for the presence in the individual of the framework of conceptual thinking in terms of a unique kind of action of reality as intelligible on the individual mind. The accounts differed in interesting respects, but the main burden remained the same. It was not until the time of Hegel that the essential role of the group as a mediating factor in this causation was recognized, and while it is easy for us to see that the immanence and transcendence of conceptual frameworks with respect to the individual thinker is a social phenomenon, and to find a recognition of this fact implicit in the very form of our image of man-in-the-world, it was not until the nineteenth century that this feature of the manifest image was, however inadequately, taken into account.

The Platonic theory of conceptual abilities as the result of the "illumination" of the mind by intelligible essences limited the role of the group, and in particular the family, to that of calling these abilities into play – a role which could, in principle, be performed by perceptual experience – and to that of teaching the means of giving verbal expression to these abilities. Yet the essentially social character of conceptual thinking comes clearly to mind when we recognize that there is no thinking apart from common standards of correctness and relevance, which relate what *I do* think to what *anyone ought to* think. The contrast between "I" and "anyone" is essential to rational thought.

It is current practice to compare the intersubjective standards without which there would be no thinking to the intersubjective standards without which there would be no such a thing as a game, and with the acquisition of a conceptual framework to learning to play a game. It is worth noting, however, that conceptual thinking is a unique game in two respects: (a) one cannot learn to play it by being told the rules; (b) whatever else conceptual thinking makes possible – and without it there is nothing characteristically human – it does so by virtue of containing a way of representing the world.

When I said that the individual as a conceptual thinker is essentially a member of a group, this does not mean, of course, that the individual cannot exist apart from the group, for example as sole survivor of an atomic catastrophe, any more than the fact that chess is a game played by two people means that one can not play chess with oneself. A group is not a group in the relevant sense unless it consists of a number of individuals, each of which thinks of himself as "I" in contrast to "others." Thus a group exists in the way in which members of the group represent themselves. Conceptual thinking is not by accident that which is *communicated* to others, any more than the decision to move a chess piece is by accident that which finds an expression in a move on a board between two people.

The manifest image must, therefore, be construed as containing a conception of itself as a group phenomenon, the group mediating between the individual and the intelligent order. But any attempt to *explain* this mediation within the framework of the manifest image was bound to fail, for the manifest image contains the resources for such an attempt only in the sense that it provides the foundation on which scientific theory can build an explanatory framework; and while conceptual structures of this framework are *built on* the manifest image, they are not definable within it. Thus, the Hegelian, like the Platonist of whom he is the heir, was limited to the attempt to understand the relation between intelligible order and individual minds in analogical terms.

It is in the *scientific* image of man-in-the-world that we begin to see the main outlines of the way in which man came to have an image of himself-in-the-world. For we begin to see this matter of evolutionary development as a group phenomenon, a process which is illustrated at a simpler level by the evolutionary development which explains the correspondence between the dancing of a worker bee and the location, relative to the sun, of the flower from which he comes. This correspondence, like the relation between man's "original" image and the world, is incapable of explanation in terms of a direct conditioning impact of the environment on the individual as such.

I have called attention to the fact that the manifest image involves two types of causal impact of the world on the individual. It is, I have pointed out, this duality of causation, and the related irreducibility, within the manifest image, of conceptual thinking in all its forms to more elementary processes, which is the primary and essential dualism of the perennial philosophy. The dualistic conception of mind and body characteristic of, but by no means an invariable feature of, *philosophia perennis*, is in part an inference from this dualism of causation and of process. In part, however, as we shall see, it is a result of the impact of certain themes present in even the earliest stages of the developing scientific image.

My primary concern in this discussion is with the question, "In what sense, and to what extent, does the manifest image of man-in-the-world survive the attempt to unite this image in one field of intellectual vision with man as conceived in terms of the postulated object of scientific theory?" The bite to this question lies, we have seen, in the fact that man is that being which conceives of itself in terms of the manifest image. To the extent that the manifest does not survive in the synoptic view, to that extent man himself would not survive. Whether the adoption of the synoptic view would transform man in bondage into man free, as Spinoza believed, or man free into man in bondage, as many fear, is a question that does not properly arise until the claims of the scientific image have been examined.

The Scientific Image

I devoted my attention in the previous sections to defining what I called the "manifest" image of man-in-the-world. I argued that this image is to be construed as a sophistication and refinement of the image in terms of which man first came to be aware of himself as man-in-the-world; in short, came to be man. I pointed out that in any sense in which this image, in so far as it pertains to man, is a "false" image, this falsity threatens

man himself, inasmuch as he, is in an important sense, the being which has this image of himself. I argued that what has been called the perennial tradition in philosophy – *philosophia perennis* – can be construed as the attempt to understand the structure of this image, to know one's way around in it reflectively with no intellectual holds barred. I analyzed some of the main features of the image and showed how the categories in terms of which it approaches the world can be construed as progressive prunings of categories pertaining to the person and his relation to other persons and the group. I argued that the perennial tradition must be construed to include not only the Platonic tradition in its broadest sense, but philosophies of "common sense" and "ordinary usage." I argued what is common to all these philosophies is an acceptance of the manifest image as the *real*. They attempt to understand the achievements of theoretical science in terms of this framework, subordinating the categories of theoretical science to its categories. I suggested that the most fruitful way of approaching the problem of integrating theoretical science with the framework of sophisticated common sense into one comprehensive synoptic vision is to view it not as a piecemeal task – e.g., first a fitting together of the common-sense conception of physical objects with that of theoretical physics, and then, as a separate venture, a fitting together of the common-sense conception of man with that of theoretical psychology – but rather as a matter of articulating two whole ways of seeing the sum of things, two images of man-in-the-world and attempting to bring them together in a "stereoscopic" view.

My present purpose is to add to the account I have given of the manifest image, a comparable sketch of what I have called the scientific image, and to conclude this essay with some comments on the respective contributions of these two to the unified vision of man-in-the-world which is the aim of philosophy.

The scientific image of man-in-the-world is, of course, as much an idealization as the manifest image – even more so, as it is still in the process of coming to be. It will be remembered that the contrast I have in mind is not that between an *unscientific* conception of man-in-the-world and a *scientific* one, but between that conception which limits itself to what correlational techniques can tell us about perceptible and introspectible events and that which postulates imperceptible objects and events for the purpose of explaining correlations among perceptibles. It was granted, of course, that in point of historical fact many of the latter correlations were suggested by theories introduced to explain previously established correlations, so that there has been a dialectical interplay between correlational and postulational procedures. (Thus we might not have noticed that litmus paper turns red in acid, until this hypothesis had been suggested by a complex theory relating the absorption and emission of electromagnetic radiation by objects to their chemical composition; yet in principle this familiar correlation could have been, and, indeed, was discovered before any such theory was developed.) Our contrast, then, is between two ideal constructs: (a) the correlational and categorial refinement of the "original image," which refinement I am calling the manifest image; (b) the image derived from the fruits of postulational theory construction which I am calling the scientific image.

It may be objected at this point that there is no such thing as *the* image of man built from postulated entities and processes, but rather as many images as there are sciences which touch on aspects of human behavior. And, of course, in a sense this is true. There *are* as many scientific images of man as there are sciences which have something to say about man. Thus, there is man as he appears to the theoretical physicist – a swirl of physical particles, forces, and fields. There is man as he appears to the biochemist, to the physiologist, to the behaviorist, to the social scientist; and all of these images are to be contrasted with man as he appears to himself in sophisticated common sense, the manifest image which even today contains most of what he knows about himself at the properly human level. Thus the conception of *the* scientific or postulational image is an idealization in the sense that it is a conception of an integration of a manifold of images, each of which is the application to man of a framework of concepts which have a certain autonomy. For each scientific theory, from the standpoint of methodology, is a structure which is built at a different "place" and by different procedures within the intersubjectively accessible world of perceptible things. Thus *the* scientific image is a construct from a number of images, each of which is *supported by* the manifest world.

The fact that each theoretical image is a construction on a foundation provided by the manifest image, and *in this methodological sense*

presupposes the manifest image, makes it tempting to suppose that the manifest image is prior in a *substantive* sense; that the categories of a theoretical science are logically dependent on categories pertaining to its methodological foundation in the manifest world of sophisticated common sense in such a way that there would be an absurdity in the notion of a world which illustrated its theoretical principles *without also illustrating the categories and principles of the manifest world*. Yet, when we turn our attention to *the* scientific image which emerges from the several images proper to the several sciences, we note that although the image is *methodologically* dependent on the world of sophisticated common sense, and in this sense does not stand on its own feet, yet it purports to be a *complete* image, i.e., to define a framework which could be the *whole truth* about that which belongs to the image. Thus although methodologically a development *within* the manifest image, the scientific image presents itself as a *rival* image. From its point of view the manifest image on which it rests is an "inadequate" but pragmatically useful likeness of a reality which first finds its adequate (in principle) likeness in the scientific image. I say, "in principle," because the scientific image is still in the process of coming into being – a point to which I shall return at the conclusion of this essay.

To all of which, of course, the manifest image or, more accurately, the perennial philosophy which endorses its claims, replies that the scientific image cannot replace the manifest without rejecting its own foundation.

But before attempting to throw some light on the conflicting claims of these two world perspectives, more must be said about the constitution of *the* scientific image from the several scientific images of which it is the supposed integration. There is relatively little difficulty about telescoping *some* of the "partial" images into one image. Thus, with due precaution, we can unify the biochemical and the physical images; for to do this requires only an appreciation of the sense in which the objects of biochemical discourse can be equated with complex patterns of the objects of theoretical physics. To make this equation, of course, is not to equate the sciences, for as sciences they have different procedures and connect their theoretical entities via different instruments to intersubjectively accessible features of the manifest world. But diversity of this kind is compatible with intrinsic "identity" of the theoretical entities themselves, that is, with saying that biochemical compounds are "identical" with patterns of subatomic particles. For to make this "identification" is simply to say that the *two* theoretical structures, each with its own connection to the perceptible world, could be replaced by *one* theoretical framework connected *at two levels of complexity* via different instruments and procedures to the world as perceived.

I distinguished above between the unification of the postulated *entities* of two sciences and the unification of the *sciences*. It is also necessary to distinguish between the unification of the theoretical *entities* of two sciences and the unification of the theoretical *principles* of the two sciences. For while to say that biochemical substances are complexes of physical particles is in an important sense to imply that the laws obeyed by biochemical substances are "special cases" of the laws obeyed by physical particles, there is a real danger that the sense in which this is so may be misunderstood. Obviously a specific pattern of physical particles cannot obey different laws in biochemistry from those it obeys in physics. It may, however, be that the behavior of very complex patterns of physical particles is related in no simple way to the behavior of less complex patterns. Thus it may well be that the only way in which the laws pertaining to those complex systems of particles which are biochemical compounds could be *discovered*, might be through the techniques and procedures of biochemistry, i.e., techniques and procedures appropriate to dealing with biochemical substances.

There is, consequently, an ambiguity in the statement: The laws of biochemistry are "special cases" of the laws of physics. It may mean: (a) Biochemistry needs no variables which cannot be defined in terms of the variables of atomic physics; (b) The laws relating to certain complex patterns of subatomic particles, the counterparts of biochemical compounds, are related in a simple way to laws pertaining to less complex patterns. The former, of course, is the only proposition to which one is committed by the identification of the theoretical objects of the two sciences in the sense described above.

Similar considerations apply, *mutatis mutandis*, to the physiological and biochemical images of man. To weld them into one image would be to show that physiological (particularly neurophysiological) entities can be equated with complex biochemical systems, and therefore, that in the

weaker sense, at least, the theoretical principles which pertain to the former can be interpreted as "special cases" of principles pertaining to the latter.

More interesting problems arise when we consider the putative place in *the* scientific image of man as conceived in behavioristics. In the first place, the term "behavioristic psychology" has more than one meaning, and it is important for our purpose to see that in at least one sense of the term, its place is not in the scientific image (in the sense in which I am using the term) but rather in the continuing correlational sophistication of the manifest image. A psychology is behavioristic in the broad sense, if, although it permits itself the use of the full range of psychological concepts belonging to the manifest framework, it always confirms hypotheses about psychological events in terms of behavioral criteria. It has no anxieties about the concepts of sensation, image, feeling, conscious or unconscious thought, all of which belongs to the manifest framework; but requires that the occurrence of a feeling of pain, for example, be asserted only on behavioral grounds. Behaviorism, thus construed, is simply good sense. It is not necessary to redefine the language of mental events in terms of behavior criteria for it to be true that observable behavior provides evidence for mental events. And, of course, even in the common-sense world, even in the manifest image, perceptible behavior is the only *intersubjective* evidence for mental events.

Clearly "behaviorism" in this sense does not preclude us from paying attention to what people say about themselves. For *using autobiographical statements as evidence for* what a person is thinking and feeling is different from simply *agreeing with* these statements. It is part of the force of autobiographical statements in ordinary discourse – not unrelated to the way in which children learn to make them – that, other things being equal, if a person says, "I am in state Ψ," it is reasonable to believe that he is in state Ψ, the probability ranging from almost certainty in the case of, "I have a toothache," to considerably less than certainty in the case of, "I don't hate my brother." The discounting of verbal and nonverbal behavior as evidence is not limited to professional psychologists.

Thus, behaviorism in the first sense is simply a sophistication within the manifest framework which relies on pre-existent evidential connections between publicly observable verbal and nonverbal

Wilfrid Sellars

behavior on the one hand and mental states and processes on the other, and should, therefore, be considered as belonging to the manifest, rather than the scientific image as I have defined these terms. Behaviorism in a second sense not only restricts its evidential base to publicly observable behavior, but conceives of its task as that of finding correlations between constructs which it introduces and defines in terms of publicly access-ible features of the organism and its environ-ment. The interesting question in this connection is: "Is there reason to think that a framework of correlation between constructs of this type could constitute a scientific understanding of human behavior?" The answer to this question depends in part on how it is interpreted, and it is import-ant to see why this is so.

Consider first the case of animal behavior. Obviously, we know that animals are complex physiological systems and, from the standpoint of a finer-grained approach, biochemical systems. Does this mean that a science of animal behavior has to be formulated in neurophysiological or biochemical terms? In one sense the answer is "obviously no." We bring to our study of animal behavior a background knowledge of some of the relevant large-scale variables for describing and predicting the behavior of animals in relation to their environments. The fact that these large-scale variables (the sort of thing that is grouped under such headings as "stimulus," "response," "goal behavior," "deprivation") are such that we can understand the behavior of the animal in terms of them is something which is not only suggested by our background knowledge, but is, indeed, *explained* by evolutionary theory. But the correlations themselves can be discovered by statistical procedures; and, of course, it *is* important to establish these correlations. Their discovery and confirmation by the procedures of behavioristics must, of course, be distinguished from their *explanation* in terms of the postulated entities and processes of neurophysiology. And, indeed, while physiological considerations may *suggest* correlations to be tested, the correlations themselves must be establishable independently of physiological consideration, if, and this is a "definitional" point, they are to belong to a dis-tinguishable science of behavior.

Thus, if we mean by "earthworm behavior-istics" the establishing of correlation in large-scale terms in respect to the earthworm and its environments, there may not be much to it, for

a correlation does not belong to "earthworm beha-vioristics" unless it is a correlation in these large-scale terms. On the other hand, it is obvious that not every scientific truth about earthworms is a part of earthworm behavioristics, unless the latter term is so stretched as to be deprived of its distinctive sense. It follows that one cannot explain everything an earthworm does in terms of earthworm behavioristics *thus defined*. Earth-worm behavioristics works within a background knowledge of "standard conditions" – conditions in which correlations in terms of earthworm behavior categories *are* sufficient to explain and predict what earthworms do in so far as it can be described in these categories. This back-ground knowledge is obviously an essential part of the scientific understanding of what earthworms do, but it is not a part of earthworm behavior-istics, but rather the application to earthworms of physics, chemistry, parasitology, medicine, and neurophysiology.

We must also take into consideration the fact that most of the interesting constructs of correla-tional behavioristics will be "iffy" properties of organisms, properties to the effect that *if* at that time a certain stimulus *were* to occur, a certain response *would be made*. Thus, to use an example from another field, we are able to correlate the fact that a current has been run through a helix in which a piece of iron has been placed, with the "iffy" property of being such that *if* an iron filing *were* placed near it, the latter *would be* attracted.

Now it may or may not be helpful, at a given stage of scientific development, to suppose that "iffy" properties of organisms are connected with states of a postulated system of entities operat-ing according to certain postulated principles. It is helpful, if the postulated entities are suffici-ently specific and can be connected to a suffi-cient diversity of large-scale behavioral variables to enable the prediction of new correlations. The methodological utility of postulational procedures for the behavioristics of lower organisms has, perhaps, been exaggerated, primarily because until recently little was known in neurophysiology which was suited to throw much light on correlations at the large-scale level of behavioristics. In human behavioristics, however, the situation has been somewhat different from the start, for an import-ant feature of characteristically human behavior is that any two successive pieces of observable behavior *essentially* involve complex, very complex, "iffy" facts about what the person *would have said or done* at each intervening moment, *if he had been asked certain questions*; and it happens that our background knowledge makes reasonable the supposition that these "iffy" facts obtain *because an inner process is going on which is, in important respects, analogous to overt verbal behavior, and each stage of which would find a natural expression in overt speech*. This is a point to which I shall return later on.

Thus it *does* prove helpful in human behavioristics to postulate an inner sequence of events in order to interpret what could *in principle* be austerely formulated as correlations between behavioral states and properties, including the *very* important and, indeed, *essential* "iffy" ones. But, and this is an important point, the postulated episodes are not postulated on neurophysiological grounds – at least this was not true until very recently, but because of our background knowledge that something analogous to speech goes on while people are sitting "like bumps on a log."

For our present purposes it does not make too much difference whether we say that human behavioristics *as such* postulates inner speechlike processes, or that whatever their contribution to explanation or discovery, they fall by definition outside behavioristics proper. Whether or not human behavioristics, as a distinctive science, includes any statements about postulated entities, the correlations it establishes must find their counterparts in the postulational image, as was seen to be true in the case of the correlations established by earthworm behavioristics. Thus, the scientific explanation of human behavior must take account of those cases where the correlations characteristic of the organism in "normal" circumstances breaks down. And, indeed, no behaviorist would deny that the correlations he seeks and establishes are in some sense the counterparts of neurophysiological and, consequently, biochemical connections, nor that the latter are special cases within a spectrum of biochemical connections (pertaining to human organisms), many of which are reflected in observable phenomena which, *from the standpoint of behavioristics*, represent breakdowns in explanation. I shall, therefore, provisionally assume that although behavioristics and neurophysiology remain distinctive sciences, the correlational content of behavioristics points to a structure of postulated processes and principles which telescope together with those of neurophysiological theory, with all the consequences which this entails. On this assumption, if we trace out these consequences, the scientific image of man turns out to be that of a complex physical system.

The Clash of the Images

How, then, are we to evaluate the conflicting claims of the manifest image and the scientific image thus provisionally interpreted to constitute *the true* and, in principle, *complete* account of man-in-the-world? What are the alternatives? It will be helpful to examine the impact of the earlier stages of postulational science on philosophy. Some reflections on the Cartesian attempt at a synthesis are in order, for they bring out the major stresses and strains involved in any attempt at a synoptic view. Obviously, at the time of Descartes theoretical science had not yet reached the neurophysiological level, save in the fashion of a clumsy promissory note. The initial challenge of the scientific image was directed at the manifest image of inanimate nature. It proposed to construe physical things, in a manner already adumbrated by Greek atomism, as systems of imperceptible particles, lacking the perceptible qualities of manifest nature. Three lines of thought seemed to be open: (1) Manifest objects are identical with systems of imperceptible particles in that simple sense in which a forest is identical with a number of trees. (2) Manifest objects are what really exist, systems of imperceptible particles being "abstract" or "symbolic" ways of representing them. (3) Manifest objects are "appearances" to human minds of a reality which is constituted by systems of imperceptible particles. Although (2) merits serious consideration, and has been defended by able philosophers, it is (1) and (3), particularly the latter, which I shall be primarily concerned to explore.

First, some brief remarks about (1). There is nothing immediately paradoxical about the view that an object can be both a perceptible object with perceptible qualities *and* a system of imperceptible objects, none of which has perceptible qualities. Cannot systems have properties which their parts do not have? Now the answer to this question is "yes," if it is taken in a sense of which a paradigm example would be the fact that a system of pieces of wood can be a ladder, although none of its parts is a ladder. Here one might say that for the system as a whole to be a

Wilfrid Sellars

ladder is for its parts to be of such and such shapes and sizes and to be related to one another in certain ways. Thus, there is no trouble about systems having properties which its parts do not have *if these properties are a matter of the parts having such and such qualities and being related in such and such ways.* But the case of a pink ice cube, it would seem clear, cannot be treated in this way. It does not seem plausible to say that for a system of particles to be a pink ice cube is for them to have such and such imperceptible qualities, and to be so related to one another as to make up an approximate cube. *Pink* does not seem to be made up of imperceptible qualities in the way in which being a ladder is made up of being cylindrical (the rungs), rectangular (the frame), wooden, etc. The manifest ice cube presents itself to us as something which is pink through and through, as a pink continuum, all the regions of which, however small, are pink. It presents itself to us as *ultimately homogeneous;* and an ice cube variegated in color is, though not homogeneous in its specific color, "ultimately homogeneous," in the sense to which I am calling attention, with respect to the generic trait of being colored.

Now reflection on this example suggests a principle which can be formulated approximately as follows:

If an object is *in a strict sense* a system of objects, then every property of the object must consist in the fact that its constituents have such and such qualities and stand in such and such relations or, roughly,
every property of a system of objects consists of properties of, and relations between, its constituents.

With something like this principle in mind, it was argued that if a physical object is *in a strict sense* a system of imperceptible particles, then it cannot as a whole have the perceptible qualities characteristic of physical objects in the manifest image. It was concluded that manifest physical objects are "appearances" *to human perceivers of* systems of imperceptible particles, which is alternative (3) above.

This alternative, (3), however, is open to an objection which is ordinarily directed not against the alternative itself, but against an imperceptive formulation of it as the thesis that the perceptible things around us "really have no color."

Against *this* formulation the objection has the merit of calling attention to the fact that in the manifest framework it is as absurd to say that a visible object has no color, as it is to say of a triangle that it has no shape. However, against the above formulation of alternative (3), namely, that *the very objects themselves* are appearances to perceivers of systems of imperceptible particles, the objection turns out on examination to have no weight. The objection, for which the British "common sense" philosopher G. E. Moore is directly or indirectly responsible, runs:

Chairs, tables, etc., as we ordinarily think them to be, can't be 'appearances' of systems of particles lacking perceptible qualities, because we *know* that there are chairs, tables, etc., and it is a framework feature of chairs, tables, etc., that they have perceptible qualities.

It simply *disappears* once it is recognized that, properly understood, the claim that physical objects do not really have perceptible qualities is not analogous to the claim that something generally believed to be true about a certain kind of thing is actually false. It is not the denial of a belief *within a framework*, but a challenge to the framework. It is the claim that although the framework of perceptible objects, the manifest framework of everyday life, is adequate for the everyday purposes of life, it is ultimately inadequate and should not be accepted as an account of what there is *all things considered.* Once we see this, we see that the argument from "knowledge" cuts no ice, for the reasoning

We know that there are chairs, pink ice cubes, etc. (physical objects); chairs, pink ice cubes are colored; are perceptible objects with perceptible qualities. Therefore, perceptible physical objects with perceptible qualities exist.

operates *within* the framework of the manifest image and cannot *support* it. It fails to provide a point of view outside the manifest image from which the latter can be evaluated.

A more sophisticated argument would be to the effect that we successfully find our way around in life by using the conceptual framework of colored physical objects in space and time, therefore, this framework represents things as they really are. This argument has force, but is vulnerable to the reply that the success of living, thinking and acting in terms of the manifest framework can be accounted for by the framework which proposes to replace it; by showing that there are sufficient structural similarities between manifest objects and their scientific counterparts to account for this success.[1]

One is reminded of a standard move designed to defend the reality of the manifest image against *logically* rather than *scientifically* motivated considerations. Thus it has been objected that the framework of physical objects in space and time is incoherent, involving antinomies or contradictions, and that therefore this framework is unreal. The counter to this objection has often been, *not* a painstaking refutation of the arguments claiming to show that the framework is incoherent, but rather something along the following lines:

We know that this collision occurred at a different place and time than that collision.

Therefore, the statement that the first collision occurred at a different place and time from the other collision *is true.*

Therefore, the statement that the two collisions occurred at different times and places *is consistent.*

Therefore, statements about events happening at various times and places are, as such, consistent.

This argument, like the one we have already considered, does not prove what it sets out to prove, because it operates within the framework to be evaluated and does not provide an external point of view from which to defend it. It makes the tacit assumption that if a framework is inconsistent, its incoherence must be such as to lead to retail and immediate inconsistencies, as though it would force people using it to contradict themselves on every occasion. This is surely false. The framework of space and time could be internally inconsistent and yet be a successful conceptual tool at the retail level. We have examples of this in mathematical theory, where inconsistencies can be present which do not reveal themselves in routine usage.

I am not, however, concerned to argue that the manifest image is unreal because ultimately incoherent in a narrowly conceived logical sense. Philosophers who have taken this line have either (a) left it at that (Hume; scepticism), or (b) attempted to locate the source of the inconsistency in features of the framework, and interpreted reality as an inadequately known structure *analogous* to the manifest image, but lacking just those features which are responsible for the inconsistency. In contrast to this, the critique of the manifest image in which we are engaged is based on logical considerations in a broader and more constructive sense, one which compares it unfavorably with a *more* intelligible account of what there is.

It is familiar fact that those features of the manifest world which play no role in mechanical explanation were relegated by Descartes and other interpreters of the new physics to the mind of the perceiver. Color, for example, was said to exist only in sensation; its *esse* to be *percipi*. It was argued, in effect, that what scientifically motivated reflection recognizes to be states of the perceiver are conceptualized in ordinary experience as traits of independent physical things, indeed that these supposed independent colored things are actually conceptual constructions which ape the mechanical systems of the real world.

The same considerations which led philosophers to deny the reality of perceptible things led them to a dualistic theory of man. For if the human body is a system of particles, the body cannot be the subject of thinking and feeling, *unless thinking and feeling are capable of interpretation as complex interactions of physical particles*; unless, that is to say, the manifest framework of man as *one* being, a *person*, capable of doing radically different kinds of things can be replaced without loss of descriptive and explanatory power by a postulational image in which he is a complex of physical particles, and all his activities a matter of the particles changing in state and relationship.

Dualism, of course, denied that either sensation or feeling or conceptual thinking could in this sense be construed as complex interactions of physical particles, or man as a complex physical system. Dualists were prepared to say that a *chair* is really a system of imperceptible particles which "appears" in the manifest framework as a "color solid" (cf. our example of the ice cube), but they were not prepared to say that man himself was a complex physical system which "appears" to itself to be the sort of thing man is in the manifest image.

Let us consider in more detail the Cartesian attempt to integrate the manifest and the scientific images. Here the interesting thing to note is that Descartes took for granted (in a promissory-note-ish kind of way) that the scientific image would include items which would be the counterparts of the sensations, images, and feelings of the manifest framework. These counterparts would be complex states of the brain which, obeying purely physical laws, would resemble and differ from one another in a way which corresponded to the resemblances and differences between the conscious states with which they were correlated. Yet, as is well-known, he denied that there were brain states which were, in the same sense, the cerebral counterparts of conceptual thinking.

Now if we were to ask Descartes, "Why can't we say that sensations 'really are' complex cerebral processes as, according to you, we *can* say that physical objects 'really are' complex systems of imperceptible particles?" he would have a number of things to reply, some of which were a consequence of his conviction that sensation, images, and feelings belong to the same family as believing, choosing, wondering, in short are low-grade examples of conceptual thinking and share its supposed irreducibility to cerebral states. But when the chips are down there would remain the following argument:

> We have pulled perceptible qualities out of the physical environment and put them into sensations. If we now say that all there really is to sensation is a complex interaction of cerebral particles, then we have taken them out of our world picture altogether. We will have made it unintelligible how things could even *appear* to be colored.

As for conceptual thinking, Descartes not only refused to identify it with neurophysiological process, he did not see this as a live option, because it seemed obvious to him that no complex neurophysiological process could be sufficiently analogous to conceptual thinking to be a serious candidate for being what conceptual thinking "really is." It is not as though Descartes granted that there might well be neurophysiological processes which are strikingly analogous to conceptual thinking, but which it would be philosophically incorrect to *identify* with conceptual thinking (as he had identified physical objects of the manifest world with systems of imperceptible particles). He did not take seriously the idea that there *are* such neurophysiological processes.

Even if he had, however, it is clear that he would have rejected this identification on the ground that we had a "clear and distinct," well-defined idea of what conceptual thinking is before we even suspected that the brain had anything to do with thinking. Roughly: we know what thinking is without conceiving of it as a complex neurophysiological process, therefore, it can't *be* a complex physiological process.

Now, of course, the same is true of physical objects. We knew what a physical object was long before we knew that there were imperceptible physical particles. By parity of reasoning we should conclude that a physical object can not *be* a complex of imperceptible particles. Thus, if Descartes had had reason to think that neurophysiological processes strikingly analogous to conceptual thinking exist, it would seem that he should *either* have changed his tune with respect to physical objects *or* said that conceptual thinking *really* is neurophysiological process.

Now in the light of recent developments in neurophysiology, philosophers have come to see that there is no reason to suppose there cannot be neurophysiological processes which stand to conceptual thinking as sensory states of the brain stand to conscious sensations. And, indeed, there have not been wanting philosophers (of whom Hobbes was, perhaps, the first) who have argued that the analogy should be viewed philosophically as an *identity*, i.e., that a world picture which includes *both* thoughts *and* the neurophysiological counterparts of thoughts would contain a redundancy; just as a world picture which included *both* the physical objects of the manifest image *and* complex patterns of physical particles would contain a redundancy. But to this proposal the obvious objection occurs, that just as the claim that "physical objects are complexes of imperceptible particles" left us with the problem of accounting for the status of the perceptible qualities of manifest objects, so the claim that "thoughts, etc., are complex neurophysiological processes" leaves us with the problems of accounting for the status of the *introspectable qualities* of thoughts. And it would seem obvious that there is a vicious regress in the claim that these qualities exist in introspective awareness of the thoughts which seem to have them, but not in the thoughts themselves. For, the argument would run, surely introspection is itself a form of thinking. Thus one thought (Peter) would be robbed of its quality only to pay it to another (Paul).

We can, therefore, understand the temptation to say that even if there are cerebral processes which are strikingly analogous to conceptual thinking, they are processes which *run parallel* to conceptual thinking (and cannot be identified with it) as the sensory states of the brain *run parallel* to conscious sensation. And we can, therefore, understand the temptation to say that all these puzzles arise from taking seriously the claim of *any* part of the scientific image to be *what really is*, and to retreat into the position that reality is the world of the manifest image, and that all the postulated entities of the scientific image are "symbolic tools" which function (something like the distance-measuring devices which are rolled around on maps) to help us find our way around in the world, but do not themselves describe actual objects and processes. On this view, the theoretical counterparts of *all* features of the manifest image would be *equally* unreal, and that philosophical conception of man-in-the-world would be correct which endorsed the manifest image and located the scientific image within it as a conceptual tool used by manifest man in his capacity as a scientist.

The Primacy of the Scientific Image: A Prolegomenon

Is this the truth of the matter? Is the manifest image, subject, of course, to continual empirical and categorial refinement, the measure of what there really is? I do not think so. I have already indicated that of the three alternatives we are considering with respect to the comparative claims of the manifest and scientific images, the first, which, like a child, says "both," is ruled out by a principle which I am not defending in this essay, although it does stand in need of defense. The second alternative is the one I have just reformulated and rejected. I propose, therefore, to re-examine the case against the third alternative, the primacy of the scientific image. My strategy will be to argue that the difficulty, raised above, which seems to stand in the way of the identification of thought with cerebral processes, arises from the mistake of supposing that in self-awareness conceptual thinking presents itself to us in a qualitative guise. Sensations and images *do*, we shall see, present themselves to us in a qualitative character, a fact which accounts for the fact that they are stumbling blocks in the

attempt to accept the scientific image as real. *But* one scarcely needs to point out these days that however intimately conceptual thinking is related to sensations and images, it cannot be equated with them, nor with complexes consisting of them.

It is no accident that when a novelist wishes to represent what is going on in the mind of a person, he does so by "quoting" the person's thoughts as he might quote what a person says. For thoughts not only are the sort of thing that finds overt expression in language, we conceive of them as analogous to overt discourse. Thus, *thoughts* in the manifest image are conceived not in terms of their "quality," but rather as inner "goings-on" which are analogous to speech, and find their overt expression in speech – though they can go on, of course, in the absence of this overt expression. It is no accident that one learns to think in the very process of learning to speak.

From this point of view one can appreciate the danger of misunderstanding which is contained in the term "introspection." For while there is, indeed, an analogy between the direct knowledge we have of our own thoughts and the perceptual knowledge we have of what is going on in the world around us, the analogy holds only inasmuch as both self-awareness and perceptual observation are basic forms of noninferential knowledge. They differ, however, in that whereas in perceptual observation we know objects as being of a certain quality, in the direct knowledge we have of what we are thinking (e.g. I am thinking that it is cold outside) what we know noninferentially is that *something analogous to and properly expressed by the sentence, "It is cold outside," is going on in me.*

The point is an important one, for if the concept of a thought is the concept of an inner state analogous to speech, this leaves open the possibility that the inner state conceived in terms of this analogy is *in its qualitative character* a neurophysiological process. To draw a parallel: if I begin by thinking of the cause of a disease as a substance (to be called "germs") which is analogous to a colony of rabbits, in that it is able to reproduce itself in geometrical proportion, but, unlike rabbits, imperceptible and, when present in sufficient number in the human body, able to cause the symptoms of disease, and to cause epidemics by spreading from person to person, there is no logical barrier to a subsequent identification of "germs" thus conceived with the bacilli which microscopic investigation subsequently discovers.

But to point to the analogy between conceptual thinking and overt speech is only part of the story, for of equally decisive importance is the analogy between speech and what sophisticated computers can do, and, finally, between computer circuits and conceivable patterns of neurophysiological organization. All of this is more or less speculative, less so now than even a few years ago. What interests the philosopher is the matter of principle; and here the first stage is decisive – the recognition that the concept of a thought is a concept by analogy. Over and above this, all we need is to recognize the force of Spinoza's statement: "No one has thus far determined what the body can do, or no one has yet been taught by experience what the body can do merely by the laws of nature, insofar as nature is considered merely as corporeal and extended" (*Ethics*, Third Part, Prop. II (note)).

Another analogy which may be even more helpful is the following: Suppose we are watching the telegraphic report of a chess game in a foreign country.

White	*Black*
P–K3	P–Q3

And suppose that we are sophisticated enough to know that chess pieces can be made of all shapes and sizes, that chess boards can be horizontal or vertical, indeed, distorted in all kinds of ways provided that they preserve certain topological features of the familiar board. Then it is clear that while we will think of the players in the foreign country as moving kings, pawns, etc., castling and checkmating, our concepts of the pieces they are moving and the moving of them will be simply the concept of items and changes which play a role analogous to the pieces and moves which take place when *we* play chess. We know that the items must have some intrinsic quality (shape, size, etc.), but we think of these qualities as "those which make possible a sequence of changes which are structurally similar to the changes which take place on our own chess boards."

Thus our concept of "what thoughts are" might, like our concept of what a castling is in chess, be abstract in the sense that it does not concern itself with the *intrinsic* character of thoughts, *save as items which can occur in patterns of relationships which are analogous to the way in which sentences are related to one another and to the contexts in which they are used.*

Now, if thoughts are items which are conceived in terms of the roles they play, then there is no barrier *in principle* to the identification of conceptual thinking with neurophysiological process. There would be no "qualitative" remainder to be accounted for. The identification, curiously enough, would be even more straightforward than the identification of the physical things in the manifest image with complex systems of physical particles. And in this key, if not decisive, respect, the respect in which they are concerned with conceptual thinking (which is the distinctive trait of man), *the manifest and scientific images could merge without clash in the synoptic view.*

How does the situation stand in respect to sensation and feeling? Any attempt at identification of these items with neurophysiological process runs into a difficulty to which reference has already been made, and which we are now in a position to make more precise. This difficulty accounts for the fact that, with few exceptions, philosophers who have been prepared to identify conceptual thinking with neurophysiological process have *not* been prepared to make a similar identification in the case of sensation.

Before restating the problem let us note that curiously enough there is more similarity between the two cases than is commonly recognized. For it turns out on reflection that just as conceptual thinking is construed in the manifest image by analogy with overt speech, so sensation is construed by analogy with its external cause, sensations being the states of persons which correspond, in their similarities and differences, to the similarities and differences of the objects which, in standard conditions, bring them about. Let me assume that this is so. But if it *is* so, why not suppose that the inner-states which *as sensations* are conceived by analogy with their standard causes, are *in propria persona*, complex neurophysiological episodes in the cerebral cortex? This would parallel the conclusion we were prepared to draw in the case of conceptual thinking.

Why do we feel that there would be something extremely odd, even absurd, about such a supposition? The key to the answer lies in noticing an important difference between identifying thoughts with neurophysiological states and identifying sensations with neurophysiological states. Whereas both thoughts and sensations are conceived by analogy with publicly observable items, in the former case the analogy concerns the *role* and hence leaves open the possibility that thoughts are radically different *in their intrinsic character* from the verbal behavior by analogy with which they are conceived. But in the case of sensations, the analogy concerns the *quality* itself. Thus a "blue and triangular sensation" is conceived by analogy with the blue and triangular (facing) surface of a physical object which, when looked at in daylight, is its cause. The crucial issue then is this: Can we define, in the framework of neurophysiology, states which are sufficiently analogous in their *intrinsic* character to sensations to make identification plausible?

The answer seems clearly to be "no." This is not to say that neurophysiological states cannot be defined (in principle) which have a high degree of analogy to the sensations of the manifest image. That this can be done is an elementary fact in psychophysics. The trouble is, rather, that the feature which we referred to as "ultimate homogeneity," and which characterizes the perceptible qualities of things, e.g., their color, seems to be essentially lacking in the domain of the definable states of nerves and their interactions. Putting it crudely, color expanses in the manifest world consist of regions which are themselves color expanses, and consist in their turn of regions which are color expanses; and so on; whereas the state of a group of neurons, though it has regions which are also states of groups of neurons, has ultimate regions which are *not* states of groups of neurons but rather states of single neurons. And the same is true if we move to the finer-grained level of biochemical process.

Nor do we wish to say that the ultimate homogeneity of the sensation of a red rectangle is a matter of each physical particle in the appropriate region of the cortex *having* a color; for whatever other difficulties such a view would involve, it does not make sense to say of the particles of physical theory that they are colored. And the principle of reducibility, which we have accepted without argument, makes impossible the view that groups of particles can have properties which are not "reducible to" the properties and relations of the members of the group.

It is worth noting that we have here a recurrence of the essential features of Eddington's "two tables" problem – the two tables being, in our terminology, the table of the manifest image and the table of the scientific image. There the problem was to "fit together" the manifest table with the scientific table. Here the problem is to fit together the manifest sensation with its neurophysiological counterpart. And, interestingly enough, the problem in both cases is essentially the same: *how to reconcile the ultimate homogeneity of the manifest image with the ultimate nonhomogeneity of the system of scientific objects.*

Now we are rejecting the view that the scientific image is a mere "symbolic tool" for finding our way around in the manifest image; and we are accepting the view that the scientific account of the world is (in principle) the adequate image. Having, therefore, given the perceptible qualities of manifest objects their real locus in sensation, we were confronted with the problem of choosing between dualism or identity with respect to the relation of conscious sensations to their analogues in the visual cortex, and the above argument seems to point clearly in the dualistic direction. The "ultimate homogeneity" of perceptible qualities, which, among other things, prevented *identifying* the perceptible qualities of physical objects with complex properties of systems of physical particles, stands equally in the way of *identifying*, rather than *correlating*, conscious sensations with the complex neural processes with which they are obviously connected.

But such dualism is an unsatisfactory solution, because, *ex hypothesi*, sensations are essential to the explanation of how we come to construct the "appearance" which is the manifest world. They are essential to the explanation of how there even *seem* to be colored objects. But the scientific image presents itself as a closed system of explanation, and *if the scientific image is interpreted as we have interpreted it up to this point the explanation will be in terms of the constructs of neurophysiology,* which, according to the argument, *do not involve the ultimate homogeneity, the appearance of which in the manifest image is to be explained.*

We are confronted, therefore, by an antinomy, *either*, (a) the neurophysiological image is *incomplete*, i.e., must be supplemented by new objects ("sense fields") which do have ultimate homogeneity, and which somehow make their presence felt in the activity of the visual cortex as a system of physical particles; *or*, (b) the neurophysiological image is complete and the ultimate homogeneity of the sense qualities (and, hence, the sense qualities, themselves) is *mere appearance* in the very radical sense of not existing in the spatiotemporal world at all.

Is the situation irremediable? Does the assumption of the reality of the scientific image lead us to a dualism of particles and sense fields, of matter and "consciousness"? If so, then, in view of the obviously intimate relation between sensation and conceptual thinking (for example, in perception), we must surely regress and take back the identification of conceptual thinking with neurophysiological process which seemed so plausible a moment ago. We could then argue that although in the absence of other considerations it would be plausible to equate conceptual thinking with neurophysiological process, when the chips are *all* down, we must rather say that although conceptual thinking and neurophysiological process are each analogous to verbal behavior as a public social phenomenon (the one by virtue of the very way in which the very notion of "thinking" is formed; the other as a scientifically ascertained matter of fact), they are also *merely* analogous to one another and cannot be identified. If so, the manifest and the scientific conception of *both* sensations *and* conceptual thinking would fit into the synoptic view as parallel processes, a dualism which could only be avoided by interpreting the scientific image *as a whole* as a "symbolic device" for coping with the world as it presents itself to us in the manifest image.

Is there any alternative? As long as the ultimate constitutents of the scientific image are particles forming ever more complex systems of particles, we are inevitably confronted by the above choice. But the scientific image is not yet complete; we have not yet penetrated all the secrets of nature. And if it should turn out that particles instead of being the primitive entities of the scientific image could be treated as singularities in a space-time continuum which could be conceptually "cut up" without significant loss – *in inorganic contexts, at least* – into interacting particles, then we would not be confronted at the level of neurophysiology with the problem of understanding the relation of *sensory consciousness* (with its ultimate homogeneity) to *systems of particles*. Rather, we would have the alternative of saying that although for many purposes the central nervous system can be construed without loss as a complex system of physical particles, *when it comes to an adequate understanding of the relation of sensory consciousness to neurophysiological process*, we must penetrate to the nonparticulate foundation of the particulate image, and recognize that in this nonparticulate image the qualities of sense are a dimension of natural process which occurs only in connection with those complex physical processes which, when "cut up" into particles in terms of those features which are the least common denominators of physical process – present in inorganic as well as organic processes alike – become the complex system of particles which, in the current scientific image, *is* the central nervous system.

Putting Man into the Scientific Image

Even if the constructive suggestion of the preceding section were capable of being elaborated into an adequate account of the way in which the scientific image could recreate in its own terms the sensations, images, and feelings of the manifest image, the thesis of the primacy of the scientific image would scarcely be off the ground. There would remain the task of showing that categories pertaining to man as a *person* who finds himself confronted by standards (ethical, logical, etc.) which often conflict with his desires and impulses, and to which he may or may not conform, can be reconciled with the idea that man is what science says he is.

At first sight there would seem to be only one way of recapturing the specifically human within the framework of the scientific image. The categories of the person might be reconstructed without loss in terms of the fundamental concepts of the scientific image in a way analogous to that in which the concepts of biochemistry are (in principle) reconstructed in terms of subatomic physics. To this suggestion there is, in the first place, the familiar objection that persons as responsible agents who make genuine choices between genuine alternatives, and who could on many occasions have done what in point of fact they did not do, simply *can not* be construed as physical systems (even broadly interpreted to include sensations and feelings) which evolve in accordance with laws of nature (statistical or nonstatistical). Those who make the above move can be expected to reply (drawing on distinctions developed in the second section above, "The Manifest Image") that the concepts in terms of which we think of a person's "character," or the fact that "he could have done otherwise," or that "his actions are predictable" would appear in the reconstruction as extraordinarily complex defined concepts not to be confused with the concepts in terms of which we think of the "nature" of NaCl, or the fact that "system X could have failed to be in state S given the same initial conditions," or that "it is predictable that system X will assume state S given these initial conditions." And I think that a reply along these lines could be elaborated which would answer *this* objection to the proposed reconstruction of categories pertaining to persons.

But even if the proposed reconstruction could meet what might be called the "free will" objection, it fails decisively on another count. For it can, I believe, be conclusively shown that such a reconstruction is *in principle* impossible, the impossibility in question being a strictly logical one. (I shall not argue the point explicitly, but the following remarks contain the essential clues.) If so, that would seem to be the end of the matter. Must we not return to a choice between (a) a dualism in which men as scientific objects are contrasted with the "minds" which are the source and principle of their existence as persons; (b) abandoning the reality of persons as well as manifest physical objects in favor of the exclusive reality of scientific objects; (c) returning once and for all to the thesis of the merely "calculational" or "auxiliary" status of theoretical frameworks and to the affirmation of the primacy of the manifest image?

Assuming, in accordance with the drift of the argument of this essay, that none of these alternatives is satisfactory, is there a way out? I believe there is, and that while a proper exposition and defense would require at least the space of this whole volume, the gist can be stated in short compass. To say that a certain person desired to do A, thought it his duty to do B but was forced to do C is not to *describe* him as one might describe a scientific specimen. One does, indeed, describe him, but one does something more. And it is this something more which is the irreducible core of the framework of persons.

In what does this something more consist? First, a relatively superficial point which will guide the way. To think of a featherless biped as a person is to think of it as a being with which one is bound up in a network of rights and duties. From this point of view, the irreducibility of the personal is the irreducibility of the "ought" to the "is." But even more basic than this (though ultimately, as we shall see, the two points coincide) is the fact that to think of a featherless biped as a person is to construe its

behavior in terms of actual or potential membership in an embracing group each member of which thinks itself as a member of the group. Let us call such a group a "community." Once the primitive tribe, it is currently (almost) the "brotherhood" of man, and is potentially the "republic" of rational beings (cf. Kant's "Kingdom of Ends"). An individual may belong to many communities, some of which overlap, some of which are arranged like Chinese boxes. The most embracing community to which he belongs consists of those with whom he can enter into meaningful discourse. The scope of the embracing community is the scope of "we" in its most embracing nonmetaphorical use. "We," in this fundamental sense (in which it is equivalent to the French "*on*" or English "one") is no less basic than the other "persons" in which verbs are conjugated. Thus, to recognize a featherless biped or dolphin or Martian as a person is to think of oneself and it as belonging to a community.

Now, the fundamental principles of a community, which define what is "correct" or "incorrect," "right" or "wrong," "done" or "not done" are the most general common *intentions* of that community with respect to the behavior of members of the group. It follows that to recognize a featherless biped or dolphin or Martian as a person requires that one think thoughts of the form "We (one) shall do (or abstain from doing) actions of kind A in circumstances of kind C." To think thoughts of this kind is not to *classify* or *explain*, but to *rehearse an intention*.

(Community intentions ("One shall . . .") are not just private intentions ("I shall . . .") which everybody has. (This is another way of putting the above-mentioned irreducibility of "we".) There is, however, a logical connection between community and private intentions. For one does not really share a community intention unless, however often one may rehearse it, it is not reflected, where relevant, in the corresponding private intention.)

Thus, the conceptual framework of persons is the framework in which we think of one another as sharing the community intentions which provide the ambience of principles and standards (above all, those which make meaningful discourse and rationality itself possible), within which we live our individual lives. A person can almost be defined as a being that has intentions. Thus, the conceptual framework of persons is not something that needs to be *reconciled with* the scientific image, but rather something to be *joined to* it. Thus, to complete the scientific image we need to enrich it *not* with more ways of saying what is the case, but with the language of community and individual intentions, so that by construing the actions we intend to do and the circumstances in which we intend to do them in scientific terms we *directly* relate the world as conceived by scientific theory to our purposes, and make it *our* world and no longer an alien appendage to the world in which we do our living. We can, of course, as matters now stand, realize this direct incorporation of the scientific image into our way of life only in imagination. But to do so is, if only in imagination, to transcend the dualism of the manifest and scientific images of man-in-the-world.

Note

1 It might seem that the manifest framework accounts for the success of the scientific framework, so that the situation is symmetrical. But I believe that a more penetrative account of the order of theories than I have been able to sketch in this essay would show that this claim is illusory. I have discussed this topic at some length in "The Language of Theories," in *Current Issues in the Philosophy of Science*, ed. Herbert Feigl and Grover Maxwell (New York, 1961).

46

From *The Blue and Brown Books*

Ludwig Wittgenstein

From "The Blue Book"

What is the meaning of a word?

Let us attack this question by asking, first, what is an explanation of the meaning of a word; what does the explanation of a word look like?

The way this question helps us is analogous to the way the question "how do we measure a length?" helps us to understand the problem "what is length?"

The questions "What is length?", "What is meaning?", "What is the number one?" etc., produce in us a mental cramp. We feel that we can't point to anything in reply to them and yet ought to point to something. (We are up against one of the great sources of philosophical bewilderment: a substantive makes us look for a thing that corresponds to it.)

Asking first "What's an explanation of meaning?" has two advantages. You in a sense bring the question "what is meaning?" down to earth. For, surely, to understand the meaning of "meaning" you ought also to understand the meaning of "explanation of meaning". Roughly: "let's ask what the explanation of meaning is, for whatever that explains will be the meaning." Studying the grammar of the expression "explanation of meaning" will teach you something about the grammar of the word "meaning" and will cure you of

Originally published in *The Blue and Brown Books* (Blackwell Publishers, Oxford, 1958).

the temptation to look about you for some object which you might call "the meaning".

What one generally calls "explanations of the meaning of a word" can, *very roughly*, be divided into verbal and ostensive definitions. It will be seen later in what sense this division is only rough and provisional (and that it is, is an important point). The verbal definition, as it takes us from one verbal expression to another, in a sense gets us no further. In the ostensive definition however we seem to make a much more real step towards learning the meaning.

One difficulty which strikes us is that for many words in our language there do not seem to be ostensive definitions; e.g. for such words as "one", "number", "not", etc.

Question: Need the ostensive definition itself be understood? – Can't the ostensive definition be misunderstood?

If the definition explains the meaning of a word, surely it can't be essential that you should have heard the word before. It is the ostensive definition's business to *give* it a meaning. Let us then explain the word "tove" by pointing to a pencil and saying "this is tove". (Instead of "this is tove" I could here have said "this is called 'tove'". I point this out to remove, once and for all, the idea that the words of the ostensive definition predicate something of the defined; the confusion between the sentence "this is red", attributing the colour red to something, and the ostensive definition "this is called 'red'".) Now the ostensive definition "this is tove" can be interpreted in all sorts of ways. I will give a few such interpretations and use English words with well established usage. The definition then can be interpreted to mean:

"This is a pencil",
"This is round",
"This is wood",
"This is one",
"This is hard", etc. etc.

One might object to this argument that all these interpretations presuppose another word-language. And this objection is significant if by "interpretation" we only mean "translation into a word-language". – Let me give some hints which might make this clearer. Let us ask ourselves what is our criterion when we say that someone has interpreted the ostensive definition in a particular way. Suppose I give to an Englishman the ostensive definition "this is what the Germans call 'Buch'". Then, in the great majority of cases at any rate, the English word "book" will come into the Englishman's mind. We may say he has interpreted "Buch" to mean "book". The case will be different if e.g. we point to a thing which he has never seen before and say: "This is a banjo". Possibly the word "guitar" will then come into his mind, possibly no word at all but the image of a similar instrument, possibly nothing at all. Supposing then I give him the order "now pick a banjo from amongst these things." If he picks what we call a "banjo" we might say "he has given the word 'banjo' the correct interpretation"; if he picks some other instrument – "he has interpreted 'banjo' to mean 'string instrument'".

We say "he has given the word 'banjo' this or that interpretation", and are inclined to assume a definite act of interpretation besides the act of choosing.

Our problem is analogous to the following:

If I give someone the order "fetch me a red flower from that meadow", how is he to know what sort of flower to bring, as I have only given him a *word*?

Now the answer one might suggest first is that he went to look for a red flower carrying a red image in his mind, and comparing it with the flowers to see which of them had the colour of the image. Now there is such a way of searching, and it is not at all essential that the image we use should be a mental one. In fact the process may be this: I carry a chart co-ordinating names and coloured squares. When I hear the order

"fetch me etc." I draw my finger across the chart from the word "red" to a certain square, and I go and look for a flower which has the same colour as the square. But this is not the only way of searching and it isn't the usual way. We go, look about us, walk up to a flower and pick it, without comparing it to anything. To see that the process of obeying the order can be of this kind, consider the order "*imagine* a red patch". You are not tempted in this case to think that *before* obeying you must have imagined a red patch to serve you as a pattern for the red patch which you were ordered to imagine.

Now you might ask: do we *interpret* the words before we obey the order? And in some cases you will find that you do something which might be called interpreting before obeying, in some cases not.

It seems that there are *certain definite* mental processes bound up with the working of language, processes through which alone language can function. I mean the processes of understanding and meaning. The signs of our language seem dead without these mental processes; and it might seem that the only function of the signs is to induce such processes, and that these are the things we ought really to be interested in. Thus, if you are asked what is the relation between a name and the thing it names, you will be inclined to answer that the relation is a psychological one, and perhaps when you say this you think in particular of the mechanism of association. – We are tempted to think that the action of language consists of two parts; an inorganic part, the handling of signs, and an organic part, which we may call understanding these signs, meaning them, interpreting them, thinking. These latter activities seem to take place in a queer kind of medium, the mind; and the mechanism of the mind, the nature of which, it seems, we don't quite understand, can bring about effects which no material mechanism could. Thus e.g. a thought (which is such a mental process) can agree or disagree with reality; I am able to think of a man who isn't present; I am able to imagine him, 'mean him' in a remark which I make about him, even if he is thousands of miles away or dead. "What a queer mechanism," one might say, "the mechanism of wishing must be if I can wish that which will never happen".

There is one way of avoiding at least partly the occult appearance of the processes of thinking, and it is, to replace in these processes any working of the imagination by acts of looking at real objects. Thus it may seem essential that, at least in certain cases, when I hear the word "red" with understanding, a red image should be before my mind's eye. But why should I not substitute seeing a red bit of paper for imagining a red patch? The visual image will only be the more vivid. Imagine a man always carrying a sheet of paper in his pocket on which the names of colours are co-ordinated with coloured patches. You may say that it would be a nuisance to carry such a table of samples about with you, and that the mechanism of association is what we always use instead of it. But this is irrelevant; and in many cases it is not even true. If, for instance, you were ordered to paint a particular shade of blue called "Prussian Blue", you might have to use a table to lead you from the word "Prussian Blue" to a sample of the colour, which would serve you as your copy.

We could perfectly well, for our purposes, replace every process of imagining by a process of looking at an object or by painting, drawing or modelling; and every process of speaking to oneself by speaking aloud or by writing.

Frege ridiculed the formalist conception of mathematics by saying that the formalists confused the unimportant thing, the sign, with the important, the meaning. Surely, one wishes to say, mathematics does not treat of dashes on a bit of paper. Frege's idea could be expressed thus: the propositions of mathematics, if they were just complexes of dashes, would be dead and utterly uninteresting, whereas they obviously have a kind of life. And the same, of course, could be said of any proposition: Without a sense, or without the thought, a proposition would be an utterly dead and trivial thing. And further it seems clear that no adding of inorganic signs can make the proposition live. And the conclusion which one draws from this is that what must be added to the dead signs in order to make a live proposition is something immaterial, with properties different from all mere signs.

But if we had to name anything which is the life of the sign, we should have to say that it was its *use*.

If the meaning of the sign (roughly, that which is of importance about the sign) is an image built up in our minds when we see or hear the sign, then first let us adopt the method we just described of replacing this mental image by some outward object seen, e.g. a painted or modelled image. Then why should the written sign plus this painted image be alive if the written sign alone was dead? – In fact, as soon as you think of replacing the mental image by, say, a painted one, and as soon as the image thereby loses its occult character, it ceases to seem to impart any life to the sentence at all. (It was in fact just the occult character of the mental process which you needed for your purposes.)

The mistake we are liable to make could be expressed thus: We are looking for the use of a sign, but we look for it as though it were an object *co-existing* with the sign. (One of the reasons for this mistake is again that we are looking for a "thing corresponding to a substantive.")

The sign (the sentence) gets its significance from the system of signs, from the language to which it belongs. Roughly: understanding a sentence means understanding a language.

As a part of the system of language, one may say, the sentence has life. But one is tempted to imagine that which gives the sentence life as something in an occult sphere, accompanying the sentence. But whatever accompanied it would for us just be another sign.

It seems at first sight that that which gives to thinking its peculiar character is that it is a train of mental states, and it seems that what is queer and difficult to understand about thinking is the processes which happen in the medium of the mind, processes possible only in this medium. The comparison which forces itself upon us is that of the mental medium with the protoplasm of a cell, say, of an amoeba. We observe certain actions of the amoeba, its taking food by extending arms, its splitting up into similar cells, each of which grows and behaves like the original one. We say "of what a queer nature the protoplasm must be to act in such a way", and perhaps we say that no physical mechanism could behave in this way, and that the mechanism of the amoeba must be of a totally different kind. In the same way we are tempted to say "the mechanism of the mind must be of a most peculiar kind to be able to do what the mind does". But here we are making two mistakes. For what struck *us* as being queer about thought and thinking was not at all that it had curious effects which we were not yet able to explain (causally). Our problem, in other words, was not a scientific one; but a muddle felt as a problem.

Supposing we tried to construct a mind-model as a result of psychological investigations, a model

Ludwig Wittgenstein

which, as we should say, would explain the action of the mind. This model would be part of a psychological theory in the way in which a mechanical model of the ether can be part of a theory of electricity. (Such a model, by the way, is always part of the *symbolism* of a theory. Its advantage may be that it can be taken in at a glance and easily held in the mind. It has been said that a model, in a sense, dresses up the pure theory; that the *naked* theory is sentences or equations. This must be examined more closely later on.)

We may find that such a mind-model would have to be very complicated and intricate in order to explain the observed mental activities; and on this ground we might call the mind a queer kind of medium. But this aspect of the mind does not interest us. The problems which it may set are psychological problems, and the method of their solution is that of natural science.

Now if it is not the causal connections which we are concerned with, then the activities of the mind lie open before us. And when we are worried about the nature of thinking, the puzzlement which we wrongly interpret to be one about the nature of a medium is a puzzlement caused by the mystifying use of our language. This kind of mistake recurs again and again in philosophy; e.g. when we are puzzled about the nature of time, when time seems to us a *queer thing*. We are most strongly tempted to think that here are things hidden, something we can see from the outside but which we can't look into. And yet nothing of the sort is the case. It is not new facts about time which we want to know. All the facts that concern us lie open before us. But it is the use of the substantive "time" which mystifies us. If we look into the grammar of that word, we shall feel that it is no less astounding that man should have conceived of a deity of time than it would be to conceive of a deity of negation or disjunction.

It is misleading then to talk of thinking as of a "mental activity". We may say that thinking is essentially the activity of operating with signs. This activity is performed by the hand, when we think by writing; by the mouth and larynx, when we think by speaking; and if we think by imagining signs or pictures, I can give you no agent that thinks. If then you say that in such cases the mind thinks, I would only draw your attention to the fact that you are using a metaphor, that here the mind is an agent in a different

sense from that in which the hand can be said to be the agent in writing.

If again we talk about the locality where thinking takes place we have a right to say that this locality is the paper on which we write or the mouth which speaks. And if we talk of the head or the brain as the locality of thought, this is using the expression "locality of thinking" in a different sense. Let us examine what are the reasons for calling the head the place of thinking. It is not our intention to criticize this form of expression, or to show that it is not appropriate. What we must do is: understand its working, its grammar, e.g. see what relation this grammar has to that of the expression "we think with our mouth", or "we think with a pencil on a piece of paper".

Perhaps the main reason why we are so strongly inclined to talk of the head as the locality of our thoughts is this: the existence of the words "thinking" and "thought" alongside of the words denoting (bodily) activities, such as writing, speaking, etc., makes us look for an activity, different from these but analogous to them, corresponding to the word "thinking". When words in our ordinary language have prima facie analogous grammars we are inclined to try to interpret them analogously; i.e. we try to make the analogy hold throughout. – We say, "The thought is not the same as the sentence; for an English and a French sentence, which are utterly different, can express the same thought". And now, as the sentences are *somewhere*, we look for a place for the thought. (It is as though we looked for the place of the king of which the rules of chess treat, as opposed to the places of the various bits of wood, the kings of the various sets.) – We say, "surely the thought is *something*; it is not nothing"; and all one can answer to this is, that the word "thought" has its *use*, which is of a totally different kind from the use of the word "sentence".

Now does this mean that it is nonsensical to talk of a locality where thought takes place? Certainly not. This phrase has sense if we give it sense. Now if we say "thought takes place in our heads", what is the sense of this phrase soberly understood? I suppose it is that certain physiological processes correspond to our thoughts in such a way that if we know the correspondence we can, by observing these processes, find the thoughts. But in what sense can the physiological processes be said to correspond to thoughts, and in what sense can we be said to get the thoughts from the observation of the brain?

I suppose we imagine the correspondence to have been verified experimentally. Let us imagine such an experiment crudely. It consists in looking at the brain while the subject thinks. And now you may think that the reason why my explanation is going to go wrong is that of course the experimenter gets the thoughts of the subject only *indirectly* by being told them, the subject *expressing* them in some way or other. But I will remove this difficulty by assuming that the subject is at the same time the experimenter, who is looking at his own brain, say by means of a mirror. (The crudity of this description in no way reduces the force of the argument.)

Then I ask you, is the subject-experimenter observing one thing or two things? (Don't say that he is observing one thing both from the inside and from the outside; for this does not remove the difficulty. We will talk of inside and outside later.) The subject-experimenter is observing a correlation of two phenomena. One of them he, perhaps, calls the *thought*. This may consist of a train of images, organic sensations, or on the other hand of a train of the various visual, tactual and muscular experiences which he has in writing or speaking a sentence. – The other experience is one of seeing his brain work. Both these phenomena could correctly be called "expressions of thought"; and the question "where is the thought itself?" had better, in order to prevent confusion, be rejected as nonsensical. If however we do use the expression "the thought takes place in the head", we have given this expression its meaning by describing the experience which would justify the *hypothesis* that the thought takes places in our heads, by describing the experience which we wish to call "observing thought in our brain".

We easily forget that the word "locality" is used in many different senses and that there are many different kinds of statements about a thing which in a particular case, in accordance with general usage, we may call specifications of the locality of the thing. Thus it has been said of visual space that its place is in our head; and I think one has been tempted to say this, partly, by a grammatical misunderstanding.

I can say: "in my visual field I see the image of the tree to the right of the image of the tower" or "I see the image of the tree in the middle of the visual field". And now we are inclined to ask "and where do you see the visual field?" Now if the "where" is meant to ask for a locality in the sense in which we have specified the locality of

the image of the tree, then I would draw your attention to the fact that you have not yet given this question sense; that is, that you have been proceeding by a grammatical analogy without having worked out the analogy in detail.

In saying that the idea of our visual field being located in our brain arose from a grammatical misunderstanding, I did not mean to say that we could not give sense to such a specification of locality. We could, e.g., easily imagine an experience which we should describe by such a statement. Imagine that we looked at a group of things in this room, and, while we looked, a probe was stuck into our brain and it was found that if the point of the probe reached a particular point in our brain, then a particular small part of our visual field was thereby obliterated. In this way we might co-ordinate points of our brain to points of the visual image, and this might make us say that the visual field was seated in such and such a place in our brain. And if now we asked the question "Where do you see the image of this book?" the answer could be (as above) "To the right of that pencil", or "In the left hand part of my visual field", or again: "Three inches behind my left eye".

But what if someone said "I can assure you I feel the visual image to be two inches behind the bridge of my nose"; – what are we to answer him? Should we say that he is not speaking the truth, or that there cannot be such a feeling? What if he asks us "do you know all the feelings there are? How do you know there isn't such a feeling?"

What if the diviner tells us that when he holds the rod he *feels* that the water is five feet under the ground? or that he *feels* that a mixture of copper and gold is five feet under the ground? Suppose that to our doubts he answered: "You can estimate a length when you see it. Why shouldn't I have a different way of estimating it?"

If we understand the idea of such an estimation, we shall get clear about the nature of our doubts about the statements of the diviner, and of the man who said he felt the visual image behind the bridge of his nose.

There is the statement: "this pencil is five inches long", and the statement, "I feel that this pencil is five inches long", and we must get clear about the relation of the grammar of the first statement to the grammar of the second. To the statement "I feel in my hand that the water is three feet under the ground" we should like to answer: "I don't know what this *means*". But the diviner would say: "Surely you know what it means. You know what 'three feet under the ground' means, and you know what 'I feel' means!" But I should answer him: I know what a word means *in certain contexts*. Thus I understand the phrase, "three feet under the ground", say, in the connections "The measurement has shown that the water runs three feet under the ground", "If we dig three feet deep we are going to strike water", "The depth of the water is three feet by the eye". But the use of the expression "a feeling in my hands of water being three feet under the ground" has yet to be explained to me.

We could ask the diviner "how did you learn the meaning of the word 'three feet'? We suppose by being shown such lengths, by having measured them and such like. Were you also taught to talk of a feeling of water being three feet under the ground, a feeling, say, in your hands? For if not, what made you connect the word 'three feet' with a feeling in your hand?" Supposing we had been estimating lengths by the eye, but had never spanned a length. How could we estimate a length in inches by spanning it? I.e., how could we interpret the experience of spanning in inches? The question is: what connection is there between, say, a tactual sensation and the experience of measuring a thing by means of a yard rod? This connection will show us what it means to 'feel that a thing is six inches long'. Supposing the diviner said "I have never learnt to correlate depth of water under the ground with feelings in my hand, but when I have a certain feeling of tension in my hands, the words 'three feet' spring up in my mind." We should answer "This is a perfectly good explanation of what you mean by 'feeling the depth to be three feet', and the statement that you feel this will have neither more, nor less, meaning than your explanation has given it. And if experience shows that the actual depth of the water always agrees with the words '*n* feet' which come into your mind, your experience will be very useful for determining the depth of water". – But you see that the meaning of the words "I feel the depth of the water to be *n* feet" had to be explained; it was not known when the meaning of the words "*n* feet" in the ordinary sense (i.e. in the ordinary contexts) was known. – We don't say that the man who tells us he feels the

visual image two inches behind the bridge of his nose is telling a lie or talking nonsense. But we say that we don't understand the meaning of such a phrase. It combines well-known words, but combines them in a way we don't yet understand. The grammar of this phrase has yet to be explained to us.

The importance of investigating the diviner's answer lies in the fact that we often think we have given a meaning to a statement P if only we assert "I *feel* (or I believe) that P is the case." (We shall talk at a later occasion of Prof. Hardy saying that Goldbach's theorem is a proposition because he can believe that it is true.) We have already said that by merely explaining the meaning of the words "three feet" in the usual way we have not yet explained the sense of the phrase "feeling that water is three feet etc." Now we should not have felt these difficulties had the diviner said that he had *learnt* to estimate the depth of the water, say, by digging for water whenever he had a particular feeling and in this way correlating such feelings with *measurements* of depth. Now we must examine the relation of the process of *learning to estimate* with the act of estimating. The importance of this examination lies in this, that it applies to the relation between learning the meaning of a word and making use of the word. Or, more generally, that it shows the different possible relations between a rule given and its application.

Let us consider the process of estimating a length by the eye: It is extremely important that you should realise that there are a great many different processes which we call "estimating by the eye".

Consider these cases:

1 Someone asks "How did you estimate the height of this building?" I answer: "It has four storeys; I suppose each storey is about fifteen feet high; so it must be about sixty feet."
2 In another case: "I roughly know what a yard at that distance looks like; so it must be about four yards long."
3 Or again: "I can imagine a tall man reaching to about this point; so it must be about six feet above the ground."
4 Or: "I don't know; it just looks like a yard."

This last case is likely to puzzle us. If you ask "what happened in this case when the man estimated the length?" the correct answer may be: "he *looked* at the thing and *said* 'it looks one yard long'." This may be all that has happened.

We said before that we should not have been puzzled about the diviner's answer if he had told us that he had *learnt* how to estimate depth. Now learning to estimate may, broadly speaking, be seen in two different relations to the act of estimating; either as a cause of the phenomenon of estimating, or as supplying us with a rule (a table, a chart, or some such thing) which we make use of when we estimate.

Supposing I teach someone the use of the word "yellow" by repeatedly pointing to a yellow patch and pronouncing the word. On another occasion I make him apply what he has learnt by giving him the order, "choose a yellow ball out of this bag". What was it that happened when he obeyed my order? I say "possibly just this: he heard my words and took a yellow ball from the bag". Now you may be inclined to think that this couldn't possibly have been all; and the *kind* of thing that you would suggest is that he imagined something yellow when he *understood* the order, and then chose a ball according to his image. To see that this is not *necessary* remember that I could have given him the order, "Imagine a yellow patch". Would you still be inclined to assume that he first imagines a yellow patch, just *understanding* my order, and then imagines a yellow patch to match the first? (Now I don't say that this is not possible. Only, putting it in this way immediately shows you that it need not happen. This, by the way, illustrates the method of philosophy.)

If we are taught the meaning of the word "yellow" by being given some sort of ostensive definition (a rule of the usage of the word) this teaching can be looked at in two different ways.

A. The teaching is a drill. This drill causes us to associate a yellow image, yellow things, with the word "yellow". Thus when I gave the order "Choose a yellow ball from this bag" the word "yellow" might have brought up a yellow image, or a feeling of recognition when the person's eye fell on the yellow ball. The drill of teaching could in this case be said to have built up a psychical mechanism. This, however, would only be a hypothesis or else a metaphor. We could *compare* teaching with installing an electric connection between a switch and a bulb. The parallel to the connection going wrong or breaking down would then be what we call forgetting the explanation, or the meaning, of the word. (We ought to talk further on about the meaning of "forgetting the meaning of a word".)

In so far as the teaching brings about the association, feeling of recognition, etc. etc., it is the *cause* of the phenomena of understanding, obeying, etc.; and it is a hypothesis that the process of teaching should be needed in order to bring about these effects. It is conceivable, in this sense, that *all* the processes of understanding, obeying, etc., should have happened without the person ever having been taught the language. (This, just now, seems extremely paradoxical.)

B. The teaching may have supplied us with a rule which is itself involved in the processes of understanding, obeying, etc.; "involved", however, meaning that the expression of this rule forms part of these processes.

We must distinguish between what one might call "a process being *in accordance with* a rule", and, "a process involving a rule" (in the above sense).

Take an example. Some one teaches me to square cardinal numbers; he writes down the row

$$1 \quad 2 \quad 3 \quad 4,$$

and asks me to square them. (I will, in this case again, replace any processes happening 'in the mind' by processes of calculation on the paper.) Suppose, underneath the first row of numbers, I then write:

$$1 \quad 4 \quad 9 \quad 16.$$

What I wrote is in accordance with the general rule of squaring; but it obviously is also in accordance with any number of other rules; and amongst these it is not more in accordance with one than with another. In the sense in which before we talked about a rule being involved in a process, *no* rule was involved in this. Supposing that in order to get to my results I calculated 1×1, 2×2, 3×3, 4×4 (that is, in this case wrote down the calculations); these would again be in accordance with any number of rules. Supposing, on the other hand, in order to get to my results I had written down what you may call "the rule of squaring", say algebraically. In this case this rule was involved in a sense in which no other rule was.

We shall say that the rule is *involved* in the understanding, obeying, etc., if, as I should like to express it, the symbol of the rule forms part of the calculation. (As we are not interested in where the processes of thinking, calculating, take place, we can for our purpose imagine the calculations being done entirely on paper. We are not concerned with the difference: internal, external.)

A characteristic example of the case B would be one in which the teaching supplied us with a table which we actually make use of in understanding, obeying, etc. If we are taught to play chess, we may be taught rules. If then we play chess, these rules need not be involved in the act of playing. But they may be. Imagine, e.g., that the rules were expressed in the form of a table; in one column the shapes of the chessmen are drawn, and in a parallel column we find diagrams showing the 'freedom' (the legitimate moves) of the pieces. Suppose now that the way the game is played involves making the transition from the shape to the possible moves by running one's finger across the table, and then making one of these moves.

Teaching as the hypothetical history of our subsequent actions (understanding, obeying, estimating a length, etc.) drops out of our considerations. The rule which has been taught and is subsequently applied interests us only so far as it is involved in the application. A rule, so far as it interests us, does not act at a distance.

Suppose I pointed to a piece of paper and said to someone: "this colour I call 'red'". Afterwards I give him the order: "now paint me a red patch". I then ask him: "why, in carrying out my order, did you paint just this colour?" His answer could then be: "This colour (pointing to the sample which I have given him) was called red; and the patch I have painted has, as you see, the colour of the sample". He has now given me a reason for carrying out the order in the way he did. Giving a reason for something one did or said means showing a *way* which leads to this action. In some cases it means telling the way which one has gone oneself; in others it means describing a way which leads there and is in accordance with certain accepted rules. Thus when asked, "why did you carry out my order by painting just this colour?" the person could have described the way he had actually taken to arrive at this particular shade of colour. This would have been so if, hearing the word "red", he had taken up the sample I had given him, labelled "red", and had *copied* that sample when painting the patch. On the other hand he might have painted it 'automatically' or from a memory image, but when asked to give the reason he might still point to the sample and show that it matched the patch he had painted. In this latter case the reason given would have been of the second kind; i.e. a justification *post hoc*.

Now if one thinks that there could be no understanding and obeying the order without a previous teaching, one thinks of the teaching as supplying a *reason* for doing what one did; as supplying the road one walks. Now there is the idea that if an order is understood and obeyed there must be a reason for our obeying it as we do; and, in fact, a chain of reasons reaching back to infinity. This is as if one said: "Wherever you are, you must have got there from somewhere else, and to that previous place from another place; and so on *ad infinitum*". (If, on the other hand, you had said, "wherever you are, you *could* have got there from another place ten yards away; and to that other place from a third, ten yards further away, and so on *ad infinitum*", if you had said this you would have stressed the infinite *possibility* of making a step. Thus the idea of an infinite chain of reasons arises out of a confusion similar to this: that a line of a certain length consists of an infinite number of parts because it is indefinitely divisible; i.e., because there is no end to the possibility of dividing it.)

If on the other hand you realize that the chain of *actual* reasons has a beginning, you will no longer be revolted by the idea of a case in which there is *no* reason for the way you obey the order. At this point, however, another confusion sets in, that between reason and cause. One is led into this confusion by the ambiguous use of the word "why". Thus when the chain of reasons has come to an end and still the question "why?" is asked, one is inclined to give a cause instead of a reason. If, e.g., to the question, "why did you paint just this colour when I told you to paint a red patch?" you give the answer: "I have been shown a sample of this colour and the word 'red' was pronounced to me at the same time; and therefore this colour now always comes to my mind when I hear the word 'red'", then you have given a cause for your action and not a reason.

The proposition that your action has such and such a cause, is a hypothesis. The hypothesis is well-founded if one has had a number of experiences which, roughly speaking, agree in showing that your action is the regular sequel of certain conditions which we then call causes of the action. In order to know the reason which you had for making a certain statement, for acting in a particular way, etc., no number of agreeing experiences is necessary, and the statement of your reason is not a hypothesis. The difference between the grammars of "reason" and "cause" is quite similar to that between the grammars of "motive" and "cause". Of the cause one can say that one can't *know* it but can only *conjecture* it. On the other hand one often says: "Surely *I* must know why I did it" talking of the *motive*. When I say: "we can only *conjecture* the cause but we *know* the motive" this statement will be seen later on to be a grammatical one. The "can" refers to a *logical* possibility.

The double use of the word "why", asking for the cause and asking for the motive, together with the idea that we can know, and not only conjecture, our motives, gives rise to the confusion that a motive is a cause of which we are immediately aware, a cause 'seen from the inside', or a cause experienced. – Giving a reason is like giving a calculation by which you have arrived at a certain result.

Let us go back to the statement that thinking essentially consists in operating with signs. My point was that it is liable to mislead us if we say 'thinking is a mental activity'. The question what kind of an activity thinking is is analogous to this: "Where does thinking take place?" We can answer: on paper, in our head, in the mind. None of these statements of locality gives *the* locality of thinking. The use of all these specifications is correct, but we must not be misled by the similarity of their linguistic form into a false conception of their grammar. As, e.g., when you say: "Surely, the *real* place of thought is in our head". The same applies to the idea of thinking as an activity. It is correct to say that thinking is an activity of our writing hand, of our larynx, of our head, and of our mind, so long as we understand the grammar of these statements. And it is, furthermore, extremely important to realize how, by misunderstanding the grammar of our expressions, we are led to think of one in particular of these statements as giving the *real* seat of the activity of thinking.

There is an objection to saying that thinking is some such thing as an activity of the hand. Thinking, one wants to say, is part of our 'private experience'. It is not material, but an event in private consciousness. This objection is expressed in the question: "Could a machine think?" I shall talk about this at a later point, and now only refer you to an analogous question: "Can a machine have toothache?" You will certainly be inclined to say: "A machine can't have toothache". All I will do now is to draw your attention to the use which you have made of the word "can" and to ask you: "Did you mean to say that all our past experience has shown that a machine never had toothache?" The impossibility of which you speak is a logical one. The question is: What is the relation between thinking (or toothache) and the subject which thinks, has toothache, etc.? I shall say no more about this now.

If we say thinking is essentially operating with signs, the first question you might ask is: "What are signs?" – Instead of giving any kind of general answer to this question, I shall propose to you to look closely at particular cases which we should call "operating with signs". Let us look at a simple example of operating with words. I give someone the order: "fetch me six apples from the grocer", and I will describe a way of making use of such an order: The words "six apples" are written on a bit of paper, the paper is handed to the grocer, the grocer compares the word "apple" with labels on different shelves. He finds it to agree with one of the labels, counts from 1 to the number written on the slip of paper, and for every number counted takes a fruit off the shelf and puts it in a bag. – And here you have a case of the use of words. I shall in the future again and again draw your attention to what I shall call language games. These are ways of using signs simpler than those in which we use the signs of our highly complicated everyday language. Language games are the forms of language with which a child begins to make use of words. The study of language games is the study of primitive forms of language or primitive languages. If we want to study the problems of truth and falsehood, of the agreement and disagreement of propositions with reality, of the nature of assertion, assumption, and question, we shall with great advantage look at primitive forms of language in which these forms of thinking appear without the confusing background of highly complicated processes of thought. When we look at such simple forms of language the mental mist which seems to enshroud our ordinary use of language disappears. We see activities, reactions, which are clear-cut and transparent. On the other hand we recognize in these simple processes forms of language not separated by a break from our more complicated ones. We see that we can build up the complicated forms from the primitive ones by gradually adding new forms.

Now what makes it difficult for us to take this line of investigation is our craving for generality.

This craving for generality is the resultant of a number of tendencies connected with particular philosophical confusions. There is –

(a) The tendency to look for something in common to all the entities which we commonly subsume under a general term. – We are inclined to think that there must be something in common to all games, say, and that this common property is the justification for applying the general term "game" to the various games; whereas games form a *family* the members of which have family likenesses. Some of them have the same nose, others the same eyebrows and others again the same way of walking; and these likenesses overlap. The idea of a general concept being a common property of its particular instances connects up with other primitive, too simple, ideas of the structure of language. It is comparable to the idea that *properties* are *ingredients* of the things which have the properties; e.g. that beauty is an ingredient of all beautiful things as alcohol is of beer and wine, and that we therefore could have pure beauty, unadulterated by anything that is beautiful.

(b) There is a tendency rooted in our usual forms of expression, to think that the man who has learnt to understand a general term, say, the term "leaf", has thereby come to possess a kind of general picture of a leaf, as opposed to pictures of particular leaves. He was shown different leaves when he learnt the meaning of the word "leaf"; and showing him the particular leaves was only a means to the end of producing 'in him' an idea which we imagine to be some kind of general image. We say that he sees what is in common to all these leaves; and this is true if we mean that he can on being asked tell us certain features or properties which they have in common. But we are inclined to think that the general idea of a leaf is something like a visual image, but one which only contains what is common to all leaves. (Galtonian composite photograph.) This again is connected with the idea that the meaning of a word is an image, or a thing correlated to the word. (This roughly means, we are looking at words as though they all were

proper names, and we then confuse the bearer of a name with the meaning of the name.)

(c) Again, the idea we have of what happens when we get hold of the general idea 'leaf', 'plant', etc. etc., is connected with the confusion between a mental state, meaning a state of a hypothetical mental mechanism, and a mental state meaning a state of consciousness (toothache, etc.).

(d) Our craving for generality has another main source: our preoccupation with the method of science. I mean the method of reducing the explanation of natural phenomena to the smallest possible number of primitive natural laws; and, in mathematics, of unifying the treatment of different topics by using a generalization. Philosophers constantly see the method of science before their eyes, and are irresistibly tempted to ask and answer questions in the way science does. This tendency is the real source of metaphysics, and leads the philosopher into complete darkness. I want to say here that it can never be our job to reduce anything to anything, or to explain anything. Philosophy really *is* 'purely descriptive'. (Think of such questions as "Are there sense data?" and ask: What method is there of determining this? Introspection?)

Instead of "craving for generality" I could also have said "the contemptuous attitude towards the particular case". If, e.g., someone tries to explain the concept of number and tells us that such and such a definition will not do or is clumsy because it only applies to, say, finite cardinals I should answer that the mere fact that he could have given such a limited definition makes this definition extremely important to us. (Elegance is *not* what we are trying for.) For why should what finite and transfinite numbers have in common be more interesting to us than what distinguishes them? Or rather, I should not have said "why should it be more interesting to us?" – it *isn't*; and this characterizes our way of thinking.

The attitude towards the more general and the more special in logic is connected with the usage of the word "kind" which is liable to cause confusion. We talk of kinds of numbers, kinds of propositions, kinds of proofs; and, also, of kinds of apples, kinds of paper, etc. In one sense what defines the kind are properties, like sweetness, hardness, etc. In the other the different kinds are different grammatical structures. A treatise on pomology may be called incomplete if there exist kinds of apples which it doesn't mention. Here we have a standard of completeness in nature. Supposing on the other hand there was a game resembling that of chess but simpler, no pawns being used in it. Should we call this game incomplete? Or should we call a game more complete than chess if it in some way contained chess but added new elements? The contempt for what seems the less general case in logic springs from the idea that it is incomplete. It is in fact confusing to talk of cardinal arithmetic as something special as opposed to something more general. Cardinal arithmetic bears no mark of incompleteness; nor does an arithmetic which is cardinal and finite. (There are no subtle distinctions between logical forms as there are between the tastes of different kinds of apples.)

If we study the grammar, say, of the words "wishing", "thinking", "understanding", "meaning", we shall not be dissatisfied when we have described various cases of wishing, thinking, etc. If someone said, "surely this is not all that one calls 'wishing'", we should answer, "certainly not, but you can build up more complicated cases if you like." And after all, there is not one definite class of features which characterize all cases of wishing (at least not as the word is commonly used). If on the other hand you wish to give a definition of wishing, i.e., to draw a sharp boundary, then you are free to draw it as you like; and this boundary will never entirely coincide with the actual usage, as this usage has no sharp boundary.

The idea that in order to get clear about the meaning of a general term one had to find the common element in all its applications has shackled philosophical investigation; for it has not only led to no result, but also made the philosopher dismiss as irrelevant the concrete cases, which alone could have helped him to understand the usage of the general term. When Socrates asks the question, "what is knowledge?" he does not even regard it as a *preliminary* answer to enumerate cases of knowledge.

From "The Brown Book"

Augustine, in describing his learning of language, says that he was taught to speak by learning the names of things. It is clear that whoever says this has in mind the way in which a child learns such words as "man", "sugar", "table", etc. He does not primarily think of such words as "today", "not", "but", "perhaps".

Suppose a man described a game of chess, without mentioning the existence and operations of the pawns. His description of the game as a natural phenomenon will be incomplete. On the other hand we may say that he has completely described a simpler game. In this sense we can say that Augustine's description of learning the language was correct for a simpler language than ours. Imagine this language:

1. Its function is the communication between a builder A and his man B. B has to reach A building stones. There are cubes, bricks, slabs, beams, columns. The language consists of the words "cube", "brick", "slab", "column". A calls out one of these words, upon which B brings a stone of a certain shape. Let us imagine a society in which this is the only system of language. The child learns this language from the grownups by being trained to its use. I am using the word "trained" in a way strictly analogous to that in which we talk of an animal being trained to do certain things. It is done by means of example, reward, punishment, and suchlike. Part of this training is that we point to a building stone, direct the attention of the child towards it, and pronounce a word. I will call this procedure *demonstrative* teaching of words. In the actual use of this language, one man calls out the words as orders, the other acts according to them. But learning and teaching this language will contain this procedure: The child just 'names' things, that is, he pronounces the words of the language when the teacher points to the things. In fact, there will be a still simpler exercise: The child repeats words which the teacher pronounces.

(Note. Objection: The word "brick" in language (1) has not the meaning which it has in *our* language. – This is true if it means that in our language there are usages of the word "brick" different from our usages of this word in language (1). But don't we sometimes use the word "brick!" in just this way? Or should we say that when we use it, it is an elliptical sentence, a shorthand for "Bring me a brick"? Is it right to say that if *we* say "brick!" we *mean* "Bring me a brick"? Why should I translate the expression "brick!" into the expression "Bring me a brick"? And if they are synonymous, why shouldn't I say: If he says "brick!" he means "brick!" . . . ? Or: Why shouldn't he be able to mean just "brick!" if he is able to mean "Bring me a brick", unless you wish to assert that while he says aloud "brick!" he as a matter of fact always says in his mind, to himself, "Bring me a brick"? But what reason could we have to assert this? Suppose someone asked: If a man gives the order, "Bring me a brick", must he mean it as four words, or can't he mean it as one composite word synonymous with the one word "brick!"? One is tempted to answer: He *means* all four words if in his language he uses that sentence in contrast with other sentences in which these words are used, such as, for instance, "Take these two bricks away". But what if I asked "But how is his sentence contrasted with these others? Must he have thought them simultaneously, or shortly before or after, or is it sufficient that he should have one time learnt them, etc.?" When we have asked ourselves this question, it appears that it is irrelevant which of these alternatives is the case. And we are inclined to say that all that is really relevant is that these contrasts should exist in the system of language which he is using, and that they need not in any sense be present in his mind when he utters his sentence. Now compare this conclusion with our original question. When we asked it, we seemed to ask a question about the state of mind of the man who says the sentence, whereas the idea of meaning which we arrived at in the end was not that of a state of mind. We think of the meaning of signs sometimes as states of mind of the man using them, sometimes as the role which these signs are playing in a system of language. The connection between these two ideas is that the mental experiences which accompany the use of a sign undoubtedly are caused by our usage of the sign in a particular system of language. William James speaks of specific feelings accompanying the use of such words as "and", "if", "or". And there is no doubt that at least certain gestures are often connected with such words, as a collecting gesture with "and", and a dismissing gesture with "not". And there obviously are visual and muscular sensations connected with these gestures. On the other hand it is clear enough that these sensations do not accompany every use of the word "not" and "and". If in some language the word "but" meant what "not" means in English, it is clear that we should not compare the meanings of these two words by comparing the sensations which they produce. Ask yourself what means we have of finding out the feelings which they produce in

different people and on different occasions. Ask yourself: "When I said, 'Give me an apple *and* a pear, *and* leave the room', had I the same feeling when I pronounced the two words 'and'?" But we do not deny that the people who use the word "but" as "not" is used in English will, broadly speaking, have similar sensations accompanying the word "but" to those the English have when they use "not". And the word "but" in the two languages will on the whole be accompanied by different sets of experiences.)

2. Let us now look at an extension of language (1). The builder's man knows by heart the series of words from one to ten. On being given the order, "Five slabs!", he goes to where the slabs are kept, says the words from one to five, takes up a slab for each word, and carries them to the builder. Here both the parties use the language by speaking the words. Learning the numerals by heart will be one of the essential features of learning this language. The use of the numerals will again be taught demonstratively. But now the same word, e.g., "three", will be taught by pointing either to slabs, or to bricks, or to columns, etc. And on the other hand, different numerals will be taught by pointing to groups of stones of the same shape.

(Remark: We stressed the importance of learning the series of numerals by heart because there was no feature comparable to this in the learning of language (1). And this shows us that by introducing numerals we have introduced an entirely different *kind* of instrument into our language. The difference of kind is much more obvious when we contemplate such a simple example than when we look at our ordinary language with innumerable kinds of words all looking more or less alike when they stand in the dictionary. –

What have the demonstrative explanations of the numerals in common with those of the words "slab", "column", etc., except a gesture and pronouncing the words? The way such a gesture is used in the two cases is different. This difference is blurred if one says, "In one case we point to a shape, in the other we point to a number". The difference becomes obvious and clear only when we contemplate a *complete* example (i.e., the example of a language completely worked out in detail).)

3. Let us introduce a new instrument of communication, – a proper name. This is given to a

particular object (a particular building stone) by pointing to it and pronouncing the name. If A calls the name, B brings the object. The demonstrative teaching of a proper name is different again from the demonstrative teaching in the cases (1) and (2).

(Remark: This difference does not lie, however, in the act of pointing and pronouncing the word or in any mental act (meaning?) accompanying it, but in the role which the demonstration (pointing and pronouncing) plays in the whole training and in the use which is made of it in the practice of communication by means of this language. One might think that the difference could be described by saying that in the different cases we point to different kinds of objects. But suppose I point with my hand to a blue jersey. How does pointing to its colour differ from pointing to its shape? – We are inclined to say the difference is that we *mean* something different in the two cases. And 'meaning' here is to be some sort of process taking place while we point. What particularly tempts us to this view is that a man on being asked whether he pointed to the colour or the shape is, at least in most cases, able to answer this and to be certain that his answer is correct. If on the other hand, we look for two such characteristic mental acts as meaning the colour and meaning the shape, etc., we aren't able to find any, or at least none which must always accompany pointing to colour, pointing to shape, respectively. We have only a *rough* idea of what it means to concentrate one's attention on the colour as opposed to the shape, or vice versa. The difference, one might say, does not lie in the act of demonstration, but rather in the surrounding of that act in the use of the language.)

4. On being ordered, "This slab!", B brings the slab to which A points. On being ordered, "Slab, there!", he carries a slab to the place indicated. Is the word "there" taught demonstratively? Yes and no! When a person is trained in the use of the word "there", the teacher will in training him make the pointing gesture and pronounce the word "there". But should we say that thereby he gives a place the name "there"? Remember that the pointing gesture in this case is part of the practice of communication itself.

(Remark: It has been suggested that such words as "there", "here", "now", "this" are the *'real proper names'* as opposed to what in ordinary life

we call proper names, and, in the view I am referring to, can only be called so crudely. There is a widespread tendency to regard what in ordinary life is called a proper name only as a rough approximation of what ideally could be called so. Compare Russell's idea of the 'individual'. He talks of individuals as the ultimate constituents of reality, but says that it is difficult to say which things are individuals. The idea is that further analysis has to reveal this. We, on the other hand, introduced the idea of a proper name in a language in which it was applied to what in ordinary life we call "objects", "things" ("building stones").

· – "What does the word 'exactness' mean? Is it real exactness if you are supposed to come to tea at 4.30 and come when a good clock strikes 4.30? Or would it only be exactness if you began to open the door at the moment the clock began to strike? But how is this moment to be defined and how is 'beginning to open the door' to be defined? Would it be correct to say, 'It is difficult to say what real exactness is, for all we know is only rough approximations'?")

5. Questions and answers: A asks, "How many slabs?" B counts them and answers with the numeral.

Systems of communication as for instance (1), (2), (3), (4), (5) we shall call "language games". They are more or less akin to what in ordinary language we call games. Children are taught their native language by means of such games, and here they even have the entertaining character of games. We are not, however, regarding the language games which we describe as incomplete parts of a language, but as languages complete in themselves, as complete systems of human communication. To keep this point of view in mind, it very often is useful to imagine such a simple language to be the entire system of communication of a tribe in a primitive state of society. Think of primitive arithmetics of such tribes.

When the boy or grown-up learns what one might call special technical languages, e.g., the use of charts and diagrams, descriptive geometry, chemical symbolism, etc., he learns more language games.

(Remark: The picture we have of the language of the grown-up is that of a nebulous mass of language, his mother tongue, surrounded by discrete and more or less clear-cut language games, the technical languages.)

Ludwig Wittgenstein

6. Asking for the name: we introduce new forms of building stones. B points to one of them and asks, "What is this?"; A answers, "This is a . . .". Later on A calls out this new word, say "arch", and B brings the stone. The words, "This is . . ." together with the pointing gesture we shall call ostensive explanation or ostensive definition. In case (6) a generic name was explained, in actual fact, as the name of a shape. But we can ask analogously for the proper name of a particular object, for the name of a colour, of a numeral, of a direction.

(Remark: Our use of expressions like "names of numbers", "names of colours", "names of materials", "names of nations" may spring from two different sources. One is that we might imagine the functions of proper names, numerals, words for colours, etc., to be much more alike than they actually are. If we do so we are tempted to think that the function of every word is more or less like the function of a proper name of a person, or such generic names as "table", "chair", "door", etc. The second source is this, that if we see how fundamentally different the functions of such words as "table", "chair", etc., are from those of proper names, and how different from either the functions of, say, the names of colours, we see no reason why we shouldn't speak of names of numbers or names of directions either, not by way of saying some such thing as "numbers and directions are just different forms of objects", but rather by way of stressing the analogy which lies in the lack of analogy between the functions of the words "chair" and "Jack" on the one hand, and "east" and "Jack" on the other hand.)

7. B has a table in which written signs are placed opposite to pictures of objects (say, a table, a chair, a tea-cup, etc.). A writes one of the signs, B looks for it in the table, looks or points with his finger from the written sign to the picture opposite, and fetches the object which the picture represents.

Let us now look at the different kinds of signs which we have introduced. First let us distinguish between sentences and words. A sentence[1]

I will call every complete sign in a language game, its constituent signs are words. (This is merely a rough and general remark about the way I will use the words "proposition"[1] and "word".) A proposition may consist of only one word. In (1) the signs "brick!", "column!" are the sentences. In (2) a sentence consists of two words. According to the role which propositions play in a language game, we distinguish between orders, questions, explanations, descriptions, and so on.

8. If in a language game similar to (1) A calls out an order: "slab, column, brick!" which is obeyed by B by bringing a slab, a column and a brick, we might here talk of three propositions, or of one only. If, on the other hand,

9. the order of words shows B the order in which to bring the building stones, we shall say that A calls out a proposition consisting of three words. If the command in this case took the form, "Slab, then column, then brick!" we should say that it consisted of four words (not of five). Amongst the words we see groups of words with similar functions. We can easily see a similarity in the use of the words "one", "two", "three", etc. and again one in the use of "slab", "column" and "brick", etc., and thus we distinguish parts of speech. In (8) all the words of the proposition belonged to the same part of speech.

10. The order in which B had to bring the stones in (9) could have been indicated by the use of the ordinals thus: "Second, column; first, slab; third, brick!". Here we have a case in which what was the function of the order of words in one language game is the function of particular words in another.

Reflections such as the preceding will show us the infinite variety of the functions of words in propositions, and it is curious to compare what we see in our examples with the simple and rigid rules which logicians give for the construction of propositions. If we group words together according to the similarity of their functions, thus distinguishing parts of speech, it is easy to see that many different ways of classification can be adopted.

Note

1 Here Wittgenstein uses "sentence" and "proposition" interchangeably for the German "*Satz*". (Edd.)

Further reading in methodology

Austin, J. L., *Sense and Sensibilia*, ed. G. J. Warnock, Oxford: Oxford University Press, 1962.
——*Philosophical Papers*, 2nd edn., ed. J. O. Urmson and G. J. Warnock, Oxford: Oxford University Press, 1970.
Ayer, A. J., *Language, Truth and Logic*, 2nd edn., London: Gollancz, 1946.
Jackson, Frank, *From Metaphysics to Ethics: A Defense of Conceptual Analysis*, Oxford: Oxford University Press, 2000.

McGinn, Colin, *Problems in Philosophy*, Oxford: Blackwell Publishers, 1993.
Ryle, Gilbert, *Dilemmas*, Cambridge: Cambridge University Press, 1960.
Sellars, Wilfrid, *Empiricism and the Philosophy of Mind*, ed. (and with a study guide) Robert Brandom, Cambridge, MA: Harvard University Press, 1997.
Wittgenstein, Ludwig, *Philosophical Investigations*, ed. G. E. M. Anscombe, London: Blackwell Publishers, 1953.

Index

Index

Index

Principle of Causal Dependence, 260–1

Principal of Causal Interaction, 252–3

Principle of the Nomological Character of Causality, 253, 260

privacy, 505

probability and probabilistic explanation, 207–14; *see also* explanation; induction

proper names, *see* meaning; names and naming; reference

properties, 21, 122

propositional attitudes, 254

propositions, 32–54, 114–21, 156, 160, 408–9, 510; conditional, 206–7; contingent and synthetic, 72, 79–85; counterfactual, 78, 206–7, 257; existential, 42, 48–9; general, 257; about the past; 420; universal, 205, 221; *see also* analyticity and synonymy; necessity and possibility

psychology, empirical, 28, 90, 227–8, 230–1, 485

purposes, *see* intention and intentionality

Putnam, Hilary, **90–6, 245–51**

Quine, W. V., 2, 62, 64, 70 n. 8, 71 n. 12, 75, 78, 79, 81, **135–43, 225–33,** 262 n. 14, 434, **450–62,** 463–72

quotation and extensionality, 8

rainbows, 202

rational reconstruction, 227, 228

Rawls, John, 3, **365–80**

realism, 103–4; metaphysical, 141

reasons and causes, 332–41, 504–5

reduction and reductionism, 225–6, 245–6, 263, 457–8, 493

reduction forms, 228; *see also* reduction and reductionism

reference, 8–17, 21, 32–54, 61–3, 90–6; indirect, 10–17

referring, *see* reference

Reid, Thomas, 194, 316, 319

relations, logical, 7, 101–10, 122

relevance, explanatory, 201–2

resentment, 301, 304, 307–8

responsibility, 301, 315–21, 438–9

rigid and nonrigid designators, 77–9, 87 n. 10, 94, 273

robots, 280

rules, 173–4, 245; and rule following, 503–4; semantical, 455–7

Russell, Bertrand, 1, **32–40,** 42–9, 73–6, 87 nn. 4 and 5, **101–11,** 117, 118, 137–8, 141, 143, 149, 150, 156, 157–70, 177, **185–9,** 226, 227, 432, 450–1, 458, 459, 509

Ryle, Gilbert, 2, 238, 239–41, 334, 431–2

Schlick, Moritz, 2, 430

science, 201–14, 225–33

scientific framework, *see* framework, the

scientific image, *see* manifest and scientific image

Searle, John R., 2, 83, **277–83**

self, the, *see* persons

self-knowledge, 315–21, 491–2; *see also* first person and first person pronouns

self-presenting states, 196

Sellars, Wilfrid, **473–96**

semantics, 232–3, 278–82, 430–3; *see also* meaning

Semmelweis, I. P., 204

sensation, 242–3, 492–3; *see also* perception

sense, *see* meaning; *Sinn*

sense data, 170, 185–7, 230, 403, 433; *see also* perception

set theory, 225–7, 228

Shoemaker, Sidney, 323

Sidgwick, Henry, 352–3, 373, 379 nn. 14 and 16, 386–7, 391

signs, 7–8, 116

Simon, Herbert, 277, 278

simplicity, 142

singular terms, *see* names and naming

Sinn, 7–17, 18 n. 10, 20, 34, 114–15, 116, 121; *see also* meaning

Sizi, Francesco, 201

skepticism, 121, 155–84, 190–1, 197–8

slavery, 374–5

Smart, J. C. C., 249

Socrates, 507

space, 105–8; *see also* time

Spinoza, Benedict, 194, 477, 483, 492

state descriptions, 452

statements, *see* propositions

states, 241–3, 246–9

states of affairs, 114–15, 316–17; *see also* facts

Stevenson, C. L., 56–7, **355–64**

Strawson, P. F., **41–54, 122–34, 301–14, 463–72**

strong AI, *see* artificial intelligence

Suarez, Francisco, 318

subjectivity, 263–9; *see also* minds and the mental

subjects, *see* reference

subsistence, 136, 143 n. 1; *see also* existence

supervenience, 255–6

syllogism, practical, 338

synonymy, *see* analyticity and synonymy

syntax, 278–82

Tarski, Alfred, 64–7, 256

tautologies, *see* analyticity and synonymy

Taylor, Charles, 254–5, 289, 293–5, 300 nn. 6, 12, and 13

testability, 201

thinking, 277–83, 491–2, 498–505

thirst, 249

thought [*Gedanke*], 19–30, 115; *see also* judgment

time, 101–2; *see also* space

Tooke, John Horne, 458

Torricelli, Evangelista, 202

translation, 142, 228–30, 232

trouser word, 443

truth, 10–11, 19–22, 25, 61–71, 438

Turing machine, 247

Twin Earth, 90–6

type–type psychophysical theory, 272

understanding and meaning, 500–3; *see also* meaning

Uniformity of Nature, 216

universals, *see* particulars and universals

utilitarianism, 326–7, 353, 367, 373–6, 377 n. 5, 378 n. 6, 382

utterer's and utterance meaning, 55–60; *see also* meaning

variables, 32–3, 141

verification and verification principle, 229, 233, 419–20, 457–8, 470; *see also* confirmation

Vienna Circle, 2, 229, 230, 231, 430

volition, *see* freedom and free will